INTERNATIONAL HANDBOOK OF
TRADE UNIONS

International Handbook of Trade Unions

Edited by

John T. Addison

Hugh C. Lane Professor of Economic Theory, University of South Carolina, Columbia, USA

and

Claus Schnabel

Professor of Economics, Friedrich-Alexander University Erlangen-Nürnberg, Germany

Edward Elgar

Cheltenham, UK • Northampton, MA, USA

Published by
Edward Elgar Publishing Limited
Glensanda House
Montpellier Parade
Cheltenham
Glos GL50 1UA
UK

Edward Elgar Publishing, Inc.
136 West Street
Suite 202
Northampton
Massachusetts 01060
USA

A catalogue record for this book
is available from the British Library

Library of Congress Cataloguing in Publication Data

International handbook of trade unions / edited by John T. Addison, Claus Schnabel.
   p. cm.
   Includes bibliographical references and index.
   1. Labor unions. 2. Labor policy. 3. Collective bargaining. 4. Comparative industrial relations. 5. Labor union members. 6. Wages. 7. International labor activities. I. Addison, John T. II. Schnabel, Claus, 1961–

HD6483.159   2003
331.88–dc21   2003049040

ISBN 1 84064 979 8 (cased)

Printed and Bound in Great Britain by MPG Books Ltd, Bodmin, Cornwall

Contents

List of contributors   *vii*

1   Introduction   1
    John T. Addison and Claus Schnabel

2   Determinants of trade union membership   13
    Claus Schnabel

3   Economic models of union behaviour   44
    Robin Naylor

4   Unions, bargaining and strikes   86
    Peter Cramton and Joseph Tracy

5   Unions and productivity, financial performance and
    investment: international evidence   118
    David Metcalf

6   Collective bargaining and macroeconomic performance   172
    Robert J. Flanagan

7   Changes over time in union relative wage effects in the UK
    and the USA revisited   197
    David Blanchflower and Alex Bryson

8   Unions and the wage structure   246
    David Card, Thomas Lemieux and W. Craig Riddell

9   Unions and innovation: a survey of the theory and empirical
    evidence   293
    Naercio Menezes-Filho and John Van Reenen

10 Trade unions as political actors   335
    Wolfgang Streeck and Anke Hassel

11 Unions and unionism around the world   366
    Jelle Visser

12 Recent changes in the industrial relations framework in the UK   415
    John T. Addison and W. Stanley Siebert

13 Europeanization of collective bargaining   461
    Dieter Sadowski, Oliver Ludewig and Florian Turk

14 Contemporary developments in and challenges to collective
    bargaining in the United States   502
    John Delaney

Index   531

Contributors

John T. Addison is Hugh C. Lane Professor of Economic Theory, University of South Carolina (USA); Professor-at-Large, Free University of Bolzano/Bozen (Italy); and Research Fellow, Institute for the Study of Labour/IZA (Germany).

David Blanchflower is Bruce V. Rauner 1978 Professor of Economics, Dartmouth College; and Research Associate, National Bureau of Economic Research (USA).

Alex Bryson is Principal Research Fellow, Policy Studies Institute; and Research Associate, Centre for Economic Performance, London School of Economics (UK).

David Card is Class of 1950 Professor of Economics, University of California, Berkeley; and Research Associate, National Bureau of Economic Research (USA).

Peter Cramton is Professor of Economics, University of Maryland (USA).

John Delaney is Associate Dean for MBA Programs and Professor of Management, Eli Broad College of Business, Michigan State University (USA).

Naercio Menezes-Filho is Assistant Professor of Economics, University of São Paulo (Brazil); and Research Associate, Institute for Fiscal Studies London (UK).

Robert J. Flanagan is Konosuke Matsushita Professor of Economics, Graduate School of Business, Stanford University (USA).

Anke Hassel is Senior Researcher, Max Planck Institute for the Study of Societies, Cologne (Germany).

Thomas Lemieux is Professor of Economics and Director of the Centre for Labour and Empirical Economic Research, University of British Columbia (Canada); and Research Associate, National Bureau of Economic Research (USA).

Oliver Ludewig is a Researcher at the Institute for Labour Law and Industrial Relations in the European Community (IAAEG), Trier (Germany).

David Metcalf is Professor of Industrial Relations and Deputy Director of the Centre for Economic Performance, London School of Economics (UK).

Robin Naylor is Professor of Economics, University of Warwick (UK)

John Van Reenen is Professor of Economics, University College London; and Research Fellow, Centre for Economic Policy Research (UK).

W. Craig Riddell is Professor of Economics, University of British Columbia (Canada); and an Associate of the Canadian Institute for Advanced Research.

Dieter Sadowski is Professor of Business Administration, University of Trier; and Director of the Institute for Labour Law and Industrial Relations in the European Community (IAAEG), Trier (Germany).

Claus Schnabel is Professor of Economics, Friedrich-Alexander University Erlangen-Nürnberg (Germany).

W. Stanley Siebert is Professor of Labour Economics, University of Birmingham (UK).

Wolfgang Streeck is Director of the Max Planck Institute for the Study of Societies, Cologne; and Professor of Sociology, University of Cologne (Germany).

Joseph Tracy is Vice President, Federal Reserve Bank of New York (USA).

Florian Turk is a Researcher at the Institute for Labour Law and Industrial Relations in the European Community (IAAEG), Trier (Germany).

Jelle Visser is Professor of Empirical Sociology, University of Amsterdam; and Scientific Director, Amsterdam Institute for Advanced Labour Studies (AIAS) (the Netherlands).

1 Introduction
John T. Addison and Claus Schnabel

This Handbook seeks to give the reader a sense of the drama in the every-day workings of modern labour markets. There is no better illustration of this than the situation confronted by the trade union. Unions have been buffeted by competitive pressures more than most other institutions. At one level – where unions are combinations in restraint of trade – this result is neither surprising nor unwelcome. But unions are more than this. The twin aims of this volume are to demonstrate the various facets of unionism and thence to address the consequences of what it is that unions do. It is then left up to the reader to form a judgement on the institution and to assess to the seriousness of union decline (or indeed otherwise) in his or her country. Necessarily, the contributors to this volume do not share a common view of the union institution or indeed its fate.

Although trade unions have long been important economic and political actors in industrialized countries, academic interest in them has been thin historically. This was especially true of the economics discipline. As late as 1975, in his short survey of the economic analysis of the union institution, Johnson (1975, p. 23) stated that '[t]he study of the behavior and effects of trade unions is not currently one of the major growth industries of the economics profession'. And yet, after surveying the union literature in the mid-1980s, Oswald (1985), Farber (1986) and Hirsch and Addison (1986) all stressed the remarkable growth of work in the area and the substantial progress that had been made in the analysis of unions and union behaviour (see also Freeman and Medoff, 1984). Subsequent advances in union research were identified by Pencavel (1991) and Booth (1995), but such has been the pace and breadth of research in recent years that presentation of a comprehensive, unified description of the current state of play is beyond the capabilities of a single author.

In the light of this embarrassment of riches, we here follow a different strategy, having commissioned chapters from the leading specialists in the field. This Handbook approach has the major advantage that the main issues can be covered in detail and within a framework that tackles different country settings and recognizes contributions from several disciplines. And although this volume will be consulted mainly by students of labour economics, industrial relations, and political science, most of the chapters are written in a rather non-technical way which should also allow non-specialists more than a glimpse of the current state of research on trade unions. In sum, the Handbook provides a detailed review and analysis of what the editors believe to be the main areas of research in the (economic) analysis of unions, ranging from the determinants and the extent of unions through analysis of their micro- and macro-economic effects to discussion of some key institutional developments at country and regional levels.

Because the existence and the power of trade unions depends on their ability to attract and nurture a loyal membership, *Claus Schnabel* leads off in Chapter 2 with a survey of the determinants of union membership. The starting point is the conventional demand and supply framework used by economists to analyse the forces that influence union membership, extended to cover the free-rider problem. The key problem for social scientists is to explain why any individual would join a union when membership is costly and where the benefits apply to all workers regardless of their union status. Recent research points to the existence of social customs and of a minimum critical mass of membership or density below which union existence is not viable, implying that a reduction in union membership caused by temporary shocks can be persistent. In short, the fall in unionization observed in many countries – and documented in Chapter 11 by Jelle Visser – may be almost irreversible. Supplementary explanations of union membership from other disciplines of social sciences are also discussed in this chapter, some of which can be incorporated in the economist's supply–demand and cost–benefit framework whereas others are more difficult to operationalize.

Schnabel's review of the international empirical evidence on the determinants of union membership shows that while there are substantial differences in the design and the results of the empirical studies, some consistent patterns do emerge. Concerning macro-determinants, for example, there is some evidence across countries that business cycle factors as well as structural developments (such as changes in the composition of the workforce) play a significant role in explaining short-run changes and long-run trends in union membership. Similarly, individual-level cross-sectional studies have identified a number of micro-determinants (such as personal, occupational and firm characteristics, earnings, attitudes, and social variables) that are associated with the unionization decision. And for their part, cross-national analyses point to the importance of institutional determinants of unionism such as the existence of union-administered unemployment insurance schemes. What is often missing, however, are attempts to integrate the macro- and micro-level findings, and it has proved difficult to build a bridge between the variety of theoretical approaches and the empirical literature on the determinants of unionization.

An important insight of recent theoretical research is that union membership and wages are determined simultaneously, and this is also stressed by *Robin Naylor* in his chapter surveying economic models of union behaviour. In a novel approach, he adapts the structure–conduct–performance framework from industrial economics to organize a review of the theory of trade unions. Focusing first on conduct (that is, the nature of union objectives and the scope of bargaining), he discusses alternative union utility functions and bargaining models. The right-to-manage outcome is shown to generate higher profits than either efficient or sequential bargaining (for a given level of union influence over the wage), so that firms will prefer to keep employment off the bargaining agenda. Naylor then turns to the issue of bargaining structure and to the literature on unionized oligopoly. He shows that in a unionized oligopoly setting there is a dominant strategy towards efficient bargaining. Furthermore, factors such as the product market structure and the nature of the external bargaining environment are important. Product market characteristics – such as the number of firms in the market – affect the outcome of wage bargaining, and Naylor demonstrates that traditional results in oligopoly theory are not always robust to the introduction of union–firm bargaining.

The bargaining process between unions and firms and the emergence of strikes are discussed in Chapter 4 by *Peter Cramton* and *Joseph Tracy*. Using non-cooperative bargaining theory and stressing the role of (the firm's) private information, they present a theoretical model that includes the union's threat choice between strikes and holdouts (that is extending an expired contract). Since negotiators have an incentive to misrepresent their private information during the bargaining process, labour disputes are interpreted as a (costly) means of communicating this private information. The model provides several insights into how the structure of the labour agreement and the prevailing economic conditions affect the bargaining outcome; for instance, strikes will be more likely after a period of uncompensated inflation and when conditions in the local labour market are tight. Furthermore, in making its threat choice between a strike and a holdout, the union must take into consideration the probability that firms will deploy replacements for striking workers. The model is shown to be consistent with empirical evidence suggesting that strike duration is counter-cyclical while strike incidence may be pro-cyclical. Cramton and Tracy use the model and its extensions to analyse several labour policies and generate predictions as to their impact on dispute incidence, dispute duration, and the settlement wage. They compare these predictions with extant empirical evidence and evaluate the efficiency and equity ramifications of labour policy. Among other things, they report that cooling-off periods do not seem to affect strike activity whereas bans on replacement workers increase strike frequency and duration as well as wages.

The pay-raising effect of union bargaining demonstrated throughout the Handbook has to be funded from somewhere – from greater productivity, or lower profits, or higher prices. In Chapter 5, *David Metcalf* examines in detail the effects of unions on productivity, profitability, and investment. He shows that it is not possible to use theory to predict unambiguously the direction of the union effect on productivity. This is because unions can either enhance productivity (by reason of their monitoring role or collective voice effects) or detract from it (via restrictive work practices and adversarial industrial relations). The empirical evidence from the six countries analysed is also mixed, confirming that both effects play a role, with different weights at different times and in different institutional settings. In contrast, the evidence on unions' effects on profits is more clear-cut, indicating that profits or financial performance are inferior in unionized workplaces, firms, and sectors. For both productivity and profitability, multi-unionism seems to deliver the worst results.

Concerning investment, rent-seeking behaviour by unions might suggest that their impact is negative, but by the same token, firms may also substitute away from expensive labour and invest more in physical capital. The empirical evidence is mixed. It does point to some clear instances of investment-reducing effects of unionism, most notably in North America. But there are also signs that union presence can boost investment in human capital, possibly offsetting the adverse impacts on investment in physical capital where observed. Metcalf stresses the important role of product market competition in both mediating and moderating any adverse union effects, and he emphasizes that cooperation between unions and management yields superior outcomes than adversarial industrial relations.

The macroeconomic effects of unions have occasioned no less controversy than their effects on firm performance. Not surprisingly the Handbook is peppered with references to the debate, and it is the direct focus of Chapter 6. Here *Robert Flanagan* examines the theory and evidence on the relationship between collective bargaining and macroeconomic performance in industrialized countries. The outcome indicators examined are the usual suspects: inflation and unemployment, a conflation of the two, wage inertia, and the misery index, amongst others. The collective bargaining variable ranges from union density/coverage through degree of centralization to extent of coordination. One important finding to emerge from Flanagan's review of the basic literature is the sensitivity of the unionism coefficient to sample period and to small changes in the institutional characterization of the country sample. Another is a tendency toward a weakening in beneficial effects of the centralization/coordination covariates in repeated cross section. The author's response to both tendencies is to look for factors that may underpin these observed changes in the relationships. Thus, for example, globalization may have removed the hump in the once nonlinear association between degree of centralization in collective bargaining and changes in inflation and unemployment. More fundamentally, however, drawing on the corporatist literature, Flanagan is concerned to show that the effect of an institution on outcomes is likely to be a function of the interactions between collective bargaining and specific policy *actions* on the part of the authorities and not just the political complexion of governments. In short, he attempts to go behind the stylized representations of the economy in which the standard models are embedded. In the same spirit, he offers an innovative discussion of how European Monetary Union may be expected to affect wage determination under unions.

In the final part of his analysis, Flanagan returns to the empirical regularity that more coordinated bargaining yields improved economic performance to ask whether encouraging greater coordination through institutional reform might be expected to deliver the macro goods. He cautions against any simplistic rejigging of institutions along these lines without greater understanding of the reasons leading contemporary economic actors to seek a greater measure of decentralization in pay bargaining. In his separate discussion of incomes policy, he notes that any such decentralization nevertheless poses an obvious challenge to an effective and necessarily evolving form of incomes policy.

In Chapter 7, *David Blanchflower* and *Alex Bryson* cover one of the most familiar areas in the economic analysis of unions, namely, their impact on relative wages. But if the topic is familiar, the authors' estimates of the course of the union wage premium – or wage gap – are brand new and fill an important gap in the empirical literature. For the USA and the UK, they offer consistent estimates of the overall wage gap through time, using the same format and procedures throughout. Estimates of the union premium by gender, age, race, broad occupational category and sector, and educational attainment are also provided for both countries; and time trends in these differentials are investigated. Next, the cyclical nature of the wage gap is examined for both countries. Finally, the authors provide estimates of the union premium in 17 other countries again using micro datasets.

What are Blanchflower and Bryson's main findings? To whet the appetite, here are just five. First, the US union premium has held up well – averaging 18 per cent – despite falling union density and coverage. The premium seems to have declined only after 1995, when the economy was booming. Second, to quote the authors, the magnitude of the US union wage differential is today a 'major liability to the future development of unionism' in that country. Third, depending on the micro data set used, the union premium in Britain averaged either 10 or 14 per cent over the sample period, but it has collapsed since the mid-1990s such that for a number of groups – for example, men and private-sector employees – the union coefficient in a log wage equation is no longer statistically significant. Fourth, for both countries the wage gap is countercyclical: as unemployment increases, the union wage premium rises. This leads the authors to speculate that the recent decline in the premium is temporary rather than a trend change in union impact. Finally, the union differential estimated for the other (17) countries examined shows that their unions, too, are able to raise wages well above the equivalent non-union wage.

Chapter 8 is given over to a detailed investigation of the effects of unions on the wage structure. Here *David Card, Thomas Lemieux*, and *Craig Riddell* provide an extensive review of the literature before offering a re-analysis of their own. The starting point is methodological, namely, a formal characterization of the potential effects of unions on wage inequality. Using a simple homogeneous worker, two-sector model, the effect on unions on the variance of wages is broken down into a 'within-sector' effect (wage dispersion is different in the union and non-union sectors) and a 'between-sector' effect (the wedge between union and non-union wages) which is always disequalizing. The model is then extended in two ways. The first complication is to introduce different skill groups. The second extension is to allow for unobserved worker heterogeneity, in recognition that selection might underpin any observed flattening of the wage structure under unionism.

If anything the early literature pointed to a disequalizing effect of unionism on the wage structure, further contributing to the hostility with which unions were often viewed. After 1975, however, the evidence increasingly pointed in an opposite direction, with negative within-sector effects dominating the positive between-sector effect. This equalizing tendency is also reported in second-generation exercises that take account of differences in union coverage and wage premia across different skill groups. And the same is true of smart studies that seek to correct for unobserved skill differences. Card, Lemieux, and Riddell give chapter and verse on this evolving literature and conclude with some important new empirical findings on the male and female wage distributions using large and comparable micro data sets for Canada, the UK, and the USA. They provide information on the raw and skill-adjusted union wage gap or premium, the standard deviation of log union and non-union wages, and a decomposition of variance (i.e. within-sector and between-sector effects). Among their most important findings are the following. First, unions always reduce wage dispersion among male workers, albeit less so when individual characteristics are controlled for. Second, unions do not reduce wage inequality among female workers, partly because unionized women are clustered in the upper end of the wage distribution, and also because their premium is not decreasing in skill level and is larger than that of males. Third, for the USA and the UK – although not Canada – the decline in unionization is associated with a *ceteris paribus* increase in wage inequality. According to the authors' estimates, the decline in the fraction of the workforce organized and in the union premium accounted for 31 (14) per cent of the growth in US wage inequality between 1973/74 and 2001 in the simple two-sector (skill-adjusted) model. For the UK, this time for the period 1983–2002, the corresponding values are 29 and 9 per cent, respectively.

The impact of trade unions on innovation is the topic of Chapter 9 by *Naercio Menezes-Filho* and *John van Reenen*. Although unions may affect innovation through their effects on relative factor prices and profitability and their stance on the introduction of new technology, recent theoretical work has focused on the possibility that unions will 'hold up' firms by expropriating sunk R&D investments through demanding higher wages. This effect may be mitigated or exacerbated by strategic incentives to compete in R&D races. In an attempt to resolve the theoretical ambiguity, Menezes-Filho and van Reenen survey recent micro-econometric studies in the areas of R&D, technological innovation, diffusion and productivity growth. While North American studies find consistently strong and negative impacts of unions on R&D, European studies generally do not uncover such negative effects. There is no consensus concerning the impact of unions on innovation, diffusion, and productivity growth. The authors conclude that the knowledge base they draw on is much thinner than in other areas of union research, which may be due to unsolved econometric problems or to institutional differences between nations in union attitudes and ability to bargain.

Although several chapters touch upon the unions and politics nexus, the analysis of *Wolfgang Streeck* and *Anke Hassel* in Chapter 10 centres on this theme. Thus, the authors first offer a typology of unions and politics along the two dimensions of political unity and politicization – a framework constructed on the basis of the historical experiences of a sample of more than a dozen countries. It is shown that the manner in which unions achieve political influence varies widely. It may occur through political exchange as when centralized unions achieve concessions from governments under incomes policy in return for wage discipline, or through repeated interaction with a given political party, or via functional representation on national economic policy councils and in the joint administration of social security schemes. Finally, there is lobbying, which is of increasing importance as the formal links between unions and (centre-left) political parties have become ever more tenuous.

Just as with the 'mechanisms', there have occurred changes through time in the union role in economic policy. Among the more recent was the abrupt diminution in that role with the dismantling of incomes policy under the challenge of monetarism. (*Vulgo*: if there was no output–inflation tradeoff to exploit, what was to be gained by negotiating with unions?) But Streeck and Hassel argue that this development was to prove more dramatic than sustained, with the recognition that the effects of monetarist policies were not independent of the structure of wage bargaining. Moreover, other union functions – such as their training capacity and potential for productivity improvement via collective voice – were often to tip the balance in favour of their continued inclusion in economic policy councils (in continental Europe if not the Anglo-Saxon OECD countries). Finally, the authors see unions as fundamental to development of the welfare state, arguing that the process of industrialization and modernization both enabled and required such public welfare provision. Specifically, they refer to a 'decommodification' of labour – meaning the extent to which society protects the individual from the market. The degree of decommodification is shown to be greatest where bargaining is centralized.

Yet the current welfare state is in retrenchment, with implications for unionism both in terms of the social wage and joint governance. Although the authors view this development as temporary, they recognize that the viability of the unions as political actors is under long-term pressure. Quite apart from the challenges of globalization, unions are less representative of the working population than heretofore. This calls into question their legitimacy as political representatives of the workforce. Moreover, the core membership is increasingly a narrow constituency. If it is to survive, corporatism has to reflect societal and not just sectional interests.

While most chapters in this Handbook draw from the experience of several countries, *Jelle Visser* in Chapter 11 ranges much further afield. He covers developments in more than 100 nations. Combining union membership data from various sources, Visser estimates the total number of union members at around 320 million. This translates into a global union density rate of 23 per cent if we exclude the one-half of the world's labour force that is involved in agricultural activities and usually not represented by trade unions. Visser discusses developments in unionism and unionization across different world regions, in most cases comparing the mid-1980s with the mid-1990s. He shows that union density has fallen substantially not only in the advanced industrialized countries of Western Europe, North America and Oceania, but also in the transition countries of Central and Eastern Europe where the new market economy is mostly non-union. Union retrenchment is also the general trend in Central and Latin America (with the notable exception of Chile after its return to democracy). In Asia the picture is more divergent, ranging from strong increases in union density in Hong Kong to dramatic membership losses in Thailand and

India, but the sheer size of the continent and the profound differences between its various parts and countries defy meaningful generalizations. The same is true for the Middle East and Africa, but despite serious data problems it becomes clear that we observe in Africa the world's lowest unionization rates. For a smaller group of countries, Visser is able to present data on the composition of unionization by sector, gender, and working hours. Among other things, this material indicates that women and part-time workers are often underrepresented in unions. Finally, he shows that although the percentage of workers covered by collective agreements can exceed the proportion unionized, union coverage no less than union density exhibits decline in many countries.

Returning to advanced industrialized economies, perhaps no other country in recent years has witnessed greater change in its industrial relations framework than the UK. In their wide-ranging chapter, *John Addison* and *Stanley Siebert* describe the dramatic developments and their consequences. Like Gaul, their treatment is in three parts. The first part charts the six major pieces of legislation – conventionally described as 'anti-union' – that were enacted by successive Conservative administrations between 1980 and 1993, and links them to the subsequent decline in unionism and to changes in firm performance and that of the macro-economy. In addition, the consequences of union decline for the wage structure are also accorded special attention. The second part examines the accession of 'New Labour' and reviews its domestic reform agenda, today largely in place. That agenda comprises two general pieces of employment and employment relations law plus a new national minimum wage. At first (and second) blush these changes do not return Britain to the mid-1970s even if they do imply an increase in union membership and rising costs for business, other things equal. For evidence of more profound change one has to turn to the third part of the story: the social policy agenda of the European Union. Almost immediately upon taking office, New Labour signed up to the Social Chapter. This means that a slew of new legislation seeking to regulate the employment relation (mostly decided by qualified majority) is now in immediate prospect. Europe is therefore set to impact the theory and practice of British industrial relations. The authors provide chapter and verse on the actual and prospective legislation.

The Europeanization of British industrial relations is one thing, the emergence of European-wide collective bargaining potentially quite another. The latter issue is the subject of Chapter 13, in which *Dieter Sadowski, Oliver Ludewig*, and *Florian Turk* argue that pan-European bargaining is at best a long way off for reasons that reflect the choices of the parties. At one level, Europeanization can be indexed by the social policy initiatives of the European Union (EU), and in particular those stemming from the uprated 'social dialogue' between the two sides of industry at European (and sectoral) level in the wake of the Maastricht Treaty. The authors characterize this process as 'Commission-driven'. The other type of Europeanization identified is 'spontaneous' initiatives: instances of cross-border collective bargaining and networks of the institutions formed by metalworker unions. These developments in turn helped form the peak organizations of labour and capital, or social partners (chief among which are UNICE/CEEP on the employer side and the ETUC on the labour side).

To establish their point that Europeanization is at this stage a fragile creature, Sadowski, Ludewig, and Turk offer the notion of an optimal bargaining area as informed by the economic theory of clubs. The goal is to determine (a) whether the actors have an interest in the Europeanization of collective bargaining, (b) the type of Europeanization that will be preferred, and (c) the topological features of the collective bargaining system that will evolve. There follows a detailed discussion of the positioning of the respective social partners and of government institutions. The conclusion of the chapter is that there is and will be an increasing European dimension of collective bargaining, but that this process does not require a 'standardization of collective bargaining and the transnational unification of social actors'. Rather, we should expect to see a centralization of information sharing, within-company bargaining in European multinationals, some wage coordination, and instances of cross-border bargaining accentuated by the eastern enlargement of the EU.

In the final chapter of this volume, *John Delaney* reviews current and likely developments in industrial relations in the United States. The picture that he paints is less than reassuring for the union movement of the world's largest economy. But could it be otherwise given the magnitude of the union wage premium (see Chapter 7), the seeming adverse effect of US unions on firm performance (see Chapters 5 and 9), and the critical mass problem associated with the long-standing decline in unionism (see Chapter 7 and also Chapters 2 and 3). The figures bear repeating: as of 2001, union density in the USA was just 13.5 per cent – 9 per cent in the private sector and 37.4 per cent in the public sector. Delaney charts the by now familiar problem of unions not being able to organize sufficient new members to offset natural attrition. In doing so, he accepts that there is no great clamour for organization from those workers that have most to gain from unionization. Is the solution for unions increased engagement of the polity? Possibly, we are told, but campaign finance reform may block this avenue. Thus far at least the exertion of political power has been used to stop changes in the law hostile to union interests, but has proved inadequate to change the law in favour of unions. The stillborn recommendations of the Dunlop Commission (1994a, 1994b) are eloquent testimony of this. In common with other observers, Delaney sees the National Labor Relations Act (NLRA) as something of a problem for the union movement. (The reasons are technical and include ineffective penalties for unfair labour practices on the part of employers, and section 8 (a) 2 of the NLRA which may remove swathes of employees from its protection.) But, reflecting his recognition of the role of market forces, Delaney does not really argue that American labour law has failed. Rather, he argues that the NLRA is becoming increasingly irrelevant to employees with the change in the nature of work and as many jobs gain supervisory and managerial duties. Unions have to address this challenge by organizing *outside of* the NLRA and by offering a different product. He is evidently thinking of a cooperative unionism, a closer partnership between management and labour, very much on the lines discussed by David Metcalf in Chapter 5.

This, then, is our product. Necessarily, it is incomplete. Space constraints have resulted in the exclusion of some countries and regions that would otherwise undoubtedly merit consideration. The most obvious omission is Japan (see the recent analysis of Tachibanaki and Noda, 2000). Note, however, that data limitations also explain the omission of nations from the country samples examined in this volume. Our response here has been to ask some contributors to state the problem and yet others to provide as much international data as possible on, say, the wage gap or density so as to provide either a resource base or a research stimulus. The effect of incomplete coverage is of course that our generalizations about the behaviour and effect of trade unions must be guarded. And even within the samples investigated here a number of caveats are required. At one level, the progression from theory to evidence is sometimes opaque, meaning that even an agreed set of findings can be consistent with very different positions. At another level, and in addition to standard problems of statistical inference – stemming in particular from the non-random distribution of union presence and lack of information on variables associated with the particular outcome indicator that are also correlated with the union measure – a certain imprecision attaches to some of the union effects charted in this Handbook. We see union effects on innovation as a notable case in point. That said, and as the chapters in this volume will make clear, theoretical work on unions is advancing, the gap between theory and measurement is closing, and the empirics are often state of the art. But note the irony: Johnson (1975), writing during the golden age of unionism, complained about the lack of union studies. Today, at a time when unionization has reached an all-time low, economists and other social scientists can claim a much better understanding of the institution.

Finally, some acknowledgments are in order. First and foremost, we are indebted to the contributors to this volume for their sustained efforts and for the tonic of some stimulating discussions. We wish also to thank Lena Koller for her invaluable technical assistance in preparing this Handbook. Last but not least we are indebted to Luke Adams at Edward Elgar who encouraged us to pursue this project.

References

Booth, Alison L. (1995), *The Economics of the Trade Union*, Cambridge: Cambridge University Press.

Dunlop Commission (1994a), *Fact-Finding Report of the Commission on the Future of Worker-Management Relations*, Washington, DC: US Department of Labor, US Department of Commerce, May.

Dunlop Commission (1994b), *Report and Recommendations of the Commission on the Future of Worker–Management Relations*, Washington, DC: US Department of Labor, US Department of Commerce, December.

Farber, Henry S. (1986), 'The Analysis of Union Behavior', in Orley Ashenfelter and Richard Layard (eds), *Handbook of Labor Economics*, Volume 2, Amsterdam: North Holland, pp. 1039–1089.

Freeman, Richard B. and James L. Medoff (1984), *What Do Unions Do?*, New York: Basic Books.

Hirsch, Barry T. and John T. Addison (1986), *The Economic Analysis of Unions*, Boston, MA.: Allen and Unwin.

Johnson, George E. (1975), 'Economic Analysis of Trade Unionism', *American Economic Review, Papers and Proceedings*, 65 (2), 23–29.

Oswald, Andrew J. (1985), 'The Economic Theory of Trade Unions: An Introductory Survey', *Scandinavian Journal of Economics*, 87 (2), 160–193.

Pencavel, John H. (1991), *Labour Markets under Trade Unionism*, Oxford: Basil Blackwell.

Tachibanaki, Toshiaki and Tomohiko Noda (2000), *The Economic Effects of Trade Unions in Japan*, New York: St. Martin's Press, London: Macmillan.

2   Determinants of trade union membership
Claus Schnabel

1. Introduction

Recent economic, sociological and political science literature contains an upsurge of theoretical and empirical work on trade union membership. Interestingly, renewed interest in the area comes at a time when in many countries, unions experience severe membership losses (see the data provided by Ebbinghaus and Visser, 2000 and by Visser in Chapter 11 of this volume). As the existence and the political and economic influence of trade unions depend on their ability to attract and nurture a loyal membership, it is important to know which workers join unions and why.

This survey starts to answer this question by sketching (in section 2) the conventional demand and supply framework used by economists to analyse the forces that influence union membership. Section 3 deals with the free-rider problem, namely why any individual would join a union when dues are costly and when the benefits apply to all workers regardless of their union status. It points to the existence of social customs and reviews corresponding theoretical models. While in general economic explanations of union membership determination are emphasized, supplementary explanations from other social sciences are discussed in section 4.

This review of the theoretical literature is followed by an overview of empirical results from time-series and cross-sectional analyses. Section 5 focuses on time-series business cycle models and attempts to identify the macro-determinants of union growth and decline. Section 6 deals with the micro-determinants of individuals' membership decision and discusses cross-sectional studies that try to provide structural explanations of unionization. Institutional determinants of unionization are investigated in section 7 by reviewing the empirical results of recent cross-national analyses. Some conclusions and directions of further research are provided in section 8.

2. The demand for and supply of unionism

Traditionally, labour economists have analysed the forces that influence union membership within a conventional demand and supply framework.[1] Beginning with Berkowitz (1954) and Pencavel (1971), union membership is considered as though it were an asset in the portfolio of an utility-maximizing worker that provides a flow of services, which are private and/or collective goods. The demand function expresses the demand of workers for union representation and services, while the supply function reflects the supply of union services.

Following standard theory, demand for union membership (U^d) can be specified as:

$$U^d = d(p, y, wdiff, z, s, t).$$

In this specification, the price p represents the costs of union membership (initiation fees and dues) relative to the price of other goods and assets, and it affects demand negatively. Wealth or permanent income y should influence union membership positively if union services are a normal good. The larger the (expected) union–non-union wage differential $wdiff$, the more likely are employees to join a union. However, since the relative wage differential cannot in general be measured directly, studies often examine the relationship of unionism with personal and industry characteristics (such as age, skills and industry concentration), which serve as proxies for the expected benefits of union representation. In addition to wage gains, net non-pecuniary benefits z from a unionized work environment such as better working conditions and grievance procedures (proxied by firm size, accident risk, etc.) can also be expected to stimulate demand for union representation. In contrast, the lower the cost of substitute services s (such as social welfare benefits), the lower demand for union services should be. Finally, individuals taste for unionism t can affect the demand for union membership. This variable is meant to reflect workers' attitudes and preferences, ideological motives, social pressure and custom, and related non-economic variables stressed by other disciplines of social science.

Although unions may not be typical profit maximizers, they face a binding budget constraint in that they must fund union organizing, services and the like, which means that they must pay attention to revenues and (opportunity) costs. Therefore the supply function of union services (U^s) can be expressed by:

$$U^s = e(p, co, cs, g).$$

Here, the revenue or price p of union services is assumed to have some positive relationship with the supply of these services whereas the costs of union organizing co and the costs of servicing existing members cs both affect supply negatively. Organizing costs involve a significant fixed-cost component and exhibit economies of scale, and they depend, *inter alia*, on industry concentration and firm size. Servicing costs are also likely to have a fixed-cost component so that collective bargaining exhibits decreasing unit costs with respect to membership, and unionism is therefore less likely in small firms. Both the costs of organizing and of servicing will be affected by employers' attitudes toward unions and collective bargaining, and they can be influenced substantially by the legal structure within which unions may operate. The last variable in the supply function stands for union goals *g* (such as maximizing membership or a certain utility function) which may affect the supply of union services in various ways.

Assuming market clearing,[2] the equilibrium level of unionism *U* is determined by:

$$U = U^d = U^s.$$

In a reduced form, *U* and *p* are functions of all other variables within the system, so that the unionism equation is given by:

$$U = f(y, wdiff, z, s, t, co, cs, g).$$

Because none of these determinants of unionism enter both the structural demand and supply equations, the sign on each in the reduced-form equation is unambiguous. Since most of these variables cannot be measured directly, however, they are often substituted for by proxy variables (such as firm size and personal characteristics) that are likely to affect unionism through more than one channel, making interpretation difficult. An advantage of this approach is that the price variable (for which data are often lacking) falls out of the model, and so empirical studies generally estimate some variant of this reduced-form equation. A difficulty with this approach is, however, that it ignores general equilibrium aspects, for instance that the benefits of union membership such as the union–non-union wage differential will not be independent of the extent of unionization.

In addition to measurement problems in the right-hand side variables of the reduced-form equation, the amount of union services *U* is also not directly observed. Assuming that the level of services is proportional to the level of unionization, direct measures of union membership, union density or bargaining coverage can be used to proxy *U*. The appropriateness of each union measure depends on the econometric design of the (cross-sectional or time-series) study, the data available and the legal framework.

3. The free-rider problem and social customs

The cost–benefit analysis of union membership determination sketched above does not take into account an important problem unions face in most countries, namely the free-rider problem. Many of the services unions provide – such as higher wages and better working conditions – accrue both to union members and non-members in the workplace. These services can be seen as public or collective goods since they are non-rival in consumption and low-cost exclusion of non-members is not possible. Hence an individual has a free-rider incentive not to join the union. The key problem for the economist is to explain why any individual would join a union when dues are costly and when the benefits apply to all workers regardless of their union status (see also Chapter 3 by Naylor in this volume).[3]

While in small groups the free-rider problem may not be insurmountable, the difficulty is to explain why large groups providing collective goods such as trade unions manage to exist despite the free-rider problem. In his path-breaking analysis of collective action, Olson (1965) argued that a large group can only have formed for two reasons: Either because membership is compulsory (this would be the case of the 'closed shop' in which union membership is a condition of employment) or because the group offers selective incentives in the form of private goods and services available only to its members (with ancillary provision of the collective good as a 'byproduct').[4] In many countries, however, closed shops are either illegal or are rarely found anymore, and the widespread presence of 'open-shop' unions (where membership is voluntary) suggests that selective incentives such as strike pay and legal support available to members may seem to be more important for joining a union.

In addition to such material selective incentives, Booth (1985) has suggested to interpret the incentive private good as being the 'reputation' utility that derives from complying with a social custom of union membership. This idea stems from Akerlof (1980, p. 749) who defines a social custom as 'an act whose utility to the agent performing it in some way depends on the beliefs or actions of other members of the community'. This takes up an argument commonly put forward by sociologists and psychologists, namely that within a community there is a set of rules and customs that are obeyed by individuals because of the sanction of a loss of reputation if the custom should be disobeyed. In the context of union membership, the social custom can be thought of as urging workers not to free-ride. Following social custom theory, Booth (1985) and Naylor (1990) have proposed models in which it is assumed that workers directly derive utility from the reputation effect of belonging to a union (and not being a 'scab'), and which show that a union can exist despite the free-rider problem if it achieves a minimum critical density. In the social custom approach, the decision to join is interdependent and – contrary to the Olson (1965) free-rider paradox – workers may be more prepared to join a union if others are joining.[5]

Within this framework, Naylor and Cripps (1993) have shown that when

workers' tastes are heterogeneous with respect to their sensitivity to reputation, stable intermediate union density is a possible equilibrium outcome.
This is an improvement of the original Booth (1985) model with homogeneous tastes where the only stable non-zero level of union density occurs
when everyone joins the union. They provide an explanation of voluntary
membership of the open-shop trade union in which the union density level
is likely to increase as a result of a reduction in union membership costs, an
increase in strike pay or an increase in individuals' sensitivity to the social
custom of union membership and the associated solidarity effects.
Extensions of the social custom model taking into account employer
behaviour in the form of management opposition to union membership
have been proposed by Naylor and Raaum (1993) and – in a game-theoretic
setting – by Corneo (1995). They show that a stable long-run equilibrium
may exist, in which strong unions persist in spite of management opposition.

In the social custom framework, Booth and Chatterji (1993) provide a
model of union membership and wage determination which predicts that
the open shop union is viable only after membership has achieved a
minimum critical density, and wages are at a sufficient level to support this.
Wage setting is modelled using the median voter framework of social
choice theory which implies that union executives will maximize the
expected utility of the median voter in order to be re-elected, and heterogeneous workers join the union if their expected utility from so doing
exceeds that from abstaining (for a given level of union-determined wages).
The model generates a simultaneous equation system: membership at the
margin is a function of the union set wage and other variables, and union
wages are a function of median membership.[6] The insight that wages and
membership are determined simultaneously, which already can be found in
related closed-shop models such as Grossman (1983), does not, however,
depend on the median voter assumption. Naylor and Raaum (1993), for
instance, do not appeal to any social choice framework like the median
voter model when simultaneously modelling wages and membership determination.

One problem of social custom models is that they leave unexplained the
formation of the social custom.[7] This is circumvented by another strand of
literature that combines a similar formal approach with the hypothesis that
unions provide pure private goods to their members instead of reputation.
Booth and Chatterji (1995) develop a theoretical model of the simultaneous determination of union wages and membership which points to the
existence of excludable private goods as an important factor motivating
workers to join unions in the absence of coercive closed-shop rules.[8] They
estimate the model for manual workers in Britain and find empirical

support for the notion that union-provided goods such as grievance procedures, influence over manning arrangements and negotiations over physical conditions are positively correlated with union density. Their results suggest that unions concerned with density will have to rely on devising excludable private goods to attract members since increasing wages alone will not increase density. In contrast, Moreton (1998, 1999) makes use of the (empirically supported) assumption that union members enjoy greater job security than do non-members in the form of a reduced probability of dismissal for reasons other than redundancy. Thus the private good of increased job security acts as a selective incentive to join the union. Less effective job protection by unions and lower union bargaining power are predicted to reduce union density.[9]

One corollary of most of the models discussed above is that a reduction in union membership caused by temporary shocks is likely to be persistent (Calmfors et al., 2001, p. 18). If membership is reduced, the process of rebuilding can be lengthy and even unsustainable since there exists a minimum critical mass of membership or density below which union existence is not viable. In the absence of coercion the open-shop union's provision of services may be crucial in obtaining its critical level of density. Union density is likely to increase with the quality of the services provided, while at the same time the size and density of the union may positively affect the provision of services due to economies of scale. If, however, union-like services are available elsewhere at lower cost or if the provision of certain welfare benefits by government substitutes for the private provision by unions (as stressed by Streeck, 1981 and Neumann and Rissman, 1984), the attractiveness of union membership will be reduced and unions may face serious problems of survival.

4.   Supplementary explanations from the social sciences

While in this survey, emphasis is laid on economic explanations of union membership determination, it should not be overlooked that social, psychological and political factors may also contribute to explaining the level and development of union membership. Sociologists and political scientists have long stressed the importance for union density of factors such as class consciousness, values, modes of production, the composition of the workforce, the political climate, the role of government incomes policies, and the centralization and cohesiveness of the labour movement (see, for instance, Beyme, 1981 and Streeck, 1981). Some of these potential determinants have been incorporated in economic models of unionization. While a full description of all contributions from the social sciences is clearly beyond the scope of this survey, several theories explaining individual behaviour will be sketched below without the pretension of exhaustiveness.[10]

Following Klandermans (1986), three theoretical and partly overlapping approaches to trade union participation can be distinguished within the social psychology, namely the frustration–aggression approach, the rational-choice approach and the interactionist approach (see also Berg, 1995, p. 155ff.). The *frustration–aggression approach* explains union membership as a result of individuals' frustration, dissatisfaction or alienation in their work situation (and membership resignation in terms of frustration with union policies). However, dissatisfaction 'is neither a necessary nor a sufficient condition for participation' (Klandermans, 1986, p. 199). Furthermore, from an economic point of view, this sort of joining and quitting behaviour could be interpreted as reflecting cost–benefit considerations and may be incorporated in standard explanations of the demand for unions.

The *rational-choice approach* interprets unionization as the outcome of a process of weighing the costs and benefits of participation (a prominent example is Crouch, 1982). Of course, such an approach also underlies economic theories of unionization, but economists often pay attention only to individual, selective costs and benefits. In contrast, social scientists try to take a broader view and point out that the decision to join a union can also be influenced by collective, social and ideological motives, which may be difficult to measure. The balance of costs and benefits, combined with expectations about the degree to which the union will be able to realize these motives, determine the actual membership decision.

In the *interactionist approach* union participation is inextricably bound up with group culture, and an individual's decision to join a union is strongly influenced by his social context, that is his living and working environment. Concerning the living environment, tradition and prevailing opinions within someone's group are important because here general beliefs are formed about unions even before the employment relationship is entered into. Starting with Booth (1985) this line of reasoning has been incorporated into the social custom models of union membership discussed in the previous chapter which in some sense blend interactionist and rational-choice explanations. Concerning the working environment, the prevailing union density in an individual's establishment or industry and the contact with the union at the workplace may play a role. While this is also recognized in some economic explanations of union membership and growth, economists have tended to concentrate on the demand side of unionism and have paid less attention to the supply side, for example the union's decision to allocate resources to the recruitment of new members.[11]

It is obvious that social scientists provide other explanations or emphasize different determinants of unionization than economists. Some of these factors can be incorporated in the economist's supply–demand and cost–benefit framework discussed above whereas others are more difficult to operationalize. It can be concluded that theories from other disciplines of the social sciences should not be neglected when analysing unionization, and the next chapters will show that many socio-political determinants have been included in empirical studies of union membership and union growth.

5.   Macro-determinants of union growth and decline: empirical results of aggregate time-series analyses

The preceding sections have identified a large number of economic, social and political variables that according to theoretical considerations can be expected to influence individuals' decisions to unionize and affect union membership growth. Empirical analyses, however, in many cases have not directly followed the lines of theoretical research. This divergence is partly due to the fact that the progress of the theoretical literature as to why employees belong to a union has been slow, and often empirical findings preceded or prompted theoretical research. In addition it reflects an eclectic approach of many empirical studies that mix economic, social and political variables. By and large, empirical analyses of union membership and growth fall within one of three approaches:[12] They either stress cyclical explanations and attempt to identify the macro-determinants of union growth and decline, or they provide structural explanations and concentrate on individual characteristics of union members as well as on sectoral and occupational factors, or they favour institutional explanations and analyse cross-national variations in institutional settings assumed to influence unionization.

Historians and labour economists have invented (and traditionally have followed) the cyclical approach which focuses on the macro-determinants of union growth and decline. This approach can be traced back at least to Commons et al. (1918) who analysed the history of the US labour movement in the nineteenth century and tried to link membership changes to the stages of the business cycle. Over the course of the twentieth century, numerous models have been developed (and estimated) that explain union growth in terms of such components of the business cycle as wage and price changes, employment growth and unemployment, and that often also include socio-political variables. Table 2.1 provides a synopsis of selected empirical time-series studies for the USA, the UK, Germany, Australia and the Netherlands, all countries for which there exists an impressive empirical literature on unionization.[13]

An early study by Ashenfelter and Pencavel (1969), examining trade union growth between 1904 and 1960, has received considerable attention and has served as the basis for much subsequent analysis.[14] The authors specify and estimate a model with the annual percentage change in trade union membership as the dependent variable and five explanatory variables that all prove to be statistically significant. Two variables that are meant to capture the movement of the relative benefits and costs of union membership to individual workers over time are the percentage change in the consumer price index and the percentage change in employment in highly unionized sectors during the current and three previous years. The positive relationship found between union growth and price inflation is interpreted as reflecting the demand for union membership as a means for catching up with previous inflation and maintaining real wages, whereas the positive impact of employment growth is said to reflect higher union organizing funds and activity as well as reduced employer retaliation efforts in tighter labour markets. Since 'it seems clear that one important determinant of union growth must be workers discontent', Ashenfelter and Pencavel (1969, p. 437) also include the unemployment rate at the pit of the preceding recession as an indicator of labour's stock of grievances, whose (positive) influence is allowed to decay with time. The level of previous union density (that is union membership as a percentage of unionizable employment) is included in the model to test (and finally confirm) the saturationist hypothesis that (p. 438) 'the greater the proportion of employment in the union sectors that is already unionized the more difficult it is further to increase union membership'. The final explanatory variable in the Ashenfelter and Pencavel (1969) model is the percentage of Democrats in the US House of Representatives, which is interpreted as a proxy for the degree of pro-labour sentiment and which is found to affect union growth positively.

The Ashenfelter and Pencavel (1969) model could be judged successful by conventional statistical criteria, fitting the data for 1904 to 1960 well and thus encouraging Sharpe (1971) to develop a similar model for Australia. Despite its good results, however, the model has not gone uncontested. Criticism has focused on the model's temporal instability, its poor predictive power and the ad hoc use and justification of explanatory variables.[15]

Among the critics were Bain and Elsheikh (1976) who proposed an alternative model in which union membership growth is a function of wage and price inflation, the level (and/or rate of change) of unemployment and the level of union density in the previous period. The authors assume that a 'threat effect' may encourage workers to unionize when prices are rising in order to defend their standard of living whereas a 'credit effect' may lead workers to unionize when money wages are rising if they (rightly or wrongly) credit such rises to unions and hope that by supporting them they will do even better in the future. Unemployment is said to affect union growth negatively by influencing the relative bargaining power of employers and unions and by affecting the propensity to become or remain a union member in various ways. The prevailing level of union density is included

Table 2.1   Selected time-series studies of trade union growth (dependent variable is membership growth except for Booth (1983) where it is union density)

Authors and sample	Price inflation	Nominal wage growth	Employment growth	Unemployment Rate	Unemployment Change	Lagged density	Politics (labour friendly)	Labour force composition	Additional variables
				Significant (insignificant) influence of key explanatory variables					
Ashenfelter/Pencavel (1969) USA 1904–60	+		+			–	+		Unemployment at the pit of the last recession: +
Bain/Elsheikh (1976) USA 1897–1970	+	+			–	–			Dummy for government actions 1937–47:+
Stepina/Fiorito (1986) USA 1911–82	(+)	+		(+)		–	(–)	–	Dummies for special periods; business failures
Bain/Elsheikh (1976) UK 1893–1970	+	+		(–/+)		–			Dummy for price rises >4%: –
Booth (1983) UK 1895–1980	(+)	+	+	(–/+)		+			
Carruth/Disney (1988) UK 1896–1984	+	–			–	(–)	(+)		
Armingeon (1989) Germany 1951–87		+	+				+		
Schnabel (1989a) Germany 1955–86	(+)	+	+	(–/+)				–	

22

Study					Other explanatory variables
Carruth/Schnabel (1990) Germany 1956–86	+	+	+	–	Dummy for labour legislation: +
Sharpe (1971) Australia 1907–69	Real wage growth	+	–	–	Dummy for labour legislation: +
Bain/Elsheikh (1976) Australia 1907–69	(+)	+	–	–	Dummy for labour legislation: +
Borland/Ouliaris (1994) Australia 1913–89	Real wage growth	+/–	–	–	Lagged membership growth: +
Van Ours (1992) Netherlands 1961–89			–	(–)	Change in labour income ratio: +
Berg (1995) Netherlands 1948–86		+	–	–	Number of strikes: + Social benefits rate: –

Note: +/– indicate that an explanatory variable exhibits a positive/negative influence on the dependent variable that is statistically significant at the 5 per cent level; insignificant results are put in parentheses.

23

to capture the conflicting 'saturation effect' (the greater difficulty of further increasing membership as density rises) and 'enforcement effect' (social coercion and the ability of unions to persuade employees to unionize, both of which increase with union density). Bain and Elsheikh (1976) estimate different specifications of this model for the UK, Sweden and (augmented by legislative dummy variables) for the USA and Australia. In most cases their explanatory variables are statistically significant and the model is able to explain union growth over long periods of time. However, the authors have had to face much the same criticisms as Ashenfelter and Pencavel (1969) concerning the selection and justification of their explanatory variables, their empirical specifications, and the structural stability and predictive power of their models.[16]

Similar cyclical models have been estimated for a variety of countries and different periods. Although the magnitude and the statistical significance (and in some cases even the sign) of estimated coefficients differ, the results show some consistent patterns indicating that union growth is procyclical.[17] From Table 2.1 it appears that employment growth and a favourable political climate enhance union growth. The same can be said for price inflation and nominal wage growth, although these variables do not show up in the estimations for the Netherlands: Here, however, van Ours (1992) detects a positive influence of the change in the labour income ratio.[18] In most empirical models unemployment tends to inhibit union growth, but it is not clear whether it is the level or the rate of change of unemployment that plays a role. A more robust result is that (with the exception of Germany) the prevailing level of union density dampens membership growth, probably reflecting a saturation effect.

Against the theoretical background sketched above, Ashenfelter and Pencavel (1969), as well as others, have interpreted these results of cyclical models mainly in terms of individuals' decisions reflecting the expected benefits and costs of union membership. This is problematic because the available explanatory variables are hardly able to measure expected benefits and costs directly.[19] Furthermore, in interpreting union growth as the aggregate of individual worker decisions, the role of employer opposition and union leadership and recruitment strategies (stressed by Visser, 1990) may be underrated.

In contrast, Bain and Elsheikh (1976, p. 62) have moved away from the traditional supply–demand framework by interpreting changes in union membership as resulting from changes in both the propensity and the opportunity to unionize, but their economic reasoning behind some key explanatory variables is questionable. For example, if prices and money wages increase at the same rate and thus real wages do not change, both a threat and a credit effect are said to enhance union growth in their model.

This is difficult to reconcile with standard economic theory (and with the absence of money illusion). If union services are a normal good, only a rise in real wages should increase demand. Interestingly, the separate effects of price and money wage inflation on union membership growth are often confirmed by the data,[20] but the absence of a good understanding of the reasons for the relationships should make us wary of placing undue emphasis on them. This is particularly true if wages and union membership are determined simultaneously (as predicted by the microeconomic models in section 3) and if there exists a simultaneous relationship between price and wage inflation and union membership growth (as proposed by the older wage-push theory of inflation).[21]

Concerning other theoretical approaches to unionization, cyclical models of union growth and decline tend to neglect the free-rider problem. Moreover, they can only provide indirect evidence on social custom explanations, by not supporting the hypothesis of a positive enforcement effect of the prevailing level of union density. Sociopolitical variables such as changes in the context of industrial relations and labour legislation are mainly taken into account in time-series models by using dummy variables or indicators of parliamentary representation, and the real impact of these factors is difficult to identify and to interpret.[22] The same can be said for the substitution hypothesis that the provision of certain welfare benefits by government substitutes at least partially for the private provision by unions, which has been tested in time-series models for the US (confirmed by Neumann and Rissman, 1984, and rejected by Stepina and Fiorito, 1986) and for West Germany (rejected by Schnabel, 1989a, 1989b).

A serious flaw of the traditional business cycle approach to union growth is the failure to separate cycle and trend. Cyclical models mainly try to explain the ups and downs of trade union membership by corresponding movements in business cycle variables whereas shifts in underlying, or secular, variables which might explain the trend in union membership are neglected. Although shifts in the occupational composition of the labour force have been included in some business cycle models (see, for example, Stepina and Fiorito, 1986, Schnabel, 1989a, 1989b), Carruth and Disney (1988) were the first to develop a time-series model which explicitly distinguishes between cyclical (short-run) and trend (long-run) factors of unionization. Their empirical model for the UK utilizes cyclical variables in the explanation of membership changes and it employs the long-run relationship between membership and employment as an error-correction mechanism which allows the identification of a long-run solution (that is steady-state union density). Carruth and Schnabel (1990) went one step further and made use of cointegration techniques in identifying a long-run equilibrium relationship in the levels of the usual business cycle variables (supplemented by a labour force composition variable) that could serve as an error-correction mechanism in the dynamic modelling of union membership for Germany. Their empirical model is able to explain the short-run dynamics and the long-run trends in membership in a satisfactory manner and it nests neatly a pure business cycle model developed for Germany by Schnabel (1989a, 1989b). Similar empirical approaches with cointegration and error-correction techniques have been undertaken, *inter alia*, by van Ours (1992) for the Netherlands and by Borland and Ouliaris (1994) and Bodman (1998) for Australia.

These sorts of time-series models based on newly developed econometric methods can be seen as an improvement on simple business cycle models because they are able to separate the cyclical short-run dynamics and the long-run secular trends affecting union membership (which might also improve the predictive power of time-series models). In doing so, they can take account of structural developments in the economy such as changes in the composition of the labour force towards women, services, etc., which are said to inhibit union growth. Even these new time-series models, however, face at least two limitations. First, aggregation problems cannot be ruled out.[23] Second, the models cannot explain within-country differences in union density and cross-country differences in the level and development of union membership and density. Here structural and institutional explanations using cross-sectional analyses occupy centre stage.

6.   Micro-determinants of union membership: empirical results of individual-level cross-sectional analyses

In addition to time-series studies, empirical research as to why individuals belong to a union has made use of cross-sectional studies that seek to explain differences in unionization across units at a point in time rather than variations over time.[24] Most of these studies tend to provide structural explanations of unionization and concentrate on individual characteristics of union members as well as on sectoral and occupational factors. Determinants of unionization are thus analysed by comparing the characteristics of union and non-union employees or firms, but with few exceptions (see Rij and Daalder, 1997; Waddington and Whitston, 1997; Visser, 2002), the process of joining a union itself is not the object of these studies.

The huge volume of cross-sectional studies of unionization can be differentiated in two dimensions, namely the unit of analysis and the dependent variable used. Starting with the former, for some countries there exist cross-sectional studies based on aggregate data for different states, regions, industries, election units, and so on. Other studies analyse unionization at the firm or establishment level.[25] The majority of cross-sectional analyses, however, focus on individual-level data of union and non-union employees.

This approach will also be pursued in the following review of the cross-sectional literature which attempts to identify major individual determinants of unionization.

The empirical studies selected for further analysis use trade union membership as the dependent variable. In the USA, however, many studies use employees' voting behaviour in NLRB elections as the dependent variable.[26] This reflects important differences between the unionization decision in the USA and in most other countries (stressed by Wheeler and McClendon, 1991). Whereas in many countries, unionization simply involves joining an existing organization which may or may not have representation rights, the decision of American workers to vote for a union also involves instituting a regime of collective bargaining, a union contract, a grievance and arbitration procedure, and so on. These differences should be kept in mind when making international comparisons, even if the empirical evidence for the USA in Table 2.2 is based on studies that use union membership as their dependent variable.

Table 2.2 provides a synopsis of individual-level cross-sectional studies of union membership. As in Table 2.1 the countries selected are the USA, the UK, Germany, Australia and the Netherlands.[27] The design and the analysis of these studies differ depending on their economic or social science motivation and the data available. Traditionally, economists have tended to interpret estimations of this sort as reduced-form membership equations deriving from the supply–demand framework and the cost–benefit considerations presented in section 2, but in recent years social custom interpretations have also been given attention. Due to space limitations only key explanatory variables are shown in Table 2.2, and similar variables are grouped together even if their definitions may not be exactly identical across studies. Although Table 2.2 reveals substantial differences in sample sizes used, variables tested and significance levels found, the results show some consistent patterns.

In most cross-sectional studies union membership has been found to be systematically related to a number of *personal characteristics* such as age, sex, race and education.[28] As Table 2.2 shows, the stylized fact of a greater propensity of males (m) to be union members is confirmed across countries. It has traditionally been interpreted as a reflection of men's greater degree of attachment to the labour force which would increase the benefits of unionization both from the point of view of workers and of unions. Research results on the relationship between age or, more appropriately, years of work experience and membership are somewhat mixed, with many estimated coefficients not being statistically significant, but in general this relationship tends to be positive or concave (increasing at a decreasing rate and possibly falling at the end). While the older US literature points to a

Table 2.2 *Selected individual-level cross-sectional studies of union membership*

Authors and sample	Significant (insignificant) influence of key explanatory variables										
	Sex	Age/work experience	Race/ nationality	Education	White collar	Part-time	Public sector	Establish-ment size	Earnings	Left-wing views	Additional variables
Scoville (1971) USA 1966; 1535 individuals	f(−)	+	negro +	(−)					+		Industry and regional dummies
Schmidt/Strauss (1976) USA 1967; 912 full-time workers	m+	(−)	white (−)	−					+		Regional dummies
Antos et al. (1980) USA 1976; 38132 blue-collar workers	f−	+	nonwhite +	−	−		+			+	SMSA: +; occupational and industry dummies
Bain/Elias (1985) UK 1975/76; 30281 individuals	m+	+/−		−	−	−		+	+/−		Union density in industry: +; regional dummies
Ingham (1995) UK 1992; 627 individuals		(−)	British (+)	(+)		−					Relatives are unionized: +; Perceived union density: +
Goerke/Pannenberg (1998) UK 1991; 517 workers		(−)	nonwhite (+)	−	−			(+)	+		Partner prefers Labour: +
Germany 1993; 1304 individuals		(−)	foreigner (+)	(−)	−			+	(+)		Partner union member: +

Study								Other variables
Windolf/Haas (1989) Germany 1980; 2510 workers	f(−)	(+)		−	−	−	+	Father is manual worker: (+); single: −; trust in union: +
Lorenz/Wagner (1991) Germany 1985; 2454 full-time workers	f−	(+)	foreigner (+)	−	−	−	+ −	Job satisfaction: (−)
Fitzenberger et al. (1999) Germany 1985/89/93; 2403 workers	f(−)	+	foreigner (−)	(−)	−	(+)	(+/−)	Married (−); industry dummies
Deery/De Cieri (1991) Australia 1987; 862 workers	m(+)	(+)		(−)	−	−	+	Spouse in union: +; negative union image: −
Christie (1992) Australia 1984; 1316 employees	f−	+		(+)	−	+		Occupational and state dummies
Berg/Groot (1992) Netherlands 1988; 2589 indiv.	m+	+/−	foreigner (−)	+	+	+	+/−	Temporary job: −; wage satisfaction: −
Netherlands 1987; 5266 workers	m+	+/−		+	+	−		Roman Catholic: −; no. of children: −

Note: +/− indicate that an explanatory variable exhibits a positive/negative influence on the dependent variable that is statistically significant at the 5 per cent level; insignificant results are put in parentheses.

higher unionization of non-whites reflecting unions' protection and egalitarian policies, international results for race and nationality are quite mixed and often insignificant (and relationships may have changed anyway over time due to tendencies of anti-discrimination and assimilation). Education is usually assumed to be negatively associated with unionism because more educated employees have greater individual bargaining power (and thus a lesser need for collective voice) and because sometimes they identify more with management than with the labour movement. As Table 2.2 indicates, in the majority of studies selected such a negative relationship shows up, but some of these results are insignificant (and in the Netherlands even a positive relationship is found).

Occupational, industrial and firm characteristics have been included with some success in most studies, indicating that the workplace context plays an important role in unionization. Not only in the selection made in Table 2.2, white-collar workers (or, more general, non-operative occupations) are usually found to be less likely to be union members than blue-collar or manual workers. This is traditionally explained by the latter having more homogeneous preferences and working conditions which make them easier to organize. Part-time workers are also less likely to be members of a union, which may reflect their lower labour force attachment. Part-time jobs are still mostly female jobs that have traditionally been considered by unions as sub-standard and not worthwhile organizing. Part-timers may also have a lower sense of shared interests with full-time colleagues at the workplace and may not expect to be in this form of employment for a long time, suggesting that they are less willing and more difficult to organize.

In contrast, union recruitment tends to be easier and less costly in large, homogeneous organizations with a bureaucratic nature and a low turnover rate, which may explain why across countries unionization is higher in the public sector than in the market sector (see the data by Visser in Chapter 11 of this volume). Similarly, the positive impact of establishment size found in most studies may reflect lower organizing costs for unions in larger units. In addition, union services may be valued most highly in large, bureaucratic organizations where workers are likely to be treated impersonally and feel a greater need for representation and protection.[29] Whether the positive effect on unionization found in both the public sector and in large establishments also reflects higher peer pressure to conform to a social custom of union membership (as suggested for large firms by Riley, 1997) can only be speculated. In addition to establishment size and workforce characteristics, strong employer resistance to unionization may also play a role at the workplace level. Although its influence is difficult to estimate empirically, there is some evidence that increased employer resistance to union representation elections in the USA (see Lawler and West, 1985; Farber, 1990) and unions' low rate of recognition in new establishments in the UK (see Disney et al., 1995; Machin, 2000) have contributed to union decline in both countries.

Cross-sectional studies that have been able to investigate the impact of various measures of *wages and earnings* on union membership either find a positive impact (which would confirm the view of unionism as a normal good) or a hill-shaped relationship: the probability of unionization first increases with earnings, and after a certain wage level it decreases again (see the graphical exposition in Lorenz and Wagner, 1991). This decrease may reflect increased employer opposition to unionization of highly-paid employees that usually occupy higher hierarchical positions in a firm. In addition, the benefits of union membership as a proportion of earnings tend to decrease as earnings rise because unions often try to reduce the dispersion of earnings, thereby favouring the workers at the bottom of the income distribution most and those at the top least (Bain and Elias, 1985). Most of these studies, however, do not control for the likely simultaneity of wage and membership determination pointed out in the theoretical literature. Notable exceptions are the simultaneous estimations by Lee (1978), Schmidt (1978) and Schmidt and Strauss (1976) for the USA and by Christie (1992) for Australia, who also deal with the union-non-union wage differential.[30] The empirical tests of the social custom model by Goerke and Pannenberg (1998) and, with firm-level data, by Booth and Chatterji (1995) also take account of this relationship. In general, the results of simultaneous analyses do not drastically alter the insights obtained from single-equation estimations of union membership.

Political and social *attitudes* of individual employees as well as their instrumentality perceptions and images of unions have been found to be significant determinants of union membership in many studies (see the survey by Riley, 1997). Employees' ideological convictions, for instance, seem to influence their unionization decision. Thus, left-wing views are associated with a higher probability of union membership (see Table 2.2). In some but not all studies, feelings of dissatisfaction with various aspects of work and pay are also found to significantly increase the probability of unionization (see Guest and Dewe, 1988; Berg and Groot, 1992). The image of the union also plays a role (cf. Deery and De Cieri, 1991), and trust in the union is associated with a higher probability of membership (cf. Windolf and Haas, 1989). Similarly, empirical evidence supports the instrumentality proposition that an employee's decision to unionize is based on his or her perception of the capacity of the union to produce the desired results (see Guest and Dewe, 1988),[31] whereas class consciousness does not seem to play an important role (cf. Deery and De Cieri, 1991). Such an instrumental view of the union role can be interpreted either in terms of social psychologists' rational choice theory or in terms of economists' cost–benefit considerations, indicating that a clear distinction between economic, social, psychological and political factors is hardly feasible and that all of these factors should be taken into account when explaining union membership.

This insight and the development of social custom models has led more and more researchers to include *social variables* into individual-level cross-sectional studies of unionization. In these studies, the influence of reference groups and key individuals such as parents and spouses on the decision maker is investigated. As can be seen from the last column in Table 2.2, a consistent finding across several countries is that if relatives or spouses are unionized, an individual is more likely to be a union member, too. Furthermore, the higher union density in the industry or perceived density in the workplace, the higher is individuals' probability of union membership. Union presence and strength at the workplace (or the existence of a works council, as found by Windolf and Haas, 1989) thus seem to be important for increasing and stabilising membership. These findings are consistent with a social custom interpretation of union membership.[32]

In general, the evidence from cross-sectional studies suggests that a wide range of personal, occupational, attitudinal and social variables play an important role in the unionization process, some of which cannot be investigated in time-series analyses. There is, however, the problem that cross-sectional analyses can only detect correlations between variables and are not able to answer questions of causality. This problem should be borne in mind when interpreting some of the significant relationships found in the empirical literature, for instance between an individual's union membership on the one hand and his left-wing views, his job satisfaction or the unionization of his spouse and relatives on the other. Furthermore, the process of joining or leaving a union and the role played by union recruitment strategies is usually not the object of individual-level studies, but it would be a promising area of further research. Despite these qualifications, there is a well-agreed-upon set of structural variables that are found to be important for explaining union membership in a firm, region or country, but it remains to be seen whether these are also able to explain international differences in unionization.

7.   Institutional determinants of unionization: Empirical results of cross-national analyses

In addition to the macro- and micro-determinants discussed above, the institutional framework in an economy and a society may also help determine the level and development of union membership or density. In principle, the costs and benefits of unionization (as well as the propensity and the opportunity to organize) can be affected by institutional variables such as union-affiliated unemployment insurance, works councils and union access to the workplace, legal protection for union organizers and union members, the centralization of collective bargaining, and the presence of left-wing governments and pro-union legislation. While some of these potential determinants (such as variations in the legislative framework) could also be investigated in the national time-series and cross-sectional studies described above, usually there is not much variation within a country in such institutions. Therefore analysing cross-national variations in institutional settings assumed to influence unionization may provide additional insights, and this approach has been favoured mainly by sociologists and political scientists (see, for example, Western, 1997; Ebbinghaus and Visser, 1999; Blaschke, 2000).

In exploiting cross-national variations in unionization, such analyses make use of three empirical approaches: They either provide cross-sectional estimations of union density across industrialized countries at a certain date (see, for example, Western, 1997; Ebbinghaus and Visser, 1999); they compare changes in union membership or density in these countries over time (Ebbinghaus and Visser, 1999; Blaschke, 2000; Visser, 2002); or they analyse a pooled time-series cross-section panel data set (Calmfors et al., 2001). In addition to institutional variables, most of the cross-national models estimated also include cyclical and structural factors as potential explanatory variables of unionization, but the evidence is mixed. Whereas Ebbinghaus and Visser (1999) report that business cycle and social structural variables are insignificant, Blaschke (2000), Calmfors et al. (2001), and Visser (2002), find that inflation, unemployment, and some measures of the composition of the labour force do play a role in explaining cross-national variations in unionization.

Concerning institutional variables, the focus is of course on institutions that may exert some influence on the recruitment or retention of union members. A likely candidate is a *union-managed unemployment insurance*, the so-called Ghent system, which currently can be found in Belgium, Denmark, Finland and Sweden (for details, see Western, 1997, Ch. 4; for a theoretical analysis, see Holmlund and Lundborg, 1999). Although union membership is not usually a prerequisite for being insured, the administration of the insurance system by union officials (who probably have some discretion in determining who is unemployed involuntarily and thus eligible for drawing benefits) may be a quasi-selective incentive for workers to become union members, and the regular contact with the union during spells of unemployment may induce them to stay in the union when unemployed. Empirical tests of this hypothesis consistently find that the presence of a union-administered unemployment insurance is an important determinant of cross-national differences in union density levels and trends (see Freeman, 1990; Western, 1997; Ebbinghaus and Visser, 1999; Blaschke, 2000; Visser, 2002).

Other institutional factors assumed to foster unionization are union security arrangements and practices of enforced membership such as the *closed shop* (Olson, 1965). Closed-shop practices, once common in the USA, the UK and Ireland, attempt to overcome the free-rider problem through coercion. But there is only weak empirical evidence that they are successful in raising union density (see Ebbinghaus and Visser, 1999 and Blaschke, 2000).[33]

Union access to the workplace, which may be secured by law or through collective agreements with employers, and the institutionalization of employee representatives such as works councils should also play a role in recruiting and keeping union members. Mandatory and voluntary systems of union access or union-dominated workplace representatives exist in many countries, but they exhibit considerable variation (for details, see Ebbinghaus and Visser, 1999). The empirical evidence on the impact of these institutions is mixed. According to Ebbinghaus and Visser (1999) and Visser (2002), union access to the workplace is a highly significant determinant of union density and membership growth, although Blaschke (2000) finds that statutory employee representation does not exert a positive influence on union development.

Some other institutional hypotheses that have been investigated in cross-national analyses also fail to receive clear empirical support. One of these concerns the (positive) relationship between unionization and the level of collective bargaining or union centralization, which is not very significant and probably not stable over time (see Western, 1997; Blaschke, 2000; Calmfors et al., 2001). The existence of leftist governments (which are sympathetic to union views on labour legislation and may enable or encourage unions to increase membership) is found to have a significant positive impact on unionization in some cross-national studies (cf. Wallerstein, 1989; Western, 1997), but it is insignificant in others (cf. Calmfors et al., 2001). This mirrors the conflicting results of including political variables in the national time-series analyses discussed in section 5.

In general, the evidence from cross-national studies suggests that in addition to economic and social structural variables, institutional factors can play a distinct role in the unionization process by affecting the framework in which individual decisions to join or leave a union are made. It should not be overlooked, however, that all cross-national analyses suffer from small sample sizes. They generally compare not more than 20 countries, and some of the institutions investigated – such as the closed shop and the

Ghent system – only exist in two to four countries. This means that the econometric results should be taken with a pinch of salt, but it does not mean that institutions are unimportant.

8. Conclusions

This survey has shown that there exists a considerable body of theoretical and empirical research on the determinants of trade union membership. While the conventional supply and demand framework of economists provides a helpful starting point for any theoretical analysis of unionization, the free-rider problem and social, psychological and political factors stressed by other disciplines of the social sciences must also be taken into account. Some of these potential determinants, which often can be interpreted in terms of costs and benefits, have been incorporated either into the traditional supply and demand framework or into new models of an individual's decision to unionize such as social custom theory. Important insights of these models are that union membership and wages are determined simultaneously, and that there exists a minimum critical mass of membership or density below which union existence is not viable.

A review of the international empirical evidence on the determinants of union membership shows that while there are substantial differences in the design and the results of the empirical studies, some consistent patterns seem to emerge. Concerning the macro-determinants analysed in time-series studies, there is some evidence across countries that business cycle factors as well as structural developments play a significant role in explaining short-run changes and long-run trends in union membership. Individual-level cross-sectional studies have identified a number of micro-determinants such as personal, occupational and firm characteristics, earnings, attitudes and social variables that are associated with the unionization decision. Cross-national analyses have pointed to the importance of some institutional determinants of unionism such as a union-affiliated unemployment insurance. What is often missing, however, are attempts to integrate macro- and micro-level findings and cyclical, structural and institutional explanations of unionization.

Similarly, it has proved difficult to build a bridge between the variety of theoretical approaches and the empirical literature on the determinants of unionization. Both strands of the literature have long developed separately, with empirical findings often preceding theoretical research. Those empirical studies that tried to relate to theoretical considerations, for instance by applying the conventional supply and demand framework, have been plagued by the lack of adequate data on key variables reflecting the costs and benefits of union membership. The gap between theoretical and empirical work seems to have narrowed with the emergence of social custom models which have prompted additional empirical research. While this research has improved our understanding of the unionization decision by identifying social custom effects, it would be desirable to include also pure private good incentives in such empirical analyses and compare their impact with that of social custom effects. Here again the lack of adequate data is a major problem. Better and richer data sets (such as representative large-scale panel data of individuals and firms) also seem to be a prerequisite for successfully integrating macro and micro approaches to unionization, but in most countries such data sets either do not exist or do not identify union members.

The impression that the strong international variation in union density as well as the substantial fall in membership and density recorded in many countries are phenomena that are not yet fully understood and the fact that the relative importance of cyclical, structural and institutional factors is heavily disputed[34] underscore that further research is needed. This research should try to integrate better the different approaches of the various disciplines of social science, it should pay more attention to the process of joining or leaving a union and to union recruitment strategies, and it should attempt to provide a more comprehensive model in which individual workers' optimizing decisions are seen in a wider perspective that pays more attention to the social and institutional background. Obviously important questions remain to be addressed before economists and other social scientists can claim a real understanding of what the determinants of union membership are.

Acknowledgement

The author would like to thank John Addison, Alan Carruth, Laszlo Goerke and Joachim Wagner for helpful comments and suggestions on a previous draft of this chapter. The usual disclaimer applies.

Notes

1. This sort of analysis is described in detail by Hirsch and Addison (1986, Ch. 2.5) and can be found in labour economics textbooks such as Ehrenberg and Smith (2000, Ch. 13) and Borjas (2000, Ch. 11).
2. Abowd and Farber (1982) point out that the market clearing assumption, while appropriate for the determination of total union membership and coverage, may be less appropriate for determining the union status of individual workers, which implies that empirical results of union choice models should be interpreted with caution.
3. In a median voter model in which workers have different reservation wages and hence different optimal points in the trade-off between an increased wage and a decreased probability of employment, Bulkley and Myles (2001) argue that joining a union instead of free-riding may be rational if it enables individuals to influence union bargaining goals and thus their own employment probability.
4. As regards unions, Olson (1965, p. 75) thought that '[i]n most cases it is compulsory membership and coercive picket lines that are the source of the union's membership'.

5. Naylor (1990) demonstrates the formal equivalence of the Booth (1985) model and the 'critical mass' or 'tipping' models developed by Schelling (1978) and discussed by Marwell and Oliver (1993); see also the 'resource mobilization' approach by Klandermans (1984).

6. The impact of tax changes or labour demand shifts in such a model is investigated by Goerke (1997).

7. Corneo (1997) tries to provide a microfoundation of the social custom approach by endogenizing the reputation effect of belonging to the union as the outcome of a signalling game among the workers. Depending on societal values, various shapes of the reputation effect may arise. If conformism prevails in the workers' community, the reputation effect increases with union density; if elitism prevails, the opposite applies.

8. A prominent example of a such an excludable private good is a union-run unemployment insurance known as the Ghent system. A formal theoretical analysis by Holmlund and Lundborg (1999) shows that the Ghent system is more conducive to unionization than a compulsory unemployment system if it is heavily subsidized by the government or if workers are strongly risk averse.

9. In a different setting, Jones and McKenna (1994) show that in the case where a union is able to offer greater employment protection for its members, employed workers join the union if the marginal benefit of protection is at least as great as union dues, and their dynamic model permits a variety of relationships between employment and membership in the adjustment to steady state.

10. Examples of psychological and socio-political approaches to unionization can be found, *inter alia*, in Crouch (1982), Klandermans (1984, 1986), Guest and Dewe (1988), Wallerstein (1989), Windolf and Haas (1989), Western (1997), Rij and Daalder (1997) and Visser (2002).

11. This is also stated by Wallerstein (1989, p. 484): 'From the traditional perspective, union growth occurs when workers organize unions. But it is equally true that union growth occurs when unions organize workers.'

12. For a similar classification see Ebbinghaus and Visser (1999), who distinguish cyclical, structural and configurational (or institutional) explanations of union growth and decline, and Calmfors et al. (2001).

13. The studies in Table 2.1 were selected for comparative purposes and for providing a general overview of this field of empirical research. In addition there exist a large number of similar time-series studies for the countries in Table 2.1 and for other economies as diverse as Italy (see, for example, Checci and Corneo, 2000), Ireland (Sapsford, 1986; Roche and Larragy, 1990) and Taiwan (Sharma and Sephton, 1991).

14. In fact, the first econometric analysis of union growth was undertaken by Hines (1964) in the context of testing theories of union wage-push. For the UK in the period 1893–1961 he estimated a simultaneous model which contained equations for the rates of change of wages, prices, and unionization. Hines, however, was not really interested in explaining union growth, and his work suffers from severe theoretical and empirical weaknesses (see Bain and Elsheikh, 1976, p. 26 ff.).

15. See, for instance, the critical assessments by Mancke (1971), Moore and Pearce (1976) and Sheflin et al. (1981).

16. See, for example, Pedersen (1978), Sheflin et al. (1981), Carruth and Disney (1988) and Visser (1990, Ch. 4).

17. See also the surveys of the empirical evidence by Riley (1997) and Calmfors et al. (2001, p. 19ff.) and the overviews for the USA by Fiorito and Greer (1982) and Chaison and Rose (1991).

18. In contrast, for Australia a real wage variable is found to affect union growth negatively by Sharpe (1971) and by Borland and Ouliaris (1994), whereas Bodman (1998) identifies a positive long-run relationship.

19. Due to lack of data, Pencavel (1971) provides one of the few time-series studies that could test (and confirm) the suspected negative influence of membership dues on unionization for the UK, whereas Schnabel (1989b) found no statistically significant effect of this variable for Germany.

20. Real wage variants have been tested (and usually rejected) by Bain and Elsheikh (1976), Carruth and Disney (1988) and Carruth and Schnabel (1990).

21. Rare examples of econometric work in the business cycle tradition allowing for simultaneity include Hines (1964), Ashenfelter and Pencavel (1969), Booth (1983) and Schnabel (1989b).

22. Discussions and (often conflicting) empirical results of such legislative and political climate variables can be found in Stepina and Fiorito (1986) for the USA, and in Armingeon (1989) and Schnabel (1989a, 1989b) for Germany. See also the controversy on the effect of the Thatcher government's labour laws on the fall in union density in the UK (cf. Freeman and Pelletier, 1990; Disney, 1990).

23. Chaison and Rose (1991, p. 37) point to the limitations of union membership data and criticise that '[a]ggregate data continue to be widely used to estimate union growth despite their tendency to obscure important and often contrasting trends, e.g., the differences between public and private sector membership growth'.

24. Obviously it is difficult to clearly distinguish between macro- and micro-determinants of unionism, and the distinction above mainly relates to the different empirical approaches applied. Time-series and cross-sectional studies and their empirical results should be seen as complements whose relationship is interpreted by Riley (1997, p. 270) as follows: 'Whilst both approaches are valuable, individual-level studies may enjoy a higher ability to detect the morphology of the causal links whose effects have been identified on a macro-level.'

25. See, for example, the interindustry analysis by Bain and Elsheikh (1979) for the UK and the interregional studies by Hirsch (1980) and Moore and Newman (1988) for the USA. Inter-establishment studies include Gregg and Naylor (1993), Booth and Chatterji (1995) and Moreton (1999) for the UK and Klodt and Meyer (1998) for Germany. A survey of older studies is provided by Fiorito and Greer (1982, Appendix 2).

26. See, for example, Farber and Saks (1980) and Farber (1990) as well as the surveys of the US literature by Fiorito and Greer (1982) and Wheeler and McClendon (1991).

27. Again, the studies in Table 2.2 were selected for comparative purposes and for providing a general overview of this field of empirical research. In addition there exist similar cross-sectional studies for the countries in Table 2.2 (surveyed by Riley, 1997) and for other countries such as Israel (Haberfeld, 1995). For helpful discussions of variables and results, see also Fiorito and Greer (1982) and Hirsch and Addison (1986, Ch. 3).

28. Marital status and number of dependents are other personal characteristics that have been examined as potential determinants of unionization (see Scoville, 1971; Bain and Elias, 1985; Berg and Groot, 1992; Fitzenberger et al., 1999), but here the evidence is usually inconclusive.

29. In addition to establishment size, many studies have also paid attention to the location of a company and have found significant effects of regional characteristics and urbanization; see, for example, the studies by Antos et al. (1980) for the USA, Bain and Elias (1985) for the UK, and Berg and Groot (1992) for the Netherlands as well as the empirical surveys by Fiorito and Greer (1982) and Riley (1997).

30. Interestingly, the three US studies disagree on the question of whether the direction of causation runs from earnings to unionization or the reverse. While Schmidt and Strauss (1976) find that earnings significantly affect unionization (whereas the reverse is not true), Lee (1978) concludes that causality runs both ways and that the union–non-union wage differential is the most important determinant of union membership for semi-skilled workers in the USA. Schmidt (1978), however, finds that the wage differential has no discernible effect on the probability of unionism; see also Hirsch and Berger (1984). Since this differential is difficult to measure correctly and does not not exist in many other countries, its impact will not be analysed in detail in this survey (but see Chapter 7 by Blanchflower and Bryson in this volume).

31. In particular, perceived union instrumentality is consistently found to be significantly related to union support in the USA; see, for instance, the studies by Farber and Saks (1980) and Deshpande and Fiorito (1989) and the survey of the US evidence by Wheeler and McClendon (1991).

32. Similarly, from his empirical analysis of Dutch workers joining or leaving the union Visser (2002, p. 425) concludes that 'social customs theory, and the hypotheses that we can derive from it, appear to stand the test'.
33. The effect of closed shop regulation can also be investigated in the federal system of the United States. While in the majority of US states the union shop is predominant (in which workers in a covered establishment must join the union), some states have passed right-to-work (RTW) laws that make mandatory union membership or dues collection illegal. Although on average these RTW states have lower levels of union density, most multivariate analyses indicate that RTW laws have little direct impact on union membership; see the surveys of empirical studies by Hirsch and Addison (1986) and by Fiorito and Greer (1982, p. 9) who conclude that '[t]he argument that RTW laws represent more symbol than substance, including the possibility of reverse causality, cannot be rejected.'
34. See, for instance, the conflicting conclusions of the cross-national analyses by Ebbinghaus and Visser (1999), Blaschke (2000) and Calmfors et al. (2001), or the widely varying explanations of the substantial decline in union density in the UK provided, *inter alia*, by Disney (1990), Freeman and Pelletier (1990), Mason and Bain (1993), Andrews and Naylor (1994), and Machin (2000).

References

Abowd, John M. and Henry S. Farber (1982), 'Job Queues and the Union Status of Workers', *Industrial and Labor Relations Review*, 35 (3), 354–367.

Akerlof, George A. (1980), 'A Theory of Social Custom, of Which Unemployment May Be One Consequence', *Quarterly Journal of Economics*, 95 (2), 749–775.

Andrews, Martyn and Robin Naylor (1994), 'Declining Union Density in the 1980s: What Do Panel Data Tell Us?', *British Journal of Industrial Relations*, 32 (3), 413–431.

Antos, Joseph R., Mark Chandler and Wesley Mellow (1980), 'Sex Differences in Union Membership', *Industrial and Labor Relations Review*, 33 (2), 162–169.

Armingeon, Klaus (1989), 'Trade Unions Under Changing Conditions: the West German Experience, 1950–1985', *European Sociological Review*, 5 (1), 1–23.

Ashenfelter, Orley and John H. Pencavel (1969), 'American Trade Union Growth: 1900–1960', *Quarterly Journal of Economics*, 83 (3), 434–448.

Bain, George S. and Peter Elias (1985), 'Trade Union Membership in Great Britain: An Individual-level Analysis', *British Journal of Industrial Relations*, 23 (1), 71–92.

Bain, George S. and Farouk Elsheikh (1976), *Union Growth and the Business Cycle: An Econometric Analysis*, Oxford: Blackwell.

Bain, George S. and Farouk Elsheikh (1979), 'An Inter-industry Analysis of Unionisation in Britain', *British Journal of Industrial Relations*, 17(2), 137–157.

Berg, Annette van den (1995), *Trade Union Growth and Decline in the Netherlands*, Amsterdam: Thesis Publishers.

Berg, Annette van den and Wim Groot (1992), 'Union Membership in the Netherlands: A Cross-Sectional Analysis', *Empirical Economics*, 17 (4), 537–564.

Berkowitz, Monroe (1954), 'The Economics of Trade Union Organization and Administration', *Industrial and Labor Relations Review*, 7 (4), 537–549.

Beyme, Klaus von (1981), *Challenge to Power: Trade Unions and Industrial Relations in Capitalist Countries*, London: Sage.

Blaschke, Sabine (2000), 'Union Density and European Integration', *European Journal of Industrial Relations*, 6 (2), 217–236.

Bodman, Philip M. (1998), 'Trade Union Amalgamations, Openness and the Decline in Australian Trade Union Membership', *Australian Bulletin of Labour*, 24 (1), 18–45.

Booth, Alison L. (1983), 'A Reconsideration of Trade Union Growth in the United Kindom', *British Journal of Industrial Relations*, 21 (3), 377–391.

Booth, Alison L. (1985), 'The Free Rider Problem and a Social Custom Model of Trade Union Membership', *Quarterly Journal of Economics*, 100 (1), 253–261.

Booth, Alison L. and Monojit Chatterji (1993), 'Reputation, Membership and Wages in an Open Shop Trade Union', *Oxford Economic Papers*, 45 (1), 23–41.

Booth, Alison L. and Monojit Chatterji (1995), 'Union Membership and Wage Bargaining when Membership is not Compulsory', *Economic Journal*, 105 (429), 345–360.

Borjas, George (2000), *Labor Economics*, 2nd edn, Maidenhead: Irwin, McGraw-Hill.

Borland, Jeff and S. Ouliaris (1994), 'The Determinants of Australian Trade Union Membership', *Journal of Applied Econometrics*, 9 (4), 453–468.

Bulkley, George and Gareth D. Myles (2001), 'Individually Rational Union Membership', *European Journal of Political Economy*, 17 (1), 117–137.

Calmfors, Lars, Alison Booth, Michael Burda, Daniele Checci, Robin Naylor and Jelle Visser (2001), 'The Future of Collective Bargaining in Europe', in Tito Boeri, Agar Brugiavini and Lars Calmfors (eds), *The Role of Unions in the Twenty-First Century*, Oxford: Oxford University Press, pp. 1–155.

Carruth, Alan and Richard Disney (1988), 'Where Have Two Million Trade Union Members Gone?', *Economica*, 55 (1), 1–19.

Carruth, Alan and Claus Schnabel (1990), 'Empirical Modelling of Trade Union Growth in Germany, 1956–1986: Traditional versus Cointegration and Error Correction Methods', *Weltwirtschaftliches Archiv*, 126 (2), 326–346.

Chaison, Gary N. and Joseph B. Rose (1991), 'The Macrodeterminants of Union Growth and Decline', in George Strauss, Daniel G. Gallagher and Jack Fiorito (eds), *The State of the Unions*, Madison, WI: Industrial Relations Research Association, pp. 3–45.

Checci, Daniele and Giacomo Corneo (2000), 'Trade Union Membership: Theories and Evidence for Italy', *Lavoro e relazioni industriali*, 7 (2), 151–186.

Christie, Virginia (1992), 'Union Wage Effects and the Probability of Union Membership', *Economic Record*, 68 (1), 43–56.

Commons, John K., David J. Saposs, Helen L. Sumner, E.B. Mittelman, H.E. Hoagland, John B. Andrews and Selig Perlman (1918), *History of Labor in the United States, I*, New York: Kelley.

Corneo, Giacomo (1995), 'Social Custom, Management Opposition, and Trade Union Membership', *European Economic Review*, 39 (2), 275–292.

Corneo, Giacomo G. (1997), 'The Theory of the Open Shop Trade Union Reconsidered', *Labour Economics*, 4 (1), 71–84.

Crouch, Colin (1982), *Trade Unions: the Logic of Collective Action*, Glasgow: Fontana Paperbacks.

Deery, Stephen and Helen De Cieri (1991), 'Determinants of Trade Union Membership in Australia', *British Journal of Industrial Relations*, 29 (1), 59–73.

Deshpande, Satish P. and Jack Fiorito (1989), 'Specific and General Beliefs in Union Voting Models', *Academy of Management Journal*, 32 (4), 883–897.

Disney, Richard (1990), 'Explanations of the Decline in Trade Union Density in Britain: An Appraisal', *British Journal of Industrial Relations*, 28 (2), 165–177.

Disney, Richard, Amanda Gosling and Stephen Machin (1995), 'British Unions in Decline: Determinants of the 1980s Fall in Union Recognition', *Industrial and Labor Relations Review*, 48 (3), 403–419.

Ebbinghaus, Bernhard and Jelle Visser (1999), 'When Institutions Matter: Union Growth and Decline in Western Europe, 1950–1995', *European Sociological Review*, 15 (2), 135–158.

Ebbinghaus, Bernhard and Jelle Visser (2000), *Trade Unions in Western Europe since 1945*, London: Macmillan.

Ehrenberg, Ronald G. and Robert S. Smith (2000), *Modern Labor Economics*, 7th edn, Reading, Mass.

Farber, Henry S. (1990), 'The Decline of Unionization in the United States: What Can Be Learned from Recent Experience?', *Journal of Labor Economics*, 8 (1), S75–S105.

Farber, Henry S. and Daniel H. Saks (1980), 'Why Workers Want Unions: The Role of Relative Wages and Job Characteristics', *Journal of Political Economy*, 88 (2), 349–369.

Fiorito, Jack and Charles R. Greer (1982), 'Determinants of U.S. Unionism: Past Research and Future Needs', *Industrial Relations*, 21 (1), 1–32.

Fitzenberger, Bernd, Isabelle Haggeney and Michaela Ernst (1999), 'Wer ist noch Mitglied in Gewerkschaften? Eine Panelanalyse für Westdeutschland', *Zeitschrift für Wirtschafts- und Sozialwissenschaften*, 119 (2), 223–263.

Freeman, Richard (1990), 'On the Divergence of Unionism among Developed Countries', in Brunetta, Renato and Carlo Dell' Aringa (eds), *Labour Relations and Economic Performance*, London, pp. 304–322.

Freeman, Richard and Jeffrey Pelletier (1990), 'The Impact of Industrial Relations Legislation on British Union Density', *British Journal of Industrial Relations*, 28 (2), 141–164.

Goerke, Laszlo (1997), 'An Open Shop, Wage Bargaining, and Taxation – A Note', *Oxford Economic Papers*, 49 (4), 651–657.

Goerke, Laszlo and Markus Pannenberg (1998), 'Social Custom, Free-Riders, and Trade Union Membership in Germany and Great Britain', DIW Discussion Paper No. 177, Berlin, December.

Gregg, Paul and Robin Naylor (1993), 'An Inter-Establishment Study of Union Recognition and Membership in Great Britain', *The Manchester School*, 6 (4), 367–385.

Grossman, Gene M. (1983), 'Union Wages, Temporary Layoffs and Seniority', *American Economic Review*, 73 (3), 277–290.

Guest, David E. and Philip Dewe (1988), 'Why Do Workers Belong to a Trade Union? A Social Psychological Study in the UK Electronics Industry', *British Journal of Industrial Relations*, 26 (2), 178–194.

Haberfeld, Yitchak (1995), 'Why Do Workers Join Unions? The Case of Israel', *Industrial and Labor Relations Review*, 48 (4), 656–670.

Hines, Albert G. (1964), 'Trade Unions and Wage Inflation in the United Kingdom 1893–1961', *Review of Economic Studies*, 31 (3), 221–252.

Hirsch, Barry T. (1980), 'The Determinants of Unionization: An Analysis of Interarea Differences', *Industrial and Labor Relations Review*, 33 (2), 147–161.

Hirsch, Barry T. and John T. Addison (1986), *The Economic Analysis of Unions*, London: Allen & Unwin.

Hirsch, Barry T. and Marc C. Berger (1984), 'Union Membership Determination and Industry Characteristics', *Southern Economic Journal*, 50 (3), 665–679.

Holmlund, Bertil and Per Lundborg (1999), 'Wage Bargaining, Union Membership, and the Organization of Unemployment Insurance', *Labour Economics*, 6 (3), 397–415.

Ingham, Mike (1995), 'Union Joining: An Empirical Test of the Social Custom Model', *Applied Economics Letters*, 2 (8), 245–247.

Jones, Stephen R.G. and C.J. McKenna (1994), 'A Dynamic Model of Union Membership and Employment', *Economica*, 61 (2), 179–189.

Klandermans, Bert (1984), 'Mobilization and Participation: Social-Psychological Expansions of Resource Mobilization Theory', *American Sociological Review*, 49 (5), 583–600.

Klandermans, Bert (1986), 'Psychology and Trade Union Participation: Joining, Acting, Quitting', *Journal of Occupational Psychology*, 59 (1), 189–204.

Klodt, Thomas and Wolfgang Meyer (1998), 'Empirical Analysis of Inter-firm Differences in Trade Union Density', Discussion Paper No. 13, Universität Hannover, Forschungsstelle Firmenpanel, July.

Lawler, John J. and Robin West (1985), 'Impact of Union-Avoidance Strategy in Representation Elections', *Industrial Relations*, 24 (3), 406–420.

Lee, Lung-Fei (1978), 'Unionism and Wage Rates: A Simultaneous Equations Model with Qualitative and Limited Dependent Variables', *International Economic Review*, 19 (2), 415–433.

Lorenz, Wilhelm and Joachim Wagner (1991), 'Bestimmungsgründe von Gewerkschaftsmitgliedschaft und Organisationsgrad', *Zeitschrift für Wirtschafts- und Sozialwissenschaften*, 111 (1), 65–82.

Machin, Stephen (2000), 'Union Decline in Britain', *British Journal of Industrial Relations*, 38 (4), 631–645.

Mancke, Richard B. (1971), 'American Tade Union Growth, 1900–1960: A Comment', *Quarterly Journal of Economics*, 85 (1), 187–193.

Marwell, Gerald and Pamela Oliver (1993), *The Critical Mass in Collective Action: A Micro-Social Theory*, Cambridge: Cambridge University Press.

Mason, Bob and Peter Bain (1993), 'The Determinants of Trade Union Membership in Britain: A Survey of the Literature', *Industrial and Labor Relations Review*, 46 (2), 332–351.

Moore, William J. and Robert J. Newman (1988), 'A Cross-Section Analysis of the Postwar Decline in American Trade Union Membership', *Journal of Labor Research*, 9 (2), 111–125.

Moore, William J. and D.K. Pearce, (1976), 'Union Growth: A Test of the Ashenfelter–Pencavel Model', *Industrial Relations*, 15 (2), 244–247.

Moreton, David (1998), 'An Open Shop Trade Union Model of Wages, Effort and Membership', *European Journal of Political Economy*, 14 (3), 511–527.

Moreton, David (1999), 'A Model of Labour Productivity and Union Density in British Private Sector Unionised Establishments', *Oxford Economic Papers*, 51 (2), 322–344.

Naylor, Robin A. (1990), 'A Social Custom Model of Collective Action', *European Journal of Political Economy,* 6 (2), 201–216.

Naylor, Robin and Martin Cripps (1993), 'An Economic Theory of the Open Shop Trade Union', *European Economic Review*, 37 (8), 1599–1620.

Naylor, Robin and Oddbjørn Raaum (1993), 'The Open Shop Union, Wages and Management Opposition', *Oxford Economic Papers*, 45 (4), 589–604.

Neumann, George R. and Ellen R. Rissman (1984), 'Where Have All the Union Members Gone?', *Journal of Labor Economics*, 2(2), 175–192.

Olson, Mancur (1965), *The Logic of Collective Action*, Cambridge, MA: Harvard University Press.

Ours, Jan C. van (1992), 'Union Growth in The Netherlands 1961–1989', *Applied Economics*, 24 (9), 1059–1066.

Pedersen, P.J. (1978), 'Union Growth and the Business Cycle: A Note on the Bain–Elsheikh Model', *British Journal of Industrial Relations*, 16 (3), 373–377.

Pencavel, John H. (1971), 'The Demand for Union Services: An Exercise', *Industrial and Labor Relations Review,* 24 (2), 180–190.

Rij, Coen van and Annelies Daalder (1997), 'The Business Cycle Theory and Individual Unionization Decisions: A Comparison of Macro- and Micro Influences on Union Membership', in Sverke, Magnus (ed.), *The Future of Trade Unionism*, Aldershot, pp. 235–248.

Riley, Nicola-Maria (1997), 'Determinants of Union Membership: A Review', *Labour*, 11 (2), 265–301.

Roche, William K. and Joe Larragy (1990), 'Cyclical and Institutional Determinants of Annual Trade Union Growth and Decline in Ireland: Evidence from the DUES Data Series', *European Sociological Review*, 6 (1), 49–72.

Sapsford, David (1986), 'Some Further Evidence on the Role of Profits in Union Growth Equations', *Applied Economics*, 18 (1), 27–36.

Schelling, Thomas C. (1978), *The Micromotives of Macrobehavior*, New York: W.W. Norton & Company.

Schmidt, Peter (1978), 'Estimation of a Simultaneous Equation Model with Jointly Dependent Continuous and Qualitative Variables: The Union–Earnings Question Revisited', *International Economic Review*, 19 (2), 453–465.

Schmidt, Peter and Robert P. Strauss (1976), 'The Effect of Unions on Earnings and Earnings on Unions: A Mixed Logit Approach', *International Economic Review,* 17 (1), 204–212.

Schnabel, Claus (1989a), 'Determinants of Trade Union Growth and Decline in the Federal Republic of Germany', *European Sociological Review*, 5 (2), 133–146.

Schnabel, Claus (1989b), *Zur ökonomischen Analyse der Gewerkschaften in der Bundesrepublik Deutschland*, Frankfurt am Main: Peter Lang.

Scoville, James G. (1971), 'Influences on Unionization in the U.S. in 1966', *Industrial Relations*, 10 (3), 354–361.

Sharma, Basu and Peter Sephton (1991), 'The Determinants of Union Membership Growth in Taiwan', *Journal of Labor Research*, 12 (4), 429–437.

Sharpe, Ian G. (1971), 'The Growth of Australian Trade Unions: 1907–1969', *Journal of Industrial Relations*, 13 (2), 138–154.

Sheflin, Neil, Leo Troy and C. Timothy Koeller (1981), 'Structural Stability in Models of American Trade Union Growth', *Quarterly Journal of Economics*, 96 (1), 77–88.

Stepina, Lee P. and Jack Fiorito (1986), 'Toward a Comprehensive Theory of Union Growth and Decline', *Industrial Relations*, 25 (3), 248–264.

Streeck, Wolfgang (1981), *Gewerkschaftliche Organisationsprobleme in der sozialstaatlichen Demokratie*, Köenigstein, Ts: Athenäum.

Visser, Jelle (1990), *In Search of Inclusive Unionism*, Deventer and Boston: Kluwer (Bulletin of Comparative Labour Relations, 18).

Visser, Jelle (2002), 'Why Fewer Workers Join Unions in Europe', *British Journal of Industrial Relations*, 40 (3), 403–430.

Waddington, Jeremy and Colin Whitston (1997), 'Why Do People Join Unions in a Period of Membership Decline?', *British Journal of Industrial Relations*, 35 (4), 515–546.

Wallerstein, Michael (1989), 'Union Organization in Advanced Industrial Democracies', *American Political Science Review*, 83 (2), 481–501.

Western, Bruce (1997), *Between Class and Market – Postwar Unionization in the Capitalist Democracies*, Princeton: Princeton University Press.

Wheeler, Hoyt N. and John A. McClendon (1991), 'The Individual Decision to Unionize', in George Strauss, Daniel G. Gallagher and Jack Fiorito (eds), *The State of the Unions*, Madison, WI: Industrial Relations Research Association, pp. 47–83.

Windolf, Paul and Joachim Haas (1989), 'Who Joins the Union? Determinants of Trade Union Membership in West Germany 1976–1984', *European Sociological Review*, 5 (2), 147–165.

3 Economic models of union behaviour
Robin Naylor

1. Introduction

Surveying the literature on the economic theory of trade unions in the mid-1980s, Oswald (1985, p. 160) observed the remarkable growth of work in the area which had occurred during the previous decade. He also stressed the change in character of this work compared to what had gone before, arguing that 'We now appear to be a little closer to a situation in which it could be said that there is an orthodox, methodologically conventional and testable theory of the trade union'. This contrasted starkly with the situation described just ten years earlier by Johnson (1975, p. 23), who wrote that the '. . . absence of a solid theoretical foundation has handicapped the economic analysis of trade unions and has surely contributed to its decline in relative attention'.

There are many reasons for the exponential growth in the theoretical literature on unions from the late 1970s. A major factor was the new emphasis on the importance of micro-foundations (and, not least, micro-foundations of labour market behaviour)[1] for macroeconomic analysis and, in that context, it is not surprising in hindsight that much of the early post-1970s work on unions focused on the issue of how to specify union preferences and constraints appropriately. For example, in his state-of-the-art survey on models of union behaviour, published in the *Handbook of Labor Economics*, Farber (1986) concentrates on two related issues. The first concerns the question of how to model union objectives and the second concerns the definition of the scope of bargaining. Indeed, as we discuss in more detail below, one of the elements of the early work which excited most attention was the interaction between theoretical and empirical investigation of these very issues.

Thirteen years after the publication of Farber's survey, in Volume III of the *Handbook*, Blau and Kahn identified two important theoretical developments in the economic analysis on trade unions compared to the early models. First, they identify developments in non-cooperative game theory as an important source of new insights into the economic modelling of unions and their effects. Second, they emphasize that the development of models of centralized bargaining has generated valuable new insights for the analysis of macroeconomic performance. We would also argue – albeit for rather different reasons – that developments in non-cooperative bargaining theory and a focus on market and institutional structure are at the heart of recent and important developments in the economic analysis of trade unions.

One of the limitations of most of the theoretical literature on unions from the late 1970s to the late 1980s was the failure to locate the analysis within a wider industrial and microeconomic context. The early literature was, doubtless inevitably, rather narrow in its scope. From the late 1980s onwards, however, the growing application of union models in various areas of economics has led to exciting developments in which barriers between labour economics and other sub-disciplines in economics (most notably with regard to industrial economics and international trade theory) have broken down, generating new common ground and new insights. In consequence, it is probably fair to say that the economic theory of trade unions has made important contributions across a broad sweep of economic analysis beyond its more natural location within the study of labour economics.

Arising from both the concerns of macroeconomists and from dialogue between labour and industrial economists, the theoretical analysis of unions has coincided with an increasing interest in labour market institutions more generally and has thereby helped restore to labour economics a concern with institutional structures, including both their implications and their origins. Pencavel (1991) has argued that the shift away from the competitive paradigm as an organizing framework for the analysis of labour markets, together with a renewed emphasis on bargaining, resonates with older traditions in labour economics, as typified by the work of Commons (1909, 1934), and holds the promise of fruitful interaction between labour economics and the study of industrial relations. These are issues to which we shall return later in this chapter (and the themes recur throughout the book).

No analysis of unions is complete without a consideration of their social, political and historical context: see for example, the classic works of Pelling (1987) and of Cole and Postgate (1963). A purely economic analysis of unions is necessarily partial. Labour economists are aware of this and of the fact that unions are complex organizations with many objectives, functions and roles. This complexity was the focus of much of the early debate on the question of how to characterize unions within an economic analysis: at least, that is, among those who thought this task possible or even desirable.[2]

To the economist, a principal role for a union is to improve workers' pay and working conditions. Most of the analysis described in the current chapter will focus on this objective of unions and on the factors which influence the union's capacity to meet its objective. To the extent that any gain for the union comes at the expense to the firm in the form of a reduction in profits, the union and the firm are regarded as having competing interests. Unions are typically thought of as attempting to capture rents from the firm. The key question then concerns the source of the rents themselves. However, to the extent that the presence of a union is able to enhance any surplus, the union and the firm can also be thought of as having complementary interests. Thus, the analysis of unions requires us to address both the conflicting and the shared interests of unions and firms.

Why might a union's presence and behaviour be surplus-enhancing? There are many possible reasons. For example, there is an extensive industrial relations literature based on the idea that unions operate to reduce conflict within the workplace. A more general framework within which to view the efficiency-enhancing role of unions is that associated with the analysis of the 'Harvard school' (see Freeman and Medoff, 1984). According to this analysis, beneficial effects of unions might lie in (1) a shock effect which reduces managerial X-inefficiency, (2) a morale effect, (3) better information and improved co-ordination between employees and management and (4) an improved use of voice in the context of potentially sub-optimal exit. The latter argument is the main contribution of the Harvard school. In the presence of public goods characteristics in the workplace, exogenous shocks and costly mobility, the analysis of Hirschman (1970) implies that the voice mechanism can enhance efficiency as the market-based mechanism of exit and search will, on its own, be sub-optimal. The argument then is that unions are potentially the best device for channelling voice. Why might this be, given that, in theory, firms could autonomously provide a voice mechanism and avoid the surplus-capturing effects of unions? One answer is that individual workers voicing grievances or preferences about workplace conditions might feel vulnerable to hostile management reaction unless protected by either an organization of their own or an independent agent. In these conditions, unions might therefore be tolerated or even encouraged and sponsored by firms and management. Prior to the development of the Harvard school's 'new view' of unions, the economics literature on the direct effects of unions on productivity had concentrated exclusively on the adverse effects associated with 'featherbedding' and other efficiency-damaging work practices.

So one can interpret unions as possessing 'two faces': one representing an efficiency-enhancing effect on production and the other reflecting the potential monopoly power of unions which enables them to capture rents through wage bargaining. However, whilst surplus-creation is a possibly important effect of unions, the bulk of the analysis we shall consider in this chapter concerns the capacity of unions to capture a share of any surplus.

Rent-capture can take various forms such as higher wages, fewer hours and better conditions. We shall focus largely on the attempt by unions to raise wages.

Our analysis can be thought of as adapting the structure–conduct–performance framework from industrial economics. Throughout, our main measure of *performance* will be the wage outcome of bargaining, though other effects of unions and bargaining will be discussed. Macroeconomists have always been interested primarily in performance as measured by variables such as employment and the responsiveness of employment to exogenous shocks (see, for example, Layard et al., 1991). The macroeconomic issue of why employment behaviour varies so much even across similar macroeconomies has led macro theorists to a particular focus on the impact of differences in bargaining structure. We argue that until the late 1980s, labour economists were significantly preoccupied with matters relating to the *conduct* of bargaining and that an appreciation of the importance of *structural* characteristics has evolved only slowly and in a somewhat disparate way.

In the analysis of industrial organization, the structure–conduct–performance approach focused on structure as a major determinant of business conduct and saw performance as shaped by the interaction of structure and conduct. Structure itself should not be seen as exogenous to economic phenomena. There is also a recognition that performance will be influenced not only by product market structure but also by interactions among markets, including the labour market. (For an important treatment of the interaction between product market structure and labour market performance, see Nickell, 1999.)

The structure–conduct–performance approach would seem to be applicable within the analysis of labour markets, especially of unionized ones. Figure 3.1 adapts the schematic representation of the structure–conduct–performance approach in Martin (2001) to the context of unionized labour markets.

The rest of this chapter is organized as follows. In the next two sections (2 and 3), we consider the nature and effects of union *conduct*, focusing on a review of the standard treatment of union objectives and of the scope of the bargaining agenda. In section 4, we emphasize the importance of the structural aspects of bargaining and, in particular, offer a survey of the burgeoning literature on unionized oligopoly – a literature which has done much to bring together researchers in industrial and in labour economics. In section 5, we offer a selected survey of the literature on the determinants of union membership as this is likely to be an important element of the bargaining structure and hence of the bargaining outcome. A short summary concludes.

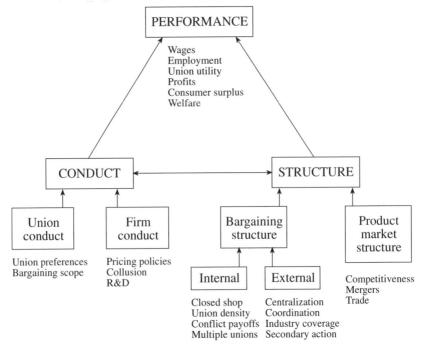

Figure 3.1   A structure–conduct–performance schema for the analysis of unionized labour markets

2.   The conduct of bargaining

In this chapter, we adapt the *structure–conduct–performance* framework from industrial organization to organize a review of the orthodox theory of trade unions. We begin by reviewing the literature on conduct, focusing first on union objectives and (in the next section) on the scope of bargaining.

As is well-known, the theoretical foundations of the economic theory of trade unions can be traced back to the work of Dunlop (1944), Leontief (1946), Fellner (1949) and Cartter (1959). In this early work, the common assumption was that a union could be modelled as an optimizing agent, facing the constraint of the employer's labour demand function. Dunlop (1944) suggested a variety of different possible specifications for a union maximand, but argued that the most reasonable objective function for a union was that of wage bill maximization, $U = wl$: where U is union utility, w is the wage per worker and l is employment. In contrast, Ross (1948) held that the very nature of trade unions militated against a simple precise representation of their objectives within a mathematical optimizing model.

There continues to be an important line of analysis investigating political models of unions though, as Booth (1995) has commented, this area of work remains relatively poorly developed (but for further discussion, see Flanagan, Moene and Wallerstein, 1993; Pencavel, 1991).

The literature on union objective functions has focused largely on either Stone–Geary or utilitarian specifications. The Stone–Geary utility function is of the form:

$$U = (w - \bar{w})^\alpha (l - \bar{l})^{1-\alpha}, \tag{3.1}$$

where α is the relative weight the union attaches to supernumerary wages, $\bar{w}$ and $\bar{l}$ are the respective reservation or 'reference' levels of wages and employment. w and l represent, respectively, the wage and employment levels after bargaining. The specification in equation (3.1) nests a number of special cases. For example, when $\alpha = 1/2$ and $\bar{l} = 0$, equation (3.1) can be interpreted as the case of rent-maximization. If, additionally, $\bar{w} = 0$ then (3.1) represents wage bill maximization. Wage rate maximization occurs when $\alpha = 1$ and $\bar{w} = 0$. Thus, an important property of the Stone–Geary function as a representation of union utility is a degree of flexibility. A second advantage is its tractability. Early models developing the Stone–Geary approach include Hersoug (1978), Oswald (1979), Corden (1981), and Stewart (1982).

A limitation of the Stone–Geary specification for the union utility function, however, is that it is ad hoc, in not being derivable from the preferences of individual union members. Dissatisfaction with the arbitrary nature of the Stone–Geary approach led to the development of union models built on more rigorous microeconomic foundations. The utilitarian utility function (or its near-neighbour, the *expected* utility function) appeared in a number of papers around the early 1980s: see, for example, Sampson (1983), Oswald (1982), Calmfors (1982) and McDonald and Solow (1981). The utilitarian utility function can be written as:

$$U = lu(w) + (m - l)u(b), \tag{3.2}$$

where $u(.)$ is the utility function of the individual union member, m is the number of union members and b is the alternative wage or the level of welfare payments to unemployed workers. It is typically assumed that $m \geq l$, and that m is fixed. Thus, the utilitarian union utility function consists of the summed utility of the l employed members plus the summed utility of any unemployed members. Under standard assumptions, equation (3.2) can be represented graphically by a downward-sloping convex indifference curve in (w, l)-space.

The utilitarian utility function, like the Stone–Geary function, captures special cases. If workers are risk-neutral, for example, then equation (3.2) is equivalent to rent-maximization. If, additionally, membership equals employment, then (3.2) collapses to the special case of wage-bill maximization. That the assumption of rent-maximization is so common in the literature perhaps stems in large part from the fact that it emerges out of both the utilitarian and Stone–Geary approaches, and yet is more general than that of wage-bill or wage-rate maximization. We also note that in contexts in which the union–firm bargain can be extended to capture firm–firm bargaining (such as in upstream–downstream bargaining in vertical markets), the additional appeal of rent-maximization is that it is formally equivalent to profit-maximization by the upstream firm (for a discussion, see Naylor, 2002).

The utilitarian utility function can be re-written as:

$$EU = \frac{l}{m}u(w) + \frac{m-l}{m}u(b), \qquad (3.3)$$

which is the same as (3.2) above, but dividing through by m in order to obtain the expected utility per union member. The interpretation is that the union objective is to maximize the expected utility of the representative member. The two representations of union utility are equivalent with identical properties so long as m – membership – is treated as fixed. If, on the other hand, membership is variable then the two functions are no longer equivalent as utilitarian utility is increasing in membership while expected utility is decreasing in membership. This is not surprising. The utilitarian function is a simple aggregation; and hence has the property of 'the more, the merrier'. In the expected utility case, in contrast, where employment is a random draw across identical members, an increase in the number of members reduces each member's chance of being employed.

Under the assumption that workers are homogeneous, employment is a random draw and, in this case, both the utilitarian and expected utility specifications possess the property that identical workers receive different outcomes ex post. Some studies attempt to generalize the utilitarian function to allow for heterogeneous members. See, for example, Farber (1978), Grossman (1983), Booth (1984), and Oswald (1985). In the last example, the combination of a median voter mechanism and a 'last-in, first-out' employment rule generates flat indifference curves. Protected from a risk of redundancy, the median union member cares only about wages.

That the utilitarian utility function is grounded in micro-foundations where the Stone–Geary function is not, has led to the former being preferred on theoretical criteria. However, it is not obvious that the micro-roots of the utilitarian model are more valid than the apparently more arbitrary Stone–Geary approach. Going back to Ross (1948), for example, and to many other more contemporary writers too, it can be argued that the union is more than simply the sum of its parts on account of its political nature. Furthermore, there are potential aggregation problems in simply summing over the utilities of individual workers in order to obtain a collective objective function. Arrow's Impossibility Theorem represents one kind of problem in this respect. Similarly, Olson (1965) – in the context of unions – has argued that collective action is not necessarily rational action even when the collective consists of individually rational actors. Finally, consider the assumption of profit-maximization, which is very generally adopted when considering the objective of firms. The assumption is not typically grounded in any micro-economic analysis of the preferences of the firm's stakeholders, broadly defined, but is more typically justified on the positive methodological principle that firms can be assumed to behave *as if* maximizing profits. A related justification is that if firms do not maximize profits they are likely to be competed out of business. We note, though, that in the case of imperfectly competitive products – which are likely to be the most relevant in the analysis of union wage effects – this mechanism does not necessarily operate strongly. Given this, one might argue that the Stone–Geary approach to union objectives is not especially ad hoc in the analysis of union-firm bargaining.

As we have indicated, depending on the precise specification of the union objective function, union preferences can be represented graphically by union indifference curves, as in Figure (3.2). From the utilitarian utility function, for example, the slope of the union indifference curve, with m fixed, is given by:

$$\frac{dw}{dl} = \frac{-[u(w) - u(b)]}{lu'(w)}.$$

Thus, the slope is negative as $w > b$ and $u'(w) > 0$. It also follows that the union indifference curve is convex under these assumptions.

But what do we know about the nature of union preferences in the real world? There have been a number of attempts to estimate parameters of the union objective function empirically. Early and important papers are those of Farber (1978), for the US bituminous coal industry, and Carruth and Oswald (1985), for the UK coal industry. Both adopt a utilitarian/expected utility framework and assume constant relative risk aversion for the underlying worker utility function. Both analyses report that the estimated values of relative risk aversion are positive and significantly different from zero, implying that workers are not risk-neutral. Under the maintained hypotheses of the empirical specifications, this result undermines the rent-maximization model of union behaviour. The maintained hypotheses include the assumption that

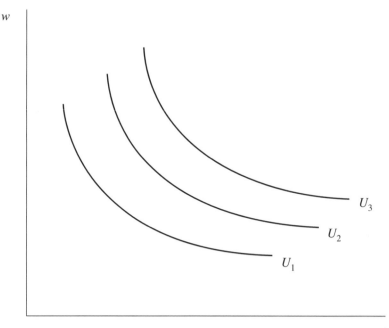

Figure 3.2   A set of convex union indifference curves

both wages and employment enter the union objective, that workers' preferences exhibit constant relative risk aversion, that union preferences are of the utilitarian/expected utility variety, and that unions are able to choose the wage level subject to the constraint that the firm is able to set employment autonomously to maximize profits given the union's wage choice. We shall discuss some of these maintained hypotheses further below.

In line with a Stone–Geary approach, Dertouzos and Pencavel (1981), analysing data for workers covered by the International Typographical Union (ITU), reject both the rent and wage-maximization models in favour of a model including reference values (i.e. supernumerary terms) for both wages *and* employment. In contrast, Pencavel (1984), using similar data but an addilog specification, found some support for the rent-maximization model for some types of union.

Surveying the empirical evidence on union objectives, Pencavel (1991, p. 91) observes that:

> Not only do the assumptions of rent and wage bill maximisation usually conflict with the data, but so does the proposition that unions care about wages only and

not about employment. On the contrary, most studies find a greater weight attached to employment, greater, that is, compared with what rent maximization would imply.

At the same time, Pencavel acknowledges the major limitations of the empirical work. These pertain not only to the various maintained hypotheses in each of the studies, but also to the conceptual and measurement problems associated with attempting to translate a theoretical model of unions into an empirical specification for the purposes of estimation. Furthermore, many of the empirical analyses have been conducted on data pertaining to very particular trade union groups: it is not obvious that the empirical estimates are relevant for other – indeed, perhaps *more typical* – trade union groups.

3.   The scope of bargaining

In the previous section, we focused on the nature of union objectives. Union preferences are potentially of interest in their own right, but how they are translated into actual wage and employment outcomes will depend, among other things, on the scope of bargaining. The scope of bargaining refers to what issues are included on the bargaining agenda; that is, the issues which are subject to bargaining between a union and a firm rather than being determined autonomously by one of the parties – typically taken to be the firm. Potentially, bargaining might cover a range of issues: from wages to employment, through work rules, and wage structure to investment and innovation decisions, to name but some.

One of the early traditions in the approach to union–firm bargaining was to assume that firms possessed the 'right-to-manage': meaning that firms could autonomously choose employment to maximize profits once wages had been set. The scope of bargaining was typically restricted to the determination of the wage level. Diagrammatically, then, the bargaining outcome would lie on the labour demand curve. If the union was all-powerful in the wage bargain, then the outcome would be where the labour demand curve is just tangential to the union indifference curve, as shown at point a in Figure 3.3. This is referred to as the case of the 'monopoly union' and is a special case of the right-to-manage model. If, on the other hand, the union has no influence over the wage, then the outcome will be the competitive equilibrium, as shown by point c. Intermediate solutions, such as depicted by point b in Figure 3.3, reflect the relative degrees of bargaining power possessed by the union and the firm.

In this right-to-manage model, the equilibrium outcome for wages and employment will depend on factors such as the relative wage preference of the union, relative bargaining power, the parameters of the labour demand

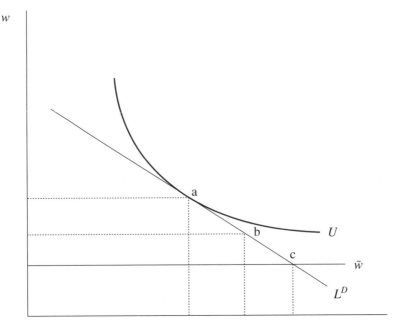

Figure 3.3   The right-to-manage model

function and the level of the reference wage. We can demonstrate this in the following simple model.

Consider equation (3.1) again, but with the simplification that $\bar{l}=0$. That is:

$$U=(w-\bar{w})^{\alpha}l^{1-\alpha}. \tag{3.4}$$

Assume that the firm is a monopolist facing linear demand given by:

$$p=a-bx, \tag{3.5}$$

where x denotes output. Assume for simplicity that the marginal product of labour is constant and set to unity as a *numeraire*. Then we can denote output and employment interchangeably by x or l. Thus, any capturable surplus stems from product market power and not from diminishing marginal returns to labour.

Given (3.5), the monopoly firm will maximize profit by choosing employment such that:

$$x = l = \frac{a - w}{2b}. \tag{3.6}$$

From (3.5) and (3.6), it is easily shown that monopoly profits are given by:

$$\pi = \frac{(a - w)^2}{4b}. \tag{3.7}$$

The right-to-manage bargaining problem can be written as:

$$w = \arg \max \ (B = U^\beta \pi^{1-\beta}), \tag{3.8}$$

where we abstract from the issue of disagreement or conflict payoffs. Substituting (3.4), (3.6) and (3.7) in (3.8) yields:

$$B = A(w - \bar{w})^{\alpha\beta} (a - w)^{2 - \beta(1 + \alpha)}, \tag{3.9}$$

where $A = 1/(2^\beta b^{1-\alpha\beta})$. Differentiating (3.9) with respect to the bargained wage gives the first order condition for the Nash wage bargain, which solves to yield:

$$w = \bar{w} + \frac{\alpha\beta}{2 - \beta}(a - \bar{w}). \tag{3.10}$$

Properties of the right-to-manage model which follow immediately from (3.10), under our assumptions include:

1. There is no union wage differential either if the union is entirely employment-oriented or if the union exerts no influence over the wage. That is, $w = \bar{w}$ if either $\alpha = 0$ or $\beta = 0$;
2. An increase in the union's relative preference for wages leads to an increase in the bargained wage. That is, $dw/d\alpha = \beta(a - \bar{w})/(2 - \beta) > 0$;
3. An increase in the union's bargaining power causes an increase in the bargained wage. That is, $dw/d\beta = \alpha(a - \bar{w})(3 - \beta)/(2 - \beta)^3 > 0$;
4. An increase in the reservation or reference wage leads to an increase in the bargained wage. That is, $dw/d\bar{w} = [2 - \beta(1 + \alpha)]/(2 - \beta) > 0$;
5. A positive shock to product demand produces an increase in the bargained wage. That is, $dw/da = \alpha\beta/(2 - \beta) > 0$; and,
6. Output and employment collapse to zero if both $\alpha = 1$ and $\beta = 1$. This has been referred to in the literature as the case of the 'Cheshire cat' union.[3] It leads us to rule out the combination of wage rate maximization and the special case of the monopoly union variant of the right-to-manage model.

Clearly, in the labour demand curve model of wage bargaining, the slope of the labour demand curve itself is an important determinant of the wage–employment outcome. It is well known from the analysis of the basic Marshallian conditions that the elasticity of the labour demand schedule will depend on factors such as the elasticity of product demand, the elasticity of substitution between (unionized) labour and other factors of production (which might include non-union labour), and the elasticity of the supply of other inputs. Two important determinants of the elasticity of product demand facing the firm are the extent of competition in the product market and the nature of union bargaining in the industry. We return to consider all of these aspects later in this chapter.

The right-to-manage model provides the framework for much contemporaneous theoretical analysis of union–firm wage bargaining. This is probably because most real-world bargaining resembles the right-to-manage bargain. However, it is despite major theoretical dissatisfaction with the model arising out of the fact that, in most cases, bargaining outcomes which lie on the labour demand curve are inefficient. With indifference curves as shown in Figure 3.3, bargained outcomes on the labour demand curve lie off the efficiency locus where union indifference curves and the firm's iso-profit curves are just tangent to one another. Along an iso-profit curve, a given level of profit can be associated with different combinations of wage and employment levels. This is shown in Figure 3.4.

From combinations of wages and employment off the efficiency locus, it is possible to move to a different combination and make at least one of the parties better off without making the other worse off. In other words, a Pareto improvement is possible. Along the contract curve, or efficiency locus, there are no further Pareto improvements. Thus, from the point of view of the firm and the union (though not necessarily for the society as a whole), bargains are efficient only if the outcome is on the efficiency locus.

Various results can be readily proved regarding the properties of the efficient bargaining model. Let us consider the efficient bargaining outcome under the same assumptions we considered above. The only difference is that both wages *and* employment are now the subject of bargaining. We know that the efficiency locus or 'contract curve' is the locus of tangency points between union indifference curves and the firm's iso-profit curves. Hence, to find the equation of the contract curve, we equate the tangencies for the union utility and iso-profit curves.

From equation (3.4), it is easily seen that the slope of the union's indifference curve is given by:

$$\frac{dw}{dl} = -\frac{\partial U/\partial l}{\partial U/\partial w} = -\frac{1-\alpha}{\alpha} \cdot \frac{w-\overline{w}}{l}. \tag{3.11}$$

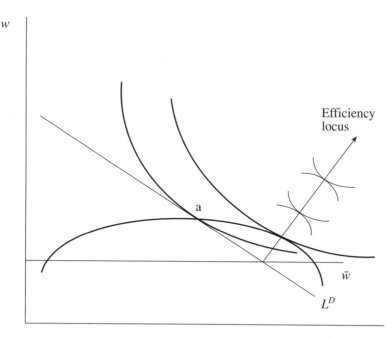

Figure 3.4   The right-to-manage model versus *efficient bargaining*

The slope of the firm's iso-profit curve is given by:

$$\frac{dw}{dl} = -\frac{\partial\pi/\partial l}{\partial\pi/\partial w} = \frac{a - 2bl - w}{l}. \tag{3.12}$$

Equating the slopes of the two curves, it follows from (3.11) and (3.12) that the equation of the contract curve is given by:

$$l = \frac{1}{2\alpha b}[\alpha(a - w) + (1 - \alpha)(w - \bar{w})]. \tag{3.13}$$

We notice from (3.13) that in the special case that $\alpha = 1/2$, it follows that employment is given by:

$$l = \frac{1}{2b}[a - \bar{w}]. \tag{3.14}$$

From (3.6) and (3.14), it follows that when $\alpha = 1/2$, employment is independent of the bargained wage outcome, w, and hence the contract curve is vertical at the competitive level of employment. More generally, from (3.13), the slope of the contract curve can be expressed as:

$$\frac{dw}{dl} = \frac{2\alpha b}{1 - 2\alpha}. \tag{3.15}$$

From (3.15), it follows that the contract curve will be positively sloped when the union is risk-averse ($\alpha < 1/2$) and negatively-sloped when the union is risk-loving ($\alpha > 1/2$). From this, it can be shown that when the union is risk-averse a rise in union bargaining power will not only lead to a rise in the bargained wage but will also cause an increase in the bargained employment outcome above the competitive level. Thus, the prediction of the efficient bargaining model is the opposite of that of the right-to-manage model in this case. A further consequence of the efficient bargaining model, not shown here, is the important wage-stickiness result demonstrated by McDonald and Solow (1981) under the assumption that the reference wage is itself relatively fixed over the cycle.

Finally, we note that, from (3.6) and (3.13), it follows that if $\alpha = 1$, so that unions care only about wages, then the equation for the contract curve coincides with that of the labour demand curve. This is because with a wage maximizing union, indifference curves are flat, as discussed in Oswald (1985).

Given that the right-to-manage and efficient bargaining models have potentially conflicting predictions about the impact of unions on employment, an important question to address is which of the models is likely to be the more valid empirically. There is a very sophisticated empirical literature addressing this issue. The reader is referred to excellent surveys by Booth (1995) and Pencavel (1991).

One of the methods for testing between the right-to-manage and efficient bargaining models has been based on the observation that only in the latter model does the alternative wage enter into the labour demand equation (compare equations (3.6) and (3.13), for example). However, there are conditions under which (1) the efficient bargaining outcome is independent of the alternative wage and (2) the right-to-manage outcome is affected by alternative wages (depending on the nature of union utility). Thus, the empirical evidence is not definitive. To the extent that a consensus has emerged, it is that there is no direct evidence that firms and unions bargain over employment, but equally there is evidence that outcomes do lie off the labour demand curve (see MaCurdy and Pencavel, 1986). One way of reconciling these conflicting pieces of evidence is through the argument that unions do influence employment – for example, through their influence on workplace rules and practices – without exerting the same degree of bargaining influence over employment as over wages. A second explanation is through the sequential bargaining model of Manning (1987). This allows for the possibility that the firm and the union bargain over both wages and employment but that, unlike in the efficient bargaining model, the union bargaining parameter is not symmetric across the two: thus, the outcome would lie off both the labour demand and contract curves (for a discussion of empirical tests based on this idea, see Andrews and Harrison, 1991).

In view of the lack of any empirically grounded consensus on the relative appropriateness of the right-to-manage and efficient bargaining models, what does economic theory suggest as the valid approach? Theory would predict that agents should not reach outcomes which are inefficient: this insight is what lies behind support for the efficient bargaining model. But if firms can dictate the scope of bargaining, why should they accede to a union's demand to bargain over employment if this leads to more efficient but less profitable outcomes? So, following closely the analysis of Dowrick (1990) – but adapted to the linear product demand structure presented above – let us consider theoretically whether the right-to-manage or the efficient bargain is the more profitable.

Assume, for simplicity, the case of a rent-maximizing trade union. Consider first the right-to-manage model. It is straightforward to show that:

$$w^{RTM} = \bar{w} + \frac{\beta}{2}(a - \bar{w}), \tag{3.16}$$

$$l^{RTM} = \frac{(2 - \beta)}{4b}(a - \bar{w}), \tag{3.17}$$

$$\pi^{RTM} = \frac{(2 - \beta)^2}{16b}(a - \bar{w})^2. \tag{3.18}$$

Correspondingly, for efficient bargaining, partial differentiation of the Nash bargaining maximand with respect to both wages and employment yields:

$$w^{EB} = \bar{w} + \frac{\beta}{2}(a - \bar{w}), \tag{3.19}$$

$$l^{EB} = \frac{1}{2b}(a - \bar{w}), \tag{3.20}$$

$$\pi^{EB} = \frac{1 - \beta}{4b}(a - \bar{w})^2. \tag{3.21}$$

Comparison of (3.18) and (3.21) reveals that profits under the right-to-manage model exceed those under efficient bargaining. It follows that if the firm is able to choose the scope of bargaining, it will keep employment off the bargaining agenda rather than allow efficient bargaining. As noted, this result is attributable to Dowrick (1990). Espinosa and Rhee (1989) have shown that, in contrast, efficient bargaining becomes the equilibrium strategy if the union–firm bargaining game is repeated infinitely. Furthermore, Bughin (1999) has shown, in the context of unionized oligopoly, efficient bargaining emerges as the equilibrium in Nash strategies when the scope of bargaining is itself the outcome of a non-cooperative game. This case is discussed further below.

So a unionized monopolist will prefer a right-to-manage outcome to an efficient bargain. But will it prefer a right-to-manage bargain over any (sequential) bargain in which the scope of the bargain covers employment? In other words, will the firm prefer to keep employment off the bargaining agenda *whatever* the degree of union influence over employment? We can show that the answer to this is: yes.

In the sequential bargain, the union and the firm bargain first over the wage and, subsequently, over the level of employment *given the prior bargained wage*. There are two differences between the sequential and the efficient bargain. In the efficient bargain, wages and employment are chosen *simultaneously* and the extent of union influence over employment is equal to that over wages. In the sequential bargain, not only are wages determined *prior* to employment but also, in the general case, the extent of union influence over wages can differ from that over employment. To solve for the sequential bargaining outcome, we proceed by backward induction, first solving the stage 2 employment bargain for a given wage level.

We assume that the product market is as defined for the right-to-manage and efficient bargain models, as represented in equation (3.5). In stage 2, then, the union and the monopoly firm bargain over employment so as to maximize the Nash-maximand given by:

$$B_2 = U^\gamma \pi^{1-\gamma}, \tag{3.22}$$

where γ represents the union's bargaining power in the employment bargain. After substitution and solving, the firm's demand for labour is given by:

$$l = \frac{a - w}{(2 - \gamma)b}. \tag{3.23}$$

We notice that (3.23) is equivalent to (3.6) – the expression for labour demand under the right-to-manage assumption – if $\gamma = 0$. Substituting (3.23) and (3.4) into the stage 1 Nash bargaining maximand and solving with respect to the wage, yields:

$$w^{SB} = \bar{w} + \frac{\beta}{2}(a - \bar{w}), \tag{3.24}$$

$$I^{SB} = \frac{(2-\beta)}{2(2-\gamma)b}(a-\bar{w}), \qquad (3.25)$$

$$\pi^{SB} = \frac{(2-\beta)^2(1-\gamma)}{4(2-\gamma)^2 b}(a-\bar{w})^2. \qquad (3.26)$$

Comparison of (3.18), (3.21) and (3.26) confirms that the sequential bargaining model nests efficient bargaining (when $\gamma=\beta$) and the right-to-manage model (when $\gamma=0$). From further comparison of (3.18) and (3.26), we can conclude that, under unionized monopoly, the firm will prefer to keep employment off the bargaining agenda *whatever* the degree of union influence over employment. In other words, the right-to-manage outcome generates higher profits than either the efficient or sequential bargains, for a given level of union influence over the wage.

4. The structure and environment of bargaining
In this section, we turn away from bargaining scope and conduct to look at issues of bargaining and product market structure. The early modern literature on the economic analysis of unions typically made the following assumptions:

1. A single union;
2. A single firm;
3. A closed shop trade union; and,
4. The existence of surplus, originating in either:

   - Diminishing marginal product of labour, or
   - Monopoly market power of the firm, or
   - Unionization of the whole industry.

The assumption that bargaining takes place between a single firm and union simplified the analysis, but implied that potentially important interactions between union–firm pairs were largely ignored. The approach was justified on the grounds that the single-union pair could be interpreted as characterizing bargaining in the context of monopoly. Thus, there was no need to examine bargaining pair interactions. A further justification was that the rents might be accruing in a competitive market where again there was no need to take account of strategic interactions across firms and unions. Rents might emerge in competitive markets in either of two settings. First, if there are diminishing returns to labour. Second, if the union has succeeded in forcing the bargained outcome on to all firms in the industry – and there is no international competition – as in this case all firms can pass on a common wage increase in the form of higher prices. In both the pure monopoly and the perfectly competitive cases, there is no analytical need to model strategic interactions and hence the single union–firm pair bargain provides the appropriate framework.

The assumption of a closed shop trade union was useful in the specification of the union objective function as it justified the common assumption that membership was at least as great as employment (see the discussion following equation (3.2) above). An exception to this assumption is the analysis of Carruth and Oswald (1987) who distinguish between 'insiders' and 'outsiders' in the context of unionization. Carruth and Oswald show that if employment exceeds membership, then union indifference curves are kinked – becoming horizontal beyond the level of membership as the union does not care about the employment of workers who are outside the union. It can be shown that this changes the properties of the standard closed shop model considerably.

In contrast to the early work – with its typical assumption of a closed shop union bargaining with a single firm – from the late 1980s there developed a deeper interest in the implications of alternative assumptions about the structure of bargaining. What do we mean by bargaining structure? In the analysis developed in this chapter, we distinguish between internal and external 'bargaining structure'. By 'internal structure' we are referring to conditions within the establishment which affect the bargain. Internal structure refers, for example, to the presence of multiple unions within the establishment and the nature of bargaining coordination across any multiple unions. Internal conditions also include factors which affect the nature of disagreement payoffs, such as the extent of union membership density within the establishment or the presence of closed shop bargaining arrangements. By *external structure*, we refer to institutional conditions characterizing the bargaining relationships across establishments. These include the extent of centralization or coordination of bargaining *across* unions and/or employers within an industry (or beyond). Accordingly, external structure depends also upon the nature of product market competition and therefore on industrial structure.

Internal Bargaining Structure

As we have seen, early union models typically adopted the assumption of a closed shop trade union in which all the firm's employees were union members. The assumption of a closed shop union was convenient for two reasons: first, in the specification of the union objective function and, second, in justifying the idea of a potentially powerful union able to capture a share of any available surplus. The early axiomatic approach to Nash bargaining did not address the issue of what factors determine the extent of union bargaining power. The Nash bargaining parameter was typically interpreted as a catch-all or proxy indicator of union bargaining strength. Thus, in empirical applications of the early theoretical models it is not unusual to see the bargaining parameter proxied by, say, union membership density.

The development and application of non-cooperative game theory provided an alternative approach to the wage-bargaining problem (see Rubinstein, 1982; Binmore, Rubinstein and Wolinsky, 1986; and Sutton, 1986). Importantly, it was shown that – in an alternating offers model with no uncertainty – the game-theoretic solution is the same as the (generalized) Nash bargaining solution associated with the more ad hoc axiomatic approach. But the game-theoretic approach has several advantages over the axiomatic approach to wage bargaining. First, there is a more formal interpretation of the Nash bargaining parameter: it represents the relative impatience of the union and the firm to reach an agreement. Second, unlike the axiomatic approach, the analysis based on non-cooperative game theory clarifies the role of both inside options (or 'conflict' or 'disagreement' payoffs) and outside options. It becomes clear that the capacity of a union to capture a share of any surplus depends both on relative impatience and on the capacity of the union to (1) impose a loss on the firm in the event of a conflict and (2) to withstand a conflict through a high disagreement payoff itself. Third, the game-theoretic approach allows one to model formally the structure of the bargaining problem; for example, specifying the nature of the disagreement payoffs of the two parties in the context of the bargaining game.

A number of important papers have applied the non-cooperative game-theoretic approach in order to analyse in a rigorous way the role of disagreement payoffs and internal bargaining structure on the bargaining outcome. Here, we consider two: the models of Horn and Wolinsky (1988a) and of Moene (1988). Such models not only illuminate our understanding of the impact of internal bargaining structure on bargained outcomes, but also suggest insights for why particular bargaining structures might develop.

Horn and Wolinsky (1988a) observe that the theoretical industrial relations literature offers various types of explanation for differences in bargaining structure. They distinguish between legal-institutional reasons and strategic explanations and proceed to develop a bargaining model which is able to offer an important insight into whether bargaining in an establishment is likely to be characterized by multiple union agreements or by a single union agreement. Horn and Wolinsky (1988a) demonstrate that if worker groups are close substitutes in production, then they will be better off combining in a single union (or, equivalently, bargaining jointly in the case of multiple unions). On the other hand, if distinct groups of workers are highly complementary, then they will do better by bargaining separately.

The intuition for these results is straightforward: if two groups of workers are highly substitutable, then they can easily be 'divided and ruled' in the event of a conflict between the firm and either of the worker groups. In other words, the firm's conflict payoff in the event of a disagreement would be higher under separate bargaining as the firm could continue production by retaining the services of the other worker group. Consequently, the firm will be highly resistant to acceding to the wage demands of either group. Conversely, if the two groups are highly complementary, then each group is powerful under separate bargaining as the firm does not then have the option of producing with just one group. Hence, its disagreement payoff is low and it concedes a higher bargained wage. For empirical analysis relating to the model, see Machin et al. (1993).

In a situation in which firms are better off under multiple union agreements, this might lead firms to organize themselves as multiple plant organizations in order to create obstacles to single union agreements. Thus, the model of Horn and Wolinsky (1988a) generates insights not only for the nature of plant-level bargaining, but also for the nature of firm structure. The analysis of Horn and Wolinsky (1988a) can be also interpreted as providing a rigorous game-theoretic intuition for the importance of both (1) the elasticity of substitution between a union's labour input and the other factors (such as capital, non-union labour or labour controlled by other unions) and (2) the elasticity of supply of these other factors.

Moene (1988) points out that the axiomatic interpretation of the Nash bargain pays insufficient attention both to strategic considerations in wage bargaining and to the nature of the underlying bargaining structure. He considers four different kinds of conflict action. These are; working-to-rule, go-slows, wild cat strikes, and official strikes/lockouts. Each action imposes a different disagreement payoff on the firm and hence a different marginal cost of employment. Moene shows that the sub-game credibility of threats depends only on the union and firm's conflict payoffs and that only one type of threat is credible. The nature of the credible threat depends on the parameters associated with the conflict outcomes (such as strike support, conflict production and conflict remuneration of workers). An important contribution of both the Moene (1988) and Horn and Wolinsky (1988a) models is that they provide an analysis of the endogenous determination of internal bargaining structure through their demonstration of the sensitivity of the bargaining outcomes to the nature of the bargaining environment. In related work, Naylor and Raaum (1993) show how bargained wages are influenced by another characteristic of the internal bargaining structure – establishment-level union density – in a model in which density affects the firm's disagreement payoff (see also Booth and Chatterji, 1995, and Ulph and Ulph, 1990, for related analyses).

External bargaining structure

As we have described, early models focused on single-firm single-union bargains and largely abstracted from issues concerning; internal bargaining structure, the nature of product market competition, and the related interactions between different bargaining units. From the late 1980s there developed a significant, albeit somewhat disparate, literature addressing the question of the interaction between bargaining and product market structure (and indeed conduct). We would argue that this was a very natural development from both empirical and theoretical perspectives.

Theoretically, it was natural to address more rigorously the question of the origin of the surplus over which bargaining takes place and to model the extent of available surplus as related to the extent of product market competition. Furthermore, research in industrial economics began to attach a significant focus to the related issues of vertical market relations and bilateral oligopoly (see, for example, Waterson and Dobson, 1996). In this context, it was natural to interpret the union–firm bargain as an example of an upstream–downstream relationship and to model the bargain as the outcome of a two-stage sequential game. At the same time as these theoretical developments, empirical analysis of the union/non-union wage differential showed the crucial influence of product market competition on the capacity of unions to raise wages (see, for example, Stewart, 1990).

We now proceed to outline a model of unionized oligopoly that will allow us to demonstrate the importance of factors such as product market structure and the nature of the external bargaining environment.

Unionized oligopoly: a simple model The assumptions of the basic model are that:

1. The product market is imperfectly competitive;
2. Cournot competition characterizes the product market;
3. Each of the (n) firms faces a local union;
4. Bargaining is decentralized to the level of the (n) union–firm pairs;
5. There is symmetry across both the firms and the unions: that is, all firms are identical, as are all unions;
6. Product demand is described by a linear demand function;
7. Firms produce a homogeneous product;
8. Unions have the objective of rent maximization;
9. Firms have the right-to-manage, so that wage-employment outcomes are on the firms' demand curves; and,
10. Returns to labour are constant, with the marginal product set to one as the numeraire.

Under these assumptions, we can specify the model as follows. Product demand is given by:

$$p = a - bX, \tag{3.27}$$

where

$$X = L = \sum_{i=1}^{n} l_i \tag{3.28}$$

represents total industry output. The representative firm i will aim to maximize profits which are given by:

$$\pi_i = (a - bL - w_i)l_i = (a - bl_i - bL_j - w_i)l_i, \tag{3.29}$$

where

$$L_j = \sum_{\substack{i=1 \\ i \neq j}}^{n} l_i. \tag{3.30}$$

From (3.29), the first-order condition for profit-maximization yields:

$$\frac{\partial \pi_i}{\partial l_i} = a - 2bl_i - bL_j - w_i = 0, \tag{3.31}$$

from which it follows that:

$$l_i = \frac{1}{2b}(a - bL_j - w_i), \tag{3.32}$$

which is, of course, firm i's Cournot best-reply function with respect to the output of the other firms.

Altogether, there are n first-order conditions of the form represented in equation (3.32) – one for each of the n union-firm bargaining pairs. Summing over these n FOCs and solving for firm i, yields:

$$l_i = \frac{1}{(n+1)b}(a - nw_i + \Sigma w_j), \tag{3.33}$$

where $\displaystyle\sum w_j = \sum_{\substack{i=1 \\ i \neq j}}^{n} w_i.$

Equation (3.33) represents firm i's sub-game perfect labour demand function. Under the assumptions of the basic unionized oligopoly model, the union–firm pair i will bargain over wages subject to this labour demand equation. The union's rent-maximizing objective is defined by:

$$U_i = (w_i - \bar{w})l_i, \tag{3.34}$$

where $\bar{w}$ is the reservation wage. The decentralized Nash bargained wage solves:

$$w_i^D = \arg\max \, [B_i = U_i^\beta \pi_i^{1-\beta}], \tag{3.35}$$

where conflict payoffs are assumed to be zero. Substituting (3.33) in (3.29) and (3.34) and subsequently solving (3.35) yields, in symmetric equilibrium, a subgame perfect Nash equilibrium bargained wage of:

$$W^D = \bar{w} + \frac{\beta}{\beta + (2-\beta)n}(a - \bar{w}), \tag{3.36}$$

under decentralized bargaining. We see immediately from equation (3.36) that, if the union has any influence over the wage level (i.e. if $\beta > 0$), then:

$$\frac{dw^D}{dn} < 0, \tag{3.37}$$

implying that an increase in the number of firms competing in the product market will have the unambiguous effect of reducing the bargained wage. This result is consistent with both the empirical analysis of Stewart (1990) and the related theoretical framework developed by Dowrick (1989). Thus, one aspect of product market structure – the number of firms competing in the market-place – can be shown to influence the nature of the bargained wage outcome. It is also, of course, straightforward in this framework to show how the bargained wage outcome varies with the type of competition in the product market. (See Nickell, 1999, for a more general discussion of the interaction between product market competitiveness and labour market outcomes.)

The model of unionized oligopoly allows for the strategic interactions which occur across bargaining units and which are ignored in the basic monopoly, competitive and monopolistically competitive models. Following on from Bulow et al. (1985), Padilla et al. (1996) showed the conditions under which wages are strategic substitutes for firms and strategic complements for unions. Under the assumptions of the basic union oligopoly model developed above, we can show that for the two-firm case ($n = 2$):

$$\frac{\partial^2 \pi_1}{\partial w_1 \partial w_2} < 0, \tag{3.38}$$

and that:

$$\frac{\partial^2 U_1}{\partial w_1 \partial w_2} > 0. \tag{3.39}$$

In other words, wages are strategic substitutes for firms and strategic complements for unions. We shall consider further the significance of this below, when we compare the decentralized bargaining outcome with that arising from centralized bargaining.

Centralized versus decentralized bargaining   We have seen that product market characteristics, such as the number of firms in the market, affect the outcome of wage bargaining. We now consider the nature of the effect of the level of bargaining on the outcome. This issue has generated significant interest since the pioneering work of Calmfors and Driffill (1988) on the relationship between bargaining centralization and coordination and bargaining outcomes (see also Boeri et al. (2001); Flanagan et al. (1993) and Chapter 6 by Flanagan in this volume). A concern with the level of bargaining has origins both in macroeconomic interest in differential performance across countries in response to adverse shocks, and also in the early econometric work on union/non-union wage differentials (see, for example, Mulvey, 1976).

Let us consider a variant of the basic unionized oligopoly model in which we now allow for the possibility that firms' products are differentiated. For simplicity, assume that $n = 2$. Our principal aim is to show how the level of bargaining affects the wage outcome. We also show the impact of the extent of product differentiation: an important characteristic of product market competition. The model follows closely the seminal paper of Horn and Wolinsky (1988b). See also Davidson (1988) for a related analysis of the importance of the level of bargaining.

With differentiated products, we can write the linear product demands for the two firms as:

$$p_1 = a - cx_2 - x_1, \tag{3.40}$$

and

$$p_2 = a - cx_1 - x_2, \tag{3.41}$$

for firm 1 and firm 2, respectively.

Decentralized bargaining   Let us suppose initially that bargaining is decentralized to the level of the individual union–firm pair. Then, following the same solution strategy as in the basic model above, the decentralized bargained wage for union–firm pair 1 can be written as:

$$w_1^D = \bar{w} + \frac{1}{4}[\beta(2 - c)(a - \bar{w}) + c\beta(w_2 - \bar{w})]. \tag{3.42}$$

From equation (3.42), we can see that, for $c > 0$ (that is, for the case of imperfect substitutability between products):

$$\frac{\partial w_1}{\partial w_2} = \frac{c\beta}{4} > 0, \tag{3.43}$$

and hence that bargained wages are strategic complements.

In symmetric equilibrium, it follows from (3.42) that the decentralized bargained wage is given by:

$$w^D = w_1^D = w_2^D = \bar{w} + \frac{\beta(2 - c)}{4 - c\beta}(a - \bar{w}). \tag{3.44}$$

We can now compare this wage outcome with that obtaining under centralized bargaining.

Centralized bargaining   Under centralized bargaining, the Nash bargained wage satisfies:

$$w^c = \arg\max \{B = (U_1 + U_2)^{\beta}(\pi_1 + \pi_2)^{1-\beta}\}, \tag{3.45}$$

and the solution to this is given by:

$$w^c = \bar{w} + \frac{\beta}{2}(a - \bar{w}). \tag{3.46}$$

We notice that the centralized bargained wage is independent of the extent of product substitutability/complementarity. It is also equal to the wage which would obtain under bilateral monopoly and, consequently, it follows that the centralized wage bargain, unlike the wage bargained under decentralization, is independent of the number of firms in the product market.

How does the centralized wage compare with the wage level bargained under decentralization? Comparison of (3.44) and (3.46) reveals that, for gross substitutes at least, the wage under centralized bargaining exceeds that under decentralization.[4] The intuition for this result lies in the strategic complementarity of the bargained wage under decentralization. To see this most clearly, consider the unions' preferred wage outcomes. These are captured in (3.44) and (3.46) under the assumption that $\beta = 1$. Substituting $\beta = 1$ into equation (3.42) gives union 1's best-reply function. This, together with the equivalent reaction function for union 2, is represented in Figure 3.5, where the bargained wage outcomes and union iso-utility – or indifference – curves are also shown. With decentralized wage bargaining, the strategic interaction between the union–firm pairs leads to wage moderation when product markets are imperfectly competitive and oligopoly profits or

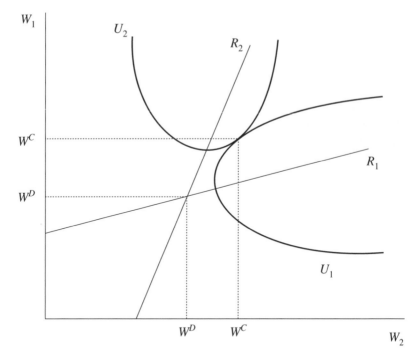

Figure 3.5   Union sub-game perfect best-reply functions

surplus can be captured. Under centralized bargaining, this wage moderation does not arise.

Horn and Wolinsky (1988b) have shown that, for $c > 0$, unions prefer centralized bargaining and firms prefer decentralized bargaining. The opposite obtains when firms produce goods which are imperfect complements
for each other. Thus, firms and unions have conflicting interests over the
level of bargaining. The prediction, then, is that the actual degree of centralization observed is likely to reflect the relative capacities of unions and
firms to shape the bargaining environment. It follows that the nature of the
bargaining arrangements should most correctly be thought of as endogenously determined. In most models – theoretical and empirical – however,
the structure of bargaining is typically taken as given.[5]

As Blau and Kahn (1999) have commented, a major advance in the economic analysis of unions centres on models of bargaining centralization
and coordination. In this chapter, we have only been able to touch on the
importance on bargaining level. We have seen how, depending on various
product market characteristics, the level of bargaining affects the equilibrium values of wages, employment, profits and union utility. We have

inferred from this that the extent to which bargaining is centralized is likely to reflect the competing interests in the bargaining agents and their capacities to shape the bargaining environment. The reader is referred to Flanagan et al. (1993) for a more thorough and detailed theoretical analysis of the impact of different bargaining structures on economic performance, and to Boeri et al. (2001) for a survey of work on the impact of bargaining centralization and coordination.

In our preceding analysis, we have assumed that decentralized bargaining occurs simultaneously across bargaining pairs. A natural extension of this approach would be to examine a leader–follower model. Such non-synchronized bargaining behaviour is observed to occur in many industries in the form of pattern bargaining. Dobson (1994) has examined this case and has shown that unions have an incentive to bargain first with a firm which either is in a weak bargaining position (in the sense of being impatient to settle) or has relatively large surplus. Again, this represents an important theoretical explanation of the possible influences on bargaining structure.

Other applications
The previous section demonstrated the important insights that can be gained from setting the bargaining problem within a unionized oligopoly model. The analysis of unionized oligopoly has generated a number of other results and shown that traditional results in oligopoly theory are not always robust to the introduction of union–firm bargaining. Here we survey some applications of the unionized oligopoly model and show that their implications are of importance both for labour economics and also for other sub-disciplines of economics.

The scope of bargaining (revisited) We saw in section 3 that firms will prefer right-to-manage bargaining outcomes to those resulting from efficient bargaining in the case of unionized monopoly. Bughin (1999) demonstrates that in a unionized oligopoly setting, there is a dominant strategy towards efficient bargaining. There is thus a prisoner's dilemma nature regarding the firms' choice of bargaining scope as profits are lower when both firms choose efficient bargaining than when both choose right-to-manage bargaining. This can be demonstrated as follows.

Consider first the case of a right-to-manage bargain in the context of a unionized duopoly. We assume that bargaining is decentralized and that each union has the objective of maximizing rents. Hence, it follows from (3.36) that, with $n = 2$, the bargained wage is:

$$w^{RTM} = \bar{w} + \frac{\beta}{4 - \beta}(a - \bar{w}), \tag{3.47}$$

and the equilibrium profits of each firm are:

$$\pi^{RTM} = \frac{4(2-\beta)^2}{9(4-\beta)^2 b}(a-\bar{w})^2. \tag{3.48}$$

Consider now an efficient (decentralized) bargain in unionized duopoly. Then, from partial differentiation of the Nash maximand with respect to the wage and employment levels, respectively, of union–firm pair 1, the first-order conditions yield:

$$w^{EB} = \bar{w} + \frac{\beta}{3}(a-\bar{w}), \tag{3.49}$$

and the equilibrium profits of each firm are:

$$\pi^{EB} = \frac{(1-\beta)}{9b}(a-\bar{w})^2. \tag{3.50}$$

Comparison of (3.48) and (3.50) confirms, as in the case of unionized monopoly, that $\pi^{RTM} > \pi^{EB}$ also for the case of unionized duopoly.

Finally, we note that whereas in the case of unionized monopoly, sequential bargaining nests both the right-to-manage and efficient bargains, this is no longer necessarily the case under unionized oligopoly. The reason for this lies in the fact that in the case of oligopoly, the strategic game played between the union–firm pairs acquires an additional strategic element in the case of the sequential bargain which is not present in the case of the efficient bargain (see Santoni, 1996).

The choice between price-setting and quantity-setting   Models of unionized oligopoly with differentiated products typically assume Cournot competition in which firms choose output. This is often justified on the grounds that firms prefer quantity to price-setting behaviour when products are gross substitutes, as demonstrated in the classic paper by Singh and Vives (1984). However, this result is established only for the case in which input (e.g. labour) prices are given. With endogenous input prices, Correa López and Naylor (2002) show that the standard result that Cournot profits exceed Bertrand profits obtains *unless* unions are both very powerful in the right-to-manage wage bargain and sufficiently wage-oriented in their utility function. The standard result can be reversed theoretically because of the fact that labour demand is less responsive to a change in wages under Cournot competition and this leads unions to bargain for higher wages than when competition in the product market is of the Bertrand type. If unions care sufficiently about wages and their bargaining power is great enough, then the fact that unions impact relatively more on wages and profits under Cournot competition can overturn the standard result.

Nevertheless, the conclusion remains that, for typical assumptions regarding the bargaining environment, it is appropriate for union-oligopoly models to proceed to assume Cournot rather than Bertrand equilibria in product markets.

Unions and entry In his classic paper, Williamson (1968) argued that unions can be used by firms as a strategic entry barrier, with union-bargained wages acting as a disincentive to entry by potential new firms. There are now a number of papers which use modern game-theoretic approaches to address the issue of the extent to which unions might enhance the profitability of firms through their role as a strategic entry deterrent. Such an approach offers one possible route for explaining the existence of unions, or at least their recognition by firms.

Vannini and Bughin (2000) use a unionized oligopoly set-up and show that, depending on the scope of bargaining, unions can represent a commitment device for firms to exert market power. Thus, firms can benefit from the presence of unions, despite the adverse effect of unions on wages. Two related papers address the issue of firm ownership and control in a unionized oligopoly. Bughin (1995) shows that strategic managerial incentives can be used to undermine union bargaining power and therefore questions the assumption of profit maximization in union–firm bargaining models. Szymanski (1994), in a duopoly model of strategic delegation and wage bargaining, shows that owners may benefit from strong unions.

In a related analysis, Naylor (2002) shows that in the presence of unions, entry does not necessarily reduce either industry profits or profits-per-firm. The intuition for the result is that increased product market competition following an increase in the number of firms is mirrored by increased labour market rivalry which induces (profit-enhancing) wage moderation. Whether the product or labour market effect dominates depends both on the extent of union bargaining power and on the nature of union preferences. A corollary of the results derived is that if the upstream agents are firms rather than labour unions, then profits are always decreasing in the number of firms, as in the standard Cournot model. However, industry profits can rise with an increase in the number of firms, with implications for the relationship between unions and the extent of product market competition.

Unions, foreign direct investment and international trade Foreign direct investment is one form of market entry which has generated growing interest from labour economists developing models of unions and bargaining. More generally, there has grown a considerable literature examining the relationship between union bargaining and international trade. In the context of discussions about the effects of globalization and regional economic integration, a growing number of studies have addressed the issue of how falling trade costs affect the capacity of unions to raise wages above non-union levels.

Driffill and van der Ploeg (1993) show that cutting tariffs has little effect on the wage set under decentralized bargaining but raises wages set by centralized unions. In a unionized duopoly model, Huizinga (1993) and Sørensen (1993) indicate that economic integration which takes two economies from complete autarky to full integration reduces bargained wages. The issue is an important one for two principal reasons. First, in a European context, the impact of integration on union wage-setting behaviour is a key determinant of the impact of the Single Market Programme (SMP) on macroeconomic performance. Second, the way in which globalization and freer international trade impact on income distribution will be mediated in part through the response of wage-setting institutions. The relationship between trade and wages is not a straightforward one. Surprisingly, there is even evidence that greater trade protection can be associated with lower wages and lower union influence on wages (see Gaston and Trefler, 1994). On the other hand, Stewart (1990) has shown that the capacity of unions to establish a wage mark-up is significantly limited in the presence of foreign competition in the product market.

The Huizinga–Sørensen result can be seen by comparing the wage that obtains in bargaining between a single firm and its union located within an autarkic economy with that which obtains when two previously autarkic countries merge, such that a unionized oligopoly replaces two internationally separate unionized monopoly firms. Under linear demand, it emerges that the wage-moderating effect of more intense product market competition dominates the wage-augmenting effect associated with market expansion. This is for the case of a discrete shift from complete autarky to full integration. More relevant to the development of the SMP, is the case of continuous integration as the marginal cost of trade diminishes with economic integration. In this case, it can be shown that small reductions in trade costs can lead unions to translate trade expansion into higher bargained wages (see Naylor, 1998, 1999). Figure 3.6 illustrates.

These models of two-way trade – or 'cross hauling' – in which both countries are unionized, build on the early work on two-way trade (e.g. Brander, 1981; Brander and Krugman, 1983) and on the partially unionized one-way trade model of Brander and Spencer (1988). A further development based on Cournot duopoly is the model of Mezzetti and Dinopoulos (1991) who show that if a domestic union is wage oriented, trade protection can lead to a fall in output and welfare. Santoni (1996) also considers the case of an international duopoly in which only the home firm is unionized: in this model, the domestic union–firm pair uses the bargained wage as a strategic variable to determine international market share. In this case, domestic

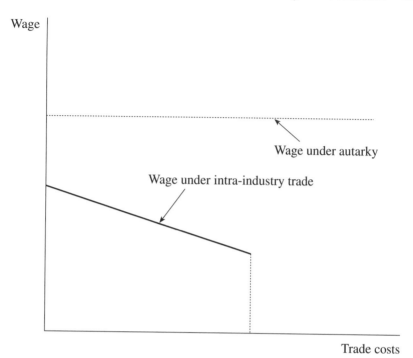

Figure 3.6   A fall in trade costs can lead to higher wages under intra-industry trade and unionized oligopoly

trade policy is shown to depend critically on both bargaining structure and on the nature of product market spillover effects. In a different setting, Danthine and Hunt (1994) analyse the impact of economic integration on wage-setting behaviour. Their key insight is based on the observation that integration renders nationally centralized bargaining inefficient as it generates international wage externalities. Other unionized oligopoly models of trade and trade policy include Fung (1995), Fisher and Wright (1999), Straume (2002) and Lommerud et al. (2002).

On the specific issue of foreign direct investment (FDI), Zhao (1995) extends the symmetric unionized oligopoly model of cross hauling in trade to that in foreign direct investment. In particular, Zhao shows that reciprocal FDI is the unique Nash perfect equilibrium and has the effect of reducing bargained wages in a model in which the incentive for FDI stems from the benefits associated with diversification. In this sense, FDI is a strategy for raising the firm's conflict payoffs in a bargaining environment in which international union cooperation is not feasible. In related work, Bughin and Vannini (1995) show how the incentives for firms to make FDI and for unions to oppose it depend on the nature of the bargaining environment. Lommerud et al. (2002) develop a unionized oligopoly model which allows for both trade in products and FDI.

This section of the chapter has surveyed some of the literature based on models of unionized oligopoly. The survey is by no means exhaustive. Rather, it is intended to give an indication of the diverse nature of the issues addressed within this expanding literature and to demonstrate the richness of the approach for researchers in various fields of economics: through the sub-disciplines of labour, industrial, international and macro economics.

5.   Explaining union membership

Firm or plant-level union membership density is likely to be an important element shaping the internal bargaining structure in the decentralized bargain. Despite this, standard theoretical models of union behaviour take the existence of the union as given and, typically, assume a closed shop union in which all workers are members of the union. In some ways, these assumptions are surprising; not least in the context of a long-standing empirical literature on the determinants of union membership (see, for example, Farber, 1983, and Chapter 2 by Schnabel in this volume). Nonetheless, there has been a growing interest in the related – but distinct – theoretical questions of why unions form and of why workers voluntarily join unions. The explanation of union existence or formation depends on an understanding not only of why workers might want to form unions but also of why firms might tolerate – or, indeed, encourage – union presence.

Management response to a demand for unionization will depend on a number of factors, including the legal environment, product market conditions and the nature of labour supply and of working conditions. Freeman and Pelletier (1990) emphasize the importance of management attitudes to unionization as a determinant of aggregate membership. The industrial relations literature has long emphasized the advantages unions can bring firms in terms of generating a more stable workplace environment for the resolution of potential conflict. Similarly, Freeman and Medoff (1984) indicate a plethora of reasons for which the existence of unions might be explained on efficiency or transactions costs grounds, as we have indicated earlier in this chapter. In what follows, however, we focus on the question of what might determine union membership in an establishment, *conditional* on union presence.[6]

The seminal work by Olson (1965) on the logic of collective action indicates the nature of the problem encountered in attempting to explain voluntary union membership. As it is typically the case that all workers (carrying out some common task) in an establishment receive a common wage, there is a dominant strategy for each worker to free-ride in avoiding the costs of union membership. In other words, union membership has the characteristics of a large numbers prisoner's dilemma. Each agent has an incentive to free-ride even though such behaviour leads to the Pareto sub-optimal outcome associated with zero membership. Without a significant number of members, there is unlikely to be a substantial union capacity to raise wages above non-union levels. So why do workers join unions in 'open shop' cases in which membership is not compulsory? Broadly, there are three main approaches to answering this question.

The first is associated with Grossman (1983) and is based on the notion of a dichotomous labour market comprising union and non-union sectors. The size of the two sectors is determined by the interaction between the demand for union membership and a wage schedule along which wages vary with membership. Membership demand is falling in union wages as higher wages imply a greater unemployment probability for members, while union wages themselves are falling in membership as the median member prefers lower wages the greater is membership. In this way, union member-ship and therefore the size of the union sector are determined endogenously with wages. Membership is voluntary but the dichotomous labour market assumption means that union plants are characterized by 100 per cent membership. For this reason, the model is probably a better characteriza-tion of North American labour markets than of European labour markets in which we observe 'open shop' plants with less than complete member-ship.

The second model of voluntary membership escapes the free-rider problem by positing that union membership buys an excludable private good, such as legal and pensions advice, the processing of grievances and unfair dismissal protection. Booth and Chatterji (1995) develop a model along these lines and assume that the union faces a budget constraint in its organizational activity. They develop a model in which wages and member-ship are determined endogenously and then they test this model empiri-cally, finding evidence that wages are increasing with membership but that membership is independent of wages. The authors conclude from this that the free-rider problem is likely to be a real threat to union bargaining power.

The third approach to explain away the free-rider problem is based on the social custom model. This model itself can be interpreted as a special case of the private incentive good model in which the private good is the accrual of 'reputation' utility associated with conformity to the social custom of union membership (see, *inter alia*, Booth, 1985; Naylor, 1989; Naylor and Raaum, 1993; Booth and Chatterji, 1993). The essential idea is as follows.

Suppose that there is a social custom invoking workers to join a trade union. Following Akerlof (1980, p. 749), a social custom is defined as: 'An act whose utility to the agent performing it in some way depends on the beliefs or actions of other members of the community'. Suppose that the community consists of both 'believers' and 'non-believers' in the social custom. Consider the utility function of a believer, b. If he or she joins the union, then:

$$U_b^J = w(\mu) + \epsilon r \mu - c, \tag{3.51}$$

where the union-bargained wage, w, is an increasing function of membership density, μ, c represents the individual membership fee, and r denotes the reputation-utility derived from conforming to the social custom of joining the union. Reputation-utility is assumed to be increasing in membership density and also to be a function of ϵ, which measures the individual's sensitivity to reputation effects. If the individual who believes in the social custom fails to join the union, then utility is given by:

$$U_b^{NJ} = w(\mu) - s, \tag{3.52}$$

and this individual forgoes the utility derived from reputation effects and also loses utility, s, associated with violating the social custom.

For a non-believer, utility from joining the union is given by:

$$U_{nb}^J = w(\mu) + \epsilon r \mu - c, \tag{3.53}$$

which is identical to that for the believer. The difference between the believer and the non-believer comes from the expression for utility associated with not joining the union. For the non-believer, this is:

$$U_{nb}^{NJ} = w(\mu) - t, \tag{3.54}$$

where t, the utility loss associated with violating the custom, is less than s – the equivalent loss incurred by believers.

We can thus establish the union-joining rules for the two types of individual. A believer will join the union so long as $U_b^J \geq U_b^{NJ}$, that is:

$$\epsilon r \mu - c \geq - s, \tag{3.55}$$

or

$$\epsilon \geq \frac{c - s}{r \mu}. \tag{3.56}$$

Similarly, a non-believer will join if:

$$\epsilon \geq \frac{c-t}{r\mu}. \tag{3.57}$$

Assume now that ϵ is distributed uniformly between ϵ_0 and ϵ_1, where $\epsilon_1 > \epsilon_0 > 0$, and that if there are both believers and non-believers in the population, then the latter group consists of the individuals with lower values of ϵ_0. In other words, belief in the social custom and sensitivity to reputation-derived utility are positively correlated.

We can represent the decision schedules – equations (3.56) and (3.57) – in (μ, ϵ)-space. Figure 3.7 shows the decision schedule for believers. The figure also includes the distribution schedule.

Suppose initially that all individuals are believers. Then from Figure 3.7, we can see that there are four stable equilibria for the level of union membership. The first occurs at point K in the figure. At K, membership is 100 per cent and this induces all individuals to join the union: equation (3.56) is satisfied. A second equilibrium occurs at L where membership is zero and this is also self-reinforcing: insufficient reputation-utility is derived to

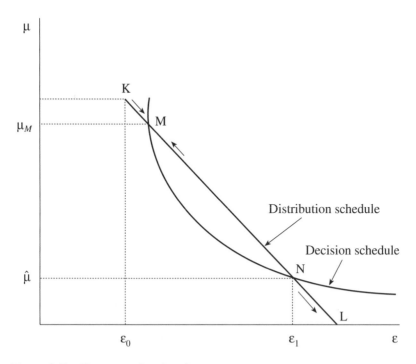

Figure 3.7   Union membership dynamics

induce any one individual to join the union. There is also a stable intermediate equilibrium at M in the diagram, where the level of membership
density is μ_M and this is self-supporting. For membership density between
100 per cent and μ_M, density falls to μ_M. For membership below μ_M but
above a critical level, $\hat{\mu}$, density rises to μ_M. The critical density level, $\hat{\mu}$, is
indicated by point N in the figure. Below $\hat{\mu}$, density falls to zero. Thus, the
critical density level has the status of a threshold level of membership.

The figure is drawn on the assumption that all individuals are believers.
If we also allow for the possibility of non-believers, then instead of a single
point equilibrium for the intermediate density solution, there is a range of
equilibrium density levels (see Naylor, 1989 for an elaboration).

This social custom model of union membership has a number of desirable properties. First, it is able to overcome the problem associated with the
free-rider incentive. Second, it generates a number of empirically testable
predictions and offers possible explanations for empirically observed phenomena. For example, an implication of the critical mass property of the
'tipping' equilibrium is that a temporary exogenous shock which causes a
decline in union membership density can have permanent effects on union
membership.

This section of the chapter has indicated three principal arguments by
which to explain the existence of voluntary union membership and has
sketched the social custom model in detail. These union membership
models can then be integrated into standard wage bargaining models and
their properties examined. Booth and Chatterji (1995) investigate the comparative static properties of a joint model of wage and membership determination. Amongst other results, they show that both membership and
bargained wages will be increasing in union bargaining power and alternative opportunities. They also show that an increase in union costs will cause
an increase in the wage but will have an ambiguous effect on membership.
For further discussion on the impact of wage–membership endogeneity, we
refer the reader to Booth and Chatterji (1993, 1995) and Naylor and
Raaum (1993).

6. Conclusions
In this chapter surveying the economic theory of the trade union, we have
necessarily been selective in our coverage of issues and models. We have
given prominence to the issue of bargaining structure and, in particular, to
the literature on unionized oligopoly. In part, this latter focus reflects our
belief that to date this important and expanding literature has been rather
disparate and diffuse. In our presentation of formal models, we have chosen
to focus on a particular set of assumptions (such as linear demand and
rent-maximizing behaviour) in order to illustrate and compare key results

in both traditional monopoly and in unionized oligopoly settings. One consequence is that we have neglected to cover some significant results in the literature; in particular, we have devoted very little attention to the issue of the robustness of results to the underlying assumptions of the models developed (see Manning, 1994; Nickell, 1999). Among the important areas of work omitted from consideration in this chapter are topics involving the interaction between unions and wage dispersion, strikes, effort and hours determination, discrimination, and efficiency.

The economic analysis of unions is as dynamic a field of economic research as it was when surveyed by Oswald (1985). Naturally enough, the approaches and the areas of concern have evolved substantially since then, with developments in non-cooperative game theory and with a growing collaboration between labour economists on the one hand, and industrial, international and macroeconomists on the other. There remains a substantial gap between the focus of much theory and the concerns of applied labour economists in the field. But the gap is narrowing and the interactions between the different fields of economics inspired by the analysis of unions and their effects is both healthy and exciting.

Acknowledgement

I am grateful to Mónica Correa López, Oddbjørn Raaum, Michele Santoni and Peter Wright for helpful discussion and to colleagues in the Department of Economics at the University of Warwick.

Notes

1. Hence, the contemporaneous growth in search models, implicit contract theory and efficiency wage theories, *inter alia*. Indeed, many of the early developments in the economic theory of the trade union originated in work focusing on macroeconomics. See, for example, Nickell (1982), Nickell and Andrews (1983), Layard et al. (1991).
2. We comment briefly below on the famous 'debate' between Ross (1948) and Dunlop (1944).
3. The fabled 'disappearing Cheshire Cat' leaves only its smile behind.
4. Vannetelbosch (1997) shows that wages are not necessarily lower under decentralized bargaining when there is private information.
5. Flanagan (1999) argues for analysis based on an understanding of the endogeneity of the level of bargaining.
6. The issue of what determines recognition is an important one. For a discussion, see Disney et al. (1995).

References

Akerlof, George E. (1980), 'A Theory of Social Custom of which Unemployment may be One Consequence', *Quarterly Journal of Economics*, 94 (4), 749–775.
Andrews, Martyn J. and Alan H. Harrison (1991), 'Testing for Efficient Contracts in Unionized Labour Markets', mimeograph, University of Manchester.
Binmore, Ken, Ariel Rubinstein and Asher Wolinsky (1986), 'The Nash Bargaining Solution in Economic Modelling', *Rand Journal of Economics*, 17 (2), 176–188.

Blau, Francine D. and Lawrence M. Kahn (1999), 'Institutions and Laws in the Labor
    Market', in Orley Ashenfelter and David Card (eds), *Handbook of Labor Economics*,
    Volume 3, Amsterdam: North Holland, pp. 1399–1461.
Boeri, Tito, Agar Brugiavini and Lars Calmfors (eds) (2001), *The Role of Unions in the
    Twenty-First Century*, Oxford: Oxford University Press.
Booth, Alison L. (1984), 'A Public Choice Model of Trade Union Behaviour and
    Membership', *Economic Journal*, 94 (376), 883–898.
Booth, Alison L. (1985), 'The Free Rider Problem and a Social Custom Model of Trade
    Union Membership', *Quarterly Journal of Economics*, 100 (1), 253–261.
Booth, Alison L. (1995), *The Economics of the Trade Union*, Cambridge: Cambridge
    University Press.
Booth, Alison L. and Monojit Chatterji (1993), 'Reputation, Membership and Wages in an
    Open Shop Trade Union', *Oxford Economic Papers*, 45 (1), 23–41.
Booth, Alison L. and Monojit Chatterji (1995), 'Union Membership and Wage Bargaining
    when Membership is not Compulsory', *Economic Journal*, 105 (429), 345–360.
Brander, James A. (1981), 'Intra-Industry Trade in Identical Commodities', *Journal of
    International Economics*, 11 (1), 1–14.
Brander, James A. and Paul Krugman (1983), 'A "Reciprocal Dumping" Model of
    International Trade', *Journal of International Economics*, 15 (3/4), 313–321, ADD.
Brander, James A. and Barbara J. Spencer (1988), 'Unionised Oligopoly and International
    Trade Policy', *Journal of International Economics*, 24 (3/4), 217–234.
Bughin, Jacques (1995), 'Unions and Strategic Managerial Incentives', *Economics Letters*, 47
    (1), 95–100.
Bughin, Jacques (1999), 'The Strategic Choice of Union-Oligopoly Bargaining Agenda',
    International Journal of Industrial Organization, 17 (7), 1029–1040.
Bughin, Jacques and Stefano Vannini (1995), 'Strategic Direct Investment under Unionized
    Oligopoly', *International Journal of Industrial Organization*, 13 (1), 127–145.
Bulow, Jeremy, John Geanakoplos and Paul Klemperer (1985), 'Multimarket Oligopoly:
    Strategic Substitutes and Complements', *Journal of Political Economy*, 93 (3), 488–511.
Calmfors, Lars (1982), 'Employment Policies, Wage Formation and Trade Union Behaviour
    in a Small Open Economy', *Scandinavian Journal of Economics*, 84 (2), 345–373.
Calmfors, Lars and John Driffill (1988), 'Bargaining Structure, Corporatism and
    Macroeconomic Performance', *Economic Policy*, 6 (1), 13–61.
Carruth, Alan A. and Andrew J. Oswald (1985), 'Miners' Wages in Post-War Britain: an
    Application of a Model of Trade Union Behaviour', *Economic Journal*, 95 (380),
    1003–1020.
Carruth, Alan A. and Andrew J. Oswald (1987), 'On Union Preferences and Labour Market
    Models: Insiders and Outsiders', *Economic Journal*, 97 (386), 431–445.
Cartter, Allan M. (1959), *Theory of Wages and Employment*, Homewood, IL: Irwin.
Cole, G.D.H. and Raymond Postgate (1963), *The Common People: 1746–1946*, London:
    Methuen.
Commons, John R. (1909), 'American Shoemakers 1648–1895: a Sketch of Industrial
    Evolution', *Quarterly Journal of Economics*, 24 (1), 39–84.
Commons, John R. (1934), *Institutional Economics*, Madison: University of Wisconsin Press.
Corden, W.M. (1981), 'Taxation, Real Wage Rigidity and Employment', *Economic Journal*, 91
    (362), 309–330.
Correa López, Mónica and Robin A. Naylor (2002), 'The Cournot–Bertrand Profit
    Differential: a Reversal Result in a Differentiated Duopoly with Wage Bargaining', mimeo-
    graph, University of Warwick.
Danthine, Jean-Pierre and Jennifer Hunt (1994), 'Wage Bargaining Structure, Employment
    and Economic Integration', *Economic Journal*, 104 (424), 528–541.
Davidson, Carl (1988), 'Multiunit Bargaining in Oligopolistic Industries', *Journal of Labor
    Economics*, 6 (3), 397–422.
Dertouzos, James N. and John H. Pencavel (1981), 'Wage and Employment Determination
    under Trade Unionism: the International Typograhical Union', *Journal of Political
    Economy*, 89 (6), 1162–1181.

Disney, Richard, Amanda Gosling and Steve Machin (1995), 'British Unions in Decline: the Determinants of the 1980s Fall in Union Recognition', *Industrial and Labor Relations Review*, 48 (3), 403–419.

Dobson, Paul (1994), 'Multifirm Unions and the Incentive to Adopt Pattern Bargaining in Oligopoly', *European Economic Review*, 38 (1), 87–100.

Dowrick, Steve (1989), 'Union–Oligopoly Bargaining', *Economic Journal*, 99 (398), 1123–1142.

Dowrick, Steve (1990), 'The Relative Profitability of Nash Bargaining on the Labour Demand Curve or the Contract Curve', *Economics Letters*, 33 (2), 121–125.

Driffill, John and Frederick van der Ploeg, (1993), 'Monopoly Unions and the Liberalization of International Trade', *Economic Journal*, 103 (407), 379–385.

Dunlop, John T. (1944), *Wage Determination under Trade Unions*, New York: Macmillan.

Espinosa, Maria and Changyon Rhee (1989), 'Efficient Wage Bargaining in a Repeated Game', *Quarterly Journal of Economics*, 104 (3), 565–588.

Farber, Henry S. (1978), 'Individual Preferences and Union Wage Determination: The Case of the United Mine Workers', *Journal of Political Economy*, 86 (5), 923–942.

Farber, Henry S. (1983), 'The Determination of the Union Status of Workers', *Econometrica*, 51 (5), 1417–1437.

Farber, Henry S. (1986), 'The Analysis of Union Behavior', in Orley Ashenfelter and Richard Layard (eds), *Handbook of Labor Economics*, Volume 2, Amsterdam: North Holland, pp. 1039–1089.

Fellner, William (1949), *Competition Among the Few*, New York: Alfred A. Knopf.

Fisher, Timothy C. G. and Donald J. Wright (1999), 'Unionised Oligopoly and Trade Liberalisation', *Canadian Journal of Economics*, 32 (3), 799–816.

Flanagan, Robert J. (1999), 'Macroeconomic Performance and Collective Bargaining: an International Perspective', *Journal of Economic Literature*, 37 (3), 1150–1175.

Flanagan, Robert J., Karl O. Moene and Michael Wallerstein (1993), *Trade Union Behaviour, Pay Bargaining, and Economic Performance*, Oxford: Clarendon Press.

Freeman, Richard B. and James L. Medoff (1984), *What Do Unions Do?*, New York: Basic Books.

Freeman, Richard B. and Jeffrey Pelletier (1990), 'The Impact of Industrial Relations Legislation on British Union Density', *British Journal of Industrial Relations*, 28 (2), 141–164.

Fung, K. C. (1995), 'Rent Shifting and Rent Sharing: a Re-examination of the Strategic Industrial Policy Problem', *Canadian Journal of Economics*, 28 (2), 450–462.

Gaston, Noel and Daniel Trefler (1994), 'Protection, Trade and Wages: Evidence from US Manufacturing', *Industrial and Labor Relations Review*, 47 (3), 574–593.

Grossman, Gene M. (1983), 'Union Wages, Temporary Layoffs and Seniority', *American Economic Review*, 73 (3), 277–290.

Hersoug, Tor (1978), 'Effects of Expansionary Policies in a Unionised Economy', mimeograph, University of Oslo.

Hirschman, Albert O. (1970), *Exit, Voice and Loyalty*, Cambridge, MA: Harvard University Press.

Horn, Henrik and Asher Wolinsky (1988a), 'Worker Substitutability and Patterns of Unionisation', *Economic Journal*, 98 (391), 484–497.

Horn, Henrik and Asher Wolinsky (1988b), 'Bilateral Monopolies and Incentives for Merger', *Rand Journal of Economics*, 19 (3), 408–419.

Huizinga, Harry (1993), 'International Market Integration and Union Wage Bargaining', *Scandinavian Journal of Economics*, 95 (2), 249–255.

Johnson, George E. (1975), 'Economic Analysis of Trade Unionism', *American Economic Review, Papers and Proceedings*, 65 (2), 23–29.

Layard, Richard, Stephen Nickell and Robin Jackman (1991), *Unemployment: Macroeconomic Performance and the Labour Market*, Oxford: Oxford University Press.

Leontief, Wassily (1946), 'The Pure Theory of the Guaranteed Annual Wage Contract', *Journal of Political Economy*, 54 (1), 76–79.

Lommerud, Kjell Erik, Frode Meland and Lars Sorgard (2002), 'Unionized Oligopoly, Trade Liberalization and Location Choice', mimeograph, University of Bergen.

Machin, Steve, Mark B. Stewart and John Van Reenen (1993), 'The Economic Effects of Multiple Unionism: Evidence from the 1984 Workplace Industrial Relations Survey', *Scandinavian Journal of Economics*, 95 (3), 279–296.

MaCurdy, Thomas E. and John H. Pencavel (1986), 'Testing Between Competing Models of Wage and Employment Determination in Unionized Markets', *Journal of Political Economy*, 94 (3), S3–S39.

Manning, Alan (1987), 'An Integration of Trade Union Models in a Sequential Bargaining Framework', *Economic Journal*, 97 (385), 121–139.

Manning, Alan (1994), 'How Robust is the Microeconomic Theory of the Trade Union?', *Journal of Labor Economics*, 12 (3), 430–459.

Martin, Stephen (2001), *Industrial Organisation: a European Perspective*, Oxford: Oxford University Press.

McDonald, Ian M. and Robert M. Solow (1981), 'Wage Bargaining and Employment', *American Economic Review*, 71 (5), 896–908.

Mezzetti, Claudio and Elias Dinopoulos (1991), 'Domestic Unionization and Import Competition', *Journal of International Economics*, 31 (1–2), 79–100.

Moene, Karl O. (1988), 'Unions' Threats and Wage Determination', *Economic Journal*, 98 (391), 471–483.

Mulvey, Charles (1976), 'Collective Agreements and Relative Earnings in UK Manufacturing in 1973', *Economica*, 43 (172), 419–427.

Naylor, Robin A. (1989), 'Strikes, Free Riders and Social Customs', *Quarterly Journal of Economics*, 104 (4), 771–785.

Naylor, Robin A. (1998), 'International Trade and Economic Integration when Labour Markets are Generally Unionised', *European Economic Review*, 42 (7), 1251–1267.

Naylor, Robin A. (1999), 'Union Wage Strategies and International Trade', *Economic Journal*, 109 (452), 102–125.

Naylor, Robin A. (2003), 'Industry Profits and Competition under Bilateral Oligopoly', *Economics Letters,* 77(2), 169–175.

Naylor, Robin A. and Oddbjørn Raaum (1993), 'The Open Shop Union, Wages and Management Opposition', *Oxford Economic Papers*, 45 (4), 589–604.

Nickell, Stephen J. (1982), 'A Bargaining Model of the Phillips Curve', Centre for Labour Economics Discussion Paper, London School of Economics.

Nickell, Stephen J. (1999), 'Product Markets and Labour Markets', *Labour Economics*, 6 (1), 1–20.

Nickell, Stephen J. and Martyn J. Andrews (1983), 'Unions, Real Wages and Employment in Britain 1951–1979', *Oxford Economic Papers*, 35 (2), 183–206.

Olson, Mancur (1965), *The Logic of Collective Action*, Cambridge, MA: Harvard University Press.

Oswald, Andrew J. (1979), 'Wage Determination in an Economy with Many Trade Unions', *Oxford Economic Papers*, 31 (3), 369–385.

Oswald, Andrew J. (1982), 'The Microeconomic Theory of the Trade Union', *Economic Journal*, 92 (367), 576–595.

Oswald, Andrew J. (1985), 'The Economic Theory of Trade Unions: an Introductory Survey', *Scandinavian Journal of Economics*, 87 (2), 160–193.

Padilla, A. Jorge, Samuel Bentolila and Juan J. Dolado (1996), 'Wage Bargaining in Industries with Market Power', *Journal of Economics and Management Strategy*, 5 (4), 535–564.

Pelling, Henry (1987), *A History of British Trade Unionism*, London: Macmillan.

Pencavel, John H. (1984), 'The Tradeoff between Wages and Employment in Trade Union Objectives', *Quarterly Journal of Economics*, 99 (2), 215–231.

Pencavel, John H. (1991), *Labor Markets under Trade Unionism*, Cambridge, MA and Oxford: Blackwell.

Ross, Arthur M. (1948), *Trade Union Wage Policy*, Berkeley: University of California Press.

Rubinstein, Ariel (1982), 'Perfect Equilibrium in a Bargaining Model', *Econometrica*, 50 (1), 97–109.

Sampson, Anthony A. (1983), 'Employment Policy in a Model with a Rational Trade Union', *Economic Journal*, 93 (370), 297–311.

Santoni, Michele (1996), 'Union-Oligopoly Sequential Bargaining: Trade and Industrial Policies', *Oxford Economic Papers*, 48 (4), 640–663.

Singh, Nirvikar and Xavier Vives (1984), 'Price and Quantity Competition in a Differentiated Duopoly', *Rand Journal of Economics*, 15 (4), 546–554.

Sørensen, Jan Rose (1993), 'Integration of Product Markets when Labour Markets are Unionised', *Recherches Economiques de Louvain*, 59, 485–502.

Stewart, Mark B. (1982), 'The Implications of the Modified Fellner–Cartter Model of Trade Union Behaviour for the Analysis of Union–Non-union Wage Differentials, mimeograph, University of Warwick.

Stewart, Mark B. (1990), 'Union Wage Differentials, Product Market Influences and the Division of Rents', *Economic Journal*, 100 (403), 1122–1137.

Straume, Odd R. (2002), 'Union Collusion and Intra-Industry Trade', *International Journal of Industrial Organization*, 20 (5), 631–652.

Sutton, John (1986), 'Non-Cooperative Bargaining Theory: an Introduction', *Review of Economic Studies*, 53 (5), 709–724.

Szymanski, Stefan (1994), 'Strategic Delegation with Endogenous Costs', *International Journal of Industrial Organization*, 12 (1), 105–116.

Ulph, Alistair and David Ulph (1990), 'Union Bargaining: a Survey of Recent Work', in David Sapsford and Zafiris Tzannatos (eds), *Current Issues in Labour Economics*, Basingstoke: Macmillan, pp. 86–125.

Vannetelbosch, Vincent J. (1997), 'Wage Bargaining with Incomplete Information in an Unionized Cournot Oligopoly', *European Journal of Political Economy*, 13 (2), 353–374.

Vannini, Stefano and Jacques Bughin (2000), 'To Be (Unionized) or Not To Be? A Case for Cost-Raising Strategies under Cournot Oligopoly', *European Economic Review*, 44 (9), 1763–1781.

Waterson, Michael and Paul Dobson (1996), 'Vertical Restraints and Competition Policy', Research Paper 12, Office of Fair Trading, London: OFT, December.

Williamson, Oliver E. (1968), 'Wage Rates as a Barrier to Entry: the Pennington Case in Perspective', *Quarterly Journal of Economics*, 82 (1), 85–116.

Zhao, Laixun (1995), 'Cross-Hauling Direct Foreign Investment and Unionized Oligopoly', *European Economic Review*, 39 (6), 1237–1253.

4   Unions, bargaining and strikes
Peter Cramton and Joseph Tracy

1.   Introduction

Labour disputes are an intriguing feature of the landscape of industrialised economies. Economists have had a long-standing interest in formulating a framework for understanding and analysing labour disputes. The development of non-cooperative bargaining theory provided the tools for a theory of collective bargaining and labour disputes. A general aim of this theoretical development is to inform policy makers of the efficiency and equity effects associated with different labour laws and institutions that govern and shape the collective bargaining process. While this new literature is still evolving, it can already offer many insights into the interplay between policy and the bargaining process. In this chapter, we will provide a sketch of this new collective bargaining theory and illustrate its ability to aid in policy analysis. We will also relate the predictions of the model to existing empirical findings in the literature.[1]

The collective bargaining process is complex and any model must of necessity involve many simplifying assumptions. Labour disputes likely arise from a wide range of causes. No model will adequately capture all of these forces. The aim of the researcher is to try and identify some of the central factors that shape the typical bargaining situation. Hicks (1932) concluded that strikes were largely the result of faulty negotiations. Ross (1948) stressed the divergent aims of the union leaders and the rank-and-file union members. Ashenfelter and Johnson (1969) formalised Ross' political model of unions into a theory of strikes.

We will focus in this chapter on another strand in the literature that stresses the role of private information. Our starting point is the assumption that the typical labour dispute arises from private information about some aspect that is critical to reaching an agreement, such as the firm's willingness to pay. Negotiators have an incentive to misrepresent their private information during the bargaining, and so some credible means of communicating this private information is necessary. Costly labour disputes serve this function. A firm with a high willingness to pay prefers to settle early at a high wage without a dispute, while a firm with a low willingness to pay prefers to endure a labour dispute in order to settle at a low wage. Labour disputes act as a signalling device for the firm's private information regarding its willingness to pay.

It is important to capture key institutional and legal features into the bargaining model. A common feature of collective bargaining in many countries is the ability of the union to continue to negotiate under an expired labour agreement. So long as the union does not call a strike, the terms and conditions of the expired agreement continue to apply during the extended period of negotiations. As we discuss below, the union has a variety of ways of putting pressure on the firm during a contract extension. This implies that unions have an important decision to make as the expiration of the agreement approaches. If a settlement cannot be reached, the union must decide between calling a strike or extending the contract – which we will call a *holdout*. Our view is that unions often find it advantageous to put pressure on the firm while continuing to work. Early research using non-cooperative bargaining models failed to recognise the union's threat choice and assumed that the union's only recourse was to call a strike (see Fudenberg et al., 1985; Hart, 1989; and Kennan and Wilson, 1989). The model's ability to explain the data is greatly improved by incorporating holdouts into the bargaining process.

In the next section of the chapter we will sketch out a basic bargaining model that includes the union's threat choice between strikes and holdouts. To start, we will assume that the threat payoffs are constant over time. Also, we will not incorporate any decision by the firm to replace striking workers. We will then extend the model to allow the threat payoffs to vary over the course of the dispute, and to allow the firm to decide whether to use temporary replacements in the event of a strike. We will then use the model and extensions to analyse several labour policies and generate predictions as to their impact on dispute incidence, dispute duration and the settlement wage. We will compare these predictions to empirical evidence in the literature, and illustrate how these empirical estimates can be used to analyse the efficiency and equity ramifications of labour policy.

2. A model of wage bargaining

A union and a firm are bargaining over the wage to be paid during a contract of duration T. We focus on a single contract negotiation.[2] We simplify the model by assuming that only the firm has any private information. The union's reservation wage – what the workers will receive during a strike – is common knowledge. If a striking worker can secure alternative employment during the strike, then the reservation wage is the non-union wage. Otherwise, the reservation wage is determined by the striking workers' access to unemployment insurance, welfare and/or other union strike benefits. Let v be the firm's value of the current union labour force working under a contract of duration T. It is common knowledge that v is drawn from the distribution F with positive density f on an interval of support $[l,$

h]. However, at the outset of the negotiations only the firm knows the realised value of v.

Negotiations begin with the union selecting a threat $\theta \in \{H,S\}$, where H indicates the holdout threat and S indicates the strike threat. The union's threat choice remains in effect until a settlement is reached. In the threat θ, the payoff to the union is x_θ and the payoff to the firm is $y_\theta(v) = a_\theta v - b_\theta$, where $a_\theta \in [0, 1]$ and $b_\theta \geq 0$. The term $1 - a_\theta$ captures the dispute cost in that threat. Define $c_\theta = (b_\theta - x_\theta) / (1 - a_\theta)$ to be the relative payment difference during the threat θ. Since the total payoff in agreement is v and the total payoff during the threat θ is $a_\theta v - b_\theta + x_\theta$, the 'pie' that the union and firm are bargaining over (the difference between the agreement and the threat payoffs) is $(1 - a_\theta)v + b_\theta - x_\theta = (1 - a_\theta)(v + c_\theta)$. We assume that the pie is positive for all $v \in [l, h]$, which implies that $c_\theta > -l$.

For now, we will not be more specific about the strike threat (x_S, $a_S v - b_S$). However, the holdout threat can be further specified. Let w^0 denote the wage under the expired labour agreement. Since during a holdout the terms and conditions of the previous labour agreement remain in force, the workers continue to be paid w^0, so $x_H = b_H = w^0$ and $c_H = 0$. We assume there is some inefficiency during a holdout, $a_H < 1$. There are several motivations for this inefficiency. First, we will show that during a holdout the workers have an incentive to slow down or 'work to rule'; that is, to work exactly according to the stipulations of the expired agreement and no more. If firms rely on 'cooperation' of the workforce for efficient production, this may be an important source of inefficiency. Second, customers and input suppliers may be reluctant to negotiate new contracts with the firm until it has a new labour agreement in effect. Third, an issue in the current negotiations may be changes to the work rules that will increase efficiency. These changes cannot be implemented until an agreement with the union is reached which stipulates the modified work rules. The precise degree of inefficiency during a holdout will turn out not to be important, so long as there is some inefficiency in this threat.

The outcome of this bargaining process between the union and the firm denoted by $<t, w, \theta>$ consists of the time of the settlement t where $t \in [0,T]$, the wage settlement w and the threat selected by the union θ. The union and firm payoffs are calculated as the sum of the threat payoffs and the agreement payoffs, weighted by the fraction of time spent in each outcome. We illustrate the union and firm payoffs in Figure 4.1 where we assume that both parties are risk neutral.

Define:

$$D(t) = \frac{1 - e^{-rt}}{1 - e^{-rT}}$$

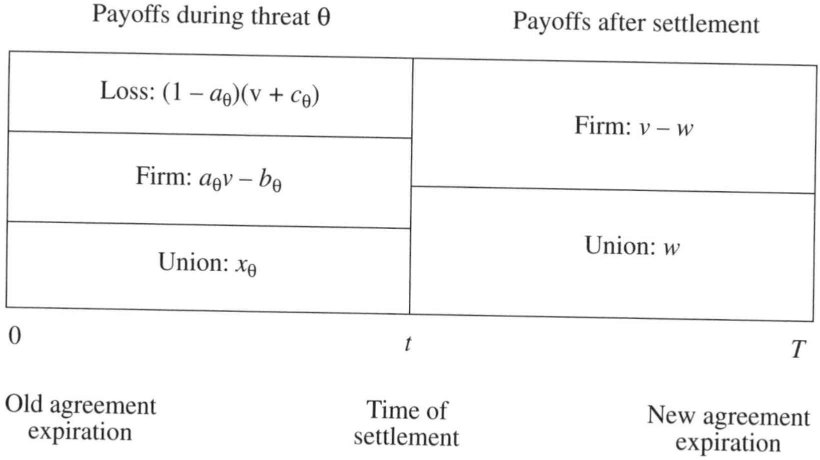

Payoffs during threat θ Payoffs after settlement

Loss: $(1 - a_\theta)(v + c_\theta)$	Firm: $v - w$
Firm: $a_\theta v - b_\theta$	
Union: x_θ	Union: w

0   t T

Old agreement   Time of   New agreement
expiration   settlement   expiration

Figure 4.1   Payoffs from bargaining outcome $\langle t, w, \theta \rangle$

to be the discounted fraction of time spent in dispute if an agreement occurs at time t. Then, given the bargaining outcome $<t, w, \theta>$, the union's payoff is:

$$U(t, w, \theta) = x_\theta D(t) + w[1 - D(t)]$$

and the firm's payoff is:

$$V(t, w, \theta) = y_\theta D(t) + (v - w)[1 - D(t)].$$

The bargaining sequence is as follows. Following the union's threat choice the union and the firm alternate in making wage offers, with the union assumed to make the initial offer. After a wage offer is made by one side, the other side has two options: (1) make a counter-offer, in which case the bargaining continues, or (2) accept the current offer, in which case the bargaining ends and labour is supplied at the offered wage for the reminder of the contract period. As in Admati and Perry (1987), a bargainer can delay responding to an offer. This assumption leads to the signalling equilibrium in which the firm signals its value through its willingness to delay the agreement. For simplicity, we assume that the minimum time between offers is arbitrarily small.

The equilibrium of this bargaining game takes a simple form. If the wage under the expired labour agreement, w^0, is sufficiently low (that is, below some indifference level $\tilde{w}$) the union decides to select the strike threat; otherwise ($w^0 \geq \tilde{w}$) the union selects the holdout threat. The indifference level wage, $\tilde{w}$, depends on r, T, F and the strike and holdout threat payoffs [(x_θ,

v_θ) for $\theta = \{S, H\}$]. A second indifference level, $m \in (l, h)$, determines the firm's response to the union's initial wage offer. If the firm's valuation is higher than this indifference level, $v > m$, the firm accepts the union's initial wage offer and an immediate settlement takes place without a dispute. Otherwise, the firm rejects the union's initial wage offer and a labour dispute begins. Whether the dispute is a strike or a holdout depends on the union's prior threat choice.

The signalling equilibrium can be characterised by three propositions from Cramton and Tracy (1992).[3]

Proposition 1.   *Let* $\theta = (x_\theta, y_\theta)$ *be the threat chosen by the union. In the limit as the time between offers goes to zero, there is a perfect Bayesian equilibrium with the following form:*

- *The union makes an immediate offer of* $w_\theta(m) = x_\theta + \frac{1}{2}(1 - a_\theta)(m + c_\theta)$, *where* $m(c_\theta) \in (l, h)$ *maximises*

(M) $$(m + c_\theta)(1 - F(m)) + \int_l^m \frac{(v + c_\theta)^2}{m + c_\theta} dF(v).$$

- *The firm accepts the offer if* $v \geq m$. *Otherwise, if* $v < m$ *the firm waits until* $(m - v)/(m + c_\theta)$ *of the contract period has passed before offering* $w_\theta(v) = x_\theta + \frac{1}{2}(1 - a_\theta)(v + c_\theta)$, *which is accepted by the union.*
- *The union's expected payoff from the threat* θ *is* U_θ, *the firm's expected payoff is* V_θ, *and the expected loss is* L_θ, *where*

$$U_\theta = x_\theta + (1 - a_\theta)(m + c_\theta)(1 - F(m))$$

$$V_\theta = a_\theta E(v) - b_\theta + (1 - a_\theta) \int_m^h (v + c_\theta) dF(v)$$

$$L_\theta = (1 - a_\theta)\left[c_\theta - (m + 2c_\theta)(1 - F(m)) + \int_l^m v dF(v) \right].$$

There are several observations that can be made based on Proposition 1. First, all wage offers are Rubinstein (1982) full information wage offers. The wage offer consists of the union's payoff in the threat θ plus half of the bargaining rents based on the firm's profitability, v.[4] Second, during a holdout the union has every incentive to impose as much inefficiency on the firm as possible. The wage increases linearly with the degree of inefficiency, $w_H(v) = w^0 + \frac{1}{2}(1 - a_H)v$. However, several factors constrain the union in its endeavour to impose inefficiencies during a holdout. The union must not take actions that will put it in violation of the expired labour agreement. This gives meaning to the expression 'work-to-rule'. Some countries give the firm the option of locking out the union. This option also limits the extent of inefficiency during a holdout. Finally, note that Proposition 1 generates a negatively sloped wage concession function. As the labour dispute continues, the union becomes more pessimistic about the firm's profitability (lowers its expectation regarding v). Since we have assumed that the threat payoffs and dispute costs remain constant during the dispute, this implies that wage offers will be a declining function of the dispute duration.[5] This result is analogous to the familiar union concession function of Ashenfelter and Johnson (1969).

For a given threat θ, we can determine how the dispute incidence and duration respond to changes in the threat payoffs and to changes in the distribution of v. The following proposition says that dispute activity increases with uncertainty. In addition, dispute activity increases when the threat θ becomes more attractive to the union (i.e. c_θ falls).

Proposition 2. *Suppose that $m(c_\theta)$ uniquely maximises* (**M**). *Dispute incidence $F(m(c_\theta))$ and dispute duration $D(v, c_\theta) = (m(c_\theta) - v) / (m(c_\theta) + c_\theta)$ increase as c_θ decreases. Likewise, dispute incidence and duration increase with a linear, mean-preserving spread of the distribution of F.*

Dispute activity depends on the amount of uncertainty about the firm's private information. Dispute incidence always exceeds one-half, and converges to one-half in the limit as this uncertainty disappears.[6] Recall that c_θ measures what the firm pays less what the union receives in the threat θ scaled by the dispute cost. Proposition 2 yields several testable predictions. For example, if a local union receives strike benefits throughout a strike from its national union (and the costs of the benefits are spread across the national membership), then this lowers c_S which should increase strike incidence and lengthen strike durations. Similarly, if workers on strike qualify for general welfare payments, this also lowers c_S and should increase strike incidence and duration.[7]

Our third proposition demonstrates that the union's threat decision depends critically on the current wage under the expired labour agreement.

Proposition 3. *If $w^0 < \tilde{w}$, the union selects the strike threat; if $w^0 \geq \tilde{w}$ the union selects the holdout threat, where*

$$\tilde{w} = x_S + (1 - a_s)(m(c_s) + c_s)[1 - F(m(c_s))] - (1 - a_H)m(0)[1 - F(m(0))]$$

and $m(c_\theta)$ maximises (**M**).

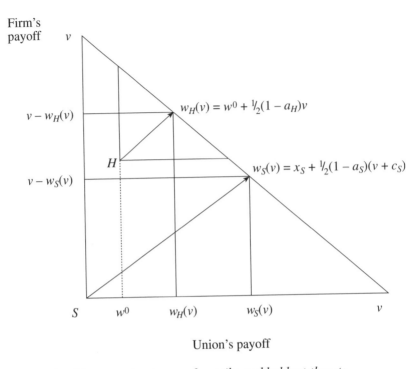

Firm's payoff

v

$v - w_H(v)$

$w_H(v) = w^0 + \frac{1}{2}(1 - a_H)v$

H

$w_S(v) = x_S + \frac{1}{2}(1 - a_S)(v + c_S)$

$v - w_S(v)$

S w^0 $w_H(v)$ $w_S(v)$ v

Union's payoff

Figure 4.2   The ex post *outcomes for strike and holdout threats*

The intuition is that the union will select the strike threat if and only if the higher bargaining costs that are associated with a strike are more than made up for by a higher wage. If the current wage under the expired labour agreement is sufficiently high, this is not the case and the union prefers the holdout threat.

This is illustrated in Figure 4.2. We have normalised the strike threat payoffs in the figure to the origin. If the strike threat (S) is selected, then the settlement occurs at the wage $w_s(v)$. Again, this settlement wage pays the union its threat value in the strike plus half of the inefficiency imposed during the strike. If the holdout threat (H) is selected, then the settlement occurs at the wage $w_H(v)$. The union will select the strike threat only if the wage differential between the strike and holdout threats compensates the union for the additional dispute costs incurred in the strike threat. As the real wage under the expired labour agreement is increased, the wage differential between the strike and holdout threats becomes smaller, but the added dispute costs from the strike are unchanged. At some point, $\tilde{w}$, as w^0 continues to increase, the union prefers to switch from the strike to the holdout threat.

The overall incidence of strikes depends not just overall on the incidence of disputes, but also on the fraction of disputes that involves a strike. As shown earlier, the level of dispute activity depends on the degree of uncertainty. The composition of disputes between strikes and holdouts depends on w^0, the threat payoffs and the location of the distribution of v. Proposition 3 provides a key insight into strike activity. For example, the model predicts that the composition of disputes will shift toward strikes in the following situations: (1) after a period of uncompensated inflation which causes the real value of w^0 to decline, and (2) when conditions in the local labour market are tight which raise the worker's reservation wages during the strike threat. Furthermore, if the level of uncertainty is relatively constant over time, then observed swings in strike incidence over time will primarily reflect shifts in the composition of disputes between strikes and holdouts.

An additional implication of Proposition 3 is that the structure of compensation in a labour agreement can affect the propensity for a strike to take place when the agreement comes up for a renewal. Whether the agreement incorporates a cost-of-living (COLA) clause and the degree of indexation built into the COLA, will affect the union's holdout threat when the agreement expires. A prediction is that following a period of unexpected inflation, renewals of non-indexed contracts will more likely involve a strike.[8] Similarly, in the USA during the concession bargaining of the mid-1980s many firms successfully negotiated lump-sum wage payments in lieu of increases in the base wage (or in return for smaller base wage increases). This switch in pay structure implies a lower real wage at the end of the agreement, and consequently a stronger incentive for the union to select the strike threat when the contract is up for renewal.

3. Extensions to the wage bargaining model

The basic model provides several important insights into how the structure of the labour agreement and the prevailing economic conditions at the time of the labour negotiations affect the bargaining outcomes. However, to do a careful study of how labour policies affect the bargaining process, it will be helpful to generalise the model in two dimensions. The first generalisation is to allow the threat payoffs to vary during the dispute. The second generalisation is to incorporate the firm's decision on whether to use replacement workers in the event of a strike.

Time-varying threat payoffs

In labour contract negotiations, threat payoffs tend to change over time as inventories or strike funds are depleted, as strikers find temporary jobs, as public assistance to strikers is triggered by passing waiting periods for benefits and as replacement workers are hired and trained. With the exception of Hart (1989), most wage bargaining models assume that the threat payoffs to the union and the firm are constant during a dispute. This is a restrictive assumption when it comes to analysing many labour policies which act to shift the threat payoffs during specific times in a dispute. Understanding how policy induced shifts in the threat payoffs affect the pattern of wage settlements and the level of dispute activity is important in evaluating the efficacy of these policies. In addition, this generalisation will also sharpen our insights into how actions undertaken by the union and the firm such as inventory accumulation affect dispute activity.

To simplify, we consider a threat that consists of two phases indexed by $\theta \in \{1,2\}$, a short-run phase (1) and a long-run phase (2) with differing payoffs in each phase. Assume that the first phase of the threat lasts until time $\tau \in [0,T]$, after which the threat shifts to the second phase for the remainder of the contract period. In some cases, the switch time τ may be determined by the firm or the union, and in other cases it may be prespecified by a labour policy. Let the discounted fraction of the pie *remaining* at time t be defined as:

$$d(t) = \frac{e^{-rt} - e^{-rT}}{1 - e^{-rT}}$$

and let $\delta = d(\tau)$. The payoffs to the union and the firm in each phase of the threat are illustrated in Figure 4.3.

A bargaining outcome, now denoted as $\langle t, w, \tau \rangle$, specifies the time of the agreement $t \in [0,T]$, the new contract wage w and the transition time between the short and long-run threats $\tau \in [0,T]$. The union's payoff is:

$$U(t, w, \tau) = \begin{cases} (1 - d(t))x_1 + d(t)w & \text{if } t \leq \tau \\ (1 - \delta)x_1 + (\delta - d(t))x_2 + d(t)w & \text{if } t > \tau \end{cases}$$

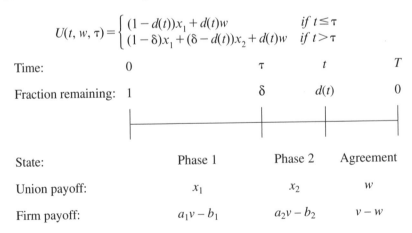

Figure 4.3   Two-phase threat payoffs

and the firm's payoff is:

$$V(t, w, \tau) = \begin{cases} (1 - d(t))(a_1 v - b_1) + d(t)(v - w) & \text{if } t \leq \tau \\ (1 - \delta)(a_1 v - b_1) + (\delta - d(t))(a_2 v - b_2) + d(t)(v - w) & \text{if } t > \tau. \end{cases}$$

The first step in the analysis is to generalise the Rubinstein (1982) full information wage offer in the presence of a two-phase threat. This generalisation is given in Proposition 4 which is from Cramton and Tracy (1994b).

Proposition 4.   *Suppose the value v is common knowledge, and the bargaining has reached time $t < \tau$ without a settlement. In the limit as the time between offers goes to zero, the full information wage at time t with a firm v is:*

$$w(t, v) = (1 - \gamma(t))w_1(v) + \gamma(t)w_2(v)$$

where:

$$\gamma(t) = \frac{e^{-rt} - e^{-rT}}{e^{-rt} - e^{-rT}}, \quad w_\theta(v) = x_\theta + \tfrac{1}{2}(1 - a_\theta)(v + c_\theta), \quad \theta \in \{1, 2\}.$$

The full-information wage from a sequence of threats is a weighted average of the full-information wages for each threat, where the weights are the fraction of the remaining discounted time spent in each threat, assuming that a settlement is never reached.

An important implication of Proposition 4 is that the settlement wage depends not only on the threat prevailing at the time of the settlement, but also on the unobserved threats that would have taken effect if the bargaining had continued. In our simple case of a two-phase threat, the settlement wage for an agreement that takes place during the short-run threat phase will be a weighted average of both the short-run threat wage and the long-run threat wage. If the time remaining until the shift in the threat is short relative to the remaining contract length, then the settlement wage is largely determined by the unobserved long-run threat. The following numerical example will illustrate this point. Suppose that the threat shift takes place after the first 30 days of the dispute (i.e. the firm's inventory runs out), the contract duration is three years and the discount rate is 10 per cent. Then at the outset of the bargaining, the long-run threat is given 97 per cent of the weight in determining the settlement wage. In this example, even if the dispute never reaches the long-run threat phase, the settlement wage is largely based on the long-run threat. So, the threat not reached can have an important influence on the wage settlement. Empirical wage specifications should take this feature of the model into consideration.

What is left to consider in a two-phase threat environment is the union's initial wage offer and the firm's response. Consider first the firm's response to the union's initial wage offer. The firm's optimal behaviour is described in Proposition 5.

Proposition 5. *Suppose the union makes an initial wage offer of* $w(m) = (1-\delta)w_1(m) + \delta w_2(m)$, *where* $\delta = (e^{-rt} - e^{-rT})/(1-e^{-rT})$. *In the subgame that follows, in the limit as the time between offers goes to zero, there is a perfect Bayesian equilibrium with the following form. If* $v \geq m$, *the firm immediately accepts the offer. If* $v_\tau \leq v < m$, *where:*

$$v_\tau = m - (1-\delta)(m+c_1)/\alpha,$$

and:

$$\alpha = 1 + \delta \frac{a_1 - a_2}{1 - a_1}$$

then the second phase is not reached; the firm waits until:

$$D(v) = \alpha \frac{m - v}{m + c_1}$$

of the contract has expired before offering:

$$w(v) = (1 - \gamma(v))w_1(v) + \gamma(v)w_2(v),$$

where $\gamma(v) = \delta/(1 - D(v))$. *If* $v < v_\tau$, *the second phase is reached; the firm waits until:*

$$D(v) = 1 - \delta \frac{v + c_2}{v_\tau + c_2}$$

of the contract has passed before making the offer $w_2(v)$. *The firm's counter-offer is accepted immediately by the union.*

To see how changes in the threat payoffs over time can affect dispute durations, consider first the case where the short-run dispute costs are low relative to the long-run dispute costs $(a_1 > a_2)$. An example would be where the firm maintains its sales in the short-run by selling off inventory. In this case, $\alpha > 1$ and we see from Proposition 5 that dispute durations are longer than for the case of constant threat payoffs, $\alpha = 1$. This is the same as Hart's (1989) result based on a screening model where the strike costs are initially low but then increase sharply when a 'crunch point' is reached. In contrast, when the short-run dispute costs are high relative to the long-run dispute costs, $\alpha < 1$ and dispute durations are shortened.

A prediction from the earlier constant threat payoff model was that settlement wages should decline with the duration of the dispute. As we will discuss later, some researchers have taken this as a central testable implication of non-cooperative bargaining models of strikes. However, a downward sloping wage/strike duration concession function is not a robust prediction from these models. In the case of constant threat payoffs, whether wages rise or fall with the dispute duration depends on where the private information exists. We have assumed that the firm had private information about its profitability and that the union's reservation wage was common knowledge. If we reverse the source of the private information, we also reverse the sign on the slope of the wage concession function. In addition, if we allow the threat payoffs to vary over the dispute, we can have an upward sloping concession function even if we maintain that only the firm has private information over its profitability. Consider the case where the short-run settlement wage is lower than the long-run settlement wage, $w_1(v) < w_2(v)$. As the dispute continues, the settlement wage is increasingly determined by the wage under the long-run threat. As a result, during the short-run threat phase the settlement wage increases with the dispute duration. These examples suggest that the slope of an estimated wage concession function is not a reliable test of non-cooperative bargaining models of labour disputes.[9]

Fixed costs and the firm's replacement decision
While we could use the model with time-varying threat payoffs to speculate on the likely impact of a policy change regarding the firm's ability to use replacement workers, a fuller treatment of the firm's replacement decision is warranted. As a first step toward incorporating the firm's replacement decision into the model, we consider adding fixed costs to the threats. Hiring replacements involves a fixed cost by the firm, so it is important to know how fixed costs affect the bargaining process.

For simplicity, consider the model with constant threat payoffs. Now assume that there are fixed costs of initiating a dispute. Let $k_{f\theta}$ and $k_{u\theta}$ be the fixed costs for the firm and the union if threat θ is initiated, and let $k_\theta = k_{f\theta} + k_{u\theta}$ be the joint fixed cost. To make these fixed costs easily comparable to the flow payoffs (e.g. v and w), each k should be thought of as the flow k over the contract period that is equivalent to the one-time fixed cost K. These fixed costs can arise from costs of shifting production, a loss of goodwill during a dispute or the costs of looking for temporary employment. An immediate settlement avoids the fixed cost k_θ.

The presence of fixed costs alters the union's initial wage offer and the firm's decision whether to accept this wage offer. However, any counteroffer by the firm is independent of the fixed costs, since after the dispute has started the fixed costs are already sunk. These changes to the model are summarised in Proposition 6, taken from Cramton and Tracy (1998).

Proposition 6.   *Let $\theta = (x_\theta, y_\theta)$ be the threat chosen by the union, where $y_\theta = a_\theta v - b_\theta$ and $c_\theta = (b_\theta - x_\theta)/(1 - a_\theta)$. In the limit as the time between offers goes to zero, there is a perfect Bayesian equilibrium with the following form:*

- *The union makes an immediate offer of $k_{f\theta} + w_\theta(m)$, where $w_\theta(m) = x_\theta + \frac{1}{2}(1 - a_\theta)(m + c_\theta)$ and $m \in [l, h]$ maximises:*

$$k_{f\theta} - k_\theta F(m) + \tfrac{1}{2}(1 - a_\theta)\left[(m + c_\theta)(1 - F(m)) + \int_l^m \frac{(v + c_\theta)^2}{m + c_\theta}dF(v) \right].$$

- *The firm accepts the offer if $v \geq m$. Otherwise, if $v < m$, the firm waits until $(m - v)/(m + c_\theta)$ of the contract period has passed before offering $w_\theta(v) = x_\theta + \frac{1}{2}(1 - a_\theta)(v + c_\theta)$, which is accepted immediately by the union.*
- *If $m > 1$, the union's expected payoff from the threat θ is U_θ, the firm's expected payoff is V_θ and the expected loss is L_θ, where:*

$$U_\theta = k_{f\theta} - k_\theta[F(m) + (m + c_\theta)f(m)] + x_\theta + (1 - a_\theta)(m + c_\theta)[1 - F(m)],$$

$$V_\theta = -k_{f\theta} - k_\theta(m + c_\theta)f(m) + a_\theta E(v) - b_\theta + (1 - a_\theta)\int_m^h (v + c_\theta)dF(v)],$$

and

$$L_\theta = k_\theta F(m) + 2k_\theta(m + c_\theta)f(m) + (1 - a_\theta)$$

$$\left[c_\theta - (m + 2c_\theta)(1 - F(m)) + \int_l^m vdF(v) \right],$$

Once a dispute is initiated, the firm's counter-offer to the union and the associated delay in making this offer are both unaffected by the fixed costs. The intuition on how the fixed costs affect the union's initial wage offer is as follows. The union's initial wage offer is designed to make the firm with profitability m indifferent to accepting the wage offer, w, or rejecting and immediately making its counter-offer, $w_\theta(m)$. This indifference relationship is given by $m - w = m - w_\theta(m) - k_{f\theta}$. Rearranging gives $w = k_{f\theta} + w_\theta(m)$. The union, then, raises its initial wage offer by the amount of the *firm's* fixed cost.

While the firm's fixed cost in the threat θ affects the union's initial wage offer, the joint fixed cost affects the probability that this offer is accepted by the firm. This is consistent with the joint cost hypothesis (Kennan, 1980; Reder and Neuman, 1980), which states that dispute incidence and duration should be inversely related to the joint cost of the dispute. Even a small fixed cost can have a sizeable impact on the likelihood of a dispute. For example, a fixed cost of roughly 1 per cent of the expected size of the pie will reduce the predicted dispute rate by 50 per cent.

The fixed cost k_θ can also affect the union's threat decision. Recall that the union selects the strike threat if $U_S > U_H$. From Proposition 6 we see that fixed costs will shift the composition of disputes since U_S depends on k_{fS} and k_{uS}. As the union's fixed cost of striking increases, U_S falls, implying a composition shift towards holdouts. An increase in the firm's fixed cost of striking typically increases U_S, implying a composition shift toward strikes. However, the observed strike incidence depends not only on the composition of disputes, but also on the likelihood that the firm accepts the union's initial wage offer. Regardless of which party bears the fixed cost, observed strike incidence declines with an increase in fixed costs due to the increased likelihood that the firm will accept the union's initial wage offer.

Now consider extending the model to incorporate the firm's decision to use replacement workers. Replacement can be thought of as a new threat $\theta = R$ with its own payoffs. If the union selects the strike threat and the firm finds the union's initial wage offer unacceptable, then the firm decides whether to hire temporary replacements at a fixed cost k_{fR}. The fixed cost k_{fR} represents the hiring and training costs associated with replacement workers. We assume that replacements have a productivity level that is some fraction $a_R < 1$ of the productivity of the union workers.[10]

To see how the firm's replacement decision affects the bargaining process, consider first the full information case where v and k_{fR} are known by both the firm and the union. The full-information settlement wages under the three threats, $w_H(v)$, $w_S(v)$ and $w_R(v)$ play a key role in determining the outcome of the bargaining. If the cost of replacement is prohibitively high or the replacement wage is higher than the strike wage, $w_R(v) > w_S(v)$, then the firm never hires replacements. The settlement wage in this case is the strike wage, $w_S(v)$, or the holdout wage, $w_H(v)$, whichever is higher.

Now suppose that the replacement wage is less than the strike wage, $w_R(v) < w_S(v)$. This wage differential gives the firm an incentive to consider hiring replacements. If the cost of replacement is not too high so that $w_S(v) - w_R(v) > k_{fR}$, then if the union selects the strike threat it will reduce its wage demand in order to prevent the firm from hiring replacements. The union offers the wage $w = k_{fR} + w_R(v) < w_S(v)$, which makes the firm indifferent between accepting or rejecting and hiring replacements. While we never see replacements hired in the full information situation, the firm's option to hire replacements can lead to lower union wage demands in the strike threat.

To observe firms hiring replacements, we need to add in some private information about the firm's fixed cost of replacing its workers. To keep things simple, suppose that the firm's replacement cost is either low or high, $k_{fR} \in \{L, H\}$, and let $p = Pr(k_{fR} = L)$ be the probability of a low replacement cost. Assume that $w_S(v) - w_R(v) \geq H$, so that the union must be concerned about replacement from both types of firms. The bargaining outcome may take the form of a pooling or a separating equilibrium. We consider each in turn.

Pooling equilibrium   If L and H are close, the union will make an initial wage offer that both types of firms will accept. In this case, the union makes the wage offer $w_L = L + w_R(v)$. This offer makes the low replacement cost firm indifferent between accepting and rejecting, and is strictly preferred by the high replacement cost firm. As in the full information case, we do not observe any replacements taking place, but the firm's option to replace reduces the union's wage demand in the strike threat. Consequently, the strike threat is less attractive to the union as a result of the firm's ability to hire replacements.

Separating equilibrium   As the gap between L and H widens, it becomes increasingly expensive for the union to buy out the replacement option for both types of firms. At some point, the union switches to the separating equilibrium where the union makes the initial wage offer $w_H = H + w_R(v)$ that makes the high cost firm indifferent between accepting and rejecting. A low replacement cost firm will reject this offer and subsequently hire replacements. The probability of observing replacements under the strike threat is p, which again is the probability that the firm has a low replacement cost. The union's expected wage is now $pw_R(v) + (1 - p)w_H = w_R + (1 - p)H$. The union's expected settlement wage is declining in the probability that the firm has a low replacement cost. Since the union only selects the strike threat if the strike wage exceeds the holdout wage by a sufficient margin, the union is less likely to select the strike threat as the replacement probability increases.

To observe both replacements and delays in settlements, we need to have private information both about v and k_{fR}. As long as the firm's decision to replace conveys only information about its fixed cost of replacement and not about v, adding the replacement decision does not upset our earlier equilibrium. Since replacement is a sunk cost, the signalling of this cost does not play a strategic role in the bargaining. In the separating equilibrium, the fraction of strikes involving replacements depends on the probability of a low replacement cost. In making its threat choice between a strike and a holdout, the union must estimate this replacement probability. If this fraction is too high, the union will select the holdout threat.

4. Policy analysis

We are now in a position to use this bargaining model and its extensions to analyse a range of labour policy issues. We will focus on the predictions that the model makes for dispute incidence and duration, the composition of disputes between strikes and holdouts and wage settlements. In the next section, we will compare these predictions with empirical findings in the literature. We will then illustrate how these empirical estimates can be used to evaluate the efficiency and equity properties of labour policies.

The most contentious labour policy issue over the past couple of decades is the right of employers to replace striking workers. We will analyse the implications for temporary replacements, leaving a discussion of permanent replacements for another occasion.[11] The firm's replacement option is expected to result in lower wage settlements for two reasons. First, if the union selects the strike threat, the model predicts that it will lower its wage demand in order to induce high replacement cost firms not to initiate replacements. Second, the replacement option reduces the attractiveness of the strike threat to the union, thereby shifting the composition of disputes to holdouts. Wage settlements are lower under the holdout threat, so a shift towards holdouts lowers the expected wage. To the extent that it takes time for the firm to hire and train temporary replacements once a dispute has begun, the replacement option makes the long-run dispute cost lower than the short-run dispute cost. From our discussion of time-varying threats, this should lead to shorter dispute durations. A ban on temporary replacement, then, should increase strike incidence both through a shift in the composition of disputes and the elimination of a source of fixed costs of strikes. In addition, a replacement ban should lead to longer dispute durations as well as higher wage settlements.

A number of Canadian provinces have at various times imposed mandatory cooling-off periods after an agreement has expired and before a strike can begin. We can use our two-phase threat model to analyse the impact of a cooling-off period. A cooling-off period is a time interval where the union only has available the holdout threat. If a union selects the strike threat, then during the first phase it is restricted to the holdout threat until the cooling-off period has been satisfied. In the second phase, the union switches to the strike threat. In practice, these cooling-off periods tend to be short (typically less than three weeks' duration). As a result, Proposition 4 indicates that cooling-off periods will leave wage settlements in the strike threat largely unaffected for those disputes that settle during the cooling-off period.[12] Since with cooling-off periods the dispute cost is higher in the second phase, Proposition 5 indicates that the settlement rate during the cooling-off period will be lower than would have occurred over this same time interval had the union selected the holdout threat. In this sense, cooling-off periods have a 'chilling' effect on the negotiations. A short cooling-off period should not significantly alter the relative attractiveness of the strike threat, so this policy will not affect the composition of disputes. The prediction, then, is that short cooling-off periods will have no impact on strike activity or wage settlements.

Unemployment benefits can also affect collective bargaining outcomes to the extent that striking workers qualify for these benefits. In the United States, eligibility for unemployment insurance (UI) benefits is determined at the state level. There are two common provisions that apply to strikes.[13] The first is the *innocent bystander* provision that allows workers displaced by a strike and who have no direct connection or financial interest in the strike to collect UI benefits. The second is the *stoppage of work* provision that allows striking workers to collect UI benefits if the firm maintains its operations at or near normal levels during the course of the strike. In addition, New York (NY) and Rhode Island (RI) allow striking workers to file for UI benefits after a waiting period has passed.[14]

The impact of UI benefits on contract negotiations depends on which provision applies and how these benefits are financed. We illustrate these points by considering two of the three types of US statutes. The clearest predictions are for an innocent bystander provision. This provision provides UI benefits to workers at the firm who are *not* involved in the strike, so x_S is unchanged. If the firm is partially or fully charged for these benefits (this depends on the degree of experience rating in the state's UI system), then b_S increases which results in an increase in c_S. Conditional on the strike threat being selected by the union, Proposition 2 indicates that strike incidence and duration should decrease. However, the increase in c_S also raises the expected wage in the strike threat making this threat relatively more attractive to the union. Therefore, an increase in b_S generates two offsetting effects: a composition shift towards the strike threat (which acts to raise the observed strike incidence), and a higher likelihood that the union's initial wage offer will be accepted conditional on the union selecting the strike threat (which acts to lower the observed strike incidence). Cramton and Tracy (1994a) find in their benchmark model that the net effect of an increase in b_S is a higher observed strike incidence. The magnitude of the effect of an innocent bystander provision on strike incidence should depend on the degree of experience rating in the UI system and the size of the UI benefits. In the extreme, if the firm is not charged for any of the UI benefits, b_S and c_S are unaffected and there should be no impact of the UI benefits on strike activity.

A distinguishing feature of the NY and RI provisions is that strikers qualify only after a substantial waiting period has elapsed. The two-phase threat model is useful for analysing the effects of these waiting periods. UI benefits increase the union's reservation wage and therefore the settlement wage during the period when strikers qualify to receive the benefits. From Proposition 4 we know that this will also increase wage settlements in a strike during the waiting period. As a result, even if most strikes settle before the qualifying period for UI benefits has been satisfied, access to UI benefits will lead to higher wage settlements.

The implications of the NY and RI UI policies for strike incidence and duration are more difficult to discern. These implications will depend on the degree of experience rating in their UI programmes, and may depend on the structure of unionisation at the firm as well as actions taken by the firm during a strike. If the UI benefits are not charged back to the firm, then access to UI benefits reduces c_S during the period when the workers qualify for the benefits. From Proposition 2, this should make strikes more frequent and last longer. However, if most or all of the benefits are charged back to firms, then the impact on strike activity depends on additional factors. If the bargaining unit covers the entire firm, then the union's gain from UI is offset by the firm's increased UI taxes, leaving c_S unchanged. In this case, UI benefits will not affect observed levels of strike activity. In contrast, if the firm has a significant number of non-union workers, then the impact of UI on c_S depends on the firm's actions during the strike. If the firm maintains operations during a strike, then only strikers receive UI benefits and $b_S = x_S$ which again leaves c_S unchanged. On the other hand, if the firm shuts down operations as a result of the strike thereby idling its entire labour force, then UI benefits will be paid out to more than just the striking workers. In this case, $b_S > x_S$ which implies an increase in c_S and a reduction in observed strike activity.

As discussed earlier, firms have an incentive to accumulate inventories ahead of the expiration of a labour agreement. However, this strategy is not feasible in many service industries where no physical good is exchanged between the firm and its customers. Examples include the airline and shipping industries. The inability to use inventories in these industries raises the dispute cost (e.g. lowers a_S) making the strike threat attractive to unions. If permissible, firms in these industries may have an incentive to arrange 'mutual aid pacts' among themselves to offset this disadvantage. The objective of these pacts is to lower the dispute cost via transfers between the member firms and the firm experiencing a strike. By raising a_S these pacts should reduce strike activity and wage settlements.[15]

Firms can attempt to offset the cost of a strike in a number of ways. As noted already, firms can use inventory to offset production losses from the strike. In addition, a firm can attempt to use its existing non-union workers (in many cases these are managers) to maintain production during the strike. This strategy tends to be more successful in industries that use a high degree of automation such as the telephone industry. Unions have an incentive to limit the firm's ability to follow this strategy by both making access to the plants difficult and by engaging in secondary picketing. To the extent that the union can increase the dispute cost in the strike threat by using these tactics, they increase the pie that is being bargained over and consequently the expected wage settlements. Not surprisingly, in many countries the labour law deals extensively with defining the boundaries of appropriate actions that the union can engage in during a strike.

Finally, other government policies not directly aimed at regulating labour negotiations can have an impact on labour disputes. For example, consider wage and price controls. The model predicts that binding wage controls will reduce strike incidence and shorten dispute durations. Suppose that a union selects the strike threat but that its optimal initial wage offer $w(m)$ exceeds the allowed increase under the wage controls. The union will have to reduce $w(m)$ to satisfy the wage controls. This increases the likelihood that the firm immediately accepts the union's initial wage offer. So, conditional on the union selecting the strike threat, with binding wage and price controls the incidence of strikes will be lower. In addition, binding wage and price controls should make the union less likely to select the strike threat. Since the initial wage offer under the strike threat is higher than the initial wage offer under the holdout threat, these controls will narrow the wage differential between the strike and the holdout threats making the strike threat less attractive. As unions substitute toward the holdout threat, the incidence of strikes is further reduced. Binding wage and price controls should also shorten average dispute durations as a direct consequence of the fact that more firms accept the union's initial wage offer. With more firms agreeing to a new contract at the outset of the bargaining, it will on average take less time for the remaining firms to signal their profitability to the union.

5.   Empirical evidence on collective bargaining and strikes

The central feature of non-cooperative bargaining models of labour disputes is the role of private information that creates uncertainty surrounding key issues in the negotiations. Labour disputes act as a credible way to signal this information. Ideally, this should be the focus of empirical tests of private information models. However, almost by definition, this is the most difficult test to carry out in the data. While there is ample anecdotal evidence supporting this view of labour disputes, formal statistical tests are difficult to construct.[16] Tracy (1986, 1987) uses the volatility of a firm's stock return as a proxy for the union's degree of uncertainty. The premise of this test is that investors and the union negotiators share the same degree of uncertainty about the firm's future profitability. In a sample of US contract negotiations between 1973 and 1977 he finds that strike incidence has a positive and significant relationship to the variance of the firm's overall stock return. Furthermore, he finds that this result is driven by the variability in the firm's excess returns and not by the variability in the market returns.[17] Higher variance in the firm's stock returns is also associated with longer strike durations. A within-sample one standard deviation increase in the stock return variability leads to an increase in the conditional strike duration by eight days (the sample average conditional strike duration is 50 days), and to an increase in the unconditional strike duration by 2.5 days (the sample average unconditional duration is 7.5 days).[18] Cramton and Tracy (1994a) examine a sample of US labour negotiations from 1970 to 1989 and find a significant relationship between a firm's stock return variance and *dispute* incidence in the 1970–81 period, but that this relationship disappears in the 1982–89 period.[19] Finally, Ohtake and Tracy (1994) report contrasting results for Japan using industry level bargaining data from 1970 to 1990. They find that the Japanese industry average dispute incidence is positively related to macro uncertainty, but negatively related to industry uncertainty.[20]

The degree to which strike incidence and duration display a cyclical pattern has received the greatest attention in the empirical literature. Early papers – such as Rees (1952) – examined the time-series properties of aggregate strike frequency. More recent work has focused on individual contract data in order to study the cyclical behaviour of strike incidence. These studies are more informative for testing bargaining models.[21] Researchers differ in their approach to testing for cyclical patterns to strike activity. These differences range from the specific choice of proxy for the business cycle and whether the cyclical variable is measured at a national or an industry/regional level.

The data generally indicate that strike duration is counter-cyclical and suggest that strike incidence may be pro-cyclical. Harrison and Stewart (1989, 1994), using Canadian data, provide the most comprehensive analysis of the cyclical behaviour of strike activity. The advantages of their studies are that they have a long time series that increases the cyclical variation in the data and they examine the robustness of their finding across several proxies for the business cycle including the choice of macro series and the level of aggregation.[22] They find that strike durations are counter-cyclic. This finding is robust to using as the cyclical proxy aggregate or industry industrial production, real GDP or the male unemployment rate. Strike incidence appears to be pro-cyclical for manufacturing contracts based on aggregate industrial production. In contrast, strike incidence for non-manufacturing contract negotiations displays no cyclical effects. When the male unemployment rate is used as the cyclical proxy, there is weak evidence that strike incidence is pro-cyclic – that is, strikes are less likely to occur in slack labour markets.[23] Controlling for aggregate industrial production, the authors find no evidence that industry-specific industrial production shifts strike incidence. Similarly, controlling for the aggregate male unemployment rate, they find no evidence that the provincial unemployment rate shifts strike incidence.

Several other studies have examined the cyclical behaviour of strike activity using data with a relatively long period of coverage. Cramton et al. (1999) also examine Canadian negotiations for the period 1967 to 1993. They control for the cycle using the provincial unemployment rate and do not find any significant relationship with either strike incidence or duration. Vroman (1989) analyses US manufacturing negotiations from 1957–84. She finds that strikes are more frequent but of shorter duration in periods of low unemployment. Finally, Ingram et al. (1993) examine 6000 British manufacturing negotiations in the 1980s and find strike incidence to increase with slackness in regional labour markets. The authors speculate that the 1980s may not be a representative decade in Britain to test for cyclical strike effects.[24]

While the evidence on procyclic strike incidence is far from definitive, it is a challenge for bargaining models to be able to explain why in 'good times' strike incidence might increase but strike durations decrease. In the traditional bargaining model where the union has only the strike threat, the incidence and duration of strikes move in tandem. However, by introducing the union's threat choice, the model can reconcile why strike incidence and duration may move in opposite directions. Assume that during an economic expansion the distribution of firm profitability, $F(v)$, shifts to the right. In addition, assume that the opportunities for striking workers to find temporary employment also improve. Proposition 2 states that the improved profitability will reduce both dispute incidence and dispute duration. That is, whether the union selects the strike or the holdout threat, the likelihood of observing a dispute falls and conditional on a dispute taking place, the expected duration of the dispute is shorter. At the same time, the enhanced temporary employment opportunities improve the union's strike payoffs but leave its holdout payoffs unaffected (the wage under the expired contract is fixed). During business expansions, then, the strike treat becomes relatively more attractive to the union than the holdout threat which shifts the composition of disputes towards strikes. As a result of the union's threat choice, there are two offsetting forces at work on the cyclical behaviour of the strike incidence – the union is more likely to select the strike threat (composition effect) and the probability of a strike is lower given that the strike threat is selected. Cramton and Tracy (1994a) show in their benchmark model that the composition effect dominates. Incorporating the union's threat decision, then, makes it possible for bargaining models to explain how strike incidence and duration can display opposite cyclical patterns.

The two-threat bargaining model also predicts that strike incidence should increase when there is uncompensated inflation over the prior contract. Uncompensated inflation lowers the real wage under the expired contract making the holdout threat less attractive. The increase in strike incidence is the result, then, of the shift in the composition of strikes. A model with only a strike threat will not generate this prediction. The real wage under the expired contract plays no significant role in a model where a strike is the union's only threat.

Several studies have controlled for measures of uncompensated inflation in the prior contract. Vroman (1989) in her study of US manufacturing contract negotiations finds a positive and significant impact of uncompensated inflation on the likelihood of a strike. Cramton and Tracy (1994a) find the same result in their study of US negotiations from 1970–89. This same pattern also shows up in Canadian contract negotiations; see Gunderson et al. (1989, 1986) and Cramton et al. (1999).

There has been little research to date that investigates the extent to which transfer payments affect strike activity. Skeels and McGrath (1997), using US data, test for the effect of union liquid assets per member on the probability of a strike.[25] They find that unions with more liquid assets available to finance strike benefits have a significantly higher strike incidence. Hutchens et al. (1989, 1992) provide the most comprehensive work on government transfer payments and collective bargaining. They examine the impact of innocent bystander, stoppage of work and the NY/RI provisions on aggregate state strike frequencies.[26] They also control for variations in the maximum UI benefit, and where possible the degree of experience rating in the state's UI programme. Their results indicate that both innocent bystander and stoppage of work provisions are associated with a higher strike frequency. They also find evidence that strike frequencies are higher in NY and RI, although the magnitude is not precisely estimated.

Several researchers have investigated whether wage and price controls have any affect on labour disputes. McConnell (1990) finds that the first stage of the Nixon wage and price controls in the USA reduced the incidence of strikes by nearly 5 percentage points (relative to an overall sample strike incidence of 13.8 per cent). She finds that the second stage of the Nixon controls had a smaller negative effect on strike incidence, but that this impact is imprecisely estimated. McConnell reports that both Nixon control periods appear to be associated with shorter strikes, but neither duration effect is well determined. Gunderson et al. (1989) report that the Canadian anti-inflation board was associated with a 4.3 percentage point reduction in strike incidence (relative to an overall sample strike incidence of 16 per cent). Using a longer time-period, Cramton et al. (1999) find that the Canadian anti-inflation board was associated with a 5.7 percentage point reduction in strike incidence and a 24 per cent reduction in strike durations.

We now turn to the empirical evidence on the impact of labour policy on the collective bargaining process, beginning with prohibitions on the use of replacement workers. The difficulty in testing predictions for replacement bans is the paucity of policy variation in the data. While several attempts have been made in the USA to pass replacement bans, none has been signed into law. Researchers have turned to Canadian data where three provinces have passed replacement bans.[27] Cramton et al. (1999) examine Canadian manufacturing and non-manufacturing contract negotiations from 1967 to 1993 and find that, following the enactment of a replacement ban, strike incidence is 12 percentage points higher, strike durations are on average 24 days longer and wage settlements are 4.4 per cent higher.[28] Gunderson et al. (1989) examine Canadian data that span a period prior to the adoption of replacement bans by British Columbia and Ontario. They find a positive but insignificant effect of Quebec's ban on strike incidence. Gunderson and Melino (1990) estimate that the impact of Quebec's replacement ban was to increase strike durations by 7 days. Finally, Budd (1996) examines Canadian manufacturing contracts from 1965–85 and discerns no significant strike incidence, duration or wage effects associated with this replacement ban.

The bargaining model indicates that the higher the union's perceived risk of replacement, the less likely it is to select the strike threat. Cramton and Tracy (1998) test this prediction using data on US contract negotiations from the 1980s. For each of the major strikes in this period, they determine if temporary or permanent replacements were hired. They estimate the probability that a firm hires replacements (conditional on the union selecting the strike threat) using a probit model that controls for the likely demographic characteristics of the union workers and local labour market conditions. Consistent with the model, they find that the higher the 'cost' of replacement, the less likely the firm is to use replacements.[29] Using this estimated probit model, they predict the replacement risk associated with each negotiation in their sample. They include this estimated replacement risk as a control variable in a probit model of the union's threat decision. The data indicate that unions facing higher replacement risks are significantly less likely to have selected the strike threat conditional on a dispute taking place.

Cooling-off periods have been mandated at some point by each Canadian province. Both the period of coverage and the length of the cooling-off period varies across provinces.[30] Cramton et al. (1999) find no significant effect of cooling-off periods on strike incidence or duration. Inconsistent with the model's prediction, they also find that 10 days of a required cooling-off period is associated with 4.2 per cent lower wage settlements. Gunderson et al. (1989) also document the lack of any effect of cooling-off periods on strike incidence.

We suggested earlier that the slope of the wage concession function is not a robust test of bargaining models. In addition, there are econometric complications involved in estimating the slope of the wage concession function. McConnell (1989) using US data, finds that wages on average decline by 3 per cent per 100 days of strikes. Card (1990b) using Canadian data finds no evidence of a negative relationship between wages and strike durations. Both studies control for bargaining unit heterogeneity and both treat the strike variables (an indicator for a strike and a measure of the strike duration) as exogenous. Jimenez-Martin (1999) using Spanish data, and Cramton et al. (1999) using Canadian data, reject this exogeneity assumption. Each of these studies finds an insignificant slope to the concession function when estimated with ordinary least squares, and a significant negative slope when estimated with instrumental variables. Care must be taken in estimating the relationship between wages and strike durations, and as we have already discussed, care must be taken in interpreting the estimated results.

A common trend across industrialised countries has been the decline in strike activity over the 1980s and 1990s from earlier decades. Aggregate measures of strike activity will overstate this decline to the extent that unionisation rates have also been receding during this period. However, even measures of strike incidence based on contract level data indicate a significant decline.[31] While changes in the economic environment may explain some of this decline, researchers also suggest an important role for labour policy. Cramton and Tracy (1998) argue that there is suggestive evidence that President Reagan's decision in August 1981 to fire the air traffic controllers after their union, the Professional Air Traffic Controllers' Organization (PATCO), called an illegal strike contributed to the decline in US strike activity. To the extent that President Reagan's action signalled a greater public acceptance for the use of replacement workers, unions have an incentive to shift from strikes to holdouts. More directly, Ingram et al. (1993) find that changes in British labour law in 1982 and 1984 (see Chapter 12 by Addison and Siebert in this volume) help to explain the decline in strike incidence in British manufacturing in the 1980s.

6. Measuring the effect of labour policy on welfare
In this section we illustrate how the estimated impacts of labour policy on strike incidence, strike durations and wage settlements can be combined to study their equity and efficiency implications. The methodology is taken from Currie and McConnell (1991). We need to assume a joint strike cost.

Cramton et al. (1999) make the conservative assumption that the joint strike costs can be estimated by the lost wages (which amount to $100 per person-day in their sample).

Labour policy can affect the efficiency with which labour agreements are renegotiated. Policies that lower the expected negotiation costs help improve bargaining 'efficiency'. We will proxy for these negotiation costs with the expected strike costs. As we have seen, labour policy can affect strike costs through its impact on the incidence and the duration of strikes. We summarise this by looking at the policy impact on the unconditional strike duration, which is calculated as the product of the probability of a strike and the expected conditional strike duration. The strike cost associated with the policy, then, is the estimated change in the unconditional strike duration due to the policy multiplied by the mean daily strike cost.

Labour policy can also have equity effects by shifting the division of the rents between the union and the firm. We capture this equity aspect of labour policy by examining the change in the wage gain due to a policy. The wage gain from a policy is measured as the change in the wage bill over the life of the contract with and without the policy. This understates the full impact of the policy to the extent that wage gains in the current contract are carried over into future contracts. In calculating the net gain from a policy, we assume that the strike cost is split equally between the union and the firm. As a result, the union's net gain is the wage gain less half the strike cost, and the firm's net loss is the wage gain plus half the strike cost.

Table 4.1 illustrates this methodology by summarising the equity and efficiency effects of cooling-off periods and replacement worker bans. These calculations are taken from Cramton et al. (1999). Cooling-off periods have no significant impact on the efficiency of contract negotiations. However, cooling-off periods shift the distribution of rents towards firms. Each week of required cooling-off is estimated to cost unions 2.6 million Canadian dollars per contract negotiation. This may be a good example of unintended policy consequences. A typical argument for cooling-off periods is that they will lower expected bargaining costs without imposing any terms on the firm or the union – that is, the policy will improve efficiency without any significant equity effects.

Looking at Table 4.1, it is easy to see why replacement legislation has been such a divisive policy issue. A ban on replacements is estimated to increase the expected bargaining cost by almost two million Canadian dollars per contract. In addition, a replacement ban is estimated to raise the expected wage gain by 3.9 million Canadian dollars per contract. This large wage gain more than offsets the higher expected strike costs for unions, implying a net gain for unions of 2.9 million Canadian dollars per contract.

Table 4.1 Estimates of the impact of labour policy on welfare

Policy variable	Percentage change in wage	Change in unconditional duration (days)	Million June 1993 C$/contract			
			Strike cost	Wage gain	Union net gain	Firm net loss
Cooling-off period (weeks)	−2.9	−0.3	−0.04 (0.04)	−2.62** (0.97)	−2.60** (0.97)	2.64** (0.97)
Prohibit replacement workers	4.4	15.1	1.93** (1.01)	3.88** (1.66)	2.91* (1.74)	−4.84** (1.74)

Notes: See Cramton et al. (1999). Standard errors are given in parentheses and reflect sampling variation in the estimated marginal effects of a policy variable on wage settlements, strike incidence and strike duration. Overall impacts are based on a mean strike incidence 0.165, a mean strike duration (D) of 59 days, a mean contract duration (l) of 822 days, a mean real wage (w) of $13.81 (June 1993 Canadian dollars), a mean bargaining unit size (n) of 1531 workers, a mean person-days lost due to strikes (d) of 76 thousand days, a mean number of hours worked per week (h) of 36, and a mean loss per strike ($L = w \cdot d \cdot h/5$) of $7.50 million, equal to the lost wages. Let D_i be the change in the unconditional strike duration. Strike costs $= C_i = L \cdot D_i/D$; wage gain $= W_i \cdot n \cdot l \cdot h/5$; union net gain $= G_i - C_i/2$; firm net gain $= -G_i - C_i/2$.
**Statistically significant at the 0.05 level, *statistically significant at the 0.10 level.

Firms are significantly worse off with a replacement ban, with an estimated net loss of 4.8 million Canadian dollars per contract.

7. Alternative bargaining models

We have focused on one simple bargaining model in which the firm signals its profitability through its willingness to postpone agreement. The advantage of the signalling model is that its equilibrium is tractable and the model is easily extended to allow other features, such as the choice of threat, more complex threats that change over time, as well as other forms of uncertainty.

A criticism of the singling model is that it imbeds a particular type of commitment: the union is unable to improve its offer while it is waiting for the firm's response. In contrast, screening models allow the union and firm to revise their offers on a particular schedule. Typically, one assumes stationary strategies, which imply that the terms of agreement critically depend on the time between offers (Gul and Sonnenschein, 1988). This is problematic for empirical work, since it suggests that the main features of interest – strike incidence, strike duration, and wages – depend critically on the parties' ability to commit to not revising offers. Indeed, disputes vanish in the limit as the time between offers goes to zero. The fact that the time between offers is unknown to the researcher poses a serious challenge in applying the theory (but see Kennan and Wilson, 1993 and 1989, for a rich analysis and discussion of the issues).

At the opposite extreme from screening models are war-of-attrition models. These models effectively make the assumption that offers cannot be revised. Compromise is not possible. Either the union's terms or the firm's terms are ultimately adopted. The party willing to postpone settlement the longest ultimately prevails.[32] The conceptual difficulty with attrition models is that compromise is a fundamental feature of collective bargaining. Although some issues may be binary, the most important, the wage, is not. As a result, attrition models provide some insight in understanding disputes, but have limited applicability to labour negotiations. In contrast to the attrition models, the ability to compromise is the primary determinant of wages in both the screening and signalling models.

We have emphasised the importance of the union's threat choice, either strike or holdout, in understanding collective bargaining data. In the theory, holdouts serve as an alternative, less destructive and safer, way for the union to put pressure on the firm. Holdouts can serve another useful purpose, enabling a union to delay negotiations until it obtains information about related bargaining outcomes in its industry (Kuhn and Gu, 1998). Holdouts of this form especially are important in situations where related bargaining pairs are negotiating simultaneously.

A limitation of the basic model outlined in this chapter is that it treats each negotiation independently. In practice, negotiations can be linked by ties across bargaining pairs on either the firm or union side. Learning from these earlier negotiations can influence current negotiations (Kuhn and Gu, 1999).[33]

A second important link in virtually all wage negotiations is the link from one contract to the next within the same bargaining unit. Union and firm bargaining relationships tend to be long-lived relative to any given contract duration. The prior contract is important, since it sets the status quo from which subsequent contracts are negotiated. Modelling a sequence of contract negotiations is difficult at best. Kennan (2001) characterises equilibrium behaviour in a setting where the firm has persistent information about its willingness to pay. The equilibrium involves information cycles that depend on the success of aggressive seller demands.

8.   Conclusion

Over the last twenty years there has been a tremendous development of both the theoretical and empirical analysis of collective bargaining. Our focus here has been on work that seeks to explain the frequent occurrence of disputes. Our view is that disputes largely are motivated from the presence of private information and the sharply conflicting interests of the union and the firm over the wage.

To make sense of the empirical findings, we have found it important to extend the basic bargaining models to include key features of collective bargaining. One such feature is the union's threat choice: whether to withhold labour services through a strike or instead to put pressure on the firm while continuing to work, which we call a holdout. In this theory, changes in strike incidence are primarily the result of changes in the composition of disputes. More strikes occur when the strike threat becomes more attractive to the union. For example, striking becomes more attractive when there has been a significant amount of uncompensated inflation during the previous contract term, since this decreases the worker's wage in the holdout threat.

The bargaining model can also be extended to address the impact of other features of collective bargaining:

- Threat payoffs that change over time, for example, as inventories or strike funds run out;
- The firm's choice to hire replacement workers;
- Links among related bargaining pairs;
- Links across contracts within the same bargaining pair.

The appropriate model to bring to the data depends in large part on the questions being asked and the institutional features of the country and industry being studied. Our focus here has been on private sector negotiations primarily in the USA and Canada. Although we suspect that many of the results apply elsewhere, it likely will be necessary to include other institutional details in interpreting collective bargaining in other country settings.

Acknowledgement

The views expressed in this chapter are those of the individual authors and do not necessarily reflect the position of the Federal Reserve Bank of New York or the Federal Reserve System.

Notes

1. There are a number of surveys of collective bargaining and strikes that provide useful background. See for example Kennan (1986), Kennan and Wilson (1993, 1990, 1989) and Card (1990a).
2. We also ignore the timing of this negotiation relative to other related contract negotiations. The model applies most directly to bargaining in the private sector.
3. Readers are referred to this article for further details and proofs.

4. The union's initial wage offer is the Rubinstein wage offer for the firm type, m, that is indifferent between accepting or rejecting. The bargaining rents are split equally between the firm and the unions since we have assumed for simplicity that both parties have the same discount rate.

5. We will have more to say about the slope of the wage concession function later in this chapter.

6. By dispute incidence we mean the likelihood that either a strike or a holdout takes place.

7. Until 1981, strikers in the United States were permitted to collect food stamps if they met the eligibility requirements. The General Accounting Office estimated that approximately $37 million was paid out to striking households in 1980; for details, see Hutchens et al. (1989).

8. If the inflation were anticipated, a non-indexed contract could factor the expected inflation into the deferred increases. In this case, we would not expect to see any differences in the likelihood of a strike between indexed and non-indexed contracts.

9. We will discuss in a later section some econometric issues that must also be taken into account when attempting to estimate the slope of the wage concession function.

10. We only consider here the decision to hire temporary replacements that are employed by the firm only until a settlement with the union is reached. In addition, we assume that the firm's decision to use temporary replacements does not affect v once a settlement is reached.

11. The model we presented only deals with a single contract negotiation and as such is not suited to analyse permanent replacements. In the United States, the incidence of temporary replacements is slightly higher than the incidence of permanent replacements (see Cramton and Tracy, 1998, p. 674).

12. From Proposition 4 it is also clear that wage settlements for observed strikes are invariant to the cooling-off period.

13. See Hutchens et al. (1989) for a detailed discussion.

14. These waiting periods are eight weeks for New York and seven weeks for Rhode Island. Rhode Island also has an innocent bystander and stoppage of work provision that if applicable, qualifies workers for UI benefits after one week.

15. Six major airlines in the US organized a Mutual Aid Pact (MAP) in October of 1958. The original agreement stipulated that a member who suffered a strike would be compensated by the other members a percentage of their 'windfall' revenues resulting from the strike. In March of 1962, the agreement was changed so that a struck member would be guaranteed at least 25 per cent of its normal operating expenses. In 1969, this percentage was raised to a sliding scale from 50 to 35 per cent depending on the length of the strike. The MAP ended in 1978 with the deregulation of the airline industry. Over its lifetime, MAP transferred more than $611 million dollars among its members (see Unterberger and Koziara, 1980).

16. The *New York Times* (October 28, 1990, p. 33) described the negotiations between New York City and its municipal workers as follows: 'At the core of the stalled New York City municipal labour talks is the union leaders' growing distrust of the claims being made about the city's financial plight. . . . Barry Feinstein, president of the 12,000-member Local 237 of the International Brotherhood of Teamsters, who is negotiating with Mr. Hill, said: "Any number of times the former administration would bring us in and say: 'This time, it's really true.' We would say, 'What makes this night different from all others?' On every occasion we were right, and the city was wrong." Mr. Feinstein called the city budget director, Philip R. Michael, "more full of it than a Christmas turkey." Mr. Michael insists his estimates are sound.'

17. This distinction is significant since variability in the excess returns reflects firm/industry uncertainty whereas variability in the market return reflects general macro uncertainty.

18. The conditional strike duration is the duration measured over actual stoppages, that is, given that a strike takes place. The unconditional strike duration includes negotiations that do not lead to strikes. The unconditional measure gives lower duration because it includes observations that are assigned a strike duration of zero days.

19. One hypothesis for why this relationship disappears is that the threat of replacements increased after President Reagan fired the air traffic controllers in August of 1981.

20. Specifically, the industry dispute incidence is positively related to the risk-adjusted market return variability and negatively related to the industry excess return variability.
21. The connection between aggregate strike frequency and aggregate strike incidence can be weak. As discussed in Harrison and Stewart (1989), not all strikes take place at contract expirations and there may be cyclical fluctuations in the number of expiring labour agreements.
22. Harrison and Stewart examine Canadian strike data from 1946–83, and contract data from 1964–88.
23. For the subset of strikes where wages are the primary issue, they find stronger statistical evidence that strike incidence falls in slack labour markets.
24. For example, when they control for legislative changes in labour law during the decade, the coefficient on the unemployment rate is reduced by two-thirds, although it is still positive and statistically significant.
25. They use liquid assets per member as a proxy for strike benefits since information on US union strike funds is not widely reported.
26. The connection to the theory would be tighter if the empirical work related to strike incidence rather than strike frequency.
27. Quebec has banned replacements since 1978 while British Columbia and Ontario introduced bans in 1993.
28. The strike incidence estimate is not precisely measured, while the strike duration and wage estimates are significant at the 10 per cent level.
29. For example, the replacement risk is declining in the average experience of union workers in that industry and with the tightness of the local labour market.
30. Cooling-off periods have varied from two days in British Columbia to 21 days in Prince Edward Island and Nova Scotia.
31. For example, in the USA strike incidence among large bargaining units (1000 and more workers) fell by roughly 50 per cent from 1970 to 1990. See Figure 1 in Cramton and Tracy (1998).
32. See Card and Olson (1995) for an application of this model to US strike data from the 1880s.
33. See Wijngaert (1994) for an analysis of holdouts in the Netherlands.

References

Admati, Anat R. and Motty Perry (1987), 'Strategic Delay in Bargaining', *Review of Economic Studies*, 54 (3), 345–364.
Ashenfelter, Orley and George E. Johnson (1969), 'Bargaining Theory, Trade Unions, and Industrial Strike Activity', *American Economic Review*, 59 (1), 35–49.
Budd, John (1996), 'Canadian Strike Replacement Legislation and Collective Bargaining: Lessons for the United States', *Industrial Relations*, 35 (2), 245–260.
Card, David (1990a), 'Strikes and Bargaining: A Survey of the Recent Empirical Literature', *American Economic Review*, 80 (2), 410–415.
Card, David (1990b), 'Strikes and Wages: A Test of an Asymmetric Information Model', *Quarterly Journal of Economics*, 105 (3), 625–659.
Card, David and Craig A. Olson (1995), 'Bargaining Power, Strike Durations and Wage Outcomes: An Analysis of Strikes in the 1880s', *Journal of Labor Economics*, 13 (1), 32–61.
Cramton, Peter and Joseph S. Tracy (1992), 'Strikes and Holdouts in Wage Bargaining: Theory and Data', *American Economic Review*, 82 (1), 100–121.
Cramton, Peter and Joseph S. Tracy (1994a), 'The Determinants of U.S. Labor Disputes', *Journal of Labor Economics*, 12 (2), 180–209.
Cramton, Peter and Joseph S. Tracy (1994b), 'Wage Bargaining with Time-Varying Threat Payoffs', *Journal of Labor Economics*, 12 (4), 594–617.
Cramton, Peter and Joseph S. Tracy (1998), 'The Use of Replacement Workers in Union Contract Negotiations: The U.S. Experience, 1980–1989', *Journal of Labor Economics*, 16 (4), 667–701.
Cramton, Peter, Morley Gunderson and Joseph Tracy (1999), 'The Effect of Collective

Bargaining Legislation on Strikes and Wages', *Review of Economics and Statistics*, 81 (3), 475–487.

Currie, Janet and Sheena McConnell (1991), 'Collective Bargaining in the Public Sector: The Effects of Legal Structure on Dispute Costs and Wages', *American Economic Review*, 81 (4), 693–718.

Durgan, J. W. and William E. J. McCarthy (1974), 'The State Subsidy Theory of Strikes: An Examination of Statistical Data for the Period 1956–1970', *British Journal of Industrial Relations*, 12 (1), 26–47.

Fudenberg, Drew, David Levine and Paul Ruud (1985), 'Strike Activity and Wage Settlements', working paper, University of California at Berkeley.

Gul, Faruk and Hugo Sonnenschein (1988), 'On Delay in Bargaining with One-Sided Uncertainty', *Econometrica*, 56 (3), 601–611.

Gunderson, Morley, John Kervin and Frank Reid (1986), 'Logit Estimates of Strike Incidence from Canadian Contract Data', *Journal of Labor Economics*, 4 (2), 257–276.

Gunderson, Morley and Angelo Melino (1990), 'The Effects of Public Policy on Strike Duration', *Journal of Labor Economics*, 8 (3), 295–316.

Gunderson, Morley, John Kervin and Frank Reid (1989), 'The Effects of Labour Relations on Strike Incidence', *Canadian Journal of Economics*, 22 (4), 779–794.

Harrison, Alan and Mark Stewart (1989), 'Cyclical Fluctuations in Strike Durations', *American Economic Review*, 79 (4), 827–841.

Harrison, Alan and Mark Stewart (1994), 'Is Strike Behavior Cyclical?', *Journal of Labor Economics*, 12 (4), 524–553.

Hart, Oliver (1989), 'Bargaining and Strikes', *Quarterly Journal of Economics*, 104 (1), 25–43.

Hicks, John R. (1932), *The Theory of Wages*, London: Macmillan Press.

Hutchens, Robert, David Lipsky and Robert Stern (1989), *Strikes and Subsidies: The Influence of Government Transfer Programs on Strike Activity*, Kalamazoo, MI: W.E. Upjohn Institute for Employment Research.

Hutchens, Robert, David Lipsky and Robert Stern (1992), 'Unemployment Insurance and Strikes', *Journal of Labor Research*, 13 (4), 337–354.

Ingram, Peter, David Metcalf and Jonathan Wadsworth (1993), 'Strike Incidence in British Manufacturing in the 1980s', *Industrial and Labor Relations Review*, 46 (4), 704–717.

Jimenez-Martin, Sergi (1999), 'Controlling for Endogeneity of Strike Variables in the Estimation of Wage Settlement Equations', *Journal of Labor Economics*, 17 (3), 583–606.

Kennan, John (1980), 'Pareto Optimality and the Economics of Strike Duration', *Journal of Labor Research*, 1 (1), 77–94.

Kennan, John (1986), 'The Economics of Strikes', in Orley C. Ashenfelter and Richard Layard (eds), *Handbook of Labor Economics*, Amsterdam, North Holland, vol. 2, pp. 1091–1137.

Kennan, John and Robert Wilson (1990), 'Can Strategic Bargaining Models Explain Collective Bargaining Data?', *American Economic Review*, 80 (2), 405–409.

Kennan, John and Robert Wilson (1993), 'Bargaining with Private Information', *Journal of Economic Literature*, 31 (1), 45–104.

Kennan, John (2001), 'Repeated Bargaining with Persistent Private Information', *Review of Economic Studies*, 68 (4), 719–755.

Kennan, John and Robert Wilson (1989), 'Strategic Bargaining Models and Interpretation of Strike Data', *Journal of Applied Econometrics*, 4 (0), S87–S130.

Kuhn, Peter and Wulong Gu (1998), 'A Theory of Holdouts in Wage Bargaining', *American Economic Review*, 88 (3), 428–449.

Kuhn, Peter and Wulong Gu (1999), 'Learning in Sequential Wage Negotiations: Theory and Evidence', *Journal of Labor Economics*, 17 (1), 109–140.

McConnell, Sheena (1989), 'Strikes, Wages, and Private Information', *American Economic Review*, 79 (4), 810–815.

McConnell, Sheena (1990), 'Cyclical Fluctuations in Strike Activity,' *Industrial and Labor Relations Review*, 44 (1), 130–143.

Ohtake, Fumio and Joseph Tracy (1994), 'The Determinants of Labour Disputes in Japan: A

Comparison with the U.S.,' in Toshiaki Tachibanki (ed.), *Labour Market and Economic Performance: Europe, Japan and the USA*, London: Macmillan, pp. 349–372.

Reder, Melvin and George Neumann (1980), 'Conflict and Contract: The Case of Strikes', *Journal of Political Economy*, 88 (5), 867–886.

Rees, Albert (1952), 'Industrial Conflict and Business Fluctuations', *Journal of Political Economy*, 60 (5), 371–382.

Ross, Arthur M. (1948), *Trade Union Wage Policy*, Berkeley: University of California Press.

Rubinstein, Ariel (1982), 'Perfect Equilibrium in a Bargaining Model', *Econometrica*, 50 (1), 97–109.

Skeels, Jack W. and Paul McGrath (1997), 'The Effect of Union Financial Strength and Liquidity on Strike Propensities', *Journal of Economics*, 23 (2), 59–71.

Tracy, Joseph (1986), 'An Investigation into the Determinants of U.S. Strike Activity', *American Economic Review*, 76 (3), 423–436.

Tracy, Joseph (1987), 'An Empirical Test of an Asymmetric Information Model', *Journal of Labor Economics*, 5 (2), 149–173.

Unterberger, S. Herbert and Edward Koziara (1980), 'The Demise of Airline Strike Insurance', *Industrial and Labor Relations Review*, 34 (1), 82–89.

Vroman, Susan (1989), 'A Longitudinal Analysis of Strike Activity in U.S. Manufacturing: 1957–1984', *American Economic Review*, 79 (4), 816–826.

Wijngaert, Rob van der (1994), *Trade Unions and Collective Bargaining in The Netherlands*, Amsterdam: Thesis Publishers.

5 Unions and productivity, financial performance and investment: international evidence
David Metcalf

1. Introduction: the issues and the countries

If the presence of a union in a workplace or firm boosts pay, financial performance is likely to be worse unless there is a roughly equivalent union effect on productivity. Any such impact on profitability may lead to higher consumer prices and is likely to cause lower investment rates, contributing to economic senescence, although when the product market is monopolistic it might under some circumstances be benign – a simple transfer from capital to labour – with no efficiency implications.

Productivity matters a lot: increased productivity is the source of higher living standards for employees, more profits for capitalists and lower prices for consumers. Similarly investment in physical and human capital is a crucial source of economic dynamism at the level of the firm as well as for the aggregate economy. Therefore the manner in which industrial relations institutions in general, and unions in particular, affect productivity, financial performance and investment is keenly important. This chapter distils evidence on such effects from six countries: USA and Canada from North America, UK and Germany from Europe and Japan and Australia from Australasia. Most of the evidence comes from cross sections of workplaces or firms because there are rather few good recent case studies. This is a pity because case studies of aircraft production (Kleiner et al., 2002) and tyre manufacturing (Krueger and Mas, 2002), which combine detailed institutional knowledge with sophisticated statistical technique, probably epitomize the direction of future research.

These six countries were chosen for two reasons. First, the vast bulk of accessible studies analysing links between unionization and productivity, investment and profits have been undertaken for these countries. It would have been nice to include some LDCs or other evidence from Africa, Asia and southern Europe but little seems to exist. Second, the system of industrial relations in these six countries varies greatly which, in principle, might be expected to lead to different union effects among the countries.

Consider Table 5.1 which summarizes the industrial relations systems on

Table 5.1 *Industrial relations characteristics in our six countries, mid-1990s*

Characteristic	USA	Canada	UK	Germany	Japan	Australia
Unionization and collective bargaining						
1. Density % [rank]	16 [18]	38 [8]	34 [10]	29 [13]	24 [16]	35 [9]
2. Coverage of collective bargaining % [rank]	18 [19]	36 [16]	47 [15]	92 [4]	21 [18]	80 [9]
Bargaining level and coordination						
3. Bargaining level [rank]	1 [16=]	1 [16=]	1.5 [14=]	2 [5]	1 [16=]	1.5 [14=]
4. Coordination [rank]	1 [16=]	1 [16=]	1 [16=]	3 [1=]	3 [1=]	1.5 [15]
Standards and protection						
5. Labour standards index	0	2	0	8	—	—
6. Employment protection legislation, stickiness index [rank]	0.7 [1]	1.1 [4]	0.9 [2]	2.6 [20]	2.3 [14]	1.2 [6]

Notes and sources: Rows 1 and 2: Percentage of employees who are union members or covered by collective bargaining, respectively. Rank refers to rank out of 19 countries. OECD *Employment Outlook* 1997, Table 3.3.

Row 3 refers to prevailing level of collective bargaining, ranging from 1 decentralized through 2 sector level to 3 centralized. Rank refers to rank out of 19 countries. OECD *Employment Outlook* 1997, Table 3.3.

Row 4 refers to the degree of coordination among employers and among unions, ranging from 1 uncoordinated to 3 coordinated. Rank refers to rank out of 19 countries. OECD *Employment Outlook* 1997, Table 3.3.

Row 5 is the aggregate score on 5 separate indices, each ranging from 0–2 (a higher score indicating greater protection) covering: working time regulations; fixed-term contracts; employment protection; minimum wage protection; employee representation rights. OECD *Employment Outlook* 1994, Table 4.8.

Row 6 measures the stickiness of employment protection legislation for regular and temporary workers. An average of 4 indices covering: regular procedural inconveniences; notice and severance pay for no fault individual dismissal; difficulty of dismissal; regulation of collective dismissal. Index runs from 0–6 on each indicator but there are few instances of numbers greater than 3. High number means most sticky. Rank refers to rank out of 27 countries. OECD *Employment Outlook* 1999, Table 2.5.

the basis of six indicators carefully constructed by OECD. In the mid-1990s union density (row 1) in Canada, Australia and UK was over double that in the USA with Japan and Germany in between. In the USA, Canada and Japan union density and coverage of collective bargaining rates (row 2) are much the same, reflecting decentralized bargaining and high density achieved via mandatory dues check-off provisions where such bargaining occurs. In the UK more employees are covered by collective bargaining than are in unions because there are lots of free-riders. In Germany and Australia collective bargaining coverage is around three times as high as union density because bargains in unionized firms get extended (*erga omnes*) to non-union enterprises.

The level of bargaining (row 3) and extent of coordination (row 4) also vary among the six countries. In the mid-1990s bargaining was decentralized to firm level in the USA, Canada and Japan. In Germany and Australia sector level bargaining predominated, although a move towards decentralization is now apparent in both countries. Even though bargaining is decentralized in Japan there is considerable coordination in bargaining strategy and tactics among both employers and unions (as there is in Germany), whereas there is much less coordination in the UK, USA and Canada although there is still some pattern bargaining in the auto and construction industries in North America.

Employment regulation by the state varies greatly among the countries. The mid-1990s labour standards index – covering working time regulations, fixed-term contracts, employment protection, minimum wage arrangements and employee representation rights ranges from eight (out of ten) in Germany to zero in the USA and UK. The more specific employment protection 'stickiness index' also demonstrates that regulations covering procedures, notice period, severance pay and rules for individual and collective dismissals are much more stringent in Germany and Japan than they are in the UK and USA.

There is now a substantial cross-country literature examining links between such industrial relations institutions and macroeconomic performance and income distribution (see for example, successive annual issues of *OECD Employment Outlook* and Chapter 6 by Flanagan in this volume). It is plausible that particular bundles of characteristics among these institutions might also affect the performance of firms and workplaces. In very broad terms, for our six countries, the USA, Canada and UK can be thought of as having low coverage, decentralized bargaining and weak labour standards, while Germany, Japan and Australia have high coverage (not Japan), less decentralized or more coordinated bargaining and stronger employment protection. There are, however, no automatic links with workplace performance. For example, strong employment protection coupled with sector level bargaining might promote security and voice leading to information sharing and more investment in human capital, thereby boosting performance. But equally decentralized bargaining with minimal standards might imply mutual gain negotiations at firm level, which could also enhance performance. We shall just have to wait and see what the evidence suggests.

Some patterns do emerge. Unions and works councils influence productivity modestly favourably in Japan and Germany respectively. In the USA, workplaces with both so-called high performance work (HPW) practices and union recognition attain superior productivity to workplaces with just recognition or just HPW practices. And in each country more intense product market competition and the evolution of cooperative industrial relations has weakened any negative associations between unions and productivity and strengthened positive ones. The vast weight of the evidence suggests that a union presence is associated with lower profitability but that the union impact is largely dependent on weak competition in the product market and the consequent surplus available for redistribution to employees. Unions appear also to lower the rate of investment in physical capital in the USA, UK and Germany – perhaps because of their impact on financial performance? – but to raise investment in human capital in the UK and USA.

But, as we shall see, such patterns must be treated cautiously. First, there is considerable heterogeneity in the findings even within countries. For example one recent, possibly idiosyncratic, US study of small entrepreneurial firms finds a strong positive link between unions and profits. And in Germany the vital information, consultation and voice role played by works councils does not yield unambiguous findings on any of the three performance measures. Second, unions are themselves heterogeneous. It seems, for example, that enterprise unions and works councils have a more positive impact on performance than multi-unionism and fragmented bargaining. Third, links between unionization and performance alter over time in response, for example, to greater competition (globalization), less adversarial relations between management and labour and modifications to the legal environment in which unions operate.

Studies in this area, including some in this survey, are sometimes incomplete. Insufficient attention is paid to product market – labour market links. Nickell (2001, p. 296) recently pointed out that 'what unions do depends on what they *can* do, and this depends on the extent of product market competition'. This link is given considerable prominence below. Next, there is rather little on process. Statistical studies typically relate institutions to outcomes but are silent on the how and why. If, for example, unions raise productivity does this come about through better quality labour, greater job satisfaction, fewer quits, better work organization or harder work? Some complementary case studies are urgently needed. Replication is also useful. The world moves on so any union impact in the more regulated UK labour market pre-Thatcher might not hold now. Similarly bargaining is becoming more decentralized in Australia and Germany and this is bound to have an effect on the role and power of unions. As heterogeneity of outcomes increases with decentralized bargaining the need for firm level studies becomes even stronger.

The chapter is organized as follows. Union effects on productivity, financial performance and investment are set out in sections 2–4 respectively. In each case the relevant theory and methods of investigation are discussed followed by evidence. We attempt to distil the weight of the evidence and provide an exemplary study for each country on each indicator, sometimes one with unexpected results. Many issues require further analysis and section 5 goes into a bit more detail on product market–labour market links, the evolution of more cooperative industrial relations and its impact, the effects of different union structures, unions' impact on investment in human capital, and the role of German works councils. Summary and conclusions are set out in section 6.

2.   Productivity
Theory and testing
Unions can influence industrial relations and personnel management for good or ill. The union impact on things like apprenticeship methods, promotion policies, work organization, wage levels and payments systems and grievance procedures will feed through into productivity. It is impossible to determine a priori whether such a union effect will raise or lower the level of labour productivity. Indeed, it is likely that productivity-enhancing union effects and productivity-detracting effects occur simultaneously, so the net effect must be a matter of careful empirical investigation. In what follows, we set out the channels by which unions might lower or raise productivity and we emphasize the limitations of and caveats to the studies reviewed.

Reasons why uniform presence may lower labour productivity   Four sets of reasons why union presence may lower labour productivity are noted. First, unions may be associated with restrictive work practices. Second, industrial action may have an adverse impact. Third, union firms may invest less than non-union firms. Fourth, if unions are associated with an adversarial style of industrial relations the consequent low trust and lack of cooperation between the parties may lower productivity.

Restrictive work practices surely lower labour productivity. Pencavel

(1977) suggests that such practices result from 'union malfeasance'. Increased security from disagreeable management decisions is more likely for union than for non-union labour. Such security may be formalized through work rules (job regulation) and unions may operate in a conventional cartel-like fashion by restricting output. Such restrictive practices take a number of forms (see e.g. Donovan Commission, 1968, Ch. 6). There may be work rules concerning, for example, pace or job demarcations. Over-manning might result from fixed gang sizes or extensive use of assistants. Capital may not be used intensively or might be poorly maintained. Finally, there may be policy overtime so that effort is restricted during normal hours in order to boost total pay via overtime working. But the scope for such practices is limited in competitive markets because the firm may go out of business. So we should expect such practices to be more prevalent in the public sector and in monopolistic product markets.

Industrial action will lower output where it occurs, but that output might be made good over time or by other firms. Such action, or the threat of it, causes uncertainty about output levels and this will tend to reduce the effectiveness of resources devoted to marketing and distribution; and company performance will be impaired if delivery dates are not met (Caves, 1980). If labour relations tend to deteriorate as plant size increases this might encourage companies to build plants smaller than would otherwise be indicated by technical economies of scale. Finally management time is diverted to problems of labour relations and away from other tasks. Particular care needs to be taken with the arrow of causation between industrial action and labour productivity. It is quite plausible that poor labour productivity reflects poor management which also causes more industrial action.

Unionized firms may invest less in capital equipment and research and development than non-union firms or the returns from such expenditure may be lower causing, in turn, less future investment (Grout, 1984a, 1984b). Shareholders and managers get locked into specific investments of plant and machinery and R&D. They are therefore vulnerable to ex post exploitation by unions. For example, capital may be kept idle because of disputes over manning levels. This lowers the rate of return to the investment thus causing under-investment. Such arguments may hold with special force to more risky investments. The impact of unions on investment is analysed in section 4.

Union presence may sometimes result in an adversarial style of industrial relations, lowering trust and cooperation. If both parties strive for their own selfish ends they may both end up worse off – in terms of labour productivity and real earnings – than if they cooperated (see Leibenstein, 1988, Ch. 5 for an intuitive but formal discussion). It is often forgotten that this point was made very forcibly by Freeman and Medoff (1984, p. 165).

Their argument was that unions would raise productivity only under very strict circumstances: 'if industrial relations are good, with management and unions working together to produce a bigger "pie" as well as fighting over the size of the slices, productivity is likely to be higher under unionism. If industrial relations are poor, with management and labour ignoring common goals to battle one another, productivity is likely to be lower under unionism'. Any such productivity-reducing effects of union presence may be compounded if multi-unionism is present in the organization.

Reasons why union presence may raise labour productivity   Five sets of reasons why labour productivity may be higher in the presence of unions are discussed. First, firms' responses to union relative wage effects may result in higher labour productivity, but this should not be interpreted as raising the welfare of society. Second, unions may play a monitoring role on behalf of the employer. Third, the familiar collective voice arguments may have favourable consequences. Fourth, it is sometimes held that a union presence may make managers less lethargic. Finally, unions should stop exploitation of labour, resulting in improved productivity.

If unions achieve a wage differential over non-union workers, firms respond by increasing the capital intensity of production and employing better quality labour, both of which raise labour productivity. But this route to higher productivity needs careful interpretation. We do not want productivity to rise because of wage push: it is not in societies' interest if unions raise wages and productivity rises because firms respond by substituting capital for labour, lowering employment and raising prices to consumers. Rather, it is the other union routes to higher productivity like monitoring and collective voice which truly raise welfare.

Pencavel emphasizes the important role played by unions in monitoring work. His arguments are related to, and anticipated, the voice and agency arguments considered below:

> The trade union may be interpreted as the employees' auditor of management, checking that the employer is fulfilling his part of the labour contract. Or when the union is given a role overseeing work performance and in disseminating wage payments to workers, its officials become the monitors of the employees. The degree to which these monitoring activities achieve a close association between productivity and rewards will determine the efficiency of the organisation. (Pencavel, 1977, p. 141)

The Donovan Commission's (1968) classic study of UK shop stewards confirmed such functions. It emphasized the shop stewards' role in communication, information and discipline and described shop stewards as lubricants rather than irritants. Although the employer does not have to operate through the union Pencavel points out that because the shop steward is drawn from the ranks of the workers, employees will be less suspicious when work operation rules are altered and there may be greater cooperation between labour and capital. Thus labour productivity may be raised because craft unions enforce standards of workmanship, and all unions may seek to prevent malingering and shirking by individuals. This favourable productivity effect may, however, be offset by the greater role now played by unions in supporting members at both internal grievance hearings and at Labour Courts.

The collective voice provided by a union may improve efficiency within the firm. First, collective voice is an information source on worker preferences which should result in an effective mix of wages and personnel policies. For example there is the standard public good (i.e. non-rival consumption) argument for collective voice to achieve the right level of health and safety provision. Without such a voice it will be under-provided. Second, collective voice may improve morale, motivation and cooperation. For example, firm-specific skills learned on the job require cooperation and this may be forthcoming if unions lessen rivalry among individuals. Likewise, unions may provide greater security against arbitrary decisions on matters like dismissal or redundancy. Thus teamwork may be enhanced. Third, the voice may improve communications leading directly to better plant layout or improved working practices – a gain in x-efficiency. Fourth, better grievance procedures may result. Fifth, voice may provide a mechanism to improve the employment contract, encouraging or discouraging, for example, performance-related pay or a less rigid workweek. These collective voice arguments are the centrepiece of the Harvard School approach to the possibility that unions may raise productivity. However, it is unclear why a union is required. A works council or some other form of consultative arrangement might do just as well. The consequences that flow from such collective voice will, in turn, also tend to raise labour productivity. Labour turnover should be reduced (over and above any lower labour turnover resulting from higher union pay). This leads to lower costs and higher returns to training and hence to greater accumulation of human capital and a more skilled workforce. Further, recruitment costs and interruption of work should both be lessened as a result of lower turnover. Similar arguments hold if voice also results in less absenteeism and greater job satisfaction.

Union presence may be associated with a shock to management and therefore to improvements in the management of labour. There are two strands to this argument, which tend to get conflated. First, there may be an impact effect of unionization. When a union initially gets recognized a firm might put better managers or equipment in place (it is a moot point as to how long the shock effect lasts and whether this argument is symmetrical when unions get de-recognized). Second, there is held to be a continuing effect: 'managerial responses to unionism that take the form of more rational personnel policies and more careful monitoring of work raise productivity by reducing organizational slack' (Freeman and Medoff, 1984, p. 164). These two potential positive effects of unionization on labour productivity may spillover to non-union firms, which may be kept on their toes in their attempts to keep unions out.

Finally, unions may counter unfair bargaining power on the employer's side. If unions stop exploitation of labour by raising wages this is socially desirable. The firm will, in turn, respond by raising the capital intensity of production, resulting in improved labour productivity.

Union presence and changes in productivity   Union presence can influence the level of labour productivity for good or ill, so unionization can also be associated with differentiated changes in labour productivity. If any of the productivity-enhancing channels discussed above, like voice, are strengthened or if restrictive practices and the like which are harmful to labour productivity are weakened, union presence will be associated with improved performance relative to the non-union sector. These dynamic forces are obviously important because the manner in which union(s) interact with management or influence investment will vary over time. For example, if managerial practices become more effective or the industrial relations climate more cooperative in union firms, then union presence will be associated with faster growth than before. Similarly, if previously the union sector invested less than the non-union sector or lagged in the adoption of new techniques, but now invests more, we would expect to see an improvement in the relative performance of the union sector. It is most unlikely that heavily unionized workplaces or industries can have permanently higher or lower productivity growth than corresponding less- or non-unionized organizations. This would imply an ever-widening gap between the two groups, which is most implausible. Thus findings for the one decade should not, for example, be extrapolated to the next.

Limitations and caveats   Pencavel (1991) notes that the ideal data to examine the net effect of unionization on productivity require: a single industry, making the assumption of a common technology among plants more plausible; a physical measure of output so as not to conflate price and quantity effects; longitudinal information for each plant; a change of union status for some plants during the period such as the granting of union recognition. A fruitful sector for such analysis is the British docklands where Evans et al. (1993) analysed productivity change in docks previously covered by the National Dock Labour Scheme, relative to non-Scheme ports, consequent on the abolition of the Scheme in 1989.

In the event, few of the studies reviewed below meet these stringent criteria. Therefore the limitations of the studies, and the caveats, must both be spelled out. These include the neglect of management, the lack of a theory of union behaviour, disregard of underlying industrial relations, failure to deal with the heterogeneity of unions and the structure of collective bargaining, the fact that the studies are time-specific, and emphasis on outcomes at the expense of processes; various measurement problems, the lack of appropriate control variables, the nature of the sample, the nature of the causal mechanisms, and the fact that there is great variation around average 'union effects'.

It takes two to tango. Any impact of unions on productivity must reflect the way in which management and unions interact. Indeed the very decision to recognise unions 'may form part of a cluster of characteristics whose effects warrant study' (Edwards, 1987). Further, the underlying model of union behaviour is seldom fully set out. This is a pity because predictions concerning the strength and direction of union productivity effects vary according to the preferred model of union behaviour. The monopoly model, for example, has different implications concerning productivity and profits to the efficient bargaining model (see Chapter 3 by Naylor in this volume).

Harvard School writers do not claim that unions mechanistically raise labour productivity. They state explicitly that this will only happen if, hand-in-hand with union recognition, there is a non-adversarial industrial relations system and competition in the product market. In Great Britain in the 1960s and 1970s unions were fragmented, there was considerable strength at shop floor level, manufacturing had overall high density and, till recently, a considerable public sector presence. Perhaps therefore we might expect a less favourable impact of unions on labour productivity in the UK at that time than (say) in the USA or Germany. And now that UK unions emphasize cooperation and partnership any union impact should have become more favourable than previously.

Unions are not homogeneous but unfortunately in many studies 'unionism remains an abstraction: one union is like every other union, one collective bargaining relationship is like all the rest' (Lipsky, 1985, p. 251). There is little attempt to capture the various forms of unionism and collective bargaining. Two examples will suffice. First, craft unions may have different consequences than general or industrial unions because craft unions have more scope for restrictive practices and are more likely to impose constraints on the growth of productivity since they will evade many of the costs associated with their protection of particular occupational interests and job territories. By contrast, an industrial union may be less likely to block technical change because a smaller proportion of its membership is displaced. Second, the structure of collective bargaining may also influence productivity outcomes. For example, multi-unionism will tend to both enlarge the number of bargaining units and increase the uncertainty inherent in the bargaining process. This could, in turn, lower labour productivity via strike activity or by in-fighting among sectional groups. The studies of the association between unions and productivity are time specific. The world moves on so any association found for the 1980s does not automatically hold in the new millennium.

Statistical analyses deal with outcomes. Case studies are a vital complement because they illuminate the processes by which unions influence productivity at the workplace level. Such case studies might incorporate (Lipsky, 1985) the history of the parties and their relationships; the customs and traditions of the worksite; the personalities, attitudes and leadership skills of the actors; negotiating tactics used by the parties; the degree of inter- and intra-organizational conflict; and the availability of various dispute resolution procedures.

Measurement problems bedevil many studies. Ideally labour productivity should be measured by a physical measure of output like tons of coal per man-shift. But as firms and industries make different things, value added per employee is often used. If gross value added per employee is used then it is necessary to control for both differences in the capital equipment and in bought-in inputs, which also contribute to value added. But this is only the beginning. Net value added per employee is the result of both quantity and price effects. There is always the danger that what is measured as higher productivity is in fact attributable to a higher price in that firm or industry. Alternatively, the existence of a union wage mark-up may cause higher costs and this, in turn, may induce higher prices – which show up as an apparently higher productivity level. More recently, some studies have sidestepped these issues by measuring productivity on a five-point ordinal scale comparing the workplace with other similar workplaces in the same industry. Union presence has also been measured in different ways. Recognition, density or the existence of a closed shop seems unproblematic. But the coverage of collective agreements used by some authors is not the same as unionization and may be inappropriate to capture the influence of union presence on labour productivity.

Selection of the sample presents problems too. For example inefficient firms might get selected out of the sample. Or unions might select inherently more productive firms to unionize. Appropriate control variables are vital to get at the true association between unions and productivity. The life cycle of plants raises particular difficulties. A negative association between union presence and productivity is spurious if it just happens that, by coincidence, unions are over-represented in 'declining' workplaces and industries which also have lower productivity. Ideally, the vintage of the workplace should be incorporated as a control. The studies of union impact on productivity often present an average union effect. But there is great variation around the average. The richness in the variety of union practices in enhancing or discouraging labour productivity, particularly concerning their interaction with management, is not always captured by these statistical studies. Finally, the arrow of causation must be examined carefully. An association does not necessarily imply causation and, anyway, causation might sometimes go 'the other way'. For example a well-organized workplace would tend to have high productivity and low strikes, producing a negative relationship between the two. But, in this case, the lower strike activity is not the cause of the higher productivity.

Evidence
On the basis of the discussion above it might be expected that unions would have a positive impact on productivity in the USA – consequent on the substantial union wage premium – and in Germany and Japan because of voice and cooperative industrial relations achieved through works councils and enterprise unions. By contrast, at least until recently, adversarial industrial relations and multi-unionism in the UK and Australia made a negative link more likely. In all countries it would be expected that more intense product market competition and moves away from antagonistic relations between management and labour towards a mutual gain system would lessen adverse union effects and enhance positive ones. Those wanting a thorough trawl of studies on unions and productivity should consult Doucouliagos and Laroche (2000) who provide evidence on nearly one hundred studies but end up emphasizing how the findings are country, time and sector specific.

In their very careful recent study of *US* unions, working practices and labour productivity, Black and Lynch (1997, p. 9) note that 'empirically, the evidence on the impact of unions on productivity is mixed'. They state that most empirical work has looked at industry level productivity and union density data or industry-specific studies: 'The range of estimates on the impact of unions on labour productivity runs from minus 3 per cent in Clark (1984) to plus 22 per cent in Brown and Medoff (1978) to no effect in Freeman and Medoff (1984)'. Further any effects may vary by sector. For example Bronars et al. (1994) state that unions are associated with higher relative productivity levels in manufacturing and lower productivity in non-manufacturing.

Black and Lynch (see Table 5.2) try and reconcile these disparate findings

Table 5.2 Unions and productivity: international evidence

Country/ Author	Sample	Indicator of productivity	Indicator of union	Controls	Results		
USA Black and Lynch (1997)	627 mfg workplaces 1993 (results confirmed in panel 1987–93)	Labour productivity (from Cobb-Douglas production function)	Recognition (plus interactions)	Information tech (4 variables) Human capital (3) High performance work systems (7) Profit sharing (2)	cf base workplace (see text) • HPW + union +20% • HPW + non-union +11% • union + no employee involvement −15%		
Canada Maki (1983)	time series 1926–78 whole economy excluding agriculture	Total factor productivity growth (tfp)	Density Strike activity	Education cycle	tfp growth (% points per year) density −1.7 strikes −1.0 during 1970s		
UK Pencavel (2003)	1484 workplaces WERS 98	Compared with workplaces in same industry % A lot better 12 Better 40 Average 43 Below average 5 Lot below average 1	Non-union (597 workplaces) Single union (322) Multiple unions joint barg. (337) Multiple unions separate barg. (228)	Workplace: size, age Workforce: % PT, F		Difference between	
						Union and non union workplaces	Separate and joint bargaining
					prob (a lot below ave)	0	0
					prob (below ave)	0	0.02
					prob (ave)	0	0.06
					prob (better than ave)	−0.01	−0.05
					prob (a lot better than ave)	−0.01	−0.03

Country Study	Sample	Value added per employee	Works council Yes/No	Control variables	Results
Germany Addison et al. (2000)	1025 mfg workplaces Hanover Panel 1994	Value added per employee	Works council Yes/No	Workplace: size, age capacity utilisation Workforce: education Technology and work organization Profitsharing Industry	estabs 101–1000 employees +, sig estabs 21–100 employees +, ns
Japan Benson (1994)	253 manufac-turing firms employing 100+ in Kansai region 1992	Compared with other firms in same industry % Much higher 4 Little higher 34 Same 40 Little lower 20 Lot lower 2	Recognition density f.t. official present	Enterprise: size, K/L ratio Workforce: % F, skilled, Non-permanent quality circle, JIT Labour practices: communications, contingent pay, other benefits Product market: competitors, expanding/ contracting	Recognition –ve (ns) but f.t. official +vc (ns)
Australia Crockett et al. (1992)	759 private sector workplaces 20+ employees AWIRS 1990	Compared with work-places in same industry % Lot higher 11 Little higher 33 Same 42 Little lower 12 Lot lower 3	Recognition density no. of unions	Workplace: size, K/L ratio capacity utilisation Workforce: composition EI, labour turnover Product market: competitors expanding/ contracting	Recognition –ve (sig at 10%) Density –ve (sig at 10%) Number of unions –ve (sig at 5%)

by interacting the union status of the establishment with other workplace practices. Essentially the aim is to distinguish between different types of labour-management relations – traditional and new – and their impact on labour productivity. This seems a very useful approach because the focus of much recent research concerns not unions and productivity but high performance work practices and productivity (see e.g. Ichniowski and Shaw (1995) and Huselid and Becker (1996) who calculate a detailed human resource management (HRM) index and analyse how changes in this index influence the performance of the firm).

The sample is over 600 manufacturing workplaces in 1993 (a panel study from 1987–93 yields very similar results). Black and Lynch construct a base case benchmark workplace which is a non-union multi-establishment plant, has profit sharing for managers but not for non-managers, no total quality management (TQM), no benchmarking, 1 per cent of employees meeting regularly about work issues, 10 per cent of non-managerial employees using computers, 1 per cent of employees in self-managed teams and mean values for age of equipment, education levels, turnover, and number of employees per supervisor. They then alter the characteristics of this benchmark to see how labour productivity changes. An old-fashioned plant with union recognition but no employee involvement does 15 per cent worse than the base case. Introducing high performance work (HPW) systems has a large and positive effect on productivity. The HPW system plant has 50 per cent of non-managers using computers, 50 per cent of workers meeting to discuss workplace issues regularly, profit sharing for non-managers, 30 per cent of workers in self-managed teams, TQM and benchmarking. And if the plant has all these HPW practices and is unionized, productivity increases 20 percentage points above the base case. Thus for US manufacturing at least:

> Unionised firms who have succeeded in moving to a more cooperative labor management relations system which gives employees more voice in decision making but at the same time links their compensation with performance have higher labor productivity. (p. 24)

Cappelli and Neumark (2001, p. 738) note that HPW practices raise employee compensation as well as productivity. This is consistent with the Black and Lynch study but causes them to emphasize an alternative conclusion, namely 'HPW practices have little effect on overall labor efficiency measured as output per dollar spent on labour'. Links between unionization and various employee involvement work/practices are discussed further in section 5.

Most studies of unions' impact compare performance (say productivity) among otherwise similar firms or workplaces that differ according to union status. An ingenious alternative approach (Pencavel, 2001) compares productivity according to the governance of the firm. The plywood mills in Washington state are of three types: classical text book (non-union) mills, traditional unionized mills and cooperative mills owned and managed by the workers. When he compares total factor productivity between cooperative mills and unionized mills Pencavel finds that productivity is 14 per cent higher in the former. It is suggested that the higher cooperative productivity reflects greater industriousness and lower levels of supervision in cooperative mills than in unionized mills. This seems consistent with the Black and Lynch study where unionized workplaces with high performance work practices such as voice and self-managed teams had higher productivity than more traditional unionized workplaces like the unionized plywood mills.

Labour economists are going 'inside the firm' more frequently now than in the past. This research method, which blends detailed knowledge of the operation of the firm with modern statistical technique, has yielded two splendid case studies on the subject of unions and productivity. These explorations overcome many of the problems associated with the cross-section studies noted above. The first deals with the impact of industrial relations variables on productivity at 'Big Plane', the largest US plane manufacturer. The second shows the dire impact of a major strike on product quality at a tyre firm.

Big Plane is the largest manufacturing exporter and the second largest manufacturing employer in the USA. Kleiner et al. (2002) analyse 18 years (1974–91) of monthly production data to assess the impact of three strikes, a 10-month long work to rule, the nature of union leadership inside the firm and the introduction of TQM on productivity. They find: 'strikes, slowdowns and union leaders influenced the productivity of this plant by large percentages and large absolute dollar amounts [but] did not have long term productivity effects, the firm was able to return to pre-event levels of production within one to four months' (p. 215). Further, introducing TQM into a low-trust industrial relations environment reduced labour productivity and increased labour costs; rather productivity was restored when TQM was abandoned after two years and the previous heavy monitoring authoritarian governance system reintroduced.

Product quality is affected by industrial relations but this link has been little studied. A skilful analysis by Krueger and Mas (2002) of the consequences of a major dispute which lasted over two years (1994–96) at the Bridgestone/Firestone tyre plant at Decatur, IL, examines this issue. It is coupled with the recall of 14.4 million tyres by Ford and Firestone. Firestone tyres were also linked to 271 fatalities and 800 injuries at the time of and immediately after the dispute. The previous contract expired in

April 1994 and employees worked without a contract for three months prior to going on strike. In negotiations Bridgestone/Firestone demanded a move from eight-hour to 12-hour shifts, as well as cutting pay for new hires by 30 per cent. Almost immediately after the 4200 workers went on strike the company began to hire replacement workers. Krueger and Mas state that the strike could have led to poor product quality in a number of ways. The replacement workers might have been under-trained. Lax supervision during the strike could have contributed to tyre defects. Discord among replacement workers, union members who crossed the picket line and returning strikers could have resulted in production defects. And workers may have been fatigued and more prone to errors because Firestone introduced a 12–hour, rotating shift to operate the plant 24 hours a day during the strike.

The evidence assembled strongly 'suggests that the strike and strife in Decatur was a major contributing factor to the production of defective tires' (p. 30). For example the analysis finds an excess number of complaints for tyres produced at Decatur in the few months before the strike began, when Bridgestone/Firestone demanded concessions, and in the period when many replacement workers and recalled union members worked side by side. It is not simply that under-trained or poorly supervised replacement workers produced defective tyres. Instead, the timing suggests that the concurrence of replacement workers and union members working side by side before the contract was settled, as well as labour strife in the months leading up to the strike, coincided with a high number of defective tyres. The stock market valuation of Bridgestone/Firestone more than halved from $16.7 billion to $7.5 billion in the four months after the recall was announced. Further, the authors estimate that more than 40 lives were lost as a result of the excessive number of problem tyres produced in Decatur during the dispute. It is hard to disagree with the authors understated conclusion that 'this episode serves as a useful reminder that a good relationship between labour and management can be in the company's interest' (p. 33).

Analysis of the impact of unions on productivity in *Canada* used a time series from 1926–78 by Maki (1983) covering the whole economy except for agriculture. The author calculates that the growth in union density during the 1970s reduced the annual growth in total factor productivity by 1.7 per cent per year and the increase in strike activity had a corresponding reduction of 1.0 per cent per year. These seem remarkably large effects.

Links between the industrial relations regime in a company or workplace and its productivity performance have long been a matter of interest and debate in the *UK*. The state of play in the 1970s and 1980s was surveyed by Metcalf (1990b). The focus of the studies of that period was manufacturing industry where the weight of the evidence suggests that around 1980, union presence was associated with lower levels of labour productivity, but that in the first half of the 1980s strongly unionized workplaces and industries had faster growth in labour productivity than their non-union counterparts. This turnaround in the productivity performance of the highly-unionized manufacturing sector was examined by Metcalf (1990a). Britain went from being bottom of the league table of productivity growth in the G-7 countries in the 1960s and 1970s to top in the 1980s (and near top in the 1990s). This was attributed to the interaction of more intense product market competition, higher levels of unemployment and the legislative onslaught against organized labour which altered management and labour practices in favour of higher productivity.

Recently, attention has concentrated on any lingering effects of multiple unionism and possible links between tougher product market competition and improved productivity performance. Multi-unionism (i.e. more than one union in a workplace) was an important feature of British industrial relations. For example in 1980, 41 per cent of establishments employing 2000 people or more had three to five unions present and a further 38 per cent had six or more present. Although there are only a small number of such plants they account for a large fraction of total employment. Oulton (1995) states that up till the 1980s the UK system of industrial relations required, particularly in large plants, 'that several different unions had to be able to reach agreement with management on changes in working methods. If they could not agree, the status quo continued. The costs of change, in terms of management time or interruptions to production, were high and the probability of no agreement at the end of the day was not negligible. It seems very likely that the greater the number of partners to a negotiation, each with the power of veto, the lower is the probability of agreement. Common sense suggests that change is likely to occur at a slower pace than in systems not suffering from these handicaps'. This was precisely the position of Bean and Crafts (1996) who concluded that the decline in multi-unionism was central to the improvement in labour productivity in the 1980s.

Two questions flow from the discussion so far. First, is there any longer any difference in productivity performance between workplaces which do and do not recognize a union? Second, do multi-union workplaces perform worse than single union workplaces and can any such disadvantages be offset if the separate unions bargain jointly? Pencavel (2003) investigates these issues (Table 5.2). His sample is drawn from the 1998 Workplace Employment Relations Survey (WERS98) and uses the subjective productivity measure where the manager compares his/her productivity performance with other workplaces in the same industry on a five-point scale. The sample size was 1484 of which 322 were single union workplaces, 337 were multi-union with joint bargaining, 228 were multi-union with separate bargaining and 597 were non-union. The control variables were percentage of labour force part-time, percentage female, and workplace size and age. The results are clear-cut. There is no difference in the productivity performance of union compared with non-union workplaces. But multi-unionism with fragmented bargaining still puts the workplace at a disadvantage. Pencavel concludes:

> By the end of the 1990s, average union–non-union differences in labour productivity appear to be negligible. Where such differences emerge, they are in establishments where fragmented bargaining occurs. Such bargaining is unusual – approximately only 7 per cent of workplaces in 1998 were characterised by fragmented bargaining. This allows the generalisation that unionism may serve as an agent permitting employees to participate in shaping their work environment without productivity suffering. (Pencavel, 2003, p. 34).

There is one important caveat to Pencavel's conclusion, discussed further in section 5, which demonstrates a remarkable difference in the link between unions and productivity when we compare monopolistic and competitive workplaces.

The *German* industrial relations system has a dual structure of employee representation. Collective agreements are negotiated between trade unions and employers' associations at industry level, while works councils watch the implementation and coordination of such agreements at workplace level. Some studies of links between employee representation and firm performance focus on works councils while others examine the union impact.

Consider first the associations between works councils and productivity. In her survey, Schedlitzki (2002) states that three out of four recent studies found a positive link between the two variables, but only one of them reported this link to be statistically significant for the whole sample (Addison et al., 2001). Due to their role as the main body for collective voice and employee involvement at the plant level, works councils might be expected to have quite a sizeable effect on the behaviour of employees and hence on their productivity. This potential impact is strengthened by the extensive set of rights formally prescribed to works councils by the Works Constitution Act 1972 and its subsequent two amendments. For example, works councils have to be informed/consulted about redundancies and the introduction of new work methods. Further, they have co-determination rights regarding social matters such as the regulation of overtime, changes in working hours, remuneration arrangements and the introduction of technical devices to monitor employee performance.

Theoretically the link between works councils and labour productivity could be either positive or negative (Addison et al., 1993). Works councils could use their rights in order to facilitate the flow of information and the introduction of new technology as suggested by Freeman and Medoff's 'collective voice' model. On the other hand, they could use their veto rights so as to delay important decisions on employment, technology and work organization issues. Any such negative impact that works councils might have on labour productivity might also occur via the 'managerial competence' hypothesis of FitzRoy and Kraft (1987). They argued, that most competent managers typically devote much attention to personnel matters, and presumably will establish effective communication and participation without the imposition of any formal institutions or regulations. Consequently, they hypothesize that works councils impose legal constraints on the internal organization of a company and so reduce the efficiency of competent managers.

A recent exemplary study measuring the link between works councils and productivity (Addison et al., 2000) used data from the Hannoveraner Firmenpanel (Hannover Firm Panel) wave in 1994. The dataset contains information on 1025 plants and is representative of the population of manufacturing establishments with at least five employees in the German federal state of Lower Saxony. The data were collected in personal interviews held with the owner or top-manager of the establishment. Productivity was measured by value added per employee and a dummy variable captures works council presence. Numerous controls were included in this study such as human capital, establishment size and age, the state of technology, the degree of market power, capacity utilization and profit-sharing schemes for employees and for management. The authors also controlled for several work organization and industry variables. The findings showed a statistically significant positive link between works councils and labour productivity only for large establishments with 101–1000 employees. For smaller establishments with 21–100 employees the link was positive but statistically insignificant. The authors speculate that the German mandatory works councils might set too high a level of employee involvement for smaller establishments and might better accord with the needs of larger plants in this regard. After also considering links between works councils and profits they conclude, that the differentiation between large and small establishments provided by the Works Constitution Act 1972 is insufficient.

Links between German trade unions and labour productivity have not been studied as much as the impact of works councils. The most thorough study (Addison et al.1989) is a cross-section analysis of 30 German industries organized by trade unions in 1983. The authors found a negative but statistically insignificant link between trade unions and labour productivity. Schnabel (1991) confirms that trade union density exerts a negative, but quantitatively small, influence on labour productivity in his survey of five German studies.

Increased international competition and moves towards decentralized bargaining have affected the German industrial relations systems recently (Hassel, 1999). Therefore, the above findings might not be representative any longer and more up-to-date studies are needed before a firm conclusion can be drawn on the relationship between works councils, unions and labour productivity.

Initial studies of the link between union recognition and labour productivity for *Japan* showed mixed results. Brunello (1992) suggested negative union effects but this finding was contradicted by Muramatsu (1984) and Morishima (1991). Fortunately the two most recent studies reach more consistent conclusions. It might be expected that enterprise unions – the norm in Japan – would be likely to enhance efficiency in the workplace or company but neither study shows this directly. Rather it is by subtle, indirect, channels – via longer tenures and the role of full-time union officials – that unions raise productivity. Tachibanaki and Noda (2000) analyse data from a panel of 404 listed manufacturing firms 1992–95 of which 350 recognize unions and 54 do not. Productivity is measured as value added per employee and the controls include firm size, the capital–labour ratio, average job tenure, average age, fraction female and the age of the workplace. Union recognition is negatively (significantly) associated with productivity but the union/tenure interaction has a positive effect. Tenure is longer in unionized firms and once tenure is above 15 years (which it is in two-thirds of their sample) the union effect becomes positive overall. The authors summarize their findings as follows:

> The larger the share of employees with longer tenures, the higher the productivity of a firm. Longer job tenures imply that they are highly experienced and skilled workers. A labour union lowers separations and thus consolidates cooperative behaviour. Such cooperative behaviour in unionized firms raises employees' work incentives, skill formation and possibly solidarity, and their loyalty to the firm as well as mutual trust (p. 78).

Benson (1994) also finds no direct significant link between recognition and productivity but notes an important role for full-time union officials (see Table 5.2). The sample is 253 manufacturing firms employing 100+ employees in the Kansai region. In each firm, productivity is measured by comparing it with other firms in the same industry. Three indicators of unions are used: recognition, density and the presence of a full-time union official at the company. Various enterprise, workforce, management, industrial relations and product market characteristics are used as controls. Firms with (a) full-time union official(s) have slightly higher levels of productivity than their non-union counterparts. This is because:

Full-time local union officials are more likely to enforce agreements and contracts relating to working conditions. They may assist management in creating a more efficient and productive working environment. Their intimate knowledge of the enterprise often means that management relies heavily on them to solve disputes, to contribute to the smooth running of the organisation and to assist in the effective management of human resources. (Benson, 1994, p. 9)

These two studies therefore suggest little or no direct impact of unions on productivity. Rather, any effects (modestly positive) come via lengthening tenures which may enhance cooperation and the role of the full-time official which Benson describes as an unpaid personnel manager. It would be interesting to know whether similar productivity-enhancing effects of unions occur in other countries too.

Compared with Japan and Germany, *Australia* probably has a less cooperative tradition of labour relations, partly influenced by multi-unionism. This resulted, according to the first Australian Workplace Industrial Relations Survey (AWIRS), in union presence being associated with lower labour productivity, but the impact of unions was rather small. Drago and Wooden (1992) conclude in their comprehensive survey that the net effect of unions on productivity is negative and that multiple unionism is associated with poorer outcomes than recognition of one single union.

The detailed study of Crockett et al. (1992) analysed data from 759 private sector workplaces employing 20+ people from the 1991 AWIRS. Productivity was measured on the subjective five-point scale comparing the respondent manager's workplace with other workplaces in the same industry. Three indicators of unionization were used: recognition, density and the number of unions (to examine the effect of multi-unionism). Various workplace, workforce, labour relations and product market controls were included. It is concluded that trade unions are associated with lower relative productivity in the Australian labour market and each union indicator has a negative sign and is significant at 10 per cent or better. But the effect of density itself is small. Rather:

The negative union effect is strongest when unionism is measured by the number of unions. Where there are several unions present, the detrimental effect on productivity is greater than if the workplace had a single union. The presence of a number of unions presumably causes demarcation problems, inter-union competition and communication problems and may be associated with possible conflicts between different union voices. (Crockett et al. 1992, p. 132).

Thus evidence from both the UK and Australia points to an adverse link between multiunionism and productivity.

3. Financial performance

The impact of unions on profitability or financial performance flows from any impact union recognition has on pay levels and productivity. If union presence boosts pay, financial performance will be worse unless there is a roughly equivalent union effect on productivity. The weight of the evidence reviewed here, focusing on the private sector, suggests a negative link between unionization and financial performance. But this association is much weaker when product markets are competitive rather than oligopolistic and industrial relations are cooperative not adversarial.

Theory and testing

If unions raise the level of wages without similarly increasing productivity the resources underpinning the higher pay level have to come from somewhere. Such union wage gains might come from lower wages for non-union workers; or from consumers via higher product prices; or from the owners of capital via lower profits. As Hirsch and Addison (1986) point out each of these routes is circumscribed by competition. Large wage differentials between similar union and non-union workers tend to be partially eroded by selective hiring, threat effects raising wages in the non-union sector and cost advantages enjoyed by non-union firms. Cost increases cannot easily be passed through to consumers in the form of higher prices unless a union has organized an entire industry or local market where exclusion of foreign and non-union competition is possible. And in many sectors competition in the product market will limit surplus profits as a source of wage gains. Therefore any union gains from potential firm profits turn largely on the existence of above-normal profits resulting from market power, government regulation, returns from fixed capital and firm-specific advantages like location and R&D returns. These channels will be briefly considered in turn.

Links between the product market and labour market are the key to the market power channel. In the short run, if the firm has some monopoly power in the product market, unions may be able to raise wages and capture a share of the economic profits associated with market power. Such a firm with market power will try to pass some of the wage push onto consumers but not all of it can be passed on in this way. In the simplest case, when the firm remains on its demand curve, the union jacks up wages and the monopolist cuts back on employment and simultaneously raises prices to consumers. This is not a simple reallocation of income from the firm to the union; this is a case where part of the union wage gains comes out of monopoly profits, but a part is paid for by the vulnerable consumer, with possible consequences for future jobs and investment. There is an alternative, but special – and probably atypical – case where the union maximizes rents and negotiates efficient contracts (see Pencavel, 1991). In such circumstances the income redistribution is benign – a simple transfer from capital to labour – and has no long-run consequences for investment and employment. The simple notion that there is a fixed level of profit some of which the unions may capture without any subsequent consequences is not correct except in this special case. Normally the monopoly firm will try to defend its profit and take corrective action by getting consumers to pay more. The end result is lower profits for the firm, but not as low as if it did not raise its prices.

Many sectors are or were previously either in state hands (nationalized industries) or regulated such that entry and price competition were simultaneously limited. This again creates a potential pot of economic profit that may be captured in part by labour. For example, in the US this happened in trucking and the airlines. In the UK the utilities were nationalized from the 1940s to the 1980s, but other also sectors experienced extensive regulation including the ports under the National Dock Labour Scheme and commercial television. It is noteworthy that unions normally opposed the privatization of the utilities and deregulation of sectors like commercial TV or legal practice. The relevant test here is whether unions made wage concessions and experienced membership losses after deregulation.

Returns on investment in physical capital or intangible capital such as R&D provide a further channel for union gains at the expense of profits. 'When the capital replacement cycle is long relative to the union's time horizon, the "surplus" that provides the return on durable and specialised capital, and that occurs only after costs are sunk, is vulnerable to capture by monopoly labor' (Hirsch and Addison, 1986, p. 210). If this is the route to lower profitability the union effect definitely lowers investment and the accumulation of capital (see also section 4 below and Chapter 9 by Menezes-Filho and van Reenen in this volume).

As recent events at Enron, WorldCom and Xerox have shown, profitability is one of the most difficult economic variables to measure. Freeman and Medoff (1984) state, for example:

> The profits reported on company balance sheets generally differ from true economic profits. They may differ in treatment of interest charges, in depreciation, in valuation of inventories or in estimation of pension fund liabilities. For tax reasons, companies often seek to report lower profits than in fact they actually earn. There are also problems in measuring the capital investments with which profits are compared. Valuing machines of different vintages is difficult; the book value reported by accountants differs from the true value of assets. Estimates rarely exist of important but nebulous forms of capital such as goodwill or reputation (pp. 181–182).

Until recently studies of industry or company profitability tended to use two 'objective' indicators. First, the return on capital was defined as business revenue less variable (usually labour) costs divided by some measure of the value of capital such as the replacement cost of plant and equipment or the gross book value of total assets. Second, the 'price–cost margin' defined as the excess of prices over variable costs. Not surprisingly these indicators have come in for criticism. It is, for example, notoriously difficult to measure the value of capital, and profits should be, conceptually, measured in present values rather than on an annual basis.

More recently some studies use an alternative ordinal scale. For example, in the UK, WERS98 defines financial performance rather than profits and uses a subjective rather than objective measure. The following question was put to managerial respondents:

> *I now want to ask you how your workplace is currently performing compared with other establishments in the same industry. How would you assess your workplace's financial performance?*

Responses were coded along a five-point ordinal scale, from 'a lot better than average' to 'a lot worse than average'. Recent British and Australian studies of the association between union presence and profits/financial performance have used this kind of measure.

Financial performance is influenced by many factors other than union presence and controls are included in statistical analyses to allow for this. Workforce controls include per cent part-time, female and skilled. Workplace characteristics include size, location and vintage. Some studies include controls for management characteristics like the extent of human resource management and the existence or otherwise of contingent pay. The nature of the product market – the number of competitors, for example – is also controlled for in some studies.

Evidence

The bulk of studies examining links between unionization and financial performance refer to just four countries and these will be considered in turn. In the *USA* empirical studies have usually found a significant negative relationship between unions and financial performance and have used a variety of financial outcome measures, including price-cost margin, net revenues per unit of capital, Tobin's q and stock market value. For example, Addison and Hirsch's (1989) review of 16 studies that used various methodologies and measures of profitability found a consistent large negative relationship between unions and financial performance. This association was confirmed by Bronars et al. (1994) using data from the 1970s and 1980s for some 300 firms. They concluded that there is fairly strong and significant evidence that the total effect of higher union coverage is to reduce profitability. They argue that this effect does not come via unions directly sharing rents but rather occurs indirectly through any union impact on impact on investment behaviour and growth. Kleiner (2001) updated the Addison and Hirsch review and similarly concluded that unions are still associated with lower profits.

The link between union recognition and shareholder wealth was analysed by Ruback and Zimmerman (1984) who found a 1.4 per cent reduction in NYSE-listed firms' stock prices on the day a petition to hold a union election is held (and a 2.4 per cent for petitions which, ex post, are successful) and a further 1.4 per cent fall on the day of a successful election, for a cumulative total loss of 3.3 per cent. Kuhn (1998) points out that, given the share of wages in costs and the average fraction of each firm's employees involved in new unionization bids, 'this loss is surprisingly consistent with a 15 per cent wage increase among newly unionised workers' (p. 1039), which is the norm for new recognitions.

Recently, however, Batt and Welbourne (2002) suggest that the association between unions and profits is more nuanced than realized. It is influenced – as elsewhere – for example, by product market competition and the degree of labour–management conflict: 'In sum, much of the evidence showing a negative relationship between unions and financial performance may be understood as a result of oligopolistic markets, mass production approaches to work organisation and conflictual labor relations in a particular historical period' (p. 10). Thus Batt and Welbourne accept the previous negative association but argue that labour and product markets have altered so fundamentally in the last decade or so that it may no longer hold – even though Kleiner's (2001) survey suggests unions are still associated with lower profits.

They point to the following developments in the 1990s. First, US firms, particularly high tech and entrepreneurial firms, have adopted much more flexible approaches to organizing work, such as HPW systems (Appelbaum and Batt, 1994) which reduce status differences between workers and managers. Next, union power has dropped significantly, with union membership falling from 24 per cent of the private sector workforce in 1973 to 10 per cent in 1995. Further, mutual gain and win–win approaches to bargaining have transformed union–management relationships in many instances, leading to greater cooperation and less zero-sum conflict.

So Batt and Welbourne revisited the relationship between unions and financial performance by drawing on evidence from 464 entrepreneurial firms at the time of their initial public offering (IPO) in 1993 and their subsequent financial performance 1993–1996 (see Table 5.3). These entrepreneurial firms

Table 5.3 Unions and financial performance: international evidence

Country/ Author	Sample	Indicator of financial performance	Indicator of union	Controls	Results
USA Batt and Welbourne (2002)	464 entrepreneurial firms at IPO 1993	• Tobin's q • change in earnings per share • change in stock price	Recognition	Firm size, age Industry Region Degree of risk	Union firm has significantly higher: • Tobin's q by 15% • earnings per share by 10% • stock price by 17%
Japan Tachibanaki and Noda (2000)	Panel of 12 mfg inds 1966–1984	Labour's share in income (wage payments ÷ total value added)	Density Disputes • number • workers involved • days lost	K:L ratio K:O ratio Concentration ratio Firm size Average age of workforce % female, graduate	+ sig association Pre oil shock density, disputes and labour's share all rising Post oil shock density, disputes and labour's share all falling e.g. 1966–1974 10% increase in no. of disputes increases labour's share by 0.9% (mean 38%)
UK Wilkinson (2000)	WERS 1998 up to 1843 workplaces	4 ordered categories subjective	recognition recognition by coverage bargaining level union strength	Workplace size, age % female, PT JCC, HRM score ESOS, incentive pay Product market (9 variables) Industry, region	No association 76 coefficients reported, only 4 significant Result holds for: • whole economy • trading sector • private trading sector • private trading sector with profit measure
Germany Addison, Schnabel and Wagner (2001)	Hanover Panel 1994 1025 mfg plants in Lower Saxony	5 ordered categories subjective • high profit dummy • index of profitability from 1 to 5	Dummy variable for works council presence	Establishment size, market share, capacity utilisation, state of production technology, profit sharing, industry dummies	sig –ve association • holds for both profit indicators and different sample sizes

are described as small and young. They are less likely to have the kind of monopoly union power, conflictual labour management relations, or rigid work rules traditionally found in large US mass-production enterprises. These IPO firms are not concentrated among high tech companies. They are split roughly equally between manufacturing and services and are located in all geographic areas within the United States. Just over one fifth report having a union at the time of the IPO. Three measures of financial performance were used: Tobin's q is the ratio of market value to book value at the initial public offering, growth in earnings per share and growth in stock price. The control variables were firm size and age, industry, region and the degree of risk at the time of the IPO.

The results are pretty remarkable. (This study was chosen as our exemplar precisely because the results are so out of line with other studies.) Union presence is associated with significantly superior financial performance on all three measures. For example, the growth in stock price was 17 per cent higher in unionized firms than non-union firms and earnings per share were correspondingly 10 per cent higher. Batt and Welbourne conclude that 'unionization does not inevitably reduce financial performance. Rather new forms of organising work and union–management relations hold the promise of maximising shareholder wealth as well as employee welfare. This is not an inevitable zero-sum trade-off' (p. 26). Thus the great weight of US studies suggest that unions reduce profits but it is just possible that changes in industrial relations and human resource management in the last decade have now weakened, or in some cases overturned, this previous stylized fact. However, if unions really do boost profits this begs the question of why firms are not asking to be unionized. The US evidence (e.g. Kleiner, 2001) demonstrates very strong continued employer resistance to unionization.

There are only a limited number of studies which have investigated the links between union presence and profitability in *Japan*. Fortunately, the two most thorough studies have used very different samples but come to identical conclusions. The exemplary study (see Table 5.3) by Tachibanaki and Noda (2000) presents evidence from a panel of 12 manufacturing industries for the period 1966–84. Profits are measured objectively, via labour's share in income, defined as wage payments divided by total value added. Union presence is indicated by either density or disputes – the number of disputes, workers involved or days lost. Controls include the capital:labour and capital:output ratios, product market competition (as measured by the concentration ratio), average firm size and workforce characteristics such as the average age of employees and the proportions female or graduate.

Union presence is associated with a higher fraction of income going to labour. Prior to the 1970s oil shock, union density, disputes and labour's share were all rising. After 1974 density, disputes and labour's share all fell. For example, for the period 1966–74 an increase in the number of disputes by 10 per cent increases labour's share by 0.9 per cent (the mean value is 38 per cent) while a 10 per cent rise in the number of workers involved in disputes is associated with a 0.27 per cent increase in labour's share. The authors interpret these findings as causal and state unambiguously that 'it is possible to conclude that the increase in labour disputes which occurred in the pre-oil crisis period raised labour shares, while the decrease during the post-oil crisis lowered them' (p. 97).

More recent evidence comes from the cross-section survey of 253 enterprises in the Kansai region, which includes Osaka, Kyoto and Kobe, by Benson (1994). Profits were measured by the rate of return on capital, indicated by pre-tax profit divided by total assets. Unionization was captured by any members present or density or the presence of a full-time union official in the enterprise. Numerous controls were included covering the characteristics of the enterprise, workforce, management practices, industrial relations and product market. Benson concludes (p. 10) that union presence reduced the probability of managers reporting a rate of return of 6 per cent or more and increased the probability that these enterprises would have lower profits. Higher wage costs in unionized firms are suggested to explain lower profitability. Union firms may not pay a higher base wage but pay higher bonuses, higher female wages and have lower annual hours.

In the 1980s virtually all *UK* studies reported a negative association between union presence and financial performance. For example Metcalf (1993) reported that eight UK studies used workplaces, firms or industries to analyse the link between profitability and unionization and all but one showed a negative association. But Wilkinson (2000, p. 3) notes that 'over the course of the 1980s this negative impact weakened such that by 1990 the overall union effect was halved as compared to 1984 and unionized establishments had lower financial performance only where the union was strong and the establishment had some product market power'. This tempering of the impact of unions was confirmed by Machin and Stewart (1996) who concluded that by 1990 unions only impacted adversely on profitability where there was a closed shop and/or weak competition in the product market. They also found that multi-unionism detracts from good financial performance. By 1990 the closed shop was outlawed in the UK and during the 1990s there was growing competition in the product market and a lower incidence of multi-unionism. It is plausible, therefore, that by now any impact of unions on financial performance has been attenuated.

The most thorough investigation of such links is by Wilkinson (2000) using the WERS98 sample (see Table 5.3). Wilkinson analysed links between financial performance and unionization using four different WERS samples and a number of different indicators of union presence and the ordinal financial performance scale noted above. Union presence was also measured in four ways: simple recognition; then the extent of collective bargaining coverage with or without recognition was added; then the level of bargaining was added – workplace, organization, industry and multiple. Finally there was a union strength measure. A strong union was defined as one with 100 per cent coverage or membership. A weak union was one with under 50 per cent coverage and membership. All remaining recognized unions were defined as medium strength. By the end of the 1990s Wilkinson states that there was no overall association between union presence and financial performance. A total of 76 coefficients are reported (four samples and 19 different union indicators) and only four (two positive, two negative) are significant at the 5 per cent level. More of the coefficients were positive (45) than negative (31). This lack of association probably reflects weaker union effects on pay and productivity.

There is little doubt that any impact of UK unions on financial performance is muted now compared with two decades ago. The 'average' results – no effects – found by Wilkinson are confirmed by both Addison and Belfield (2000) and McNabb and Whitfield (2000). As Bryson and Wilkinson (2002, p. 17) put it: 'the absence of general union effects on financial performance implies that the negative influence of unions on performance identified by previous studies has diminished in the 1990s'. But some residual union effects do remain when different tests are done. First, Pencavel (2003) shows that multi-unionism continues to have adverse consequences for financial performance. Second, unions have a very different effect on profits (and productivity) when the product market is monopolistic compared with when it is competitive (Metcalf 2003). When there are five or fewer competitors, unions are associated with significantly worse financial performance but union recognition has no such impact when the product market is more competitive. Third, Wilkinson finds that it is weak unions which have negative associations, while medium and strong unions have a positive link with performance. This hints that where a union is recognized it is – at least when considering financial performance – better to have an encompassing union rather than one where under half the workforce belong.

When examining the characteristics and influences of unions and works councils on profitability in *Germany* it is important to bear in mind the unique features of the dual system of cooperative industrial relations. First, pay settlements take place at the industry level and are therefore decoupled from participatory and other factors at the plant level (Hassel, 1999). This means that work councils are excluded from the negotiation and settlement of wage agreements with the employer unless the firm explicitly authorizes work agreements of such type (Addison et al., 1996). Rather, works councils focus on their extensive rights covering information, consultation and co-determination at the plant level. Second, in order to ensure cooperation at plant level, the Works Constitution Act of 1972 has precluded any strike activity initiated by works councils. The legislation even 'enjoins the employer and works council to work in a spirit of mutual trust'. Third, although works councils are formally independent of unions, in practice the two institutions are intertwined. Works councils feed trade unions with members, reserve seats for union members and supervise the implementation of collective agreements, and trade unions support and help works councils in their local bargaining function. The bulk of the literature analysing the link between institutions and profits in Germany has focused on works councils rather than unions.

Bearing in mind that works councils are neither allowed to strike nor to bargain on wages, it seems reasonable to predict a positive impact on profitability as suggested by the collective voice model. During the 1990s there was considerable interest in studies measuring and evaluating the link between works councils and profitability. This was mostly a reaction to the debate on the transferability of the German model of mandatory works councils initiated by the Dunlop Commission (1994) in the United States. In the event, various studies surveyed by Schedlitzki (2002) reported a negative impact of works councils on profitability. Addison et al. (1996) similarly argue that 'the works council is a classic vehicle for the expression of collective voice, [but] 'the dual system of industrial relations in Germany by no means excludes the possibility that works councils are rent-seeking agencies' (p. 579).

The most recent and thorough study measuring the link between works councils and profitability is by Addison et al. (2001). They used 1994 data from the Hannoveraner Firmenpanel that was collected in personal interviews by Infratest Sozialforschung. The dataset is representative of all manufacturing establishments in Lower Saxony, and contains information on 1025 plants. Top management was asked to rate the establishment's current profitability on an ordinal scale from 'very good' to 'very bad'. The authors measured works council presence via a dummy variable. Further, detailed establishment controls were included such as size, the market share of the most important product line, capacity utilization, profit sharing for the workforce and for management, the state of production technology and industry.

The results show a statistically significant negative association between works councils and profitability and confirm a previous detailed study (Addison et al., 2000) which concluded that among both small and large establishments, works councils are associated with significantly lower profitability. In many ways the consistent empirical finding that the existence of a works council lowers profits is something of a surprise. Works councils do not formally bargain and cannot initiate a strike, and they express the collective voice of the employees. So what is the mechanism by which they adversely impact on financial performance? Two channels have been put forward. Fitzroy and Kraft (1987) suggest that works councils are themselves linked to various legal provisions which constrain competent managers – and such constraints are not present when there is no council. Alternatively, Addison et al. (2001) show that although councils do not formally bargain they may engage in rent-seeking behaviour and achieve a higher wage level than counterpart firms without a council.

Empirical evidence on the impact of unions on profitability is quite scarce and rather inconclusive. Huebler and Jirjahn (2001) measured the effect of collective bargaining coverage on the rent-seeking behaviour of works councils and hence on the impact of works councils on firm performance. They found that works councils in establishments covered by collective agreements were less likely to be engaged in rent-seeking activities and therefore less likely to impact negatively on firm performance. In a nutshell, where there is collective bargaining the works council engages less in rent seeking than it would do without collective bargaining. This emphasizes, again, how important it is to examine the institutional framework in which unions operate.

4.   Investment

Capital accumulation is the key to long-run growth. Therefore the impact of unions on investment is a matter of great importance. In this section we examine the routes by which unions might influence investment, and the evidence that exists on this issue for our six countries 'but there is surprisingly little empirical research analysing unions' impact on investment' (Odgers and Betts, 1997, p. 19). The arguments typically refer to investment in new technology and process innovations, but could also be used to analyse any effect unions might have on investment in research and development (see Chapter 9 by Menezes-Filho and van Reenen in this volume); on product improvements through design, marketing, advertising and after-sales service; and on human capital where a few studies are now appearing and assume greater importance with the growth of the knowledge economy (these are analysed in section 5). A further dimension (not analysed here) concerns 'where to invest' which influences closure and relocation decisions, especially in multi-establishment organizations.

Theory

Rent-seeking behaviour by unions suggests a negative impact on investment. By contrast the traditional on-the-demand curve approach implies union firms substitute away from expensive labour and invest more.

The presence of a union in a workplace might inhibit investment either directly or indirectly in the rent-seeking model. The direct effect occurs if a union delays the installation of new machinery, perhaps because the union representatives are not content with associated organizational changes such as modifications to shift patterns or any required easing of skill demarcations. Further, inflexible work rules might mean that the investment is not used to its full capacity, effectively adding to the cost of installation.

Indirect union effects are set out formally by Grout (1984a, 1984b). When a firm invests in a new project, unionized workers may capture ('tax') some of the returns in the form of higher pay because, once the capital is installed or the R&D done, the process cannot easily be reversed thereby weakening the firm's bargaining position (see also Chapter 9 by Menezes-Filho and van Reenen in this volume). This 'holdup' reduces the profit incentive for new investment thereby depressing the overall investment rate. It was shown in section 3 that the union may be able to appropriate rents accruing from monopoly power in the product market. The argument here is that, in addition, the union is able to capture quasi-rents from capital that represent some of the normal competitive return to capital. If part of the competitive return is captured by unions, firms will reduce investment in capital (see Odgers and Betts, 1997 for more details). Hirsch (1992) describes this behaviour as 'rational myopia' because unions' members have a lack of interest in wages far into the future. Any such rational myopia can lead to opportunistic behaviour by the union.

There is an offsetting force. In the traditional on-the-demand curve model the union-set wage is exogenous and the firm adjusts along the demand curve. Therefore a higher union wage stimulates investment because the firm substitutes away from expensive labour. In this case union activity raises investment (although the positive substitution effect might be attenuated by a negative scale effect), but recall that higher investment consequent on wage push does not necessarily raise social welfare (see section 2).

As the rent-seeking model predicts unions have a negative effect on investment but the traditional substitution approach predicts a positive impact, the issue cannot be decided theoretically: any impact of unions on capital accumulation is an empirical matter.

Evidence

Studies of the impact of unionization on investment in the *USA* reach a remarkably consistent conclusion – a union presence reduces investment.

The classic studies are by Hirsch (1990, 1991) dealing with union effects on physical capital accumulation. The 1990 study (see Table 5.4) used detailed data from 315 American firms and matched investment and other firm/sector information spanning 1970 to 1980 to union density in 1972. The evidence suggested that unionization reduced investment by more than 20 per cent in the typical union firm. Around half this effect was a consequence of the rent-seeking activity described in the theory section above and the other half came via the reduced profitability associated with unions. Hirsch's second study had even more observations and covered a later period and got similar results. More recently Hirsch (1992), Bronars and Deere (1993) and Bronars et al. (1994) have each reached the same conclusion using different data sets: at firm level, higher levels of unionization are associated with lower investment rates. For example Bronars et al. (1994) state that a 10 per cent increase in unionization decreases the R&D/sales ratio by around 4 per cent in manufacturing, the advertising/sales ratio by some 6 per cent in manufacturing and a bit less in non-manufacturing.

Results from a detailed study by Odgers and Betts (1997) for *Canada* mirror those from the USA. The data set contains observations for 18 Canadian manufacturing industries on profits, taxation, investment, capital stock, employment, union membership, imports and exports and the study uses a balanced panel of 378 industry/year observations 1967–87. The impact of unions on investment (as on productivity) seems rather large in Canada. An industry with an average unionization rate experiences a reduction in its gross investment rate of 18–25 per cent relative to a similar non-union industry. The corresponding reduction of net investment is put at 66–74 per cent. It is a nice question how Canadian unionized manufacturing industry survives given such large effects.

Hirsch found that the steepest declines in US investment occurred at low levels of unionization. This non-linear impact of unions on investment is replicated for Canada and the UK. Odgers and Betts (1997) suggest that one reason for this non-linear effect is 'a plateau effect in union bargaining power' such that if firms cannot easily substitute one type of labour for another 'a union representing any of these types of labour can extract most of the quasi-rents by threatening to strike. . . it follows that a relatively small component of a firm's workforce could extract most of the quasi-rent for itself' (p. 34). An alternative explanation is that the voice effects of an encompassing union are more beneficial than those generated by partial coverage.

UK evidence is fully surveyed in Metcalf (1993) and is mixed. Denny and Nickell (1992, 1991) get the most clear-cut union effects (see Table 5.4). Their sample is drawn from manufacturing industries and incorporates

Table 5.4 Unions and investment: international evidence

Country/Author	Sample	Indicator of investment	Indicator of union	Controls	Results
USA Hirsch (1990)	315 firms data 1970–80	Investment rate	Density	Concentration ratio Firm growth rate Vintage Industry import %	Unionization reduced investment by 20% in the typical unionized firm half effect directly half effect via lower profits
Canada Odgers and Betts (1997)	18 mfg industries 1967–1987	Investment rate gross net	Density	Strike activity Import share Accelerator Cost of capital	Compared with non-union industry, one with average density reduces investment rate by: gross 18–25% net 66–74%
UK Denny and Nickell (1992)	73 3-digit mfg industries 1980–84 incorporating WIRS80 and WIRS84 data	Investment rate	Recognition density	Industry demand Prices Technical progress Pay Expected growth	Recognition −ve Density +ve 100% density not sufficient to offset recognition effect

Japan Benson (1994)	253 mfg firms with 100+ employees in Kansai region	Labour's share in total costs Labour's share % % of firms <10 3 10–20 24 21–40 41 41–60 25 61+ 6	Recognition density f.t. official	See Table 5.1	Recognition associated with higher K-intensity: reduces [raises] probability of capitalisation rate less than 60% [above 60%]
Germany Addison et al. (1993)	101 mfg establishments in Niedersachsen and Baden-Württemberg 1990–91	investment rate • gross • net	Work council present	Capacity utilisation Firm size Export: sales ratio Hours of overtime Product innovation	Presence of works councils lowers investment: • gross by 20–33% (sig) • net by 1–11% (ns)

information on industrial relations variables from the first two Workplace Industrial Relations Surveys (WIRS80 and WIRS84). They find, for 1980–84 – before unions were tamed – that union recognition depressed investment, but that this adverse effect was offset as density rose. However, even 100 per cent density did not completely counter the negative recognition effect. By implication, they point out that the worst possible situation is union recognition but with only a small fraction of the workforce being union members. Voice effects are also apparent. Where many workers are covered by joint consultative councils (whether in union or non-union workplaces) investment rates are higher.

Union density in *Germany* tends to be negatively related to investment in capital and in R&D. Likewise the presence of a works council tends to reduce the investment or innovation rate. But these links between mechanisms of employee representation and investment are almost all non-significant (see Schedlitzki, 2002, for a full survey). One exception is the study of Addison et al. (1993) which gets quite clear-cut effects. The sample was 101 manufacturing firms in Niedersachsen and Baden-Württemberg. After controlling for other factors which might influence the investment rate – like capacity utilization and product innovation – the authors find that an establishment with a works council has a gross investment rate between a fifth and a third below a counterpart firm without a council. The impact on net investment is also negative but much weaker.

Benson (1994) is one of the few who have analysed the links between unions and investment in *Japan*. The definition of union presence and controls were as set out in section 2 dealing with productivity. There was no available evidence on investment rates so, instead, Benson used labour's share in total cost arguing that (1–labour's share) measures capital intensity which 'reflects capital investment in the long run'. The evidence suggests that union recognition goes hand-in-hand with greater capital intensity. There is no evidence that unions siphon off returns to capital or impose restrictions on the use of capital – under 6 per cent of managers claimed that unions constrained them in the introduction of new technology. Rather, capital–labour substitution was sometimes promoted by the union because introduction of new technology often replaced dirty, dangerous or repetitive work. If this latter explanation is correct it suggests that 'holdup' in Japan is not the problem it is in the USA and Canada.

5.   Extensions

Many of the issues raised in sections 2–4 are worthy of more detailed investigation. In this section we examine five such matters. Links between the product market and the labour market show the crucial role that competition plays in moderating any union effects. Similarly, in both the USA and

UK, cooperative industrial relations between capital and labour are shown to yield superior outcomes to adversarial relations. Union structures matter too: multi-unionism is associated with worse productivity and financial performance than a single union or enterprise unions. The long-run health of any enterprise depends on sufficient investment. While findings on links between unions and capital investment are mixed, it is shown here that a union presence boosts investment in human capital in both the USA and UK. Finally, the unique dual structure of industrial relations in Germany is discussed. The information, consultation and voice role of works councils does seem to raise productivity but these institutions also engage in rent-seeking activities similar to unions in the other countries analysed here.

Links between the product market and the labour market
Links between the product market and the labour market have not received sufficient attention in many of the studies surveyed in sections 2–4. The intensity of competition has a profound affect on what unions can do (see also Chapter 3 by Naylor in this volume). It is well known that non-competitive product markets permit unions to raise wages. But unions can capture product market rents in forms other than wages: 'For example, they can impose rigidities in the workplace to reduce the pace of work [which] may discourage innovation and result in lower productivity growth' (Nickell, 2001, p. 296).

The 1998 British WERS permits this matter to be investigated thoroughly because it contains information on the number of competitors faced by each workplace. Metcalf (2003) has analysed how variation in product market competition influences the impact of unions on labour productivity, quality of product service and financial performance. The results are summarized in Table 5.5 and demonstrate the crucial role played by product market competition in determining union influence. The nationally representative sample covered around 1200 workplaces in the trading sector. In the survey, productivity, service quality and financial performance are defined by the familiar five-point scale and this was collapsed to the probability that a workplace was above average on the indicator. Unionization was defined by recognition and numerous workplace and workforce controls included.

When no account is taken of product market competition, unionization has a modest negative impact on each of the three variables. But it will be seen that the results are driven by the non-competitive sector. Thus when there are just one to five competitors the probability of above average labour productivity is 14 per cent lower for a unionized workplace than its non-union counterpart. But when there are six or more competitors the

Table 5.5 Union recognition and workplace performance

Indicator	Sample	Union indicator	Control variables	Union effect Probability of above average when union recognised	
Labour productivity Compared with establishments in same industry	WERS 1998 trading sector 1153 workplaces with 25+ employees	Recognition	HRM (9 variables) % female % skilled private/public pay of local LM workplace size industry	whole sample 1–5 competitors 6+ competitors	−4.5% −14.0% 0.6%
Quality of product service Compared with establishments in same industry	as above 1262 workplaces	Recognition	As above	Whole sample 1–5 competitors 6+ competitors	−8.5% −8.5% −6.6%
Financial performance Compared with establishments in same industry	as above 1195 workplaces	Recognition	As above	Whole sample 1–5 competitors 6+ competitors	−8.2% −12.4% 7.4%

Source: Metcalf (2003).

corresponding figure is 0.6 per cent (not statistically significant). And when there is little product market competition the likelihood of above average financial performance is 12.4 per cent lower for a union than non-union workplace, yet the corresponding figure is 7.4 per cent higher with a more competitive product market.

If replicated for other countries results like this have profound implications for the future of unions. Blanchard (2001, p. 295) has noted that across OECD countries 'rents are getting smaller, leading to less room for rent extraction . . . this decrease in attractiveness [of unions to members] is reflected, in nearly all countries, by decreased membership and support'. More intense product market competition implies a corrosion of the impact of union recognition in the workplace which suggests that in the longer term unions may need to find a different role if they are to prosper.

Role of, and unions links' with, management
Our focus is on links between unionism and productivity, performance and profitability. Of course, performance is affected by numerous factors other than unionization – that is why so many control variables are included in the studies analysed in sections 2–4. But there is one factor, so far inadequately discussed, which may both dominate and itself affect any impact unions have on performance, namely management. The debate in the management literature turns on whether or not those firms and workplaces with high-involvement management (HIM) practices such as job flexibility, team working and minimal differences in status will universally outperform those without and/or the importance of aligning such HIM practices to the business or competitive strategy of the firm in order to achieve superior performance. In his exhaustive survey, Wood (1999) states that the evidence on both issues is mixed and that it is too early to draw general conclusions on the importance of management practices and strategy. For us a narrower issue is important. If relations between management and unions are cooperative does the workplace have a superior performance to those with adversarial relations? This is an important matter. It should, for example, be remembered (see section 2) that Freeman and Medoff (1984) held that superior performance is contingent on cooperation between labour and capital.

We have evidence on this issue for both the USA and UK and it is remarkably consistent. Section 2 noted the USA manufacturing evidence. Black and Lynch (1997) showed that there was a hierarchy for productivity performance. A traditional workplace with union recognition but no employee involvement does worse. In the middle are non-union plants with high performance work (HPW) systems, but superior productivity performance is achieved by establishments with *both* HPW practices and union recognition. Analogous evidence for the UK is set out in Table 5.6 (for more details see Metcalf, 2003). A HRM workplace with no union has a superior productivity and financial performance to a unionized workplace with no HRM. But when the workplace with union recognition also has the various HRM practices its performance is much enhanced, indeed in the case of labour productivity growth the best performing workplaces are those with both HRM and recognition.

Another way of analysing the influence of cooperative industrial relations is to study partnerships. As espoused by the British TUC (1998) partnership agreements include mutual recognition of the roles of management and the union, joint commitment to the success of the business and job security, open information sharing, continuous improvement in the quality of working life and adding value. The spread of such agreements has been rapid. For example Gall (2000) states that there were 748 new recognitions agreements in the five-year period beginning in 1995 and of these 150 are partnership agreements. Further, many previous recognitions have been transformed into similar agreements. The impact of such partnerships in British workplaces is set out in Table 5.6. A workplace is defined as having a partnership when a union negotiates pay and management negotiates with, or consults, the union(s) on recruitment, training, payment systems, handling grievances, staff planning, equal opportunities, health and safety and performance appraisals. It will be seen that such designs significantly raise the probability of above-average financial performance and both the level of and change in labour productivity. These are potentially important findings. Union recognition with partnership yields substantially better economic and industrial relations outcomes than union recognition without partnership.

Union structure and organization
The nature of workplace unionism varies considerably both within and among countries. For example in some workplaces union membership is or was compulsory (defined as a union shop in the USA and a closed shop in the UK). In other, typically larger, workplaces multiple unions exist side-by-side to represent the interests of different groups like craft and less skilled employees. Such multiple unionism is a distinctive feature of industrial relations in Australia and the UK. By contrast, in Japan enterprise unions are the norm – one union for one enterprise. It is worth considering briefly some links between union organization and workplace performance outcomes. For example how does productivity or financial performance compare under enterprise unionism versus multi-unionism?

Multiple unionism is generally held to be detrimental to performance because of the greater difficulty of reaching agreement among the parties,

Table 5.6   Workplace governance and performance

Outcome	HRM workplace, no union recognition	Union recognition, no HRM	HRM workplace with union recognition	Marginal effect of partnership
1. Percentage with financial performance above-average for industry	86	40	76	32.2*
2. Percentage with labour productivity above average for industry	75	43	70	31.7*
3. Percentage with labour productivity increased over past 5 years	89	73	95	51.9**

Notes:
1. Outcomes 1–3 probit regressions. Statistical analysis based on approximately 1300 workplaces.
2. Outcomes 1–3 are from 5–point scale and refer to probability of the workplace being in the top two categories. For example 86 per cent of managers in the HRM workplaces believe that their workplace has above average (for the industry) financial performance, compared with 40 per cent for union workplaces.
3. Definition of independent variables:
   HRM: Formal strategic plan on human resources, with employee relations manager involved in formulation; personality or performance tests in recruitment, or recruitment based on skills, qualifications, experience and motivation only; most employees in largest occupational group trained in job other than their own; individual- or group-performance-related pay.
   Other controls: Union recognition; joint consultative committee; employee involvement viz some form of financial involvement i.e. profit-related pay, employee share ownership or deferred profit-sharing, *and* either a quality circle or employee suggestion scheme; partnership viz union negotiates pay and management negotiates with, or consults union on recruitment, training, payment systems, handling grievances, staff planning, equal opportunities, health and safety and performance appraisals; collective dispute in previous year; variety in work of largest occupational group; growing market; more than half the workforce in managerial, professional or technical occupations; workplace under 10 years old; proportion of workers female; private sector; level of most recent pay increase compared with similar employees in locality; size of workplace and industry.
4. Definition of benchmark workplaces:
   HRM: No union recognition, all HRM variables and all other variables at weighted means.
   Union recognition: Union recognition and all other variables at weighted means.
5. *Partnership*: Defined as where union negotiates pay and management negotiates with, or consults union on recruitment, training, payment systems, handling grievances, staff planning, equal opportunities, health and safety and performance appraisals. Such partnerships significantly raise the probability of above average performance on the financial performance, productivity level, productivity growth and relations between managers and workers.

Source: 1998 Workplace Employment Relations Survey, Management Questionnaire. Nationally representative sample of all workplaces with 10+ employees in trading sector.

communication and demarcation problems and inter-union competition. Bean and Crafts (1996) go as far as to suggest that the decline of multi-unionism in the UK in the 1980s was the key alteration in industrial relations contributing to the raising of Britain's productivity growth. Pencavel (2003) provides the most up-to-date analysis for the UK. He first compares union with non-union workplaces, then goes on to contrast multi-union workplaces with joint bargaining (where the multiple unions sit around a 'single table') and those with separate bargaining. He finds that, overall, union recognition is associated with lower financial returns. When there is multi-unionism, if bargaining is fragmented the workplace is over 5 per cent less likely to have better than average financial performance compared to a joint bargaining workplace. Likewise, for labour productivity, although there is no overall association between union presence and labour productivity, when there are multi-unions, workplaces with fragmented bargaining have a 4 per cent lower probability of being better/lot better than average compared with those with joint bargaining. He concludes that:

> On average, by the late 1990s, unionism per se has negligible effects on productivity; the state of labour relations is the key variable associated with productivity and, in Britain, workplaces with fragmented bargaining are associated with poorer productivity. With respect to financial performance, unions tend to reallocate an organization's rents towards workers and this occurs more substantially in fragmented bargaining workplaces. (Pencavel, 2003, p. 34).

This conclusion is replicated in Australia where Crockett et al. (1992) state that 'where there are several unions present, the detrimental effect on productivity is greater than if the workplace had a single union'.

This evidence begs the question as to why management was prepared to recognize multiple unions in the first place. Presumably it reflects either incompetence, possibly motivated by divide-and-rule tactics, or an inability to control the growth of such multi-unionism because the costs of doing so would have been greater than the benefits. It is noteworthy that alterations in the political climate in both the UK and Australia yielded a reduction in fragmented bargaining in recent years.

In Japan, enterprise unionism is the normal type of union organization such that there is one union in one firm. All regular and permanent employees – blue collar, white collar and sales – who do not occupy managerial positions join the union which organizes in the one firm. Tachibanaki and Noda (2000) state that this imparts 'common goals' among management and employees particularly in overcoming economic crises facing a firm:

> Enterprise unionism [is] one of the sources of a relatively better performance of firms in Japan because it encourages cooperative behaviour of unions towards

management . . . unions want to work in close cooperation with management because they believe that a cooperative attitude produces an ultimate benefit to them. A more direct interest in the overall performance of the firm is ultimately more beneficial to employees than adversarial behaviour. (p. 97)

On this basis we might expect that a union presence would be associated with superior productivity and investment performance and possibly even better financial performance than non-union counterparts. In the event, as we showed in sections 2–4, while capital accumulation rates are higher in unionized workplaces both productivity and profit levels are modestly lower. However, the direct productivity effect is offset by a favourable indirect effect stemming from longer tenures and, in some enterprises, the presence of a full-time union official who acts as an unpaid personnel manager. So, it may be that enterprise unions actually have rather similar links with performance to traditional western unions.

Investment in human capital

The presence of a union might influence investment in human capital in the workplace over and above any more traditional effect on investment in physical capital or R&D. Such investment in the incidence and amount of training could be higher where a union is recognized for the following reasons. First, unions might widen their bargaining agenda to include investment in human capital, a way of raising employees' living standards in the longer run. Second, unions provide a voice thereby lowering labour turnover which, in turn, increases the incentives of both the employer and employee to invest as they will reap a return over a longer period. Third, the lower labour turnover in unionized workplaces implies greater job security and employees will feel less threatened by alterations to working practices which may flow from investment in human capital. Finally, a unionized workplace is more likely to have a formal procedure to identify training needs and to implement them. It is possible, but unlikely, that these routes which boost the accumulation of human capital may lead investment in training above what is socially or privately optimal.

Alternatively, some arguments point in the opposite direction. First, if unions raise wages compared with similar non-union workers the firm may not be able to afford to invest in human capital. Second, seniority is an important (objective) factor in promotion decisions in unionized workplaces, which may reduce the incentive of employees to invest in training. Third, Green et al. (1999) point out that, in Britain for example, greater aggregate investment in human capital in the last two decades has occurred at a time when unions have become much weaker. As good arguments can be advanced to suggest unions might either increase or decrease investment in human capital, the issue can only be settled empirically.

There is quite a large body of empirical research investigating the relationship between training and unionism for the USA. Booth et al. (2001) summarize it as follows:

> Some of the early studies find a negative impact of unions on training (e.g. Duncan and Stafford, 1980). More recent studies, however, find that the probability of receiving on-the-job training and the amount of work-related training received are higher for unionized workers than non-unionized ones (e.g. Lynch, 1992). An exception is the study by Lynch and Black (1998), which uses data from a 1994 representative survey of US establishments and reports no statistically significant impact of unionization on either the provision of formal training or the proportion of workers receiving it. It should be noted that this study concentrates on a rather specific set of formal training programmes, including computer literacy training, teamwork or problem solving training, literacy, numeracy or basic training, and sales or customer service training. (p. 4)

British evidence (Booth, 1991, Claydon and Green, 1994) also points to a positive impact of union presence on training investments. Recently Green et al. (1999) used nationally representative samples to analyse both the incidence and intensity of training. Unionized establishments and workers are more likely to provide and receive training than their non-union counterparts and this impact holds with even more force for the intensity of training. Consider, for example, non-manual workers. A unionized workplace provided nearly an extra day of training during the previous year (the sample average is 2.7 days so this is a large effect). Likewise unionized workers received an extra 0.34 hours of training in the previous week (sample average 1.3 hours). Related work (Arulampalam and Booth, 1997) suggests that these positive union effects hold more strongly for women than men. Booth et al. (2001) also suggest that the payoff to such training is greater for union workers than non-unionists. For union men the post-training wage was 21 per cent higher than the pre-training wage, but the corresponding increase for non-unionism was only 4 per cent. This is an important finding because it contradicts the often-stated notion that egalitarian or seniority-based union wage policies reduce the return to investing in human capital.

Works councils and employee involvement in Germany
The German industrial relations system is well known for its unique dual-structure of employee representation. Collective agreements are negotiated between trade unions and employers' associations at the industry level, while works councils watch the implementation and coordination of such agreements in the workplace. Theoretically, works councils are pure agents of employee representation because legislation forbids them engaging in

any form of industrial action or negotiating wage agreements. Reality looks a bit different as trade union members very often dominate works councils so the line between the rent-seeking behaviour of trade unions and the voice function of works councils is often blurred.

Generally, works councils constitute the most important collective voice institution in Germany. They were legally established in 1920, but the current form and legal basis has its origin in the Works Constitution Act, passed in 1972 (Mueller-Jentsch, 1995). This Act prescribes an extensive set of information, consultation and co-determination rights to the works council. Employers have to inform works councils on the current and future economic situation of the firm, on reductions in operations and introduction of new work methods. Further, works councils have to be consulted on issues such as dismissals, personnel planning, and changes in equipment. Additionally, works councils have co-determination rights on social and personnel matters. These rights were extended by the Works Constitution Reform Act passed in 2001. The new legislation facilitates the creation of works councils in small firms, widens the functions of the works council and lowers the thresholds used to determine the size of the works councils and the number of full-time works councillors.

Some studies have analysed the incidence of works councils. For example Sadowski, Junkes and Lindenthal (2001) state that only a fifth of eligible plants use their right to form a works council, but that such plants employ some two-thirds of all eligible employees. The probability of a works council being present increases with plant size, age of firm and with the share of workers and that it decreases with the share of part-time and female workers. There is also evidence (Addison et al., 1997) that works councils are less likely to exist where the firm or workplace has well developed direct or indirect participation mechanisms.

In broad terms, recent evidence suggests that works councils increase productivity, reduce profitability, and have a negative but insignificant impact on investment and innovation (Addison et al., 2001, 1993; Frick, 1996; Frick and Sadowski, 1995. See Frege, 2002, for a useful critique of these studies). The behaviour of works councils can probably be best explained via a mixture of the monopoly union model and the collective voice model. The monopoly model explains the negative relationship between works councils and profits, by suggesting that the extensive set of legal rights prescribed to works councils, the domination of trade union members and the indirect impact on wage determination jointly foster rent-seeking behaviour on the part of works councils. Further, the collective voice model proposes that the provision of a formal collective voice for the workforce will improve the working climate, reduce labour turnover and tend to raise productivity.

Until the early 1990s, the German model of centralized bargaining was famous for its high degree of consensus, social cohesion, few disputes, competitiveness and high levels of training (Hassel, 1999). But this system is facing pressure from international competition and moves to decentralize. Hassel (1999) suggests that a steady erosion of the dual structure and therefore the decrease in the incidence of works councils and trade union presence is quite likely in the near future. In the face of a potential future 'representation gap', it is worth investigating what could or already does substitute the works council as the formal plant-level institution of employee representation. In recent years, new forms of employee representation, also known as 'employee involvement (EI) programmes', have emerged in Germany. Those programmes allow employees to participate in the decision-making of a company. Several US and UK studies have suggested a positive relationship between such EI programmes and establishment profitability, so employers might consider those programmes as possible substitutes for works councils in terms of employee representation.

Schedlitzki (2002) has investigated the impact of works councils and EI programmes on establishment profitability and the interaction between those two forms of employee representation. The theoretical underpinnings are based on the 'managerial competence' hypothesis (FitzRoy and Kraft, 1985), which argues that competent managers will provide employee representation on their own initiative, yielding higher profits because they do without the legal complexity and rent-seeking behaviour of works councils. Competent managers are assumed to know about the efficiency of EI programmes and to implement them. Consequently, presence of EI programmes is defined as a proxy for the presence of competent managers. This permits the 'managerial competence' hypothesis, the interaction of works councils and EI programmes and their impact on establishment profitability to be studied.

The research used data from the third wave of the Hannover Firm Panel, which is representative of the manufacturing industry in Lower Saxony. It confirmed the 'managerial competence' hypothesis: there is a negative impact of works councils, and a positive impact of EI programmes, on establishment profitability. When both a works council and an EI programme were present in a workplace profitability was lower compared to a workplace with just EI. It was concluded that the competent managers do better without works councils so in future, employers may focus on EI programmes as the major vehicle for employee representation. Such a move would be congruent with recent US evidence (Kleiner and Freeman, 2000, p. 223) which suggests that EI 'has no adverse effects or a slight positive effect on the bottom line' while simultaneously workers report that EI has a 'strong [positive] effect on their working lives'.

6.   Summary and conclusions

If the presence of a union in a workplace or firm raises the pay level, unless productivity rises correspondingly, financial performance is likely to be worse. If the product market is uncompetitive this might imply a simple transfer from capital to labour with no efficiency effects, but is probably more likely to lead to lower investment rates and economic senescence. Therefore the impact of unions on productivity, financial performance and investment is extremely important. This chapter distils evidence on such effects from six countries: USA, Canada, UK, Germany, Japan and Australia. These countries were chosen for two reasons. First, the bulk of the evidence is for them. Second, they have very different systems of industrial relations on dimensions like density, coverage and level of collective bargaining, coordination, labour standards, employment protection, union structures and voice mechanisms. In principle, this diversity should contribute to understanding where unions have favourable or unfavourable effects. The unit of analysis in this chapter switches between sectors, firms and workplaces. There is an urgent need for comparative analysis of union effects using international data with standardized measures of unionization and performance.

It is not possible to use theory to predict unambiguously any union effect on productivity because unions can both enhance and detract from the productivity performance of the workplace or firm. Union presence may lower labour productivity via: restrictive work practices; industrial action; causing the firm to invest less; and if adversarial industrial relations lowers trust and cooperation. Alternatively labour productivity may be beneficially higher in the presence of a union if: unions may play a monitoring role on behalf of the employer; collective voice provided by the union has favourable consequences; unions may make managers less lethargic; and unions stop exploitation of labour.

The evidence indicates that, in the USA, workplaces with both high performance work systems and union recognition have higher labour productivity than other workplaces. And a case study of bitter adversarial industrial relations at a tyre plant showed what a dreadful effect this had on the quality of the product. In the UK, previous negative links between unions and labour productivity have been eroded by greater competition and more emphasis on 'partnership' in industrial relations but there is a lingering negative effect of multi-unionism, just as there is in Australia. In Germany, the weight of the evidence suggests that the information, consultation and voice role of works councils enhances labour productivity in larger firms. Finally, in Japan, unions also tend to raise labour productivity via the longer job tenures in union workplaces which makes it more attractive to invest in human capital and through the unpaid personnel manager role played by full-time enterprise union officials in the workplace. These results emphasize that there is no one generalized or average productivity effect of unions – it all depends on the quality of management and unions. As decentralization of bargaining spreads, so any union effects become more varied.

Unions will reduce profits if they raise pay and/or lower productivity. Unions might capture surplus profits in monopolistic or regulated sectors. Alternatively they may siphon off returns which belong to sunk investments in physical capital or R&D, which would have serious consequences for the long-run health of the union sector. The evidence is pretty clear cut: the bulk of studies show that profits or financial performance is inferior in unionized workplaces, firms and sectors than in their non-union counterparts. This may, in turn, influence the rate of growth of employment and closures in union compared with non-union firms and workplaces. But the world may be changing. A recent study of small USA entrepreneurial firms found a positive association between unions and profits and in the UK the outlawing of the closed shop, coupled with a lower incidence of multi-unionism has contributed to greater union–management cooperation such that recent studies find no association between unions and profits. There is something of a paradox in this evidence. In Japan and Germany, known for cooperative labour relations and proper employee voice, unions or works councils are linked to inferior financial performance. By contrast, this traditional stylized fact – unions lower profits – may no longer hold in the UK and, possibly, the USA. This suggests that more intense product market competition inhibits unions' ability to cream off (previous monopoly) profits. To the extent that any union effects are weaker than previously, employees' affinity with the union may also crumble, implying that unions' survival may depend on them embracing a different – representational – role to their more traditional collective bargaining role.

Unions can influence investment in physical capital both positively and negatively. Any positive effect occurs when the firm invests more to substitute away from expensive union labour. The negative impact comes if a union delays the installation of new machinery or captures returns properly due to (sunk) investment. North American and German evidence suggests that unionization reduces investment by around one fifth compared with the investment rate in a non-union workplace. In both Canada and the USA this effect is even felt at low levels of unionization. The UK evidence is mixed: the most thorough study also finds that union recognition depresses investment, but this adverse effect is offset as density rises. The exception is Japan where union recognition goes hand-in-hand with greater capital intensity.

Finally, it is worth remembering that any union impact on financial performance not only affects investment in physical capital but may also influence the rate of growth of employment and the probability that the workplace or firm closes as between union and non-union organization. A survey of studies on employment and closures would require a separate paper. In very broad terms US and UK evidence (see for example Bryson, 2001; Kleiner and Freeman, 1999) suggests that any union impact on profits has little or no association with closure – unions may cannily focus on monopoly profit and know just how far to push. But employment in union workplaces grows (falls) some 3 per cent p.a. less (faster) than that in non-union workplaces. This has serious implications both for the displaced members themselves and for future union membership.

More detailed investigation of some issues shows: the vital role of product market competition in both mediating and moderating any adverse union effects; that management–union cooperation yields superior outcomes to adversarial relations; multi-unionism confers worse productivity or profitability than a single union or enterprise union; a union presence boosts investment in human capital, possibly offsetting any adverse impact on investment in physical capital; while German works councils, with their consultation/voice role, do raise productivity they also lower profits.

Acknowledgement

I acknowledge, with thanks, efficient research assistance by Doris Schedlitzki who is the joint author of the material on Germany; and very helpful comments on an earlier draft from Alex Bryson, Sue Fernie, Rafael Gomez, Morris Kleiner, John Pencavel and the editors of this Handbook. This paper is produced under the Leverhulme Trust funded Programme on 'The Future of Unions in Modern Britain' being undertaken in the Centre for Economic Performance at the LSE.

References

Addison, John T. and Clive Belfield (2000), 'The Impact of Financial Participation and Employee Involvement on Financial Performance: A Re-estimation using the 1998 WERS', *Scottish Journal of Political Economy*, 47 (5), 571–583.

Addison, John T. and Barry T. Hirsch (1989), 'Union Effects on Productivity, Profits and Growth: Has the Long Run Arrived?', *Journal of Labor Economics*, 7 (1), 72–105.

Addison, John T., Joachim Genosko and Claus Schnabel (1989), 'Gewerkschaften, Produktivitaet und Rent Seeking', *Jahrbücher für Nationalökonomie und Statistik*, 206 (2), 102–116.

Addison, John T., Kornelius Kraft and Joachim Wagner (1993), 'German Works Councils and Firm Performance', in Bruce E. Kaufman and Morris M. Kleiner (eds), *Employee Representation: Alternatives and Future Directions*, Madison, WI: University of Wisconsin Press for IRRA pp. 305–338.

Addison, John T., Claus Schnabel and Joachim Wagner (1996), 'German Works Councils, Profits and Innovation', *Kyklos,* 49 (4), 555–582.

Addison, John T., Claus Schnabel and Joachim Wagner (1997), 'On the Determinants of Mandatory Works Councils in Germany', *Industrial Relations*, 36 (4), 419–445.

Addison, John T., W. Stanley Siebert, Joachim Wagner and Xiangdong Wei (2000), 'Worker Participation and Firm Performance: Evidence from Germany and Britain', *British Journal of Industrial Relations,* 38 (1), March, 7–49.

Addison, John T., Claus Schnabel and Joachim Wagner (2001), 'Works Councils in Germany: Their Effects on Establishment Performance', *Oxford Economic Papers*, 53 (4), 659–694.

Appelbaum, Eileen and Rose Batt (1994), *The New American Workplace: Transforming Work Systems in the United States*, Ithaca, NY: Cornell ILR Press.

Arulampalam, Wiji and Alison Booth (1997), 'Who Gets Over the Training Hurdle? A Study of the Training Experiences of Young Men and Women in Britain', *Journal of Population Economics*, 10 (2), 197–218.

Batt, Rose and Theresa Welbourne (2002), 'Performance Growth in Entrepreneurial Firms: Revisiting the Union–performance Relationship', in Jerome A. Katz and Theresa Welbourne (eds), *Research Volume on Entrepreneurship*, Vol. 5, JAI Press, pp. 1–29.

Bean, Charles and Nicholas Crafts (1996), 'British Economic Growth since 1945: Relative Economic Decline . . . and Renaissance?' in Nicholas Crafts and Gianni Toniolo (eds), *Economic Growth in Europe since 1945*, Cambridge: Cambridge University Press, Centre for Economic Policy Research, pp. 131–172.

Benson, John (1994), 'The Economic Effects of Unionism on Japanese Manufacturing Enterprises', *British Journal of Industrial Relations*, 32 (1), March, 1–21.

Black, Sandra and Lisa Lynch (1997), 'How to Compete: the Impact of Workplace Practices and Information Technology on Productivity', NBER Working Paper 6120, August.

Blanchard, Olivier (2001), 'Final Remarks', in Tito Boeri, Agar Brugiavini and Lars Calmfors (eds), *The Role of Unions in the Twenty-first Century*, Oxford: Oxford University Press, pp. 292–295.

Booth, Alison (1991), 'Job-related Formal Training: Who Receives it and What is it Worth?', *Oxford Bulletin of Economic and Statistics*, 53 (3), 281–294.

Booth, Alison, Marco Francesconi and Gylfi Zoega (2001), 'Unions, Training and Wages: Evidence for British Men', mimeo, University of Essex, August.

Bronars, Stephen and Donald R. Deere (1993), 'Unionisation, Incomplete Contracting and Capital Investment', *Journal of Business*, 66 (2), January, 117–132.

Bronars, Stephen, Donald R. Deere and Joseph S. Tracy (1994), 'The Effects of Unions on Firm Behaviour: An Empirical Analysis Using Firm-Level Data', *Industrial Relations*, 33 (4), October, 426–451.

Brown, Charles and James Medoff (1978), 'Trade Unions in the Production Process', *Journal of Political Economics*, 86 (3), 355–378.

Brunello, Giorgio (1992), 'The Effect of Unions on Firm Performance in Japanese Manufacturing', *Industrial and Labor Relations Review*, 45 (3), April, 471–487.

Bryson, Alex (2001), 'Employee Voice, Workplace Closure and Employment Growth', Policy Studies Institute Discussion Paper 6.

Bryson, Alex and David Wilkinson (2002), *Collective Bargaining and Workplace Performance*, Employment Research Series 12, Department of Trade and Industry.

Cappelli, Peter and David Neumark (2001), 'Do "High Performance" Work Practices Improve Establishment Level Outcomes?', *Industrial and Labor Relations Review*, 54 (4), July, 737–775.

Caves, Richard (1980), 'Productivity Differences Among Industries', in Richard Caves and Lawrence Krause (eds), *Britain's Economic Performance*, Washington DC: Brookings Institution.

Clark, Kim (1984), 'Unionisation and Firm Performance: The Impact on Profits, Growth and Productivity', *American Economic Review*, 74 (5), December, 893–919.

Claydon, Tim and Francis Green (1994), 'Can Trade Unions Improve Training in Britain?', *Personnel Review*, 23 (1), 37–51.

Crockett, Geoffrey, Peter Dawkins, Paul Miller and Charles Mulvey (1992), 'The Impact of Unions on Workplace Productivity in Australia', *Australian Bulletin of Labour*, 18 (2), June, 119–141.

Denny, Kevin and Stephen Nickell (1991), 'Unions and Investment in British Manufacturing Industry', *British Journal of Industrial Relations*, 29 (1), 113–122.

Denny, Kevin and Stephen Nickell (1992), 'Unions and Investment in British Industry', *Economic Journal*, 102, 874–887.

Donovan Commission (1968), 'Royal Commission on Trade Unions and Employers Associations', Report, Cmnd 3623, London: HMSO.

Doucouliagos, Chris and Patrice Laroche (2000), 'What Do Unions Do to Productivity? A Meta Analysis', mimeo, GREFIGE, Université Nancy 2.

Drago, Robert and Mark Wooden (1992), 'The Australian Workplace Industrial Relations Survey and Workplace Performance', *Australian Bulletin of Labour*, 18 (2), June, 142–169.

Duncan, Greg and Frank Stafford (1980), 'Do Union Members Receive Compensating Differentials?', *American Economic Review*, 70 (3), 355–371.

Dunlop Commission (1994), *Commission on Future of Worker–management Relations: Fact Finding Report*, Washington DC: US Department of Labor and US Department of Commerce, May.

Edwards, Paul (1987), *Managing the Factory*, Oxford: Blackwell.

Evans, Neil, Donald Mackay, Mike Garratt and Philip Sutcliffe (1993), 'The Abolition of the Dock Labour Scheme', *Employment Department Research Series*, No. 14, September.

FitzRoy, Felix and Kornelius Kraft (1985), 'Unionisation, Wages and Efficiency – Theories and Evidence from the US and Germany', *Kyklos*, 38 (4), 537–554.

FitzRoy, Felix and Kornelius Kraft (1987), 'Efficiency and Internal Organization: Works Councils in West German Firms', *Economica*, 54 (4), 493–504.

Freeman, Richard and Morris Kleiner (1999), 'Do Unions Make Enterprises Insolvent?', *Industrial and Labor Relations Review*, 52 (4), July, 510–527.

Freeman, Richard and James Medoff (1984), *What Do Unions Do?*, New York: Basic Books.

Frege, Carola (2002), 'A Critical Assessment of the Theoretical and Empirical Research on Works Councils', *British Journal of Industrial Relations*, 40 (2), June, 221–248.

Frick, Bernd (1996), 'Co-determination and Personnel Turnover', *Labour*, 10 (2), 407–430.

Frick, Bernd and Dieter Sadowski (1995), 'Works Councils, Unions and Firm Performance', in Friedrich Buttler, Wolfgang Franz, Ronald Schettkat and David Soskice (eds), *Institutional Frameworks and Labor Market Performance – Comparative Views on the US and German Economies*, London: Routledge, pp. 46–81.

Gall, Gregor (2000), 'In Place of Strife?', *People Management*, 14 September, 26–30.

Green, Francis; Stephen Machin and David Wilkinson (1999), 'Trade Unions and Training Practices in British Workplaces', *Industrial and Labor Relations Review*, 52 (2), January, 179–195.

Grout, Paul A. (1984a), 'Investment and Wages in the Absence of Legally Binding Labour Contracts: a Nash Bargaining Approach', *Econometrica*, 52 (2), March, 449–460.

Grout, Paul A. (1984b), 'A Theoretical Approach to the Effect of Trade Union Immunities', *Economic Journal*, Conference Papers, 95, 96–101.

Hassel, Anke (1999), 'The Erosion of the German System of Industrial Relations', *British Journal of Industrial Relations*, 37 (3), 483–505.

Hirsch, Barry T. (1990), 'Innovative Activity, Productivity Growth and Firm Performance: Are Labor Unions a Spur or a Deterrent?', *Advances in Applied Micro-Economics*, Vol. 5, Greenwich, CT: JAI Press, 69–104.

Hirsch, Barry T. (1991), *Labor Unions and the Economic Performance of Firms*, Kalamazoo, MI: W.E. Upjohn Institute for Employment Research.

Hirsch, Barry T. (1992), 'Firm Investment Behavior and Collective Bargaining Strategy', *Industrial Relations*, 31 (Winter), 95–121.

Hirsch, Barry T. and John T. Addison (1986), *The Economic Analysis of Unions*, Boston, MA: Allen & Unwin.

Huebler, Olaf and Uwe Jirjahn (2001), 'Works Councils and Collective Bargaining in Germany: The Impact on Productivity and Wages', IZA Discussion Paper, No. 322, Bonn.

Huselid, Mark and Barry Becker (1996), 'High Performance Work Systems and Firm Performance: Cross-sectional Versus Panel Results', *Industrial Relations*, 35 (4), 400–422.

Ichniowski, Casey and Katherine Shaw (1995), 'Determinants of the Adoption of Productivity-enhancing Work Practices', *Brookings Papers on Economic Activity*, 1–65.

Kleiner, Morris (2001), 'Intensity of Management Resistance: Understanding the Decline of Unionization in the Private Sector', *Journal of Labor Research*, 22 (3), Summer, 519–540.

Kleiner, Morris and Richard Freeman (2000), 'Who Benefits Most From Employee Involvement: Firms or Workers?', *American Economic Review*, 90 (2), May, 219–223.

Kleiner, Morris; Jonathan Leonard and Adam Pilarski (2002), 'How Industrial Relations Affect Plant Performance: the Case of Commercial Aircraft Manufacturing', *Industrial and Labor Relations Review*, 55 (2), January, 195–219.

Krueger, Alan and Alexandre Mas (2002), 'Strikes, Scabs and Tread Separations: Labor Strife and the Production of Defective Bridgestone/Firestone Tires', Working Paper 461, Industrial Relations Section, Princeton University, January.

Kuhn, Peter (1998), 'Unions and the Economy: What We Know and What We Should Know', *Canadian Journal of Economics*, 31 (5), 1033–1056.

Leibenstein, Harvey (1988), *Inside the Firm*, Cambridge, MA: Harvard University Press.

Lipsky, David B. (1985), 'Comment', *Industrial and Labor Relations Review*, 38 (2), January, 250–253.

Lynch, Lisa M. (1992), 'Private Sector Training and the Earnings of Young Workers', *American Economic Review*, 81 (1), 299–312.

Lynch, Lisa M. and Sandra Black (1998), 'Beyond the Incidence of Employer-provided Training', *Industrial and Labor Relations Review*, 52 (1), 64–81.

Machin, Stephen and Mark Stewart (1996), 'Trade Unions and Financial Performance', *Oxford Economic Papers*, 48 (2), 213–241.

Maki, Dennis (1983), 'The Effects of Unions and Strikes on the Rate of Growth of Total Factor Productivity in Canada', *Applied Economics*, 15 (1), 29–41.

McNabb, Robert and Keith Whitfield (2000), 'The Impact of Financial Participation and Employee Involvement on Financial Performance: A Reply', *Scottish Journal of Political Economy*, 47 (5), November, 584–590.

Metcalf, David (1990a), 'Industrial Relations and the "Productivity Miracle" in British Manufacturing Industry in the 1980s', *Australian Bulletin of Labour*, 16 (2), June, 65–76.

Metcalf, David (1990b), 'Union Presence and Labour Productivity in British Manufacturing Industry', *British Journal of Industrial Relations*, 28 (2), July, 249–266.

Metcalf, David (1993), 'Industrial Relations and Economic Performance', *British Journal of Industrial Relations*, 31 (2), June, 255–283.

Metcalf, David (2003), 'Trade Unions' in Paul Gregg and Jonathan Wadsworth (eds), *The State of Working Britain*, 2nd edn, Macmillan.

Morishima, Motohiro (1991), 'Information Sharing and Firm Performance in Japan', *Industrial Relations*, 30 (1), 37–61.

Mueller-Jentsch, Walter (1995), 'Germany: From Collective Voice to Co-management', in Joel Rogers and Wolfgang Streeck (eds), *Works Councils – Consultation, Representation and Cooperation in Industrial Relations*, Chicago: University of Chicago Press, pp. 53–78.

Muramatsu, Kuramitsu (1984), 'The Effect of Trade Unions on Productivity in Japanese Manufacturing Industries', in Masahiko Aoki (ed.), *The Economic Analysis of the Japanese Firm*, Amsterdam: Elsevier, pp. 103–123.

Nickell, Stephen (2001), 'Final Remarks', in Tito Boeri, Agar Brugiavini and Lars Calmfors (eds), *The Role of Unions in the Twenty-first Century*, Oxford: Oxford University Press, pp. 296–297.

Odgers, Cameron and Julian Betts (1997), 'Do Unions Reduce Investment? Evidence from Canada', *Industrial and Labor Relations Review*, 51 (1), October, 18–36.

Oulton, Nicholas (1995), 'Supply Side Reform and UK Economic Growth: What Happened to the Miracle?', *National Institute Economic Review*, 154, November.

Pencavel, John (1977), 'Distributional and Efficiency Effects of Trade Unions in Britain', *British Journal of Industrial Relations*, 15 (2), July, 137–156.

Pencavel, John (1991), *Labor Markets Under Trade Unionism*, Oxford: Basil Blackwell.

Pencavel, John (2001), *Worker Participation: Lessons from Worker Co-ops of the Pacific Northwest*, New York: Russell Sage Foundation.

Pencavel, John (2003), 'The Surprising Retreat of Union Britain', in Richard Blundell, David

Card and Richard Freeman (eds), *Seeking a Premier League Economy*, Chicago: University of Chicago Press for NBER.

Ruback, Richard and Martin Zimmerman (1984), 'Unionization and Profitability: Evidence from the Capital Market', *Journal of Political Economy*, 92 (6), 1134–1157.

Sadowski, Dieter, Joachim Junkes and Sabine Lindenthal (2001), 'Gesetzliche Mitbestimmung in Deutschland: Idee, Erfahrungen und Perspektiven aus oekonomischer Sicht', *Zeitschrift für Unternehmens- und Gesellschaftsrecht*, 30 (1), 110–145.

Schedlitzki, Doris (2002), 'German Works Councils, Employee Involvement Programmes and their Impact on Establishment Profitability', CEP Working Paper No. 1191, LSE.

Schnabel, Claus (1991), 'Trade Unions and Productivity: The German Evidence', *British Journal of Industrial Relations*, 29 (1), 15–24.

Tachibanaki, Toshiaki and Tomohiko Noda (2000), *The Economic Effects of Trade Unions in Japan*, Basingstoke: Macmillan Press.

TUC (Trade Union Congress) (1998), 'Promoting Best Practice Through Workplace Partnership: Case Studies', *Briefing*, 7 September.

Wilkinson, David (2000), 'Collective Bargaining and Workplace Financial Performance in Britain', mimeo, Policy Studies Institute, April.

Wood, Stephen (1999), 'Human Resource Management and Performance', *International Journal of Management Review*, 1 (4), 367–413.

6 Collective bargaining and macroeconomic performance
Robert J. Flanagan

1. Introduction

Labour unions emerge in virtually all countries, irrespective of stage of development or ideological orientation, as the main vehicle of collective representation of worker interests. But the institutional arrangements through which unions seek to improve the lives of their members vary widely across countries. Moreover, few unions can restrict the consequences of their actions to their members. In most countries, union wage increases spread to non-members through a variety of mechanisms, including threat effects and legal extension. To the extent that union wage impacts exceed productivity impacts, unions will also alter the prices of the products that their members produce, thereby influencing the welfare of consumers.

The ultimate influence of collective bargaining on third parties is through its impact on macroeconomic performance. Concerns over the effects of unregulated collective bargaining on unemployment, inflation and the resilience of national economies in the face of macroeconomic shocks frequently motivate actual or threatened government interventions into the collective bargaining process. This chapter evaluates theory and evidence on the relationship between collective bargaining and macroeconomic performance in industrialized countries. One clear theme from research on this question is that the impact of collective bargaining on macroeconomic performance varies with the strikingly diverse collective bargaining arrangements found around the world. A second theme is that knowledge of these arrangements alone is no longer sufficient to provide reliable predictions on macroeconomic outcomes. The aggregate effects of collective bargaining increasingly appear to depend on interactions between features of collective bargaining systems and the economic and political environment in which they operate.

This chapter reviews the variation in key industrial relations institutions in industrialized countries (section 2), explains the key findings on how collective bargaining systems influence the unemployment, the real wage level, the price level and the distribution of income (section 3), discusses how changes in the economic and political environment alter these findings over time (sections 4 and 5), and evaluates public policy toward the macroeconomic effects of unions (section 6).

2. Collective bargaining systems

Research into the effect of collective bargaining on macroeconomic performance exploits the rich variation in collective bargaining systems found among industrialized countries. Chapter 11 by Visser in this volume documents international variations in *union membership* and *coverage*, the most widely cited measures of union presence.[1] As will become apparent, these measures by themselves provide a poor guide to the macroeconomic impact of unions. Collective bargaining arrangements vary substantially among countries with a given degree of unionization, and Table 6.1 provides data on some of the arrangements believed to have a greater influence on macroeconomic outcomes.[2]

Measures of *bargaining structure* describe the level at which collective bargaining occurs (columns 1 and 2 of Table 6.1). In *decentralized* systems (typical of North America and Japan), collective bargaining negotiations occur between an employer and representatives of employees in a company or plant. Most countries with decentralized bargaining also have considerable non-union pay determination (through company or plant level human resource management decisions). *Intermediate* bargaining systems (common in continental Europe) establish an industry-wide floor for working conditions through negotiations between an industry-wide union and employers' association. *Centralized* bargaining (common at times in Scandinavian countries) involves negotiations between nationwide labour and employer federations to establish a national wage increase.[3]

Many countries exhibit important differences between the form and substance of collective bargaining, however. For a given bargaining level, countries may differ in the extent to which collective bargaining is effectively *coordinated* (Soskice, 1990). As collective bargaining in Japan illustrates, even decentralized bargaining systems may produce significant bargaining coordination when employers and unions establish a pattern settlement that is widely accepted. On the other hand, centralized collective bargaining arrangements often include significant bargaining at the industry and local levels over the distribution of the central agreement. These less centralized rounds of bargaining can potentially produce outcomes that differ from the central bargain. Columns 3 and 4 in Table 6.1 provide data on bargaining coordination. Measures of bargaining coordination are now viewed as more informative than measures of bargaining level in analysing the macroeconomic impacts of collective bargaining.

When collective bargaining threatens macroeconomic performance, governments often consider policy actions to counter the threats. Columns

Table 6.1   Characteristics of industrial relations systems

	Bargaining level[a] (scale)		Bargaining coordination[b]		Government involvement[c]	
	1980	1994	1980	1994	1977–80	1990–92
Australia	2+	1.5	2+	1.5	10	10
Austria	2+	2+	3	3	6	6
Belgium	2+	2+	2	2	4	4
Canada	1	1	1	1	2	2
Denmark	2+	2	2.5	2+	11	5
Finland	2.5	2+	2+	2+	8	8
France	2	2	2–	2	3,5	3
Germany	2	2	3	3	3	3
Italy	2–	2	1.5	2.5	3	3,7
Japan	1	1	3	3	4	4
Netherlands	2	2	2	2	6	6
New Zealand	2	1	1.5	1	10	10
Norway	2	2+	2.5	2.5	9	5
Sweden	3	2	2.5	2	5	8
Switzerland	2	2	2+	2+	3	3
United Kingdom	2	1.5	1.5	1	2,11	2
United States	1	1	1	1	2	2

Notes:
[a]   Bargaining level: (1) Plant or company bargaining; (2) Industry bargaining; (3) Centralized bargaining.
[b]   Bargaining coordination: Range is from uncoordinated bargaining (=1) to highly coordinated bargaining (=3).
[c]   Government involvement: (1) Uninvolved in wage setting; (2) Establishes minimum wage(s); (3) Extends collective agreements; (4) Provides economic forecasts to bargaining partners; (5) Recommends wage guidelines or norms; (6) Negotiates wage guidelines with unions; (7) Imposes cost-of-living adjustment; (8) Formal tripartite agreement for national wage schedule without sanctions; (9) Same as (8) but with sanctions; (10) Arbitrator imposes wage schedules without sanctions on unions; (11) Imposes national wage schedule with sanctions; (12) Imposes wage freeze and prohibits supplementary local bargaining.

Sources: Bargaining level, bargaining coordination: OECD (1997), p. 71.
Government involvement: Golden, Lange and Wallerstein (1997).

5 and 6 of Table 6.1 provide information on the nature of government interventions into the collective bargaining process in various countries. A more extensive discussion of government policy interventions appears in section 6.[4]

3.   Bargaining, contracts and outcomes

How and why might the characteristics of collective bargaining systems listed in Table 6.1 influence a country's macroeconomic performance? Research into these questions reveals a healthy interaction between theory and evidence. This section reviews the literature on *unilateral* linkages between the collective bargaining characteristics and macroeconomic outcomes such as aggregate wage and price inflation, the price level, the real wage level, and unemployment. As will become apparent, many of the early correlations between institutional characteristics and macroeconomic outcomes have turned out to be fragile. Section 4 therefore reviews theoretical advances that indicate that the macroeconomic effects of collective bargaining systems are likely to be contingent on details of their economic and political environment. Indeed, important changes in the economic and political environment of bargaining over the past 30 years may account for the fragility of the early empirical results.

Unionization

In both micro and macro studies, union membership or coverage have been used to proxy the degree of monopoly power in labour markets. Economic theory predicts that other things equal, the union relative wage advantage and the relative price of products made by union labour are directly related to the extent of unionization. Linking unions to ongoing money wage or price inflation requires changes in bargaining power (signalled by changes in unionization). Studies conducted in a Phillips curve framework found that the rate of change of union membership significantly influenced aggregate nominal wage changes, after holding constant the effects of unemployment and inflation. In the United Kingdom, the union membership variable was more strongly correlated with money wage movements than the unemployment rate (Hines, 1964).

This approach also yielded two implications that seemed contrary to fact: (1) collective bargaining should not influence macroeconomic outcomes during periods of stable unionization; and (2) the decline of union density rates in most industrialized countries since 1980 should have produced a diminution of union influence on the economy.[5] These problems seemed quite salient as countries with different collective bargaining procedures varied in their economic adjustments to the supply shocks of the 1970s. Analyses gradually shifted to details of collective bargaining systems that might explain the different outcomes in the face of stable or declining unionization.

Bargaining structure and coordination

Early studies emphasized the relationship of bargaining *level* to macroeconomic outcomes but subsequently acknowledged the superiority of bargaining *coordination*, which is not completely determined by bargaining level. The earliest analyses of the effects of bargaining structure/coordination on macroeconomic outcomes assumed completely unionized, closed economies with profit-maximizing employers and unions that maximized a utility function including the real wage and employment levels of union members. (See Chapter 3 by Naylor in this volume for details on the modelling of union utility functions.) These analyses show that the impact of bargaining arrangements on the aggregate real wage *level* and unemployment depend on (1) whether the arrangements lead unions to internalize various external effects of their bargaining and (2) how the arrangements influence the relative bargaining power of labour and management. Consider each in turn.[6]

The crux of the externality argument is that in more coordinated bargaining arrangements, negotiators know that wage increases will affect (for example) the price level that their members subsequently face and will modify wage demands accordingly. Conversely, with uncoordinated, decentralized bargaining, each negotiator can reasonably discount the effect of a small settlement on the general price level and increase members' real wages by pressing for large money wage increases. (Note the importance of the distinction between the effect of negotiations on the general consumer price level and producer price of the products made by union labour.) When different unions represent work groups that are complements in production, there should be a negative relationship between the real wage level and bargaining coordination, so that highly coordinated systems produce lower real wages and less unemployment.

The crux of the bargaining power argument concerns the effect of bargaining arrangements on the elasticity of the demand curve for union labour. Union bargaining power declines when wage increases threaten significant employment losses for union members. Decentralized bargaining structures tend to face highly elastic demand curves, since customers can easily shift their purchases to other companies if a collective bargaining settlement raises wages at one company.

Combining the two arguments, Calmfors and Driffill (1988) postulate a non-linear ('hump-shaped') relationship between bargaining structure and the real wage, with the industry-level bargaining arrangements found in many continental European countries providing the highest real wage and unemployment rates. (Although Calmfors and Driffill originally emphasized the role of bargaining level, the argument extends easily to bargaining coordination arrangements.) Note that both of these arguments provide predictions about real wage *levels*, and hence unemployment levels, not the rates of change of money wages that are frequently the focus of policy discussions.

Both the monotonic and the non-linear (hump-shaped) hypotheses have received empirical attention of varying degrees of formality. Most studies test for relationships between indices of bargaining centralization or coordination and the real wage level and/or the unemployment rate. The measurement of the crucial bargaining level and coordination variables presents many difficulties. Many studies simply rank sample countries by degree of centralized bargaining, and the implication of comparable institutional differences between countries with adjacent rankings is difficult to defend. More fundamentally, in most countries (particularly those with centralized bargaining) there are multiple tiers of bargaining, and negotiators at the industry and firm level lack the incentives of central negotiators to internalize externalities.

In particular, all centralized systems experience wage drift, the difference between actual earnings increases and the increases required by central agreements. Drift is particularly significant in the centralized Scandinavian collective bargaining systems, where it has ranged from 30 to 60 per cent of total earnings increases. Whether it is sufficient to rely on measurements of the official bargaining level depends on whether central negotiators can anticipate and allow for subsequent wage drift. Evidence from Scandinavian countries indicates that lower levels of bargaining may weaken but not completely offset the ability of central federations to influence overall wage growth (Hibbs and Locking, 1996; Holmlund and Skedinger, 1990; Holden, 1990). Measures of bargaining coordination require even more subjective judgements.

Evidence

The arguments outlined thus far address the effects of collective bargaining arrangements on the average real wage level, and hence the average unemployment rate (net of cyclical influences), in a country. (Later in this section we address the effect of institutional arrangements on the cyclical responsiveness of wages.) Table 6.2 reports the findings of several representative studies in this tradition, which nevertheless differ somewhat in their indicators of macroeconomic performance, measures of institutional structure, time periods, and controls.[7]

The Bruno and Sachs (1985) study predates many of the theoretical ideas reviewed above and is something of a bridge between older studies in the corporatist tradition (discussed in section 4 below) and subsequent studies of the influence of bargaining structure. Bruno and Sachs find that relatively corporatist countries experienced smaller increases in inflation and in a 'misery index' (defined as the rise in inflation minus the slowdown in growth) between 1965–73 (pre oil shock) and 1973–80 (post oil shock). Their corporatism index includes but is not limited to a measure of collective bargaining level. Subsequently, Layard et al. (1991) and Nickell (1997) each find that countries with relatively coordinated collective bargaining arrangements experience relatively low equilibrium unemployment rates. They also find that increases in union membership and coverage tend to raise unemployment. Each of these studies finds a linear relationship between their measures of macroeconomic performance and institutional structure.

Calmfors and Driffill (1988) find some support for their hypothesis of a non-linear (hump-shaped) relationship between bargaining level and changes in macroeconomic performance between 1965–73 and 1974–85. Soskice (1991) later stressed the importance of bargaining coordination over bargaining level and found a linear relationship between coordination and macroeconomic performance. (The sensitivity of empirical results to small changes in the institutional characterization of the small sample of industrialized countries is a disturbing characteristic of much of this literature. Soskice's conclusions emerged after changing the institutional description of only two countries, for example.) Subsequent research indicates that whether a linear or non-linear relationship prevails indeed depends on the choice of institutional measure. One recent literature review concluded: 'When broader coordination measures are used, there is support for a monotonic negative relationship between the degree of coordination and unemployment, with higher coordination leading to lower unemployment. . . . When centralisation measures are used, one tends instead to find a hump-shaped relationship.' (Calmfors et al., 2001, p. 93).

The macroeconomic shocks that initiated the long rise of unemployment beginning in the 1970s cannot by themselves explain the variations in unemployment that eventually emerged in industrialized nations. At the same time, institutional characteristics of countries that explain cross-country unemployment differences cannot explain the general rise in unemployment. Many of these institutional characteristics were in place long before the rise of unemployment, and as unemployment increased, institutional changes that occurred in some countries should have mitigated unemployment growth. Many students of unemployment increasingly believe that the evolution of unemployment in a country can only be understood by an appraisal of the interactions between macroeconomic shocks and a country's institutions. The idea is that some labour market institutions may

Table 6.2 Collective bargaining institutions and macroeconomic performance: representative findings

Study	Performance measure	Institutional measure	Findings
Bruno and Sachs (1985)	Change in inflation Change in misery index	Corporatism index Corporatism index	Linear negative relationship Linear negative relationship
Calmfors and Driffill (1988)	Change in unemployment Change in employment Change in Okun index[a]	Bargaining level Bargaining level Bargaining level	Nonlinear relationship Nonlinear relationship Nonlinear relationship
Layard et al. (1991)	Unemployment Union coverage	Bargaining coordination Linear positive relationship	Linear negative relationship
Nickell (1997)	Unemployment	Bargaining coordination Union density Union coverage	Linear negative relationship Linear positive relationship Linear positive relationship
OECD (1997)	Level, change in unemployment Level, change in employment Level, change in Okun index[a]	Union density Union coverage Bargaining level Bargaining coordination	See text

Note: [a]Inflation rate plus the unemployment rate.

179

turn a shock into persistent unemployment, while others may quickly dissipate the initial unemployment (Bertola et al., 2002; Blanchard and Wolfers, 2000). Consistent with earlier studies, this approach confirms that high union density or coverage worsens the effect of a macroeconomic shock on subsequent unemployment, while coordinated bargaining arrangements mitigate the effect on unemployment.

Most of the studies discussed above are based on single cross-sections or limited panel data, and other research questions the durability of the findings over time. Pooling data for 1980, 1990 and 1994, the OECD (1997, Ch. 3) study finds that countries with relatively centralized/coordinated bargaining systems have lower unemployment and inflation and that higher union coverage rates are associated with higher unemployment and inflation. For individual years, however, significant correlations are elusive, and there is some indication that correlations are weakest of all for the mid-1990s. Nor was there empirical support for a non-linear relationship between these performance measures and either bargaining level or coordination by the 1990s. Using 1993 data, moreover, Forslund and Krueger (1994) were unable to reproduce the bargaining coordination results of Layard et al. (1991). The question of why correlations between collective bargaining institutions and macroeconomic performance might weaken over time is addressed below in section 4.

Contractual details
The contents of collective bargaining contracts are as varied as the arrangements that produce them. For example, the scope of collective bargaining agreements decreases with the centralization of negotiations. In the interest of reaching agreement, national negotiations cover issues, such as wages and hours, which are common to all workplaces and generally avoid plant- or company-specific issues such as work rules, safety, and technical change. Irrespective of bargaining level, contracts also vary in duration and in the extent to which they protect workers from unforeseen events that may arise during the contract period. These details can contribute to the inertia of nominal wages in the face of macroeconomic shocks.

Longer contract periods economize on negotiating costs but leave workers vulnerable to the consequences of unforeseen economic developments. Even if all contracts were renegotiated at the same time, there is evidence from the USA that long-term collective bargaining agreements reduce wage flexibility. Multi-year agreements typically provide for a wage increase in the first year of the agreement, deferred wage increases in later years, and (in some instances) cost-of-living adjustments (COLAs) that adjust wages to price increases. First-year union wage increases are about as sensitive to labour market conditions as non-union wages. However, the responsiveness of first-year increases is muted by the rigidities introduced by fixed, deferred pay increases, which are not contingent on macroeconomic conditions in the years in which they take effect. As a result, average union nominal wage changes are less sensitive to labour market conditions than non-union wage changes because of the drag of deferred wage increases (Flanagan, 1976). COLAs make average union wages more responsive than non-union wages to changes in consumer prices. Wage indexation rarely provides complete compensation for price increases, so this aspect of contracts does not rule out real wage adjustments, although it may retard them. At various times, wage indexation has also been an important element of many wage adjustments in Denmark, Italy and Norway.

When the negotiations of multi-year collective bargaining agreements are not synchronized, the problem of wage inertia becomes more serious. With staggered contract expiration dates, (elected) union negotiators will worry that their members will suffer both real and relative wage losses if they reduce wage demands in the face of adverse macroeconomic shocks and unions that negotiate later do not follow their example. Staggered contract models predict a very slow adjustment of money wages to new prices, higher real wages and higher unemployment than with synchronised bargaining (Jackman, 1985; Taylor, 1980). Staggered collective bargaining contracts with complete indexation of wages to prices would be even worse.[8]

There is some evidence that coordination of bargaining produces greater cyclical wage flexibility as well as the real wage moderation discussed above. Layard et al. (1991) estimated a structural model of wage and price determination on time-series and cross-section data as part of their study of unemployment differentials among industrialized countries during 1983–88. In part of the study, they examined the effect of various labour market institutions, including measures of bargaining level and coordination, on parameters of the model. They found that employer and union coordination are more likely to raise the sensitivity of wages to unemployment than centralized bargaining arrangements.

Pay compression
Equality is a public good that only encompassing organizations can deliver. Perhaps one should not be surprised that the most robust correlation to emerge from cross-section studies of the effects of collective bargaining systems is an inverse relationship between wage dispersion and the level of collective bargaining. The relationship also emerges in studies of institutional change. Wage dispersion in Sweden narrowed with the adoption of centralized bargaining arrangements in the mid-1950s and then widened

following the adoption of more decentralized arrangements in 1984. In contrast, Norway adopted increasingly centralized bargaining arrangements in the late 1980s, and the pay structure narrowed (Kahn, 1998). Furthermore, countries with centralized bargaining experienced the smallest increase in inequality during the 1980s and 1990s (Gottschalk and Smeeding, 1997).

This robust correlation goes to links between collective bargaining arrangements and the long-term growth of a country rather than the medium-term macroeconomic adjustments that have been stressed so far. A key question is whether pay compression policies establish disincentives to invest in human capital or otherwise retard productivity growth. The answer depends on how the pay compression is produced.

Consider two approaches to producing lower pay dispersion: (1) Equal pay for equal work; (2) Equal pay for unequal work. At various times, the 'solidaristic' wage policies of some Scandinavian labour federations have incorporated each of these approaches. Approach (1) involves the elimination of inter-plant and inter-industry wage differentials for a given skill, as might occur in a perfectly-informed labour market with zero search costs. Moene and Wallerstein (1997) have shown that when plant-level productivity varies with the age of a plant's capital stock, policy (1) will raise productivity growth by accelerating job destruction in relatively inefficient plants and job creation in new, efficient plants. This process is attenuated when wages vary with plant efficiency in a decentralized bargaining setting. On the other hand, policy (2) raises the usual concerns regarding incentives.

A study of the effects of the solidaristic wage policy of Swedish unions documents the disparate effects of these two policies. These unions originally implemented policy (1) in the mid-1950s. In the late 1960s, however, the implementation drifted into policy (2), narrowing wage differentials by gender, age, and skill. *Ceteris paribus*, the original 'equal pay for equal work' implementation was associated with higher productivity growth, while the policy (2) approach reduced productivity growth (Hibbs and Locking, 1995). Pay compression mechanisms are merely one way in which a collective bargaining system may affect long-term growth rates. For a discussion of other mechanisms, see Chapters 5 and 10.

Taking stock
With the exception of the results on pay dispersion, the fragility of the cross-section correlations between characteristics of collective bargaining systems and macroeconomic outcomes over time is impressive. Assuming accurate measurement of the institutional variables, no features of the theories supporting these relationships can be invoked to explain the weakening correlations. On the other hand, the models generating these fragile

predictions are rather stylized representations of modern economies. The next section examines the effects of relaxing the more austere assumptions and provides some insights into the fragility of some of the empirical results discussed in this section.

4.   Economic and Political Environment of Bargaining

Everywhere in the world, unions bargain in open economies that often have significant non-union sectors, and most economies have become more open and more non-union since 1980. Moreover, the data in columns 5 and 6 in Table 6.1 indicate that governments are rarely neutral about the outcomes of collective bargaining. By assuming fully unionized, closed economies, the earliest models of the effects of bargaining structure on macroeconomic performance failed to address the effects of some of the most important changes in the economic environment of the past 30 years. Contrary to an earlier literature on corporatism, these models also implicitly assume that the prevailing political environment does not influence the macroeconomic effects of collective bargaining.

Globalization and non-union employment

The growth of international trade and of non-union employment in many countries over the past 30 years have two effects that tend to erode the predictions emerging from analyses of closed, fully unionized economies. First, unionized domestic firms now compete with foreign firms and/or non-union firms for sales in domestic markets. If goods made by foreign or non-union producers are substitutes, domestic firms encounter difficulty in trying to pass on pay increases to consumers. Competition from imports and non-union firms effectively increases the elasticity of demand facing employers in industry-wide bargaining units and circumscribes their ability to pass on wage increases without incurring employment losses.

Second, consumer prices, but not producer prices, now include the prices of goods made abroad so that the foreign trade and non-union production that encourages greater wage restraint in countries with industry-level bargaining may reduce wage restraint in countries with centralized bargaining in the unionized sector. In these countries, negotiated wage increases will produce smaller increases in consumer prices (which include the prices of imported and non-union goods and services) than in producer prices. The real consumption wage increases even when the real producer wage does not (Danthine and Hunt, 1994). With economic integration and non-union competition, macroeconomic outcomes become more or less independent of bargaining coordination. Therefore, the growth of trade and non-union employment may help to explain weakening correlations between institutional structure and macro outcomes.

Corporatism

The corporatist hypothesis represents the earliest effort by social scientists to incorporate the effects of the *political* environment on the macroeconomic effects of collective bargaining. The basic idea is that 'corporatist' institutional arrangements, which facilitate bargaining between labour, management, and the government, produce implicit or explicit 'social contracts' in which unions restrain wage demands in exchange for policy concessions from the government.

Corporatism is vulnerable to definitional quibbles. Students of corporatism rarely agree on the exact list of corporatist institutions or on whether one defines corporatism by a set of institutions or a process through which organized interest groups participate in policy bargaining or formulation. The literature produced numerous national corporatism indices constructed by aggregating such diverse information as bargaining structure, centralization of authority within the labour movement, concentration of union and employer organizations, union density, dispute settlement procedures, etc. The resulting indices are rankings of countries, and hence are susceptible to criticisms expressed in the review of the bargaining structure literature. Despite the diverse inputs to corporatism indices, they are highly intercorrelated.[9] Austria and the Scandinavian countries rank high, while the United States and the United Kingdom rank low on all measures of corporatism. Disagreements occur over the ranking of countries in the middle range of corporatism indices.

Notwithstanding the imprecision, an early corporatist literature correlated these measures with macroeconomic indicators such as inflation and unemployment (or the misery index – the sum of the two variables) across a small sample of industrialized countries. Studies rarely included additional control variables. A study of country cross sections for the 1960s, 1970s and 1980s by Crouch (1990) provides a useful guide to the main findings. Crouch finds significant correlations between all three measures of economic performance and an index of corporatism based on the authority of the dominant union federation in each country over its member unions (not the centralization of bargaining). The results reveal two patterns that emerge in other studies of corporatism and of bargaining structure. First, the strength of the correlations varies by decade, with the weakest results in the 1960s, the strongest in the 1970s, and intermediate in the 1980s. Second, the correlations are quite sensitive to the exact list of industrialized countries included in the study. The addition or subtraction of data for Spain and Switzerland had dramatic effects on the strength of the correlations.

One could cite several other studies providing correlations between measures of corporatism and macroeconomic performance, but even if taken at face value, the results present a daunting interpretive problem: which elements of the index account for the correlation? The process of institutional aggregation involved in constructing these measures provides opportunities for significant errors of interpretation. The exact institutions and mechanisms responsible for a correlation are difficult to identify, and there is a danger of attributing influence to elements of an index that have no impact at all. Moreover, the results on measures of corporatism share the fragility of the results on bargaining level and coordination. Recent work by the OECD (1997) indicates that the correlations have weakened over time.

As originally stated, the corporatist concept offered weakly specified hypotheses that paid scant attention to the motivations and capabilities of the main actors in the collective bargaining and public policy drama. Taking the hypothesis to data involved often-subjective measurements and fragile findings that seemed to dissipate over time. Yet, the corporatist theme that the macroeconomic impact of collective bargaining institutions may vary with the nature of government institutions has merit if the interests of and interactions between the respective institutions are carefully specified. Subsequent contributions have explored the interaction between collective bargaining and specific fiscal and monetary policy actions more carefully.

Fiscal policy
The corporatist literature frequently lists pro-labour governments and centralized collective bargaining as key elements of corporatist economies on the grounds that such governments are more likely to induce union cooperation by delivering pro-labour policies (Garrett, 1998; Crouch, 1990). Upon close examination, however, the broad proposition that a pro-labour government facilitates superior macroeconomic outcomes or even is good for the long-term health of a nation's labour movement turns out to be ambiguous. The outcomes of union–government interactions instead depend on the specific policies adopted by the government.

Consider first the macroeconomic stance of a pro-labour government. The key choice is between accommodative or non-accommodative policies. Unions clearly prefer the former policies, because they mitigate the employment issues associated with a negotiated real wage increase. But if a government adopts an accommodative fiscal (or exchange rate) policy, what is the effect on wage demands? Suppose that a government aggressively pursues an employment target by increasing public employment and other expenditures whenever employment falls below the target. The policy effectively lowers the elasticity of labour demand facing a centralized union, and results in a higher real wage in equilibrium (Calmfors and Horn, 1985;

Calmfors, 1982). Contrary to the corporatist claim, the pro-labour (accommodative) fiscal policy produces more, not less real wage pressure.

Nor is it clear that the micro policies of pro-labour governments necessarily enhance union welfare. Indeed, the general political orientation of a government (stressed by the corporatist literature) is less important than the exact policies that pro-labour governments use to influence union fortunes. A pro-labour government might try to enhance the institutional security of labour by passing legislation that facilitates union recognition and collective bargaining procedures. Such legislation may increase real wage pressure in an economy. (This mechanism also works in reverse: governments may also pass legislation that demonstrably reduces the institutional security of unions, as has occurred in the United Kingdom – see Chapter 12 by Addison and Siebert in this volume – and New Zealand.)

Alternatively, a pro-labour government might pass legislation providing benefits and regulations (e.g. governing dismissals, occupation health and safety, pensions, etc.) sought by unions. Such legislation will simultaneously improve working conditions and make it more difficult for unions to differentiate their employment conditions from those of non-union employers. Legislation effectively provides working conditions that used to be unique to union contracts to all workers irrespective of union status. Workers have less reason to join unions and the presence of a friendly government does not enhance union power.

In sum, the effect of pro-labour governments on union wage demands depend on the specific fiscal policies adopted by the government. Contrary to corporatist arguments, some empirically important fiscal policies would enhance the ability of maximizing unions to raise real wages. In these cases, the wage restraint quid pro quo claimed in the corporatist literature seems to rest on fiscal policy inducing a shift in the union utility function. To date, no careful testing of this possibility has occurred.

The idea that the macroeconomic impact of a collective bargaining system depends in part on the stance of monetary policy has persisted in various forms for over fifty years. John Hicks (1955, p. 391) argued that the early postwar period was characterized by a Labour Standard in which 'monetary policy adjusts to the equilibrium level of money wages so as to make it conform to the actual level', rather than the other way around. In his view, compliant central banks regularly accommodated negotiated wage (and subsequent price) increases by increasing the money supply sufficiently to maintain production and employment. One can read into this view an early expression of the idea that in formulating wage demands, unions interact *strategically* with the relevant central bank, so that the outcomes of collective bargaining might be quite different if central banks refused to accommodate pay increases.

Non-accommodation pledges by central banks lack credibility in countries where central banks lack independence from elected politicians, whose re-election prospects often rest on high employment. A credible non-accommodation stance by a central bank requires institutional independence from political authorities. The German Bundesbank and the US Federal Reserve provide two leading examples. Empirical studies have document that countries with independent central banks have lower inflation (Alesina and Summers, 1993).

How is the view that collective bargaining cum compliant central banks produces a Labour Standard altered when a country has an independent, non-accommodating central bank? With a credible non-accommodation commitment from the central bank, unions understand that the bank will not increase the nominal money supply to accommodate price increases stimulated by negotiated money wage increases. That is, the real money supply will decline with such price increases, reducing the demand for labour. How different collective bargaining systems respond to this knowledge becomes the central question.

In highly centralized or coordinated systems, negotiators understand that settlements influence the price level, irrespective of the monetary regime. Because the bargain covers all production, raising money wage demands raises the price level, but cannot increase real wages, irrespective of the policy stance of the central bank. Given their potential to influence the price level, however, central negotiators may be particularly sensitive to signals sent by the central bank.

For collective bargaining systems with an intermediate level of bargaining coordination (e.g. Germany) an independent central bank may produce more wage restraint. Here, negotiators for industrial unions understand that industry money wage settlements will induce smaller increases in the national price level, so that money wage pressure can advance real wages. Unions effectively trade some employment loss for a real wage gain. The tradeoff worsens with an independent central bank that does not alter the nominal money supply to accommodate the price increase. The real money supply falls, and employment falls more than it would with an accommodating central bank. If an independent central bank literally targets the price level it will contract the nominal money supply, producing a downward shift in the labour demand curve and further employment losses. Negotiators have incentives to avoid these employment losses by mitigating their money wage demands.

In decentralized or uncoordinated bargaining systems, central bank threats are less likely to produce wage restraint, however, because negotiators are (1) unlikely to believe their decisions will influence the price level and (2) likely to be concerned about losing their relative wage position.

Decentralized negotiators effectively face a prisoner's dilemma. Cross-section evidence seems roughly consistent with these arguments, indicating that independent central banks appear to produce the greatest improvement in macroeconomic performance in relatively coordinated collective bargaining systems (Hall and Franzese, 1998).

The foregoing arguments rest on the assumption that a country's central bank targets inflation. The argument loses force to the extent that a central bank instead targets the exchange rate, as has been true in a number of countries. Prior to the European Monetary Union, for example, the German Bundesbank arguably set European monetary policy. While the Bundesbank targeted inflation, other European central banks effectively targeted their exchange rate in order to align their currencies with the deutsche-mark. Thus, a central bank's choice of a nominal anchor can have an important impact on the outcome of wage bargaining. A shift from targeting the exchange rate to targeting inflation, for example, should induce greater wage restraint in countries with all but the least centralized bargaining arrangements.

5. Application: The European Monetary Union

With the development of a common currency area, such as the European Monetary Union, countries lose the ability to use monetary policy (interest rate adjustments) or exchange rate policy to counter domestic macroeconomic shocks. A regional central bank (e.g. the European Central Bank or ECB) establishes interest rate policy, and the common currency fixes exchange rates among community members. How are these developments likely to affect collective wage determination?

Clearly, the shift from a domestic to a regional central bank alters the wage determination game between unions and the central bank discussed in the previous section. Even nationally centralized collective bargaining systems are now comparatively decentralized with respect to the regional central bank. Since national wage decisions have a comparatively smaller influence on the regional price level targeted by a regional central bank, even centralized national unions may assume that their bargaining activities are less likely to provoke a central bank response than when they faced a national central bank. In countries in which the central bank had targeted inflation, wage pressure may increase. This would include Germany, where the Bundesbank clearly targeted inflation, but would exclude countries that tied their currency to the Bundesbank, effectively requiring their central banks to target the exchange rate. When targeting the exchange rate, central banks cannot react to negotiated wage increases. The overall implication is that the shift to the ECB implies somewhat higher real wages and unemployment.

A more challenging set of implications flows from the loss of monetary and exchange rate policies to offset domestic macroeconomic shocks. With the loss of these policy instruments, adjustments to macroeconomic shocks require changes in labour costs. While some labour cost variation may be achieved via cyclical variations in the social charges paid by employers,[10] the greater need for more flexible labour cost adjustments is also likely to focus attention on details of collective bargaining agreements. While there appears to be considerable resistance to nominal wage cuts on both sides of the labour market (Bewley, 1999), some features of collective bargaining contracts contribute additional elements of wage inflexibility. For example, section 3 described how long contract durations contribute to significant nominal wage rigidity in the face of changing unemployment and how indexation arrangements limit real wage flexibility.[11] The need for greater labour cost flexibility may therefore raise the demand for either shorter contract durations or wage provisions that are indexed to macroeconomic conditions. The prospects for the development of 'social contracts' between collective bargaining parties and the government are examined in the following section.

6. Policy approaches to union macroeconomic impacts

Virtually all governments at some point have introduced policies to limit the macroeconomic consequences of collective bargaining. Most policies have not been informed by the research reported in this chapter. Indeed, many policy efforts predate these research developments.

Institutional design

The strongest policy implications of the research on collective bargaining and macroeconomic performance concern the design of collective bargaining and public policy institutions. Probably the most cited finding in this research is that coordinated bargaining systems produce superior macroeconomic outcomes, and some observers recommend greater coordination of pay determination where greater labour cost flexibility is desired (as in the new EMU). Yet the implication that superior macroeconomic performance will follow the development of more coordinated bargaining institutions should be treated with caution. Even taking the research results at face value, one must recognize that the strongest results were obtained for earlier time periods, and the correlations appear to have weakened by the 1990s. This chapter has addressed changes in the economic environment that may account for the fragility of the results.

A second difficulty with institutional redesign proposals is that they follow the literature in assuming that collective bargaining institutions are exogenous and tend to be frozen in time. This stance is clearly not tenable for bargaining structures and union representation. Over the past 20 years, bargaining structures have decentralized in many countries (see Calmfors et al., 2001; Hartog and Theeuwes, 1993; Katz, 1993). Some Scandinavian countries abandoned centralized bargaining. New Zealand abandoned a longstanding arbitration system for a system of individual employment contracts. In the USA, industry-wide and other multi-employer bargaining arrangements gave way to company- and plant-level bargaining. Declining unionization and the consequent growth of non-union employment, discussed elsewhere in this volume, has supplemented the trend toward less centralized and less coordinated bargaining.[12]

Some of these changes appear to be reactions against the adverse economic consequences of earlier, more centralized, institutional frameworks. Changes in the legal framework of collective bargaining removed direct and indirect government protections of union power in New Zealand and the United Kingdom. Employers instigated decentralization measures in Sweden and Germany as old arrangements delivered inefficient cost levels or structures.

Contrary to the literature that emerged in the 1970s and 1980s, at the turn of the twenty-first century relatively high transactions costs appear to be associated with centralized bargaining structures. This paradox may reflect the fact that some of the more important propositions of this literature follow from a model (fully unionized, closed economies) that accords poorly with the increasing integration of industrialized nations. Without a clearer understanding of why private and public decisions are now altering some features of collective bargaining systems toward greater decentralization of pay determination, recommendations to redesign institutions to achieve greater coordination in pay determination seem premature.

Incomes policy
The belief that collective bargaining could initiate or sustain inflation informed early postwar applications of incomes policies in many industrialized nations. Countries with high union density and/or coverage assumed that bargaining produced upward labour cost pressure. Countries with a substantial non-union sector, such as the USA, assumed that wage spillovers from the union to the non-union sector threatened price stability. Countries therefore introduced incomes policies either to prevent the emergence of inflation at high employment or, during periods of inflation, to reduce inflationary expectations. A wide variety of incomes policy formulations emerged.

A first generation of incomes policies in the 1950s and 1960s stated a wage rule, exceptions to that rule, and a price rule. The wage rule generally depended on the current economic environment. Countries seeking to prevent an outbreak of inflation might state that wage increases should not exceed the rate of productivity growth, so that prices would not increase because of labour cost developments. Policies applied during periods of significant inflation would instead set wage targets that took some account of current inflation but tried to alter expectations and wind inflation down. Price rules could generally be deduced from the wage rule, through the links between costs, productivity and prices. At times, policies included exceptions to the wage rule to facilitate reallocation of labour resources or address distributional concerns (Ulman and Flanagan, 1971).

A later generation of incomes policies resembled earlier corporatist ideas by establishing multilateral negotiations between labour, management, government officials and other economic interest groups over the growth of incomes. In such 'social contract' negotiations, governments often offered policy concessions (in the form of tax reductions, wage indexation, or legislation supporting the institutional position of unions) in exchange for wage restraint (Flanagan et al., 1983).

Unlike most of the later research on links between collective bargaining and macroeconomic outcomes, the application of incomes policies rarely rested on concerns that a specific set of institutional arrangements was inflation prone. Instead, virtually all industrialized western countries adopted such policies at one time or another between 1950 and 1980. This provided the opportunity to observe whether incomes policies were more effective under some institutional arrangements than others. Yet detailed comparative studies revealed that the effectiveness of the policies was at best short-lived and often produced unintended consequences that exacerbated the original macroeconomic problems (Calmfors et al., 2001; Flanagan et al., 1983; Ulman and Flanagan, 1971, pp. 75–79).

There appear to be several reasons for the failure of this policy approach. Perhaps the most important is compliance risk – a prisoner's dilemma faced by every union contemplating compliance with the wage rule of an incomes policy in all but the most coordinated bargaining systems. The members of a union that complies with a government wage target suffer both real and relative wage losses if other unions do not comply. While the price level would be lower, and all unions would be at least as well off if they complied with the target, no individual union has an incentive to do so.

Various approaches to countering compliance risk were offered or proposed. In the 'social contract' approach of the second generation of policies, governments often offered explicit quid pro quos for accepting the risk. As the earlier discussion of interactions between collective bargaining and political environment clarifies, a key question is whether a government can deliver its side of the bargain while maintaining its macroeconomic objectives.[13] Several academic proposals to use the tax system to give firms or workers incentives to moderate wage and price increases also emerged. Tax-based incomes policies (TIPs) in principle provide both compliance incentives and allocational flexibility (since firms could rationally exceed the guideline and incur the tax if warranted by economic circumstances). The details can be difficult to design, however, and efforts to implement such proposals are extremely rare.[14]

By the 1980s, incomes policies were out of favour, and many governments shifted to a non-accommodative monetary and or fiscal stance in the face of union wage pressure. Nevertheless, the renewed emphasis on labour cost flexibility raised by the EMU may stimulate further experiments. The exact content and effectiveness of such efforts remains a matter of speculation, given the reduction in the power and influence of unions in most industrialized countries. With declining unionization and more decentralized bargaining the number of parties that require representation to formulate an effective policy would seem to be large, raising the barriers to successful negotiations.

7. Conclusions

This chapter has reviewed the theoretical and empirical research on the relationship between the characteristics of collective bargaining systems and macroeconomic performance in industrialized countries. (Whether the results established in the research apply to developing nations remains an under-explored area of study.) Some features of a collective bargaining system appear to influence macroeconomic outcomes, and some do not. The extent of union representation or coverage seems much less important than specific bargaining arrangements, for example.

Considered as a whole, however, this body of research almost inadvertently (through the fragility of some of the results) implies that the influence of collective bargaining on macroeconomic performance is more conditional than is commonly acknowledged. Many of the most prominent results concerning the effects of bargaining level and coordination abstract from important features of the economic and political environment in which bargaining occurs. These conditioning features include the openness of the economy, the importance of the non-union sector, and the independence of a country's central bank and its policy rule. (At the same time, the effect of a pro-labour government on macroeconomic outcomes appears more ambiguous than is sometimes claimed.) As those environments have changed, the correlations have weakened. Exploring specific hypotheses on how interactions between characteristics of a collective bargaining system and its economic and political environment influence macroeconomic performance remains a rich area for additional research.

The research discussed in this chapter requires institutional variance to achieve identification and has always been limited by the fact that (a) the requisite data are available for less than two dozen industrialized countries and (b) the limited time-series variation in institutional characteristics. Future research will be even more challenging if a convergence of collective bargaining institutions further limits institutional variance. Convergence is implied by a 'survival of the fittest (least costly) institutions' hypothesis, but to date, research simply does not support the notion that history has produced a single set of equilibrium labour market institutions. Yet the growing importance of market forces in the wake of greater economic integration may increase the pressure for such convergence. Research into the endogeneity of the collective bargaining arrangements that the research discussed in this chapter take as given would also deepen our understanding of the prospects for convergence. Such studies should consider a reversal of the question that motivated this chapter: Can macroeconomic performance influence collective bargaining arrangements?

Endnotes

1. Most countries offer much more limited statistical descriptions of the employer side of collective bargaining relationships. Since official statistical agencies rarely survey employers about the extent to which pay and other working conditions are influenced by collective bargaining, there are no reliable measures of the exact number or proportion of firms working on a non-union basis.
2. The table and related discussion draw on material in Flanagan (1999).
3. During much of the twentieth century, quasi-judicial arbitration procedures established wages in Australia and New Zealand. In some of its variations, this system provided another approach to centralized pay determination.
4. Missing from Table 6.1 are measures of the extent of 'corporatist' institutions in a country. This topic is sufficiently extensive that it receives separate treatment in section 3.
5. One can also challenge the adequacy of union density or coverage variables as measures of market power on a variety of grounds (Flanagan, 1999, pp. 1165–1166).
6. Readers may wish to consult the detailed reviews of this literature in Calmfors (1993), Calmfors et al. (2001), Flanagan (1999), and Moene et al. (1993). Comparative data on bargaining structure appear in Calmfors and Driffill (1988, p. 18), OECD (1997, p. 71), and Calmfors et al. (2001, p. 92).
7. For synopses of several other studies, see OECD (1997, p. 67) and Calmfors et al. (2001, p. 94).
8. Bargaining level and synchronization are not synonymous. Not only do centralized bargaining systems have multiple tiers of bargaining, but 'pattern bargaining' in which key settlements are emulated in many subsequent negotiations can evolve in decentralized bargaining systems.
9. Teulings and Hartog (1998) provide a thorough discussion of the construction of the various measures and find that the correlation between the most commonly adapted indices ranges from 0.7 to 0.9. Other compilations of indices of corporatism and bargaining structure may be found in Calmfors and Driffill (1988, p. 18), OECD (1997, p. 71), and Calmfors et al. (2001, p. 92).
10. For example, Finland and Sweden have recently considered the use of 'buffer funds', which support a constant benefit stream with cyclical variations in social charges.
11. Democratic decision processes may also limit the ability of some unions to adjust contract provisions to changing macroeconomic conditions. For example, several US unions

only gave up fixed wages for pay contingent on organizational performance in the early 1980s, when the job security of median union voters was threatened (Flanagan, 1993).

12. One should not draw broad policy conclusions from single cases, but the USA, with one of the most uncoordinated wage-setting systems found among industrialized nations, experienced the lowest unemployment rates of any OECD country during the long expansion of the 1990s.

13. Moreover, Colin Crouch's remark that 'corporatism places enormous reliance on the capacity of organizations to regulate their members' captures the difficulties confronting bargaining institutions attempting to deliver on their commitments in social contracts (Crouch, 1985, p. 138).

14. The earliest formulations of tax-based incomes policies appear to have emerged in socialist countries as central planners tried to limit the growth of the wage bill in state-owned enterprises.

References

Alesina, Alberto and Lawrence H. Summers (1993), 'Central Bank Independence and Macroeconomic Performance', *Journal of Money, Credit and Banking*, 25 (2), 151–163.

Bertola, Giuseppe, Francine D. Blau and Lawrence M. Kahn (2002), 'Comparative Analysis of Labor-Market Outcomes: Lessons for the United States from International Long-run Evidence', in Alan B. Krueger and Robert Solow (eds), *The Roaring Nineties: Can Full Employment Be Sustained?* New York: Russell Sage Foundation, pp. 34–61.

Bewley, Truman. F. (1999), *Why Wages Don't Fall During a Recession*, Cambridge, MA: Harvard University Press.

Blanchard, Olivier and Justin Wolfers (2000), 'The Role of Shocks and Institutions in the Rise of European Unemployment: the Aggregate Evidence', *Economic Journal*, 110 (462), C1–C33.

Bruno, Michael and Jeffrey D. Sachs (1985), *Economics of Worldwide Stagflation*, Cambridge, MA: Harvard University Press.

Calmfors, Lars (1982), 'Employment Policies, Wage Formation and Trade Union Behaviour in a Small Open Economy', *Scandinavian Journal of Economics*, 84 (2), 345–373.

Calmfors, Lars (1993), 'Centralization of Wage Bargaining and Macroeconomic Performance: A Survey', *OECD Economic Studies*, (21), 161–191.

Calmfors, Lars and John Driffill (1988), 'Bargaining Structure, Corporatism and Macroeconomic Performance', *Economic Policy*, 3 (6), 13–61.

Calmfors, Lars and Hendrik Horn (1985), 'Classical Unemployment, Accommodation Policies and the Adjustment of Real Wages', *Scandinavian Journal of Economics*, 87 (2), 234–261.

Calmfors, Lars, Alison Booth, Michael Burda, Daniele Checchi, Robin Naylor and Jelle Visser (2001), 'The Future of Collective Bargaining in Europe', in Tito Boeri, Agar Brugiavini and Lars Calmfors (eds), *The Role of Unions in the Twenty-First Century*, Oxford University Press, pp. 1–134.

Crouch, Colin (1985), 'Conditions for Trade Union Wage Restraint', in Leon Lindberg and Charles Maier (eds), *The Politics of Inflation and Economic Stagnation*, Washington, DC: Brookings Institution, pp. 105–139.

Crouch, Colin (1990), 'Trade Unions in the Exposed Sector: Their Influence on Neo-corporatist Behaviour', in Renato Brunetta and Carlo Dell'Aringa (eds), *Labor Relations and Economic Performance*, New York: New York University Press, pp. 68–91.

Danthine, Jean Pierre and Jennifer Hunt (1994), 'Wage Bargaining Structure, Employment and Economic Integration', *Economic Journal*, 104 (424), 528–541.

Flanagan, Robert J. (1976), 'Wage Interdependence in Unionized Labor Markets', *Brookings Papers on Economic Activity*, 3 (2), 635–673.

Flanagan, Robert J. (1993), 'Can Political Models Predict Union Behaviour?', in Robert J. Flanagan, Karl O. Moene and Michael Wallerstein (eds), *Trade Union Behaviour, Pay Bargaining, and Economic Performance*, Oxford: Clarendon Press, pp. 5–45.

Flanagan, Robert J. (1999), 'Macroeconomic Performance and Collective Bargaining: An International Perspective', *Journal of Economic Literature*, 37 (3), 1150–1175.

Flanagan, Robert J., David W. Soskice and Lloyd Ulman (1983), *Unionism, Economic Stabilization, and Incomes Policies: European Experience*, Washington, DC: Brookings Institution.

Forslund, Anders and Allan B. Krueger (1994), 'An Evaluation of the Swedish Active Labour Market Policy: New and Received Wisdom', National Bureau of Economic Research Working Paper No. 4802, Cambridge, MA, July, 1994.

Franzese, Robert and Peter Hall (2000), 'Institutional Dimensions of Coordinated Wage Bargaining and Monetary Policy', in Torben Iversen, Jonas Pontusson and David Soskice (eds), *Unions, Employers and Central Banks: Wage Bargaining and Macro-economic Policy in an Integrating Europe*, Ann Arbor: University of Michigan Press, pp. 191–223.

Garrett, Geoffrey (1998), *Partisan Politics in the Global Economy*, Cambridge: Cambridge University Press.

Golden, Miriam A., Peter Lange and Michael Wallerstein (1997), 'Reinterpreting Postwar Industrial Relations: Comparative Data on Advanced Industrial Societies', unpublished manuscript.

Gottschalk, Peter and Timothy M. Smeeding (1997), 'Cross National Comparisons of Earnings and Income Inequality', *Journal of Economic Literature*, 35 (2), 633–687.

Hall, Peter and Robert Franzese (1998), 'Central Bank Independence and Coordinated Wage Bargaining', in Torben Iversen, Jonas Pontusson and David Soskice (eds), *Unions, Employers and Central Banks: Wage Bargaining and Macro-Economic Policy in an Integrating Europe*, Ann Arbor: University of Michigan Press, pp. 37–63.

Hartog, Joop and Jules Theeuwes (eds) (1993), *Labour Market Contracts and Institutions: A Cross-National Comparison*, Amsterdam: North-Holland.

Hibbs, Douglas A. and Hakan Locking (1995), 'Wage Dispersion and Productive Efficiency: Evidence for Sweden', FIEF WP 128, Stockholm.

Hibbs, Douglas A. and Hakan Locking (1996), 'Wage Compression, Wage Drift and Wage Inflation in Sweden', *Labour Economics*, 3 (2), 109–141.

Hicks, John (1955), 'Economic Foundations of Wage Policy', *Economic Journal*, 65 (259), 389–404.

Hines, Albert G. (1964),'Trade Unions and Wage Inflation in the United Kingdom, 1893–1961', *Review of Economic Studies*, 31 (4), 221–252.

Holden, Steinar (1990), 'Wage Drift in Norway', in Lars Calmfors, (ed.), *Wage Formation and Macroeconomic Policy in the Nordic Countries*, Oxford: Oxford University Press.

Holmlund, Bertil and Per Skedinger (1990), 'Wage Bargaining and Wage Drift: Evidence from the Swedish Wood Industry', in Lars Calmfors (ed.), *Wage Formation and Macroeconomic Policy in the Nordic Countries*, Oxford: Oxford University Press.

Jackman, Richard (1985), 'Counterinflationary Policy in a Unionised Economy with Nonsynchronized Wage Setting', *Scandinavian Journal of Economics*, 87 (2), 357–378.

Kahn, Lawrence M. (1998), 'Against the Wind: Bargaining Recentralization and Wage Inequality in Norway, 1987–91', *Economic Journal*, 108 (448), 603–641.

Katz, Harry C. (1993), 'The Decentralization of Collective Bargaining: A Literature Review and Comparative Analysis', *Industrial and Labor Relations Review*, 47 (1), 3–22.

Layard, Richard G., Stephen J. Nickell and Richard Jackman (1991), *Unemployment: Macroeconomic Performance and the Labour Market*, Oxford and New York: Oxford University Press.

Moene, Karl O. and Michael Wallerstein (1997), 'Pay Inequality', *Journal of Labor Economics*, 15 (3), 403–430.

Moene, Karl O., Michael Wallerstein and Michael Hoel (1993), 'Bargaining Structure and Economic Performance', in Robert J. Flanagan, Karl O. Moene and Michael Wallerstein (eds), *Trade Union Behaviour, Pay Bargaining, and Economic Performance*, Oxford: Clarendon Press, pp. 63–131.

Nickell, Stephen (1997), 'Unemployment and Labor Market Rigidities: Europe versus North America', *Journal of Economic Perspectives*, 11 (3), 55–74.

OECD (1997), *Employment Outlook*. Paris: OECD.

Soskice, David (1990), 'Reinterpreting Corporatism and Explaining Unemployment: Co-ordinated and Non-coordinated Market Economies', in Renato Brunetta and Carlo

Dell'Aringa (eds), *Labour Relations and Economic Performance*, New York: New York University Press, pp. 170–211.

Soskice, David (1991), 'Wage Determination: The Changing Role of Institutions in Advanced Industrialized Countries', *Oxford Review of Economic Policy*, 6 (4), 36–61.

Taylor, John B (1980) 'Aggregate Dynamics and Staggered Contracts', *Journal of Political Economy*, 88 (1), 1–23.

Teulings, Coen and Joop Hartog (1998), *Corporatism or Competition? Labour Contracts, Institutions and Wage Structures in International Comparison*, Cambridge: Cambridge University Press.

Ulman, Lloyd and Robert J. Flanagan (1971), *Wage Restraint: A Study of Incomes Policies in Western Europe*, Berkeley: University of California Press.

7 Changes over time in union relative wage effects in the UK and the US revisited
David G. Blanchflower and Alex Bryson

1. Introduction

Union density has been in decline in the United States and Britain for two decades now (Appendix Table 7A.1). It is often asserted by commentators that trade unions are outmoded institutions, shunned by employers and unable to reach a new generation of workers imbued with individualist values that are at odds with the ethos underpinning unionism. But the propensity of individuals to join unions is not simply a question of 'desire' or ideological commitment. More broadly, one can think of union membership as a good – a product or service to be purchased. Employees derive utility from this good, as they would other services or products. In the case of union membership, this utility can be psychological. For example, the decision to purchase membership may be due to the desire to conform to a social norm and thus maintain one's reputation among co-workers. It may also be driven by instrumentalism, wherein employees think they have something tangible to gain from membership, either in terms of better wages, improved non-pecuniary terms of employment, or they may see it as insurance against arbitrary employer actions. So, benefits may accrue to the individual, but they come at a cost. Employees will purchase membership if the benefits outweigh the costs. A shift in the propensity to purchase union membership may reflect a shift in individuals' perceptions of the costs and benefits attached to membership. It does appear though that the cost of union membership is generally low. Reynolds et al. (1999, p. 406) estimate that the fee required for membership is equivalent to roughly two hours' pay per month while the cost of industrial action accounts for less than 1 per cent of working time for the typical union worker. Neither has risen substantially over time.

What of the benefits of membership? Perhaps the most visible and most significant is the union wage premium or wage gap. The most obvious way of measuring the value of union membership to employees is to estimate the extent to which members' wages are higher than those of similar non-members. This union wage premium arises because unions bargain on members' behalf for wages that are above the market rate. In the literature what is usually estimated is the difference between the ceteris paribus earnings of union members and those of non-members. That is, how much would wages change if an individual moved from non-union to union status or vice-versa, holding constant their individual and workplace characteristics. There has been speculation that the intensification of competition since the 1980s, coupled with a diminution of union bargaining strength, has prevented unions from obtaining the sort of wage premium they achieved in the past. This is the issue we investigate in this chapter.

If the costs of membership have remained constant or risen, while the wage benefits of membership have fallen, this might help explain the reticence of employees to join unions. However, evidence to date is only suggestive of a declining union wage premium: there are few studies estimating the union wage premium with consistent time-series data and recent studies use techniques which were not used in earlier analyses. This gap in the evidence is filled by the remainder of this chapter. In particular, we consider how much the premium varies by country, across groups and through time. These issues are examined using broadly comparable time series data for the United States and the United Kingdom.[1] The evidence suggests that there has been some constancy in the premium for most of the post-war years in both countries, although the level of the differential has been somewhat higher in the USA than in the UK. We find evidence that the union wage premium has declined steadily in both countries since the mid-1990s as the economies entered unprecedented boom periods and labour markets tightened dramatically.[2] In addition, some evidence is presented on the size of the wage premium in 17 other countries drawn from three continents – Australia, Austria, Brazil, Canada, Chile, Cyprus, Denmark, France, Germany, Italy, Japan, the Netherlands, New Zealand, Norway, Portugal, Spain and Sweden.

2. Background

There are two ways unions can affect wages in the economy (Farber, 2001). The first is the direct effect on the wages of workers in jobs where wages are set through collective bargaining. This may affect non-members' and members' wages. The second level is the impact that the presence of unions has in the economy: this can change the level and distribution of wages generally. In theory, these general equilibrium effects may both raise and reduce the level of aggregate wages in the economy. Since it is not possible to observe the counterfactual (wages in the absence of unions) this union effect is not easily estimable. The union–non-union wage differential (the wage gap), defined as:

$$\Delta = \frac{W_u - W_n}{W_n}, \tag{7.1}$$

is estimable because we observe the wages of members (W_u) and non-members (W_n). Provided differentials are small, this expression is usefully approximated by:

$$\Delta \approx \Delta_u - \Delta_n, \tag{7.2}$$

which says that the measured union wage gap is approximately equal to the difference in the proportional effects of unions on the union and non-union wage. The union wage gap in equation (7.1) can be usefully approximated by the difference in log wages, implying that:

$$\Delta \approx \ln(W_u) - \ln(W_n). \tag{7.3}$$

The union wage gap may reflect the direct effect of unions on the wages of unionized workers, and the offsetting effects on non-union workers. Of course, there may be endogenous selection into union status arising for two reasons. First, there is 'worker choice' in which workers only choose membership if the union wage is greater than the wage available to the individual outside the union. It is often assumed that workers with a lower underlying earning capacity have more to gain from membership than higher quality workers, in which case this selection process will understate the union wage premium. The second selection process arises through 'queuing', since not all workers desiring union employment can find union jobs. Under this model, union employers may choose the best of the workers among those desirous of a union job. This employer selection implies a positive bias in the union premium but, a priori, it is not clear whether this bias is greater or less than the negative bias implied by worker selection. Either way, if there is endogenous selection, the membership mark up estimated using standard cross-sectional regression techniques 'can be interpreted as the average difference in wages between union and non-union workers, but it can not be interpreted as the effect of union membership on the wage of a particular worker' (Farber, 2001, p. 11).

Causal inference is problematic because, where workers who become members differ systematically from those who do not become members in ways which might affect their earnings, independent of membership, we cannot infer the non-union wage for union members simply by comparing union members' wages with those of non-members. In the literature for the United States, the problem of selection bias is usually tackled by modelling union status determination simultaneously with earnings and estimating an econometric model that takes account of the simultaneity. This usually involves a Heckman estimator where the earnings function and union status determination function are assumed to have errors that are jointly normal. This technique relies on untestable exclusion restrictions whereby variables assumed to affect union status have no direct effect on earnings. In his review of the literature, H. Gregg Lewis (1986) concluded that, because of these arbitrary functional form assumptions and untestable exclusion restrictions, results from these studies were unreliable. Estimates of the union wage gap using simultaneous equation methods tend to produce large and unstable estimates. Panel estimates, which involve making use of data on the same individuals over time and observing how wages change as individuals alter their union status have problems of misclassification and measurement error which tend to result in estimates of the impact of unions that are *downward* biased. Lewis (1986) takes the view that the most appropriate way to estimate the impact of unions on wages is using ordinary least squares (OLS). He suggests OLS may produce an upper bound estimate of the true impact of unions because 'such estimates suffer from upward bias resulting from the omission of control variables correlated with the union status variable' (Lewis, 1986, p. 9). The assumption is that some of the wage gap attributed to union membership is, in fact, attributable in part to the characteristics of members, their jobs and their employers which would give them higher wages than non-members in any case. In practice, as we note above and as other studies indicate (Farber, 2001; Robinson, 1989), bias in cross-sectional OLS estimation due to unobserved heterogeneity may both upwardly or downwardly bias the 'true' impact.[3] Here, our primary concern is with changes in the union wage premium over time. We do not seek to control for the potential endogeneity of union membership. Rather, we adopt the standard approach to estimation of the union–non-union wage gap using individual-level data and estimating by OLS. That is:

$$\ln W_{it} = X_{it}\beta + \delta U_{it} + \epsilon_{it}, \tag{7.4}$$

where subscript *it* indexes individuals over time, X_{it} is a vector of worker, job and workplace characteristics, U_{it} is a dummy variable indicating union membership, and ϵ_{it} is a random component. The parameter δ represents the average proportional difference in wages between union and non-union workers adjusted for worker and workplace characteristics, and it is the regression-adjusted analogue of Δ. In our work, we assume that any bias in our estimates of the δ over time arising through unobserved heterogeneity remains constant over time.

The vast majority of work estimating the effects of union membership on relative wages has been based on US data. The definitive empirical works in this area are by H. Gregg Lewis, (1963, 1986), the father figure of this literature.[4] The first of his two books measured the effects of unions using relatively aggregated data at the industry level, backed up by case study evidence. In the 1986 volume, Lewis examined approximately 200 studies that had used micro-data to estimate the effect of unions. He concluded that it was not possible to use 'macro' data to estimate the union wage gap and that methodologically estimating an OLS equation with wages on the left, and union status on the right with a group of controls, was probably the best way to estimate the size of the effect. Panel estimates had problems of misclassification and measurement error while simultaneous equation methods suffered from poor identification due to a lack of suitable instruments. Lewis (1986) found that the overall impact of unions in the US economy was approximately 15 per cent and showed relatively little variation across years – varying between 12 per cent and 19 per cent between 1967 and 1979.

Subsequent work confirmed constancy of the differential until the 1990s. For example, Hirsch and his co-authors have produced a series of papers estimating changes in the differential over time and concluded there has been some decline in the premium in recent years (e.g. Hirsch and Schumacher, 2002; Hirsch and Macpherson, 2002; Hirsch et al., 2002). Bratsberg and Ragan (2002) examine the trend in the private sector union wage differential in the USA, 1971–99, and conclude that dispersion in the wage premium across industries has substantially declined as the US economy has become more competitive but that there has been only a modest decline in the average premium. Bratsberg and Ragan thus confirmed the stability of the union premium over time noted in Linneman et al. (1990), while observing some evidence of a decline in the premium at the end of the 1990s.

There are reasons to believe that the union wage gap might vary with the business cycle. If the union premium comes from employers sharing rents, it is plausible that the premium will be higher when those rents are higher, in which case the wage gap would be pro-cyclical. Alternatively, unions may insulate their members from the downward wage pressures workers in general face in more difficult times, in which case the wage gap may be counter-cyclical. In an interesting paper, Grant (2001) used panel data on individuals from the CPS from 1975 to 1993 to examine the cyclicality of union and non-union wages over time. He found that the union coefficients in the non-union sector for the two periods 1975–81 and 1983–93 were always pro-cyclical and generally similar in the two periods. In contrast in the union sector Grant found strong pro-cyclicality in the first period, confirming earlier evidence in Moore and Raisian (1980), but weak or no pro-cyclicality in the union sector in the second period. We come back to this issue later since we find evidence of a counter-cyclical wage gap in the USA and UK in the 1990s.

Raphael (2000) used a sample of workers displaced by plant closings from the 1994 and 1996 Current Population Survey Displaced Workers Supplement files to estimate the effects of union membership on weekly earnings. When models were estimated using the entire sample of displaced workers, longitudinal estimates of the union earnings effect were found to be similar in magnitude to estimates from cross-sectional regressions. In models estimated separately by skill group, the author found some evidence of positive selection into unions among workers with low observed skills and negative selection into unions among workers with high observed skills. Finally, Wunnava and Okunade (1996) used data for men from the Panel Survey of Income Dynamics and found an overall union wage premium of about 12 per cent for the 1980s, which is a good deal lower than reported in most other studies and possibly driven by measurement error in the union status variable. In response to fluctuations in local labour market conditions, proxied by the local unemployment rate, they found a much more flexible wage-setting process in the non-union sector relative to the union sector. The long-term effect of unemployment on non-union real wages suggested an approximate 0.6 per cent decline for every one percentage point increase in unemployment, but the long-term effect of unemployment on real wages of union members was negligible. Wunnava and Okunade's estimates of the union wage premium ranged between 11.6 to 12.3 per cent for the sample period. Union wages were found to be insensitive to short-run fluctuations in local labour market conditions, and counter-cyclical in nature.

In the UK there have been approximately 30 studies, some based on establishment data[5] and others on individual data (including some using linked employer–employee data).[6] It needs to be pointed out at the outset that industrial relations are rather more complex in Britain than they are in the United States. For example, in Britain many more non-members work in workplaces that are covered by union agreements and, conversely, more union members are employed in workplaces where unions are not engaged in pay bargaining than is true for the USA. There is, correspondingly, a multi-faceted literature in the UK which has investigated the free-rider problem (see Booth and Bryan, 2001; Hildreth, 2000) as well as the importance of union recognition (Blanchflower, 1984; 1986), multiple unionism (Machin et al., 1993) and closed shops (Metcalf and Stewart, 1992; Blanchflower et al., 1989; Stewart, 1987). (There are one or two papers in the USA also on the role of coverage, including Budd and Na, 2000, and Schumacher, 1999.) Because we are interested in the benefits accruing to individuals through their membership, this is not the path we will follow here: our main focus is a comparative one involving the benefits of union *membership* on wages.

The recent spate of studies that have looked at the impact of union membership on wages has been occasioned by a growing belief that the union wage premium may be falling in Britain. Some argue that a decline in the average union premium is consistent with diminishing union influence over pay setting. There is certainly evidence pointing in that direction. First, case studies suggest the scope of bargaining has narrowed substantially in companies that continue to bargain with unions (Brown et al., 1998). Second, pay settlements in the private sector during 1997/98 were no greater where trade unions were involved than in their absence (Forth and Millward, 2000b). Third, even where managers say employees have their pay set through workplace-level or organization-level collective bargaining, union representatives and officials are either not involved or are only consulted in a substantial minority of cases (Millward et al., 2001). But there is also evidence to the contrary. For example, unions continue to have a substantial effect on pay structures, bringing up the wages of the lowest paid and thus narrowing pay differentials across gender, ethnicity, health and occupation (Metcalf et al., 2001). These studies, which indicate union effects despite substantial declines in union density, might suggest that those unions that have survived are the stronger and, as such, better able to command a wage premium (thus raising the 'batting average' of unions). Here we briefly review what studies to date have told us about the size of the union wage premium over time and across workers.

The consensus in the earlier literature was that the mean union wage gap was approximately 10 per cent (Blanchflower, 1999). Despite the rapid decline in union density experienced in the UK since 1979, there was evidence to suggest that the gap remained roughly constant from 1970 – the year for which the earliest estimate is available (Shah, 1984) – to 1995 (see Blanchflower, 1999). However, there is some dispute on this question, with some studies pointing to trends in either direction. For instance, establishment-level analyses indicated that the union wage premium in the early 1980s was most evident where unions were strong, as indicated by the presence of a closed shop (Stewart, 1987). This premium seems to have declined in the second half of the 1980s, a trend which has been attributed to a decline in the incidence and impact of the closed shop, coupled with unions' inability to establish differentials in new workplaces (Stewart, 1995). On the other hand, Andrews et al. (1998a) find the bargaining coverage differential over the period 1975–94 moved counter-cyclically, with an underlying upward trend which they attribute to the decentralization of pay bargaining. In addition to cross-sectional estimates, there has been a series of papers producing estimates for this period based on longitudinal data for Britain using the British Household Panel Survey (Machin, 2001; Swaffield, 2001; Blanchflower, 1999; Hildreth, 1999). As noted earlier, and as both Lewis (1986) and Freeman (1984) pointed out, these estimates tend to be below the estimates obtained by OLS because of a downward bias induced by measurement error in the classification of union status. As also noted earlier, OLS estimates may be upwardly biased if unobserved heterogeneity accounts for some of wage variation attributed to union membership. Thus, for example, in Blanchflower (1999) the OLS estimate for the years 1991–93 was 10.6 per cent compared with 3.7 per cent when a full set of people fixed effects were included.[7] As Freeman (1984, p. 24) has suggested, it may well be that the cross-section and fixed effect or 'panel' estimates of the impact of unions on wages 'bound the true impact of unionism'.

Studies using individual pay data covering the first half of the 1990s also suggested that, while the union effect was persisting, the premium declined for some workers (Blanchflower, 1999; Hildreth, 1999). For example, Hildreth (1999, p. 7) argues that stability in the union premium for blue-collar male workers in 1991–95 compared with a declining premium for their white-collar counterparts may reflect their respective abilities to maintain their bargaining power. The picture emerging from research through to 1998/99 is suggestive of a more widespread decline in the premium. Machin's (2001) analysis of longitudinal data from the British Household Panel Survey indicates that, although there was a wage gain for people moving into union jobs in the early 1990s, this had disappeared by the late 1990s. Booth and Bryan (2001) using linked employer–employee data for 1998 also found no significant wage premium. Bryson (2002) finds a membership premium for covered workers, but it is much smaller than the 10 per cent common in the literature. Furthermore, the premium is confined to employees in older workplaces and those with high union density. Forth and Millward (2000a) find the premium was confined to workers in workplaces with high bargaining coverage or multiple unions.

It would be hasty to assert, on the basis of this evidence alone, that unions' ability to secure better than market rates for their workers has declined since the 1980s because methodological and data differences across studies make comparisons extremely difficult (Andrews et al., 1998b). It is even more difficult to establish what has happened to the trend over time. As Lanot and Walker (1998, p. 343) note: 'the existing literature says little about how the differential has changed over time. Different studies at different times have different specifications and there are so few studies it is difficult to take a view of whether there is any systematic movement over time'. For instance, using standard regression techniques deployed in most studies, Booth and Bryan (2001, p. 12) identify a membership premium of roughly 10 per cent. Bryson reports a similar regression-adjusted premium for the private sector (2002, p. 25). However, in both cases, the authors lay emphasis on the results they obtain through the use of other techniques (instrumental variables in the case of Booth and Bryan and propensity score matching in Bryson's case).

The disaggregated pattern of results reported by Lewis (1986) for the USA appear to be broadly repeated for the UK. The main exception is that the wage gap in the UK appears to be larger for females than it is for males (see Blanchflower, 1999; Main, 1996). We explore this issue in more detail below.

In what follows a series of estimates for the union wage gap since 1973 are presented. What is the size of the union wage gap in the UK and the USA in the twenty-first century? How much has it changed in the years since 1980, which is the end-point for Lewis' 1986 study? How much do the estimates vary by gender, race and across the public and private sectors? How large is the wage gap in other countries? In the following three sections, micro-data on individuals are used to estimate log hourly earnings equations first for a group of 17 countries and then for the USA and the UK. In the case of the USA and the UK, data are available over time that allow us to examine the time series properties of the union wage premium. Clearly, one would wish to examine the extent to which unions are able to influence the total compensation package including fringe benefits. Unfortunately, relatively little is known about the extent to which unions are able to influence fringe benefits, primarily because of a lack of suitable data. Such literature as does exist – most of which is for the USA – suggests that these effects are large (see Freeman and Medoff, 1984, for the USA; and Renaud, 1998, for Canada). For Britain, Forth and Millward (2000a) find unions enhance pension and sick pay provision in similar circumstances to those where they affect pay. But our data files do not contain information that permit us to examine this issue over time.

Before moving to estimating union wage gaps, it is appropriate to place these results in the wider context of the changes in the labour market experience of the two countries over the last couple of decades; specifically, in terms of unemployment and employment, wage inequality, real wage growth and union density. This allows for some appreciation of the climate in which unions have been operating.

1. Unemployment was generally higher in the USA than it was in the UK from 1965 to 1980. The picture reversed itself in the later period, 1980–99. In 2000 and 2001 the unemployment rate in the UK was below that of the United States, averaging 3.4 per cent and 4.4 per cent, respectively (see Appendix Table 7A.1). Both employment and the size of the labour force increased rapidly over the period 1990–2000 in the USA. Over this period, employment in the USA increased by 14 per cent while the labour force increased by 12 per cent.[8] The UK experienced smaller growth along both

of these dimensions, with respective growth rates of 7 per cent and 3 per cent.[9]

2. Levels of earnings and wage inequality are high in the USA and the UK compared with most other countries, and especially so in comparison with most European countries (Blanchflower, 2000). There was substantial growth in earnings inequality in the 1970s and 1980s in the USA. Since the early 1970s earnings in the USA have become much more unequal between more-skilled and less-skilled workers as well as between workers with high and low levels of education and those with many years of labour market experience compared to those with few. For example, in 1979 male college-educated workers earned on average 30 per cent more than male high-school-educated workers. By 1995 this premium for college-educated workers had risen to about 70 per cent (Blanchflower, 2000). Earnings inequality declined in the UK in the 1970s but increased in the 1980s. Only Britain and the United States have continued to experience a rapid rise in inequality into the 1990s, albeit at a slower rate than had occurred in the 1980s. There is much less evidence of rising wage inequality in other countries (see the various contributions to Freeman and Katz, 1995). Blanchflower (2000), for example, found that from 1973–94/95 at the lower part of the distribution, the earnings of the median worker rose a lot in comparison to the worker at the first decile *only* in the UK and the USA from a group of 15 countries (Australia, Austria, Belgium, Canada, Finland, France, Germany, Italy, Japan, the Netherlands, New Zealand, Norway, Sweden, the UK and the USA). Appendix Table 7A.2 presents four measures of inequality for most of these countries at various points in time, using data from the Luxembourg Income Study. The measures reported are the Gini coefficient as well as the 90/10, 80/20 and 90/50 differentials. The table confirms the high levels of inequality in the US and the UK compared to other countries.

3. In the United States real wage growth has been much greater at the top of the earnings distribution than at the bottom. In the hundred years to 1973, real average hourly earnings rose by 1.9 per cent a year. Between 1973 and 1997, CPI-deflated real wages have *fallen* by about 0.4 per cent a year. The combination of flat average wages and rising inequality means that large numbers of American workers have experienced stagnation or even absolute declines in their real earnings in recent decades. And workers at the low end of the earnings distribution have suffered the most, particularly those in the lowest decile. For example, the real hourly earnings of high-school-educated males fell by 20 per cent from 1979 to 1993.[10] In contrast, there has been considerable growth in real earnings at the top of the earnings distribution. Senior managers and executives have experienced large increases in real earnings over the last couple of decades, and especially so when total compensation including stock options are included. In contrast

to the United States, in most OECD countries (including the UK) there has been strong real earnings growth across the wage distribution. For only one or two countries (New Zealand and Australia) has a rise in earnings inequality implied weak growth or even declining real wages for workers at the bottom half of the earnings distribution.[11] The low-paid in most industrial countries have experienced real earnings growth over the last two decades (see OECD, 1996). In a comparison of seven OECD countries (Australia, Canada, France, the Netherlands, Sweden, the UK and the USA), using data from the Luxembourg Income Study for the 1980s, Gottschalk (1993) shows that only in the USA did the inequality of family income rise more than the inequality of earnings. In these countries, government actions through social expenditures mitigated somewhat the impact of increasing wage inequality.

4. Union density rates declined steadily in the US from 1970.[12] In Britain density increased in the 1970s and then declined dramatically. Appendix Table 7A.1 provides the background data. Since 1991, there has been a decrease in union membership of 1.3 million, a fall over the ten-year period of 15 per cent. The fall in union membership has been steeper for men than for women over the past decade: union density for men was 42 per cent in 1991 and 29 per cent in 2001, whereas that for women was 32 per cent in 1991 and 28 per cent in 2001. There has been an even more pronounced decline in unionization in Australia, where union density was 45.6 per cent in 1986 but only 28.1 per cent in 1998. Moreover, Australian union density continues to fall, with the latest estimate being 24.5 per cent.[13] The decline in density has also been pronounced in Japan and Austria. Some countries, including Denmark, Finland and Sweden, actually experienced *increases* in density over the period (for a discussion, see Blanchflower and Freeman, 1992; Blanchflower, 1996; Ebbinghaus and Visser, 1999, 2000; see also Chapter 11 by Visser in this volume).

Section 3 sets the scene by presenting evidence on the size of union wage premia in 17 countries. In section 4 we make use of data from the Current Population Survey (CPS) to obtain estimates of the impact of trade unions on hourly earnings for the USA. In section 5, data from the UK Labour Force and British Social Attitudes Surveys are used for direct comparison with the US experience. Section 6 discusses the cyclical nature of the wage gap in the USA and UK, and section 7 presents our conclusions.

3.   Union wage differentials around the world

Over the past couple of decades there has been a growing body of literature estimating the size of the union wage gap outside the UK and the USA. There are a number of studies for Canada which suggest that the union wage gap is in the 10–15 per cent range (Donald et al., 2000; Kuhn and Sweetman, 1999, 1998; Lemieux, 1998; DiNardo and Lemieux, 1997; Doiron and Riddell, 1994; Robinson and Tomes, 1984; MacDonald and Evans, 1981). This estimate appears to have remained fairly constant over time.[14] Renaud (1998) provided the first empirical evidence of the impact of unions on benefits and total compensation in Canada using micro data from the Canadian General Social Survey (GSS) of 1989. His results suggest that the Canadian unions increased total compensation by 12.4 per cent, compared to an impact of 10.4 per cent on wages. Even though the union impact on total compensation is 2 per cent greater than the impact on wages, given that benefits comprise only about 6 per cent of total compensation in this sample, the percentage impact of unions on benefits is estimated to be 45.5 per cent. This latter estimate implies a very substantial impact of unions on benefits in Canada, as large or larger than estimates for the USA.

In Australia the range is generally estimated to be between 7 and 17 per cent, with most estimates at the lower end of the range.[15] Blanchflower and Machin (1996) provide estimates of union wage premia for Australia using the 1989/90 Australian Workplace Industrial Relations Survey (AWIRS90) where the establishment is the unit of observation. They found significant wage differentials for labourers and unskilled workers of 15.6 per cent but no evidence of significant differentials in respect of plant and machine operators, sales and personal service workers, clerks, tradespersons, para-professionals or professionals – along with evidence of a negative differential for managers. More recently, Miller and Mulvey (1996) have reported evidence that union premia in Australia are small. Using individual level data from the 1993 Survey of Training and Education, they calculate the union wage effect to be 2.6 per cent for men and 1.6 per cent for women. Wooden (2001, p. 2) takes exception to this result and argues that previous research has understated the impact of unions 'by focusing on differences across individuals rather than differences across bargaining units'. Using data on 11 840 individual workers from 1357 workplaces in the 1995 Australian Workplace Industrial Relations Survey (AWIRS95), Wooden showed that simply including a union membership dummy produces insignificant differentials for both men and women.[16] However, Wooden found that at those workplaces where the majority of workers were covered by collective agreements a strong union presence conferred a wage advantage of the order of 15 to 17 per cent to members and non-members alike relative to workers in workplaces where collective agreements had not been negotiated and where union wage effects were found to be small and insignificant. This does seem to make some sense because in Australia, union negotiated agreements and awards typically apply to both members and non-members within the same workplace, and in the case of awards, to all workers within the same industry. Further, Wooden and Bora (1998) use the AWIRS95 data file and find that the wage premium associated with union membership in unionized workplaces (compared with non-union work-places) is as high as 7.7 per cent. They found this was only the case where (a) all workers at the workplace were union members and (b) where the union was relatively 'active'. (An 'active union' is defined as one in which the senior delegate from the union with most members spends one hour or more each week on union activities, and where a general meeting of members is held at least once every six months or delegates meet regularly with management.)

Moll (1993) estimated the 1985 union premium in South Africa at 24 per cent for black blue-collar workers (19 per cent for black males and 31 per cent for black females) and 13 per cent for whites. Schultz and Mwabu (1998) found that among male African workers in the bottom decile of the wage distribution, union membership was associated with wages that were 145 per cent higher than those of comparable non-union workers; among those in the top decile, the differential was 19 per cent. For South Korea, Park (1991) obtained estimates of 4.2 per cent for men and 5 per cent for women. Wagner (1991) found significant positive union effects for blue-collar workers in Germany, while Schmidt (1995) found small but significant wage differentials of less than 6 per cent. Neither Schmidt (1995) nor Schmidt and Zimmermann (1991) were able to find evidence of significant union wage gaps in Germany for male workers.

In Table 7.1 we estimate union wage gaps for *seventeen* countries from three continents – Australia, Austria, Brazil, Canada, Chile, Cyprus, Denmark, France, Germany, Italy, Japan, the Netherlands, New Zealand, Norway, Portugal, Spain and Sweden.[17] The data used are from the 1994–99 International Social Survey Program (ISSP).[18] The dependent variable is the log of earnings/wages/income with the exact measure used being variously defined across countries but consistent over time. Included in each equation is a restricted set of controls: age, age squared, years of schooling, sector, hours and union status. The samples are restricted to employees only. The small number of controls will imply that the estimated union effects reported here are biased. Given that the same controls are used in each country in each year, our best hope is that such biases are constant over space and time. The quality and size of the data files are not comparable to those we use below for the USA and the UK, and for that reason the reader should be cautious in interpreting these cross-country results. The (unweighted) average differential across these countries is 12.1 per cent.

Countries appear to fall into three groups. The first group of just two countries has a wage differential in excess of 20 per cent, namely, Brazil (40

Table 7.1   Union wage gaps for various countries, 1994–99

Country	Years	Union coefficient	N	Comments
Australia	1994, 98 & 99	.118*	1703	
Austria	1994, 95, 98 & 99	.150*	1404	
Brazil	1999	.337*	803	No education or private
Canada	1997–99	.083*	1682	sector dummies
Chile	1998, 99	.159*	951	No private sector dummy
Cyprus	1996–98	.137*	1272	
Denmark	1997–98	.159*	1058	
France	1996–98	.029	2738	
Germany	1994–99	.037	4115	
Italy	1994, 98	−.003	578	
Japan	1994–96, 98, 99	.258*	2505	
Netherlands	1994 & 95	−.006	1291	
New Zealand	1994–99	.099*	2784	No private sector dummy
Norway	1994–99	.073*	4666	
Portugal	1998–99	.179*	970	
Spain	1995, 97–99	.069*	1490	No private sector dummy
Sweden	1994–99	−.002	3619	

Notes:
Dependent variable is the log of earnings which is variously defined. * indicates statistically significantly different from zero at the .05 level or better. Controls are age, age squared, years of schooling, private sector, hours and union status. Sample restricted to employees. Germany includes East and West.
Dependent variable defined as follows:

Australia	Yearly income in Australian $
Austria	Respondent's personal net income per month in Austrian schilling
Canada	In what range would your own personal income fall in Canadian $
Chile	Respondent's monthly net income in CLP
Cyprus	Monthly gross earnings before taxes in Cyprus pounds
Denmark	Respondent's earnings per year before taxes in DKK
France	Respondent's monthly earnings in francs
Germany	Respondent's net earnings per month after taxes and social insurance in DM
Ireland	Weekly gross income before taxes and social insurance in Pounds
Italy	Respondent's net income per month in thousands of lire
Japan	How much did you earn yourself last year before taxes in thousands of yen.
Netherlands	Respondent's income after taxes in guilder
New Zealand	Yearly income from all sources before tax in NZ $
Norway	Personal gross income before taxes and allowances in 1997, incl. retirement benefits. etc.
Portugal	Respondent's monthly average net income in escudos
Spain	Respondent's monthly earnings in pesetas
Sweden	Approximate income per month before taxes in SEK.

Source: ISSP, 1994–99.

Table 7.2(a)   Union density rates in European countries, 1950–98 (wage
and salary workers)

	1950	1960	1970	1975	1980	1985	1990	1995	1998
Austria	62	60	57	53	52	52	47	41	39
Denmark	56	62	63	69	79	78	75	77	76
France	30	24	20	22	22	19	14	10	10
Germany (West)	38	35	32	35	35	34	32		
Germany							36	29	26
Italy	45	28	37	48	50	42	39	39	38
Netherlands	43	42	37	38	35	28	24	24	23
Norway	45	52	50	52	55	56	56	55	55
Portugal					52		40	30	25
Spain					30	8	10	12	18	17
Sweden	67	71	67	73	78	82	82	88	86

Sources: Ebbinghaus and Visser (2000); Blanchflower (1996)

Table 7.2(b)   Union density rates in non-European OECD countries

	1970	1980	1990	1993
Australia	44.2	49.9	40.8	35.0
Canada	31.0	36.1	35.8	37.4
Japan	34.7	30.8	25.2	24.2
New Zealand	40.8	47.7	45.5	30.1

Source: Blanchflower (1996).

per cent) and Japan (29 per cent). The second group of ten countries have
more modest, but still material, differentials of around 10 per cent –
Australia (13 per cent), Austria (16 per cent), Canada (9 per cent), Chile (17
per cent), Cyprus (15 per cent), Denmark (17 per cent), New Zealand (10
per cent), Norway (8 per cent), Portugal (20 per cent) and Spain (7 per
cent). Trade unions in the final group of five countries have no measured
impact on the wage – France, Germany, Italy, the Netherlands and Sweden.
In these countries, the union wage gap is zero primarily due to the fact that
unions are also able to control wage outcomes in the non-union sector.

Panels (a) and (b) of Table 7.2, which report union density rates for these
countries and chart how they have changed over time, suggest a helpful way
of classifying the observed differences in wage premia.

1. Two countries with dramatic declines in density – Austria and Japan – have estimated differentials in double digits. (Below we shall show the UK and the USA are similar.) In the case of Austria, it seems that a big increase in inequality accompanied this decline in unionization (see Appendix Table 7A.2). Australia and New Zealand have declining density and a positive union wage differential, although it should be noted that the decline in unionization in New Zealand is a very recent phenomenon (see Maloney and Savage, 1996; Maloney, 1998). Portugal also has declining unionization rates and a sizeable wage gap (see Blanchflower, 2001).

2. The distinguishing feature of the group of countries that have union wage premia of zero – Germany, Italy, the Netherlands and Sweden – is high levels of both union membership and coverage, and unions' ability to influence wage setting in the non-union sector by extension of collectively bargained rates. (France is an exception in that it has very low union membership rates but approximately 100 per cent coverage.) It is also clear from Appendix Table 7A.2 that, with the exception of Italy, income inequality is low in these countries.

3. Four countries with significant differentials – Canada, Denmark, Norway and Spain – have all had constant or rising levels of union density over the last few decades.[19]

4. Little is known about the labour market in Cyprus or Chile. According to our ISSP files, union density averaged 62 per cent and 10 per cent, respectively, in the two countries over the sample years.

5. The large estimate for Brazil is based on a single year of data with few controls and less than 1000 observations and should be interpreted with caution.

We now turn to an examination of union wage premia in the USA and the UK, for which countries we have better quality data and more data points. The data will also permit us to examine movements in differentials over time.

4.   Union wage differentials for the United States

Table 7.3 presents estimates of the wage gap using separate log hourly earnings equations for each of the years from 1973 to 1981 using the National Bureau of Economic Research's (NBER) May Earnings Supplements to the Current Population Survey (CPS)[20] and for the years since then using data from the NBER's Matched Outgoing Rotation Group (MORG) files of the CPS.[21] The MORG data for the years 1983–95 were previously used in Blanchflower (1999).[22] For both the May and the MORG files a broadly similar, but not identical, list of control variables is used, including a union status dummy, age and its square, a gender dummy, education, race and hours controls plus state and industry dummies.[23]

Table 7.3   *Union coefficients in a log hourly wage equation for the USA,*
1973–2001

	All sectors		Private sector	
Year	Imputed + Non-imputed	Non-imputed only	Imputed + Non-imputed	Non-imputed Only
1973	.132	.132	.120	.120
1974	.136	.136	.129	.129
1975	.141	.141	.134	.134
1976	.144	.144	.136	.136
1977	.174	.174	.168	.168
1978	.172	.172	.171	.171
1979	.121	.154	.119	.142
1980	.130	.163	.124	.157
1981	.116	.149	.118	.151
1983	.151	.178	.160	.192
1984	.158	.186	.169	.202
1985	.150	.176	.160	.191
1986	.151	.172	.160	.183
1987	.146	.170	.152	.182
1988	.145	.169	.145	.175
1989	.139	.164	.146	.176
1990	.133	.158	.132	.162
1991	.124	.149	.124	.154
1992	.140	.165	.146	.176
1993	.145	.170	.149	.179
1994	.135	.170	.126	.168
1995	.126	.161	.124	.166
1996	.125	.160	.126	.169
1997	.126	.160	.123	.163
1998	.113	.147	.105	.149
1999	.103	.148	.096	.156
2000	.092	.126	.092	.134
2001	.091	.132	.087	.141

Notes and Sources: Dependent variable is the log hourly wage.
a. 1973–1981 May CPS, $n = 38\,000$ for all sectors, and $n = 31\,000$ for the private sector.
   Controls comprise age, age^2, male, union, years of education, two race dummies, 28 state
   dummies, usual hours, private sector and 50 industry dummies. For 1980 and 1981 sample
   sizes fall to approx. 16 000 because from 1980 only respondents in months four and eight
   in the outgoing rotation groups report a wage. Since the May CPS sample files available
   to us do not include allocated earnings in 1973–81, the series in columns 2 and 4 are
   adjusted upward by the average bias of 0.033 found by Hirsch and Schumacher (2002)
   using these May CPS data for 1979–81.
b. Matched Outgoing Rotation Group files of the Current Population Survey (MORGs),
   1983–2001. Controls comprise usual hours, age, age^2, four race dummies, 15 highest
   qualifications dummies, male, union, 46 industry dummies, four organizational status
   dummies, and 50 state dummies. Sample is non-agricultural workers working at the time
   of interview, aged at least 16 years. For 1989–95 allocation flags are either unreliable (in
   1989–93) or not available (1994 to August 1995). For 1989–93, the gaps are adjusted
   upward by the average imputation bias during 1983–88 (.031 in column 3). For 1994–95
   the gap is adjusted upward by the bias during 1996–98 (.046 in column 3).

The first and third columns of Table 7.3 report the union coefficient in log hourly earnings equations for the total sample and the private sector, respectively. Hirsch and Schumacher (2002) have recently shown that there is what they call a 'match bias' in union wage gap estimates due to earnings imputations.[24] They show that this bias arises because currently 30 per cent of workers in the Current Population Survey have earnings imputed using a 'cell hot deck' method. This means that wage gap estimates are biased *downward* when the attribute being studied (e.g. union status) is *not* a criterion used in the imputation. They show that standard union wage gap estimates such as reported in Blanchflower (1999) are understated by about 3 to 5 percentage points as a result of including individuals who have had their earnings imputed. By construction, the individuals with imputed earnings have a union wage gap of zero; hence omitting them raises the size of the union wage gap. Unfortunately, it is not a simple matter to exclude those individuals with imputed earnings in a consistent way over time.[25] Here we follow the procedure suggested by Hirsch and Schumacher (2002). All allocated earners are identified and excluded for the years 1983–88 and 1996–2001 in the MORG files. For 1989–95, allocation flags are either unreliable (in 1989–93) or not available (1994 to August 1995). For 1989–93, the gaps are adjusted upward by the average imputation bias during 1983–88. For 1994–95, the gap is adjusted upward by the bias during 1996–98. Because the May CPS sample files available to us do not include allocated earnings in 1973–81, the series are adjusted upward by the average bias (of 0.033) found by Hirsch and Schumacher using these May CPS data for 1979–81. Time-consistent estimates of union wage gaps, with match bias removed, are presented for 1973–2001 in the second and fourth columns of Table 7.3 for the economy as a whole and for the private sector, respectively. These estimates are larger than those reported in the first and third columns of the table, which included individuals with imputed earnings.[26] In each year there are approximately 160 000 observations for the US economy and 130 000 for the private sector in the MORG; in the May files, sample sizes are approximately 38 000 and 31 000 respectively until 1980 and 1981 when sample sizes fall to approximately 16 000 and 13 000, respectively, as from that date on only respondents in months four and eight in the outgoing rotation groups report a wage.

Table 7.4 reports the estimated wage gaps derived by taking the antilogs of the coefficients in (the second and fourth columns of) Table 7.3 and deducting one. Separate results are reported for the economy as a whole as well as the private sector. Results obtained by Hirsch and Schumacher (2002) are also reported in the final column of the table. A number of facts emerge:

1. On average the wage differential over the period is approximately 18 per cent. This compares with an average of just over 14 per cent when similar calculations are performed using the first and third columns of Table 7.3 which include workers with imputed wages.[27]

2. The size of the union wage gap or mark-up is the same in the private sector as it is in the economy as a whole.

3. There appears to be a decline in the size of the differential since 1995, as the US economy entered a boom period. We later examine this issue in more detail as we find similar results in the UK.

4. The private sector differentials we report in the second column of Table 7.4 are smaller than those obtained by Hirsch and Schumacher (2002) in the third column of the table. Why? It appears the answer is because of the sensitivity of the union coefficient to changes in the controls. We illustrate this by pooling the MORG files, excluding those with imputed earnings data, for the six years 1996–2001 for the public and private sectors combined. The union coefficient changes in the following manner as controls are added:

CPS MORG: 1996–2001 (n=663 564)

1. No controls except time	.321
2. + age, age^2 + male	.203
3. + race (4)	.202
4. + education (15)	.191
5. + usual hours	.183
6. + organizational status (4)	.201
7. + state dummies (50)	.169
8. + industry dummies (50)	.145
9. + 8 1-digit occupation dummies	.157
10. replace 8 occupation dummies with 85 2-digit occupation dummies	.185
11. Hirsch/Schumacher specification	.199
(Age, age^2, male, race (4), education (15), marital status (6), occupation (8), industry (9), region (8))	

Only including time as a control (1996=0, 1997=1,..., etc.) produces a coefficient of .321. Progressively adding controls that are correlated with union status reduces the coefficient to .145 in line 8, which is the specification we use in Tables 7.3 and 7.4. In row 11 we report the specification used by Hirsch and Schumacher (2002), which includes many fewer controls than used in our preferred specification in line 8. There is a large literature supporting the inclusion of controls for local labour market characteristics (e.g. Blanchflower and Oswald, 1994) and industry characteristics (e.g. Blanchflower et al., 1996). Adding occupation dummies, especially at the two-digit level, appears to *raise* the size of the differential by approximately

Table 7.4   *Union wage gap estimates for the USA, 1973–2001 (%)*
          (excludes workers with imputed earnings)

	All sectors	Private sector	Private sector
	Blanchflower/Bryson (%)	Blanchflower/Bryson (%)	Hirsch/Schumacher (%)
1973	14.1	12.7	17.5
1974	14.6	13.8	17.5
1975	15.1	14.3	19.2
1976	15.5	14.6	20.4
1977	19.0	18.3	23.9
1978	18.8	18.6	22.8
1979	14.1	16.3	19.7
1980	17.7	17.0	21.3
1981	16.1	16.3	20.4
1983	19.5	21.2	25.5
1984	20.4	22.4	26.2
1985	19.2	21.0	26.0
1986	18.8	20.1	23.9
1987	18.5	20.0	24.0
1988	18.4	19.1	22.6
1989	17.8	19.2	24.5
1990	17.1	17.6	22.5
1991	16.1	16.6	22.0
1992	17.9	19.2	22.5
1993	18.5	19.6	23.5
1994	18.5	18.2	25.2
1995	17.4	18.0	24.5
1996	17.4	18.4	23.5
1997	17.4	17.7	23.2
1998	15.8	16.1	22.4
1999	16.0	16.9	22.0
2000	13.4	14.3	20.4
2001	14.1	15.1	20.0
1973–2001 average	18.0	18.4	22.4

Notes: Wage gap estimates calculated taking anti-logs and deducting 1. Columns 1 and 2 are taken from Table 3. Column 3 is taken from column 5 of Table 4 of Hirsch and Schumacher (2002).
Source: Data for 1973–81 are from the May CPS Earnings Supplements, and for 1983–2001 from the monthly CPS-ORG earnings files. The Hirsch and Schumacher (2002) sample includes employed private sector nonagricultural wage and salary workers aged 16 years and above with positive weekly earnings and non-missing data for control variables (few observations are lost). The wage gap reported in column 3 is the coefficient on a

dummy variable for union membership in a regression where the log of hourly earnings is the dependent variable. The control variables included are years of schooling, experience and its square (allowed to vary by gender), and dummy variables for gender, race and ethnicity (3), marital status (2), part-time status, region (8), large metropolitan area, industry (8), and occupation (12). Because the sample does not include allocated earnings in 1979–81, the 'not corrected' series are adjusted upwards by the average bias found by Hirsch and Schumacher (2002) during 1979–81 of 0.33 in column 3. All three columns include only workers reporting earnings. All allocated earners are identified and excluded for the years 1973–88 and 1996–2001. For 1989–95 allocation flags are either unreliable (in 1989–93) or not available (1994 through August 1995). For 1989–93, the gaps are adjusted upward by the average imputation bias during 1983–88 (.031 in column 3). For 1994–95 the gap is adjusted upward by the bias during 1996–98 (.046 in column 3).

4 percentage points, confirming the point made by Hirsch and Schumacher (1998).[28] Our view is that it is not appropriate to include occupation controls here as they are likely nothing more than slices (deciles/percentiles?) of the wage distribution itself. In private correspondence, Barry Hirsch has disagreed with this view and argued that occupation dummies should be included because they reflect large differences in skill not controlled for by years of schooling and age. Given that there is a large variation in individual union status within broad occupation groups, his view is that they may be an appropriate control. There is no simple way to resolve this issue – it is a substantive point that does influence the *level* of the differential although it appears to have little effect on the *time-series properties* of the differential. We have simply agreed to disagree on this one and let the reader decide. As ever, the truth probably lies somewhere in between!

The results reported in Table 7.4 are broadly comparable to the estimates obtained by H. Gregg Lewis (1986) in his Table 9.7, which summarized the findings of 165 studies for the period 1967–79. Lewis concluded that during this period the US mean wage gap was approximately 15 per cent. His results are as follows:[29]

Year	# studies	mean estimate (%)
1967	20	14
1968	4	15
1969	20	13
1970	8	13
1971	20	14
1972	7	14
1973	24	15
1974	7	15
1975	11	17
1976	7	16
1977	10	19
1978	7	17
1979	3	13

The estimates for the first six years are prior to our starting point in Table 7.4. It does appear that the unweighted average for this first period, 1967–72, of 14 per cent is slightly below the 16 per cent of the second interval, 1973–79. The estimates for the later period are very close to those we obtained in Table 7.4 – which also average 16 per cent – and appear to have the same time-series pattern. In part, the low number Lewis obtained for 1979 is explained by the fact that the 1979 May CPS file included allocated earners and hence the estimates were not adjusted for the *downward* bias caused by the imputation of the earnings data.[30]

Table 7.5 uses the same pooled MORG file as we used above to examine the sensitivity of the union coefficient to changes in controls for the years 1996–2001, but this time to measure disaggregated union wage gaps. The first row entry of column 1 presents the union coefficient of .145 obtained from specification 8 above, which included a full set of controls except occupation. The coefficient is exponentiated in column 4 giving an overall differential of 15.6 per cent. Reading down that column, estimates for males and females and the public and private sectors are broadly the same,[31] and union wage effects are higher for the young and the least educated, non-whites, part-timers, manual workers, and non-manufacturing. These results are similar to those found by Lewis (1986), who concluded that the gap was greater for blacks than whites; in services than in manufacturing; for construction than for other non-manufacturing; for blue-collar workers than for white-collar; and for private- than for public-sector workers. As do we, Lewis concluded that the estimates for men and women were approximately the same. Further, Lewis found that the wage gap fell as years of schooling, establishment or firm size and industry unemployment rates rose. For age, years of experience and years of seniority the gap at first fell and then increased. The robustness of Lewis's results were broadly confirmed by Jarrell and Stanley (1990) using meta-analysis, although their mean estimate of the wage gap for the period was a little lower than that obtained by Lewis. There is very little new under the sun!

Columns 2 and 3 of Table 7.5 report the results of including both a union variable and a union*time interaction term. In all cases, the interaction term is negative and significant, implying for all groups a significant decline in the size of the premium between 1996 and 2001. The penultimate two columns attempt to enumerate the scale of these declines. In the fifth column headed 'Wage gap 1996' the union*time term is set to zero and the union coefficient is exponentiated (i.e. for row 1 antilog $(0.167 - [0.012*0])$ minus $1 = 18.2$ per cent). In the next column the same exercise is performed for the end year of 2001 when time $= 5$. Hence, in this case the calculation for row 1 is antilog $(0.167 - [0.012*5])$ minus $1 = 11.3$ per cent, implying an

Table 7.5 Disaggregated estimates for the USA, 1996–2001

	Union coefficient	Union	Union*Time	Wage gap (%)	Wage gap 1996 (%)	Wage gap 2001 (%)	Decline 1996–2001 (%)
All (663 564)	.145	.167	−.012	15.6	18.2	11.3	6.90
Male (333 188)	.143	.161	−.012	15.4	17.5	10.6	6.90
Female (330 376)	.135	.152	−.012	14.5	16.4	9.6	6.80
Age <40 (360 458)	.160	.179	−.013	17.4	19.6	12.1	7.50
Age >=40 (303 106)	.128	.142	−.010	13.7	15.3	9.6	5.70
White (514 330)	.143	.161	−.013	15.4	17.5	10.1	7.40
Non-white (149 234)	.175	.192	−.011	19.1	21.2	14.7	6.50
Public sector (116 771)	.134	.144	−.007	14.2	15.5	11.5	4.00
Private sector (546 793)	.150	.167	−.012	16.2	18.2	11.3	6.90
Manual worker (171 688)	.246	.254	−.006	27.9	28.9	25.1	3.80
Non-manual worker (491 876)	.114	.134	−.013	12.1	14.3	7.1	7.20
Manufacturing (107 562)	.093	.105	−.009	9.7	11.1	6.2	4.90
Non-manufacturing (556 002)	.162	.182	−.014	17.6	20.0	11.9	8.10
High education (180 106)	.086	.115	−.019	9.0	12.2	2.0	10.20
Medium education (194 827)	.131	.145	−.010	14.0	15.6	10.0	5.60
Low education (288 631)	.199	.211	−.009	22.0	23.5	18.1	5.40
Full-time (496 727)	.123	.154	−.013	13.1	16.6	9.3	7.30
Part-time (166 837)	.205	.224	−.008	22.8	25.1	20.2	4.90

Notes: 'High education' = at least a bachelor degree; 'Medium education' = some college including an associates' degree; 'Low education' = high school graduate or below. Manufacturing = SIC codes 100–392. Manual = occupation codes 503–889 + farm workers (477–489). Sample is all sectors. Controls are 46 industry dummies, 50 state dummies, age, age squared, 15 highest qualification dummies, four organization type dummies, usual hours, four race dummies, gender dummy and a time trend. Numbers of observations in parentheses.

overall decline of just under 7 percentage points in the differential between 1996 and 2001. The decline has been greatest over the period among the most highly educated and in services (see the summary results in the final column of the table). But all groups have experienced a substantial decline in the wage premium. In 1996, the premium was above 15 per cent for all but three of the 17 worker types. In 2001, it was below 15 per cent for all but three of the worker types.

Is the relatively high differential in the USA an artefact of sample selectivity? In Blanchflower and Freeman (1992) it was argued that this is not the correct way to interpret the data and this is still our view. The reasons given, which are still relevant, were as follows:

1. Evidence within the USA tends to reject the notion that union wage effects are large when union density is small. Union wage differentials tend to be greater, the greater the extent of unionization in the sector (see Lewis, 1986; Freeman and Medoff, 1984), presumably because this gives unions greater bargaining power.
2. If selectivity were the major cause of the estimated large effects of unionism on wages in the USA, similar differences in other labour market outcomes should be expected, which is not the case.
3. Third, the fact that employers as well as workers affect union density makes the direction of the selectivity effect uncertain (Farber, 2001). One might well argue that selectivity operates to bias downward union wage effects as employers fight hardest against unions that have the most potential for raising wages and accept unions when they have the least potential.
4. Massive employer opposition to unions in the USA, but not elsewhere, is consistent with the union demand for higher wages being greater in the USA than in other countries.

All of this does not deny the possibility that our estimates may be contaminated by the reverse effects of density on wage differentials. But any such potential contamination is unlikely to reverse the finding that union wage differentials are relatively high for similar workers in the USA relative to other countries.

An obvious question to ask is: why has union membership and union employment been in decline given the relative constancy of the union wage premium in the years up to 1995? The level of the differential – at around 18 per cent – is still very high by international standards. The United States decides union membership through an adversarial electoral process at plant level, which has evolved into a system where management has a greater say in unionization outcomes than it does in other countries. The benefit to employers in removing unions from the workplace often outweighs the costs of doing so. The costs to unions in organizing recruitment drives is high: Farber and Western (2001) estimate that in order to match the rate of union organizing seen in the 1970s, unions would have to organize 374 000 private sector employees a year, which is much more than is currently being achieved (99 000). Their lower-bound estimate of the cost of doing so is $575.5 million per year, or about $64 per union member.[32] Bender (1997) has further argued that the loss of economies of scale in union organizing is an important factor in explaining union decline. It is much harder for employers in other countries to get rid of unions than it is in the USA. Even in the UK there are only a very few examples of union de-recognition (Millward et al., 2000). Employers are unable to hide from a union; they have no place to go. The decline in US unionism seems to have been driven by employer opposition, fuelled by more competitive product markets, increased international trade and a favourable legal environment, as a result of which there have been smaller economic rents to be shared with workers than was true in the past.[33] Linneman et al. (1990, p. 51) have gone even further and suggested that the evidence of a relatively constant aggregate union wage premium is a 'statistical artifact'. High premium industries, they show, have been increasing their union wage premia and losing employment shares and hence membership of trade unions. Union wage premia in private services, they argue, have held constant or fallen. They argue that even though unions have been hurt by exogenous factors, which have created shifts in demand from goods to service-producing industries, they have been hurt most by the rising wage premia. Supporting evidence for this view is presented by Freeman (1988), who found a positive correlation between the union wage gap and a proxy for managerial opposition to unions, namely, the number of unfair labour practices per worker in NLRB elections. Farber (1990) also concludes that the decline was principally a result of increased employer opposition to unions along with lower demand for union services by workers.

The results in this chapter suggest that the union wage differential in the USA is comparatively high, although there is now some, admittedly weak, evidence of countries with even larger effects (see above). However, it is unclear how much weight should be placed on the latter estimates, which are based on small sample sizes. The decline in union density in the USA does not appear to be an aberration but is structurally rooted in what unions do on the wage front. Whereas in the 1950s and 1960s the large differentials that US unions gained were probably economically justified given the United States' role as world economic leader, the increased differentials that emerged in the 1970s still appear to be a major liability to the future development of unionism in that country.

5.   Union wage differentials for the United Kingdom

Evidence to date is merely suggestive of a declining union wage premium: there are few studies estimating the union wage premium with consistent time-series data, and recent studies use techniques which were not used in earlier analyses.[34] This gap in the evidence is filled by analyses of the union wage premium over the period 1985–2001 presented in Table 7.6. We use two data sources: the Labour Force Survey (LFS) for the UK, and the British Social Attitudes Surveys (BSAS). The LFS estimates tend to be above the BSAS estimates, but in both series there has been a decline in the log hourly union wage premium since 1994 (with the BSAS estimate for 1997 being an outlier, perhaps due to the much smaller sample that year).[35] Although the premium remains roughly 10 per cent in the 2000 LFS, it falls to a statistically insignificant 5 per cent in BSAS 2000, and falls even further in 2001. Both series are based on standard specifications for each separate year (detailed in the notes to Table 7.6). In identifying the union effect over time, we make what we think is the reasonable assumption that any bias in our estimates arising through unobserved heterogeneity is constant over time.

Table 7.7 presents log hourly wage estimates for the United Kingdom based on pooled years from the LFS.[36] It adopts the same format and methodology as the CPS estimates presented in Table 7.5. The purpose is to show the variation in the membership premium across types of worker, and how the downward trend in the premium since the mid-1990s has affected each group. The fourth column of row 1 shows that, for the period 1993–2000, the hourly union wage premium across the economy was 9.9 per cent ($n = 105\,112$). This figure is the exponentiated coefficient based on the point estimate of .094 in the first column. This point estimate for the union coefficient changes as follows as controls are added:

UK – LFS files: 1993–2000 (n = 105 000)

1. No controls except time	.279
2. +age, age^2 + male	.185
3. +race	.185
4. +education	.118
5. +workplace size	.074
6. +region dummies	.097
7. +industry dummies	.094
8. +1 digit occupation dummies	.103
9. +2 digit occupation dummies	.104

Table 7.6   Time-series estimates of union wage gaps, UK

	LFS		BSA	
	Percentage wage gap	No. of observations	Percentage wage gap	No. of observations
1985			3.5	768
1986			11.1	1418
1987			7.9	1277
1989			6.3	1329
1990			6.3	1167
1991			4.8	1097
1993	14.9	8391	11.4	1032
1994	17.5	8301	13.7	1345
1995	14.6	9008	13.1	1359
1996	14.8	9029	7.3	1432
1997	11.4	18227	17.7	506
1998	12.2	18409	11.0	1336
1999	10.2	17357	9.5	1271
2000	10.3	16132	5.0	1426
2001			4.4	1417

Sources: Data in the first two columns are from the UK Labour Force Surveys. The controls comprise industry dummies, region dummies, age, age squared, highest qualification dummies, workplace size dummies, usual hours, race dummies, and a gender dummy. Data in the last two columns are from the British Social Attitudes Surveys. Controls are gender, age, ethnicity, qualifications, manual worker, full-time worker, establishment size, public sector, manufacturing, and region. The BSAS estimates for 1994 and 1995 exclude the public sector dummy because this was not available in that year, while the 1991 estimates exclude the ethnic minority dummy due to the low number of valid cases with ethnicity in that year. In both series, the dependent variable is the log of the hourly wage. In the BSAS this is derived from the annual banded earnings data by taking the mid-point of the respondent's earnings band and dividing this by continuous hours worked. (The earnings band for the top-coded highest earners is closed by introducing an upper ceiling which is 1.5 times the lower band.) Before 1996, the BSAS hours worked question did not explicitly mention overtime hours. The hours denominator used here explicitly includes overtime hours from 1996 onwards. No BSAS surveys were conducted in 1988 and 1992.

The coefficient falls with the addition of new controls, particularly at stages 2 and then at stage 5 when workplace size is introduced. However, it rises a little in stages 6 and 7, pointing to the fact that unobserved heterogeneity can both upwardly and downwardly bias estimates of the union wage premium. As was found above for the USA, the addition of 1- or 2-digit occupation dummies *increases* the size of the estimated union effect. However, in contrast to the USA, the size of the union effect does not rise as we move from 1-digit to 2-digit occupation dummies.

Table 7.7 *Disaggregated estimates for the UK, 1993–2000*

	Union coefficient	Union	Union*Time	Wage gap (%)	Wage gap 1993 (%)	Wage gap 2000 (%)	Decline 1993–2000 (%)
All (105112)	.094	.133	−.009	9.9	14.2	6.3	7.9
Male (51544)	.035	.090	−.013	3.6	9.4	−1.4	10.8
Female (53568)	.147	.168	−.005	15.8	18.3	13.7	4.6
Age <40 (56527)	.095	.147	−.013	10.0	15.8	4.4	11.4
Age >=40 (48585)	.090	.110	−.005	9.4	11.6	7.3	4.3
White (100921)	.094	.130	−.009	9.9	13.9	6.0	7.9
Non-white (4191)	.093	.189	−.022	9.7	20.8	1.3	19.5
Public sector (29712)	.127	.104	−.005	13.5	11.0	6.6	4.4
Private sector (75000)	.052	.097	−.011	5.3	10.2	0.9	9.3
Manual worker (32569)	.157	.200	−.010	17.0	22.1	12.7	9.4
Non-manual worker (72490)	.066	.124	−.008	6.8	13.2	6.2	7.0
Manufacturing (20491)	.041	.104	−.016	4.2	11.0	−2.4	13.4
Non-manufacturing (84621)	.107	.141	−.008	11.3	15.1	8.0	7.1
High education (16237)	.037	.054	−.004	3.8	5.5	2.2	3.3
Medium education (74632)	.095	.144	−.012	10.0	15.5	4.9	10.6
Low education (13903)	.122	.160	−.010	13.0	17.4	8.3	9.1
Full-time (76968)	.060	.094	−.008	6.2	9.9	3.0	6.9
Part-time (27932)	.148	.174	−.006	16.0	19.0	13.4	5.6

Notes: 'High education' = at least a bachelor degree; 'Medium education' = some qualifications below degree level; 'Low education' = no qualifications. Sample is all sectors. Time coded from zero in 1993 to eight in 2000. Controls comprise 61 industry dummies, 18 region dummies, qualifications, 40 highest qualification dummies, six workplace size dummies, usual hours, eight race dummies, gender dummy and a time trend, age, age squared.
Source: Authors' calculations using pooled UK Labour Force Surveys, 1993–2000.

Returning to Table 7.7, the entries in the fourth column show that the union premium is highest among manual workers, part-timers, and women. These are all groups with traditionally low earnings. Conversely, the premium is lowest among the traditionally higher paid, namely, men and the highly educated. In the same way as described for the US data in Table 7.5, the fifth and sixth columns of Table 7.7 use the information generated by a union*time interaction – the data are reported in columns 2 and 3 – to show the premium in 1993 and 2000 for the whole economy and for seventeen sub-groups of employees. In the whole sample, the wage gap dropped from 14.2 per cent in 1993 to 6.3 per cent in 2000. What is remarkable is the evidence of a large fall in the wage premium across most types of worker, indicated by the sub-group regressions. In 1993 only one group of employees (the highly educated) had a premium well below 10 per cent. In 2000, all but three out of the 17 types of worker had a premium below 10 per cent. Those worse affected were manufacturing workers, men, private sector workers and non-whites, all of whom had no significant premium by 2000.

Table 7.8 performs a similar task to Table 7.6, this time presenting differences in the union wage premium for Britain – the BSAS excludes Northern Ireland – but based on pooled years from the BSAS 1985–2001.[37] The first column shows that, for the period 1985–2001, the hourly union wage premium across the economy was around 9 per cent. This point estimate for the union coefficient changes as follows as controls are added:

BSAS files: 1985–2001 (n = 17 934)

1. No controls except categorical time dummies	.196
2. + 5 age dummies + female	.149
3. + 7 education dummies	.108
4. + full-time status + manual	.111
5. + 6 workplace size dummies	.068
6. + 6 region dummies	.082
7. + manufacturing dummy	.087

The coefficient falls with the addition of new controls from stages 1 to 3, rises a little when full-time and manual status are controlled for, then falls substantially with the workplace size dummies, as happened with LFS. Again, as with the LFS, the coefficient rises with region and industry dummies. The sub-group analysis in the first column of Table 7.8 shows that, over the whole period, the wage premium was highest among manual workers, part-timers, those with low or no qualifications and women, again reflecting the LFS findings.

Table 7.8   Disaggregated estimates of the union hourly wage premium in Britain, 1985–2001

	M(1): 1985–2001 (%)	M(2): 1993–95 (%)	M(3): 1999–2001 (%)
Whole sample	9.1 (17934)	12.2 (3756)	5.1 (3947)
Men	6.1 (8969)	11.5 (1829)	1.8 (1898)
Women	11.2 (8965)	11.6 (1927)	7.5 (2049)
Age <45 years	9.4 (12082)	11.6 (2557)	2.4 (2681)
Age 45+ years	8.2 (5852)	13.0 (1199)	10.1 (1266)
Private sector	7.1 (10463)	10.1 (696)	3.6 (2811)
Public sector	10.0 (4748)	14.7 (337)	10.6 (1136)
Manual worker	15.0 (6925)	19.2 (1406)	11.7 (1410)
Non-manual	5.6 (11009)	8.4 (2350)	2.0 (2537)
Manufacturing	9.6 (3973)	13.1 (742)	10.0 (770)
Non-manufacturing	8.5 (13961)	12.1 (3014)	4.3 (3177)
High education	4.7 (5694)	8.5 (1166)	−0.9 (1443)
Medium education	9.4 (6545)	10.6 (1489)	8.1 (1503)
Low education	11.3 (5536)	17.5 (1056)	9.0 (965)
Full-timer	8.0 (14237)	11.9 (2952)	3.3 (3065)
Part-timer	14.6 (3697)	15.0 (804)	13.7 (882)

Notes:
a. Coefficients are exponentiated, depicting the difference in log gross hourly wages between members and non-members, expressed as a percentage of non-members' wages. Figures in parentheses are the number of observations in the model.
b. The figures are derived from the union membership dummy coefficient in pooled regressions for the years stated. Specification M(1) pools the data for 1985–2001 and (where the sub-groups do not preclude their inclusion) they contain the following controls: gender, age, qualifications, manual worker, full-time worker, establishment size, manufacturing, region, grouped year dummies. M(2) is the same as M(1), but excluding the grouped year variables, for the period 1993–95; M(3) performs the same calculation for the most recent period, 1999–2001.
c. Surveys in 1994 and 1995 did not collect information on sector, so M(2) for public and private sector equations is run for the 1993 data only. We tested the sensitivity of results to the inclusion of a public sector dummy in models. Where significant, these are reported in the text.
d. All estimates are based on unweighted data.
e. The dependent variable is the log of the hourly wage. Using the mid-point methodology, this is derived from the annual banded earnings data by taking the mid-point of the respondent's earnings band and dividing this by continuous hours worked. (The earnings band for the top-coded highest earners is closed by introducing an upper ceiling which is 1.5 times the lower band.) Before 1996 the BSAS hours worked question did not explicitly mention overtime hours. The hours denominator used here explicitly includes overtime hours from 1996 onwards.
f. No surveys were conducted in 1988 and 1992.

Source: Authors' calculations using pooled British Social Attitudes Surveys, 1985–2001.

The simplest way to show the impact of the declining union premium across types of worker in BSAS is to estimate the premium for each group before the decline occurred (1993–95), and then again at the end of the period (1999–2001). These estimates are presented in the last two columns of Table 7.8. In 1993–95, only two types of worker (non-manuals and the highly qualified) had a union premium of less than 10 per cent. By 1999–2001, eleven types of worker had a premium of less than 10 per cent. For five types of worker (men, younger workers, those in the private sector, non-manuals, and the highly educated) the membership premium was no longer statistically significant.

Across the economy as a whole, the membership premium fell from 12.2 per cent in 1993–95 to 5.1 per cent in 1999–2001. What is interesting is the way that the premium collapses for some workers. For instance, there has always been a ranking in the premium according to educational attainment, with membership raising the wages of the least qualified most. This is apparent in the second column for the period 1993–95. But what is striking is that, by 1999–2001, the premium for the highly qualified is flattened. Similarly, full-timers saw their premium plummet to a barely statistically significant ($t = 1.97$) 3.3 per cent, while the premium held up well for part-timers. The premium has also held up well in the public sector, among older workers, and among manual workers, but it has all but collapsed in the private sector, among younger workers, and among non-manuals.

The case of male workers is unique. The table shows that, whereas the premium was similar for men and women in the mid-1990s, it was considerably lower for men than for women by the end of the period. However, the picture changes on introducing a public sector control. As note c to the table points out, the public sector dummy was omitted from the results presented because it was not available for the 1994 and 1995 surveys. However, we re-ran all estimates including the public sector dummy for years where the public sector dummy was available to check the sensitivity of our results. Calculating the premia for men and women for 1993 only produces results similar to the 1993–95 pooled estimates but, with the public sector added to the pooled 1999–2001 analysis, the male union premium is estimated to be 6.3 per cent, while that for women is 5.7 per cent. Thus, once the public sector control is included, men's and women's membership premium is not significantly different in the later period. This is because the public sector dummy is negative and significant in the case of men, but non-significant in the case of women. The explanation is straightforward. Because public sector employment and unionization are highly correlated, in the absence of a public sector control the union membership dummy is picking up the negative wage differential of public sector workers among men. For women, the addition of the public sector control makes no difference because there is no negative public sector wage differential among women.

6.   The cyclical nature of the wage gap in the USA and the UK

Figure 7.1(a) plots the point estimates of the union wage premium for the USA, taken from the first column of Table 7.4, against unemployment for 1973–2001. Figure 7.1(b) does the same for Britain for 1985–2001, using the data from the last column in Table 7.6. In both countries the premium is counter-cyclical. Seperate regressions were then run for each country with the union premium as the dependent variable – using the data from Table 7.4 for the USA and Table 7.6 for the UK (when there were observations in a single year from both the LFS and the BSAS, the average of the two was used) for the years 1973–2001. The data for the two countries were they pooled to establish the effects of unemployment, time and country on the

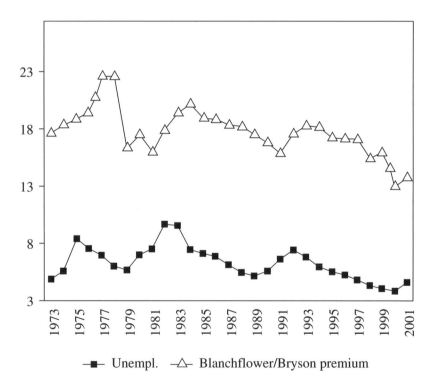

Figure 7.1a   Movements in the wage premium in the USA, 1973–2001

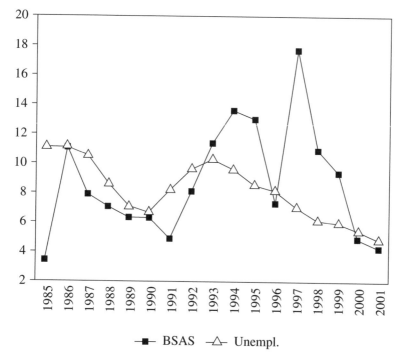

Figure 7.1b   Movements in the wage premium in Britain, 1985–2001

premium. The US dummy was positive and highly significant. The one-year lag on the unemployment rate was significantly positive (*t*-statistics are in parentheses) whether a lagged dependent variable was excluded (equation 7.5) or included (equation 7.6). The contemporaneous level of unemployment was never significant and is excluded in the equations reported below. When the time trend – significant in one equation – was replaced by the union density rate that variable was insignificant and the other results were the same:

$$\text{Premium}_t = 1.465 + .930 \text{ Unemployment}_{t\text{-}1} - .084\text{time} + 8.717\text{US} \qquad (7.5)$$
$$\quad (1.07) \quad (4.54) \qquad\qquad\qquad (1.74) \qquad (10.56)$$
$$\quad (N = 42, R^2 = .773)$$

$$\text{Premium}_t = -0.691 + .407\text{Premium}_{t\text{-}1} + .780 \text{ Unemployment}_{t\text{-}1} - .048\text{time} + 5.300\text{US}$$
$$\quad (0.30) \quad (3.28) \qquad\qquad (3.64) \qquad\qquad\qquad (0.94) \qquad (4.04)$$
$$\quad (N = 42, R^2 = .803)$$
$$\qquad\qquad\qquad\qquad\qquad\qquad\qquad\qquad\qquad\qquad\qquad (7.6)$$

These regressions support the notion that the union wage premium is counter-cyclical, moving positively with changes in the (lagged) unemployment rate. Thus, as unemployment falls, as it has done since 1995, the union wage premium falls; and as unemployment rises the wage premium rises. As the economy moves into boom the differential falls, and as it moves into recession the premium rises: unions are better for workers in slumps than they are in booms. Further, the insignificance of the time trend implies the premium is untrended. So, contrary to what some commentators, particularly British ones, have been suggesting, it seems the recent decline in the union wage premium is not necessarily a secular decline, but a decline induced by favourable labour market conditions. What this suggests is that, when demand for labour is strong, employees are less reliant on unions to bargain for better wages because market wages rise anyway. However, when market conditions are less favourable to workers, the premium rises because union bargaining cushions members from market fluctuations. So, although there are indications that the benefits of membership – as measured by the wage premium – have declined since the mid-1990s, this may be a cyclical phenomenon. The premium may rise again in the face of deteriorating economic conditions currently being experienced at the time of writing (October 2002). Furthermore, although it is possible that a decline in the net benefits of membership has induced a decline in union density, trends in the wage premium can only help explain falling density since the mid-1990s, since the premium was fairly stable before that point. In the years up to 1995 this could be a batting average effect. As union density declines, the more powerful unions are the ones that remain. The weaker batsmen are removed from the batting order so the team's average rises. Another possibility, of course, is that a high union/non-union wage differential provides an incentive for employers to try and reduce union power. The fact that the differential remained more or less constant in both the UK and the USA for so long is a puzzle, particularly given the rapid declines in union membership in both countries. The evidence is not consistent with the widely-held view that union power has been emasculated.

7. Conclusions

This chapter has attempted to address the question: 'What do unions do on the wage front?' The answer in the cases of both the USA and the UK is that, despite declining membership numbers, unions are able to raise wages substantially over the equivalent non-union wage. Unions in other countries, such as Australia, Austria, Brazil, Canada, Chile, Cyprus, Denmark, Japan, New Zealand, Norway, Portugal and Spain, are also able to raise wages by significant amounts. In countries where union wage settlements frequently spill over into the non-union sector (e.g. France, Germany, Italy, the Netherlands and Sweden) there is, as one might expect, no significant union wage differential. The estimates from the seventeen countries we examined averages out at 12 per cent.

Time series evidence from both the USA and the UK suggests three interesting findings. First, the union differential in the USA is higher on average than that found in the UK (18 per cent compared with 10 per cent). Second, the union wage premium in both countries was untrended in the years up to the mid-1990s. Third, in both countries the wage premium has fallen in the boom years since 1994/95. It is too early to tell whether the onset of a downturn in 2002 will cause the differential to rise again or whether there is a trend change in the impact of unions. It is our view that the most likely explanation for what has happened is that the tightening of the labour market has resulted in a temporary decline in the size of the union wage premium. Time will tell whether the current loosening of the labour market, that is occurring in both countries, will return the union wage premium to its long-run values of 10 per cent in the case of the UK and 18 per cent in the case of the USA. On the basis of past experience it seems likely that they will.

Appendix

Appendix Table 7A.1 Union density and unemployment in the UK and the USA, 1964–2001

	Union density (%)		Unemployment rate (%)	
	USA	UK	USA	UK
1964	29.3	44.1	5.2	
1965	28.9	44.2	4.5	
1966	28.4	43.6	3.8	
1967	28.3	43.7	3.8	
1968	28.2	44.0	3.6	
1969	28.0	45.3	3.5	
1970	27.8	48.5	4.9	
1971	27.2	48.7	5.9	2.4
1972	26.6	49.5	5.6	2.7
1973	26.6	49.3	4.9	1.9
1974	26.2	50.4	5.6	1.9
1975	24.6	51.7	8.5	2.9
1976	24.5	52.0	7.7	3.9

Appendix Table 7A.1   (continued)

	Union density (%)		Unemployment rate (%)	
	USA	UK	USA	UK
1977	24.1	53.6	7.1	4.2
1978	23.4	54.3	6.1	4.1
1979	24.4	54.5	5.8	3.8
1980	23.3	52.8	7.1	4.8
1981	21.7	49.9	7.6	7.6
1982	21.0	47.9	9.7	9.0
1983	20.3	46.7	9.6	9.9
1984	19.1	45.3	7.5	10.1
1985	18.2	44.0	7.2	10.3
1986	17.7	42.8	7.0	10.5
1987	17.3	42.8	6.2	9.4
1988	17.0	42.2	5.5	7.6
1989	16.6	41.5	5.3	5.9
1990	16.3	40.1	5.6	5.5
1991	16.3	38.2	6.8	7.6
1992	16.0	36.1	7.5	9.2
1993	16.0	35.4	6.9	9.7
1994	15.7	33.9	6.1	8.8
1995	15.1	32.3	5.6	7.6
1996	14.7	31.5	5.4	7.0
1997	14.2	30.4	4.9	5.3
1998	14.1	29.9	4.5	4.5
1999	14.0	29.6	4.2	4.2
2000	13.6	29.5	4.0	3.6
2001	13.5	29.1	4.8	3.2

Notes and sources:
a. USA: The 1983–2000 Current Population Survey Outgoing Rotation Group (CPS–ORG)
    earnings files, the May 1973–81 CPS earnings files, and the Directory of National Unions
    and Employee Associations, various years. Hirsch, Macpherson and Vroman (2001).
    2001 number from BLS:
    (http://stats.bls.gov/news.release/union2.nr 0.htm), non-agricultural wage and salary
    workers.
b. UK: 1964–92, Visser (1996) and Golden, Lange, and Wallerstein (1997). From 1995,
    source is Brook (2002). Figures for 1993 and 1994 are authors' interpolations using
    overlap in the Visser and Brook series in 1991 and 1992 for the UK and Britain. UK
    figures are union density among employees in employment. UK unemployment is based
    on the ILO definition.

Appendix Table 7A.2   Income inequality measures

		Gini coefficient	Percentile ratio (90/10)	Percentile ratio (90/50)	Percentile ratio (80/20)
Australia	1981	0.281	3.93	1.86	2.48
	1985	0.292	3.97	1.87	2.55
	1989	0.304	4.19	1.94	2.59
	1994	0.311	4.33	1.95	2.76
Austria	1987	0.227	2.89	1.62	1.98
	1995	0.277	3.73	1.79	2.33
Belgium	1985	0.227	2.73	1.62	1.96
	1988	0.232	2.77	1.63	1.97
	1992	0.224	2.76	1.62	1.96
	1997	0.255	3.26	1.73	2.16
Canada	1971	0.316	4.79	1.89	2.70
	1975	0.289	4.27	1.80	2.44
	1981	0.284	4.05	1.83	2.42
	1987	0.283	3.89	1.84	2.35
	1991	0.281	3.78	1.82	2.33
	1994	0.285	3.87	1.85	2.39
	1997	0.291	4.01	1.86	2.45
	1998	0.305	4.13	1.88	2.51
Denmark	1987	0.254	3.22	1.60	2.12
	1992	0.236	2.85	1.55	2.02
	1995	0.263	3.18	1.63	2.19
	1997	0.257	3.15	1.62	2.18
Finland	1987	0.209	2.59	1.51	1.86
	1991	0.210	2.63	1.53	1.83
	1995	0.226	2.68	1.59	1.90
	1979	0.293	3.47	1.87	2.22
	1981	0.288	3.40	1.88	2.25
	1984	0.292	3.46	1.93	2.27
	1989	0.287	3.46	1.82	2.24
	1994	0.288	3.54	1.91	2.23
Germany	1973	0.271	3.22	1.81	2.12
	1978	0.264	3.11	1.78	2.06
	1981	0.244	2.89	1.79	2.03
	1983	0.260	3.11	1.79	2.10
	1984	0.249	3.01	1.71	2.06
	1989	0.247	2.94	1.70	1.99
	1994	0.261	3.18	1.74	2.10

Appendix Table 7A.2   (*continued*)

		Gini coefficient	Percentile ratio (90/10)	Percentile ratio (90/50)	Percentile ratio (80/20)
Italy	1986	0.306	4.05	1.97	2.51
	1991	0.289	3.76	1.85	2.49
	1995	0.342	4.77	2.02	2.76
Netherlands	1983	0.260	2.94	1.86	2.10
	1987	0.256	2.94	1.82	2.07
	1991	0.266	3.02	1.73	2.11
	1994	0.253	3.15	1.73	2.15
Norway	1979	0.223	2.76	1.58	1.88
	1986	0.233	2.92	1.62	1.96
	1991	0.231	2.79	1.58	1.90
	1995	0.238	2.83	1.57	1.95
Spain	1980	0.318	4.37	2.02	2.60
	1990	0.303	3.96	1.97	2.46
Sweden	1975	0.215	2.73	1.53	1.92
	1981	0.197	2.43	1.51	1.76
	1987	0.218	2.71	1.51	1.89
	1992	0.229	2.78	1.59	1.91
	1995	0.221	2.61	1.56	1.76
UK	1969	0.267	3.23	1.84	2.17
	1974	0.268	3.41	1.76	2.21
	1979	0.270	3.53	1.80	2.34
	1986	0.303	3.79	1.94	2.53
	1991	0.336	4.67	2.06	2.95
	1995	0.344	4.57	2.10	2.84
US	1974	0.318	4.92	1.90	2.65
	1979	0.301	4.67	1.86	2.64
	1986	0.335	5.71	2.04	3.04
	1991	0.336	5.55	2.06	3.03
	1994	0.355	5.85	2.15	3.11
	1997	0.372	5.57	2.14	3.03

Source: Luxembourg Income Study; downloadable at
http://www.lisproject.org/keyfigures/ineqtable.htm
All figures relate to disposable income.

Appendix Table 7A.3   *Log hourly earnings equations for the USA,*
                          1996–2001

	(1) All	(2) Private sector	(3) Public sector	(4) Men	(5) Women
Union	.145	.150	.134	.143	.135
	(85.18)	(68.85)	(47.03)	(61.85)	(52.97)
Age	.045	.045	.0478	.055	.036
	(173.5)	(158.2)	(73.14)	(143.3)	(103.7)
Age^2	−.0005	−.0005	−.0005	−.0006	−.0004
	(146.5)	(134.5)	(60.64)	(120.7)	(88.30)
Male	.151	.157	.123	n/a	n/a
	(126.0)	(116.5)	(47.33)		
State government	−.145	n/a	−.141	−.149	−.147
	(36.41)		(34.01)	(25.71)	(26.58)
Local government	−.131	n/a	−.138	−.137	−.133
	(34.79)		(34.04)	(25.40)	(24.85)
Private for profit	−.077	.080	n/a	−.031	−.120
	(21.04)	(30.47)		(6.14)	(22.89)
Private non-profit	−.165	n/a	n/a	−.222	−.157
	(39.94)			(34.81)	(6.42)
Black	−.009	−.012	−.009	−.015	−.004
	(7.20)	(7.93)	(2.99)	(7.71)	(2.09)
American Indian	−.052	−.082	.015	−.075	−.032
	(9.66)	(12.25)	(1.65)	(9.51)	(4.36)
Asian or Pacific Islander	−.101	−.105	−.079	−.120	−.075
	(31.61)	(30.27)	(10.04)	(26.62)	(16.89)
Hispanic	−.112	−.125	−.033	−.130	−.090
	(50.42)	(51.81)	(5.89)	(42.21)	(28.17)
Usual hours	.004	.005	.002	.003	.005
	(76.00)	(76.70)	(11.65)	(40.77)	(63.43)
N	663 564	546 793	116 771	333 188	330 376
R^2	.4655	.4609	.4546	.4581	.4436
Adjusted R^2	.4654	.4607	.4540	.4579	.4434

Notes: All equations also include time 15 schooling dummies, 50 state dummies and 50 industry dummies. Excluded categories are federal government and white. Private sector excludes the self-employed. *t*-statistics are given in parentheses.

Source: CPS Matched Outgoing Rotation Group (MORG) files.

Appendix Table 7A.4   *Log hourly earnings equations for the UK, 1993–2000*

	(1) All	(2) Private sector	(3) Public sector	(4) Men	(5) Women
Union	.094	.052	.127	.035	.147
	(28.07)	(11.41)	(24.54)	(7.25)	(31.73)
Age	.066	.068	.053	.088	.046
	(94.43)	(84.34)	(35.89)	(85.55)	(48.90)
Age^2	−.0007	−.0007	−.0006	−.0009	−.0005
	(82.43)	(73.25)	(31.91)	(74.99)	(43.10)
Male	.181	.195	.158	n/a	n/a
	(55.90)	(49.81)	(28.20)		
Black Caribbean	−.076	−.116	−.020	−.128	−.047
	(4.61)	(5.26)	(0.85)	(4.87)	(2.27)
Black – African	−.191	−.189	−.186	−.272	−.134
	(7.67)	(5.81)	(5.17)	(7.27)	(4.12)
Black – other	−.122	−.105	−.133	−.210	−.072
	(3.30)	(2.11)	(2.55)	(3.75)	(1.49)
Indian	−.101	−.122	−.045	−.094	−.107
	(7.96)	(8.23)	(1.85)	(5.23)	(6.05)
Pakistani	−.110	−.165	.067	−.143	−.043
	(4.94)	(6.43)	(1.57)	(4.91)	(1.28)
Bangladeshi	−.264	−.395	−.121	−.364	.005
	(6.09)	(7.89)	(1.43)	(6.86)	(0.07)
Chinese	−.033	−.018	−.067	−.076	.010
	(0.99)	(0.46)	(1.12)	(1.39)	(0.25)
Other race	−.030	−.021	−.034	−.049	−.022
	(1.98)	(1.17)	(1.38)	(2.19)	(1.10)
11–19 employees	.082	.076	.078	.101	.060
	(14.51)	(11.74)	(6.44)	(11.24)	(8.47)
20–24 employees	.091	.083	.080	.106	.072
	(12.18)	(9.35)	(5.68)	(8.98)	(7.57)
Don't know but <25	.040	.031	.049	.066	.003
	(3.38)	(2.25)	(2.06)	(3.82)	(0.16)
25–49 employees	.118	.116	.090	.135	.096
	(22.34)	(18.82)	(8.32)	(16.64)	(14.05)
Don't know but >24	.083	.084	.049	.100	.062
	(6.49)	(5.37)	(2.06)	(5.66)	(3.42)
>=50 employees	.177	.183	.127	.203	.149
	(43.03)	(38.83)	(13.99)	(31.93)	(28.49)
N	105112	75000	29712	51544	53568
R^2	.4537	.4524	.4256	.4487	.4273
Adjusted R^2	.4530	.4514	.4230	.4472	.4259

Notes: All equations also include time, 40 schooling dummies, 19 region dummies and 60 industry dummies. Excluded categories are one to ten employees and white. Private sector excludes the self-employed. *t*-statistics are given in parentheses.

Source: Labour Force Survey files.

Appendix Table 7A.5   *Log hourly earnings equations for Britain,*
1985–2001

	(1) All	(2) Private sector	(3) Public sector	(4) Men	(5) Women
Union	.087	.069	.095	.059	.106
	(12.30)	(6.50)	(6.69)	(6.29)	(9.88)
Age 25–34	.272	.280	.258	.310	.239
	(23.83)	(19.59)	(11.27)	(19.85)	(14.37)
Age 35–44	.363	.374	.335	.455	.276
	(30.61)	(24.90)	(14.41)	(28.54)	(15.76)
Age 45–54	.370	.377	.362	.462	.281
	(29.73)	(23.42)	(15.22)	(27.34)	(15.43)
Age 55 or more	.375	.384	.339	.427	.309
	(24.91)	(19.43)	(12.02)	(22.20)	(13.18)
Female	−.261	−.286	−.240	n/a	n/a
	(34.44)	(26.98)	(18.46)		
Full-time	.126	.169	.064	.021	.127
	(10.99)	(10.31)	(3.46)	(0.51)	(10.38)
Manual	−.255	−.250	−.277	−.287	−.225
	(29.55)	(22.53)	(16.09)	(25.38)	(16.59)
10–24 employees	.108	.089	.081	.082	.123
	(7.98)	(5.35)	(2.63)	(4.34)	(6.58)
25–99 employees	.146	.159	.063	.141	.151
	(12.02)	(10.48)	(2.20)	(8.28)	(8.88)
100–499 employees	.182	.211	.097	.205	.158
	(14.56)	(13.46)	(3.35)	(11.85)	(8.88)
500 or more employees	.257	.317	.117	.279	.231
	(19.38)	(17.94)	(4.02)	(15.40)	(12.05)
Manufacturing	.062	.047	.115	.067	.044
	(7.55)	(4.74)	(3.08)	(7.07)	(2.87)
N	17934	10463	4748	8969	8965
R^2	.51	.53	.55	.50	.49

Notes: All equations also include five categorical time dummies, seven highest
qualification dummies, and six region dummies. Excluded categories are aged 18–25 years
and one to nine employees. Confined to employees in employment working ten or more
hours per week. Public/private sector status unavailable in 1994/95, so these two years are
excluded from the public and private sector equations. *t*-statistics are given in parentheses.

Source: British Social Attitudes Surveys 1985–2001.

Acknowledgement

We thank John Addison, Dan Feenberg, Barry Hirsch, David Metcalf and Mark Wooden for helpful discussions and John Addison also for encouraging us to write this chapter. We wish to thank the Economic and Social Research Council for their financial assistance (grant R000223958). We thank the BSAS team – particularly Katarina Thomson – at the National Centre for Social Research for providing the BSAS data. We acknowledge the Department of Trade and Industry, the Economic and Social Research Council, the Advisory, Conciliation and Arbitration Service and the Policy Studies Institute as the originators of the 1998 Workplace Employee Relations Survey data, and the Data Archive at the University of Essex as the distributor of the WERS data. None of these organizations or individuals bears any responsibility for the authors' analysis and interpretations of the data.

Notes

1. Some of the estimates are for Great Britain which excludes Northern Ireland. Estimates are similar whichever geographical area is chosen.
2. We have no micro-data since 2001 when labour markets loosened and the unemployment rate started to rise again in the United States.
3. Wessels (1994) has cogently argued that OLS will not necessarily provide an upper limit estimate. His argument is that, provided a union has a certain degree of bargaining power, union-won increases in the wage that lead the firm to hire more able workers will be followed by further union actions to raise the wage. Knowing this and given repeated bargains, the firm will not necessarily hire more able workers.
4. Kaufman (2002) discusses the extent to which this empirical work on union wage determination fits the various economic models of union wage determination that have been developed since the work of Dunlop and Ross. His conclusion is pessimistic.
5. See Forth and Millward (2000b), Blanchflower and Machin (1996), Machin et al. (1993), Metcalf and Stewart (1992), Blanchflower and Oswald (1990), Blanchflower et al. (1990), Stewart (1990, 1991, 1995, 1987), Blanchflower (1986, 1984), .
6. See Bryson (2002), Forth and Millward (2000b), Booth and Bryan (2001), Millward et al. (2001), Swaffield (2001), Machin (2001), Forth and Millward (2000a), Blanchflower (1999), Hildreth (2000, 1999), Andrews et al. (1998a, 1998b), Lanot and Walker (1998), Main (1996), Main and Reilly (1992), Murphy et al. (1992), Blanchflower (1991), Blackaby et al. (1991), Yaron (1990), Green (1988), Symons and Walker (1988), Shah (1984), and Stewart (1983).
7. Unfortunately the BHPS data file is very small in size with only around 4000 workers present in consecutive waves and hence there are very few individuals that change status from year to year. This means there are severe limitations to using BHPS to compare the sensitivity of union wage gap estimates to differences in methodology as in Andrews et al. (1998b).
8. Source: *Statistical Abstract of the US, 2002*, Table no. 567 downloadable at http://www.census.gov/prod/2002pubs/01statab/stat-ab01.html
9. Source: UK Office of National Statistics. Downloadable from http://www.statistics.gov.uk/statbase/TSDtimezone.asp
10. Freeman (1995) and Mishel and Bernstein (1994) report declines of this magnitude.
11. For more information on changes in real wages, see OECD (1996) and Katz et al. (1995) for the UK, the USA, France and Japan.
12. Interestingly enough, Canada with many of the same firms and trade unions as the USA

has not seen declines in density: 1970 = 31 per cent, 1980 = 36.1 per cent; 1990 = 35.8 per cent; 1993 = 37.4 per cent (see Visser, 1996).

13. We thank Mark Wooden for providing us with these numbers.
14. Further examples of studies for Canada are Simpson (1985), who found 11 per cent for 1974; Grant et al. (1987) who reported 12–14 per cent for 1969 and 13–16 per cent for 1970.
15. Australian studies include Kornfeld (1993), who found 7–10 per cent for young people between 1984 and 1987; Mulvey (1986), who obtained estimates of 7 per cent for women and 10 per cent for men using a 1982 sample; Christie (1992) who obtained an estimate of 16.6 per cent using OLS and 17.2 per cent using simultaneous equation methods with 1984 data; and Blanchflower and Freeman (1992) who report 8 per cent for the period 1985–87.
16. In note 35 below we make use of individual level data from a similar survey undertaken in the UK, namely, the 1998 Workplace Employee Relations Survey.
17. In Blanchflower (1996) union wage gap estimates were obtained based on similar data and specifications for the following countries (in per cent, * indicates not significantly different from zero):
   Australia (9.2), Austria (14.6), Canada (4.8*), Germany (3.4), Ireland (30.5), Israel (7.0*), Italy (7.2), Japan (47.8), Netherlands (3.7*), New Zealand (8.4), Norway (7.7), Spain (0.3*), Switzerland (0.8*). The very large estimate for Japan appears to arise because of the lack of controls for workplace/firm size. Some of the estimates are based on only a few hundred observations and so care has to be taken in interpreting these results.
18. Details of the ISSP surveys, data and manuals are available at www.issp.org. The data files are also available through ICPSR at the University of Michigan at http://www.icpsr.umich.edu.
19. Troy (2000) has argued that union density in Canada has remained as high as it has due to the expanded role of the public sector and quasi-public sector organizations (particularly in health care). Troy shows that private sector density – in contrast to that in the public sector – has declined albeit at a somewhat slower rate than in the USA.
20. The May extracts of the CPS extracts in Stata format from 1969–1987 are available from the NBER at http://www.nber.org/data/cps_may.html.
21. Hirsch et al. (2002) have compared union wage gap estimates obtained from the BLS quarterly Employment Cost Index (ECI) constructed from establishment surveys and from the annual Employer Costs for Employee Compensation (ECEC) with those obtained using the CPS. They find that union/non-union wage trends in the three series 'are consistent neither with each other nor with the CPS', and ultimately conclude that 'we find ourselves relying most heavily on results drawn from the CPS' (Hirsch et al., 2002, p. 23).
22. There was no CPS survey with wages and union status in 1982.
23. Following Mincer, it is more usual to include a term in potential experience rather than a direct measure of age. We use education, however, for reasons of comparability as the CPS Outgoing Rotation Group files from 1993 report qualifications rather than years of schooling.
24. We do not deal here with a further problem identified by Card (1996) of misclassification of self-reported union status in the CPS, first identified by Mellow and Sider (1983). Card concludes that about 2.7 per cent are false positives and 2.7 per cent are false negatives. Given that there are more non-union workers than union workers, this means the union density rate is biased upwards. See Farber (2001) for a discussion and a procedure to adjust the union density rate for error. In 1998, the observed private sector rate of 9.7 per cent translates to an adjusted rate of 7.4 per cent (the figures for 1973 were 25.9 per cent and 24.5 per cent respectively).
25. The number of wage observations followed by the percentage imputed in parentheses (hourly + non-hourly paid) in the NBER MORG are given below. Note in 1995, allocation information is only available on one-third of wage observations, hence the small sample.

1979 171745 (16.5%)	1987 180434 (13.5%)	1995 55967 (23.3%)
1980 199469 (15.8%)	1988 173118 (14.4%)	1996 152190 (22.2%)
1981 186923 (15.2%)	1989 176411 (3.7%)	1997 154955 (22.2%)
1982 175797 (13.7%)	1990 185030 (3.9%)	1998 156990 (23.6%)
1983 173932 (13.8%)	1991 179560 (4.4%)	1999 159362 (27.6%)
1984 177248 (14.7%)	1992 176848 (4.2%)	2000 161126 (29.8%)
1985 180232 (14.3%)	1993 174595 (4.6%)	2001 171533 (30.9%)
1986 179147 (10.7%)	1994 170865 (0%)	

26. We thank Barry Hirsch for helpful discussions on these issues. All errors are ours of course and not his!
27. Bratsberg and Ragan (2002) found an average premium in the private sector of 16.8 per cent, 1971–99, using a set of control variables similar to those used by Hirsch and Schumacher (2002).
28. There was essentially no difference in the results when two-digit occupation dummies were replaced with three-digit dummies (results not reported).
29. There is a dissonance between the estimates Lewis offers by way of summary in his introductory chapter and those given in his Table 9.7 which are produced here (Lewis, 1986, p. 9).
30. Lewis (1986) had 35 studies using the CPS, 1970–79; 16 studies using the 1967 Survey of Economic Opportunity; 25 studies using the Panel Study of Income Dynamics, 1967–78; 15 studies using Michigan Survey Research Center survey data other than the PSID, including the 1972–73 Quality of Employment Survey; 22 studies using the National Longitudinal Surveys of 1969–72; and eight studies exploiting other sources.
31. Full equations for the USA as a whole as well as disaggregations by gender and broad sector are reported in Appendix Table 7A.3.
32. Even activism on this scale would yield a steady state private sector unionization rate of just 6.4 per cent (Farber and Western, 2001).
33. For further discussion on this point, see Blanchflower and Freeman (1992).
34. Blanchflower (1999) estimated union wage premia for the UK using the same methods as used here for the period 1983–94 using data from the same sources as used here plus the British Household Panel Survey for 1991–93 and the 1983 General Household Survey and found evidence of a constancy of the differential at approximately 10 per cent.
35. Further support for the proposition that the BSAS 1997 point estimate is an outlier comes from the authors' calculations of the log hourly wage premium using the same methodology (unweighted estimates of the mid-point earnings) for individual level data from the Workplace Employee Relations Survey 1998, the fieldwork for which spanned 1997 and 1998. The raw membership premium is .226 (25.4 per cent). This shifts with the addition of controls as follows: + demographics = .121; + job = .114; + establishment = .076; + geographical = .091. In short, these estimates also point to a premium of around 10 per cent in 1997/98.
36. Full equations for the economy as a whole, private and public sectors, and for men and women are reported in Appendix Table 7A.4.
37. Full equations for the economy as a whole, private and public sectors, and for men and women are reported in Appendix Table 7A.5.

References

Andrews, Martyn J., David N.F. Bell and Richard Upward (1998), 'Union Coverage Differentials: Some Estimates for Britain Using the New Earnings Survey Panel Dataset', *Oxford Bulletin of Economics and Statistics,* 60 (1), 47–78.

Andrews, Martyn J., Mark B. Stewart, Joanna K. Swaffield and Richard Upward (1998), 'The Estimation of Union Wage Differentials and the Impact of Methodological Choices', *Labour Economics,* 5 (4), 449–474.

Bender, Keith A. (1997), 'The Changing Determinants of U.S. Unionism: An Analysis Using Worker-Level Data', *Journal of Labor Research,* 18 (3), 403–423.

Blackaby, David H., P.D. Murphy and Peter J. Sloane (1991), 'Union Membership, Collective Bargaining Coverage and the Trade Union Mark-Up for Britain', *Economics Letters*, 36 (2), 203–208.

Blanchflower, David G. (1984), 'Union Relative Wage Effects: A Cross-Section Analysis Using Establishment Data', *British Journal of Industrial Relations*, 22 (3), 311–332.

Blanchflower, David G. (1986), 'What Effect Do Unions Have on Relative Wages in Great Britain?', *British Journal of Industrial Relations*, 24 (2), 196–204.

Blanchflower, David G. (1991), 'Fear, Unemployment and Pay Flexibility', *Economic Journal*, 101 (406), 483–496.

Blanchflower, David G. (1996), 'The Role and Influence of Trade Unions in the OECD', Report to the Bureau of International Labor Affairs, Washington, DC: US Department of Labor, August.

Blanchflower, David G. (1999), 'Changes Over Time in Union Relative Wage Effects in Great Britain and the United States', in Sami Daniel, Philip Arestis and John Grahl (eds), *The History and Practice of Economics: Essays in Honour of Bernard Corry and Maurice Peston*, Volume 2, Cheltenham, UK and Northampton, MA: Edward Elgar, pp. 3–32.

Blanchflower, David G. (2000), 'Globalization and the Labor Market', Report to the Trade Deficit Review Commission, downloadable at http://www.ustdrc.gov.

Blanchflower, David G. (2001), 'Unemployment, Well-Being and Wage Curves in Eastern and Central Europe', *Journal of Japanese and International Economies*, 15 (4), 364–402.

Blanchflower, David G. and Richard B. Freeman (1992), 'Unionism in the U.S. and Other Advanced OECD Countries', *Industrial Relations*, 31 (1), 156–179, reprinted in Mario Bognanno and Morris M. Kleiner (eds), *Labor Market Institutions and the Future Role of Unions*, Oxford: Blackwell, pp. 56–79.

Blanchflower, David G. and Stephen Machin (1996), 'Product Market Competition, Wages and Productivity: International Evidence from Establishment Level Data', *Annales d'Economie et de Statistique*, 41/42, 220–253.

Blanchflower, David G. and Andrew J. Oswald (1994), *The Wage Curve*, Cambridge, MA: MIT Press.

Blanchflower, David G., Andrew J. Oswald and Martha Garrett (1990), 'Insider Power and Wage Determination', *Economica*, 57 (226), 143–170.

Blanchflower, David G., Andrew J. Oswald and Peter Sanfey (1996), 'Wages, Profits and Rent Sharing', *Quarterly Journal of Economics*, 111 (1), 227–251.

Booth, Alison L. and Mark L. Bryan (2001), 'The Union Membership Wage-Premium Puzzle: Is There A Free Rider Problem?', Working Paper, Institute for Social and Economic Research, University of Essex.

Bratsberg, Bernt and James F. Ragan (2002), 'Changes in the Union Wage Premium by Industry – Data and Analysis', *Industrial and Labor Relations Review*, 56 (1), 65–83.

Brook, Keith (2002), 'Trade Union Membership: An Analysis of Data from the Autumn 2001 LFS', *Labour Market Trends*, 110 (7), 343–354.

Brown, William, Simon Deakin, M. Hudson, C. Pratten and Paul Ryan (1998), *The Individualisation of Employment Contracts in Britain*', Employment Relations Research Series 4, London: Department of Trade and Industry.

Bryson, Alex (2001), 'Union Effects on Workplace Governance, 1983–1998', PSI Discussion Paper No. 8, London: Policy Studies Institute.

Bryson, Alex (2002), 'The Union Membership Wage Premium: An Analysis Using Propensity Score Matching', Discussion Paper No. 530, Centre for Economic Performance, London School of Economics.

Budd, John W. and I-G. Na (2000), 'The Union Membership Wage Premium for Employees Covered by Collective Bargaining Agreements', *Journal of Labor Economics*, 18 (4), 783–807.

Card, David (1996), 'The Effect of Unions on the Structure of Wages: A Longitudinal Analysis', *Econometrica*, 64 (4), 957–979.

Christie, Virginia (1992), 'Union Wage Effects and the Probability of Union Membership', *Economic Record*, 68 (200), 43–56.

DiNardo, John and Thomas Lemieux (1997), 'Diverging Male Wage Inequality in the United

States and Canada, 1981–1988: Do Institutions Explain the Difference?', *Industrial and Labor Relations Review*, 50 (4), 629–651.

Doiron, Denise J. and Craig W. Riddell (1994), 'The Impact of Unionization on Male–Female Earnings Differences in Canada', *Journal of Human Resources*, 29 (2), 504–534.

Donald, Stephen G., David A. Green and Harry J. Paarsch (2000), 'Differences in Wage Distributions between Canada and the United States: An Application of a Flexible Estimator of Distribution Functions in the Presence of Covariates', *Review of Economic Studies*, 67 (4), 609–633.

Ebbinghaus, Bernhard and Jelle Visser (1999), 'When Institutions Matter: Union Growth and Decline in Western Europe, 1950–1995', *European Sociological Review*, 15 (2), 135–158.

Farber, Henry S. (1990), 'The Decline of Unionization in the United States: What Can Be Learned from Recent Experience', *Journal of Labor Economics*, 8 (1), Part 2, January, pp. S75–S105.

Farber, Henry S. (2001), 'Notes on the Economics of Labor Unions', Working Paper 452, Princeton University Industrial Relations Section.

Farber, Henry S. and Bruce Western (2001), 'Accounting for the Decline of Unions in the Private Sector, 1973–1998', *Journal of Labor Research*, 22 (3), 459–486.

Farber, Henry S. and Bruce Western (2002), 'Ronald Reagan and the Politics of Declining Union Organization', *British Journal of Industrial Relations*, 40 (3), 385–402.

Forth, John and Neil Millward (2000a), 'The Determinants of Pay Levels and Fringe Benefit Provision in Britain', NIESR Discussion Paper No.171, London: National Institute for Social and Economic Research.

Forth, John and Neil Millward (2000b), 'Pay Settlements in Britain', NIESR Discussion Paper No.173, London: National Institute for Social and Economic Research.

Freeman, Richard B. (1984), 'Longitudinal Analyses of the Effects of Trade Unions', *Journal of Labor Economics*, 2 (1), 1–26.

Freeman, Richard B. (1988), 'Contraction and Expansion: The Divergence of Private Sector and Public Sector Unionism in the United States', *Journal of Economic Perspectives*, 2 (2) 63–88.

Freeman, Richard B. (1995), 'Are Your Wages Set In Beijing?', *Journal of Economic Perspectives*, 9 (3), 15–32.

Freeman, Richard B. and Lawrence Katz (eds) (1995). *Differences and Changes in Wage Structures*. Chicago: University of Chicago Press for NBER.

Freeman, Richard B. and James L. Medoff (1984), *What Do Unions Do?*, New York: Basic Books.

Golden, Miriam, Peter Lange and Michael Wallerstein (1997), 'Union Centralization Among Advanced Industrial Societies: An Empirical Study', dataset available at http://www.shelley.polisci.ucla.edu/data.

Gottschalk, Peter (1993), 'Changes in Inequality of Family Income in Seven Industrialized Countries', *American Economic Review*, 83 (2), 136–142.

Grant, Darren (2001), 'A Comparison of the Cyclical Behavior of Union and Nonunion Wages in the United States', *Journal of Human Resources*, 36 (1), 31–57.

Grant, E. Kenneth, Robert Swidinsky and John Vanderkamp (1987), 'Canadian Union–Nonunion Wage Differentials', *Industrial and Labor Relations Review*, 41 (1), 93–107.

Green, Francis (1988), 'The Trade Union Wage Gap in Britain: Some Recent Estimates', *Economics Letters*, 27 (2), 183–187.

Hildreth, Andrew K.G. (1999), 'What Has Happened to the Union Wage Differential in Britain in the 1990s?', *Oxford Bulletin of Economics and Statistics*, 61 (1), 5–31.

Hildreth, Andrew K.G. (2000), 'Union Wage Differentials for Covered Members and Non-Members in Great Britain', *Journal of Labor Research*, 21 (1), 133–147.

Hirsch, Barry T. and David A. Macpherson (2002), *Union Membership and Earnings Data Book: Compilations from the Current Population Survey (2002 Edition)*. Washington, DC: Bureau of National Affairs.

Hirsch, Barry T. and Edward J. Schumacher (1998), 'Unions, Wages, and Skills', *Journal of Human Resources*, 33 (1), 201–219.

Hirsch, Barry T. and Edward J. Schumacher (2002), 'Match Bias in Wage Gap Estimates Due To Earnings Imputation', mimeograph, Trinity University, available at www.trinity.edu/bhirsch/ or www.ssrn.com.

Hirsch, Barry T., David A. Macpherson and Wayne G. Vroman (2001), 'Estimates of Union Density by State', *Monthly Labor Review*, 124 (7), 51–55.

Hirsch, Barry T., David A. Macpherson and Edward J. Schumacher (2002), 'Measuring Union and Non-Union Wage Growth: Puzzles in Search of Solutions', paper presented at the 23rd Middlebury Economics Conference, *Changing Role of Unions*, Middlebury, Vermont, April.

Jarrell, Stephen B. and T. D. Stanley (1990), 'A Meta-Analysis of the Union–Nonunion Wage Gap', *Industrial and Labor Relations Review*, 44 (1), 54–67.

Katz, Lawrence, Gary Loveman and David G. Blanchflower (1995), 'A Comparison of Changes in the Structure of Wages in Four OECD Countries', in Richard B. Freeman and Lawrence F. Katz (eds) *Differences and Changes in Wage Structures*, Chicago: University of Chicago Press for NBER, pp. 25–65.

Kaufman, Bruce E. (2002), 'Models of Union Wage Determination: What Have We Learned Since Dunlop and Ross?', *Industrial Relations*, 41 (1), 110–158.

Kornfeld, R. (1993), 'The Effects of Union Membership on Wages and Employee Benefits: The Case of Australia', *Industrial and Labor Relations Review*, 47 (1), 114–128.

Kuhn, Peter (1998), 'Unions and the Economy: What We Know; What We Should Know', *Canadian Journal of Economics*, 31 (5), 1033–1056.

Kuhn, Peter and Arthur Sweetman (1998), 'Wage Loss Following Displacement: The Role of Union Coverage', *Industrial and Labor Relations Review*, 51 (3), 384–400.

Kuhn, Peter and Arthur Sweetman (1999), 'Vulnerable Seniors: Unions, Tenure, and Wages Following Permanent Job Loss', *Journal of Labor Economics*, 17 (4), 671–693.

Lanot, Guy and Ian Walker (1998), 'The Union/Non-Union Wage Differential: An Application of Semi-Parametric Methods', *Journal of Econometrics*, 84 (2), 327–349.

Lemieux, Thomas (1998), 'Estimating the Effects of Unions on Wage Inequality in a Panel Data Model with Comparative Advantage and Non-Random Selection,' *Journal of Labor Economics*, 16 (2), 261–291.

Levy, P. A. (1985), 'The Unidimensional Perspective of the Reagan Labor Act', *Rutgers Law Journal*, 19 (2), 269–390.

Lewis, H. Gregg (1963), *Unionism and Relative Wages in the United States*, Chicago: University of Chicago Press.

Lewis, H. Gregg (1986), *Union Relative Wage Effects: A Survey*, Chicago: University of Chicago Press.

Linneman, Peter D., Michael L. Wachter and William H. Carter (1990), 'Evaluating the Evidence on Union Employment and Wages', *Industrial and Labor Relations Review*, 44 (1), 34–53.

MacDonald, G.M. and J.C. Evans (1981), 'The Size and Structure of Union–Non-Union Wage Differentials in Canadian Industry', *Canadian Journal of Economics*, 14 (2), 216–231.

Machin, Stephen (2001), 'Does It Still Pay To Be In Or To Join A Union?' Working Paper, University College London.

Machin, Stephen, Mark B. Stewart and John Van Reenen (1993), 'The Economic Effects of Multiple Unionism', *Scandinavian Journal of Economics*, 95 (3), 279–296.

Macpherson, David A. and James B. Stewart (1990), 'The Effect of International Competition on Union and Non-Union Wages', *Industrial and Labor Relations Review*, 43 (4), 434–446.

Main, Brian (1996), 'The Union Relative Wage Gap', in Duncan Gallie, Roger D. Penn and Michael J. Rose (eds), *Trade Unionism in Recession*, Oxford: Oxford University Press, pp. 216–243.

Main, Brian and Barry Reilly (1992), 'Women and the Union Wage Gap', *Economic Journal*, 102 (410), 49–66.

Main, Brian and Barry Reilly (1993), 'The Employer Size-Wage Gap: Evidence for Britain', *Economica*, 60 (238), 125–142.

Maloney, Tim (1997), *Benefit Reform and Labour Market Behaviour in New Zealand*, Institute of Policy Studies, Victoria University, Wellington, New Zealand.

Maloney, Tim (1998), *Five Years After: The New Zealand Labour Market and the Employment Contracts Act*, Institute of Policy Studies, Victoria University, Wellington, New Zealand.

Maloney, Tim and John Savage (1996), 'Labour Markets and Policy', in Brian Silverstone, Alan Bollard and R. Lattimore (eds), *A Study of Economic Reform: The Case of New Zealand*, Amsterdam: Elsevier Science, pp. 173–213.

Mellow, Wesley and H. Sider (1983), 'Accuracy of Response in Labor Market Surveys: Evidence and Implications', *Journal of Labor Economics*, 1 (4), 331–344.

Metcalf, David and Mark B. Stewart (1992), 'Closed Shops and Relative Pay: Institutional Arrangements or High Density?', *Oxford Bulletin of Economics and Statistics*, 54 (4), 503–516.

Metcalf, David, Kristine Hansen and Andy Charlwood (2001), 'Unions and the Sword of Justice: Unions and Pay Systems, Pay Inequality, Pay Discrimination and Low Pay', *National Institute Economic Review*, 176 (2), 61–75.

Miller, Paul and Charles Mulvey (1996), 'Unions, Firms Size and Wages', *Economic Record*, 72 (217), 138–152.

Millward, Neil, Alex Bryson and John Forth (2000), *All Change At Work?*, London: Routledge.

Millward, Neil, John Forth and Alex Bryson (2001), *Who Calls the Tune at Work? The Impact of Unions on Jobs and Pay*, York: Joseph Rowntree Foundation.

Mishel, Lawrence and Jared Bernstein (1994), *The State of Working America, 1994–95*, Economic Policy Institute series. Armonk, NY: M.E. Sharpe.

Moll, Peter G. (1993), 'Black South African Unions: Relative Wage Effects in International Perspective', *Industrial and Labor Relations Review*, 46 (2), 245–262.

Moore, William J. and John Raisian (1980), 'Cyclical Sensitivity of Union/Non-Union Relative Wage Effects', *Journal of Labor Research*, 1 (1), 115–132.

Mulvey, Charles (1986), 'Wage Levels: Do Unions Make a Difference?', in J. Niland (ed.), *Wage Fixation in Australia*, Sydney: Allen and Unwin, pp. 203–216.

Murphy, Philip D., Peter Sloane and David H. Blackaby (1992), 'The Effects of Trade Unions on the Distribution of Earnings: A Sample Selectivity Approach', *Oxford Bulletin of Economics and Statistics*, 54 (4), 517–542.

OECD (1996), *Employment Outlook*, Paris: Organization of Economic Co-operation and Development.

Park, Alison, John Curtice, Katarina Thomson, Lindsay Jarvis and Catherine Bromley (2001), *British Social Attitudes, The 18th Report: Public Policy, Social Ties*, London: Sage Publications.

Park, Young-Bum (1991), 'Union/Non-Union Wage Differentials in the Korean Manufacturing Sector', *International Economic Journal*, 5 (4), 79–91.

Raphael, Stephen (2000), 'Estimating the Union Earnings Effect Using a Sample of Displaced Workers', *Industrial and Labor Relations Review*, 53 (3), 503–521.

Renaud, Stephane (1998), 'Unions, Wage and Total Compensation in Canada – An Empirical Study', *Relations Industrielles – Industrial Relations*, 53 (4), 710–729.

Reynolds, Lloyd, Stanley H. Masters and Culletta H. Moser (1999), *Labor Economics and Labor Relations*, 11th edn, Upper Saddle River, NJ: Prentice Hall.

Robinson, Chris (1989), 'The Joint Determination of Union Status and Union Wage Effects: Some Tests of Alternative Models', *Journal of Political Economy*, 97 (3), 639–667.

Robinson, C. and N. Tomes (1984), 'Union Wage Differentials in the Public and Private Sectors: A Simultaneous Equations Specification', *Journal of Labor Economics*, 2 (1), 106–127.

Schmidt, Christoph (1995), 'Relative Wage Effects of German Unions', mimeograph, Selapo, University of Munich.

Schmidt, Christoph and Klaus F. Zimmermann (1991), 'Work Characteristics, Firm Size and Wages', *Review of Economics and Statistics*, 73 (4), 705–710.

Schultz, T. Paul and Germano Mwabu (1998), 'Labor Unions and the Distribution of Wages and Employment in South Africa', *Industrial and Labor Relations Review*, 51 (4), 680–703.

Schumacher, Edward J. (1999), 'What Explains Wage Differences between Union Members and Covered Non-Members?', *Southern Economic Journal*, 65 (3), 493–512.

Shah, A. (1984), 'Job Attributes and the Size of the Union/Non-Union Wage Differential', *Economica*, 51 (204), 437–446.

Simpson, Wayne (1985), 'The Impact of Unions on the Structure of Canadian Wages: An Empirical Analysis with Microdata', *Canadian Journal of Economics*, 18 (1), 164–181.

Stewart, Mark B. (1983), 'Relative Earnings and Individual Union Membership in the United Kingdom', *Economica*, 50 (198), 111–125.

Stewart, Mark B. (1987), 'Collective Bargaining Arrangements, Closed Shops and Relative Pay', *Economic Journal*, 97 (385), 140–156.

Stewart, Mark B. (1990), 'Union Wage Differentials, Product Market Influences and the Division of Rents', *Economic Journal*, 100 (403), 1122–1137.

Stewart, Mark B. (1991), 'Union Wage Differentials in the Face of Changes in the Economic and Legal Environment', *Economica*, 58 (230), 155–172.

Stewart, Mark B. (1995), 'Union Wage Differentials in an Era of Declining Unionisation', *Oxford Bulletin of Economics and Statistics*, 57 (2), 143–166.

Swaffield, Johanna K. (2001), 'Does Measurement Error Bias Fixed-Effects Estimates of the Union Wage Effect?', *Oxford Bulletin of Economics and Statistics*, 63 (4), 437–457.

Symons, Elisabeth and Ian Walker (1988), 'Union/Non-Union Wage Differentials, 1979–1984: Evidence from the UK Family Expenditure Surveys', mimeograph, Keele University.

Troy, Leo (2000), 'U.S. and Canadian Industrial Relations: Convergent or Divergent?', *Industrial Relations*, 39 (4), 695–713.

Visser, Jelle (1996), 'Unionisation Trends Revisited', Working Paper, University of Amsterdam.

Visser, Jelle and Bernhard Ebbinghaus (2000), *Trade Unions in Western Europe Since 1945*, in P. Flora (ed.), no 2 'The Societies of Europe' Series, London: Macmillan Reference and Gower Dictionaries, pp. 841 and xxli, with CD-Rom.

Wagner, Joachim (1991), Gewerkschaftsmitgliedschaft und Arbeitseinkommen in der Bundesrepublik Deutschland – Eine ökonometrische Analyse mit Inividualdaten', *ifo-Studien*, 37 (2), 109–140.

Wessels, Walter J. (1994), 'Do Unionized Firms Hire Better Workers?', *Economic Inquiry*, 32 (4), 616–629.

Wooden, Mark (2001), 'Union Wage Effects in the Presence of Enterprise Bargaining', *Economic Record*, 77 (236), 1–18.

Wooden, Mark and Bijit Bora (1998), 'Workplace Characteristics and Their Effects on Wages: Australian Evidence', *Australian Economic Papers*, 38 (3), 276–289.

Wunnava, Phanindra V. and Albert A. Okunade (1996), 'Countercyclical Union Wage Premium? Evidence for the 1980s', *Journal of Labor Research*, 17 (2), 289–296.

Yaron, G. (1990), 'Trade Unions and Women's Relative Pay: A Theoretical and Empirical Analysis Using UK Data', Applied Economics Discussion Paper No. 95, Oxford University: Institute of Economics and Statistics.

8 Unions and the wage structure

David Card, Thomas Lemieux and W. Craig Riddell

1. Introduction

This chapter discusses the impact of unions on the *wage structure* – the way in which wages vary systematically with characteristics such as education, age, gender, or occupation. Do unions widen or narrow pay differentials between the skilled and unskilled, between men and women, or between blue-collar and white-collar workers? Is the net effect of unions to increase or decrease overall wage inequality? These questions have long intrigued social scientists. Recently, they have attracted renewed interest as analysts have struggled to explain the rise in earnings inequality in several industrialized countries. The fact that two of the countries with the largest declines in unionization – the USA and the UK – also experienced the biggest increases in wage inequality raises the question of whether these two phenomena are linked. If so, how much of the growth in earnings inequality can be attributed to the fall in union coverage?

The impact of unions on the wage structure depends on the industrial relations system – the social, political, legal, institutional and economic environment in which unions operate. Countries vary widely in their industrial relations systems, and these differences potentially affect both the goals of unions, and their ability to achieve these goals. In some countries unions exert considerable influence on the political process. By supporting minimum wage or pay equity legislation, for example, unions may be able to alter the wage structure in the economy. Unions also affect the wage structure directly through collective bargaining. This influence in turn depends on the extent of union organization in the labour force, and the extent to which collectively bargained wage structures are legally imposed or voluntarily adopted by employers outside of the 'covered' sector. For these reasons, the mechanisms through which unions alter the wage structure and the magnitude of these impacts are likely to vary across countries.

Assessing the impact of unions on the wage structure raises the familiar, but nonetheless difficult, challenge of determining an appropriate counterfactual. We can observe the wage structure at a particular point in time, but we cannot observe what the wage structure would look like without unions, or with a different level of union organization and influence. Some form of modelling is required to estimate the counterfactual. There are a number of possible approaches to this problem. Most progress has been made in cases where the non-union wage structure provides an arguably appropriate benchmark for the wage structure in the absence of unions. Comparisons over time and across countries have also been useful. The former are most compelling when there have been substantial changes in union strength, while the latter are most informative when otherwise similar countries differ substantially in the extent of union organization.

In this chapter we focus on assessing the influence of unions on the wage structures of three countries – Canada, the UK and the USA. These are the countries about which the most is currently known. In part this is because of data availability. More importantly, however, in these countries the non-union wage structure provides a plausible counterfactual. In all three countries there is a relatively clear distinction between the union and non-union sectors, and there is generally no legal mechanism to extend collective bargaining provisions to the non-union sector. If the unorganized sector is to serve as a benchmark for wage-setting in the absence of unions, it is crucial to be able to precisely identify those workers whose wages are unaffected by *direct* union influence. Second, in these countries the non-union sector is relatively large. The relative size of the non-union sector reduces, but does not eliminate, concern that union wage patterns may *indirectly* influence wages in the non-union sector through market or non-market spillover mechanisms. Third, in these three countries the main way that unions influence wages is through collective bargaining. In other countries where unions have a substantial effect on wage policies through lobbying and direct political involvement, the non-union wage structure is unlikely to provide a good estimate of the wage structure in the absence of unions.

After briefly reviewing patterns of unionism and collective bargaining coverage in industrialized countries, the next section lays out a framework for measuring the effect of unions on wage inequality, under the assumption that the non-union wage structure is an appropriate counterfactual. Then, we present a review of the literature on unionism and wage inequality, focusing on contributions written since 1975. The last section of the chapter presents a comprehensive re-analysis of the link between unions and wage inequality in the USA, Canada, and the UK, using micro datasets from the three countries.

2. Union membership and collective bargaining coverage

Two commonly used measures of union influence are union membership and collective agreement coverage, expressed as a proportion of paid (wage and salary) workers. There exist large cross-country differences not only in the levels of these measures, but also in the gap between the two.[1] In Canada and the USA, the differential between coverage and membership is small, typically 1–2 percentage points. In the UK, the gap is somewhat larger, but nonetheless much smaller than in many European countries. The differential between membership and coverage depends on a number of features of a country's industrial relations and wage-determination system. These cross-country differences are important for understanding the impact of unions on the wage structure.

In Canada and the USA, union representation and collective bargaining are regulated by an elaborate legal framework – the 'Wagner Act' model. In this system, workers who meet the statutory definition of an employee have the right to union representation and collective bargaining. The procedures for defining appropriate bargaining units and for certifying bargaining representatives are administered by a quasi-judicial body, often referred to as a Labour Relations Board. Once a group of workers chooses to be represented by a union (usually by majority vote or a card-signing system), the union becomes the exclusive bargaining representative of all employees in the bargaining unit, including those who choose not to formally join the union. Nearly all bargaining units cover a subset of the workers at a single firm – for example, the United Automobile Workers represent the production non-supervisory workers at Ford plants in the USA. The UK has also recently adopted the Wagner Act model, although traditionally its system of union recognition and collective bargaining was more informal.[2]

In contrast to the USA, Canada, and the UK, where highly decentralized firm-by-firm bargaining is the norm, centralized bargaining between unions and groups of employers in an industry or region is the usual case in Australia and many European countries. In some countries these agreements set legally binding minimum pay levels for all employers. As a consequence, there is no logical connection between union membership and collective agreement coverage, and the gap between the two can be substantial. The extreme case is France, where 95 per cent of workers were estimated to be covered by collective agreements in the late 1990s, yet union membership is approximately 10 per cent (see Chapter 11 by Visser in this volume). In other countries, such as Germany, industry-wide contracts are not necessarily binding on all employers, but a majority of employers traditionally adhere to the contracts. In either environment it is difficult or impossible to make a meaningful distinction between the union and non-union sectors.

Furthermore, only a small minority of workers in Continental Europe and Australia has their wages set outside the umbrella of collective bargaining. The case of the Scandinavian countries is particularly instructive. In Finland, Sweden, and Norway powerful confederations of trade unions have organized a large percentage of the labour force, leaving only a small minority of paid workers outside the covered sector. Wage patterns for these workers are unlikely to be representative of the labour force as a whole, and also are likely to be strongly influenced by patterns in the organized sectors. Thus the non-union wage structure will not provide a suitable benchmark for comparison with the union wage structure. The Scandinavian trade unions have pursued strongly egalitarian ('solidaristic') wage policies, and these countries are characterized by wage differentials across skill groups and occupations that are small by international standards. One might be tempted to attribute the compressed wage structure to union wage policies, but these countries are also characterized by close ties between union confederations and social democratic political parties with a highly egalitarian bent. Separating the direct and indirect effects of unions on the wage structure would be a difficult task in these circumstances.

There are two additional reasons for focusing on Canada, the UK and the USA. As we document later in the chapter, the UK experienced a steep decline in union coverage in the 1980s and 1990s. In contrast, Canada and the USA experienced more moderate reductions in the extent of union organization. Thus we may be able to use the different experiences of these three countries to learn about the effects of changes in union coverage on the wage structure. Similarly, there is a substantial gap between Canada and the USA in union density – coverage in Canada is approximately double that of the USA. Since labour markets are otherwise fairly similar in the two countries, the gap provides another opportunity to examine the impact of unions on the wage structure.

3. Unions and the structure of relative wages

The impact of unions on wage structures in countries such as Canada, the UK and USA is determined by two factors: which workers are covered by unions; and how unions alter the pay of those who are covered. To illustrate these forces, consider the effect of unions on the average wage gap between men and women. The economy-wide average wage for either gender is a weighted average of the gender-specific means in the union and non-union sectors:

$$W_m = \alpha_m \, W_m^{\,U} + (1 - \alpha_m) \, W_m^{\,N}, \tag{8.1}$$

$$W_f = \alpha_f \, W_f^{\,U} + (1 - \alpha_f) \, W_f^{\,N}, \tag{8.2}$$

where W_m denotes the average wage of men, $W_m^{\,U}$ is the average wage of men in the union sector, $W_m^{\,N}$ is the average wage of men in the non-union sector, α_m is the fraction of male workers covered by union agreements, and we employ similar notation for women using the subscript f. Combining these equations, the gender wage gap is:

$$W_m - W_f = W_m^N - W_f^N + \alpha_m (W_m^U - W_m^N) - \alpha_f (W_f^U - W_f^N). \quad (8.3)$$

The final two terms in this expression are the average *wage gains* for men and women associated with the presence of unionism (Lewis, 1963). These are the products of the extent of union representation (α_m and α_f) and the respective union *wage gaps* ($W_m^U - W_m^N$) and ($W_f^U - W_f^N$).

The influence of these two factors can be seen most clearly by considering the special cases in which union coverage of men equals that of women ($\alpha_m = \alpha_f = \alpha$) and in which the union relative wage effect is the same for both genders. In the case of equal coverage:

$$W_m - W_f = W_m^N - W_f^N + \alpha [(W_m^U - W_m^N) - (W_f^U - W_f^N)], \quad (8.4)$$

so that unions narrow the gender wage gap if the union wage impact for women exceeds that for men, and vice versa. In the case where the union wage impact is the same for both men and women, we obtain:

$$W_m - W_f = W_m^N - W_f^N + (\alpha_m - \alpha_f)[W_m^U - W_m^N], \quad (8.5)$$

so that unions narrow the gender wage gap if female coverage exceeds that of males, and vice versa. The two effects may operate in the same direction, as would be the case if the union wage gap is greater for men than women and union coverage is also greater for men, or they may act in opposite directions. Indeed, using Canadian data from the 1980s, Doiron and Riddell (1994) concluded that unions raise the wages of women more than of men but collective agreement coverage is greater for males. In this case the net effect – which they estimate to be approximately zero for Canada in the 1980s – depends on the magnitudes of these offsetting factors.

The importance of the two factors may also change over time. For example, the rise of unionism in the public sector in many countries has resulted in more rapid growth (or less decline) of union coverage among women than among men. Other things being equal, this development contributes to narrowing the gender wage differential. Even and Macpherson (1993) estimate that the narrowing of the gender unionization differential between 1973 and 1988 accounts for approximately one-seventh of the narrowing of the male–female earnings gap that took place in the USA during that period. Doiron and Riddell (1994) obtain similar results for Canada during the decade of the 1980s.

As this discussion makes clear, the impact of unions on the structure of relative wages depends on both which types of workers tend to be unionized and on how union relative wage impacts vary across different groups of workers. There are large research literatures on both questions, and these are reviewed elsewhere in this volume. Our focus in this chapter is on how these two phenomena combine to influence the structure of relative wages among workers who differ by gender, skill and other characteristics.

Unions and the dispersion of wages

In addition to assessing the impact of unions on the relative wages of different groups, we are also interested in the effects of unions on economy-wide wage inequality. Indeed, there has been substantial recent debate about the sources of rising earnings inequality in several industrialized countries, and the extent to which changes in labour market institutions may have contributed to these developments.[3]

A useful starting point for discussing the impacts of unions on earnings inequality is a simple two-sector model. Let W_i^N be the log wage of individual i if employed in the non-union sector and let W_i^U be the log wage of the same individual when employed in the union sector. Assume that:

$$W_i^N = W^N + e_i^N, \tag{8.6}$$

$$W_i^U = W^U + e_i^U, \tag{8.7}$$

where W^N and W^U denote the mean log wages in the non-union and union sectors, and e_i^N and e_i^U are random error terms with conditional means of zero, i.e. $E(e_i^N | \text{non-union}) = 0$ and $E(e_i^U | \text{union}) = 0$. Finally, assume that in the absence of unionization, current union members would receive the same average wage as non-union workers: in other words, that in the absence of unions, the mean wages in both sectors would be the same. The observed union–non-union differential in mean wages is:

$$\Delta_w = W^U - W^N. \tag{8.8}$$

Under the assumptions we have made, this is also the expected wage gain that a non-union worker would receive if she could obtain a union job, and the expected wage loss that a union worker would suffer if he moved to the non-union sector. The mean log wage of all workers is:

$$W = (1-\alpha)\, W^N + \alpha\, W^U = W^N + \alpha\, \Delta_w. \tag{8.9}$$

As before, the second term in equation (8.9), the product of the union coverage rate and the union relative wage effect, is the average wage gain associated with unionism.

In addition to affecting the mean level of wages, unions can potentially influence the intra-sectoral distribution of wages. Let $\text{Var}(e_i^N) = V^N$ and

$\mathrm{Var}(e_i^U) = V^U$ denote the variances of log wage outcomes for individuals in the non-union and union sectors, respectively. The union–non-union variance gap is denoted by:

$$\Delta_v = V^U - V^N. \tag{8.10}$$

The overall variance of log wages is given by:[4]

$$V = V^N + \alpha\,\Delta_v + \alpha\,(1-\alpha)\,\Delta_w^{\,2}. \tag{8.11}$$

The effect of unions on the variance of wages, relative to what would prevail if all workers were paid according to the current wage structure in the non-union sector, is:

$$V - V^N = \alpha\,\Delta_v + \alpha\,(1-\alpha)\,\Delta_w^{\,2}. \tag{8.12}$$

The first term on the right-hand side of this equation is a 'within-sector' effect associated with the fact that wage dispersion is different in the union and non-union sectors. The sign of this effect depends on the sign of Δ_v. The second term is a 'between-sector' effect, arising because unions insert a wedge between the average pay of union and non-union workers that is always disequalizing.

Two features of union wage policy contribute to the within-sector effect: standardization of pay within establishments and firms and standardization of wages across firms in a common product market. Standardization of pay within firms arises because unions replace wage-setting based on managerial discretion with wage rates attached to a job or job classification rather than an individual. This characteristic of union wage policy was noted in many studies carried out by institutional labour economists in the 1940s and 1950s. For example, Slichter et al. (1960, p. 602) state that 'the influence of unions has clearly been one of minimizing and eliminating judgement-based differentials in pay for individuals employed on the same job' and of 'removing ability and performance judgements as a factor in individual pay for job performance'. Unions have also attempted to achieve standard wage rates across firms or establishments in a common product market – to 'take wages out of competition'. As noted by Slichter et al. (1960, p. 606) 'wage standardization within an industry or local product market is the most widely heralded union wage policy'. These two features of union wage policy can be expected to reduce wage dispersion in the union sector relative to the non-union sector.

While this simple model provides a useful starting point for discussing the impact of unions on the distribution of earnings, it does not incorporate differences in the extent of union coverage or the size of the union wage effect across different workers. To incorporate these factors it is useful to assume that workers can be classified into homogeneous skill groups – for example, categories based on detailed levels of education and labour market experience.[5] Let $W_i^N(c)$ represent the log wage that individual i in skill group c would earn in the non-union sector, and let $W_i^U(c)$ denote the log wage for the same individual if employed in a union job. As before, assume that:

$$W_i^N(c) = W^N(c) + e_i^N, \tag{8.13}$$

$$W_i^U(c) = W^U(c) + e_i^U, \tag{8.14}$$

where $W^N(c)$ and $W^U(c)$ are the mean non-union and union log wages for individuals in skill group c, respectively, and that the random terms satisfy the conditions

$$E(e_i^N) = E(e_i^U) = E(e_i^N \mid \text{non-union}) = E(e_i^U \mid \text{union}) = 0. \tag{8.15}$$

The union–non-union gap in average wages for workers in skill group c is:

$$\Delta_w(c) = W^U(c) - W^N(c), \tag{8.16}$$

and the union–non-union variance gap for skill category c is:

$$\Delta_v(c) = V^U(c) - V^N(c), \tag{8.17}$$

where $V^U(c) = \mathrm{Var}\,(e_i^U \mid c)$ and $V^N(c) = \mathrm{Var}\,(e_i^N \mid c)$ denote the variances of log wage outcomes for individuals in skill group c in the union and non-union sectors, respectively. Denoting the fraction of skill group c that is covered by union agreements as $\alpha(c)$, the mean log wage of all workers in skill category c is:

$$W(c) = W^N(c) + \alpha(c)\Delta_w(c), \tag{8.18}$$

where the second term is the average wage gain associated with unionism for skill group c. The variance of log wage outcomes for workers in skill group c is:

$$V(c) = V^N(c) + \alpha(c)\Delta_v(c) + \alpha(c)(1-\alpha(c))\Delta_w(c)^2. \tag{8.19}$$

As in a model with homogeneous workers, unions exert both a 'within-sector' effect and a 'between-sector' effect on the variance of wages among the subset of workers in skill group c.

Using equation (8.19), the variance of log wages across all skill groups can be written as

$$
\begin{aligned}
V &= \mathrm{Var}[W(c)] + \mathrm{E}[V(c)] \\
&= \mathrm{Var}[W^N(c) + \alpha(c)\Delta_w(c)] + \mathrm{E}[V^N(c) + \alpha(c)\Delta_v(c) + \alpha(c)(1-\alpha(c))\Delta_w(c)^2] \\
&= \mathrm{Var}[W^N(c)] + \mathrm{Var}[\alpha(c)\Delta_w(c)] + 2\mathrm{Cov}[W^N(c),\, \alpha(c)\Delta_w(c)] \\
&\quad + \mathrm{E}[V^N(c)] + \mathrm{E}[\alpha(c)\Delta_v(c)] + \mathrm{E}[\alpha(c)(1-\alpha(c))\Delta_w(c)^2],
\end{aligned}
\tag{8.20}
$$

where expectations (denoted by E[ ]), variances (denoted by Var[ ]), and covariances (denoted by Cov[ ]) are taken over the skill categories. In contrast, if all workers were paid according to the wage structure in the non-union sector, the variance of wage outcomes would be:

$$
V^N = \mathrm{Var}[W^N(c)] + \mathrm{E}[V^N(c)].
\tag{8.21}
$$

Thus the effect of unions on the variance of wage outcomes, relative to what would be observed if all workers were paid according to the wage structure in the non-union sector, is:[6]

$$
\begin{aligned}
V - V^N &= \mathrm{Var}[\alpha(c)\Delta_w(c)] + 2\mathrm{Cov}[W^N(c),\, \alpha(c)\Delta_w(c)] \\
&\quad + \mathrm{E}[\alpha(c)\Delta_v(c)] + \mathrm{E}[\alpha(c)(1-\alpha(c))\Delta_w(c)^2].
\end{aligned}
\tag{8.22}
$$

This expression can be compared to equation (8.12), the equivalent expression when union coverage rates, relative wage differentials, and variance gaps are the same for all skill groups. The final two terms in equation (8.22) are analogues of the 'within-sector' and 'between-sector' effects discussed previously; when there are many skill groups these are simply averaged across groups. The two additional terms in equation (8.22) reflect variation in the union coverage rate $\alpha(c)$ and/or the union wage effect $\Delta_w(c)$ across skill groups. The first is a positive component that arises whenever the union wage gain $\alpha(c)\Delta_w(c)$ varies across groups. The second is a covariance term that may be positive or negative, depending on how the union wage gain varies across the wage distribution. If union coverage is higher for less-skilled workers, or if the union wage impact is higher for such workers, then the covariance term will be negative, enhancing the equalizing effect of unions on wage dispersion.

The magnitude – indeed, even the direction – of the effect of unions on wage dispersion may change over time as changes occur in union coverage rates or the relative wage differentials of particular groups. Later in this chapter we examine the changes that have taken place in the components of equation (8.22) in Canada, the UK and the USA during recent decades.

The effect of unobserved skills

Equation (8.22) has to be modified if the union and non-union workers in a given skill group have different productivity levels and would earn different wages even in the absence of unionization. Such a phenomenon will arise when workers have productivity-related characteristics that are known to employers but not observed by the researcher, and when the unobserved characteristics are correlated with union status. As before, assume that workers are classified into skill categories on the basis of *observed* characteristics, and suppose that:

$$W_i^N(c) = W^N(c) + a_i + e_i^N, \tag{8.23}$$
$$W_i^U(c) = W^U(c) + a_i + e_i^U, \tag{8.24}$$

where a_i represents an unobserved skill component, and $E(e_i^N \mid \text{non-union}) = E(e_i^U \mid \text{union}) = 0$. Note that a_i is assumed to shift wages by the same amount in the union and non-union sectors. Let:

$$\theta(c) = E[a_i \mid \text{union}, c] - E[a_i \mid \text{non-union}, c] \tag{8.25}$$

represent the difference in the mean of the unobserved skill component between union and non-union workers in group c. The mean wage gap between union and non-union workers in skill group c then includes the true union wage premium and the difference attributable to unobserved heterogeneity:

$$E[W_i^U(c) \mid \text{union}] - E[W_i^N(c) \mid \text{non-union}] = \Delta_w(c) + \theta(c). \tag{8.26}$$

Taking account of differences in unobserved productivity-related characteristics between union and non-union workers, the difference between the variance of wages in the presence of unions and in the counterfactual situation in which all workers are paid according to the non-union wage structure is:

$$\begin{aligned}
V - V^N &= \text{Var}[\alpha(c)\Delta_w(c)] + 2\text{Cov}[W^N(c), \alpha(c)\Delta_w(c)] \\
&\quad + E[\alpha(c)\Delta_v(c)] + E\{\alpha(c)(1-\alpha(c))[(\theta(c) + \Delta_w(c))^2 - \theta(c)^2]\}. \tag{8.27}
\end{aligned}$$

Only the last term of this equation, which reflects the gap in mean wages between union and non-union workers with the same observed skills in the presence and absence of unions, differs from equation (8.22), the expression that applies when $\theta(c) = 0$ for all groups.

The relatively simple form of equation (8.27) depends crucially on the assumption that unobserved skills are rewarded equally in the union and non-union sectors. The formula needs to be extended if unobserved skills are rewarded differently in the union and non-union sectors.[7]

4. A review of the literature on unions and inequality

Until recently, most economists believed that unions tended to raise inequality. For example, Friedman (1956) argued that – principally on the basis of Marshall's laws of derived demand – craft unions will be more successful in raising the wages of their members than industrial unions. Following this logic, Friedman concluded:

> If unions raise wage rates in a particular occupation or industry, they necessarily make the amount of employment available in the occupation or industry less than it otherwise would be – just as any higher price cuts down the amount purchased. The effect is an increased number of persons seeking other jobs, which forces down wages in other occupations. Since unions have generally been strongest among groups that would have been high-paid anyway, their effect has been to make high-paid workers higher paid at the expense of lower-paid workers. Unions have therefore not only harmed the public at large and workers as a whole by distorting the use of labor; they have also made the incomes of the working class more unequal by reducing the opportunities available to the most disadvantaged workers. (Friedman, 1962, p. 124)

As this quote makes clear, Friedman posited two channels for the disequalizing effect of unions. One is the 'between-sector' effect identified in the two-sector model – unions create a gap in wages between otherwise similar workers in the union and non-union sectors. The other is a hypothesized positive correlation between the union wage gain and the level of wages in the absence of unions – that is, an assumption that the covariance term in equation (8.22) is positive.

Even economists more sympathetic to unions than Friedman echoed this view. For example, Rees (1962) suggested that 'theory and evidence' both predict unions will have a bigger effect on high-skilled workers. Noting that union membership (as of 1950) was concentrated among workers in the upper half of the earnings distribution, Rees concluded that the overall effect of unions was probably to increase inequality. Not all scholars accepted this position. Following their detailed analysis of the evolution of the wage structure in several industries, Reynolds and Taft (1956, p. 194) concluded that:

> Summing up these diverse consequences of collective bargaining, one can make a strong case that unionism has at any rate not worsened the wage structure. We are inclined to be even more venturesome than this, and to say that its net effect has been beneficial.

Much of the reasoning behind this position was based on evidence of unions negotiating 'standard rates' that resulted in greater uniformity of wages within and across establishments.

Evidence on these questions was scanty and inconclusive until the widespread availability of microdata in the 1970s. Stieber (1959) examined the effect of unions in the steel industry and concluded that during the 1947–60 period collective bargaining did not flatten the wage distribution. In an interesting contribution, Ozanne (1962) tabulated data for McDormick Deering (a farm machine company) over the period 1858 to 1958. During this century, many different unions unionized the same plant. He found no tendency for unions per se to reduce or increase intra-firm wage inequality. Skill differentials narrowed during some regimes and they widened during other periods. However, there was a general tendency for industrial unions to lower skill differentials, and for craft unions to raise them. In his classic study of union relative wage effects, Lewis (1963) examined the correlation between estimates of the union wage differential and wage levels. He concluded that unionism increased the inequality of average wages across industries by 2 to 3 percentage points.

Some contrary evidence appeared in the late 1960s and early 1970s. Stafford (1968), Rosen (1970) and Johnson and Youmans (1971) found that unions compress the wage structure by raising wages of less skilled workers relative to their more skilled counterparts, while Ashenfelter (1972) found that that unions contributed to the narrowing of the black–white wage gap. Nonetheless, in a survey written in the mid-1970s, Johnson (1975, p. 26) concluded that 'union members generally possess characteristics which would place them in the middle of the income distribution, . . . so that unionism probably has a slight disequalizing effect on the distribution of income.'

Since that time a series of studies has substantially altered the prevailing view. Table 8.1 summarizes the first generation of post-1975 studies. The top panel presents studies based on aggregate data. Hyclak (1979) analysed the determinants of inequality in wage and salary income in urban labour markets and found that higher union coverage is associated with lower earnings inequality, at least for males as a group and also for black males. Hyclak (1980) found a negative relationship between the state mean of union density and the percentage of families with low earnings. These studies suggested that, controlling for other influences, earnings tend to be more equally distributed in more heavily unionized urban areas and states, at least for men. However, they provide no insight into the mechanisms that produce this negative relationship.

Hirsch (1982) carried out a cross-sectional study at the industry level using a model that allows for the joint determination of earnings, earnings dispersion and union coverage. He concluded that the equalizing effects of unions

Table 8.1 Studies of the impact of unionization on wage inequality

Study	Country	Nature of data	Findings
(a) Aggregate data			
Hyclak (1979)	USA	1970 Census data on wage and salary income by SMSA	A 10 per cent increase in union density reduced the Gini coefficient by 0.58 per cent for men and .64 per cent for black men. No significant relationship was found for all women or black women.
Hyclak (1980)	USA	1950, 1960, 1970 Census data on family income by state	Each 1 per cent increase in state union density reduced the fraction of families earning below $3000 in 1970 by 3 per cent. Similar results for 1950 and 1960.
Hirsch (1982)	USA	1970 Census data by 3-digit industries	Each percentage point of union coverage lowered the variance of log earnings by 0.015 points.
Plotnick (1982)	USA	Time series of CPS data for men	Each percentage point of unionization lowered variance of log earnings by 0.065 points.
Metcalf (1982)	UK	1972, 1973, 1978 New Earnings Survey Data	Union coverage narrowed the pay structure by occupation and race but increased it by industry.
(b) Individual data			
Freeman (1980)	USA	CPS data on male wage and salary workers in private sector, May 1973, 1974, 1975. Firm data on expenditures for employee compensation	Union workers had 15 per cent lower standard deviation of log earnings than comparable non-union workers. Unionism reduced blue-collar/white-collar differential by 10 per cent. These effects produced a 2–3 per cent reduction in inequality among comparable workers. The net reduction in wage dispersion was greater in manufacturing than non-manufacturing industries.

Freeman (1982)	USA	BLS Industry Wage Survey data on individuals in 9 industries	Standard deviation of log wages in union sector was on average 22 per cent lower than in non-union sector.
Freeman (1984)	USA	Longitudinal data before and after unionization: May 1974–75 CPS, NLS of men 1970–78, PSID 1970–79, QES 1973–77	Workers who joined unions experienced declines in standard deviation of earnings of .03 to .09 points relative to workers who left unions.
Meng (1990)	Canada	LMAS data on adult men, 1986	Standard deviation of hourly wages in manufacturing was 24 per cent lower in union than in non-union sector. Differential in non-manufacturing was 16 per cent.
Freeman (1993)	USA	CPS longitudinal matched data on men, 1987–88	20 per cent of the increase in the standard deviation of male log earnings between 1978 and 1988 was attributable to declining unionization.
Gosling and Machin (1995)	UK	1980, 1984, 1990 Workplace Industrial Relations Survey	For semi-skilled workers, the decline in unionization explained around 15 per cent of the growth in the variance of log wages between 1980 and 1990.

on earning inequality are larger in both manufacturing and non-manufacturing industries when allowance is made for the joint determination of union coverage and wage dispersion. Metcalf (1982) also looked at the dispersion of wages across industries in the UK (without controlling for the joint determination of earnings and union coverage) but concluded that union coverage widened the pay structure across industries. Metcalf also shows, however, that the coefficient of variation of weekly earnings is lower in the union than in the non-union sector, and that unions narrow pay structure by occupation and race.

The studies in the lower panel of Table 8.1 are all based on individual micro data. These studies follow the important contribution by Freeman (1980), which first laid out the two-sector framework. Freeman also used establishment-level data to study the impact of unionism on the wage gap between blue-collar and white-collar workers in the organized sector. Since few white-collar workers are unionized, this exercise extends the simple two-sector model to incorporate a 'between group–within sector' effect analogous to the 'between' and 'within' effects in the basic two-sector model.

The key finding in Freeman's study – and a result that was largely unanticipated by earlier analysts – is that the 'within-sector' effect of unions on wage inequality is large and negative, especially in manufacturing. Freeman attributed the compression of wages in the union sector to explicit union policies that seek to standardize wages within and across firms and establishments. He also found that unions substantially narrow the wage differential between blue-collar and more highly paid white-collar employees within the organized sector. These two equalizing effects more than offset the 'between-sector' effect that runs in the other direction. In non-manufacturing industries, Freeman concluded that the net impact of unions was smaller, reflecting both a smaller 'within-sector' effect and larger 'between-sector' effect.

Meng (1990), using Canadian data, confirmed that wage dispersion is lower in the union sector than the non-union sector under 'North American' collective bargaining institutions. Indeed, numerous studies have found that wage differences between different demographic and skill groups are lower, and often much lower, in the union sector than in the non-union sector.[8] The residual variance of wages within demographic and skill groups is also generally lower in the union sector.

Analysis of longitudinal data by Freeman (1984) confirmed the finding of lower wage inequality in the union sector, even controlling for individual worker effects. In particular, Freeman documented that wage dispersion tends to fall when workers leave non-union for union jobs and to rise when they move in the opposite direction. The impact of unions on wage dispersion estimated from longitudinal data is, however, smaller than comparable estimates using cross-sectional data. This lower estimate appears to be at least partly due to measurement error in union status.

Freeman (1993) reaches the same conclusion that unionism reduces wage dispersion using more recent longitudinal data from the 1987–88 CPS. On the basis of his longitudinal estimates, he concludes that declining unionization accounts for about 20 per cent of the increase in the standard deviation of male wages in the USA between 1978 and 1988. Using a more sophisticated econometric approach (see the discussion of Card, 1996, below), Card (1992) also concludes that the drop in unionization explains around 20 per cent of the increase in wage inequality during the 1980s.

Gosling and Machin (1995) reach a similar conclusion that the fall in unionization accounts for around 15 per cent of the increase in male wage inequality among semi-skilled workers in Britain between 1980 and 1990. They use wage data at the establishment level from the 1980, 1984, and 1990 Workplace Industrial Relations Survey (WIRS). One drawback of the WIRS is that it only provides limited information on workers' skills and on within-establishment wage dispersion.

Second generation studies
The studies summarized in Table 8.1 significantly altered views regarding the relationship between unionization and wage inequality, but they tell an incomplete story. On the one hand, the first wave of post-1975 studies focused on male private sector workers.[9] On the other hand, these studies essentially ignored variation in the union coverage rate and the union wage effect across different types of workers.

The studies reported in Table 8.2 use variants of the framework underlying equation (8.22) to develop a more complete picture of the effect of unions. To set the stage for these studies, it is helpful to look directly at how the union wage gap and the extent of union coverage vary across the wage distribution. Figures 8.1–8.3 provide some simple evidence on the variation in the union wage gap for men and women in the USA, Canada, and the UK in the early 1990s. These graphs plot mean wages for unionized workers in a given skill group (defined by narrow age and education categories) against the corresponding means for non-union workers with the same skill level. Using our earlier notation, the figures plot $W^U(c)$ against $W^N(c)$ for skill groups based on age and education.[10]

Observe first that if union workers with a given level of age and education have the same average wages as non-union workers, then all the points in these graphs will lie on the 45-degree line. On the other hand, if the union wage gap $\Delta_w(c)$ is positive, then the points will lie above the 45-degree line. Moreover, if $\Delta_w(c)$ is larger for lower wage workers, then the points will tend to be further above the 45-degree line for low-wage skill groups (on the left

Table 8.2 'Second generation' studies of the impact of unions on the wage structure

Study	Country	Nature of data	Findings
DiNardo and Lemieux (1997)	USA and Canada	1981 and 1988 Men only. CPS data (US) and LFS data (Canada)	In 1981 unions reduced the variance of wages by 6 per cent in the USA and 10 per cent in Canada. In 1988 unions reduced the variance of wages by 3 per cent in the USA and 13 per cent in Canada. Wage dispersion grew faster in the USA relative to Canada for age/education groups with larger relative declines in unionization.
DiNardo, Fortin and Lemieux (1996)	USA	1979–88 CPS data	Shifts in unionization explained 15–20 per cent of rising wage inequality for men, 3 per cent for women. Shifts in unionization explained up to one-half of the rise in the wage gap between male high school graduates and dropouts.
Machin (1997)	UK	1983 GHS and 1991 BHPS	About 40 per cent of the rise in the variance of log wages of men was attributable to the decline in unionization.
Bell and Pitt (1998)	UK	1982–93 FES Supplemented with NCDS, GHS and BHPS	Approximately 20 per cent of the increase in the standard deviation of log male wages during the 1980s was due to declining union density.
Card (2001)	USA	1973/74 and 1993 CPS data	Unionization rates fell for less educated men and women but were stable (men) or rising (women) for college graduates. Union densities rose in the public sector. Shifts in unionization explained 10–15 per cent of the rise in male wage inequality, none of the rise for women. Relative shifts in unionization explained one-half or more of the greater rise in male inequality in the private sector.
Gosling and Lemieux (2001)	USA and UK	1983 and 1998 CPS data (US) GHS and LFS data (UK)	Unionization fell faster in the UK than the USA. Shifts in unionization explained up to one-third of the rise in male wage inequality in the UK and up to 40 per cent of the rise in male inequality in the USA. Shifts in unionization explained very little of the rise in wage inequality for women in USA or UK.

side of the graph) than for high-wage groups (on the right). This is in fact the case for US men. The best-fitting line relating $W^U(c)$ to $W^N(c)$ is also shown in the figure, and lies above the 45-degree line but with a slope of less than 1.

Interestingly, the same pattern is true for men in Canada and the UK, as shown in Figures 8.2a and 8.3a. For age–education groups with low average wages (e.g. less-educated and relatively young men) the mean union wage tends to be substantially higher than the mean non-union wage, while for groups with high average wages (e.g. middle-age college or university graduates) the mean union wage is not too much above the mean non-union wage. Thus, in all three countries $\Delta_w(c)$ is larger for low-wage men than high-wage men, suggesting a potential role for unions to significantly reduce wage inequality. As we discuss in the next section, one caveat to this conclusion is that there may be important *unobserved* skill differences between union and non-union workers in different age–education groups that tend to exaggerate the apparent negative correlation between wages in the non-union sector and the union wage gap.

For women, the patterns of union wages relative to non-union wages are also remarkably similar in the three countries. Unlike the patterns for men, however, the union wage gaps for women are roughly constant. Thus, unions do not seem to 'flatten' the wage differences between older and younger women, or between more and less educated women, relative to the non-union sector.

Although the data in Figures 8.1–8.3 pertain to the early 1990s, similar plots from other years suggest that the basic patterns have been very stable in all three countries over the past 20–30 years. Contrary to the predictions of Friedman (1956) and others, the union–non-union wage gap for men tends to be highest for the least skilled workers, and to be relatively small (or even negative) for highly skilled men. The union gap for women, on the other hand, tends to be stable or only slightly declining with skill level.

Another key feature that determines the effect of unions on wage inequality is the variation in union coverage. Figures 8.4–8.6 show the fractions of union members among male and female workers in the USA, Canada and the UK, by hourly wage. (We plot union membership rates in the USA and UK although collective bargaining coverage patterns are generally similar). For the USA, we show union densities in 1973–74, 1984, 1993, and 2001. For the UK, the earliest available data are for 1983: thus we show union densities in 1983, 1993, and 2001. Similarly, individual micro data with wages and union status are only available for Canada starting in the 1980s, so we have plotted union densities by wage level for 1984, 1993 (actually, an average of 1991 and 1995), and 2001.

Several important conclusions emerge from these figures. First, in all three countries, union membership rates of men tend to be highest for

(a) US men, 1993

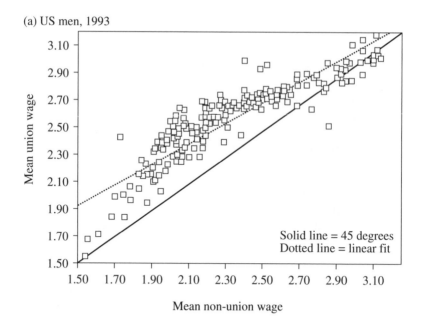

(b) US women, 1993

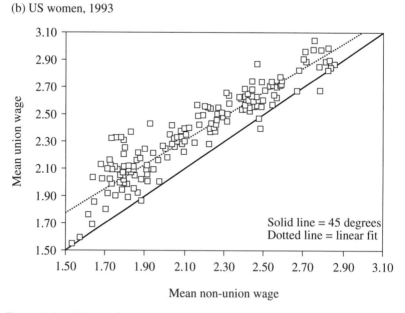

Figure 8.1   Union relative wage structure in the United States, 1993

(a) Canadian men, 1991–95

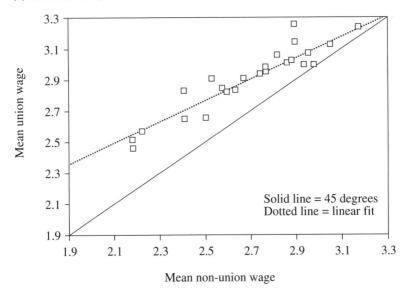

(b) Canadian women, 1991–95

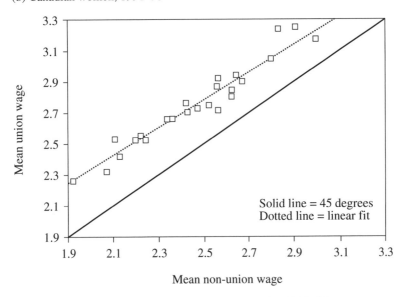

Figure 8.2 Union relative wage structure in Canada, 1991–95

(a) UK men, 1993

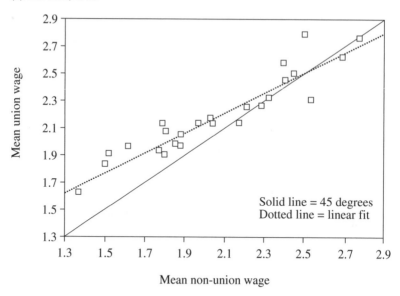

(b) UK women, 1993

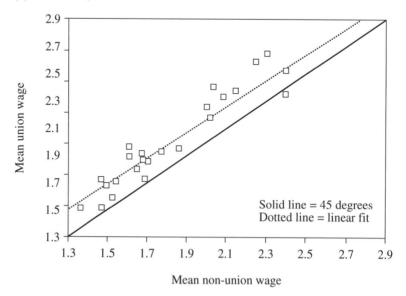

Figure 8.3   Union relative wage structure in the United Kingdom, 1993

(a) US men

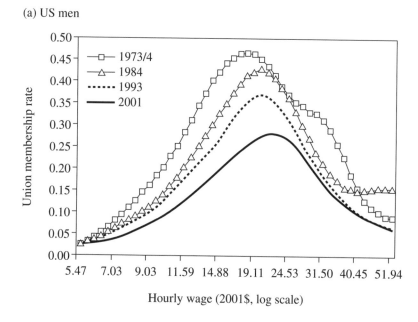

Hourly wage (2001$, log scale)

(b) US women

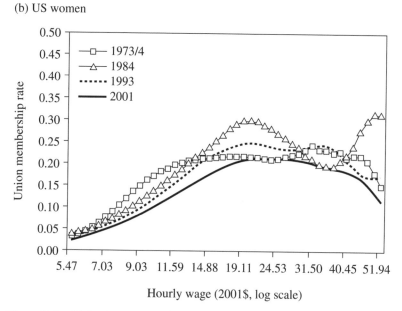

Hourly wage (2001$, log scale)

Figure 8.4   Unionization rate by wage level, United States

(a) Canadian men

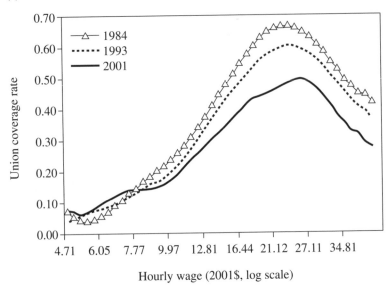

(b) Canadian women

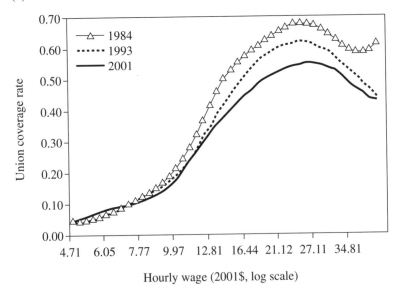

Figure 8.5   Unionization rate by wage level, Canada

(a) UK men

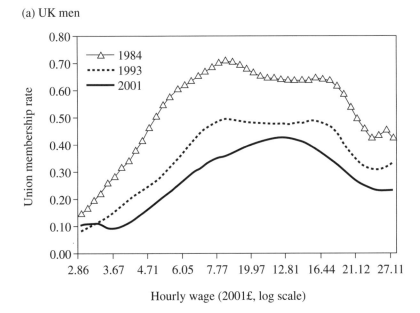

Hourly wage (2001£, log scale)

(b) UK women

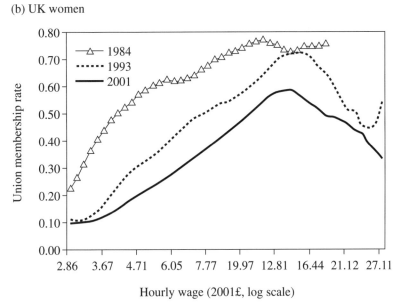

Hourly wage (2001£, log scale)

Figure 8.6   Unionization rate by wage level, United Kingdom

workers near the middle or upper middle of the wage distribution, and lower at the bottom and top of the wage distribution. Despite the higher union wage premiums for men at lower skill levels, low rates of union membership among the least skilled men substantially moderate any potential redistribution effects of unions. Second, unionization rates of women in the USA and Canada are not much lower for the highest-wage groups than for those in the middle of the wage distribution. Coupled with the fact that the union wage gaps are roughly constant across different wage groups, these patterns suggest that unions may actually widen wage inequality across skill groups for women. In the UK, there is more of a fall-off in union membership among the highest-paid women, suggesting that unionization may have a greater potential equalization effect for women there.

A third important feature of Figures 8.4–8.6 is the obvious decline in unionization rates over time. The declines are most evident for men in the USA and UK, but there are also substantial declines among Canadian men, and smaller reductions among women in the three countries. We discuss the impacts of these changes in more detail later in this chapter.

With this background, we turn to a brief discussion of the studies in Table 8.2. The first, by DiNardo and Lemieux (1997), uses a reweighting technique to construct estimates of the sum of the terms in equation (8.22) for men in the USA and Canada in 1981 and 1988. DiNardo and Lemieux also present a slightly different decomposition of the net contribution of unionization to the overall variance of wages in each country and year. They estimate that in 1981, the presence of unions reduced the variance of male wages by 6 per cent in the USA and 10 per cent in Canada. The corresponding estimates in 1988 are 3 per cent in the USA and 13 per cent in Canada. Thus, they estimate that changing unionization patterns contributed to the rise in US wage inequality in the 1980s, but worked in the opposite direction in Canada. Their decompositions also show that in both countries, unions lower the variation in wages within and between groups, with a larger net effect within skill groups.

A related study, by DiNardo et al. (1996), examined both men and women in the USA in 1979 and 1988. They (henceforth, DFL) use the reweighting technique applied by DiNardo and Lemieux. DFL do not report the effects of unions on the levels of wage inequality in either year, but instead focus on explaining the rise in wage inequality over the 1979–88 period. For men, their methods suggest that shifts in unionization account for 10–15 per cent of the overall rise in wage dispersion in the 1980s, with most of the effect concentrated in the middle and upper half of the wage distribution. For women, on the other hand, the estimated contribution of changing unionization is very small. DFL also estimate that falling unionization explains about one-half of the rise in the wage premium between men with a high school diploma and dropouts, and about a quarter of the rise in the college–high school wage gap for men.

The study by Bell and Pitt (1998) uses DFL's method to analyse the impact of declining unionization on the growth in wage inequality in Britain. Their main analysis is based on Family Expenditure Survey Data (FES) that only contains a proxy for union status (whether there are deductions from pay for union dues). They also analyse data from the National Child Development Study (NCDS), the British Household Panel Survey (BHPS) and the General Household Survey (GHS) that contain direct measures of union membership. Depending on the data source used, they find that between 10 and 25 per cent of the increase in male wage inequality (measured by the standard deviation of or the 90–10 gap in log wages) can be explained by the fall in unionization. Machin (1997) reaches similar conclusions using the 1983 GHS and 1991 BHPS data.

The next study in Table 8.2, by Card (2001), examined the contribution of unions to wage inequality among US men and women in 1973–74 and in 1993. Card reports estimates based on the simple two-sector formula (equation (8.12), and on a variant of equation (8.22) obtained by dividing workers into 10 equally-sized skill groups, based on predicted wages in the non-union sector. Two key findings emerge from this analysis. First, the presence of unions is estimated to have reduced the variance of men's wages by about 12 per cent in 1973–74 and 5 per cent in 1993. Overall, shifts in unionization can explain about 15–20 per cent of the rise in male wage inequality in the 1973–93 period. Second, although the within-group variance of wages is lower for women in the union sector than the non-union sector (i.e. $\Delta_v(c)$ is on average negative), this equalizing effect is counteracted by a positive between-group effect, so overall unions had little net effect on wage inequality among US women in 1973–74 or 1993.

Card (2001) also conducted separate analyses of the effects of unions on men and women in the public and private sectors in 1973–74 and 1993. The trends in unionization were quite different in the two sectors, with *rises* in union membership in the public sector for both men and women, and declines in the private sector. Nevertheless, comparisons of the patterns of union wage gaps by skill group suggest that unions affect the wage structure very similarly in the two sectors, with a strong tendency to 'flatten' wage differences across skill groups for men, and less tendency for flattening among women. Overall, Card's estimates imply that unions reduced the variance of men's wages in the public sector by 12 per cent in 1973–74 and 16 per cent in 1993. In the private sector, where union densities declined, the union effect fell from 9 per cent in 1973–74 to 3 per cent in 1993. An interesting implication of these estimates is that differential trends in unionization among men in the public and private sectors can potentially explain a large share (up to 80 per cent) of the greater rise in wage inequality in the private sector. The estimated effects of unions on women's wage inequality are all close to zero, except in the public sector in 1993, when the effect is about -5 per cent.

The final study in Table 8.2, by Gosling and Lemieux (2001), examined the effects of unions (and other factors) on the rise in wage inequality in the USA and the UK between 1983 and 1998, using the DFL reweighting method. Gosling and Lemieux do not report estimates of the cross-sectional effects of unionization. However, their estimates suggest that in both the USA and the UK, unions have a much smaller equalizing effect on female wage inequality than male inequality. They estimate that shifts in union coverage among men in the UK can explain up to one-third of the rise in wage inequality there between 1983 and 1998, while in the USA the decline in unions can explain up to 40 per cent of the rise in inequality. Consistent with findings in DFL and Card (2001) they conclude that changes in unionization had little net effect on female wage inequality in either country.

Studies that correct for unobserved skill differences
A potential problem with estimates of the equalizing effect of unions based on equations (8.12) or (8.22) is that union workers may be more or less productive than otherwise similar non-union workers. In this case, comparisons of the mean and variance of wages for union and non-union workers with the same observed skills confound the true 'union effect' and unobserved differences in productivity. Traditionally, economists have argued that union workers are likely to have higher unobserved skills than their non-union counterparts (Lewis, 1986). This prediction arises from the presumption that in a competitive environment, unionized employers will try to counteract the effect of above-market wage scales by hiring the most productive workers. If total productivity of worker i consists of an observed component p_i and another component a_i that is observed by labour market participants but unobserved by outside data analysts, and if an employer who if forced to pay a union wage W^U hires only those workers with $p_i + a_i > W^U$, then p_i and a_i will be *negatively* correlated among those who are hired. Workers with the lowest observed skills will only be hired if they have relatively high unobserved skills, whereas even those with below-average unobserved skills will be hired if their observed skills are high enough. This view suggests that the 'flattening' of the wage structure in the union sector arises from selectivity bias, rather than from the wage policy of unions per se.

If unions really flatten the wage structure, however, then there is another side to the story, since highly skilled workers gain less from a union job. A worker with observed productivity skills p_i and unobserved skills a_i can expect to earn $p_i + a_i$ in a competitive labour market. Such a worker will only take a union job paying W^U if $p_i + a_i < W^U$. In this case, union members are negatively selected: workers with the highest observed skills will only accept a union job if their unobserved skills are low. This view also implies that the wage structure in the union sector will appear 'flatter' than the non-union wage structure. Combining the two sides of the market, one might expect union workers with low unobserved skills to be positively selected, since for these workers the demand side is the binding constraint, whereas unionized job holders with high unobserved skills are negatively selected, since for these workers the supply side constraint is the more serious constraint.

Some evidence of this 'two-sided' view of the determination of union status was developed by Abowd and Farber (1982), who used information on workers who reported that they would prefer a union job, as well as on those who held union jobs, to separate the roles of employer and employee choice. They found that workers with higher experience were less likely to want a union job (consistent with the idea that wages for highly experienced workers were relatively low in the union sector), but were more likely to be hired for a union job, conditional on wanting one (consistent with the idea that employers try to choose the most productive workers).

The three studies in Table 8.3 all attempt to assess the effect of unions on the wage structure, while recognizing that union workers may be more or less productive than otherwise similar non-union workers. The studies by Lemieux (1993) and Card (1996) measure the wage outcomes of job changers who move between the union and non-union sectors, distinguishing between workers in groups defined by observed productivity characteristics. A limitation of these studies is that they implicitly assume that the rewards for unobserved ability are similar in the union and non-union sectors. Lemieux (1998) adopts a more general approach that allows the union sector to flatten the returns to unobserved ability relative to the non-union sector.

Lemieux (1993) studies men and women in Canada in the late 1980s, and reports separate estimates of the effect of unions for three different observed skill categories (high, medium, and low) in the public and private sectors separately, and in the overall economy. For men, his results show that unionized workers from the lowest skill group are positively selected (i.e. they have higher unobserved skills than do non-union workers in the same group), whereas those in the upper skill groups are negatively selected. This result – which is consistent with a simple two-sided selection model – echoes a similar finding in Card (1996) for US men in the late 1980s.[11] An implication of this pattern is that the between-group 'flattening effect' of

Table 8.3 Longitudinal estimates of the effect of unions on the wage structure

Study	Country	Nature of data	Findings
Lemieux (1993)	Canada	LMAS longitudinal data on men and women in private and public sectors 1986–87	Unionized men with low observed skills tended to have higher unobserved skills than their non-union counterparts, whereas unionized men with high observed skills tended to have lower unobserved skills than non-union workers. This pattern also held for women in the private sector. Unionized women in the public sector had higher unobserved skills than non-union workers at all skill levels. Unions reduced the within-sector variance for both men and women. Unions reduced the overall variance of male wages by 14.5 per cent but increased the variance of female wages by 4.1 per cent.
Card (1996)	USA	CPS longitudinal matched data on men, 1987–88	Unionized men with low observed skills tended to have higher unobserved skills than their non-union counterparts, whereas unionized men with high observed skills tended to have lower unobserved skills than non-union workers. Unions reduced the overall variance of male earnings in 1987 by 7 per cent.
Lemieux (1998)	Canada	LMAS longitudinal data on men, 1986–87	Unions lowered the returns to permanent unobserved skill characteristics. The variance of wages around the expected mean, accounting for observed and permanent unobserved skill characteristics, was lower in the union sector. Unions reduced the overall variance of wages by 17 per cent.

274

unions documented in Figures 8.1a and 8.2a is somewhat exaggerated, although there is still evidence that unions raise wages of low-skilled men more than those of high-skilled men. Lemieux also examines the changes in the variance of wages, and concludes that some of the apparent reduction in variance in the union sector may be due to selectivity, rather than to a within-sector flattening effect. Unfortunately, this inference is confounded by the potential selectivity of the group of union status changers, and the fact that the variability of wages may be temporarily high just before and just after a job change. Overall, Lemieux concludes that the presence of unions lowers the variance of male wages in Canada in the late 1980s by about 15 per cent. A similar calculation for US men, based on Card (1996), shows a 7 per cent effect. These effects are somewhat smaller than corresponding estimates that fail to correct for unobserved heterogeneity.

As one might suspect given the patterns in Figures 8.2 and 8.5, Lemieux's findings for women in Canada are very different to those for men. In particular, neither the cross-sectional nor longitudinal estimates of the union wage gaps show a systematic flattening effect of unions. Coupled with the fact that union coverage is lower for less-skilled women, these results imply that unions raise the between-group variance of wages for women. This effect is larger than the modest negative effect on the within-group variance, so on net Lemieux's results imply that unions raised wage dispersion among Canadian women.

Lemieux (1998) presents an estimation method that accounts for the potential 'flattening' effect of unions on the returns to individual skill characteristics that are constant over time but unobserved in conventional data sets. Using data on men who were forced to change jobs involuntarily, he concludes that unions tend to 'flatten' the pay associated with observed and unobserved skills. Moreover, the variance of wages around the expected level of pay is lower in the union sector. As a result of these tendencies, Lemieux's results imply that unionization reduced the variance of wages among Canadian men by about 17 per cent – not far off the estimate in his 1993 study.

5. Unions and wage inequality in the USA, UK and Canada: An update
Data sources and background
In this section we update and extend the existing literature on the effect of unions on wage inequality for the USA, UK and Canada using data up to 2001. There are several important motives underlying our new analysis. First, unionization rates have declined steeply in the USA and UK over the past two decades. It is interesting to check whether this decline has resulted in a more modest effect of unions on wage inequality in the early 2000s. On

a related point, several studies mentioned in section 4 have shown that falling unionization contributed to the steep increase in wage inequality in the USA and UK in the 1980s. Wage inequality did not change much, however, during the 1990s in the USA (Card and DiNardo, 2002). This leads to the natural question of whether the evolution of the impact of unionization on wage inequality can account for some of this slowdown in the growth in wage inequality.

Finally, it is now possible to use large and very comparable micro data sets to look at the impact of unionization on wages in the USA, UK and Canada. All three countries conduct large-scale monthly labour force surveys to measure the unemployment rate and other related statistics in a timely fashion. In the USA, the Current Population Survey (CPS) has been asking questions about wages and union status on an annual basis since 1973, and on a monthly basis (for sample members who are rotating out of the sample – the so-called 'outgoing rotation group' or ORG) since 1983.

Similar questions were added to the UK's Labour Force Survey (UKLFS) in 1993, and to the Canadian Labour Force Survey (CLFS) in 1997. Since 1997, it is therefore possible to compare much more accurately the extent of wage inequality and the effect of unions on wage inequality in the three countries. Estimates of the role of unionization in cross-country differences in wage inequality are no longer significantly affected by survey differences, or by the limitations of small sample sizes.

In our empirical work we nonetheless want to provide a perspective that is as broad as possible on the role of unions in wage inequality over the last two or three decades for both men and women in the three countries. Our most recent data point is 2001 for which comparable data are available in all three countries.[12] We then go back to 1993, which is the earliest year for which comparable CPS and UKLFS data are available. For Canada we cover a similar point in time by combining two relatively small Surveys on Work Arrangements (SWA) that were conducted as supplements to the November CLFS in 1991 and 1995. These surveys both ask questions about wages and collective bargaining coverage that are comparable to the questions in the latest CLFS.

In the UK, the only large survey of individuals that contains information on both wages and unionization prior to 1993 is the 1983 General Household Survey (GHS).[13] A large-scale survey on union membership and wages (Survey of Union Membership, SUM) was also conducted for 1984 in Canada as a supplement to the CLFS. We use these two surveys, along with data from the OGR supplements of the 1984 US CPS, as reference points for the early 1980s. Finally, for the USA only, we augment the data from the early 1980s, early 1990s, and 2001 with data from the May 1973 and 1974 CPS. From 1973 to 1981, the May CPS supplements asked the same questions about wages and union membership that were later used in the ORG supplements. One difference, however, is that unlike the ORG supplement, the May supplement does not ask about union coverage. For the sake of consistency, we look at the effect of union membership on wages in the United States.

Although data on both union membership and 'union presence' are available in our UK data sources, we focus on the impact of union membership on wages in Britain, because the available measures of 'union presence' do not appear to be a satisfactory measure of actual coverage.[14] In the 2001 UKLFS, for example, a high fraction of workers who are not union members and report that a union is 'present in their workplace' nevertheless report that their wages and working conditions are not determined by a collective agreement.

Canada is in an opposite situation since the 1991 and 1995 SWA asked only one question about union membership or coverage, instead of asking the questions separately as was done in the 2001 CLFS and the 1984 SUM. For consistency reasons we therefore use union coverage as our measure of unionization in Canada. This choice has little effect on the results since only about 2 per cent of wage and salary workers who are not union members are covered by a collective agreement.[15]

To arrive at the final estimation samples, we process the various data sets in the same way as in Card (2001) for the USA, Gosling and Lemieux (2001) for the UK, and DiNardo and Lemieux (1997) for Canada. Generally speaking, our samples include only wage and salary workers age 16 to 64 (15 to 64 in Canada) with non-allocated wages and earnings (except in 1984 and 2001 in Canada). We use hourly wages for workers who are paid by the hour and compute an average hourly earnings for the other workers by dividing weekly earnings by weekly hours (or earnings for a longer time period divided by the corresponding measure of hours). We also exclude workers with very low or very high hourly wage values.[16] Sample weights are used throughout except in the 1983 GHS for which sample weights are not available.

To implement the techniques developed in section 3, we divide workers in each sample into skill groups, based on age and educational attainment. The number of skill groups used varies across data sets, however, depending on the sample size and the ways that age and education are coded in public use files. For example, in Canada age is only reported in 10-year categories in the 1984 SUM and the 1991–95 SWA (a total of 5 categories for workers aged 15 to 64) and education can only be consistently coded into 5 categories through time. Thus we only use 25 skill groups for Canada. We use the same number of skill groups for the UK (five age and five education groups) to have a reasonable number of observations (in the 100–200 observation range) in each cell. We are able to use a much larger number of cells in the USA because of much larger sample sizes and finely coded age and education categories. We have re-analysed the US data using about the same number of skill groups as in Canada and the UK and find that this has little impact on our results.

Results

Some of the main patterns in our data have been noted already in the discussion of Figures 8.1–8.6. Tables 8.4, 8.5 and 8.6 summarize a variety of facts about unionization and the structure of wages for the USA, Canada, and the UK, respectively. Starting with the USA, the first row of Table 8.4 confirms the steep decline in unionization rates during the past three decades. As illustrated in Figures 8.4a and 8.4b, however, these aggregate figures hide a sharp difference between men and women. Between 1973 and 2001, the unionization rate of women declined only about 2 points, from 14 to 12 per cent, while it fell much more for men, from 31 to 15 per cent. This sharp male–female difference has much to do with the gradual shift of unionization from the private to the public sector. For instance, Card (2001) shows that for both men and women, unionization rates declined by about 50 per cent in the private sector between 1973 and 1993. During the same period, however, unionization rates increased sharply in the public sector. Women in general, and unionized women in particular, are much more concentrated in the public sector than their male counterparts. As a result, the shift of unionization from the private to the public sector was relatively beneficial to women in terms of their unionization rates.

The trends in unionization in Canada between 1984 and 2001 (Table 8.5) are remarkably similar to those in the USA. The male unionization rate declined by 14 percentage points, even more than the 9 percentage point decline in the USA over the same period.[17] As in the USA, the decline for women was more modest (4 percentage points).

Our results for the UK reveal a very rapid decline in the extent of unionization. Between 1983 and 2001, the unionization rate fell by 27 percentage points (from 57 to 30 per cent) for men and by 14 percentage points for women. As in the USA and Canada, the differential trends in the male and female unionization rates are closely linked to the relative shift of unionization from the private to the public sector (Gosling and Lemieux, 2001). These changes are compounded by the fact that privatizations moved a significant number of male workers from the unionized public sector (i.e. the former nationalized industries) to the much less organized private sector (Gosling and Lemieux, 2001).

Another development evident in Tables 8.4–8.6 is the convergence of the extent of union organization among men and women. By 2001, the male and female unionization rates were more or less equal in all three countries. This unprecedented situation marks a major departure from the historical pattern of greater unionization among men.

The next set of rows in Tables 8.4–8.6 shows the evolution of both the raw union wage gap and the wage gap adjusted for differences in the relative distribution of characteristics (or skills) in the union and non-union sectors. In terms of the notation of section 3, the unadjusted and adjusted union wage gaps represent estimates of Δ_w and $E[\Delta_w(c)]$, respectively. As in the case for the unionization rates, the estimated wage gaps show a remarkably similar pattern across the three countries. In all three countries the unadjusted wage gap is larger for women than for men. The adjusted wage gaps are uniformly smaller than the unadjusted gaps, and in all three countries, the divergence has increased over time, implying that union membership and coverage rates have fallen more for relatively unskilled workers.

Like the unadjusted union wage gap, the adjusted wage gap is typically larger for women than for men. The male–female difference in the adjusted gaps is less pronounced than the gender gap in the unadjusted gap. This is consistent with Figures 8.4 to 8.6 that show that unionized women are more highly concentrated in the upper end of the skill distribution than unionized men. As a result, controlling for the skill composition of the workforce reduces the union wage gap more for women than for men. The larger adjusted wage gaps for women and the relative concentration of female union members at the high end of the wage distribution mean that the disequalizing effect of unions on between-group inequality is larger for women than men in all three countries.

Another trend that is shared by all three countries is a gradual decline in the adjusted union wage gap, by 5 to 10 percentage points (depending on gender and country) between the early 1980s and 2001. Since the rate of unionization also declined sharply during this period, the average impact of unions on wages has declined dramatically over the last two decades. For example, the adjusted union wage gain for UK males went from 9.2 percentage points in 1983 (unionization rate of .57 times the adjusted gap of .162) to 1.7 percentage points in 2001 (.307 times .045). This also means that any disequalizing effect of unions on between-group inequality declined sharply during this period.

The next rows in Tables 8.4 to 8.6 report measures of wage dispersion within the union and non-union sectors. Once again, the results are remarkably consistent across countries. As first documented in Freeman (1980), the standard deviation of wages is *always* smaller in the union than in the non-union sector. Moreover, the gap between the standard deviation in the union and non-union sectors is always larger for men than for women. One reason for this male–female difference is that, for women, union wage gaps

Table 8.4 Effect of unions on wage structure of US workers, 1973–2001

	1973/74		1984		1993		2001	
	male	female	male	female	male	female	male	female
Fraction union members	0.307	0.141	0.236	0.141	0.185	0.132	0.149	0.121
Mean log wages (2001$):								
Non-union workers	2.646	2.270	2.573	2.276	2.535	2.337	2.667	2.457
Union workers	2.841	2.499	2.866	2.605	2.838	2.686	2.899	2.761
Union gap (unadjusted)	0.196	0.230	0.293	0.329	0.304	0.349	0.233	0.305
Union gap (adjusted)	0.185	0.220	0.208	0.228	0.210	0.210	0.156	0.149
Standard deviation log wages:								
Non-union workers	0.553	0.442	0.563	0.467	0.594	0.515	0.601	0.538
Union workers	0.354	0.383	0.363	0.408	0.399	0.444	0.417	0.460
Union gap	−0.198	−0.059	−0.199	−0.058	−0.194	−0.071	−0.184	−0.077
Variance decomposition:								
Overall variance	0.258	0.195	0.289	0.223	0.331	0.270	0.340	0.289
Two-sector model								
Within-sector effect	−0.055	−0.007	−0.044	−0.007	−0.036	−0.009	−0.028	−0.009
Between-sector effect	0.008	0.006	0.015	0.013	0.014	0.014	0.007	0.010
Total effect	−0.047	0.000	−0.028	0.006	−0.022	0.005	−0.021	0.001

Model with skill groups

Within-sector effect	-0.022	-0.006	-0.020	-0.007	-0.018	-0.009	-0.013	-0.009
Between-sector effect	0.007	0.004	0.010	0.008	0.012	0.011	0.004	0.008
Dispersion across groups	-0.011	0.001	-0.007	0.000	-0.008	-0.003	-0.006	-0.005
Total effect	-0.026	0.000	-0.017	0.001	-0.014	-0.001	-0.015	-0.007
Sample size	43189	30500	77910	69635	71719	69723	55813	55167
Number of skill groups	180	180	343	343	244	246	245	246

Note: Samples include wage and salary workers age 16–64 with non-allocated hourly or weekly pay, and hourly wages between $2.00 and $90.00 per hour in 1989 dollars.

281

Table 8.5 *Effects of unions on wage structure of Canadian workers, 1984–2001*

	1984		1991/1995		2001	
	male	female	male	female	male	female
Fraction union workers	0.467	0.369	0.408	0.353	0.330	0.317
Mean log wages (2001$)						
Non-union workers	2.658	2.365	2.661	2.452	2.728	2.495
Union workers	2.987	2.793	2.972	2.851	2.964	2.853
Union gap (unadjusted)	0.330	0.428	0.311	0.398	0.236	0.358
Union gap (adjusted)	0.251	0.321	0.204	0.275	0.153	0.226
Standard deviation log wages:						
Non-union workers	0.528	0.446	0.514	0.465	0.501	0.463
Union workers	0.343	0.368	0.362	0.380	0.386	0.395
Union gap	−0.185	−0.078	−0.152	−0.084	−0.115	−0.068
Variance decomposition:						
Overall variance	0.231	0.218	0.233	0.227	0.229	0.224
Two-sector model						
Within-sector effect	−0.075	−0.023	−0.054	−0.025	−0.034	−0.019
Between-sector effect	0.027	0.043	0.023	0.036	0.012	0.028
Total effect	−0.048	0.019	−0.031	0.011	−0.021	0.009

Model with skill groups

Within-sector effect	−0.041	−0.027	−0.033	−0.028	−0.025	−0.022
Between-sector effect	0.017	0.022	0.010	0.017	0.006	0.012
Dispersion across groups	−0.014	0.014	−0.002	0.014	0.001	0.013
Total effect	−0.037	0.009	−0.025	0.002	−0.017	0.003
Sample size	17737	15356	17981	18323	24003	23703
Number of skill groups	25	25	25	25	25	25

Note: Samples include wage and salary workers age 15–64 with allocated hourly or weekly pay (except in 1991–95), and hourly wages between $2.50 and $44.00 per hour in 2001 dollars.

Table 8.6 Effects of unions on wage structure of UK workers, 1983–2001

	1983		1993		2001	
	male	female	male	female	male	female
Fraction union workers	0.570	0.426	0.392	0.337	0.307	0.285
Mean log wages (2001£):						
Non-union workers	1.843	1.416	2.036	1.705	2.170	1.873
Union workers	2.053	1.685	2.224	2.047	2.306	2.167
Union gap (unadjusted)	0.210	0.269	0.188	0.342	0.135	0.294
Union gap (adjusted)	0.162	0.195	0.131	0.184	0.045	0.137
Standard deviation of log wages:						
Non-union workers	0.532	0.412	0.586	0.499	0.588	0.510
Union workers	0.382	0.399	0.438	0.475	0.442	0.468
Union gap	−0.150	−0.013	−0.148	−0.024	−0.146	−0.043
Variance decomposition:						
Overall variance	0.216	0.183	0.293	0.268	0.303	0.266
Two-sector model						
Within-sector effect	−0.078	−0.004	−0.059	−0.008	−0.046	−0.012
Between-sector effect	0.011	0.018	0.008	0.026	0.004	0.018
Total effect	−0.067	0.013	−0.051	0.018	−0.042	0.006

Model with skill groups

Within-sector effect	−0.034	−0.023	−0.031	−0.028	−0.032	−0.025
Between-sector effect	0.009	0.011	0.006	0.008	0.002	0.005
Dispersion across groups	−0.026	0.009	−0.016	0.012	−0.013	0.010
Total effect	−0.050	−0.003	−0.041	−0.008	−0.042	−0.010
Sample size	4435	3512	4009	4139	7548	8113
Number of skill groups	25	25	25	25	25	25

Note: Samples include wage and salary workers aged 16–64 with non-missing hourly or weekly pay, and hourly wages between £1.50 and £50.00 per hour in 2001 pounds.

are roughly constant across different skill groups while, for men, they are systematically lower for high-wage workers (Figures 8.1 to 8.3). This suggests that, relative to the non-union wage distribution, unions compress the wage distribution relatively more for men than for women.

The lower parts of Tables 8.4 to 8.6 show the various elements of the variance decompositions discussed in Section 3. Recall that in the simple two-sector model of equation (8.12), the effect of unions on the variance of wages is the sum of the within-sector effect, $\alpha \Delta_v$, and the between-sector effect, $\alpha (1-\alpha) \Delta_w^2$. Once again, the results are remarkably consistent across countries and time periods. For men, unions always reduce wage dispersion since the within-sector effect *always* dominates the between-sector effect. Relative to the overall variance, the compression effect ranges from 31 per cent in the UK in 1984, when the unionization rate was 57 per cent, to 6 per cent in the USA in 2001 (unionization rate of 15 per cent). More generally, the compression effect of unions tends to be positively correlated with the extent of unionization, which is consistent with equation (8.12).[18]

Relative to men, the within-sector effect for women is smaller for the reasons mentioned earlier. On the one hand, since the unionization rate α is lower for women than for men, unions reduce wage inequality for a smaller fraction of the workforce. Second, the gap between the variances (or standard deviations) in the union and non-union sectors (Δ_v) is much smaller for women than men. Both elements of the within-sector effect $\alpha \Delta_v$ are thus lower (in absolute value) for women than men. By contrast, the union wage gap is systematically larger for women than men. This yields a larger between-sector effect $\alpha (1-\alpha) \Delta_w^2$ that in later years of our analysis dominates the equalizing within-sector effect. Consistent with Card (2001) and Lemieux (1993), unions thus tend to increase the variance of wages among women.

The final set of rows in Tables 8.4 to 8.6 show the elements of the variance decomposition when we distinguish between skill groups using the framework of equation (8.22). Starting with men, controlling for characteristics systematically reduces the magnitude of both the within- and between-sector effects. It is easy to see why this happens in the case of the between-sector effect. As shown previously, adjusting for characteristics reduces the union wage gap and thus the between-group effect. In other words, part of the measured between-sector effect in the simple two-sector calculation is a spurious consequence of the fact that union workers are more skilled, on average, than non-union workers.

A similar reasoning can be used to understand why the within-group effect also declines when characteristics are controlled for. Recall from Figures 8.4 to 8.6 that union workers are more concentrated in the middle and upper part of the wage distribution than non-union workers. This suggests that union workers have more homogenously distributed skills than their non-union counterparts. Part of the lower dispersion of wages in the union sector is thus a spurious consequence of the fact that union workers are more homogenous.

Interestingly, adjusting for characteristics also reduces the magnitude of the between-sector effect for women but *increases* (or leaves unchanged in the USA) the magnitude of the within-group effect. The latter finding means that union women are not more homogenous (in terms of their skills) than their non-union counterparts, which is consistent with the evidence reported in Figures 8.4 to 8.6. Once worker characteristics are taken into account, the within-group effect tends to dominate the between-group effect for both men and women. This suggests that the large male–female differences in the measured effect of unions on wage dispersion from a simple two-sector decomposition are overstated by ignoring differences in the distribution of skill characteristics in the union and non-union sectors.

Recall from equation (8.22) that the effect of unions on the variance of wages also depends on the variance and covariance terms $\mathrm{Var}[\alpha(c)\Delta_w(c)] + 2\mathrm{Cov}[W^N(c),\ \alpha(c)\Delta_w(c)]$. Those two terms indicate how unionization changes the distribution of average wages across the different skill groups. As highlighted in our discussion of Figures 8.1–8.3, the wage gap $\Delta_w(c)$ is systematically lower for high-wage men, inducing a *negative* covariance between $W^N(c)$ and $\alpha(c)\Delta_w(c)$. By contrast, the wage gap for women is not typically lower for high-wage groups, and the higher unionization rate for those groups induces a *positive* covariance between $W^N(c)$ and $\alpha(c)\Delta_w(c)$.

The results in Tables 8.4 to 8.6 are broadly consistent with this prediction. As expected, unions tend to reduce wage dispersion across skill groups for men (except in recent years in Canada where the effect is essentially zero). Also as expected, unions tend to increase wage dispersion across skill groups for women in Canada and the UK. In the USA, however, unions have little effect on female wage dispersion across skill groups from 1973 to 1993, and actually reduce wage dispersion in 2001. A natural explanation for the difference between the USA on the one hand, and Canada and the UK, on the other, is that the union wage gap for US women tends to decline slightly with higher non-union wages (Figure 8.1b). This lowers the covariance between $W^N(c)$ and $\alpha(c)\Delta_w(c)$ for US women relative to the other two countries.

Once all three factors are taken into consideration, our calculations show that unions systematically reduce the variance of wages for men. By contrast, the effect for women tends to be small and positive (more inequality). This is quite similar to the pattern of results we found with the two-sector model, though the magnitude of the effects tends to be smaller when we control for workers' characteristics.

Unions and differences in the trends in wage inequality

To what extent can changes in the strength of unions explain the evolution of wage inequality over time and the differences in inequality across countries? In light of the results of Table 8.4 to 8.6, we look at this question for men only since unions appear to have little effect on wage inequality for women.[19] Starting with the USA, Table 8.4 shows that the variance of male wages increases from 0.258 to 0.340 (change of 0.082) between 1973/74 and 2001. During the same period, the effect of unions on the variance of wages computed using the simple two sector model declines from −0.047 to −0.021 (change of 0.026). If this effect had remained constant over time, overall wage inequality would have grown by 31 per cent less (0.026/0.082) than it actually did. The contribution of unions to the growth of inequality remains important though smaller (14 per cent) when estimates of wage compression effects that control for characteristics are used instead.

The results for the UK are qualitatively similar. Between 9 per cent (based on the model that controls for workers' characteristics) and 29 per cent (two-sector model) of the 0.087 growth in the variance of wages between 1983 and 2001 can be accounted for by the decline in union compression effects. Furthermore, in both the USA and UK union wage compression effects remained relatively constant between 1993 and 2001. In particular, the effects computed in the model with workers' characteristics are essentially unchanged during this period. This is consistent with the pattern of change in the overall variance of wages that grew much more rapidly before than after 1993.

As in the USA and UK, the union wage compression effect has been steadily declining for Canadian men since 1984. Unlike the USA and UK, however, overall inequality remained very stable over time. This suggests that overall inequality would have actually declined if union wage compression effects had remained at their 1984 levels. Several developments may have offset the pressures toward increased inequality associated with the decline in union strength. The real minimum wage in Canada rose from the mid-1980s to the late-1990s, in contrast to the USA where the real minimum wage was approximately constant over this period (Kuhn, 2000). In addition, there is some evidence that the much more rapid growth in educational attainment in Canada compared to the USA during the 1980s and 1990s reduced the tendency for widening earnings differentials between less-educated and more-educated workers (Murphy et al. 1998).

Turning to cross-country differences in wage inequality, first note that in 1983/84 the variance of wages was lowest in the UK (0.216) followed by Canada (0.231) and the USA (0.289). By contrast, union wage compression effects (adjusted for differences in characteristics) were highest in the UK (−0.050), followed by Canada (−0.037) and the USA (−0.017). The pattern of cross-country differences in wage inequality is thus consistent with the pattern of union wage compression effects. For instance, differences in union wage compression effects account for 45 per cent of the UK-USA difference in the variance of wages. By 2001, the USA-UK difference in the variance of wages is down to 0.037 (0.340–0.303), while the USA-UK difference in the union compression effect is 0.027. This indicates that over 70 per cent of the USA-UK gap in wage inequality can now be explained by union wage compression effects. In 2001, however, union wage compression effects cannot account for the much lower variance of wages in Canada.

In summary, union wage compression effects help explain a reasonable fraction of the secular growth in male wage inequality and of cross-country differences in male wage inequality. One exception is the surprising lack of growth in male wage inequality in Canada relative to the other two countries. An assessment of the relative importance of the various influences on wage inequality among Canadian men is a worthwhile subject for future research.

6. Conclusion

What is the effect of unions on pay differentials and wage inequality? Until the late mid-1970s, the consensus among economists was that '. . . unionism probably has a slight disequalizing effect on the distribution of income' (Johnson, 1975, p. 26). This prevailing view was substantially altered by the landmark paper by Freeman (1980). Subsequent studies that used different data and more sophisticated econometric methods confirmed Freeman's finding that, overall, unions tend to reduce wage inequality among men. Indeed, our new empirical work indicates that this finding is very robust across countries (USA, UK and Canada) and time periods (from the early 1970s to 2001).

Interestingly, an equally robust finding that emerges from this work is that unions *do not* reduce wage inequality among women. In all three countries, this important male–female difference in the impact of unionism is due to a combination of three factors. First, unionized women are more concentrated in the upper end of the wage distribution than their male counterparts. Second, the union wage gap is larger for women than for men. Third, the union wage gap is larger for lesser- than higher-skilled men, while this is not the case for women.

Another important conclusion is that the impacts of unions on the wage structure in the USA, Canada, and the UK have followed remarkably similar trends over the last two decades. In all three countries, the unionization rate and the union wage differential have declined substantially since the early 1980s. For men, this has resulted in smaller effects of unions on wage inequality in all three countries that help account for a significant fraction of the growth in wage inequality in the USA and UK.

Notes

1. See Chapter 11 by Visser in this volume for data on union membership and collective agreement coverage in various countries in the mid-1980s and late-1990s.
2. See Chapter 12 by Addison and Siebert in this volume for a review of recent changes in the collective bargaining framework in the UK.
3. See, for example, the Symposium on Wage Inequality in the *Journal of Economic Perspectives*, vol. 11, no. 2, Spring 1997.
4. The equation follows from the standard decomposition of a variance into within-sector and between-sector components.
5. This presentation follows Card (1992), Lemieux (1993) and Card (2001). Although the exposition is in terms of skill groups, the same principles apply to any situation in which groups of workers can be ordered according to their average wage.
6. Of course, as noted previously, unions may alter the wage structure in the non-union sector.
7. Lemieux (1998) presents a model in which unobserved attributes are rewarded differently in the union and non-union sectors.
8. See Lewis (1986) for a review of US studies and Simpson (1985) and Lemieux (1993) for Canadian evidence.
9. The lone study that included data for women (Hyclak, 1979) found no significant relationship between female earnings inequality and union coverage in urban labour markets.
10. The US plots are based on skill groups defined by years of education (10 categories) and two-year intervals of age (25 categories). Due to data limitations, the Canadian and UK plots are based on much broader age and education groups. The data underlying these figures are explained in more detail in the next section.
11. Hirsch and Schumacher (1998) use data on test scores and find that union members with high measured skills have relatively low test scores.
12. For the UK, we only use the LFS for the Fall semester since wage and unionization data are not available for other semesters. In Canada, we use the LFS data from November 2001 (all rotation groups have wage and unionization data) since the earlier SWA 1991 and 1995 data sets were also collected in November (December in 1984 SUM). Data for all months are used in the 1984, 1993 and 2001 CPS.
13. Blanchflower and Bryson (Chapter 7 in this volume) use UKLFS data from 1985 to 1991 to estimate the union wage premium during this period. Unfortunately, the available samples (about 1000 observations a year) are too small to conduct a detailed analysis of the impact of unionization on wage inequality for a large number of skill groups as we do here.
14. The UKLFS has asked a question about union coverage similar to the ones in the CLFS and ORG CPS since 1996 only. Both the 1993 UKLFS and the 1983 GHS ask about union membership and union presence in the workplace.
15. More precisely, 2.4 per cent of male workers and 1.9 of female workers are covered but not members of a union in the 2001 CLFS. The two different concepts of unionization also yield very similar union wage gaps and variance gaps. For example, when union membership is used the unadjusted wage gaps are 0.235 and 0.361 for men and women, respectively, compared to 0.236 and 0.358 (Table 8.5) when union coverage is used instead.
16. The cutoff points are $2 and $90 (1989 dollars) for the USA, $2.5 and $44 (2001 dollars) for Canada, and £1.50 and £50.00 (2001 pounds) for the UK. Note also that we exclude Northern Ireland from the UK samples because union membership data is not available from Northern Ireland in the 1993 UKLFS.
17. However, because the extent of union organization in Canada is about double that in the

USA, the drop in unionization in Canada is smaller in proportional terms. For example, unionization of Canadian men fell by 29 per cent between 1984 and 2001, versus a decline of 37 per cent among US men.

18. The derivative of the compression effect with respect to the unionization rate is $\Delta_v +$ $(1 - 2\alpha) \Delta_w^2$. It is negative (higher negative effect on the variance when the unionization rate increases) as long as the within-group effect (Δ_v) dominates the between-group effect $((1 - 2\alpha) \Delta_w^2)$.

19. DiNardo et al. (1996), Card (2001) and Gosling and Lemieux (2001) all reach the same conclusion that declining unionization explains very little of the increase in wage inequality among women in the USA or UK.

References

Abowd, John M. and Henry S. Farber (1982), 'Job Queues and the Union Status of Workers', *Industrial and Labor Relations Review*, 35 (3), 354–367.

Ashenfelter, Orley (1972), 'Racial Discrimination and Trade Unionism', *Journal of Political Economy*, 80 (3), 435–464.

Bell, Brian D. and Michael K. Pitt (1998), 'Trade Union Decline and the Distribution of Wages in the UK: Evidence from Kernel Density Estimation', *Oxford Bulletin of Economics and Statistics*, 60 (4), 509–528.

Card, David (1992), 'The Effects of Unions on the Distribution of Wages: Redistribution or Relabelling?', NBER Working Paper 4195, Cambridge: MA: National Bureau of Economic Research.

Card, David (1996), 'The Effects of Unions on the Structure of Wages: A Longitudinal Analysis', *Econometrica*, 64 (4), 957–979.

Card, David (2001), 'The Effect of Unions on Wage Inequality in the U.S. Labor Market', *Industrial and Labor Relations Review*, 54 (2), 296–315.

Card, David and John E. DiNardo (2002), 'Skill Biased Technological Change and Rising Wage Inequality: Some Problems and Puzzles', NBER Working Paper 8769, Cambridge, MA: National Bureau of Economic Research.

DiNardo, John and Thomas Lemieux (1997), 'Diverging Male Wage Inequality in the United States and Canada, 1981–88: Do Institutions Explain the Difference?', *Industrial and Labor Relations Review*, 50 (4), 629–651.

DiNardo, John, Nicole M. Fortin and Thomas Lemieux (1996), 'Labor Market Institutions and the Distribution of Wages, 1973–1992: A Semi-Parametric Approach', *Econometrica*, 64 (5), 1001–1044.

Doiron, Denise J. and W. Craig Riddell (1994), 'The Impact of Unionization on Male–Female Earnings Differences in Canada', *Journal of Human Resources*, 29 (2), 504–534.

Even, William E. and David A. Macpherson (1993), 'The Decline of Private Sector Unionism and the Gender Wage Gap', *Journal of Human Resources*, 28 (2), 279–296.

Freeman, Richard B. (1980), 'Unionism and the Dispersion of Wages', *Industrial and Labor Relations Review*, 34 (1), 3–23.

Freeman, Richard B. (1982), 'Union Wage Practices and Wage Dispersion Within Establishments', *Industrial and Labor Relations Review*, 36 (1), 3–21.

Freeman, Richard B. (1984), 'Longitudinal Analyses of the Effects of Trade Unions', *Journal of Labor Economics*, 2 (1), 1–26.

Freeman, Richard B. (1993), 'How Much has Deunionization Contributed to the Rise of Male Earnings Inequality?', in Sheldon Danziger and Peter Gottschalk (eds), *Uneven Tides: Rising Income Inequality in America*, New York: Russell Sage Foundation, pp. 133–163.

Friedman, Milton (1956), 'Some Comments on the Significance for Labor Unions on Economic Policy', in David McCord Wright (ed.), *The Impact of the Union*, New York: Kelley and Millman, pp. 204–234.

Friedman, Milton (1962), *Capitalism and Freedom*, Chicago: University of Chicago Press.

Gosling, Amanda and Thomas Lemieux (2001), 'Labor Market Reforms and Changes in Wage Inequality in the United Kingdom and the United States', NBER Working Paper 8413, Cambridge, MA: National Bureau of Economic Research.

Gosling, Amanda and Stephen Machin (1995), 'Trade Unions and the Dispersion of Earnings in British Establishments', *Oxford Bulletin of Economics and Statistics*, 57 (2), 167–184.

Hirsch, Barry T. (1982), 'The Interindustry Structure of Unions, Earnings and Earnings Dispersion', *Industrial and Labor Relations Review*, 36 (1), 22–39.

Hirsch, Barry T. and Edward J. Schumacher (1998), 'Unions, Wages, and Skills', *Journal of Human Resources*, 33 (1), 201–219.

Hyclak, Thomas (1979), 'The Effect of Unions on Earnings Inequality in Local Labor Markets', *Industrial and Labor Relations Review*, 33 (1), 77–84.

Hyclak, Thomas (1980), 'Unions and Income Inequality: Some Cross-State Evidence', *Industrial Relations*, 19 (Spring), 212–215.

Johnson, George (1975), 'Economic Analysis of Trade Unionism', *American Economic Review*, 65 (2), 23–28.

Johnson, George E. and Kenwood C. Youmans (1971), 'Union Relative Wage Effects by Age and Education', *Industrial and Labor Relations Review*, 24 (2), 171–179.

Kuhn, Peter (2000), 'Canada and the OECD Hypothesis: Does Labour Market Inflexibility Explain Canada's High Level of Unemployment?', in W. Craig Riddell and France St-Hilaire (eds), *Adapting Public Policy to a Labour Market in Transition*, Montreal: Institute for Research on Public Policy, pp. 177–209.

Lemieux, Thomas (1993), 'Unions and Wage Inequality in Canada and the United States', in David Card and Richard B. Freeman (eds), *Small Differences That Matter: Labor Markets and Income Maintenance in Canada and the United States*, Chicago: University of Chicago Press, pp. 69–107.

Lemieux, Thomas (1998), 'Estimating the Effects of Unions on Wage Inequality in a Panel Data Model with Comparative Advantage and Non-Random Selection', *Journal of Labor Economics*, 16 (2), 261–291.

Lewis, H. Gregg (1963), *Unionism and Relative Wages in the United States*, Chicago: University of Chicago Press.

Lewis, H. Gregg (1986), *Union Relative Wage Effects: A Survey*, Chicago: University of Chicago Press.

Machin, Stephen (1997), 'The Decline of Labour Market Institutions and the Rise in Wage Inequality in Britain', *European Economic Review*, 41 (3–5), 647–657.

Meng, Ron (1990), 'Union Effects on Wage Dispersion in Canadian Industry', *Economics Letters*, 32 (4), 399–403.

Metcalf, David (1982), 'Unions and the Dispersion of Earnings', *British Journal of Industrial Relations*, 20 (2), 163–169.

Murphy, Kevin M., W. Craig Riddell and Paul M. Romer (1998), 'Wages, Skills and Technology in the United States and Canada', in Elhanan Helpman (ed.), *General Purpose Technologies and Economic Growth*, Cambridge, MA: MIT Press, pp. 283–309.

Ozanne, Robert (1962), 'A Century of Occupational Wage Differentials in Manufacturing', *Review of Economics and Statistics*, 44 (3), 292–299.

Plotnick, Robert D. (1982). 'Trends in Male Earnings Inequality', *Southern Economic Journal*, 48(3), 724–732.

Rees, Albert (1962), *The Economics of Trade Unions*, Chicago: University of Chicago Press.

Reynolds, Lloyd G. and Cynthia H. Taft (1956), *The Evolution of Wage Structure*, New Haven, CT: Yale University Press.

Rosen, Sherwin (1970), 'Unionism and the Occupational Wage Structure in the United States', *International Economic Review*, 11 (2), 269–286.

Simpson, Wayne (1985), 'The Impact of Unions on the Structure of Canadian Wages: An Empirical Analysis with Microdata', *Canadian Journal of Economics*, 28 (1), 164–181.

Slichter, Sumner H., James J. Healy and E. Robert Livernash (1960), *The Impact of Collective Bargaining on Management*, Washington, DC: Brookings Institution.

Stafford, Frank P. (1968), 'Concentration and Labor Earnings: Comment', *American Economic Review*, 58 (1), 174–181.

Stieber, Jack (1959), *The Steel Industry Wage Structure*, Cambridge, MA: Harvard University Press.

9 Unions and innovation: a survey of the theory and empirical evidence
Naercio Menezes-Filho and John Van Reenen

1. Introduction

The role of trade unions in the economy has always been the subject of intensive debate. Traditionally, the theoretical literature emphasized the role of unions in distorting relative prices and the empirical studies concentrated on the determinants of union membership and on the effect of unions on wages and profitability. More recently however, economists have focused on the role of unions as 'taxing' the returns on sunk capital and on the design of efficient contracts, whereas applied economists shifted their attention to the long-term effects of unions, that is, on investment, technology and productivity growth.

The reason for this shift of emphasis is clear. If the presence of strong unions led the firms to reduce capital and R&D (research and development) investments then unionized firms would tend to lose market share. In turn this would mean that the unionized sector would shrink and eventually trade unions would disappear from the economy.[1] In a closed economy unions could organize an entire industry in order to avoid withering away, but this option is unavailable in an open economy, where a unionized industry will be undermined by competition from countries with weaker unions.[2] Some commentators have contrasted the high R&D and dynamic innovation of the USA (where unions are weak) with the relatively lower R&D and slower innovation of Europe (where unions are strong) and drawn the conclusion that unionized labour markets may be at the heart of Europe's problems. If, on the contrary, the presence of unions leads to increase in innovation and productivity (or are at least neutral), then their long-term prospects are brighter.

In this chapter we will review the literature on the effects of unions on innovation. We will take a broad view of innovation and include both the key inputs to the innovation process – R&D expenditures – as well as the outputs of the 'knowledge production function' – innovation, diffusion and finally, productivity growth. Moreover, we intend to carefully evaluate the literature outside the United States, where many of the previous surveys have concentrated. This survey will not address the 'macro' literature about institutions and performance (the reader is referred to Layard and Nickell,

1999, and Chapter 6 by Flanagan in this volume, for a more detailed treatment). Nor will we look at unions and the diffusion of 'managerial innovations' (such as decentralization and delayering).

The structure of the survey is the following. We start with a review of the papers that theoretically model the relationship between unions and innovation. We then focus on empirical issues, such as measurement, aggregation and the econometric problems that arise when the researcher investigates the effects of unions on the different aspects of innovation. We proceed with a survey of the results of the papers that have estimated the impact of unions on R&D, innovation, technological diffusion and productivity growth. In the final section we offer some concluding remarks.

In short, the effects of unions on innovation are generally ambiguous both in theory and in empirical practice. There does, however, seem to be some emerging consensus that there is a negative association between unions and R&D in North America. This is not the case for Europe where no such stable relationship is found. We discuss reasons for this in the conclusion, but suggest it is due to different bargaining institutions between the Old and New Worlds.

2.   Theoretical models of the impact of unions on innovation

There are several theoretical mechanisms through which unions might have an effect on innovative activity. These mechanisms include: (1) direct effects ('Luddism'), (2) relative price effects, (3) profitability, (4) 'hold-up' problems and (5) strategic R&D. Over the last two decades there has been much emphasis placed on the hold-up problem after the seminal article by Grout (1984), but recent theoretical interest has focused on strategic R&D issues.

2.1   Direct effects: 'Luddism'

Unions have long had reputations for attempting to block the introduction of new technologies and being the institutional heirs to the Luddites.[3] This may be because of the fear of job losses, organizational change or work intensification following new technology. For example, the British unions representing the print-workers for the national newspapers were renowned for the long-standing opposition to the introduction of computerized typesetting. This changed only when the owners of these newspapers (led by Rupert Murdoch) closed down their production shops in central London and moved completely to a new location in the east of London. Were this example generally true, unions would be a direct break on technological diffusion.

Some companies use their inventions in their own establishments since there are some complementarities between usage and invention – an innovating firm may know more about the pros and cons of its new device than a rival.[4] If such a firm knows that there is a truculent labour force downstream that may block the introduction of new technology, this is likely to depress R&D activities upstream (or at least lead to its licensing out the technology).

On the other hand, there are several reasons why unions may actually be able to boost productivity – for example, by reducing grievances and staff turnover or by improving morale and training. This is the *collective voice* of unionism highlighted by Freeman and Medoff (1984). This may make the introducing of new technology more attractive in unionized settings. Indeed, survey evidence of union attitudes usually finds considerable support for the introduction of new technology.[5] It is often remarked that unions take a more pro-productivity stance in Continental Europe and Japan where industrial relations are co-operative than in countries that have more adversarial industrial relations (such as the USA and the UK). This may be one reason for expecting a different relationship between union power and innovation across different countries.

2.2 Relative factor price effects

There is a straightforward relative factor price effect of the union mark-up on any substitute factor of production. Consider a simple two-factor model where there is a choice between labour and new technological capital. An increase in the relative price of labour (through union wage increases) will cause substitution of high tech machines for workers, for a given level of output (i.e. along an isoquant). On the other hand, a union-driven increase in costs will mean higher average costs, causing lower overall production (a shift to a lower isoquant) and therefore less need for all factors, including labour. The impact of unions via their wage effects will depend on the balance between the substitution and the scale effects, so that even in a purely static neo-classical model, the direction of the union relative price effect is ambiguous.

2.3 Unions and profitability under imperfect financial markets

There is a consensus in the empirical literature that unions, on average, reduce profitability (e.g. Menezes-Filho, 1997). There are two routes by which this occurs. First, and most importantly, unions increase the overall compensation for their members – see Chapter 7 by Blanchflower and Bryson in this volume. Second, unions may lower the level of productivity through featherbedding, industrial action and by creating a more antagonistic climate of industrial relations – see Chapter 5 by Metcalf in this volume. The productivity impact of unions is more ambiguous, however, as unions may increase productivity in some settings, for example by discouraging turnover (see Freeman and Medoff, 1984, and sub-section 2.1 above). Nevertheless, even if there were a positive effect of unions on productivity it would not seem to empirically outweigh the union wage mark-up.

The lower profitability in unionized firms does not necessarily reduce investment in R&D. In principle, if unions merely redistribute excess profits from shareholders to workers then there may be no effect on R&D. Unions would act as a pure rent-sharing device and other factors would still be used at their efficient levels. Optimal investment decisions would still be made with respect to the fundamentals (see Modigliani and Miller, 1958). Unfortunately, in a world where there are imperfect capital markets, firms will sometimes find themselves financially constrained in their investment decisions. This is likely to be a particular problem for R&D investments due to its inherent high risk, the fact it cannot be collateralized (as it is mainly composed of human assets) and the deep informational asymmetries between inventors and investors.[6] Companies may be very reluctant to turn to external finance to raise money for innovation, as potential investors will demand information to demonstrate the value of the R&D. This information could 'leak out' to rival firms and be used imitate the invention, undermining its value. There is ongoing controversy regarding the extent of financial constraints, but empirically many researchers have found supporting evidence that the financial constraints seem to bite more tightly for R&D than other forms of investment (see the survey in Bond and Van Reenen, 2002).

2.4 'Hold-up' problems
Grout (1984) built on Simons' (1944) model of the negative impact of unions on investment because of their appropriation of quasi-rents from investment. The mechanism is quite simple when extended to R&D as a specific form of investment. R&D has a large element of sunk cost (about 90 per cent of R&D is current expenses on staff costs and materials). Once an R&D investment is in place and an innovation has successfully been introduced, it is possible for a union to 'hold up' the shareholders by demanding higher wages.[7]

Figure 9.1 gives the extensive form of a simple game to show this possibility. In stage I the firm chooses R&D ('high' or 'low') and in stage II the union chooses the wage ('high' or low'). The union would like to commit to a low wage strategy conditional on the firm choosing high R&D. This way the pie is bigger (10 compared to 8) and both parties can gain (both get a pay-off of 5 as opposed to 4). However, the union cannot credibly commit to a low wage strategy in advance; because once the R&D investment is sunk there exists a strong temptation to deviate from any agreement. It is clear that the union's best response at stage II is always to play a high wage strategy. The firm knows this to be the case in stage I, and will always

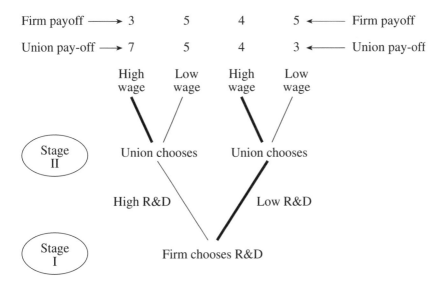

Firm payoff ⟶ 3   5   4   5 ⟵ Firm payoff

Union pay-off ⟶ 7   5   4   3 ⟵ Union pay-off

High wage   Low wage   High wage   Low wage

Stage II   Union chooses   Union chooses

High R&D   Low R&D

Stage I   Firm chooses R&D

Note: This is the extensive form of a two-stage game. At stage I the firm chooses R&D (simplified to be either 'high' or 'low') and at stage II the union chooses wages (again either 'high' or 'low'). Solving backwards the union will always pick 'high' wages at stage II. Knowing this firm will always choose a low R&D strategy (sub-game perfect equilibrium). This leaves union with pay-off of 4 and firm with pay-off of 4. Both parties would be strictly better off with a (high R&D, high wage) equilibrium where each party would receive a pay-off of 5. Unfortunately, although this is Pareto optimal it is not a sub-game perfect Nash equilibrium.

Figure 9.1   Unions and R&D investment: the 'hold-up' problem

choose a low R&D policy. The only sub-game perfect equilibrium therefore is the (low R&D, high wage) outcome.

This game has the form of a prisoner's dilemma and, as usual, there may be many ways 'out' of the dilemma by changing the structure of the game. Grout himself suggested that the first best could be achieved if unions and firms could get together and bargain over investment as well as wages. This is a common and intuitive result. It is symmetrical to the contrast between the 'right to manage' union model (where there is bargaining only over the wage) and the efficient bargaining model (where there is bargaining over both wages and employment). The latter is Pareto efficient and the former is not (e.g. Leontief, 1946).

Unfortunately this 'solution' to the Grout model faces a similar problem to the 'efficient bargaining over employment' model. Explicit union bargaining over employment is seldom empirically observed. Bargaining over the introduction of new technology or investment is still rarer, and bargaining over R&D itself is almost *never* seen. One response to this criticism is the argument that some kind of 'implicit' bargaining takes place over other instruments. It is difficult to see how this would practically come about. With employment, one could imagine that effort bargaining (e.g. over manning levels) gets us some way towards the efficient solution,[8] but there seems little analogous mechanism for an implicit bargain over R&D.[9]

A version of the implicit contract argument is that the long-term labour contracts, such as those in large Japanese companies, act as a kind of commitment device. Japanese workers can effectively commit themselves not to appropriate the rents from innovation. Unfortunately, this is certainly not the case in Britain and the United States where contracts are more short term (three years generally being the maximum). Ulph and Ulph (1989) have suggested that this may be a reason for the differential effects of unions on innovation across different countries. Even when contracts are more durable, however, commitments are likely to be difficult to sustain when there is uncertainty and significant informational asymmetries between the players.

Another related 'escape route' from the hold-up problem is to notice that the game between unions and firms is repeated over time rather than being a one-shot game. Van der Ploeg (1987), for example, stressed the damage to a union's reputation in seeking to expropriate a firm's quasi-rents from innovation.

An important element of these models will be the degree to which unions discount the future. It is quite likely that the time horizons for unions are lower than the time horizons for firms, because unions do not hold property rights in jobs. High turnover or the control of the union by senior members who are looking to retirement will lower the discount factor of the union vis-à-vis the firm. This is one of the insights of Baldwin (1983). She also shows that, in the presence of union demands for sharing the returns from long-lived capital investment, investors may choose a self-enforcing counter-strategy of investing in less efficient plant and equipment or, alternatively, to try and extend the union's time horizon.

Addison and Chilton (1998) focus on the possibility of efficient investment and employment outcomes in explicitly repeated games. They first follow Espinosa and Rhee (1989), assuming the following structure: first the firm chooses capital which then remains fixed. There follows a repeated game where union chooses wages and the firm sets employment, conditionally on the wage chosen. In this framework, Espinosa and Rhee (1989) show that, so long as the discount factor is sufficiently close to one, there exist equilibria where neither the firm nor the union will be tempted to deviate, because they would find the punishment too harsh. The resulting equilibria will encompass the monopoly union and the fully efficient bargaining models as particular cases that result from certain discount rates.

Addison and Chilton (1998) also extend this model to allow the firm to choose capital at the beginning of each sub-game. Capital flexibility, besides raising the punishment the firm can impose on a deviating union (as in Baldwin, 1983), also weakens the union's punishment of the firm that cheats, introducing the possibility of opportunistic behaviour on the part of the firm as well and making the efficient outcome depend crucially on the firm's discount factor.

In some cases (e.g. US shipbuilding) the assumption that the repeated game will go on forever[10] breaks down when unions are clearly in an 'end-game' situation of a sector in terminal decline (e.g. Lawrence and Lawrence, 1985). In this case, the firm knows that the union will pay non-cooperatively in the final sub-game and this will unravel the incentive to cooperate in previous sub-games.

Another implication of the hold-up model is that firms may take action to mitigate the degree to which they can be expropriated in other ways. Bronars and Deere (1991) suggest that firms may alter their financial structure (e.g. leveraging up the debt–equity ratio to increase the risk of bankruptcy) to reduce the incentive of unions to expropriate the innovative rents. Bronars et al. (1994) emphasize the incentive to license out technology rather than develop it in-house.

It has been observed that firms could also 'hold up' the sunk investments of workers in training and that this will lead to an under-investment in human capital. In this model, unions could act to prevent the hold-up problem by making the firm honour its commitments. This may lie behind the positive impact of unions on training that is often observed (e.g. Green et al., 1998).

2.5 Strategic R&D

There is a more recent body of theoretical literature that has cast doubt on the robustness of the negative impact of unions on R&D through the 'hold-up' mechanism. This literature notes that R&D is mainly performed by large firms who operate in oligopolistic industries. The strategic interactions of these firms is critical to modern game-theoretic models of R&D, but are wholly absent in Grout's model, which is in the context of a monopolistic firm facing a single union. The introduction of strategic interaction undermines the analytical clarity of the Grout result.

In a strategic R&D game, firms invest in R&D at the first stage of the game in the knowledge that they will be competing against each other at the second stage of the game. Investments in R&D can shift the advantages at this second stage in various ways. Much theoretical effort has been expended analysing the role of market structure in affecting firms' R&D decisions: this was the focus of interest of Schumpeter's work and reappears in the modern endogenous growth literature (e.g. Aghion and Howitt, 1992). For example, consider the R&D incentives of a monopolist facing a potential entrant in an R&D game. Assume that R&D is determined by a first price sealed bid auction where the firm that bids the most (i.e. spends the most on R&D) will certainly obtain an innovation with infinitely lived patent protection.[11] In this case the current monopolist will have a greater incentive to invest in R&D than the challenger and will always invest most in R&D so long as the innovation is 'non-drastic' (i.e. both firms will be able to remain in the market post-innovation and earn positive profits). The reason for this result is that if the challenger wins the innovation and enters the market there will be a duopoly. Since joint industry profits in a duopoly will never exceed monopoly profits, the monopolist always has an additional incentive to bid harder in the R&D auction than the potential entrant. This is sometimes known as the 'efficiency effect' as monopoly is privately more efficient for the industry players than a duopoly.

A more realistic alternative to an auction model of R&D is a patent race where there is some uncertainty over who will win the race (this is still a one-shot tournament model). Firms invest in R&D and draw a chance of winning the race from a known, but stochastic, probability distribution. The more R&D is performed the greater is the chance of winning, but unlike the auction model, success is not guaranteed. The efficiency effect still exists in this game (giving the high market share firm an incentive to win) but there are also counterbalancing effects. In particular the current monopolist receives a stream of rents before the innovation occurs and he or she will be reluctant to see these replaced. The challenger does not have any current rents and the 'replacement effect' will therefore make the challenger more likely to spend more on R&D.

Ulph and Ulph (1994, 2001) have established many results in the context of a patent race in R&D, a Cournot duopoly in the product market and separate firm specific unions. In particular they find two interesting results when there is 'ex post' bargaining (i.e. no bargaining over R&D at the first stage, but bargaining with unions over wages and sometimes employment at the second stage):

1. When the union bargains only over the wage ('right to manage'), there is an unambiguously negative effect of union power on R&D (a generalization of the Grout result).
2. When the union bargains over employment and the wage, an increase in union power can actually *increase* R&D.

The second result is surprising and occurs in a setting when the union is not 'too powerful' and places a high weight on jobs (vis-à-vis wages) in the utility function. In such a situation, the first-order effect of an increase in union power is to increase employment and therefore market share. This increase in market share enhances the incentive to do more R&D due to the threat of losing this high share (this is like the efficiency effect discussed above). Some of the empirical literature has found support for this prediction (e.g. Menezes-Filho et al., 1998b).

2.6 Summary of theory
The upshot of this brief theoretical overview is that, although there are many reasons to suspect that increases in union power may reduce the incentive to invest in innovation this is not a foregone conclusion. There are some countervailing incentives and ultimately the sign and direction of the union effect is an empirical question.

There is not a standard 'R&D equation' as there is a standard human capital earnings equation, so most empirical researchers have not investigated structural models. This is probably wise as there is no consensus in the R&D literature (or in fact, in the larger investment literature) over the appropriate empirical form for an R&D equation.[12] We now turn to these empirical issues.

3. Empirical issues in the relationship between innovation and unions
In this section we mainly focus on empirical issues relating to innovation, as the econometric problems related to the union variables are covered extensively elsewhere in this volume.

3.1 The measurement of innovation
The standard measure of innovation is *R&D* (research and development expenditures). This is the early stage of the knowledge production function. Since R&D is an input measure (like fixed investment expenditure) it cannot measure the quality of the research. 'Innovative outputs' would include patents and headcounts of innovations. These innovative outputs should give rise to higher productivity in the firm who first uses them and in subsequent firms as the innovation diffuses around the economy. There are a multitude of measures of diffusion such as the adoption of computers or of other micro-electronic technologies (such as robots, numerically controlled (NC) machines, computer assisted design (CADCAM), etc.). On average, these diffusion measures should be reflected in *indirect* measures of productivity (such as TFP, total factor productivity).

R&D has the great advantage over other *direct* innovation measures in that it is a continuous variable with a monetary value attached. It is more intuitive to think of $2 million of R&D as twice as important as $1 million of R&D, whereas the comparison of a firm with two patents as opposed to one patent is not so obvious (see below).

R&D also has the advantage that most countries have official R&D surveys that are published on an industry-wide basis at fairly regular time intervals. There is now a series that compares R&D expenditure at the industry level across a wide range of OECD countries (the OECD's ANBERD dataset) from the early 1970s onwards. This data is starting to be used extensively by researchers.[13] Although there are cross-national differences, most nations have a version of the Frascati Manual's definition of R&D, which aids comparability across countries.

Firm or establishment level comparisons of R&D are more difficult. US accounting regulations ensure that all firms listed on the stock market that perform 'material amounts' have to declare their R&D expenditure. By contrast, even the larger publicly-listed British firms have only had to report R&D since 1989.[14] In most other countries the reporting of R&D remains a voluntary item in the company accounts. Apart from the restrictions in sample size, this leads to selectivity issues as the sample of firms who are voluntarily reporting R&D are a non-random sample of the population.[15] This is one reason why most published work in this area has been on US firms.

A further problem with R&D is that most small and medium-sized firms, even in high-tech industries, report zero or very low levels of R&D. This is partly because the fixed costs of R&D mean that they are genuinely not performing any R&D. But it is also likely to be because smaller firms are pursuing informal research activities that are not captured by the formal R&D measures in the company accounts or in government statistics.

Patenting and innovation count data seeks to overcome this problem, as these measures are available, in principle, for all firms in the economy. The problem with patent or innovation counts is one of 'apples and oranges' – are we comparing like with like when we add up the patent numbers? Researchers who have investigated the value of patents using renewal fees have argued that the valuation is extremely heterogeneous with many 'duds' (i.e. zero value patents) and a few bonanzas. Pakes (1986), for example, uses renewal fees to estimate the distribution of the value of patents and finds a huge amount of variability. It is possible to weight the counts by other measures to reflect differential valuations – for example Bloom and Van Reenen (2002) weight by number of citations. The importance of these adjustments has not yet been fully investigated in the union and R&D literature.

Patents are judged by the relevant Patent Office, an external arbitrator of value.[16] Innovation measures have the further problem that they may be subjective – managers will always tend to systematically overestimate how 'innovative' they are.[17] This is why more objective expert-based surveys, such as the SPRU (Science Policy Research Unit) innovations dataset are desirable (see Geroski, 1990).

A third problem with counts of patents or innovations is the econometric problem that appears when highly non-linear variables are used as dependent variables. In this case, the use of Ordinary Least Squares will lead to misleading results (for example, the distribution of the error terms will take on a number of discrete values and OLS standard errors will be incorrect). Recent developments in the analysis of count data models that allow for fixed effects and dynamic adjustment have extended our ability to look into these issues (see Blundell et al., 1999, and below).

3.2 Aggregation

In our survey we consider studies at the establishment, firm and industry level. In general, the lowest level of aggregation is generally preferred from an econometric point of view, but there are several factors to take into consideration.

First, the appropriate level will partially depend on where bargaining takes place. In the USA and Japan, wage bargaining is overwhelmingly at the firm or establishment level. In Germany wage bargaining focuses at the industry level, so there could be a stronger argument for industry-level studies. In the UK private sector, wage bargaining (where it exists) is mainly at the firm or establishment level, although in the 1970s industry-level bargaining was predominant. The effects of unions may go beyond their wage effects however, which establishes the case for looking at a lower level of aggregation. For example, the impact on technical diffusion may be different depending on the activities of unions at different plants within the same firm.

Second, there is an argument for aggregation if measurement is likely to be very poor at the micro level. Grouping can smooth out some of the measurement error in the micro-series that disguises the true relationship between variables (see Grunfeld and Griliches, 1960).

Finally, the establishment level may be too disaggregated since large firms usually have R&D labs on separate sites and the R&D decisions will be generally on a company-wide basis. The appropriate level is more likely to be the impact of company-wide variables on company-wide R&D.

3.3 Unobserved Heterogeneity

Consider the basic equation for the R&D of a firm:

$$\ln R\&D_{it} = \alpha UNION_{it} + \beta' x_{it} + u_{it} \qquad (9.1)$$

where i denotes firm, t time period, R&D is R&D expenditure (usually normalized by some measure of size, such as sales or employment), *UNION* is an indicator of union power, x is a vector of controls and u is the error term.

There are a large number of controls that need to be included in x to avoid omitted variable bias. Most researchers have included measures of size, market structure and capital intensity, as these variables are likely to be correlated with both union status and R&D. For example, since larger firms perform more R&D and are more likely to recognize unions, a failure to control for size would leave to a spurious positive association of unions and R&D. Unions would falsely appear to be stimulating innovation.

Matters become more complex, however, with some of the variables known to affect R&D. Technological opportunity and 'appropriability', for example, are important drivers of innovative activity (see Cohen and Levin, 1989), yet these are hard to quantify at the firm level. Industry dummies may capture some of this, but if technological opportunity or appropriability vary over time, or if a firm spans several sectors (as most large firms do) then industry dummies will not solve the problem. Menezes-Filho et al. (1998b) for example, find that the failure to control for age and sector-level technological conditions (industry R&D intensity and patent intensity) severely biases the union coefficient downwards.

One obvious variable to consider is profitability. Consider including a measure of profitability or cash flow in equation (9.1). If there are cash flow constraints on R&D then this variable is likely to have a positive sign in the R&D equation. If the union impact of R&D is purely through reducing profitability (see section 2.3 above), then the inclusion of profitability should drive any negative union impact to zero. Otherwise, some decomposition of the union effect into 'finance' vs 'non-finance' aspects can be attempted (see, for example, Hirsch, 1992, and Bronars et al., 1994). Although suggestive, the interpretation of the cash flow variable is difficult in any investment equation, as it may just signal future profitable opportunities in the industry.[18] Consequently this method is not without its problems.

A natural approach in a panel data setting (i.e. where the same firms are observed at several points of time) is to consider controlling for fixed effects. This will generally involve a variance decomposition of the error term in equation (9.1) into a time invariant firm specific fixed effect (η_i) which can be correlated with the observables in an arbitrary manner, a set of time dummies (τ) which do not vary across firms in a given time period and a truly idiosyncratic effect which is uncorrelated with all the other variables in the model (v_{it}).

$$u_{it} = \eta_i + \tau + v_{it} \qquad (9.2)$$

The technological opportunities of a firm probably do not vary too dramatically over time so may be captured fully by the firm dummies[19] or by taking differences (first differences or longer differences) of equation (9.1). The problem here is that union status does not vary dramatically over time so there is likely to be considerable attenuation bias from this method (see Freeman, 1984). This will tend to bias the union effect towards zero. Comparison of first differences with longer differences and within group estimators would be helpful in this regard because long differenced estimators suffer less attenuation bias than first differenced estimators.

A related problem is the fact that R&D also does not vary much over time so, even in the absence of any measurement error for the unions variable, including fixed effects unnecessarily will cause a large loss in efficiency (see Griliches and Mairesse, 1997). Practically speaking, it is a difficult job to decide whether the different results of OLS compared to fixed effects are due to true unobserved heterogeneity or rather caused by the low time series variation of the key variables of interest.[20]

3.4 Endogeneity of union status

In equation (9.1) union status may not be exogenous for a variety of reasons. Combining equation (9.1) with equation (9.2) will reduce some of the endogeneity bias. For example, if highly skilled environments are conducive to R&D but not to unions then this will impart a downwards bias to the coefficient on unions. In other words we may falsely conclude that unions had a negative effect on R&D if we do not properly control for skills. If the skill composition is stable over time, however, it will be controlled for by the fixed effect. On the other hand if both R&D and union density are pro-cyclical then the union coefficient will be biased upwards and we may mistakenly believe unions have a positive impact on R&D. If these cyclical effects are purely macro-economic, the bias can be removed by the inclusion of time dummies from equation (9.2).

Unfortunately, there may be other shocks that equation (9.2) cannot deal with. For example, improved expectations of firm-specific business conditions may boost R&D and union density. If this is the case there will be a positive bias to the coefficient on unions and we are left with the usual problems of finding a valid instrumental variable for unionization. Such an instrument must be correlated with union status, but uncorrelated with the shock in equation (9.1). Standard instrumentation strategies (e.g. first differenced GMM) of using suitably lagged endogenous variables as instruments are unlikely to be convincing because of the low time series variation in union status discussed above.

Menezes-Filho et al. (1998b) use industry union density at the time of the firm's start-up as an instrument for present union density, without significant changes in their results. Conditions at the time of firm-start up are unlikely to be correlated with the current shocks to R&D. Addison and Wagner (1994) explore data variation across countries in similar industries to (effectively) use unionization in Germany as an instrument for industry union density in the UK.

3.5   Heterogeneity of the union effect

Theory strongly suggests that the impact of unions is likely to be different according to several factors, such as the scope of bargaining (wages/employment/technology, wages/employment or wage only), the bargaining priorities of unions (e.g. the weight given to wages relative to jobs in the union utility function), the bargaining power of unions and the state of product market competition. Several studies have investigated one or all of these interactions with the union status variable (see below). Other studies have empirically examined how the union effect differs across different industries without specifying the reasons for this heterogeneity.

3.6   Non-linearities in the union effect and R&D disclosure

The large number of plants and firms reporting zero R&D raises several econometric issues. If the problem is pure censoring then the appropriate strategy for equation (9.1) is to estimate a Tobit model. If the zeros are actually related to non-random selection, because of the choice over whether or not to disclose R&D, then a sample selection model is more appropriate (Heckman, 1979). Natural instruments in the selection equation are R&D accounting regime shifts, which have affected different firms in different ways (see Menezes-Filho et al., 1998b).

There should be no presumption that the impact of unions on innovation is linear. Some of the theoretical models of strategic R&D discussed above actually have direct implications that the union impact will be non-linear (i.e. positive at low levels of union power but negative at high levels of union power).

3.7   Magnitude of the union effect on innovation

The many empirical difficulties of measuring the union effect have led most researchers to focus on the qualitative issue of whether there is an effect of unions on innovation or not. The economic (as opposed to statistical) object of interest, however, is whether the magnitude of the union effect is large or small. This is particularly difficult for the innovation or diffusion measures, as these dependent variables are usually discrete and difficult to compare across studies. R&D and total factor productivity are more satisfactory in this respect as, in principle, they are quantitative measures that can be compared across studies even from different countries in different time periods.

In the survey in the next section we include the quantitative size of the union effect wherever available. It is noticeable that the size of unions effect on R&D is often very large in the North American studies. This is rather surprising given the other more fundamental reasons for performing R&D, such as the underlying science base.

4.   Survey of existing empirical work

In this section we will first look at two 'example studies' in the USA and UK (see Table 9.1). The first two columns are taken from Table 4 in Hirsch (1992). His measure of unionization uses categorical variables depending on the level of density. It is clear that the unionized firms perform substantially less R&D than non-unionized firms. Dropping profitability in column (2) increases the magnitude of the union effect, but not by a large amount, suggesting that negative association is not driven by the reduction in profits caused by union presence.

The third column is an example UK study taken from Menezes-Filho et al. (1998b). As with Hirsch there is also a large, significantly negative coefficient on union density. By contrast to the US study, however, including other covariates in column (4) reverses the sign on the union variable and renders it insignificant. The important control variables are industry technological opportunity measures (R&D and patent intensity) and firm age. The authors interpret this as evidence that unions are generally found in older firms and in low-tech sectors, so that the negative association of R&D with unionization is not causal. Many of the same variables are in both studies and take similar signs: for example older firms perform less R&D and more capital intensive firms do more R&D. The differences between the studies is not caused by different specifications or covariate set: Menezes-Filho et al. (1998b) took Hirsch's data and estimated identical specifications to their own and still found significant negative union effects in the USA but no significant effects in the UK. Therefore, the differential union impact on R&D is more likely to be driven by different institutions surrounding bargaining in the two countries.

To put these results in a wider context, we have surveyed all the existing published work of which we are aware concerning the effects on unions on innovation, in Tables 9.2 to 9.5. We have arranged our survey in four parts, according to which measure of innovation is used as the dependent variable. Following the 'knowledge production function' approach, we examine R&D first in Table 9.2. Headcount measures of innovation are in Table 9.3 and indicators of diffusion are in Table 9.4. Finally, Table 9.5 includes measures of productivity growth.

Table 9.1   The determinants of investment in R&D: two example studies
from the USA and the UK

	(1)	(2)	(3)	(4)
	US firms Hirsch (1992)		UK firms Menezes-Filho et al., (1998)	
	Dependent variable is ln(R&D expenditure)		Dependent variable is ln(R&D/Sales)	
Union density <30%	−0.281	−0.292	—	—
	(9.10)	(9.42)		
Union density between 30% and 60%	−0.315	−0.34	—	—
	(9.78)	(10.56)		
Union density above 60%	−.438	−.462	—	—
	(12.25)	(12.91)		
Union density	—	—	−0.470	0.139
			(2.37)	(.586)
Profits	1.692	—	—	—
	(7.37)			
Lagged ln(R&D stock)	0.545	0.55	—	—
	(49.56)	(49.8)		
Ln(capital)	0.171	0.153	—	0.442
	(7.13)	(6.4)		(4.02)
Ln(labour)	0.361	0.377	—	Quadratic in
	(14.52)	(15.11)		employment
Age/100	−0.163	−0.189	—	—
	(4.47)	(5.19)		
Firm born after 1979	—	—	—	0.999
				(5.07)
Industry earnings	0.706	0.733	—	1.627
	(6.73)	(6.95)		(2.29)
Industry R&D/Sales	—	—	—	0.381
				(5.15)
Other variables	Firm growth, industry growth, industry concentration, industry imports imports and industry unionization		None	Market share, industry patents per employee, firm skills
Industry and time dummies	yes	yes	yes	yes
Sample selection correction	no	no	yes	yes
N	4176	4176	339	339

Note: Coefficients estimated by OLS and *t*-statistics underneath in parentheses. The base for columns (1) and (2) is union density = zero.

4.1 R&D expenditures

A survey of the papers that studied the relationship between unions and R&D can be found in Table 9.2. There are 13 papers in all. The six US studies all tend to find significant negative effects of unions on R&D whether at the firm level (e.g. Hirsch, 1992) or the industry level (Allen, 1988). The union effect falls slightly after controlling for profitability, suggesting that labour unions depress R&D both through a reduction in profitability (sub-section 2.3) and also through non-profit related mechanisms (such as hold up). The only Canadian study (Betts et al., 2001) reaches a similar conclusion with, if anything, even more damaging effects of unions on R&D than the US studies. Most of the studies interpret the union effect as being due to the 'hold-up' phenomenon (sub-section 2.4 above).

The European studies generally find no statistically significant linear effects of unions on R&D, once one controls for other factors correlated with union power. The two British studies at the industry level (Ulph and Ulph, 1989, and Addison and Wagner, 1994) both find that the union impact can be positive or negative depending on the precise industry under study. Menezes-Filho et al. (1998b) present results from different samples at the firm-level and at the establishment-level, which tell a similar story (as discussed in the previous section). There is a negative raw correlation between R&D intensity and unionization but this becomes statistically insignificant when one controls for proxies for the age of the enterprise and technological opportunity. Schnabel and Wagner (1992a and 1994) also find no statistically significant association of R&D with union density in their cross section of German industries in the early 1980s.[21] Schnabel and Wagner (1994) find that works councils have a positive association with R&D and union density has a negative impact with R&D. Their interpretation is that there is a non-linear effect of union power on R&D: the 'presence of a works council is positive for R&D if union density is not too high' (Schnabel and Wagner, 1994, p. 501).

Many of the studies examining the impact of unions on R&D use panel data where the same firms are observed over time. It is therefore possible, in principle, to control for fixed effects by examining the impact of *changes* in unionization on *changes* in R&D. When this has been attempted, the union effect tends to fall into insignificance even in the US studies. This could be indicative of the fact that the negative union effect is spurious and driven by some other unobserved variables (such as managerial quality). However, both unionization and R&D have very little time series variation and, as discussed above, this will tend to cause both attenuation bias and large standard errors, which may disguise any true causal effects of unions on R&D.

The models of strategic R&D discussed in section 2 imply that the union

Table 9.2 Unions and R&D

Authors	Methodology	Data	Indicators of technical changes & unionization	Controls	Results
Addison and Wagner (1994)	Least Median Squares regression of British R&D/value added against union density in Britain, use German information on density to control for endogenity	38 British industries 1989; 18 matched UK–German industries	Percentage of workers in a union from the Labour Force Survey. R&D/value added	German R&D/value added	Positive association between unions and R&D in 'low tech' industries; argued that this is due to endogeneity of unionization. When German R&D entered in a UK R&D equation no significant effect of unions
Allen (1988)	OLS regressions of industry R&D/output by industry of origin and industry of use	74 US industries 1973–1975	1973–1975 average union density. R&D/output	1972 concentration ratio	Negative and significant R&D intensity 17% lower in unionized industries
Betts, Odgers and Wilson (2001)	Least Squares dummy variables, R&D/value added	13 Canadian industries in production sector 1968–1986	Union density. R&D/value added	Import share, Herfindahl Index of industrial concentration, growth of sales, profits	Unions have a significant and negative effect on R&D even after controlling for fixed effects; size is larger than in USA; union density rising from 25th to 75th percentile associated with a fall in R&D of 40%

Study	Method	Sample	Data	Other variables	Findings
Bronars and Deere (1993)	Log (R&D/capital) regressions	600 US firms (firm specific averages over sample period)	Percentage of industry who are members of trade union weighted by firm's sales across these three digit industries. R&D/fixed capital	Sales, industry dummies, sales growth, concentration, median firm size in industry	One standard deviation in unionization rate associated with a 51.1% fall in R&D/capital
Bronars, Deere and Tracey (1994)	R&D/Sales ratio averaged over time: averages are taken within two distinct sub-periods: 1975–1978 and 1979–1982	120–130 US firms 1979–82; 130–150 firms 1975–78	Various: e.g. Bureau of Labor Statistics contract data matched to Compustat firms, Hirsch's survey, CPS industry averages. R&D/sales	Sales growth, concentration, industry dummies, capital–labour ratios, investment/–sales ratios	Unionization has generally a negative effect, although this is only strong in manufacturing (10% increase in unionization associated with a 3.5–5% fall in R&D); effect not significant when industry effects included or estimates in first differences
Connolly, Hirsch and Hirschey (1986)	R&D/Sales regressions and market value including R&D as explanatory variable. Is rate of return to intangible capital lower in union firms?	367 firms from US Fortune 500 in 1977	Industry level union density. R&D/Sales	Concentration market share, advertising/sales, growth, diversification	Unions have consistently negative effects on R&D/Sales; they reduce the rate of return to R&D as measured on the stock market. Increasing unionization from 0 to mean reduces R&D by 32%

Table 9.2 (continued)

Authors	Methodology	Data	Indicators of technical changes & unionization	Controls	Results
Hirsch (1991)	Regressions of R&D on union coverage	452 US firms; 4327 observations between 1968–1980	The proportion of a firm's North American work-force covered by a collective bargaining agreement in 1972 and 1978 (retrospective questioning in 1987). Firm specific R&D lagged stock of R&D as a control; R&D/sales.	Labour, capital, firm growth, industry wages, concentration, imports, profits	Consistently negative in all specifications, especially in drugs and medicines. Fixed effects and 2SLS models severely reduce union effect
Hirsch (1992)	R&D regressions of R&D on union coverage	706 US firms; 5841 observations 1972–80	As in Hirsch (1991)	As in Hirsch (1991) plus age of firm	Always a negative effect of unions on R&D
Menezes-Filho, Ulph and Van Reenen (1998b)	Log(R&D/sales) regression with correction for selectivity of R&D disclosure	Panel of 446 UK firms 1983–90	R&D as reported in company accounts. Union recognition and union density.	Age, size, skills, market share, capital intensity, industry R&D, industry patents/worker, industry wage, non-random R&D disclosure	Raw correlation between unions and R&D significantly negative, but insignificant when including all controls; some evidence of non-linearity (positive at low density levels, negative at high density levels).

Study	Method	Data	Measurement of unionism and R&D	Controls	Results
Menezes-Filho, Ulph and van Reenen (1998b) – cont.	Tobit regression of R&D/ expenditure and R&D employees/total employment	Cross-section of up to 826 British establishments in 1990	Union recognition, union density. R&D as reported by survey of plants	Age, size, skills, industry R&D/sales, industry wage, industry patents/worker, single site	Raw correlation between unions and R&D significantly negative, but insignificant when including all controls; some evidence of non-linearity; negative impact for plants where there was no wage bargaining.
Schnabel and Wagner (1992a)	Robust regression techniques as well as OLS regressions	29 German industries 1983–1984	Union density not observed but predicted based on characteristics from individual level membership equation. R&D/Sales and % of R&D workers in total employment	Wages, concentration, firm size, capital intensity, rate of profit, capital vintage, sales growth	No significant association
Schnabel and Wagner (1994)	Least Median Squares	26 German industries in 1984/85	Union density not observed but predicted based on characteristics from individual level membership equation. R&D/Sales	Quadratic in firm size, average wage, profitability, concentration	No significant association

Table 9.2 (continued)

Authors	Methodology	Data	Indicators of technical changes & unionization	Controls	Results
Schnabel and Wagner (1994)	Tobit	31 German establishments in two states 1989	Union density and Works Council. R&D/sales	Quadratic in firm size, average wage, profitability, concentration	Union power has non-linear effect: works councils (highly correlated with union density) had a positive and significant effect, but union density negative and significant.
Ulph and Ulph (1989)	OLS regression	33 British industries in 1972 and 1978	Percentage of workforce covered by a union agreement; percentage of workforce covered by a local agreement. R&D/sales	Concentration, high-tech sector dummy	Union measures have a positive effect in low-tech industries, but a negative effect in high-tech industries

effect on R&D may exhibit non-linearities. Menezes-Filho et al. (1998a) explicitly test for these and do find some evidence consistent with the theory. They find an 'inverted U' relationship whereby small increases in union density can actually have a positive effect on R&D, although there is a negative and significant impact at higher levels of union power (this is also the interpretation of Schnabel and Wagner, 1994, of their results in German establishments). Furthermore, this pattern is only true of establishments where there is some bargaining over employment. When unions only bargain over wages the union impact is uniformly negative. This is consistent with some of the models of unions and strategic R&D discussed in sub-section 2.5 above.

A similar pattern is not exhibited in the North American studies. A reanalysis of the Hirsch data or the Betts et al. (2001) study reveals a pretty uniformly negative impact of unions on R&D.

4.2   Innovation

We are only aware of five econometric studies examining the impact of union power on counts of innovations (the output of R&D) (see Table 9.3). Again, two US studies (Acs and Audretsch, 1988, and Hirsch and Link, 1987) find significant negative effects, whereas the European studies generally find insignificant effects. Schnabel and Wagner (1992b) find no significant effects of unions in their sample of German establishments. Both the Geroski (1990) and Blundell et al. (1999) studies use the UK SPRU panel that contains scientists' identification of major innovations between 1945 and 1983. Geroski uses the innovations data at the industry level whereas Blundell et al. use it at the firm level. The Blundell et al. (1999) study is the most sophisticated attempt to control for fixed effects using a variety of methods.[22] Although unionization does tend to be more robustly negative in this study than in the UK R&D studies surveyed above, the measure of unionization is defined at the 2–3 digit industry level rather than at the firm level, so unionization could be reflecting some other industry level factors.

4.3   Diffusion

A wide variety of countries are represented in Table 9.4 that contains results from 12 studies examining the impact of unions on the diffusion of new technologies (USA, Canada, Australia, Britain and Germany). The results vary widely from the negative and significant in Australia (Drago and Wooden, 1994) to positive and often significant in the UK (e.g. Machin and Wadhwani, 1991). There are often positive raw correlations between unions and diffusion, but unionization usually becomes insignificant when other variables such as higher wages and training are included in the covariate set (e.g. Keefe, 1991).[23]

Table 9.3   Unions and direct measures of innovation

Authors	Methodology	Data	Indicators of technical changes & unionization	Controls	Results
Acs and Audretsch (1988)	OLS regression of count of total number of innovations normalized on employment	US Small Business Administration Dataset; 247 4-digit industries in 1982	Union density. Innovations collected from trade journals	Capital, advertising, concentration, industry growth and skills	Negative and significant union effect
Blundell, Griffith and Van Reenen (1999)	Dynamic count data model of innovation counts, allows for fixed effects through either 'pre-entry stock' method or nonlinear General Method of Moments	UK Firm level panel data 1972–82; Science Policy Research Unit (SPRU) innovations (1945–82) data and Datastream company accounts	Two-digit industry union density. Science Policy Research Unit's (SPRU) innovation dataset (survey of scientists, engineers and other experts covering 1945–83).	Lagged innovations, market share, capital, concentration, imports, time dummies, fixed effects	Unions have negative effect on innovation, significance varies in different specifications
Geroski (1990)	Innovations counts using OLS and within groups (i.e. inclusion of industry dummies for fixed effects)	73 British manufacturing industries; two pooled cross section 1970–74 and 1975–79	Percentage of workers coverage by a collective bargain (NES). Average number of innovations from Science Policy Research Unit (SPRU) innovations.	Industry concentration, share of firms that entry and exit the industry, growth, imports, exports, size	Negative but insignificant

316

Hirsch and Link (1987)	Ordered probits of response to question on product innovation	315 New York manufacturing firms in 1985	Binary variable if firm density over 50%. Question relating to company's comparative advantage in product innovation.	Size, concentration, profitability, foreign competition, labour management relations, R&D	Unions have significant and negative effect
Schnabel and Wagner (1992b)	Probits of product innovation	78 German establishments in 1990	Presence of works councils, extent of wage drift. Product innovation.	Number of employees	Positive but insignificant effect

Table 9.4 Unions and technological diffusion

Authors	Methodology	Data	Indicators of technical changes & unionization	Controls	Results
Benvignati (1982)	Probits of adoption, probits of being 'pioneer' mill (if mill had adopted any advanced machinery of above average speed)	241 US textile mills	Union = 1 if 10% or more of production workers are members of a union. Important textile machinery (any one of 33 different types)	Size, concentration, 4-digit industry	Unionized mills significantly more likely to be pioneers; positive but insignificant effect on adoption
Betcherman (1988)	OLS regressions on three measures of technology	536 Canadian firms 1980–85 (Working with Technology Survey)	Union present or not? Expenditure on computers (and as a % of sales) 1980–85; % of employees using technology in 1985.	Size, industry, region, ownership type	Negative but insignificant effect
Borghans and ter Weel (2002)	Logit analysis where the dependent variable is whether an individual uses a computer or not	c. 2500 individuals in the Skill Survey of Employed British workers, 1997	Whether an individual covered by a collective bargaining agreement; membership of union. Computer use	Education, age, gender, marital status	Positive and significant effect of union coverage (interpreted as union wage effect) and negative interaction of coverage with membership
Chennells and van Reenen (1997)	Wage and technology equation across 3 different skill groups;	Pooled cross section of c.992 British establishments in 1984	Dummy for union recognition at the workplace. Has	Size, industry, single site, UK owned, employers' association,	Unions have no significant effect on technology once one

	Method	Sample	Variables		Results
	allow unions to affect both wages and technology adoption	and 1990 (WIRS)	workplace been affected by introduction 'of major new plant, equipment (involving microelectronics)' over the previous three years? Computer presence and age of plant.	skills, gender, payment by results, local unemployment	controls for wages and other factors
Drago and Wooden (1994)	Probits of technological adoption	802 Australian establishments (AWIRS) in 1990	UNION – any union members in workplace; DELEGACT – whether union delegates active in expressing concerns to management; Union density. Has workplace been affected by introduction 'of major new plant, equipment or office technology' over the previous two years	Wages, size, capacity utilisation, financial performance, demand, foreign ownership, organizational change, joint consultative committee	Unions have a generally negative (and significant) effect. This is mitigated by (a) 'active' unions (DELEGACT) (b) very high levels of union density
Fitzroy and Kraft (1990)	Weighted least squares and Tobit treating unionization as endogenous	57 small and medium sized German firms in 1979	Proportion of sales accounted for by products introduced within the last 5 years. Union density interacted with presence	Industrial concentration, batch production dummy, capital, total employment, occupational proportions, exports, capital held by	Union power has negative and significant effect (but works council and union density are only included as an interaction). Results

Table 9.4 (continued)

Authors	Methodology	Data	Indicators of technical changes & unionization	Controls	Results
			of a works council	managers, urban area dummy, incentive pay, profits.	when union power treated as exogenous are not presented.
Kelley and Brookes (1991)	Probit of whether the establishment uses programmable automation	757 US metalworking establishments in 1987	Union recognition. Computerized automation	Wages, organizational complexity (factor combining size and multi-plant), machining employment share, other computer use, small batch output and other organizational features	Negative but insignificant (but wages included), union highly correlated with multi-plant firms
Keefe (1991)	Seven different probits for seven types of advanced manufacturing technology	260 US plants in seven industries	Union = 1 if majority of workers in the establishment are covered by a collective bargaining agreement. Seven technologies including numerically controlled machine tools (NC), machine centre (MC), Computerised	Wages, training, shiftwork, plant size (number of employees)	Unions have significant negative effect on CADCAM and CNC; unions have a significant positive effect on ROBOTS variable

320

Study	Method	Sample	Technology variables	Other variables	Result
			Numerical Control (CNC), Direct Numerical Control (DNC), CADCAM, FMS		
Latreille (1992)	Probit	418 British establishments 1984	Manual union recognition; presence of micro-electronics in production process	Size, foreign ownership, few competitors, profit-sharing, industry imports, industry sales (level and growth),	Positive and significant effect of unions
Lintner et al. (1987)	OLS regressions	133 UK mechanical engineering plants 1983–84	Union recognition and density by blue collar/white collar (binary dummy). Adoption of CADCAM (Computer Aided Design and Manufacturing Equipment), CNC and flexible manufacturing systems	Number of employees in establishment, flexibility of investment, region	No significant effect of unions
Taymaz (1991)	OLS regressions	US engineering industries 1979–83 (42 observations)	Collective bargaining coverage for all workers and production workers only. Share of numerically controlled machine tools as percentage of all machine tools	Total employment, proportion of technicians, average firm size, capital/labour ratio, variance of industry growth rate, work in progress	Unions have no significant effect

Table 9.4 (continued)

Authors	Methodology	Data	Indicators of technical changes & unionization	Controls	Results
Machin and Wadhwani (1991)	Probits of incidence of advanced technical change	British establishments in 1984 (WIRS)	Union recognized at workplace dummy and union density. Has workplace been affected by introduction 'of major new plant, equipment (involving microelectronics)' over the previous three years?	Wages, size, capacity utilisation, financial performance, demand, foreign ownership, organizational change, joint consultative committee	Unions have a positive association with the adoption of new technology but this association is not significant after controlling for wages and joint consultative committees ('voice')

Table 9.5   Unions and productivity growth

Authors	Methodology	Data	Indicators of technical changes & unionization	Controls	Results
Allen (1988)	Ordinary least squares	74 US industries (3 and 4 digit). 1972–83	Percentage of workers organized. Average output (physical units) per employee hour	R&D, concentration	Insignificant negative (levels). Insignificant positive (changes)
Clark and Griliches (1984)	Ordinary least squares	924 US line of business 1975–79	Union recognition. Real sales	R&D, capital utilisation, revenues	Insignificant positive
Freeman and Medoff (1984)	Ordinary least squares	79 US industries (3-digit): 1958–76 450 US industries (4-digit): 1958–78 State by industry cells: 1972–77	Percentage of workers unionized. Average annual value added per worker	None	Insignificant negative
Gregg et al. (1993)	GMM (but unionization treated as exogenous)	328 UK firms 1984–89	Union recognition. Real sales growth	*Firm Level:* Labour, capital, market share, borrowing ratio, competition *Industry level:* hours worked, price of materials	Between 1985–87 there is no union effect; between 1988–89 there is a positive and significant union effect especially for firms that de-recognised unions and/or faced increased competition

Table 9.5 (*continued*)

Authors	Methodology	Data	Indicators of technical changes & unionization	Controls	Results
Hirsch (1991)	Ordinary least squares	531 US firms between 1968–80	Firm-level union coverage in 1977. Real value added growth	*Firm Level:* Size, labour, capital, R&D *Industry level:* sales, energy usage, trade	Strong negative correlation; Remains negative after firm-level controls; Weakly negative after industry dummies; Insignificantly positive after correcting for firm specific serial correlation in the error term
Hirsch and Link (1984)	Ordinary least squares	19 US manufacturing industries (2-digit) 1957–73	Union density in 1958. Total factor productivity growth	R&D/sales, market concentration	Negative effect of the levels and the changes in union density
Link (1981)	Ordinary least squares	51 major manufacturing firms in the US	Percentage of workers unionized. Avg. annual rate of change in total factor productivity	Different measures of R&D	Negative (significant at 10%) impact of unions
Link (1982)	Ordinary least squares	97 US firms in the chemical, machinery and petroleum industry	Percentage of workers unionized. Avg. annual rate of change in total factor productivity	Different measures of R&D	Negative impact of unions

Study	Method	Data	Dependent/Independent variables	Control variables	Results
Maki (1983)	Annual time series regression	US non-agricultural manufacturing sector between 1926 and 1978	Aggregate union membership (level and change). Total factor productivity growth.	Strikes, median education	Negative effect of the level of density (long term effect) and positive effect of change in density (shock effect)
Mansfield (1980)	Ordinary least squares	20 US manufacturing industries (2-digit) between 1948–66.	Union density in 1953. Avg. annual rate of change in total factor productivity	Different measures of R&D	Negative in all specifications
Menezes-Filho et al. (2002)	Ordinary least squares	222 Brazilian manufacturing firms	Firm-level union density in 2000. Real value added growth: 1995–2000	Firm employment, capital, market share, product market competition, industry dummies	No effect in the linear specification. Strong evidence of non-linearity (positive at low density levels, negative at high density levels)
Nickell et al. (1992)	GMM (but unionization treated as exogenous)	122 UK firms 1975–86	Proportion of manual employees covered by trade union agreement. Real sales growth	Firm employment, capital, market share, borrowing ratio, industry concentration, import penetration	Between 1975–78 union effect is negative; between 1979–84 union effects is positive; between 1985–86 union effect is negative. All effects are significant
Nickell and Layard (1999)	Ordinary least squares	20 OECD countries	Union density, union coverage, coordination of bargaining. Labour productivity, TFP	Tax, employment protection, replacement rate, benefit duration	No effect in all specifications

There are two serious problems with most of these studies. First, the measures that they use are usually quite crude – a simple binary dummy for the adoption of a particular technology is most common. Unlike R&D which can be measured in a currency, there is no natural numeraire to compare the intensity of use of a technology. Second, the studies are generally cross-sectional which limits the amount of information available and prevents the authors from even attempting to control for fixed effects.

4.4   Productivity growth

Unions may have an impact upon either the level and/or the growth of productivity. If it is the level of unionization that is included in the productivity growth regression, than what is being estimated is the union impact on productivity growth. If, on the other hand, a measure of changes in unionization is included as a regressor, then its estimated coefficient will capture the impact of unions on the level of productivity, since this specification can be seen as a first-differences transformation of one relating the level of productivity to the level of unionization (perhaps to eliminate some fixed effects).

The interpretation of the findings is also interesting in these two cases. The effect of unionization on productivity growth could be the result of its impact on innovations or on the level of R&D expenditures, which would then be transmitted to changes in productivity growth. The impact of unionism on the level of productivity may reflect a 'collective voice' effect (e.g. unions may lower turnover, Freeman and Medoff, 1984) or a 'shock' effect, with managers adopting a more efficient structure of production as a reaction to unionism (see Hirsch and Link, 1984). It is important to note that the effects of unions on the 'levels' and the 'changes' of productivity need not go in the same direction. Finally, the interpretation of the impact of unions on productivity growth may also depend on the specific institutional framework surrounding the bargaining process, which obviously varies across countries, but may also vary for the same country over time (such as the UK in the 1980s).

The results of the studies that examined the relationship between unionism and productivity growth are contained in Table 9.5. These studies are concentrated in the USA and in the UK, although some evidence is becoming available for less developed countries. The first US studies (Mansfield, 1980 and Link, 1981) found a negative union density effect on the average annual rate of change in total factor productivity. Maki (1983), using time series data from Canada, found a positive union effect on the level of productivity and a negative one on productivity growth. Allen (1988), using industry level data, found the same, but both effects were found to be statistically insignificant. Hirsch and Link (1984) found both effects negative (and statistically significant). Hirsch (1991), in one of the most complete US studies to date, used firm level panel data to find a negative effect of unionism on productivity growth, but this effect was found to be weak when industry effects were controlled for and insignificant when corrected for firm-specific serial correlation in the error term. Therefore, it seems that there is a relative consensus in the US literature of a negative union impact on productivity growth, but this is also subject to the criticism that unionism may in fact be picking up other unobserved effects.

It is also important to note that, for most of the studies, R&D is included on the right-hand side of the productivity regressions as an extra covariate. It would be interesting to examine the results excluding R&D from the equation, as that would allow the researcher to uncover the indirect impact of unions on productivity via R&D.

In the UK, the interpretation of the results is clouded by the weakening of the trade unions in the 1980s, due to the legal and political changes under Mrs Thatcher's government. For example, Nickell et al. (1992) and Gregg et al. (1993) find significant *positive* effects of the level of unionism on the growth of productivity at the beginning and in the end of the 1980s, respectively. They interpret this as reflecting the fact that during the 1980s managers in unionized firms were able to assert their 'right to manage' and introduce organizational changes that had been resisted by the unions when they were stronger in the 1970s. Additional evidence is presented by the Nickell et al. (1992) study that finds a *negative* effect of the level of union density on productivity growth in the late 1970s when it is argued that unions were becoming stronger due to a favourable legislative environment. Gregg et al. (1993) also found that the rise in productivity in the late 1980s was stronger among the unionized firms that de-recognized unions in some of their plants, suggesting also a negative effect of unionism on the *level* of productivity. So the interpretation of the UK studies is that unions have a negative effect on the level of productivity, but not on the growth of productivity (which is consistent with the absence of a significant negative union effect on R&D in the UK).

Outside the USA and UK, the literature is far scantier. In what seems to be the first study in Latin America, Menezes-Filho et al. (2002) find that there is a negative but insignificant correlation between unionism and productivity growth in Brazil in the 1990s. However, when the authors allow for a non-linear relationship they find that at low union density levels, an increase in union density tends to increase the rate of productivity growth, but at a decreasing rate, just as Menezes-Filho et al. (1998b) found with UK R&D intensity.

5.   Conclusions

There is a general view that unions tend to retard innovation for a wide variety of reasons. In this chapter we have examined the different theories that could lead to union power changing the incentive and abilities of firms to innovate. Although there are many ways in which unions could indeed slow down technological advance, there are also circumstances in which unions could foster new technology, so that a blanket condemnation in the absence of rigorous empirical evidence is unwarranted.

We have examined over forty separate empirical studies of the impact of unions on innovation as measured by four different indicators: R&D, innovation headcounts, technology diffusion and productivity growth. In our view, there is a reasonable consensus in the empirical literature of the impact of unions on some economic measures. Unions have a clear positive effect on wages and a clear negative effect on profitability. There are no grounds for such a consensus on the impacts of unions on innovation. The sign, size and statistical significance of the association of unions with innovation vary dramatically from study to study. However, there do appear to be some patterns that have emerged.

First, the North American (overwhelmingly US) studies find consistently negative impacts of unions on R&D. At face value this is extremely damaging to the US union movement. R&D is the basis of growth and if unions damage R&D they are undermining their own long-term survival chances, as well as damaging the few remaining industries where they remain strong.

Second, the European studies do not find that unions generally reduce R&D. Interestingly, this statement is true not just in the Continental European countries with 'co-operative' industrial relations (like Germany) but also in the UK where relations are usually described as 'adversarial'. The raw negative correlation can be accounted for by the fact that unions are found in older firms and low-tech industries. This difference between the UK and US studies does not appear to be driven by differences in specification. It is more likely to reflect differences in institutions. One hypothesis would be that UK unions place a higher weight on jobs than wages in their utility functions than their US counterparts (see Naylor, Chapter 3 of this volume, for a discussion of economic models of the trade union). The fact that the union wage mark-up is about twice as large in the USA as in the UK is consistent with this hypothesis. Placing a greater emphasis on jobs than wages should mitigate the size of the union tax on R&D and may even help some firms boost their R&D spend in some models. It may also be a reason why European unionization (even in the UK) is higher than in the USA.

A third finding is that there does appear to be a mildly negative association of union power with productivity growth, especially at higher levels of union density. This is less strong than the US R&D evidence, but does seem to emerge from most of the studies (although it is often difficult to interpret, as in the UK studies of the 1980s). This should be a serious cause for concern. Many firms do not depend upon formal R&D for their survival (at least not their own R&D), but all firms will rely on their own productivity growth if they are to prosper in the longer run. Productivity growth in firms depends not only on technology, but also on 'innovation' more widely, including innovation in new organizational forms (decentralization, delayering, performance pay, just-in-time production, team-working, etc.). Unions are often suspicious of these organizational changes and resist them more than new technologies (Daniel, 1987).

Finally, we should end with some methodological points. The knowledge base we draw on is much thinner in this area than in other areas of union research. There have been fewer systematic attempts to deal with the well-known problems of endogeneity and fixed effects. Is the negative union effect on R&D in the North America studies really causal or does it reflect some further unmeasured influence on both unions and R&D? Is there really a non-linear union effect or is it just another reflection of measurement error in the union density variable? There is also a need to expand the samples of countries under study that are still very Anglo-Saxon biased. With the growth of cross-European datasets on innovation and micro-data sets in developing countries, data availability is no longer an excuse. The important issue of the effect of labour market institutions on innovation and growth needs to spread its empirical net wider and deeper.

Acknowledgement

We would like to thank our co-authors in other work on the economic impact of unions, especially Steven Machin and David Ulph. We have also benefited from helpful discussions with David Metcalf over these issues. Responsibility for all errors remains our own.

Notes

1. This is suggested by the title of Addison and Hirsch's (1989) paper: the 'long-run' has arrived for US unionism.
2. This may be a reason why unions are often in the forefront of lobbying for greater protection from foreign trade (they have a common interest with their employers in this regard).
3. The original Luddites claimed to be led by one Ned Ludd, also known as 'King Ludd', who is believed to have destroyed two large stocking-frames that produced inexpensive stockings undercutting those produced by skilled knitters and whose signature appears on a 'workers' manifesto' of the time. Whether or not Ludd actually existed is historically unclear. The movement spread rapidly throughout England in 1811, with many wool and cotton mills being destroyed, until the British government suppressed them harshly (including making 'machine breaking' a capital crime, and executing 17 men in 1813).
4. Of course this will not always be the case. When Edison invented the phonograph in 1877 he envisioned several uses for it such as preserving the words of dying people, recording

books for blind people, announcing clock time and teaching spelling. Other entrepreneurs created jukeboxes to use the phonograph but Edison objected this debasement of his invention. It was only after about twenty years that Edison reluctantly conceded that the main use of the phonograph was for recorded music.

5.   For example, an analysis of over 2000 establishments from the British Workplace Industrial Relations Survey (WIRS) concluded:

> Overall, our results showed, first, that when it came to the introduction of particular changes involving advanced technology at the workplace, the general reaction of the workers affected was favourable. Second, in the cases where either shop stewards or full time officers [i.e. union officials] became involved, they tended to support the change even more strongly than their members. (Daniel, 1987, p. 264).

6.   See Arrow (1962) for a classical analysis of these problems.
7.   Empirical evidence tends to show a positive impact of new innovations on wages (see Van Reenen, 1996, for example, or the survey in Chennells and Van Reenen, 2002).
8.   McDonald and Solow (1981) made this 'implicit bargaining' argument but Johnson (1990) showed that in the context of a formal theoretical model that wage and effort bargaining would not reach the efficient bargaining solution (although it would get the partners closer to the Pareto Efficient outcome).
9.   Ulph and Ulph (2001) show that the incompleteness of the union/firm contract (that may induce under-investment in R&D) may actually compensate for the socially inefficient over-investment induced by the R&D tournament among firms (for the latter effect see Beath et al., 1995).
10.   Or, more realistically, end with a small and commonly known finite probability in every sub-game.
11.   This is the model of Gilbert and Newbery (1982); formally it is a one-shot tournament R&D game with no uncertainty and two players.
12.   See Bond and Van Reenen (2002) for an overview of the investment and R&D literature. Structural models of unions and R&D would constitute interesting new research.
13.   For example see Carlin et al. (2001), Griffith et al. (2000) or Machin and Van Reenen (1998).
14.   Under the accounting regulation SSAP(13) Revised.
15.   See Bound et al. (1984) for an early discussion of this.
16.   Although there is the problem that budgetary cutbacks in the Patent Office can alter the time series of patents, so that it may take longer to get a patent granted (see Griliches, 1998). There is also the issue that the standard for patents may have slipped over time (such as the granting of patents for 'business process innovations', such as Amazon's 'click and pick' web-site).
17.   The EU has currently developed a programme to measure firm-level innovation using the Oslo definition, which is subjective. It is becoming more useful now, as it is possible to compare this measure over time.
18.   For a discussion over the interpretation of cash flow in R&D equations see Bond et al. (1999).
19.   This is equivalent to the 'within groups' transformation that involves subtracting the firm-specific time series mean from each observation.
20.   This will be less of a problem for some measures like TFP or diffusion that show more time series variation. One must ask, however, whether the time series variation in TFP is due to technology or other non-technology related factors such as the state of the business cycle.
21.   A disadvantage of their data is that they do not observe union density at the industry level, but have to predict density from industry characteristics using the coefficients from individual level union membership regressions.
22.   It introduces the method of conditioning on pre-entry stocks of innovation counts and with a non-linear dynamic GMM model with fixed effects.
23.   Borghans and ter Weel (2002) use unionization as an instrumental variable for wages in a computer use equation. Unfortunately, the absence of a significant correlation between

unions and technology adoption (conditional on wages) does *not* guarantee the validity of this identification strategy.

References

Acs, Zoltan and David Audretsch (1988), 'Innovation in Large and Small Firms: An Empirical Analysis', *American Economic Review*, 78 (4), 678–690.

Addison, John T. and Barry T. Hirsch (1989), 'Unions Effects on Productivity, Profits and Growth: Has the Long Run Arrived?', *Journal of Labor Economics*, 7 (1), 72–105.

Addison, John T. and J. Chilton (1998), 'Self-Enforcing Union Contracts: Efficient Investment and Employment', *Journal of Business*, 71 (3), 349–369.

Addison, John T. and Joachim Wagner (1994), 'UK Unionism and Innovative Activity: Some Cautionary Remarks on the Basis of a Simple Cross-Country Test', *British Journal of Industrial Relations*, 32 (1), 85–98.

Aghion, Philippe and Peter Howitt (1992), 'A Model of Growth through Creative Destruction', *Econometrica*, 60 (2), 323–351.

Allen, Steve (1988), 'Productivity Levels and Productivity Change under Unionism', *Industrial Relations*, 27 (1), 94–113.

Arrow, Kenneth (1962), 'Economic Welfare and the Allocation of Resources for Invention', in Richard Nelson (ed.), *The Rate and Direction of Inventive Activity*, Princeton, NJ: Princeton University Press, pp. 609–625.

Baldwin, Carliss Y. (1983), 'Productivity and Labour Unions: an Application of the Theory of Self-Selection Contracts', *Journal of Business*, 56 (2), 155–185.

Beath, John, Yannis Katsoulacos and David Ulph (1995), 'Game-Theoretical Models of Innovation', in Paul Stoneman (ed.), *Handbook of Innovation*, Oxford: Basil Blackwell, pp. 150–187.

Benvignati, Anita (1982), 'Inter-firm adoption of capital goods innovations', *Review of Economics and Statistics*, 64 (2), 33–335.

Berman, Eli, John Bound and Zvi Griliches (1994), 'Changes in the Demand for Skilled Labor within US Manufacturing Industries: Evidence from the Annual Survey of Manufacturing', *Quarterly Journal of Economics*, 109 (2), 367–398.

Betcherman, George (1988), 'Technological Change and its Impacts: Do Unions Make a Difference?', *Proceedings of the 1987 Annual Meetings of the Canadian Industrial Relations Society*, Quebec: Laval University, pp. 65–78.

Betts, Julian R., Cameron W. Odgers and Michael K. Wilson (2001), 'The Effects of Unions on R&D: An Empirical Analysis using Multi-Year Data', *Canadian Journal of Economics*, 34 (3), 785–806.

Bloom, Nicholas and John Van Reenen (2002), 'Patents, Real Options and Firm Performance', *Economic Journal*, 112 (March), C97–C116.

Blundell, Richard, Rachel Griffith and John Van Reenen (1999), 'Market Structure and Innovation: Evidence from British Manufacturing Firms', *Review of Economic Studies*, 66 (3), 529–554.

Bond, Steven and John Van Reenen (2002), 'Micro-econometric Models of Investment and Employment', in James Heckman and Edward Leamer (eds), *Handbook of Econometrics*, vol. 6. Amsterdam: North Holland, forthcoming.

Bond, Steven, Dietmar Harhoff and John Van Reenen (1999), 'Investment, R&D and Financial Constraints in Britain and Germany', Institute for Fiscal Studies Working Paper No. 99/5.

Borghans, Lex and Bas ter Weel (2002), 'Computers, Skills and Wages', mimeo Maastricht University.

Bound, John, George Cummins, Zvi Griliches, Bronwyn Hall and Adam Jaffe (1984), 'Who does R&D and Who Patents?', in Zvi Griliches (ed.), *R&D, Patents and Productivity*, Chicago: Chicago University Press, pp. 130–167.

Bronars, Steven and Donald Deere (1991), 'The Threat of Unionisation, the Use of Debt and the Preservation of Shareholder Equity', *Quarterly Journal of Economics*, 106 (1), 231–253.

Bronars, Steven and Donald Deere (1993), 'Unionisation, Incomplete Contracting and Capital Investment', *Journal of Business*, 66 (1),117–132.

Bronars, Steven, Donald Deere and John Tracy (1994), 'The Effects of Unions on Firm Behavior: An Empirical Analysis using Firm Level Data', *Industrial Relations*, 33 (4), 426–451.

Carlin, Wendy, Andrew Glyn and John Van Reenen (2001), 'Export Market Performance of OECD Countries: an Empirical Examination of the Role of Cost Competitiveness in an OECD Panel of Industries', *Economic Journal*, 110 (468), 1–35.

Chennells, Lucy and John Van Reenen (1997), 'Technical Change and Earnings in British Establishments', *Economica*, 64 (256), 587–604.

Chennells, Lucy and John Van Reenen (2002), 'Technical Change in the Structure of Employment and Wages: A Survey of the Microeconometric Evidence' in Nathalie Greenan, Yannic L'Horty and Jacques Mairesse (eds), *Productivity Growth, Inequality and the Digital Economy*, Cambridge, MA: MIT Press, pp. 175–224.

Clarke, Kim and Zvi Griliches (1994), 'Productivity Growth and R&D at the Business Level: Results from the PIMS Data Base' in Zvi Griliches (ed.), *R&D, Patents and Productivity*, Chicago: University of Chicago Press, pp. 393–416.

Cohen, Wesley and Richard Levin (1989), 'Empirical Studies of Innovation and Market Structure', in Richard Schmalensee and Frank Willig (eds), *The Handbook of Industrial Organization*, vol. 1, Amsterdam: North-Holland, pp. 1059–1107.

Connolly, Richard, Barry Hirsch and Mark Hirschey (1986), 'Union Rent Seeking, Intangible Capital and the Market Value of the Firm', *Review of Economics and Statistics*, 68 (4), 567–577.

Daniel, William W. (1987), *Workplace Industrial Relations and Technical Change*, Washington D.C.: Policy Studies Institute.

Drago, Richard and Mark Wooden (1994), 'Unions, Investment and Innovation: Australian Evidence', *Applied Economics*, 26 (6), 609–615.

Espinosa, Maria P. and Changyong Rhee (1989), 'Efficient Wage Bargaining as a Repeated Game', *Quarterly Journal of Economics*, 104 (3), 565–588.

Fitzroy, Felix and Kornelius Kraft (1990), 'Innovation, Rent-Sharing and the Organization of Labour in the Federal Republic of Germany', *Small Business Economics*, 2 (4), 95–103.

Freeman, Richard (1984), 'Longitudinal Analysis of the Effect of Trade Unions', *Journal of Labor Economics*, 2 (1), 1–26.

Freeman, Richard (1992), 'Is Declining Unionism of the US Good, Bad or Irrelevant?', in Larry Mishel and Paula Voos (eds), *Unions and Economic Competitiveness*, Economic Policy Institute, pp. 143–169.

Freeman, Richard and James Medoff (1984), *What Do Unions Do?*, New York: Basic Books.

Geroski, Paul (1990), 'Innovation, Technological Opportunities and Market Structure', *Oxford Economic Papers*, 42 (3), 586–702.

Geroski, Paul (1995), *Market Structure, Corporate Performance and Innovative Activity*, Oxford: Oxford University Press.

Gilbert, Richard and David Newberry (1982), 'Preemptive Patenting and the Persistence of Monopoly', *American Economic Review*, 72 (3), 514–526.

Green, Francis, Stephen Machin and David Wilkinson (1998), 'Trade Unions and Training Practices in British Workplaces', *Industrial and Labor Relations Review*, 52 (4), 179–195.

Gregg, Paul, Steve Machin and David Metcalf (1993), 'Signal and Cycles? Productivity Growth and Changes in Unions Status in British Companies: 1984–1989', *Economic Journal*, 103 (419), 894–907.

Griffith, Rachel, Steve Redding and John Van Reenen (2000), 'Mapping the Two Faces of R&D: Productivity Growth in a panel of OECD industries', CEPR Discussion Paper No. 2457.

Griliches, Zvi (1998), *R&D and productivity: The Econometric Evidence*, Chicago: Chicago University Press.

Griliches, Zvi and Jacques Mairesse (1997), 'Production Functions: The Search for Identification', in Stephen Strom (ed.), *Essays in Honour of Raynar Frisch*, Cambridge: Econometric Monograph Series, pp. 231–266.

Grout, Paul A. (1984), 'Investment and Wages in the Absence of Binding Contracts: a Nash Bargaining Approach', *Econometrica*, 52 (2), 449–460.

Grunfeld, David and Zvi Griliches (1960), 'Is Aggregation Necessarily Bad?', *Review of Economics and Statistics*, XLII (1), 1–13.

Heckman, James (1979), 'Sample Selection Bias as a Specification Error', *Econometrica*, 47 (1), 153–161.

Himmelberg, Charles and Bruce Petersen (1994), 'R&D and Internal Finance: A Panel Study of Small Firms in High-Tech Industries', *Review of Economics and Statistics*, 76 (1), 38–51.

Hirsch, Barry T. (1991), *Labor Unions and the Economic Performance of US Firms*, Kalamazoo, MI: Upjohn Institute.

Hirsch, Barry T. (1992), 'Firm Investment Behavior and Collective Bargaining Strategy', *Industrial Relations*, 31 (Winter), 95–121.

Hirsch, Barry T. and Albert N. Link (1984), 'Unions, Productivity and Productivity Growth', *Journal of Labor Research*, 5 (Winter), 29–37.

Hirsch, Barry T. and Albert N. Link (1987), 'Labor Union Effects on Innovative Activity', *Journal of Labor Research*, 8 (Fall), 323–332.

Johnson, George E. (1990), 'Work Rules, Featherbedding and Pareto-optimal Union–Management Bargaining', *Journal of Labor Economics*, 8 (2), S237–259.

Keefe, James H. (1991), 'Do Unions Influence Technological Progress?', *Industrial and Labor Relations Review*, 44 (2), 261–274.

Kelley, Mark and Harold Brookes (1991), *The State of Computerized Automation in US Manufacturing*, Cambridge, MA: MIT Press.

Latreille, Paul (1992), 'Unions and the Inter-establishment Adoption of New Technologies in the British Private Manufacturing Sector', *Oxford Bulletin of Economics and Statistics*, 54 (1), 31–49.

Lawrence, Charles and Robert Lawrence (1985), 'Manufacturing Wage Dispersion: An End Game Interpretation', *Brookings Papers on Economic Activity*, 1, 4–116.

Layard, Richard and Steve Nickell (1999), 'Labor Market Institutions and Economic Performance', in Orley Ashenfelter and David Card (eds), *Handbook of Labor Economics*, vol. 3C, Amsterdam: Elsevier, pp. 267–312.

Leontief, Wassily (1946), 'The Pure Theory of the Guaranteed Annual Wage Contract', *Journal of Political Economy*, 54 (2), 76–79.

Link, Albert (1981), 'Basic Research and Productivity Increase in Manufacturing: Additional Evidence', *American Economic Review*, 71 (5), 1111–1112.

Link, Albert (1982), 'Productivity Growth, Environmental Regulations and the Composition of R&D', *Bell Journal of Economics*, Autumn, 548–554.

Lintner, Victor, Mikheal J. Pokorny, Michael M. Woods and Michael R. Blinkhorn (1987), 'Trade Unions and Technical Change in the UK Mechanical Engineering Industry', *British Journal of Industrial Relations*, 25 (1), 19–29.

Machin, Steve and John Van Reenen (1998), 'Technology and Changes in the Skill Structure: Evidence from Seven OECD Countries', *Quarterly Journal of Economics*, 113 (4), 1215–1244.

Machin, Steve and Sushil Wadhwani (1991), 'The Effects of Unions on Organizational Change, Investment and Employment', *Economic Journal*, 101 (407), 324–330.

Maki, Dennis (1983), 'The Effect of Unions and Strikes on the Rate of Growth of Total Factor Productivity in Canada', *Applied Economics*, 15 (February), 29–41.

Mansfield, Edward (1980), 'Basic Research and Productivity Increase in Manufacturing', *American Economic Review*, 70 (5), 863–873.

McDonald, Ian and Robert Solow (1981), 'Wage Bargaining and Employment', *American Economic Review*, 71 (3), 896–908.

Menezes-Filho, Naercio A. (1997), 'Unions and Profitability over the 1980s: Some Evidence on Union–Firm Bargaining in the UK', *Economic Journal*, 107 (442), 651–670.

Menezes-Filho, Naercio A., David Ulph and John Van Reenen (1998a), 'The Impact of Unions on R&D: Empirical Evidence', *European Economic Review*, 42 (3–5), 919–930.

Menezes-Filho, Naercio A., David Ulph and John Van Reenen (1998b), 'R&D and Union

Bargaining: Evidence from British Companies and Establishments', *Industrial and Labor Relations Review*, 52 (1), 45–63.

Menezes-Filho, Naercio A., Helio Zylbertajn, Jose Chahad and Elaine Pazello (2002), 'Trade Unions and the Economic Performance of Brazilian Establishments', mimeo, University of São Paulo.

Millward, Neil, Mark Stevens, Steven Smart and William R. Hawes (1992), *Workplace Industrial Relations in Transition*, Aldershot: Dartmouth Publishing Company.

Modigliani, Frank and Marcus Miller (1958), 'The Cost of Capital, Corporation Finance and the Theory of Investment', *American Economic Review*, 48 (3), 261–297.

Nickell, Steve, Sushil Wadhwani and Martin Wall (1992), 'Productivity Growth in UK Companies', *European Economic Review*, 36 (3–5), 518–536.

Pakes, Ariel (1986), 'Patents Options: Some Estimates of the value of holding European Patent Stocks', *Econometrica*, 54 (4), 755–784.

Schnabel, Claus and Joachim Wagner (1992a), 'Unions and Innovative Activity in Germany', *Journal of Labor Research*, 13 (8), 393–406.

Schnabel, Claus and Joachim Wagner (1992b), 'Unions and Innovations: Evidence from Germany', *Economics Letters*, 39, 369–373.

Schnabel, Claus and Joachim Wagner (1994), 'Industrial Relations and Trade Union Effects on Innovation in Germany', *Labour*, 8 (3), 489–503.

Simons, Herbert (1944), 'Some Reflections on Syndicalism', *Journal of Political Economy*, 52 (1), 1–25.

Stewart, Mark (1995), 'Union Wage Differentials in an Era of Declining Unionisation', *Oxford Bulletin of Economics and Statistics*, 57 (2), 143–166.

Taymaz, Eli (1991), 'The Impact of Trade Unions on the Diffusion of Technology: The Case of NC Machine Tools', *British Journal of Industrial Relations*, 29 (2), 305–312.

Ulph, Alistair and David Ulph (1989), 'Labour Markets and Innovation', *Journal of Japanese and International Economics*, 3 (3), 403–423.

Ulph, Alistair and David Ulph (1994), 'Labour Markets and Innovation: Ex Post Bargaining', *European Economic Review*, 38 (3–5), 195–210.

Ulph, Alistair and David Ulph (2001), 'Strategic Innovation with Complete and Incomplete Labor Market Contracts', *Scandinavian Journal of Economics*, 103 (2), 265–282.

Van der Ploeg, Rik (1987), 'Trade Unions, Investment and Employment', *European Economic Review*, 31 (6), 1465–1492.

Van Reenen, John (1996), 'The Creation and Capture of Economic Rents: Wages and Innovation in a Panel of UK Companies', *Quarterly Journal of Economics*, CXI (443), 195–226.

10 Trade unions as political actors
Wolfgang Streeck and Anke Hassel

1. Introduction

Modern trade unions act in two arenas: the state and politics on the one hand, and the labour market and collective bargaining on the other. The relative importance of their economic and political activities differs between countries and world regions, as well as historically and between types of unions. So do the way and the extent to which union action in the two arenas is coordinated.

The dominant kind of trade union as it emerged from the second postwar settlement after 1945 recognizes the primacy of the liberal-democratic state and of parliamentary democracy, just as it accepts private property and the principal rules of a – socially embedded and regulated – market economy. Most unions after 1945 no longer claimed a right or reserved the option to overthrow the government of the state through a political strike. In this they paid tribute to the superior legitimacy of free elections, as compared to 'direct action' of the organized working class. Today more or less explicit constitutional law makes it illegal for unions in most liberal democracies to call a strike in order to put pressure on the elected parliament, and most trade unions have accepted this as legitimate. In return liberal democratic states allow unions – within the limits of usually complex legal rules – to strike in the context of disputes with employers and in pursuit of collective agreements on wages and working conditions.

In the nineteenth century, syndicalist traditions of the trade union movement aimed at replacing the emerging national state with directly elected councils of workers, called *sovjets* in Russian and *Räte* in German. Anarcho-syndicalist unions, which in countries like Spain survived into the twentieth century, pursued direct democracy of producers as an alternative to both the bureaucratic territorial state and the capitalist market economy. Such projects, however, came to naught and were eventually abandoned in exchange for the legal and constitutional recognition of collective bargaining and rights for unions to act as organized interest groups within liberal democracy. While many unions still keep a distance from 'bourgeois democracy' and claim for themselves a special political status above that of a mere lobbying group, this mainly reflects the memory of the class society of the past in which the dominant political cleavage was that between capital and labour.

Well into the 1980s and 1990s, European unions in particular launched or were involved in political campaigns on a variety of matters not directly related to their members' economic interests, such as international peace or free abortion. In this they drew on a broad concept of worker interests informed by traditional visions of class conflict and by a syndicalist sense of rivalry with the state over the legitimate representation of workers, not just as workers but also as citizens. Especially in Europe, unions continued for a long time to be expected by their members and officials, and also by intellectuals and public opinion, to be leaders in a general movement for social progress, far beyond economic matters in a narrow sense. To an extent this is still the case and unions often find it difficult to reject expectations of this sort. Nevertheless, most unions have in recent decades increasingly concentrated their political activities on objectives related to those pursued in collective bargaining, such as general economic policy, industrial and labour market policy, the public provision of economic infrastructure, including training and education, social welfare policy and the 'social wage', and not least the legal framework for collective bargaining, workplace representation, and trade unionism in general.

As political actors within the constitutional framework of liberal democracy trade unions can use various channels of influence. The most important of these are still unions' traditional relations to political parties. In all democratic countries unions are in some form of alliance with a major party of the Left or the Centre-Left, such as the SPD in Germany, the Labour Party in Britain, or the Democratic Party in the United States. Often such relations go back to common origins in the nineteenth or twentieth centuries, in the context of a 'labour movement' organized in a political and an economic wing. Similar relations sometimes exist with Catholic parties of the Centre-Right. In countries where collective bargaining is less firmly established, or a purely economic pursuit of member interests is for other reasons less promising, unions may be dominated by allied parties, like in Italy or France. Mostly, however, the relationship is more balanced and unions may exercise considerable influence over their political allies, serving as a recruiting ground for party officials, contributing money to fund election campaigns or cover the current costs of party organization, and mobilizing their members to vote for the party in general elections. Unions may increase their political clout if they can credibly threaten to shift their support to a competing party, for example from a social-democratic to a centre-right party. This, however, requires not just a high degree of political and ideological independence but also a suitable political opportunity structure. While the German DGB may sometimes ally itself with the Christian-Democratic Party if the Social Democrats disregard its demands, the British TUC has no other party than Labour to turn to as the British Conservatives will not deal with them.

Important sources of political strength of unions are parastate public institutions of functional representation that include unions in their governance structures. Examples are social security or labour market policy funds under the shared control of unions, employers and, in some cases, the state. Even where such funds are governed by law, they enable unions to influence the implementation of public policies. They also offer employment opportunities for union activists and opportunities for membership recruitment. Governments trying to control the political power of unions or to retaliate for unions not supporting their policy may sometimes undertake to eliminate functional representation and replace it with state control.

Most economists regard unions as economic actors, especially as labour market monopolists. Political scientists, by comparison, treat unions as interest groups, emphasizing their political activities and their relations to political parties. For industrial relations scholars, the political activities of unions are an aspect, of different importance in different countries, of their participation in tripartite industrial rule making. Historical-institutionalist approaches look at the ways in which unions evolved in opposition to the modern state and in alliance with political parties of the working class or of religious minorities; past origins are drawn upon to explain present differences in unions' political status and political strategies. Students of neo-corporatism consider unions as institutionalized interest groups with more or less corporatist organizational characteristics and acting more or less in concert with the government; to them industrial relations is one arena among others where selected interest organizations are institutionalized and endowed with special rights and obligations by the state. Theorists of collective action make little difference between political and economic activities as in either case, organizations must find ways of offering outside inducements to rational individuals to overcome inherent free-rider problems.

2. Historical origins of union political behaviour

Union political behaviour today is shaped by the economic, political and legal conditions in which unions first organized (Streeck, 1993a). Whether unions became reformist or radical depended on two factors: 'first the nature of the social class system before industrialization; second the way economic and political elites responded to the demands of workers for the right to participate in the polity and economy' (Lipset, 1982, p. 1). Modern unions evolved in symbiosis with the nation-state, which first contested and later protected their right to organize. Liberal and interventionist state traditions, conditioned in part by the time and pace of industrialization, shaped the organizational form of trade unions as well as their relationship to political parties. Early patterns of union involvement in politics, as distinguished from collective bargaining with employers, not only affected the extent to which national unions achieved control over their local and sectoral constituents, but also prefigured the eventual relationship between industrial relations and state social policy in the constitution of mature nation-states.

More specifically, in liberal environments where the general extension of the right to vote preceded or coincided with the onset of industrialization, unions remained independent from political parties and hostile to political ideologies. This went together with organizational fragmentation and an overwhelming preference for industrial over political action. Over time in such countries, union political independence evolved into a pattern of primarily voluntary and particularistic, as opposed to statutory and universalistic, regulation of employment conditions, accompanied by a pattern of state abstention from social policy or intervention in labour law. By comparison, in states that took an active and, usually, authoritarian role in the industrialization of their societies, unions typically had to struggle for universal suffrage as a precondition for the achievement of effective organizing rights; this often resulted in their subordination to an allied political party, as well as in their politicization and centralization. With improved economic and legal opportunities for collective bargaining, political unions of this sort more or less managed to escape from party tutelage while not losing their capacities for political action and centralized coordination. When union-friendly political parties were voted into government, such unions had the opportunity to combine encompassing collective bargaining with a political quest for a universalistic social policy, engaging in industrial and political action simultaneously and deploying one in support of the other. For example, just as unions could use their influence on social policy to improve their position in relation to employers in collective bargaining, they could draw on their role in collective bargaining to defend their independence from allied parties and, by extension, the state. In particular, joint understandings with employers on the range of issues to be regulated 'voluntarily' by collective agreement rather than by government statute, constituted an important resource for political unions defending their jurisdiction against state intervention.

In early industrializing countries with a relatively liberal political system, repression of unionism was weak and union organizing rights were comparatively easily gained (Bartolini, 2000, p. 244ff; Crouch, 1993). The first British unions were occupational associations of a highly skilled labour aristocracy ('craft unions'). Being able to achieve their economic objectives on their own by relying on their strong position in the market, unions of this sort had no demands on the state apart from non-interference in their organizing activities, which were typically based on the closed shop and included control over skill formation. In particular, they had little need for government social policy as they preferred to negotiate their wages and benefits directly with their employers and were prosperous enough to build their own social insurance funds on a voluntary basis. General unions of unskilled 'mass workers' emerged much later and although they commanded considerably less market power, they had to organize and act under political, institutional and ideological conditions that for a long time continued to be controlled by their predecessors.

Craft unions originally had no need for political action as liberal support for union organizing rights was all they required from the state. When later, after long hesitation, British unions did resolve to engage in continuous political activity, they set up the Labour Party as their extended arm funded and formally controlled by the Trades Union Congress (von Beyme, 1977). As predicted by the opponents of direct union engagement with politics, unions often turned out unable to make the parliamentary Labour Party follow its directions. Given that British unions never developed a coherent socialist ideology, however, this did not matter much as long as Labour remained committed to free collective bargaining and did not stray from a core welfare-state agenda. Moreover, their low degree of politicization protected British unions from the political divisions that tore apart union movements on the European Continent.

In the USA, by comparison, craft unions were even more conservative and maintained their dominance over the union movement even longer than in Britain (Lipset and Marks, 2000; Friedmann, 1998; Katznelson and Zolberg, 1986). Well into the 1920s the mainstream of American trade unionism remained hostile to state intervention in the economy, not to mention a statutory social policy securing benefits for workers that well-organized craft unions were able to secure on their own through collective bargaining. The unskilled unions of the CIO that grew in strength only under the New Deal in the 1930s soon turned into business unions and after the Second World War at the latest, also relied on non-political collective bargaining as their principal mode of action. A slightly different approach was taken only by the union of automobile workers (UAW) which, with little success, held on to its demand for a universalistic social policy of the federal government, in particular with respect to the provision of health insurance. The only lasting result of the New Deal was the close relationship it established between American trade unions and the Democratic Party of the then President, Franklin D. Roosevelt.

In Continental Europe the relationship between unions and political parties, and subsequently between collective bargaining and social policy, was quite different from the Anglo-American world (Kendall, 1975). Sweden is the main example of a country where delayed industrial development, with the associated lack of opportunities for a successful pursuit of worker interest through the market, resulted in unions being founded by a political party of the Left rather than, like in Britain, the other way around. While in Sweden just as in Britain, unions were corporate members of the political party of the working class, in stark contrast to Britain this meant subordination of the former to the latter. It was only after collective bargaining had become firmly established in the late 1930s, under the Saltsjöbaden national agreement with the employers, that Swedish unions gained autonomy from the primacy of the party inside the labour movement. This in turn came after the Socialist Party had become the hegemonic force of Swedish politics when in the early 1930s it broke a wildcat strike of construction workers that threatened to undermine the government's reflation programme. Continuing Socialist dominance within Swedish unions resulted in a political division of the Swedish union movement as white-collar workers refused to join the Socialist blue-collar unions and set up their own federation after 1945 (Fulcher, 1991).

Political unionism proved even more divisive in countries where, unlike Sweden, national politics included a strong Catholic element or where the First World War led to a split in the political party of the working class. In Italy and France, Socialist, Communist and Catholic parties founded their own unions, setting in motion protracted conflicts between and among unions and parties over trade union unity, with unions periodically joining together and then again breaking apart (Friedmann, 1998; Ebbinghaus, 1995; Valenzuela, 1994). Politicization and party-political control of trade unions was favoured in Italy by slow industrialization and by weak institutions of collective bargaining and a dominant role of the national state in the economy, with strong clientelism and centralism. To escape instrumentalization for party-political purposes, for example in elections or in conflicts over the composition of the national government, Italian unions made several attempts after 1945 to merge across political divisions. Immediately after the war national federations were founded in Italy and France that included the former Socialist, Communist and Catholic unions. But these soon broke up, mainly under American pressure aimed at isolating the Communists and ending their alleged control over the united union movement. In Italy, several attempts at reuniting the union movement were made beginning in the 1970s, but always failed earlier or later when party strategists utilized industrial relations as an additional political arena, or when unions required political patronage to score a success in collective bargaining. In France, the joint effects of syndicalist and liberal-republican political traditions and weak labour market institutions created a similar effect of dominance over unions by political parties – in particular the Communist party – and of union polarization. In contrast to Italy, unions did not benefit from the social unrest of the late 1960s, but lost much of their importance and most of their members in subsequent years.

Political unionism took a different path in Germany where industrial development was faster than in Sweden, Italy and France and where political repression hit the working-class party more than the unions (Mommsen and Husung, 1985). Already early in the twentieth century, Socialist unions were formally conceded strategic independence by the leadership of the Social-Democratic Party. A contributing factor may have been the early existence of a strong Catholic union movement associated with the Centre Party. Like Socialists, Catholics were suspected by the Bismarckian state of internationalist loyalties, which made them, too, a target of state repression. After the First World War, the Social-Democratic and the Centre Parties together became the pillars of the Weimar Republic and the unions associated with them coexisted more or less peacefully. A Communist union wing emerged inside the Socialist, or General, unions but never achieved political relevance. The Nazis suppressed all unions in 1933. After 1945, Socialist and Catholic unions set aside their differences and founded the DGB as an independent *Einheitsgewerkschaft* not organizationally affiliated to any political party.

That the DGB, unlike the CGIL in Italy or the CGT in France, remained united may be explained by the insignificance of its Communist element, due to the confinement of German Communism in the second postwar German state, the DDR. Formal party-political independence, however, does not prevent the DGB, from maintaining a particularly cordial relationship with the Social-Democratic Party (SPD). At the same time, however, it allows it to manoeuvre between the SPD and the Christian-Democratic Union (CDU/CSU), which grew out of the former Centre Party with its traditional pro-union element. While the great majority of their officials sympathize with the SPD and presumably carry its membership card, German industrial unions try to ensure that at least one member of their national executive is a member or confidant of the CDU/CSU. There are also some union officials that are members of the post-Communist PDS, which after German unity absorbed the – few – Communist elements of West German unions before 1989.

In Belgium, the Netherlands and Switzerland, the labour–capital cleavage was cut across by conflicts between church and state. In a battle over political control, two competing sets of worker organizations and social milieus developed, one under the leadership of the party in the Socialist movement and one under the control of religious leaders in the Christian workers' movement (Ebbinghaus, 1995, p. 83). In contrast to Austria and

Germany, in the 'consociational' countries religious cleavages became institutionalized. Complex party–union relations combining religious and political cleavages split the trade union as well as the party systems and gave rise to complicated consensus-orientated political arrangements.

In Japan, both unions and working-class political parties were outlawed for a long time under the authoritarian developmental state of the decades after the Meiji Restoration. Parliamentary democracy and free collective bargaining became safely institutionalized only after 1945. Unionization proceeded rapidly in the immediate postwar period and in 1947, the Socialist Party took over the national government, only to be removed from office shortly thereafter by the American military command, on the eve of a general strike. Subsequently the national trade union confederation divided along political lines and national unionism for many decades remained a site of arcane ideological disputes between rapidly changing factions of the radical Left, unrelated to the realities of the workplace. There employers and the government succeeded in establishing the principle of enterprise unionism. While this responded to strong interests of workers to have a say at their workplace, especially with respect to the protection of 'lifetime' employment, it also de-politicized trade unionism and cut off the experience of workers at the workplace from the ideological disputes between national trade union centres, which were mainly on matters of war and peace and on the desirability of a fast transition to Communism. National trade union centres continued to reconfigure rapidly through most of the postwar years, without visible impact on industrial relations at the workplace. Enterprise unionism and the practical irrelevance of their politicized national confederations corresponded to the absence of a public welfare state in the Japanese political economy and its internalization into the industrial relations and the employment policy of large companies. While Japanese unions were often effective in representing their members at the workplace, there was for a long time little opportunity for them for political action in support of their activities in collective bargaining, not to speak of tripartite political exchange at national level between unions, employers, and the government. It was only in the 1980s with the formation of Rengo – a new 'moderate' trade union confederation ideologically not committed to the Left – that Japanese industrial relations, focused as they are on the workplace and the enterprise, became to some extent institutionally reconnected to politics and political activities.

In conclusion, the relationship between trade unions and political parties, and the political arena as a whole, can be classified by two structural dimensions that evolved in the course of nation-building and state formation in the nineteenth and twentieth century: the degree of political unity and the degree of politization of trade unions (see Figure 10.1).

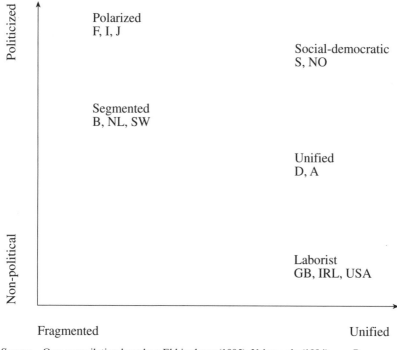

Polarized
F, I, J

Social-democratic
S, NO

Segmented
B, NL, SW

Unified
D, A

Laborist
GB, IRL, USA

Politicized

Non-political

Fragmented   Unified

Source: Own compilation based on Ebbinghaus (1995); Valenzuela (1994); von Beyme (1977).

Figure 10.1   Union–party relations

Political unity exists in countries where political differences within trade unions have not led to organizational fragmentation. The degree of politization describes the extent to which trade unions are active in the political arena. Politically unified trade unions are the less politicized the more dominant they historically were in relation to political parties. Dominant unions tend to be politically unified but fragmented along industrial, occupational or enterprise lines. Politically fragmented trade unions are always highly politicized. The more politicized trade unions are, whether politically fragmented or not, the more encompassing they are in industrial terms.

Union–party relationships have remained remarkably stable since the Second World War. Political cleavages were organizationally frozen early in both political party and trade union systems. Still, there are long-term tendencies towards unification of unions and mutual independence between parties and unions. Unification was most pronounced in Germany and

Austria, where the entire trade union structure was reorganized immediately after the war. Religious and political segmentation lost in importance in the Netherlands, Switzerland and Italy, less so in France and Belgium. Union–party links have generally become weaker over time, with trade unions and political parties responding to the evolution of their respective industrial and political environments.

3.   Unions in the political process

Trade unions may achieve political influence by converting industrial into political power (Pizzorno, 1978). *Political exchange* of this sort occurs where centralized unions command strong bargaining power; where the outcomes of collective bargaining are decisive for macroeconomic performance, in particular with respect to monetary stability and employment; and where the political survival of the government depends on such performance. Also, unions may insert themselves in the political process through *privileged links* with an allied political party, which may enable them to achieve their industrial objectives more effectively and efficiently through political instead of industrial means. Where such links do not exist or have attenuated, unions must try to achieve political influence through electoral support for the party most sympathetic to their demands. Third, union political power may derive from institutionalized collective representation on bipartite or tripartite parastate or parafiscal agencies, such as labour market or social security boards. Presence on such forums of *functional representation* may enable unions to control the implementation of public policies or even veto changes in government policy. Functional representation is less formalized in regional, sectoral or international policy networks that often include unions to enhance their legitimacy or mobilize expertise. Finally, unions may like other interest groups lobby parliament and government in the preparation of legislation and policy decisions; here it is important for unions, like lobbyists in general, to provide lawmakers with technical information and, if necessary, influence public opinion in favour of their preferred policies.

Political exchange

Until the end of the 1970s, economic policy in postwar democratic capitalism was conducted on the premise that social stability and the electoral fortunes of the government depended on politically guaranteed full employment. Keynesian methods of macroeconomic management, however, increased the bargaining power of unions as these no longer needed to worry about unemployment resulting from excessive wage settlements. Rising worker militancy fuelled by high growth, inflation and secure employment prospects made governments dependent on unions willing to act as 'managers of industrial discontent' (Flanders, 1970) and help them restore monetary stability without having to retreat from their commitment to full employment. In this situation, centralized and broadly based encompassing unions (Olson, 1982) were in a position to offer governments wage moderation in exchange for favourable social policies, such as higher pensions, or for improved institutional conditions for unions in the industrial relations system, like extended participation rights at the workplace or centralization of collective bargaining.

Conversion of industrial into political power under what came to be referred to as neo-corporatist incomes policies enabled unions to get a wide variety of concessions from governments, including industrial, regional and educational policy programmes, and to wield extensive power over public policy (Lehmbruch, 1984; Schmitter, 1977; Headey, 1970). But it also required unions to discipline their members and make them forgo short-term for long-term benefits. To the extent that member militancy reflected collective and symbolic as much as individual and material grievances, the transformation of direct action in political negotiations involved a trade-off of expressive identities against instrumental interests (Pizzorno, 1978). Unions engaging in neo-corporatist political exchange thus faced a double risk of member opposition and uncontrolled militancy on the one hand and member de-motivation and apathy on the other. On the part of government, the concessions offered to unions in return for wage moderation may in effect only have moved problems into the future, via growing deficits in the public budget. At the same time, while the price paid by governments for union cooperation was often high, control of union leaders over their rank-and-file remained tenuous at best and frequently unions turned out unable to deliver the wage moderation for which they had collected political concessions.

'Democratic class struggle' and party linkages
Corporatist political exchange in principle worked also with conservative parties, provided these were still committed to the postwar political orthodoxy of politically guaranteed full employment. However, where as in Scandinavia social-democratic parties had achieved hegemonic control of the state, another conversion of industrial into political strength of trade unions became possible under which unions could increasingly rely on political means to achieve their objectives. According to Korpi (1983) this explains why the most successful trade unions of their time had the lowest strike rates in the Western world, especially in comparison to the United States with its very intense industrial conflict. Sweden in particular was a country where class conflict, far from having subsided or 'withered away', had been transposed into the political arena, where it was possible to extend the achievements of the labour movement, not just to union members, but

to society as a whole. As Swedish unions turned into a popular movement closely identified with Swedish society and the Swedish people, they were able to organize an unmatched 80 per cent of the workforce.

In the 1960s and 1970s the 'Swedish model' seemed to offer a generalizable vision of democratic-socialist progress under a close alliance between powerful unions and a hegemonic socialist party (Stephens, 1979). Subsequently, however, traditional union–party links weakened even in Sweden, where an important contributing factor was the rise of politically unaffiliated white-collar unionism. In the United Kingdom after the failure of the Labour government under Callaghan in the 1979 'winter of discontent', the Labour Party began to regard its political dependence on the TUC as an electoral liability and gradually extricated itself from it. In Germany in the 1990s, the SPD on several occasions distanced itself publicly from the unions, in the belief that this would improve its electoral fortunes. Generally centre-left political parties today take care not to appear as extended arms of trade unions whose membership base is shrinking and whose policies are perceived by a growing share of the public as serving only union members, sometimes at the expense of the rest of society. Nevertheless, social-democratic parties still require the votes of the union constituency and thus make considerable efforts to gain union support, especially before elections and during election campaigns (Western, 1997; Taylor, 1993).

As social-democratic parties must broaden their electoral appeal in a society that is becoming more and more heterogeneous, unions can no longer take it for granted that they will necessarily adopt and carry out the policies unions prefer (Taylor, 1989). Increasingly, therefore, unions must apply political pressure to make social-democratic parties take their interests into account. Such pressure is likely to be most effective if unions can credibly threaten to divert their support, and the votes of their members, to a competing party. In addition to the actual existence of such a party, this depends on the extent to which union members and constituents follow the recommendations of their leaders when casting their votes. As electorates tend to become increasingly volatile, neither parties nor union leaders can be certain to what extent unions will in fact be able to deliver their members' votes; indications are that this capacity has been declining in recent years. The situation is similar for other large organizations, such as churches or sports associations.

Growing voter volatility increases the importance of campaign contributions and financial support generally. Depending on a country's campaign spending laws, unions may invest considerable sums of money to ensure that social-democratic parties first support their policies and then win the election. For example, in Germany the trade union confederation DGB mobilized an unprecedented amount of indirect campaign contributions during the election campaign of 1998, to extract from the SPD a commitment to undo certain labour market reforms passed by the last Kohl government and to enable Schröder to win the election, also with the support of the union vote. A similar effort was made in 2002 to ensure Schröder's re-election, after the Red–Green government had closed ranks with the unions on labour market and social security reform.

Functional representation
In many Continental-European countries trade unions and employers are represented on national economic policy councils, which were set up in the interwar years or after 1945, to provide for regular meetings and discussions between labour, business and the government. For instance, the Netherlands created a tripartite Social and Economic Council after the Second World War and similar bodies exist in Belgium and Austria. Some of these have, usually narrowly circumscribed, constitutional rights to advise the government or the parliament on matters of economic policy, or to be heard on current legislation. Moreover, trade unions, usually together with employers and sometimes also with the government, sit on the boards of a variety of quasi-public or parafiscal agencies administering labour market policy or social insurance programmes. In part such agencies were created at an early time when national states incorporated in their compulsory social insurance programmes the friendly societies and mutual aid funds founded for their members by unions and small business associations in the nineteenth century. Not to be pushed aside, unions, sometimes supported by employers, insisted on being given a role in the administration of the newly-created agencies, which in countries like Germany subsequently came under the 'self-government' of the 'social partners'. Bipartite and tripartite bodies of this kind emerged in particular in the so-called Bismarck countries where social insurance was funded through contributions of workers and employers rather than by general taxes, with the parafiscal agencies collecting and administering such contributions providing for representation of those paying them.

Although involvement in the administration of social security programmes sometimes offered unions rich opportunities for patronage, it is questionable how much political power unions derived from it. In countries where public unemployment benefit is administered by the unions, under the so-called Ghent system, they use this as a device for recruiting and retaining members. This indirectly contributes to union power (Ebbinghaus, 2002; Rothstein, 1992). However, levels of benefit and contributions are universally fixed by law, and unions and employers, far from having a veto, can influence them only through the legislature. The same, with appropriate modifications, seems to apply also to the national economic councils that have survived from the postwar years, or to an institution like the Economic and Social Committee of the European Union.

Unlike formal participation in state councils or quasi-public agencies, informal inclusion of unions in sectoral, regional and international policy networks seems to have become increasingly important in recent years. New forms of governance below, within and above the national state depend on bringing together all concerned parties to collect expertise, provide for mutual information on policy preferences, and increase as much as possible the legitimacy of jointly devised policies. Rather than conflict, policy networks emphasize cooperation in the pursuit of common objectives and the improvement of collective infrastructures that cultivate joint comparative advantage. Although policy networks have no constitution and there are no formal rights to inclusion, in most cases care is taken to ensure that unions participate, both to gain the general support of their members and to tap their expertise with respect to industrial development, training and skill formation, employment, labour law, work organization and the like (Marin and Mayntz, 1991).

Lobbying
As the links between unions and centre-left political parties have become more tenuous, and formalized functional representation tends to be pre-empted by legislative activism and state intervention, unions trying to influence political decisions seem to depend more than ever on classical lobbying of parliament and government. Especially in international environments, but also in national politics, the opportunities for unions to exercise political influence seem to be becoming similar to those of any other interest group, from farmers to environmentalists. In most countries, unions have established procedural rights to be heard by parliamentary committees and like bodies on impending decisions close to their concerns; sometimes those rights exceed those of other groups. Still, unions used to acting directly through collective bargaining or through political exchange based on their bargaining strength, through a closely related socialist party within an encompassing labour movement, or through legally based functional representation, may not be particularly good at shaping legislation from the outside or making their cause attractive to the general public. Also, in many countries unions not carry much favour in postindustrial media politics. Not least, unions that have traditionally relied on organizing, mobilizing and negotiating skills may take time to build up a capacity convincingly to present expert knowledge to bureaucrats and legislators, and a pleasant appearance to the general public. Here business firms and business associations command considerable advantage over unions in their present condition.

4. Unions and economic policy

Trade unions emerged in conflict with the economic liberalism of the nineteenth century as they tried to protect their members from the fluctuations of the market economy. Partly in response to union pressures, national governments in the first half of the twentieth century assumed responsibility for stabilizing the economy and promoting economic growth and employment. Moreover, in the First World War, governments intervened deeply in national economies, only to discover that economic mobilization and the governance of the war economy required the collaboration of union leaders. In many countries these came to be co-opted in positions of quasi-public authority. Also enlisted soldiers had to be promised a better life in a fairer society upon their return from the battlefields, which entailed a commitment to lasting state intervention in the economy.

The first postwar settlement after 1918 involved concessions of 'industrial democracy' and the acceptance of free collective bargaining in many industrialized countries. However, national governments proved unable to stabilize their economies without causing high unemployment, and in many countries the Great Depression ended liberal democracy and free trade unionism and brought authoritarian regimes into power. A new labour inclusive settlement based on a Keynesian full employment policy, which first took shape in the New Deal in the United States and under the British war cabinet, became the cornerstone of the political economy of the West after 1945. The democratic capitalism of the 'Golden Age' entailed not only the legal recognition of trade unions and the rise of the modern welfare state, but also the promise of an economic policy in line with the fundamental interest of workers in full employment.

Keynesianism and the second post-war settlement

The Keynesian revolution in economic thought held out the prospect of full employment secured through creation of aggregate demand by public authorities, rather than through reduction of costs by private enterprises under the pressure of competition. The Keynesian scenario, which was based on the assumption that nominal wages were rigid and could not easily be adjusted, was attractive for governments since it integrated strong trade unions and collective bargaining as an empirical fact into economic theory. Keynesian ideas strengthened the role of the state in economic policy by holding it responsible for providing for counter-cyclical demand whenever the economy required new stimulus.

In theory, Keynesianism did not entail trade union participation in economic policy, nor did it require detailed economic planning. In practice, however, many European governments after 1945 tried to plan their economies to avoid a repetition of the politically disruptive economic crisis of the interwar years. In France, the country where planning became most formalized, union influence on the plan was low. Neither government nor business was interested in discussing economic policy with trade unions (Barbash, 1972, p. 149). In other European countries, planning was conceived as a policy instrument that was deliberately meant to integrate the labour movement, especially in order to moderate wage demands. In such countries, economic planning was used to constrain free collective bargaining. In the UK, planning took place in the framework of the National Economic Development Council (NEDC) under a Labour government. Trade unions were initially willing to participate but were quickly disillusioned by the complexity of the problems and by the expectation of the government that they would in return settle for lower wages.

In other countries, consultation on economic policy took place outside formal councils. Coordination between trade union collective bargaining and government economic policy was based on a more informal shared understanding of the macroeconomic interaction of wage setting and economic policy. The Swedish Rehn–Meidner model of 'active manpower policy' was developed in cooperation between trade unions and the governing Social Democratic party, but not in a formal consultation structure. Governments encouraged trade union wage restraint by offering growth-enhancing public policies (Lange and Garrett, 1985).

Economic policy problems in postwar Europe were unlike those in the interwar years. In the first decade after the war, wage growth was moderate and capital stocks were being built up. After demobilization and recovery had been achieved, 'the main difficulty of the post-war economies was not slack demand, relative overproduction or insufficient investment, but an ungovernable tendency of demand to outrun the economy's capacity to meet it without inflation and price rise' (Postan, 1967, p. 19). Instead of having to stimulate demand, governments soon faced the task of containing inflationary pressure. At the same time, they remained committed to full employment and free collective bargaining.

As a consequence, Western governments soon found themselves facing a trilemma between full employment, price stability and free collective bargaining, in which any two could be achieved only by sacrificing the third. The tradeoff between unemployment and price stability – the so-called Phillips curve – depended on the conduct of collective bargaining. Under the institutional conditions of a regulated labour market and free collective bargaining, any decrease in unemployment would lead to an increase in inflationary pressure (Flanagan et al., 1983; Ulman and Flanagan, 1972, p. 2–4). Macroeconomic policy had to deal with the question of how to accommodate the effects of free collective bargaining without reducing employment.

In this situation, incomes policies were considered a promising potential instrument to shift the Phillips curve downwards and preempt inflationary pressure. At first, in the 1960s, incomes policies included the control of prices and wages. After price controls were dropped due to insuperable problems of implementation, governments issued recommendations or ordered wage freezes. At the same time unions were included in consultation with governments on how to resolve balance of payment and other economic difficulties.

Economic management became far more difficult in the late 1960s when labour unrest broke out in a large number of countries, often in opposition to trade union wage restraint. By that time, the experiments with incomes policies were widely seen as a failure. Nevertheless, when the postwar political economy was put to the test of the devaluation of the US dollar and the first oil shock in the early 1970s, many governments turned to incomes policies again. Lacking alternatives, they approached trade unions for voluntary tripartite concertation with the aim to control wage expectations. Throughout the 1970s, there were frequent attempts to find cooperative approaches of governments and trade unions to deal with the problem of stagflation. In most countries, public expenditure rose in order to compensate for job losses and provide for the unemployed, but also to provide a demand stimulus for the economy.

The rise of monetarism
At the end of the 1970s, governments' approach to economic policy changed drastically. Hesitation in the 1960s and 1970s to use monetary policy to dampen inflation was reduced by the success of the 'German model'. The German Bundesbank switched to a restrictive monetary policy in 1974. At the end of the decade, unemployment and inflation in Germany were far below the European average. Moreover, the US government shifted its economic adjustment strategy in 1978/79, among other things adopting a new policy of deregulation. The Federal Reserve Bank responded to the second oil shock with sharp increases in interest rates and, given the international nature of financial markets, forced the rest of the industrialized world to follow. In the UK, the newly elected Conservative government in 1979 based its economic strategy on tight monetary policy and labour market deregulation. The attempt by the French socialist government in 1982 to stimulate growth by encouraging wage rises and increasing public expenditure failed within only a few months. In addition the European monetary system, set up in 1978, aimed at keeping exchange rate fluctuations within a narrow band and thereby made adjustment through currency devaluation much more difficult.

The shift in economic policy was accompanied by changes in economic thought. Whereas previously the Philips curve was widely accepted in economic theory – not on theoretical grounds but on the basis of empirical facts – rational expectations theory questioned the tradeoff between inflation and unemployment. In the long run, according to the new consensus in macroeconomics, it was impossible to generate employment by allowing for higher inflation. Inflation was to be fought by tighter monetary policies. Imbalances in the real economy, such as unemployment, had to be dealt with by improving competitive conditions on the markets for goods and labour. To create employment, policy makers should focus on the supply side of the economy and on flexible adjustment of the labour market.

The new trend in economic policy potentially undermined government cooperation with unions. Deregulation threatened the role of trade unions in the labour market. Rather than negotiating joint economic adjustment policies that combined wage restraint with economic policies beneficial for labour, monetarism aimed at disciplining labour by increasing unemployment. According to Scharpf, only in a Keynesian economic environment did governments depend on the willingness of trade unions to engage in voluntary wage restraint. If the government switched to a monetarist strategy, wage restraint no longer required trade union cooperation. Rather, excessive wage settlements were immediately punished by unemployment. Unemployment, unlike inflation, is experienced, not as a collective evil, but as an individual risk. Trade unions have to respond to rising economic insecurity and lower their wage claims (Scharpf, 1991).

As it turned out, the effect of monetarist policies on the role of trade unions was not as straightforward as anticipated. Previous studies had pointed out that the economic performance of countries varied with the level of centralization of wage bargaining institutions. In the classic version of the argument, the effects of wage bargaining institutions were determined by two countervailing forces. Where centralized unions were in control of wage formation for the economy as a whole, they were forced to internalize the negative effects of excessive wage settlements. In these cases, trade union behaviour in wage setting was more responsive to changes in the economy and therefore had a positive impact on economic performance. At the same time, the bargaining power of trade unions was higher in centralized wage bargaining structures. In decentralized bargaining systems a local wage push by trade unions would be disciplined by competing non-union companies. As a result, the relationship between economic performance and the centralization of wage bargaining would take the shape of a hump (Calmfors and Driffill, 1988; see also Chapter 6 by Flanagan in this volume).

Elsewhere in the literature a linear relationship is assumed between wage bargaining centralization and economic performance, with performance improving with increasing centralization or coordination (Soskice, 1990; Dell'Aringa and Sameh, 1992). In decentralized wage bargaining systems, wage formation is said to depend on the conditions in local labour markets for particular skills. Moreover, since wage structures are embedded in social norms about fair relativities, even in decentralized wage formation relative wages tend to be rigid.

Building on these arguments, it was shown that wage bargaining institutions also interacted with monetary policy (Iversen, 1999; Hall and Franzese, 1998). In countries with decentralized wage bargaining, a commitment of monetary authorities to a restrictive policy would have less of an impact on trade unions since local wage bargainers would not perceive their wage settlements to be influential with respect to monetary policy. Only in centralized wage bargaining are trade unions able to take into account the responses of monetary authorities that their wage settlements might trigger. In countries with more centralized wage bargaining, unions are therefore expected to be more responsive towards tight monetary policies (see Chapter 6 by Flanagan in this volume). In empirical studies it was shown that countries with sectoral wage bargaining tended to adjust better to a monetarist environment. Countries with decentralized wage formation showed the worst performance (Traxler et al., 2001; Iversen, 1999). Also, the interplay between the Bundesbank's restrictive monetary policy and sectoral wage bargaining institutions in Germany was seen as contributing to the relative success of the German economy in the 1970s and 1980s (Streeck, 1994). Thus tight monetarist economic policy seemed in principle compatible with regulated labour markets and centralized wage bargaining.

In line with these arguments about the persisting importance of wage bargaining institutions for economic performance, the postwar tradition of concertation and trade union involvement in economic policy survived the turn to monetarism in many countries. While restrictive monetary policies were eventually adopted in all advanced industrialized countries, this was not accompanied by universal labour market deregulation and trade union exclusion. Only in the Anglo-American OECD countries, with the exception of Ireland, did the labour-inclusive postwar political economy disappear in the 1980s and 1990s. In the USA, Canada, New Zealand, Australia and the UK where labour inclusion and economic planning had always been alien to the political system, the turn to neo-liberalism and monetarism excluded unions from economic policy making.

In Continental Europe, by comparison, many governments in the 1980s opted for negotiating wage restraint with unions and employers when facing the challenges of tight money, fiscal austerity, and attacks on their currencies in international financial markets. A new wave of 'social pacts' revived national traditions of concertation (Ebbinghaus and Hassel, 2000; Fajertag and Pochet, 2000). Pacts also became an important policy instrument in the transition countries of Eastern Europe (Schmitter and Grote, 1997). In all these cases, monetarism improved the bargaining position of governments vis-à-vis trade unions. In Europe, the Maastricht Treaty and the subsequent Stability Pact imposed tight ceilings on inflation and public spending. The Single European Market liberalized product markets and intensified competition. Governments not only acted under tighter constraints, but they were also in a better position to convey this to domestic interest groups.

5.   Unions and the Welfare State

Trade unions played a major role in welfare state development by promoting democratization and the evolution of social rights as a core element of citizenship. Industrialization and modernization both enabled and required public welfare provisions. They undermined pre-industrial sites of solidarity such as the extended family, the church and the guilds by advancing social mobility, urbanization and market exchange. As the expansion of markets tended to destroy the social community on which markets are based, social policy had to re-embed the market economy into society. An obvious source of provision for the needy was the state, which developed bureaucratic organizations to deal with the new demands (Flora and Alber, 1981).

The evolution of the welfare state coincided with the emergence of democratic forms of state legitimacy. The provision of collective welfare through public expenditure became a principal means for governments to secure the support of an increasing group of voters. Expansion of the franchise moved the political agenda towards the institutionalization of social rights. Full citizenship became based, not just on equality before the law, but also on social equality (Marshall, 1965). At the same time, social policy often preceded full democratization and in fact was used to pre-empt it. Also, early democracies were often slow to introduce comprehensive welfare systems because political power was captured by small property owners campaigning for lower taxation rather than higher welfare provisions (Esping-Andersen, 1992, p. 99).

While the expansion of the welfare state was a universal phenomenon in the twentieth century, there are marked differences between different types of welfare state. Welfare regimes can be distinguished by the degree to which they protect the individual from the market and the social status of individuals in economic hardship or when their employment changes (Esping-Andersen, 1990). 'Decommodification' of labour can take different forms and entail different sorts of entitlement in cases of sickness, unemployment, disability and the like.

Three welfare regimes were identified in a seminal study (Esping-Andersen, 1990). Decommodification is strongest in the social-democratic regime with universal provision of a wide range of entitlements. Social-democratic welfare states were designed to secure high standards for all, and not just to support the needy. Their political project was equality between the classes. Status differences between manual and white-collar workers were eradicated within a universal insurance system, although benefits continued to be based on accustomed earnings. Exemplary cases are the Scandinavian countries of Sweden, Norway, Finland and Denmark. At the other end, a liberal welfare regime developed in the Anglo-Saxon countries and in a country like Switzerland. Here welfare provisions are minimal and means-tested, and the state encourages market solutions by subsidizing private welfare schemes. Public schemes are universal but provisions are too low for status maintenance.

Third, in conservative welfare states social security is provided mainly by the state and the share of the market is minimal. Provisions and entitlements are, however, not as comprehensive as in the social-democratic welfare regime; the emphasis is not on equality but on the preservation of social status. Redistributive effects are therefore negligible. Conservative welfare states are primarily to be found on the European continent.

Many countries combine elements of different welfare regimes. The Danish welfare state has liberal elements combined with social-democratic ones. In the poorer countries of southern Europe, a mix of liberal and conservative elements can be found. Different combinations indicate different relative importance of conflicting goals in social security provision: equality, the maintenance of status differentials, and market reliance.

Unions and the Evolution of the Welfare State
Trade union demands for social security collided and interacted with the demands of other political actors in country-specific political constellations. Nation and state building, industrialization and political cleavage structuration coincided with trade union organization and the evolution of welfare states (Rokkan, 1968). Welfare state intervention owes its origins 'to an epoch that antedates labor's emergence as a real political force' (Esping-Andersen, 1994, p. 139). Thus the evolution of the welfare state took place in interaction between labour movements and groups like farmers and business. While the presence of strong farming communities often worked against welfare state expansion (Gourevitch, 1986), business could occasionally be drawn on labour's side. Several studies show a shared interest of employers' associations and trade unions in the expansion of specific forms of social security provision (Mares, 2000; Swenson, 1997). For instance, unemployment insurance also serves interests of employers as

it preserves the skills of workers during economic downturns (Mares, 2000). The actual design of unemployment benefits – whether they are based on taxation or on a comprehensive or narrowly defined occupational insurance scheme – depended on the relative power and the strategic behaviour of trade unions, employers and the government.

Trade unions were highly influential with respect to the direction of welfare state evolution in different countries. While expansion of social security was an obvious goal for all unions, more radical unions pressed for a political solution beyond capitalism, in which social security would be part of a socialist economic order. Reformist labour movements supported voluntaristic provision of social security by friendly societies rather than the state.

The type of social security provision trade unions demanded varied substantially with the type of trade unionism and its interaction with other political forces. A key factor was the mix of craft and industrial trade unionism at the time of the first period of social security expansion in the latter half of the nineteenth century. Craft unions preferred particularistic solutions. Not least to protect their own organizations, they insisted on providing social security themselves rather than letting the state take over their role. Thus they often experienced the growth of the welfare state as expropriation and dilution of their own social security provisions. In countries where originally unemployment benefits, sickness pay and similar forms of social insurance were provided by organizations of skilled workers, craft union dominance impeded the development of universalistic social security programmes with high levels of equality. Since the craft unions in the Anglo-Saxon countries were also less politicized than the more encompassing unions of continental Europe, they did not have the political clout to press for comprehensive social security. But even in Denmark the craft-oriented labour movement blocked social democratic initiatives for an active labour market policy like in Sweden and Norway. In the United States and the United Kingdom, craft unions preferred occupational over universal benefits.

Industrial unions, by comparison, had a broader and more heterogeneous membership and were under pressure from their majority of low-skilled members to even out occupational differentials. As political unions, they also were better able to bargain with central governments. In countries where industrial unions became dominant, a wide range of social benefits are more likely to be provided by the state, achieved through political mobilization instead of collective bargaining and on the basis of universal rights of citizenship. In Sweden, unions pursued the levelling of status and pay differentials between blue- and white-collar workers in social security as well as in pay bargaining.

Political fragmentation of trade unions in continental Europe under-mined support for a social-democratic welfare state. The persistence of the religious cleavage in countries with segmented union–party relations shaped the normative orientation of policy makers vis-à-vis the provision of social security. Strong ties between Christian-democratic parties and trade unions encouraged policies based on the subsidiarity principle. This emphasized the traditional role of women and the family and tended to work against universal and comprehensive social security provisions. Political conflict between communist and Christian trade unions had a similar effect. In Austria and Germany, the origins of the welfare state reach back to a period of political division and oppression. Social security provision developed along the line of status differentials and this changed only slowly in the postwar period after the restructuring of the trade unions.

There is a close interaction and correlation between the organization of wage bargaining and the evolution of the welfare state, mediated by the degree of centralization of trade unions and their politicization. The more encompassing and centralized trade unions were initially, the more they were able to influence the political economy both in wage bargaining and in social policy. The decommodification of welfare regimes is highly corre-lated with the centralization of wage bargaining (see Figure 10.2).

Unions and mature welfare states

As welfare states matured after the Second World War, the interaction between unions and the welfare state and between social policy, collective bargaining and the labour market changed. Over time, trade unions learned to use the welfare state and its expanding provisions to stabilize the income of their members. While political exchange between governments and trade unions entailed wage restraint on the side of the unions, it often provided for the expansion of social security benefits by the government.

At the same time, welfare state regimes increasingly affected the perfor-mance of labour markets and trade unions grew dependent on the welfare state. First, the welfare state became a big employer. In the mid-1990s, the social service economy accounted for one quarter of total employment in Sweden (Esping-Andersen, 1996). In the social-democratic welfare states, female labour market participation increased with the increase in employ-ment of the social security sector.

Second, the welfare state reduced employment by offering incentives to older workers to leave the labour market for early retirement. Participation rates of men above 55 declined on average in the EU by 27 percentage points, from 81 to 54 per cent, between 1970 and 1995. Beginning with the 1970s when governments were no longer able to guarantee full employment,

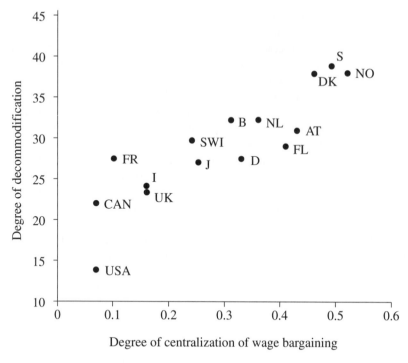

Source: Esping-Andersen (1990), Iversen (1999); own calculations.

Figure 10.2   Decommodification and centralization of wage bargaining

early retirement and similar policies were developed to take care of redundant workers. Early retirement was popular with older workers, and therefore with trade unions whose membership gradually grew older on average (Ebbinghaus, 2001).

Third, social security expansion raised the price of labour. In insurance-based welfare states, non-wage labour costs have exploded since the early 1970s. Since early retirement programmes and disability pensions are paid out of contributions of those employed, unit labour costs increased while wages remained stagnant. As non-wage labour costs began to make national economies non-competitive, employers and governments had to seek massive productivity increases, which often resulted in even more publicly-funded early retirement.

The welfare state in retreat

Since the early 1980s the welfare state has been in retreat. Only a few governments, especially in Britain and the USA, attempted to cut back on social security spending. But ageing, low employment and public debt forced welfare states to restructure. The Treaty of Maastricht and the subsequent Stability and Growth Pact had similar consequences for European welfare states.

The retreat of the welfare state has ambivalent implications for trade unions. To the extent that trade unions were embedded in the welfare state, retrenchment is a threat to their established role in social policy. Where trade unions participate in the administration of welfare state programmes, this has come under criticism in recent years, like for example in Austria, France, Germany and the Netherlands. Whereas in some cases employers have pressed for change, in others governments have taken the initiative and tried to curtail the role of the 'social partners' in the governance of the welfare state. In Austria and Italy this was seen as an attack on trade unionism as such and has led to a call for protest strikes, in particular to the first general strike for two decades in Italy in 2002 (Ebbinghaus, 2002).

On the other hand, restructuring of the welfare state expanded the space for collective bargaining (Myles and Pierson, 2001; Schludi, 2001; Swank, 2001; Ebbinghaus and Hassel, 2000). For instance, the gradual retrenchment of pay-as-you-go pension schemes on the European continent has opened up opportunities for bargaining on occupational pensions. In the Netherlands, France and Sweden have existed for a long time. They negotiated supplementary pensions increased in importance with the cutback of universal state pension schemes. In other countries where trade unions had no tradition of negotiating private pensions, they have started to do so. The German pension reform of 2001 introduced new voluntary private pension funds to supplement declining public benefits. This has led to collective agreements on funded occupational pension schemes and the conversion of parts of the wage into insurance contributions (Ebbinghaus, 2002).

Trade union inclusion in economic policy and social security provision survived in Western Europe mainly because of the close connection between the mature welfare state and the labour market. For many governments it became apparent in the 1980s and 1990s that labour market deregulation in mature welfare states is politically risky and expensive. Mature welfare states not only offer multiple veto points to social groups undertaking to obstruct deregulation and retrenchment (Pierson, 1998). Social security provision has also become a main source of legitimacy for governments in an unstable world economy. In many countries, in particular on the European continent, trade unions have used their influence on the welfare state to take redundant workers out of the labour market rather than make them unemployed. Unemployment is still seen by the public and by policy makers as the main benchmark for economic policy. Even in countries with liberal welfare states where trade unions are not involved in the design and administration of social securing programmes, the politics of retrenchment were difficult for neo-liberal governments like those of Ronald Reagan in the USA, and Margaret Thatcher in the UK (Pierson, 1994).

6.   New challenges

In the last two decades of the twentieth century, new challenges arose for organized labour in the politics of advanced industrialized countries. The architecture of the world economy had changed fundamentally since the early 1970s with the breakdown of the Bretton Woods system and the rise of international capital markets. Economic liberalization, privatization and deregulation spread across the world, and protected niches of employment in state-run industries were eradicated. In Europe, the Single European Market, Monetary Union and the Stability and Growth Pact cemented the turn to austerity and tight monetarism. Labour markets became more volatile, insecure and heterogeneous. Party systems underwent fundamental changes as they dissociated themselves from traditional class cleavages (Kitschelt, 1997). Trade union membership declined and in many countries the cohesion of the trade union movement as a political actor is in doubt.

Transnational economic policy
With economic internationalization, the interdependence between national economies has increased. National economic policies produce stronger external effects than before and they are more than ever subject to international regulation. Increasingly, international agencies and supranational bodies regulate or, for that matter, deregulate market access and trade and capital flows. Intergovernmental bodies that operate in an international space derive their legitimacy from the cooperation of sovereign governments. Union influence on them is generally low. Neither the International Monetary Fund nor the World Trade Organization provide opportunities for union participation.

The internationalization of capital markets
The internationalization of capital markets puts a premium on price stability. Under flexible exchange rates the value of a currency depends on the rate of inflation and the current account balance. National monetary and fiscal policy makers therefore have to take the effects of wage inflation on the exchange rate into account. As the ability of governments to

tolerate wage inflation is diminished, unions come under pressure to cooperate in adjusting national labour markets to the new international constraints.

At the same time, governments have reasons to seek new forms of cooperation with trade unions in their effort to adjust to the new economic environment. In particular in countries where labour markets are still highly regulated and the role of trade unions in wage formation is strong, governments try to persuade trade unions to accept voluntary wage restraint. Depending on unions' ability to mobilize electoral pressure, governments have an incentive to preempt union opposition through negotiations. The interest of governments in tripartite agreements on wages and welfare state reform opens new opportunities for trade union political influence. In countries where trade unions are weak in political, institutional and organizational terms, governments increasingly tend to exclude them from political decision making.

Europeanization

In the European Union the process of economic and monetary integration has made a tight monetary policy and fiscal austerity an international obligation for member states. The Maastricht Treaty and the Stability and Growth Pact have tied the hands of national governments. Economic governance, as envisaged by the French government, is underdeveloped in comparison to the role of the autonomous European Central Bank.

Still, European integration has always entailed an element of social partnership and tripartism. Like most of the Continental European member states, the EU has a tripartite Economic and Social Committee on which unions are represented. Moreover, the European Union has long been committed to 'social dialogue' between business and labour (Falkner, 1998), and the European employment strategy emphasizes the inclusion of unions at the supranational as well as the national level.

As of now the impact of European social policy has remained limited. European social policy directives, written with more or less involvement of the European Trade Union Confederation, cover only narrow issues and do not substantially affect national labour or social legislation. European-wide collective bargaining is a long way off and indeed seems unlikely ever to materialize (see Chapter 13 by Sadowski, Ludewig and Turk in this volume). Despite the preferential treatment of the social partners by the European Commission, the European political system is much more pluralist than corporatist (Streeck, 1992). A large number of trade unions, associations, lobby groups, firms and regions have a variety of choices of different paths of access to the political centre, and policy making is organized around a complex interplay between the national and European level.

European decision makers have a variety of interest groups to deal with, trade unions being only one among many (Streeck, 1993b).

Trade unions as political actors

In postwar Europe and beyond, unions were included in national politics as representatives of the working class as a whole. In the 1970s in particular, their membership grew and so did their political influence. However, deep changes in the composition of trade union membership have taken place since. In most countries, union membership has declined substantially and its structure became stuck in the golden era of welfare state expansion. By the end of the twentieth century, the average union member was older than the average employee; more likely to be a blue-collar worker than a white-collar worker; male rather than female; and employed in manufacturing rather than in services (see Chapter 2 by Schnabel and Chapter 11 by Visser in this volume). In particular, the increase in female and service sector employment is not reflected in trade union membership. Such imbalances are likely to have long-term negative effects on the political legitimacy of trade unions. For example, established rights of unions to be represented on public committees and administrative boards may be increasingly challenged by a sceptical public.

Even more important, the political interests of unions will naturally be defined by their remaining core membership. The massive expansion of early retirement in the 1980s and 1990s reflected the demands of older trade union members. Trade unions in Italy, where up to 50 per cent of union members are retired, campaign for pensioners rights at the expense of young workers (Ebbinghaus, 2002). Despite the effort of many trade unions to broaden their membership base, unions as political actors are likely to be increasingly defined as a pressure group for a narrow constituency of skilled manual workers. This will make it difficult for them to defend the political status they achieved in the postwar period, which is still reflected in many of the core institutions of democratic capitalism.

Present tendencies towards deregulation of advanced political economies may, however, be overstated. In many European countries trade unions are still strong (Ross and Martin, 1999). They generally continue to be regarded by many governments as indispensable participants in national social pacts for wage moderation and employment. On the other hand, even where postwar corporatism is not disappearing, it is changing under pressures on governments to strengthen economic incentives and ensure that the costs of the organized pursuit of collective interests are borne by those who also reap the benefits, rather than by the public-at-large.

Acknowledgement

We would like to thank Marco Hauptmeier for his help in searching and compiling substantial parts of the literature as well as the editors for very helpful comments.

References:

Barbash, Jack (1972), *Trade Unions and National Economic Policy*, Baltimore MD, and London: John Hopkins Press.

Bartolini, Stefano (2000), *The Political Mobilization of the European Left, 1860–1980*, Cambridge: Cambridge University Press.

Beyme, Klaus von (1977), *Gewerkschaften und Arbeitsbeziehungen in kapitalistischen Ländern*, Munich: Pieper.

Calmfors, Lars and John Driffill (1988), 'Bargaining Structure, Corporatism and Macroeconomic Performance', *Economic Policy*, 6, pp. 13–61.

Crouch, Colin (1993), *Industrial Relations and European State Traditions*, Oxford: Clarendon Press.

Dell'Aringa, Carlo L. and Manuela Samek (1992), 'Industrial Relations and Economic Performance', in Tiziano Treu (ed.), *Participation in Public Policy-Making. The Role of Trade Unions and Employers' Association*, Berlin: De Gruyter, pp. 26–58.

Ebbinghaus, Bernhard (1995), 'The Siamese Twins: Citizenship Rights, Cleavage Formation, and Party–Union Relations in Western Europe', *International Review of Social History*, 40, Supplement 3, pp. 51–89.

Ebbinghaus, Bernhard (2001), 'The Political Economy of Early Retirement in Europe, Japan and the USA', in Bernhard Ebbinghaus and Philipp Manow (eds), *Comparing Welfare Capitalism. Social Policy and Political Economy in Europe, Japan and the USA*, London: Routledge, pp. 76–101.

Ebbinghaus, Bernhard (2002), 'Trade Unions Changing Role: Membership Erosion, Organisational Reform, and Social Partnership in Europe', *Industrial Relations Journal*, Annual Review 2001/02 (special issue).

Ebbinghaus, Bernhard and Anke Hassel (2000), 'Striking Deals. The Role of Concertation in the Reform of the Welfare State', *Journal of European Public Policy*, 7 (1), pp. 44–62.

Esping-Andersen, Gøsta (1990), *The Three Worlds of Welfare Capitalism*, Princeton, NJ: Princeton University Press.

Esping-Andersen, Gøsta (1992), 'The Three Political Economies of the Welfare State', in Kolberg, Jon Eivind (ed.), *The study of Welfare State Regimes*, London, NY: M.E. Sharpe, pp. 92–123.

Esping-Andersen, Gøsta (1994), 'The Emerging Realignment between Labor Movements and Welfare States', in Marino Regni (ed.), *The Future of Labor Movements*, London: Sage, pp. 133–149.

Fajertag, Guiseppe and Philippe Pochet (2000), *Social Pacts in Europe: New Dynamics*, Brussels: OSE-ETUI, pp. 9–40.

Falkner, Gerda (1998), *Towards a Corporatist Policy Community: EU Social Policy in the 1990s*, London: Routledge.

Flanagan, Robert, David W. Soskice and Lloyd Ulman (1983), *Unionism, Economic Stabilization, and Incomes Policies. European Experience*, Washington DC: Brookings Institution.

Flanders, Alan (1970), *Management and Unions: the Theory and Reform of Industrial Relations*, London: Faber.

Flora, Peter and Jens Alber (1981), *The Development of the Welfare State in Europe and America*, London: Transaction Books.

Friedmann, Gerald Carl (1998), *State-Making and Labor Movements: France and the United States 1876–1914*, Ithaca, NY: Cornell University Press.

Fulcher, James (1991), *Labor Movements, Employers and the State. Conflict and Co-operation in Britain and Sweden*, Oxford: Clarendon Press.

Gourevitch, Peter Alexis (1986), *Politics in Hard Times. Comparative Responses to International Economic Crises*, Ithaca, NY: Cornell University Press.

Hall, Peter A. and Robert J. Franzese (1998), 'Mixed Signals: Central Bank Independence, Coordinated Wage Bargaining and European Monetary Union', *International Organization*, 52 (3), pp. 505–535.

Headey, Bruce W. (1970), 'Trade Unions and National Wage Policies', *Journal of Politics*, 32 (2), pp. 407–439.

Iversen, Torben (1999), *Contested Economic Institutions. The Politics of Macroeconomics and Wage Bargaining in Advanced Democracies*, Cambridge and New York: Cambridge University Press.

Katznelson, Ira and Aristide R. Zolberg (1986), *Working-Class Formation. Nineteenth-Century Patterns in Western Europe and the United States*, Princeton, NJ: Princeton University Press.

Kendall, Walter (1975), *The Labor Movement in Europe*, London: Allen Lane.

Kitschelt, Herbert (1997), 'European Party Systems: Continuity and Change', in Martin Rhodes, Paul Heywood and Vincent Wright (eds), *Developments in West European Politics*, London: Macmillan, pp. 131–150.

Korpi, Walter (1983), *The Democratic Class Struggle*, London: Routledge.

Lange, Peter and Geoffrey Garrett (1985), 'The Politics of Growth: Strategic Interaction and Economic Performance 1974–1980', *Journal of Politics*, 47 (3), pp. 792–827.

Lehmbruch, Gerhard (1984), 'Concertation and the Structure of Corporatist Networks', in John Goldthorpe (ed.), *Order and Conflict in Contemporary Capitalism*, Oxford: Oxford University Press, pp. 60–80.

Lipset, Seymour Martin (1982), 'Radicalism or Reformism: The Sources of Working-class Politics', *American Political Science Review*, 77 (1), pp. 1–18.

Lipset, Seymour Martin and Gary Marks (2000), *It Didn't Happen Here: Why Socialism Failed in the United States*, New York, London: W.W. Norton.

Mares, Isabela (2000), 'Strategic Alliances and Social Policy Reform: Unemployment Insurance in Comparative Perspective', *Politics & Society*, 28 (2), pp. 223–244.

Marin, Bernd and Renate Mayntz (eds) (1991), *Policy Networks. Empirical Evidence and Theoretical Considerations*, Frankfurt: Campus Verlag.

Marshall, Thomas H. (1965), *Class, Citizenship, and Social Development*, New York: Anchor Books.

Mommsen, Wolfgang J. and Hans-Gerhard Husung (1985), *The Development of Trade Unionism in Great Britain and Germany, 1880–1914*, London: George Allen & Unwin.

Myles, John and Paul Pierson (2001), 'The Comparative Political Economy of Pension Reform', in Paul Pierson (ed.), *The New Politics of the Welfare State*, Oxford: Oxford University Press, pp. 305–333.

Olson, Mancur (1982), *The Rise and Decline of Nations: Economic Growth, Stagflation and Social Rigidities*, New Haven, CT: Yale University Press.

Pierson, Paul (1994), *Dismantling the Welfare State? Reagan, Thatcher, and the Politics of Retrenchment*, Cambridge: Cambridge University Press.

Pierson, Paul (1998), 'Irresistible Forces, Immovable Objects: Post Industrial Welfare States Confront Permanent Austerity', *Journal of European Public Policy*, 5 (4), pp. 539–560.

Pizzorno, Alessandro (1978), 'Political Exchange and Collective Identity', in Colin Crouch and Alessandro Pizzorno (eds), *The Resurgence of Class Conflict in Western Europe since 1968*, Vol. 2, London: Macmillan, pp. 277–298.

Postan, Michael M. (1967), *An Economic History of Western Europe*, London: Methuen.

Rokkan, Stein (1968), 'Nation-building, Cleavage Formation and the Structuring of Mass Politics', *Comparative Studies in Society and History*, 10 (2), pp. 173–210.

Ross, George and Andy Martin (eds) (1999), *The Brave New World of European Labor. European Trade Unions at the Millennium*, New York: Berghahn Books, pp. 1–25.

Rothstein, Bo (1992), 'Labor Market Institutions and Working Class Strength', in Sven Steinmo, Kathleen Thelen and Frank Longstreth (eds), *Structuring Politics. Historical Institutionalism in Comparative Analysis*, New York: Cambridge University Press, pp. 33–56.

Scharpf, Fritz W. (1991), *Crisis and Choice in European Social Democracy*, Ithaca, NY: Cornell University Press.

Schludi, Martin (2001), 'The Politics of Pension in European Social Insurance Countries', MPIfG Discussion Paper, Cologne: Max Planck Institute for the Study of Societies.

Schmitter, Philippe C. (1977), 'Modes of Interest Intermediation and Models of Societal Change in Western Europe', *Comparative Political Studies*, 10 (1), pp. 7–38.

Schmitter, Philippe C. and Jürgen R. Grote (1997), 'The Corporatist Sisyphus: Past, Present and Future', EUI Working Papers in Political and Social Sciences, Florence: European University Institute.

Soskice, David (1990), 'Wage Determination: the Changing Role of Institutions in Advanced Industrialized Countries', *Oxford Review of Economic Policy*, 6 (4), pp. 36–61.

Stephens, John D. (1979), *The Transition from Socialism to Capitalism*, London: Macmillan.

Streeck, Wolfgang (1992), 'From National Corporatism to Transnational Pluralism: European Interest Politics and the Single Market', in Tiziano Treu (ed.), *Participation in Public Policy-Making. The Role of Trade Unions and Employers' Associations*, Berlin: De Gruyter, pp. 97–126.

Streeck, Wolfgang (1993a), 'The History of Unions in Western Europe', *Encyclopaedia Britannica*, Chicago: Encyclopaedia Britannica, pp. 953–956.

Streeck, Wolfgang (1993b), 'The Rise and Decline of Neocorporatism', in Lloyd Ulman, Barry Eichengreen and William T. Dickens (eds), *Labor and an Integrated Europe*, Washington DC: Brookings Institution, pp. 80–101.

Streeck, Wolfgang (1994), 'Pay Restraint Without Incomes Policy: Institutionalized Monetarism and Industrial Unionism in Germany', in Ron Dore, Robert Boyer and Zoe Mars (eds), *The Return to Incomes Policy*, London, New York: Pinter, pp. 117–140.

Swank, Duane (2001), 'Political Institutions and Welfare State Restructuring: The Impact of Institutions on Social Policy Change in Developed Democracies', in Paul Pierson (ed.), *The New Politics of the Welfare State*, Oxford: Oxford University Press, pp. 197–237.

Swenson, Peter (1997), 'Arranged Alliance: Business Interests in the New Deal', *Politics and Society*, 25 (1), pp. 66–116.

Taylor, Andrew J. (1989), *Trade Unions and Politics: A Comparative Introduction*, London: Macmillan.

Taylor, Andrew J. (1993), 'Trade Unions and the Politics of Social Democratic Renewal', in Richard Gillespie and Willie E. Patterson (eds), *Rethinking Social Democracy in Western Europe*, London: Frank Cass, pp. 133–155.

Traxler, Franz, Sabine Blaschke and Bernhard Kittel (2001), *National Labour Relations in Internationalized Markets*, Oxford: Oxford University Press.

Ulman, Lloyd and Robert J. Flanagan (1971), *Wage Restraint: A Study of Incomes Policies in Western Europe*, Berkeley, Los Angeles, London: University of California Press.

Valenzuela, J. Samuel (1994), 'Labor Movements and Political Systems: Some Variations', Marino Regini (ed.), *The Future of Labor Movements*, London: Sage, pp. 53–101.

Western, Bruce (1997), *Between Class and Market. Postwar Unionization in the Capitalist Democracies*, Princeton, NY: Princeton University Press.

11 Unions and unionism around the world
Jelle Visser

1. Introduction

Most of our theories and research on industrial relations and trade unions are derived from a limited set of countries and experiences. Because of data limitations, comparative studies are usually limited to the 20 odd industrialized market economies. This has two disadvantages. First, our views and generalizations are likely to be biased by a 'western' or 'industrialized economy' view. Second, cross-national comparative analysis typically suffers from a small-N problem. Our predictions about the development of trade unions, and the propositions that underlie them, would gain in stature if tested in as many different national and industrial settings as possible (Verma et al., 2002). It is in this spirit, that I have tried to expand beyond the usual in this chapter.

This survey covers developments of trade unions and unionization from 103 countries, together making up 2.5 billion of the three billion people who, according to the most recent estimate of International Labour Organization, form the world's labour force (ILO, 1998, p. 1). The total number of union members can be estimated at around 320 million people: 91 million in China, 65 million in Russia, Ukraine and Belarus, 61 million (74 million if retired and unemployed workers are included) in Europe (33 countries), 38 million in Asia (16 countries), 14 million in Africa (28 countries), 24 million in North America (Canada, the USA and Mexico) and 29 million in Central and Latin America (19 countries).[1]

If we exclude the one half of the word's labour force involved in agricultural activities, the global union density rate can be put at 23 per cent. In other words, towards the end of the twentieth century between one-fifth and one-quarter of the 1.3 billion people on earth who supplied labour for production or services outside agriculture joined a trade union. Unionization rates are, and used to be, higher in Russia (58 per cent) and China (42 per cent), average in Europe (26 per cent) and South America (25 per cent), and lower in Africa (16 per cent), North America (13 per cent) and Asia (10 per cent). These regional figures hide large cross-national variations in labour markets, political conditions, labour relations and union activity.

In this chapter I shall discuss developments in unionism and unionization across different world regions. Most of the data presented are national aggregates. Relatively greater attention will be given to union density, defined as the ratio of union membership to potential membership, as a summary measure of union presence in society. Although the union density rate captures some aspects of union bargaining power – it is probably more difficult to replace striking workers in the short run when most of the firm's or industry's workers are unionized – as a full measure it is inadequate (Flanagan, 1999). We cannot get the complete picture 'without studying labour and association laws, collective bargaining practices, organizational charters, public roles of labour', and 'without understanding how workers are convinced to stay, pay, and, if needed, to act' (Visser, 1992, p. 22). It is useful to recall that small unions can be very effective in organizing work stoppages and that union membership and strike incidence do not necessarily move in the same direction (Shalev, 1992). Case studies show that large unions are not always effective in organizing workers in the workplace, though it is unlikely that permanently ineffective unions will attract large memberships on a voluntary basis. If large variations or swings in unionization rates are observed, we can almost be certain that something in the legal-political, social or economic environment of union organizing has changed. In this sense, the union density statistic provides a useful comparative indicator in industrial relations research (Bain and Price, 1980).

For measuring up the bargaining power of unions it matters whether union organizations are concentrated or fragmented; united or entangled in political and jurisdictional rivalry; subservient to other interests (of employers, political parties, governments or public agencies) or politically and financially independent; led by weak and undemocratic leaders or placed on a lively democratic and professional footing. The social composition of membership – what sections of society and what parts of the labour market do the unions represent? – is another telling indicator. Furthermore, the conditions external to the unions – product demand, the state of the labour market, political and legal support – cannot be ignored when one tries to make up the balance of union bargaining strength.

Finally, membership is only one indicator of union presence. Other indicators of relevance are: bargaining coverage, i.e. the share of workers covered by labour contracts negotiated by one or more trade union(s); election results in employee works councils, staff representation bodies or workers' chambers; union representation in advisory, consulting and legislative councils, and union standing in public opinion (Calmfors et al., 2001; Lipset, 1986). Whereas union density is closer to measuring potential union bargaining pressure, the other measures, especially bargaining coverage, is closer to measuring the effectiveness of unions in providing and defending minimum standards of income and employment protection in labour markets. Between the two measures there exists a considerable difference, as will be seen in the final section of the chapter.

2.   Comparing union membership

In discussing trends I shall try to compare the mid-1980s with the mid-1990s or, where possible, some later year, thus covering a period of ten to fifteen years. 1985 has been chosen as a matter of convenience. In work for the ILO Labour Report (ILO, 1997a), a global survey of representatives of governments, unions and employers was conducted from which it was possible to derive data for 1995 and ten years earlier (Visser, 1997). This has been the most important source for this chapter, together with updates from statistical offices, secondary sources, ILO-field offices, the Data Handbook on European Unions (Ebbinghaus and Visser, 2000), the on-line database of the OECD and Golden and Wallerstein (1995) on organizational data for the non-European members of the OECD.

The choice of 1985 as the base year has the advantage that it precedes the recent acceleration in globalization and liberalization of world markets, including the opening of the command economies of Russia and Central and Eastern Europe, the creation of a Single Market (1992) and Monetary Union in Western Europe, Mercosur and NAFTA in the Americas, the recent rounds of trade liberalization and the establishment of the WTO. Going back further in time increases the difficulty of comparison and data collection. Where longer and annual time-series data do exist, for instance in the case of Western Europe and North America, we find that 1985 was not an exceptional year. In many countries it is in fact close to the post-1945 average (Ebbinghaus and Visser, 2000; Golden et al., 1999). Many governments in Western Europe had tried to establish cooperative relationships with the unions in response to the wave of worker militancy of the late 1960s and the monetary instability, inflation and the oil shocks of the 1970s. The years between 1968 and 1979 had been 'exceptional' years of growth in support and membership for European trade unions (Regini, 1992; Baglioni, 1990). The disinflation policies and sharply rising unemployment rates of the 1980s meant that trade unions in industrial market economies were losing some of their political and industrial clout, and some of their membership (Shalev, 1992; Visser, 1991).

In order to assure comparability, over time and across countries or world regions, I use two baselines for calculating density rates: the non-agricultural labour force (density A) and the formal sector of employment for wages or salaries, including agriculture (density B). These approximations of the *potential* membership seem either too broad or too narrow for a true measurement of union membership among *eligible* workers. Ideally, workers who are not legally permitted to join a trade union should be excluded from the calculation of the density statistic. In many countries, senior civil servants, the armed forces, police officers, security staff, teachers or domestic servants are not permitted to join a union or denied the right of bargaining and strike action (for an overview see ILO, 1997a). As Chang and Sorrentino (1991) have observed, union eligibility shifts across time and countries. Consequently, the strict application of such a criterion for calculating union density rates would make comparison across countries and time extremely difficult.

In the calculation of both density rates we exclude full-time students, persons occupied solely in domestic duties in their own households, inmates of institutions, retired persons, persons living on their own means, and persons wholly dependent on others (ILO, 1998, p. 245). I have tried to calculate membership figures net of spouses, students, the self-employed and pensioners where such groups are included in the union's membership in significant numbers. For example, in the late 1990s some 11 million retired workers had retained their membership in trade unions in Western Europe, with a share varying from 8 per cent of the total membership in the UK to 50 per cent in Italy (calculated from Ebbinghaus and Visser, 2000).

The advantage of using the non-agricultural labour force as the denominator in calculating union density rates (density A) is that we have reasonably comparable data for all countries (ILO, 1998, 1996; World Bank, 1995, 1996).[2] The main disadvantage is that we thus include many categories of workers that do not belong to the target population of the trade unions and are usually difficult to organize. I mention owners, the self-employed and unpaid family workers in commercial, personal and household services. Restricting our definition to people who work for wages and salaries, including agriculture (in density B), yields a potential membership closer to the target population as is prescribed in most legal statutes and union by-laws.

3.   The size and rise of the informal sector

In developing countries people who, formally and regularly, work for wages are often only a minority of those who depend on paid labour for their living. According to the most recent estimate of the ILO (1998, p. 6), the informal sector accounts for the bulk of employment in urban areas in most developing countries. Calculated as a proportion of the non-agricultural labour force, the size of the informal sector, including the unemployed, the self-employed and family workers, varies from 20 per cent in the OECD (but double that size in Mexico, Turkey, Greece, Italy and Spain, partly due to high unemployment), 33 per cent in the new economies of South-East Asia, 44 per cent in Central America, 55 per cent in Latin America, Sub-Saharan Africa and China, and over 80 per cent in India.[3] In the 1990s the informal sector has been growing at the expense of formal employment in all developing countries, partly as a consequence of strategies of casualization and informalization in response to more intense global competition and trade union organizing (ILO, 1998, pp. 16, 19, 22, 25 and 163ff.).

The ILO World Employment Report 1998–1999 divides the informal sector in three subcategories: small or micro enterprises for the most dynamic element, which is often an extension of the formal sector through subcontracting and putting-out arrangements, sometimes through networks organized by global parent companies; the household production sector consisting of mainly unpaid female labour, often seasonal and mostly with very poor labour conditions; and the independent services provided by domestic helpers, street vendors, cleaners, casual labourers, and other self-employed workers, again with female over-representation. Many are wage labourers, though often without the classic features of the wage relation, as analysed by Marx or Marshall (van der Linden, 2001). The difference with the formal sector is mostly institutional: the absence of written or formal contracts and the lack of legal protection (ILO, 1998, p. 168). In other words, the exclusion of the informal sector introduces an arbitrary element in comparing union representation around the world, because it reflects the policy choices of unions, firms and governments to leave a particular part of the economy unrepresented or create a non-protected sector so that market forces can operate freely. Hence, when comparing unionization rates in different regions, it is necessary to take account of the relative size and the growth of the informal sector.

It is comforting to know that the use of either baseline does not affect the ranking of countries by level of unionization. Across the 80 countries for which both rates can be calculated, density rates A and B highly correlate (Pearson r = .93; for the 30 OECD member states r = .99) (see Figure 11.1). Moreover, as might be expected there appears to be a significant relationship between the relative size of the formal sector (as a percentage of the non-agricultural labour force) and the level of unionization in 1995: r = .55 (n = 102) (see Figure 11.2). I do not make a claim about causality. A large formal sector, based on broadly covering labour laws, prudent policies or economic success in the past, may help unions to organize and prevent the opening-up of a space for an informal non-union sector. It has been argued that sectoral collective bargaining and broadly covering collective labour agreements, applicable to non-union firms, lower employer hostility and makes the union organizing task less arduous if unions can also find ways to overcome the free-rider problem (Freeman, 1986; Teulings and Hartog, 1998). On the other hand, the informal sector might be small, because politically powerful unions may have been effective in defending and implementing collective statutes, labour laws and public policies, even in an open trade environment (Rodrik, 1998).

4.   The meaning and counting of membership
When comparing union membership and union organization across countries, it is often objected that 'membership' and 'organization' do mean

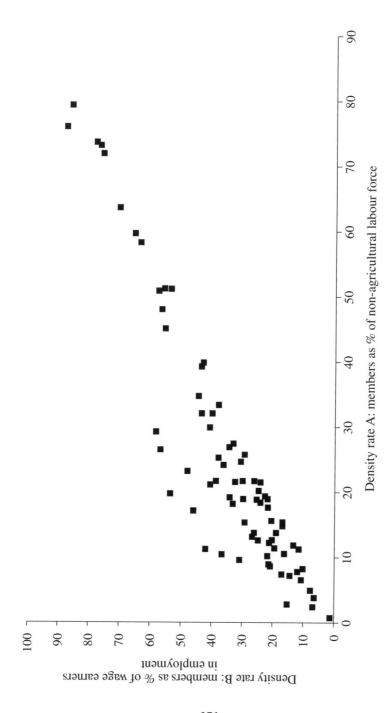

Figure 11.1   Density rate A and B

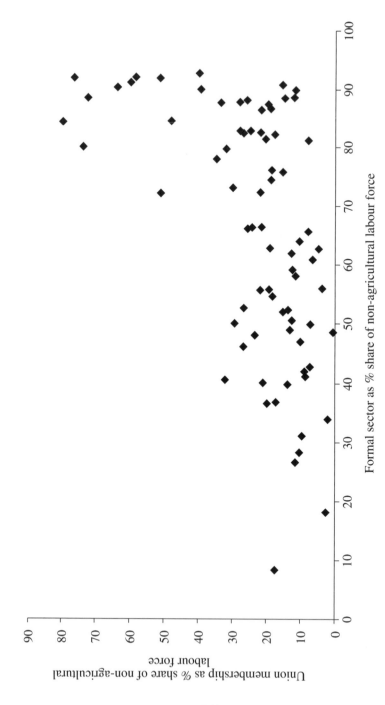

Figure 11.2 Formal sector and unionization

different things in different places and at different times. Union membership involves variable degrees of sacrifice, costs and rewards. The often-cited example in Europe is France where union membership is sometimes taken to mean active engagement in the union and may be coterminous of people elected in various representative functions on a union ticket (Rosanvallon, 1988). Elsewhere, but also according to the rulebooks of French unions, membership implies no other obligation than the monthly payment of dues, preferably, from the point of view of the unions, through automatic withdrawals, possibly in direct transfer from the wage cheque by the employer. Do such differences render the cross-national comparison of membership statistics invalid or useless? Not quite, if combined with the necessary contextual information, union membership statistics usefully reveal differences in union organizing strategies and effectiveness.

Similarly, some union members may derive hugely important personal benefits from their membership, varying from various kinds of insurance, preferential job treatment or higher wages (relative to non-members), while other unions may offer no tangible benefits but a moral or ideological sense of belonging. It is important to be aware of such variations, often hidden in complex legal and organizational practices. Comparative research in Europe has shown that density rates are 20 to 30 percentage points higher if unions, rather than the state, assess unemployment insurance claims even where the insurance itself is fully subsidized and non-members have legally the same entitlements as members (Ebbinghaus and Visser, 1999; Holmlund and Lundborg, 1999; Rothstein, 1992).[4] Few unions have maintained a closed shop and in many countries the law upholds 'the right not to join', but compulsory membership upon taking the job has been common in some occupations (printers, dockworkers). In a few countries the concept of a 'voluntary paying member' is alien, as union revenues are raised through a kind of tax or levy on wages, sales or enterprises, perhaps even unknown to the worker.[5]

What is a trade union and who counts as a union member? Applied to industrial market economies I have proposed the definition of the Australian Bureau of Statistics: 'an organisation, consisting predominantly of employees, the principle activities of which include the negotiation of pay and conditions of employment for its members' (Visser, 1991, p. 99). That definition did include management staff unions and professional associations, even when collective bargaining was not their main activity. This may be the case, either because these groups possess other means for the promotion of their interests, or because they cannot (yet) get the employer to recognize them. The widest coverage, in this particular sense, is found in Europe, especially in Northern Europe, where managers and professional groups like artists, doctors, architects, lawyers, church ministers or soccer players, have formed their own unions and employee associations. In the USA, against a background of general union decline, the rate of unionization among professionals has doubled from 9 to 19 per cent since the late 1950s with large advances among teachers, nurses, physicians, psychologists, social workers, librarians, and speech therapists (Lipset and Katchanovski, 1999). Once these professional associations may have been an alternative to labour unions (Blum et al., 1971; Lipset, [1962] 1967), but this is no longer the case as more and more professional associations adopt union objectives and methods, including the strike weapon. Following national usage, I include such organizations in my count, if possible excluding those members who work on their own account.[6]

The proposed definition is less adequate when applied to developing countries. Following my previous observations on the informal sector and the ambiguous status of many types of wage labour, it would seem advisable to include the self-employed and other such groups. The density A statistic may therefore be the more appropriate measure. Thus, I have tried to include 'self-employed workers' unions' and their members in places like India (though statistical coverage is extremely poor). The 'membership' covered by works councils is not counted.[7]

The application of these criteria demands a fair amount of judgement and knowledge. As usual, the devil is in the detail. Where we have information on all trade unions in a particular country, for instance through a survey or register of associations, it is usually possible to judge which organization is or is not a trade union according to our definition. If the data are taken from reports or estimates from union federations, one cannot take for granted that all unions that would satisfy the definition are covered. Where union federations are divided politically and compete for recognition, seats on councils, public approval or money, there are likely to be rival and often grossly exaggerated membership claims (Ebbinghaus and Visser, 2000; Valenzuela, 1992).

These problems would seem to be solved when union membership statistics are derived from labour force survey data, provided the survey questions asked are clear and consistent. We have now solid survey data on union membership, on an annual or biennial basis, for the United States (from 1973), Canada (1984–), Australia (1976–), South Africa (1985– however with some misrepresentation because of the omission of hostels), the United Kingdom (1989–), Ireland (1992–), the Netherlands (1992–), Iceland (1993–) and Sweden (1994–). In Norway a survey was conducted in 1994. This method has clear advantages for research, allowing individual-level analysis and the calculation of detailed union density rates, for instance, by sex, race, employment status, industrial branch, enterprise size, educational attainment, level of earnings or other characteristics.[8]

The second and more common method is a compilation of membership statistics from questionnaires completed by individual unions or trade union federations. In many countries this is the task of an official registrar, government office, central statistical bureau, one or more federations of trade unions, or independent research centres. This kind of data has advantages when studying membership developments in relation to union type, membership concentration, inter-union competition, union politics and union ideology. One of the main drawbacks is varying statistical coverage, the identification of small and unregistered unions, administrative arrears, and the misrepresentation of paying membership. Official registration does not always help either, because it is sometimes used as a means to hinder the formation of newly emerging unions by denying recognition (examples abound in East Asia, Africa or Latin America before the recent tide of democratization). Union membership data are inevitably based on self-reporting: by individual workers or employers in the case of labour force or enterprise surveys; by union officials in the case of administrative data. The results may be biased because of memory failure, outdated files, financial interest or deliberate misrepresentation. Usually, density rates from labour force surveys are slightly lower that the series derived from administrative sources, even after correction for persons not in the labour force (i.e. retired workers), though trends tend to be similar. Besides the differences in the methods used, survey and administrative data may vary in the timing of measurement and the definitions of the labour force.

5.   Divergence in Europe

With the help of Table 11.1 we can take a closer look at developments in Western Europe. In these 18 countries, total union membership among wage and salary earners in employment stood near 39 million in the late 1990s, three million less than in 1985. The aggregate union density rate (B) in the European Union (all countries in the Table except Iceland, Norway and Switzerland) fell from 37.3 per cent in 1985 to 29.5 per cent in 1997. Absolute membership numbers fell by 8 per cent, the European Union's aggregate density rate by 20 per cent.

This decline is mainly driven by developments in the larger member states, i.e. the United Kingdom, France, Germany since unification in 1990, and Italy, to a lesser extent. Since the mid-1980s unionization levels dropped by 34 per cent in the United Kingdom, 28 per cent in France, 27 per cent in Germany (since 1990) and 11 per cent in Italy. We can compare this with developments in the other G7 economies: a 25 per cent decline in the USA and Japan, and 9 to 13 per cent less, depending on the series, in Canada. Current density levels of G7 nations vary from 38 per cent in Italy and 31 per cent in the UK to 13 per cent in the USA and 10 per cent in France.

Table 11.1   Union membership and density in Western Europe since 1985

Country	Period		Members*		t1=1	Density A**		t1=1	Density B***		t1=1
	t1–t2		t1	t2		t1	t2		t1	t2	
Iceland	85–98		83.0	106.1	1.28	76.8	76.1	0.99	78.3	87.4	1.12
	lfs 93–99		105.0	108.2	1.03				87.9	83.7	0.95
Sweden	85–98		3247.9	3050.4	0.94	79.5	79.3	1.00	81.5	85.7	1.05
	lfs 94–98		2922.0	2892.0	0.99				83.7	81.3	0.97
Finland	85–98		1427.2	1443.7	1.01	66.6	73.2	1.10	69.1	76.1	1.10
Denmark	85–99		1726.5	1816.0	1.05	69.2	72.0	1.04	78.2	75.4	0.96
Norway	85–97		1001.5	1103.7	1.10	53.0	51.2	0.97	57.5	55.6	0.97
	lfs 94			1048.8						57.0	
Belgium	85–95		1461.9	1611.1	1.10	49.0	51.0	1.04	50.7	53.4	1.05
Ireland	85–97		451.4	482.3	1.07	40.4	34.7	0.86	56.3	44.4	0.79
	lfs 94–97		422.6	472.8	1.12				48.3	43.5	0.90
Luxembourg	87–95		75.0	85.0	1.13	48.1	39.9	0.83	49.7	42.9	0.86
Italy****	85–98		6125.5	5481.5	0.89	29.6	25.3	0.85	42.5	38.0	0.89
Austria	85–99		1419.6	1209.3	0.85	46.3	33.4	0.72	51.6	38.0	0.74
Germany W	85–90		7892.8	8013.8	1.02	29.0	27.7	0.96	34.3	32.1	0.94
Germany	91–98		11969.4	8326.9	0.70	32.7	21.7	0.66	35.9	26.2	0.73
UK	85–97		9738.9	7015.5	0.72	36.3	24.7	0.68	45.9	30.5	0.66
	lfs 89–98		8839.0	7257.0	0.82	31.9	25.6	0.80	39.0	30.7	0.79
Netherlands	85–99		1290.2	1631.0	1.26	23.6	21.6	0.91	28.7	24.1	0.84
	lfs 92–99		1459.0	1661.0	1.14				25.2	24.5	0.97

Switzerland	85–99	808.9	729.6	0.90	25.4	18.9	0.74	28.6	21.7	0.76
Portugal	86–95	1434.0	800.0	0.56	40.3	18.8	0.47	51.4	25.1	0.49
Greece	85–95	664.0	430.0	0.65	23.3	12.4	0.53	37.5	20.9	0.56
Spain	85–97	672.4	1582.6	2.35	6.1	10.5	1.73	9.3	16.4	1.76
France	85–98	2443.0	2000.0	0.82	11.2	8.2	0.73	13.9	10.0	0.72
EU 15	**85–97**	**40070.3**	**36869.7**	**0.92**	**29.3**	**22.8**	**0.78**	**37.3**	**29.5**	**0.79**

Notes:
* = without retired, unemployed and self-employed members (in the case of the UK and Ireland a 10 per cent discount is applied);

** = unemployed members included in Sweden, Iceland, Denmark, Finland and Belgium (the five countries where the unemployed retain membership for reasons of insurance);

*** = unemployed members excluded;

**** = Italian membership and density rates are based on the membership in the three main federations and exclude an estimated 10–20 per cent members of non-affiliated unions.

lfs = calculated from labour force survey

In many (but not all) smaller countries – i.e. Finland, Denmark, Iceland, Ireland, the three Benelux countries, and most prominently in Spain – membership increased, in some cases the membership gains in the 1990s (Spain, Ireland and the Netherlands) made up for the losses of the earlier decade.[9] But even in the smaller economies of Europe a rise in aggregate union density was rare.

The most remarkable feature in Western Europe is the degree of disparity in unionization levels. In spite of common legal-political, social and economic developments, further promoted by the European Union and the Single Market, the position of the unions, as indicated by unionization rates, is very diverse and shows no signs of convergence. Between 1985 and 1995 the coefficient of variation of these density rates has risen from .405 in 1985 to .565 in 1995. Strong union movements tend to grow stronger and weak union movements weaker, presumably because stronger unions can devote more resources to organizing and the custom of union membership is more easily sustained (Checchi and Visser, 2002; Visser, 1992; see also Chapter 2 by Schnabel in this volume). Thus, while common developments – the rise in unemployment since the late 1970s, the shift towards services, the halt of public sector growth, the increased use of flexible contracts – tend to halt union growth, differences in institutions such as sectoral collective bargaining, workplace organization, and union provision of insurance may explain why there is increased divergence (Visser, 2002; Ebbinghaus and Visser, 1999; Lange and Scruggs, 1999; Western, 1997).

We tend to find a North–South divide, with higher levels of organization in the North. This appears to be associated with less divisions between different union centres or peak federations, more cooperation within the union movement under the leadership of comprehensively organized Social Democratic federations, stable and pervasive collective bargaining and bipartite relationships with highly organized employers' associations, widespread workplace organization and routine company bargaining recognized by employers (Golden et al., 1999; Iversen, 1999; Traxler, 1994; Visser, 1990). In Southern Europe, we tend to find more rivalry between different union centres, more dependence on rival political parties and contingent government support, more fragmentation, less stable and shallower collective bargaining arrangements, and, with the exception of Italy, a more limited and fragile form of union presence in the workplace. In the continental centre of Western Europe we find a mix of these institutional elements, whereas voluntary arrangements prevail in Britain and Ireland.

In the Eastern half of Europe the state of the unions is far more turbulent and fragile. The transition to the market economy and a more voluntary-based union membership went together with sharply rising unemployment rates, falling wages, huge losses of membership and intense inter-union rivalry (Crowley and Ost, 2001; Vaughan-Whitehead, 2000; ILO, 1997b; Standing, 1997; Ost, 1996; Mason, 1995; Weinstein, 1995; Clarke and Fairbrother, 1994; MacShane, 1994). Before the disintegration of the Soviet Union the official membership number was put at 140 million (Mason, 1995) or twice the combined membership of the unions in Belarus, Ukraine, and the Russian Federation in the mid-1990s (see Table 11.2). In 1990 the official unions declared their independence of the Communist Party and the state, but they hung on to their considerable financial and property resources. Reform of the official unions may be unrealistic; a survey of enterprise union presidents in 1993 showed that 95 per cent 'considered themselves to be part of the senior management of the enterprise and none believed that trade unionism had a future' (Clarke and Fairbrother, 1994, pp. 387–388).

In Russia the first independent workers' organizations developed during 1987 in response to Gorbachev's attempt to mobilize shop-floor pressure in support for '*perestroika* from below'. Further mobilization took place in the context of the Democrats and Conservative Fronts in 1989 and the miners' strikes during the summer of the same year. Some of the new independent unions associated with commercial groups and made use of the tax advantages available to trade unions. The official unions appear to have kept the powers of patronage in the workplace and independent unions have been kept weak by fierce opposition from the new entrepreneurs.

In Central and Eastern Europe it is not untypical to find four to six rival union centres, each struggling for a declining share of the membership pie (Mason, 1995). (The Westeuropean average is two or three federations.) MacShane (1994) distinguishes four types: newly created, anti-Communist, nationalistic or free market unions such as *Solidarity* in Poland, *Fratia* in Romania, *Prodkepa* in Bulgaria, *Sotsprof* in Russia, or *Liga* in Hungary; former Communist trade unions who have been taken over by a post-Communist leadership, as in the case of the *KOS* federation in Czechoslovakia, which in 1993 was split up in a Czech and Slovak federation; the reformed Communist unions, which started to change in the 1980s and accepted western style pluralism, as for instance *MSzOSz* in Hungary and *CITUB* in Bulgaria; and the inheritors of the Communist unions, as are *OPZZ* in Poland, the *Federation of Independent Unions* in the Russian Federation, and some small Communist unions in the Czech and Slovak Republics. Further splits, based on politics and personalities, occurred in 1990s. Membership is concentrated in the traditional (usually public) sectors of the economy and collective bargaining tends to be decentralized with a minor role for industry or sector organizations.

Comparing Table 11.2 with Table 11.1 it would appear that in most transition countries unionization is still more extensive than in Western Europe. However, where we have recent data (Poland, Hungary, Slovenia), we

Table 11.2 *Union membership and density in transition countries since 1985*

Country	Period	Members*		t1 = 1	Density A**		t1 = 1	Density B***		t1 = 1
	t1 – t2	t1	t2		t1	t2		t1	t2	
Russian Fed.	85–98	70000.0	40000.0	0.57	91.4	58.2	0.64	100.0	63.1	0.63
Azerbaijan	85–95	2522.3	1706.7	0.68	84.9	73.7	0.87	86.3	77.6	0.90
Belarus	85–95	5355.4	4134.2	0.77	101.0	91.9	0.91	100.0	91.9	0.92
Ukraine	85–96	26000.0	21850.0	0.84	100.0	99.3	0.99	–	–	
Bulgaria	91–95	2200.0	1500.0	0.68	62.0	37.7	0.61	62.3	–	
Romania	91–95	4000.0	3100.0	0.78	50.7	34.1	0.67	52.8	–	
Slovakia	90–95	1920.0	1150.0	0.60	73.8	50.9	0.69	78.7	57.3	0.73
Czech Rep.	90–95	3820.0	1886.0	0.49	79.6	39.2	0.49	78.8	43.4	0.55
Slovenia	98	–	300.0		–	32.0		–	40.0	
Hungary	85–98	3000.0	1000.0	0.33	74.1	27.6	0.37	74.1	33.2	0.45
Estonia	89–95	580.0	166.6	0.29	82.9	24.1	0.29	82.5	36.1	0.44
Lithuania	98	–	221.0		–	12.7		–	25.0	
Poland	89–99	6300.0	2700.0	0.43	47.1	18.5	0.39	60.0	24.2	0.40

Notes: as in Table 11.1.

observe further decline and low density rates, comparable with Southern Europe. In Poland, the birthplace of the first independent union movement *Solidarity* in 1980, which became a major force in the disintegration of Communism, the rate of unionization (B) fell from 47 per cent in 1989 to 18.5 per cent in 1999, and unions are now entirely concentrated in the residual state sector, where there is less than 30 per cent of employment (Meardi, 2002, p. 84). Other sources put union density even lower (Ost, 2002, p. 42). Within a highly decentralized and fragmented environment of union organizing and collective bargaining, also characteristic for the Baltic states and Hungary and Slovenia, the new market economy of the 1990s is mostly non-union (Dovydeniene, 2002; Frege, 2002; Neumann, 2002).

6. Union decline in liberal market economies
The USA, Canada, the UK and, since the 1990s, Australia and New Zealand can be classified as liberal market economies, contrasting with the coordinated market economies of Northern and continental Europe (Hall and Soskice, 2001). The absence of sectoral employers' associations and sectoral wage bargaining, decentralization and fragmentation are among the defining characteristics of union organizations and industrial relations in North America. This has proved to be a setting for union decline (Freeman, 1986). In the 1950s US unions organized one-third of wage and salary earners in employment, in 1985 that proportion had been halved, in 2000 it has further decreased to 13 per cent (Table 11.3). Crossing the Northern border we find that Canadian workers are more prone to unionize, but in the 1990s Canadian unions, too, witnessed a slow decline. According to the 2000 labour force survey, union density (B) had dropped just under 30 per cent, down from 34.6 per cent in 1985 (Macredie and Pilon, 2001).

In an attempt to explain the US–Canada gap in unionization, Troy (2000) argues that this is mostly a result of the larger size of the public sector in Canada, but he overlooks the fact that union decline in the market sector in Canada, though far from negligible, has been slower than in the USA. Riddell (1993) has shown that differences in the composition of the labour force can explain only as much as 15 per cent of the US–Canada gap in unionization. Public opinion towards the unions is more negative in the US case (Lipset, 1986), though Freeman and Rogers (1999) have been able to demonstrate that there is a considerable demand among US workers for some kind of union or union-like representation. The US case suggests that union decline has a self-perpetuating element insofar it has caused an inward-looking focus on servicing existing members and an adverse impact on organizing priorities and resources (Rose and Chaison, 2001). In recent years, the leadership of American unions has made an attempt to reverse present trends by giving more attention, and devoting more resources, to membership drives.

Australia and New Zealand are losing their traditional characteristic of unionized economies fast. Under the award system, introduced in the early years of the twentieth century, compulsory arbitration played an important role in generalizing collective agreements to entire sectors and blanketing workers into union membership. In the 1980s and 1990s the system started crumbling. In Australia the rate of unionization has fallen from 46 to 25 per cent in 15 years. The decline began long before the legal changes and suggested that fewer workers could resist the temptation of a free ride. The haemorrhage did not stop when the main Australian unions entered into a series of high-level agreements ('Accords') with the Labour Party in the 1980s and stepped up coordination within their ranks. The 1997 Workplace Relations Act, introduced by the Conservative government, steers a different course. The Act encourages enterprise bargaining and prohibits closed shops and discriminatory advantages for union members.

'The removal of external legitimisation of unions through legislative mechanisms has been the dominant factor in the decline of New Zealand unions' (Harbridge and Honeybone, 1996, p. 440). In New Zealand attempts to encourage enterprise bargaining and move away from dependence upon the occupationally driven multi-employer national award system started in the 1980s, under the Labour government (Walsh, 1989). The Conservative government elected towards the end of the decade moved quickly to deregulate the labour market. The enactment of the Employment Contracts Act of 1991 saw the end of a 90-year tradition of state protection of union organization and collective bargaining. The new system prohibited compulsory union membership and promoted individual contracting over collective bargaining (Cramford et al., 1996; Hince and Vranken, 1991). Union density dropped from around 44 per cent to under 18 per cent (Harbridge et al., 2001). The new political situation may give New Zealand's unions some breathing space. The Labour/Alliance coalition government, elected in 1999, is more favourable to unions and seeks to promote fairness and bargaining in good faith.

7. Asian variations
The sheer size of Asia and the profound differences between its various parts defy meaningful generalizations regarding industrial relations and union organization. Following Thomas et al. (1985) we may distinguish between three trajectories of economic, political and union development: the New Industrializing Countries of East Asia (Japan, South Korea, Hong Kong, Singapore and Taiwan), the five followers or 'Tigers' of South-East Asia (Philippines, Indonesia, Malaysia, Thailand, and Vietnam), and the

Table 11.3 Union membership and density in North America and Oceania since 1985

Country	Period	Members*		$t1=1$	Density A**		$t1=1$	Density B***		$t1=1$
	$t1-t2$	$t1$	$t2$		$t1$	$t2$		$t1$	$t2$	
Australia	85–96	2793.0	2450.0	0.88	40.9	28.3	0.69	49.5	34.7	0.70
	lfs 86–00	*2593.9*	*1901.0*	*0.73*	*36.5*	*20.2*	*0.55*	*45.6*	*24.7*	*0.54*
Canada	85–98	3730.0	4010.0	1.08	30.2	26.9	0.89	37.6	34.2	0.91
	lfs 85–00	*3435.0*	*3740.0*	*1.09*				*34.6*	*29.9*	*0.87*
New Zealand	85–99	683.0	302.4	0.44	52.5	17.6	0.34	53.1	21.4	0.40
USA	*lfs 85–00*	*16996.1*	*16258.0*	*0.96*	*15.2*	*11.7*	*0.77*	*17.4*	*13.0*	*0.75*

Notes: as in Table 11.1.

383

large and populous economies of China, the Indian subcontinent and South Asia. West Asia, the Arab countries and the Middle East will be discussed in relation to Northern Africa and the Eastern Mediterranean.

In the 1990s the labour markets of East Asia lost their abundance and gradually became tighter due to labour-intensive industrialization. Together with the move towards democracy, this ought to have improved the conditions for union organizing. The opposite economic conditions are found in South Asia. In India and Pakistan, for instance, import substitution industrialization strategies had dominated until the 1980s but were abandoned for more export-oriented policies, together with a liberalization of restrictions to finance, industry and trade, in the 1990s. The unions tended to operate through political channels and restrict their activities to the formal (i.e. public and protected) sector. Economic liberalisation has reduced their traditional political leverage (Kuruvilla et al., 2001).

Studies of the union situation in East and South-East Asia agree on the weak structure of industrial relations, the extreme decentralization of collective bargaining (mitigated in Japan through the practice of annual wage rounds), the strict state controls and repression in order to preempt or prevent the development of autonomous trade unions, and the discouragement of anything but enterprise unionism (Kuruvilla et al., 2001; Thomas et al., 1995; Jacoby, 1993; Galenson, 1992; Deyo, 1989). In contrast, a political tradition of union organization, influenced by the fact that British colonial rulers legalized trade unions long before they accepted political parties, had dominated in the Indian sub-continent.

The rate of unionization (density B) in East Asia lies within a band of 12–25 per cent of the employed wage earners, with Japan and Hong Kong (until 1997) towards the higher and South Korea towards the lower end (Table 11.4). Taiwan is a case apart, the massive surge in unionization is mostly related to a new health insurance provision which was channelled through occupational or craft unions; when this facility was withdrawn, in 1994, the rise in membership stopped and turned into decline (Chi-Sen, 1998; Hwang, 1996). Unions have lost terrain in Japan year after year since 1949 when, following a wave of support, the militant Japanese unions organized 55 per cent of the Japanese wage earners. One reason for the decline in the past 20 to 30 years is that employment in the industrial large-firm sector has been falling and that the Japanese enterprise unions hardly organize at all outside these firms (Tsuru and Rebitzer, 1995). Union density rates fell in the 1990s in Singapore even before the onslaught of the recent Asian crisis, in spite of a tight labour market and a long tradition of social dialogue and tripartite relationships between the unions, employers and the government.

In contrast, unionization rates rose in Hong Kong in anticipation of the

Table 11.4 Union membership and density in South and South-East Asia since 1985

Country	Period	Members		$t1=1$	Density A		$t1=1$	Density B		$t1=1$
	$t1-t2$	$t1$	$t2$		$t1$	$t2$		$t1$	$t2$	
Taiwan	85–98	1549.0	3135.9	2.02	22.2	26.5	1.19	32.5	50.1	1.54
Philippines	85–96	2117.0	3587.0	1.69	18.4	21.7	1.18	24.1	29.9	1.24
Hong Kong	85–96	367.6	624.3	1.70	14.1	19.6	1.38	16.8	22.3	1.33
Japan	85–00	12417.5	11539.0	0.93	22.8	17.8	0.78	28.8	21.5	0.75
Singapore	85–98	201.1	272.8	1.36	17.0	15.4	0.91	20.6	16.9	0.82
South Korea	85–99	1004.4	1481.0	1.47	8.5	7.8	0.92	12.4	11.8	0.95
Malaysia	86–95	605.8	706.3	1.17	13.5	11.2	0.83	13.5	11.7	0.87
Indonesia	95	–	1000.0		–	2.4		–	7.0	
Thailand	85–99	234.4	100.0	0.43	3.3	0.7	0.21	3.3	1.4	0.42
China	85–97	85258.0	91310.0	1.07	59.4	42.2	0.71	–	–	
Sri Lanka	85–94	1565.4	1613.4	1.03	48.6	41.8	0.86	–	–	
Bangladesh	85–95	1090.0	1720.7	1.58	15.3	7.5	0.49	–	–	
Pakistan	87–94	880.9	984.2	1.12	6.4	4.0	0.63	–	–	
India	80–91	5917.0	4256.0	0.72	6.6	2.8	0.42	–	15.2	

Notes: as in Table 11.1

reunion with the Republic of China (Levin and Wing-Kai Chiu, 1994) and in South Korea between 1987 and 1990 when newly organizing union federations played an important role in bringing the end to a 30-year history of authoritarian rule and repression by the ex-military generals (Lim and Hwang, 1999). Unionization in South Korea peaked in 1989, when close to 20 per cent of all employed workers joined a union. However, in the 1990s many members walked away in disappointment; management remained hostile, unions were ineffective outside the shrinking large-firm sector, and unemployment was on the rise even before the Asian crisis of 1999. By the end of the decade, union density had fallen to 12 per cent (Kuruvilla et al., 2001; Lim and Hwang, 1999; Young-Ki, 1998).

It has been noted that in South Korea, organized labour gained much less than it contributed to democratization (Song, 2002, p. 209). In 1993, under pressure of popular, students' and workers' protest, there were democratic elections for the presidency. Under international pressure and pending membership of the OECD, the law on restriction of union pluralism was lifted (Evans, 1998, p. 10).[10] But South Korean industrial relations are still an unfriendly environment for unions, with many legal restrictions, limited legal encouragement of enterprise bargaining and discouragement of sectoral bargaining, poorly financed union federations, with dues paid to local enterprise unions, and rival union centres (Lim and Hwang, 1999). Attempts at consensus-building dialogue, modelled after tripartite talks in Western Europe have failed and ended with a walk-out of the radical union federation in 1999 (Song, 2002, pp. 220–221).

With the partial exception of the Philippines, where unionization rates soared following the fall of the Marcos regime, the union density figures suggest a weakening of unions in the Tiger economies of South-East Asia (I have no information concerning Vietnam). In Malaysia and Thailand unions have retrenched from already low levels. In Indonesia, independent unionism was severely repressed under the New Order regime of Suharto and has a fledgling existence since (Greenfield, 2000; Manning, 1995). In each of these cases union organizations are extremely fragmented and operating in a local and decentralized setting, trying to steer a course between patronage and repression. Union membership in the public sector tends to be prohibited. In Malaysia the large presence of migrant workers is an obstacle, especially since labour law offers no protection to migrants (Ali, 1995). In Thailand recurrent state repression is the main issue. The assorted enterprise unions organized some 400 000 members in peak years between 1980 and 1991, but they were weakened after the military retook power in 1991. Strikes were outlawed and in 1995 union membership had dwindled to an estimated 100 000 dues paying members, or 1.4 per cent of wage employment in the private sector (Manusphaibool, 1998, p. 82).

Collective bargaining was also interrupted and Thailand does not ratify the relevant ILO conventions. In Indonesia, independent unions did regain their organizing rights after the fall of the Suharto regime. In a mixture of state control, repression and paternalism, the old unions had been under the obligation to cooperate with management but were also expected to fulfil the duty of assisting workers, as individuals, by presenting their grievances to the labour courts and the labour department (Greenfield, 2000).

My data for South Asia (Bangladesh, India, Pakistan, and Sri Lanka) are less robust. They indicate that, with a possible exception for Sri Lanka, unionization is patchy, that the trade unions operate only in a small part of the economy and that unions have retrenched further in the 1990s. The informal economy is overwhelming and according to most observers the official unions hardly put in any effort at organizing. Density rates (B) of the formal wage earner class present therefore a misleading picture, but density rates (A) suggest that only a small and declining part of the economy is organized (Blowmik, 1998). Various researchers claim that employers have responded to union organization by the casualization and informalization of labour (Ghose, 1999; Breman, 1996). Bhattacherjee and Chaudhuri (1994, p. 459) use wage data between 1960 and 1986 to show that the policy of Indian plant-based unions to protect the wage standards in the traditional industries has accelerated the development of a low-pay sector that 'became more vulnerable to competitive forces and could no longer count on the traditional "wage-welfare" functions provided by party-based unions'.

Indian trade unions, with few exceptions, have historically concentrated on advancing the interests of those on whom the law confers the rights to engage in industrial action, and have ignored unorganized workers without this right (Harriss-White and Gooptu, 2000, p. 106; Blowmik, 1998, pp. 158–159). Despite their narrow membership base, these unions sometimes prospered in terms of influence on government policy due to an import substitution industrialization policy, highly protective labour legislation, and close connections between union federations and political parties. From the days of independence, the union movement has split along party lines, later adding ethnic and region cleavages, and in most cases 'there were no ambiguities in the chain of command from party to union' (Bhattacherjee, 2002, p. 319). Based on the study of Chatterjee (1980), Bhattacherjee (2002, p. 312) assesses the position of the Indian National TUC, which is closely related to the Congress Party, as follows: 'when confronted between patronage of the ruling party and genuine worker support, the INTUC usually opted for the former'. The multiplicity of unions and the exposure to the exertions of political parties, state manipulation and employer opposition invited political mediation of disputes. 'Labour protests tend to remain localized, small-scale, and focused on immediate employers – reflecting the structural characteristic of the labour market and employment relations' (Harriss-White and Gooptu, 2000, p. 109).

In China the once direct relationship between unions, state and party has been weakened and is now mediated by surrogate bureaucracies and regional power brokers (Hong and Warner, 1998). The giant All-Chinese Federation of Trade Unions (ACFTU) monopoly, with more than half a million affiliated, mostly local unions, had been crippled in its role of translating party policy into the workplace, following Lenin's conveyor-belt doctrine. Since the opening of Chinese markets to foreign capital, starting in the late 1970s and intensified after the economic reforms of 1992 and 1994, the powers of the local enterprise unions have been diluted as managerial authority has grown. In the non-state sector the position of the unions vis-à-vis management is weak and their role problematic (Hong and Warner, 1998, p. 94). The official attempt to 'evolve' a distinctly Asian, non-conflicting model of labour–management collaboration appears to have surrendered to a practice that is more close to the western multinationals' style of shunning the trade union. The ACFTU, while still charged with the role of cushioning agitation, but unable to deliver the goods in the workplace, suffers from a 'credibility crisis' (Hong and Warner, 1998, p. 123). Currently, most enterprise unions operate in the state sector and union representation in the foreign investment enterprise sector has remained low, somewhere between one-tenth and one-third of the workforce, in spite of enabling legislation in larger establishments with 25 or more staff (Kuruvilla et al., 2001).

8.   Africa and the Middle East

It is hard to make general statements about developments in North Africa, the Middle East and the Eastern Mediterranean, because we have too few observations and the observations that we have show divergent patterns. We have no data for the Arab countries. Here, the study of trade union organization should concentrate on the position of migrants and the role of transregional migration over long distances. We have now, for Western Europe, a comparative and historical study about trade unions, immigration policies and immigrant workers covering the 1960s to 1990s (Penninx and Roosblad, 2000). That study nicely shows that unions faced three consecutive dilemmas over the immigration issue: whether to prevent or accept immigration; whether to organize immigrants or keep them outside the movement; and whether to engage in special policies, helping immigrants to overcome their handicaps in the labour market, or stick to a more formal concept of equal treatment. It turns out that different answers were given, though European mainstream unions did nearly always accept, if not endorse immigration and organize immigrant workers in their ranks.

In Northern Africa unions are very weak, with density rates (A) under 10 per cent in Morocco and Tunisia (see Table 11.5). Trade unions in Egypt have a stronger membership base, but they operate under state control and are loosing terrain (Galenson, 1994). The Turkish data suggest strong growth in the 1980s, when repression eased, but need further research. The figures released by the Turkish Federation of Employers suggest a small decline in unionization in the exposed sector of the economy between 1988 and 1996. There is no dispute about the rout of Israel's trade union movement following the change in the National Health Insurance Law and the electoral defeat of the Labour Party in the Histadrut in 1994. The Histadrut, Israel's only union confederation, had been formed in the 1920s as a surrogate for a state organization which did not yet exist at the time and had assumed many of its functions, varying from immigrant settlement and housing to social and medical insurance. In the not-so-distant past, every adult employee and their relatives had obtained health insurance by signing up as a member (Galin, 1994). In the late 1990s unionization had dropped to 30 per cent (Nathanson and Associates, 2002).

During the 1980s and 1990s most African economies have been declining. Colonial economic policy had left a legacy of dependence on primary commodity exports, poorly developed infrastructure, and limited linkages between rural and urban sectors. Ethnic and sometimes religious rivalries in post-colonial Africa constituted potent divisive forces making for civil war and social disintegration. The ravages of war, periodic refugee inflows, mass poverty, hunger and the HIV/AIDS epidemic have crippled many economies from the Horn of Africa to Africa's West Coast. As was mentioned before, the majority of the workforce is now (under)employed in the informal sector. For instance, of around one hundred million people living in the ten core countries of Southern Africa, the potential labour force is estimated at less than one-third, while only one in ten is formally employed. For comparative reasons, density rates (A), measuring union membership as a share of the labour force outside agriculture, are to be preferred.

The struggle for independence usually made for close relationships between unions and political parties. Ever since the days of independence, nationalist politics dictated that workers and unions tone down or repress their demands. Examples where one-party governments control the main union federations and repress or outlaw independent unions are easily found in Ghana, Nigeria, Uganda or Zambia. The Cold War left a particularly debilitating mark on African trade unions. In many countries, e.g. Angola, Mozambique, Congo, Uganda, Kenya, unions were prostrated by the fight between rival international union federations under American or Communist influence, and by the response of nationalist governments that tried to prohibit union links with the outside world.

Table 11.5 *Union membership and density in Middle East and North Africa since 1985*

Country	Period	Members		$t1=1$	Density A		$t1=1$	Density B		$t1=1$
	$t1-t2$	$t1$	$t2$		$t1$	$t2$		$t1$	$t2$	
Malta	85–97	53.0	80.5	1.52	44.9	59.6	1.33	47.3	65.1	1.38
Cyprus	85–95	144.9	161.0	1.11	62.7	47.9	0.76	66.0	56.5	0.86
Egypt	85–95	2720.6	3313.1	1.22	38.9	21.7	0.56	42.7	38.8	0.91
Turkey	87–99	1594.6	2988.0	1.87	16.3	21.7	1.33	28.1	32.5	1.16
Israel	85–98	1850.0	450.0	0.24	99.1	18.9	0.19	100.0	30.0	0.30
Jordan	88	212.0	–		27.6	–		–	–	
Syria	85–96	437.3	644.9	1.47	20.7	21.1	1.02	–	–	
Tunisia	94	–	220.0		–	8.9		–	–	
Morocco	94	–	290.0		–	4.9		–	–	

Notes: as in Table 11.1

Unsurprisingly, we observe in Africa the world's lowest unionization rates (A) (see Table 11.6). In Eritrea, Ethiopia, Uganda, Lesotho, Mauritania, Guinea, Gabon, Morocco and Tunisia, unions organize less than 10 per cent of the workforce outside agriculture. The highest unionization rates are found in relatively prosperous Mauritius, Tanzania and Kenya in the East, Namibia, Zambia, and South Africa in the South, and Ghana and Senegal in the West. Unfortunately, we have very few time-series data. They suggest that there was a decline in Uganda, Zambia and Kenya – in each case related to the opening of the economy to foreign markets (Fashoyin, 1992, 1997). Only in South Africa and Zimbabwe did unions made significant gains (Baskin, 1996a and 1996b; Standing et al., 1996; Schiphorst, 1995). There are different accounts on the developments of union membership in Nigeria, Africa's most populous country. Observers agree on a sharp decline in the 1980s, following the closure of the Nigerian Congress of Labour by the government (Damachi, 1992). Several unions lost half or more of their membership, also on account of the fall in employment, petroleum exports and prices. In the first half of the 1990s there appears to have been some recovery and unions have moved away from their traditional adversarial approach (Fashoyin, 1995).

Unions in Zimbabwe, Namibia, South Africa, Botswana, and Niger, to name the most prominent examples, were in the forefront of the struggle for democracy. In the final decade of the struggle against apartheid, union membership in South Africa more than doubled. Legal restrictions on union organizing were relaxed in 1979 and 1981, and progressive unions, combined in the new federation COSATU, organized black alongside white workers while fighting for the political and civil rights of black people. The growth of COSATU during the 1980s contrasted with the decline of the exclusively white trade unions (Macun and Frost, 1994). Union growth came to a halt in the mid-1990s, partly as a consequence of the decline in mining and manufacturing, the traditional union strongholds. COSATU served as regional role model and gave direct assistance to unions in Namibia, Zambia, Zimbabwe and Swaziland. Trade unions in Zimbabwe were in the forefront of the failed campaign to dislodge Mugabe, but in Namibia, South Africa, Botswana and Swaziland union–party coalitions were continued, despite internal tensions. In Malawi unions played a role in unseating the neo-colonial dictator Banda.

9. Central and Latin America
Recent development of industrial relations union organization in Latin America must be judged against three developments: the breakdown of conventional model of inward-oriented development based on import-substituting industrialization and its replacement by structural adjust-

Table 11.6 *Union membership and density in Africa since 1985*

Country	Period t1 – t2	Members t1	Members t2	t1 = 1	Density A t1	Density A t2	t1 = 1	Density B t1	Density B t2	t1 = 1
Mauritius	85–95	98.4	106.0	1.08	34.8	25.8	0.74	34.8	29.2	0.84
Tanzania	95	–	469.6		–	19.2		–	34.2	
Kenya	85–95	700.0	500.0	0.71	41.9	18.3	0.44	41.9	33.3	0.79
Eritrea	95	–	18.0		–	5.2		–	–	
Ethiopia	95	–	152.2		–	4.1		–	–	
Uganda	89–95	101.5	62.6	0.62	7.8	3.8	0.49	10.2	6.8	0.67
Namibia	95	–	106.0		–	29.9		–	40.8	
Zambia	85–95	320.1	273.1	0.85	36.1	29.3	0.81	40.0	58.2	1.46
South Africa	85–98	1391.4	3202.0	2.30	15.5	21.2	1.37	17.7	40.5	2.28
	lfs 94		2616.1						31.3	
Botswana	95	–	59.0		–	15.6		–	20.5	
Zimbabwe	85–95	161.9	250.0	1.54	11.6	14.8	1.28	11.6	16.7	1.44
Malawi	95	–	75.0		–	11.9		–	13.4	
Mozambique	95	–	190.0		–	11.3		–	42.2	
Swaziland	95	–	21.0		–	10.4		–	36.8	
Lesotho	95	–	36.0		–	7.2		–	14.4	
Ghana	95	–	670.0		–	21.2		–	–	
Senegal	95	–	184.0		–	19.7		–	53.8	
Cameroon	95	–	250.0		–	14.6		–	–	

Cape Verde	95	–	15.2		–	14.0	–	–
Nigeria	82–95	3000.0	3520.0	1.17	20.0	13.3	–	–
Côte d'Ivoire	95	–	300.0		–	13.2	–	–
Mali	95	–	102.8		–	12.4	–	–
Mauritania	95	–	15.0		–	2.7	–	–
Guinea	95	–	13.3		–	2.6	–	–
Gabon	95	–	5.4		–	1.9	–	–

Notes: as in Table 11.1

ment and trade liberalization (Bresser Pereira, 1993); the end of the state-corporatist and populist models and concomitant forms of state–unions relations; and the informalization of employment and livelihood strategies and social organization (Koonings et al., 1995).

Typically, the established unions in South America were tied to government parties through clientelism. The rise of the 'bureaucratic-authoritarian' regimes, with state-sponsored unions and political incorporation of labour, dates from the 1930s (O'Donnell, 1973). But organized labour was marginalized politically after several military coups in Brazil (1964), Argentina (1966 and 1976), Chile (1973) and Uruguay (1973). In Brazil, beginning in the late 1970s, vigorous new trade unions succeeded in sidestepping the tightly controlled trade union system set up under Várgas and preserved by the military. These unions played an active part in the transition to democracy in the 1980s.

Epstein (1989, p. 63) suggests that in the mid-1980s the growth and mobilization power of the new union movement in Brazil 'forced the recognition of organized workers as a major political actor', similar to what was to happen in South Africa. 'Alone in the states of Southern America, the trade unions in Brazil still have a capacity to organize workers and to exert a powerful influence upon workplace activities', write Beynon and Ramalho (2000, p. 219) in the Socialist Register of 2001. This assessment contrasts with more sceptical account concerning the traditional unions and the difficulty to replace the old union tax by voluntary subscriptions (Smith, 1995). Until the end of the military dictatorship (1964–85), Brazilian unions were subject to restrictive corporatist laws, modelled after Italian fascism in the 1930s. The overall system evolved with weak links to the workplace and was more characterized by the provision of services and favours rather than by labour militancy. The principle function of the trade unions was to administer social welfare programmes, and strikes were prohibited. The unions were financed by a tax of one day's pay per annum for each worker (Galenson, 1994). This system fell apart even before 1985 and already in the late 1970s a kind of 'new unionism' emerged, very critical of the officially recognized unions. Its leaders were frequently harassed and arrested. Unfortunately, the data about Brazil are scant and allow only a quantitative estimate of the degree of unionization for the early 1990s (see Table 11.7).

In Central America unionization rates (A) in 1995 vary between less than 5 per cent in Guatemala to around 25 per cent in Nicaragua. The case of Cuba is special, with obligatory enrolment in the union in many (formal) sectors of the economy. All Central American countries, including Cuba, for which we have time series share the experience of union decline (Rama, 1995). Union decline is especially pronounced in Mexico, where union

Table 11.7   Union membership and density in Latin America since 1985

Country	Period	Members		t1 = 1	Density A		t1 = 1	Density B		t1 = 1
	t1 – t2	t1	t2		t1	t2		t1	t2	
Cuba	85–95	2892.8	2771.5	0.96	65.4	63.6	0.97	68.9	70.2	1.02
Antigua	95	9.0	14.4	1.60	–	–		–	55.4	
Nicaragua	95	–	280.5		–	23.3	0.93	–	48.2	
Domin. Rep.	89–95	360.0	450.1	1.25	18.9	17.6	0.93	42.8	18.9	0.44
Mexico	91–97	7000.0	4000.0	0.57	31.0	13.9	0.45	29.1	16.6	0.57
Costa Rica	85–95	138.6	138.6	1.00	22.9	13.7	0.60	20.5	19.4	0.95
Panama	91–95	90.0	90.0	1.00	–	11.3		–	20.8	
Honduras	94	–	105.9		–	8.6		–	20.8	
El Salvador	85–95	78.6	102.6	1.31	7.9	6.5	0.83	9.8	10.7	1.09
Guatemala	85–94	65.2	88.6	1.36	7.7	4.8	0.63	9.4	7.7	0.82
Brazil	91	–	15205.0		–	32.1		–	43.5	
Guyana	95	–	70.0		–	28.8		–	–	
Argentina	86–95	3262.0	3200.0	0.98	48.7	25.4	0.50	67.4	50.5	0.72
Bolivia	94	–	276.1		–	17.1		–	46.4	
Venezuela	88–93	1700.0	1153.1	0.68	25.9	15.3	0.59	29.8	17.1	0.57
Chile	85–98	361.0	600.0	1.66	11.6	13.1	1.13	23.1	26.7	1.15
Uruguay	88–93	222.0	151.2	0.68	19.9	12.6	0.64	31.2	20.3	0.65
Ecuador	95	–	300.4		–	10.3		–	21.7	
Paraguay	95	–	108.8		–	9.6		–	31.0	
Peru	91	–	442.0		–	8.9		–	21.2	
Colombia	85–95	877.0	840.0	0.96	11.2	7.3	0.66	24.9	17.1	0.69

Notes: as in Table 11.1

membership as a proportion of the labour force outside agriculture fell from 31 to 14 per cent in the 1990s.

Union retrenchment is also the general trend in South America. The only exception is Chile, where the unions gained more members with the return to democracy. Ten years into the Pinochet dictatorship, unions had dwindled to one-third of their strength in 1973, the year of the coup. At that time, Chile's trade unions organized one-third of the non-agricultural labour force, their strongest position ever since they had been legally recognized in the 1920s (Campero, 2002). In the 1980s unions began to recover and around 1991 membership covered one-sixth of the non-agricultural labour force (Frías and Ruiz-Tagle, 1995). But unionization rates have slipped since. As was mentioned before, we have no data to evaluate the position of Brazilian unions in the 1990s. In Argentina, traditionally a highly unionized economy, the position of the unions was slipping fast, with a drop in density (A) from 49 to 25 per cent (or from 67 to 51 of the wage earners in the formal sector). A similar retrenchment is observed in Venezuela (from 26 to 15 per cent), Uruguay (20 to 13 per cent) and Colombia (11 to 7 per cent). We have no time series data for Ecuador, Paraguay, Bolivia and Peru, but in each of these countries union density is or was very low.

10. Social composition and within-nation variation in density rates

The social composition of trade unions is an important indicator in its own right. Unions are hard-pressed to organize workers in the informal sector. Blowmik (1998) estimates that less than 1 per cent of all registered union members in India come from its huge informal labour force. There is some informal organizing outside the official unions, for instance among textile workers in Gujarat (Breman, 1996) or among groups of self-employed women workers (Hensman, 2001), but numbers are extremely limited. The consequence is that women, while over-represented in the informal sector, will be under-represented in the unions.

In Africa and South America, official trade unions are hardly present outside the government and large-firm sector. In the United States, trade union membership is concentrated among government employees and the traditional manufacturing and mining industries. In Europe, too, public employees and those in large firms provide the bulk of the union membership. However, some European union organizations, for instance in Denmark and Italy, have been quite successful in recruiting workers in the small-firm sector. There are various attempts to organize the growing number of self-employed workers. In Western Europe, unions tend to retain the membership and represent the interests of pensioners. In rare cases – notably in Northern Europe and in Belgium – the unemployed, and workers with precarious employment, are highly unionized.

From Table 11.8 we learn that the share of female membership varies from a low 10–15 per cent in places like India, Ghana and South Korea to 50 per cent or more in the welfare states of Northern Europe. (Unfortunately, our data on female membership cover only few countries and do not include Central or Latin American countries or the transition economies.) It is worth noting that since the early 1980s, nearly all of growth in membership in EU unions has come from women. Thanks to the strong presence of female workers in the public sector and in professions like teaching and nursing, the gender gap in unionization is narrowing, even disappearing in the Nordic countries.

Part-time employment has increased in recent decades. Part-time jobs are still mostly female jobs and have traditionally been considered by trade unions as sub-standard jobs. Unfortunately, we have only scattered recent data for some countries. We observe that in Sweden there is hardly a difference in the union density rate of full-time and part-time workers. The fact that most part-time jobs in Sweden are standard (half-time) jobs in the public sector matters greatly. In other countries the unionization rates of full- and part-time workers are far apart, with Japan as the most extreme case. In Japan, part-time work is distinguished less by shorter working hours than by marginal status in the company and the labour market. An analysis of the Dutch labour force sample survey data of 1997 showed that it is the flexibility of the job, interpreted as absence of job protection and low job tenure, which matters, since it decreased the probability of union membership in a large measure (Visser, 2002).

For two countries – the United States and South Africa – labour survey data permit the calculation of density rates by sex and race. In both countries, we observe that black workers have a higher propensity to join than white workers. In South Africa, black women join unions in equal numbers to black men, whereas there is still a significant gender gap in unionization among whites. In the United States, the gender gap has also narrowed more among black than among white workers.

Finally, looking at the density rates in the last columns of Table 11.8, we observe that private sector rates are always lower than public sector rates. Reading this table we should recognize that the public sector, due to differences in welfare state development or state involvement in the economy and measured in terms of its employment share, is about twice as large in Europe and South America than in the United States, Japan or East Asia.

The most extreme cases with very low unionization rates in the private sector are the United States, Poland and France. Differences are also very large in India and China, and in South America, although exact figures on private sector unionization are lacking. Density rates in manufacturing tend to be much higher than in the private sector as a whole, confirming

Table 11.8 Composition of union membership and density rates by sector, gender, working hours and race (in per cent)

Country	Year	Share female members	Density		Density		Density: manufacturing	Density	
			Male	Female	Full-time	Part-time		Private	Public
Austria	1998	31.8	44.0	26.8	–	–	57.0	29.8	68.5
Belgium	1991	–	–	–	–	–	100.0	45.3	67.0
Denmark	1997	48.5	73.4	78.0	–	–	94.0	–	–
Finland	1989	50.5	69.3	75.4	–	–	80.0	64.6	85.7
France	1993	33.0	13.0	7.0	–	–	9.0	4.4	24.7
Germany	1997	31.2	29.8	17.0	–	–	45.0	21.9	56.3
Germany – West	1990	26.2	38.1	18.6	–	–	48.0	27.7	56.6
Great Britain	1999	43.7	31.0	28.0	34.0	20.0	30.0	19.0	60.0
Ireland	1997	37.9	44.3	42.6	–	–	47.0	–	74.1
Italy	1997	–	–	–	–	–	39.0	35.8	43.1
Netherlands	1997	25.7	33.0	17.0	31.0	13.0	33.0	19.0	45.0
Norway	1995	48.7	57.0	58.0	62.0	36.0	62.0	44.0	79.0
Spain	1997	–	–	–	–	–	24.0	14.5	32.0
Sweden	1997	57.0	83.2	89.5	90.0	83.0	100.0	77.0	93.0
Switzerland	1988	18.2	35.5	12.1	–	–	34.0	22.4	70.6
Canada	2000	46.9	30.6	29.2	31.6	22.2	34.1	18.4	70.1
United States	1999	39.2	16.1	11.4	15.4	6.7	16.0	9.4	37.3
black			20.7	15.1					
white			15.8	10.8					
Australia	1998	41.6	30.0	25.8	34.0	12.0	35.0	24.0	55.0
New Zealand	1999	–	–	–	–	–	25.0	–	–
Japan	1995	27.4	27.0	16.0	29.4	2.2	–	22.0	67.5

Country	Year							
Korea, Rep. of	1998	15.0	15.3	5.4	–	–	–	–
Malaysia	1988	30.0	15.3	7.5	–	–	–	–
Poland	1999	–	–	–	–	–	10.0	80.0
Israel	1997	50.0	–	–	–	–	25.0	50.0
South Africa	1994	29.0	32.4	29.3	–	48.0	–	39.6
black			35.1	36.0				
white			26.9	16.5				
Ghana	1995	10.0	–	–	–	–	–	–
Argentina	1995	–	–	–	–	–	–	66.0
Bolivia	1994	–	–	–	–	–	–	60.0
Brazil	1991	–	–	–	–	–	–	66.0
Chile	1995	–	–	–	–	–	–	33.0
Paraguay	1995	–	–	–	–	–	–	50.0
Venezuela	1995	–	–	–	–	–	–	33.0
China	1998	–	–	–	–	–	–	90.0
India	1995	12.0	–	–	–	–	–	40–50

Source: own calculation from ILO database and Ebbinghaus and Visser (2000).

that the Achilles' heel of union organizing lies in commercial and personal services, and in the decline or informalization of manufacturing employment.

Finally, international data on unionization rates by social status (white-collar/blue-collar), occupation or profession is patchy. In Europe, blue-collar workers lost their majority in the union movement some time ago (Visser, 1990). This is in large part due to the expansion of public sector unions (including health and education). Union density among white-collar staff is three times higher in the public than in the private sector (Lipset and Katchanovski, 1999; Visser, 1990). In the private sector and within manufacturing the unionization gap between blue- and white-collar workers has remained. Among manual workers the propensity to join unions is two to three times higher. According to BLS data of 1996, the union density rate among white-collar staff in the United States is half (11 per cent) the rate among blue-collar workers (23 per cent). Lipset and Katchanovski (1999, p. 4) report a similar result, based on another survey: 14 versus 30 per cent. In Canada, due to the larger public sector, the gap is narrower: 28.6 per cent white-collar against 37.5 per cent for manual workers in 1997 (Akyeampong, 1997, p. 49). In North America, the UK and also in the Netherlands manual levels have fallen, whereas white-collar unionization rates have hardly changed or slightly increased on account of strong upsurges in unionization of professions like teaching and nursing. Among white-collar employees gender differences in union density of white-collar employees have disappeared, in stark contrast with the situation of one or two generations ago (Lipset and Katchanovski, 1999, p. 9).

11.   Bargaining coverage and union representation in collective bargaining

The final section of this survey directs its attention to bargaining coverage, i.e. the share of employed wage and salary earners covered by collective agreements or statutes resulting from union–management negotiations. This measure captures an important aspect of the effectiveness of unions in defending or regulating minimum standards of income and related terms of employment for employees.

In the first instance, the influence of unions is determined by the willingness of management or employer associations to negotiate with them. This is by no means a given and depends to a large extent on the legal framework for labour relations and the political or industrial pressure that unions can mobilize. Enabling legislation has large effects on the ability of unions to perform their functions.

A crucially important means of extending union presence comes under the heading of extension or *erga omnes* mechanisms. These ensure that collectively bargained wages act as binding minima for all contracts in the relevant firm, occupation or sector. *Erga omnes* can be achieved in a number of ways. Legal extension of national or regional agreements by act of the labour minister, parliament, decree, or court ruling are mechanisms that are in use (Traxler, 1994). Such legal mandatory extension provisions are used in Western Europe, Australia and South Africa.

The collection of coverage data faces problems comparable to the ones we encounter in the case of union density (see Traxler, 1994, for a summary of data, measurement problems, and sources). Survey data, based on questionnaires of individual workers, may be problematic in countries with *erga omnes* provisions, as workers may not know that they are covered. Enterprise surveys are probably of greater use. Other useful sources are surveys of labour inspectorates and administrative data from registrars. In general, measurement precision is less in the case of bargaining than in the case of union membership. Time series data are also less available (but see Ochel, 2001, for an attempt based on the assembly of knowledge-of country experts). The coverage data in Table 11.9 have been pieced together from various sources (see references in the table).

Table 11.9 shows that in the European Union, 73 per cent of all employees are covered by collective bargaining, varying from a high 99 per cent in 'corporatist' Austria to a low 36 per cent in the 'liberal' United Kingdom. European coverage rates tend to be high compared to the rest of the world, with the exception of Australia (66 to 80 per cent) (Peetz, 1998), Argentina (73 per cent) (ILO, 1997a), South Africa (49 per cent) (Standing et al., 1996) and – if the data are to be believed – the Czech Republic and Hungary (ILO, 1997b). Very low coverage rates, suggesting the existence of a large non-union sector, are found in South-East Asia, North America and New Zealand.

Comparison with earlier data indicates that between 1985 and 1995 collective bargaining has held its place in most European countries, but that there was a significant reduction in coverage in the United Kingdom (Brown, 1993) and Switzerland (Prince, 1994), and some erosion in Germany (Hassel, 1999). Bargaining coverage under the award system has decreased in Australia and was in 1998 estimated to lie between 65 and 80 per cent (Peetz, 1998). In New Zealand, the legal changes of the early 1990s triggered a reduction of the coverage of collective contracts in half, from slightly more than 50 per cent of all employees in 1989/90 to under 25 per cent in 1999/2000 (Harbridge and Walsh, 2001). The USA, Canada and Japan also witnessed a decline in coverage.

As Figure 11.3 shows, the result of various extension provisions is that the coverage of collective agreements can easily exceed union representation measured by union density (B). Between the two variables – coverage and density – the correlation is weak: $r = 0.43$ for the 28 countries in Figure

Table 11.9   Union density, bargaining coverage and union centralization

Country	Period	Union density rates		Bargaining coverage rate	
Austria	(85–99)	52	38	99	99
Finland	(85–98)	69	76	95	95
France	(85–98)	14	10	87	95
Belgium	(85–95)	51	53	90	90
Sweden	(85–98)	82	86	86	89
Netherlands	(85–99)	29	24	80	85
Italy	(85–98)	43	38	85	82
Spain	(85–97)	9	16	70	78
Germany (West)	(85)	34		78	
Germany	(98)		26		73
Portugal	(86–95)	51	25	70	71
Norway	(85–97)	58	56	70	70
Denmark	(85–99)	78	75	74	69
Switzerland	(85–99)	29	22	53	37
United Kingdom	(85–97)	46	31	64	36
EU (15)	*(85–97)*	*37*	*29*	*78*	*73*
Czech Republic	(90–95)	79	43	–	55
Hungary	(85–98)	74	33	–	51
Turkey	(87–99)	28	32	–	25
Australia	(85–96)	50	35	85	80
Canada	(85–98)	38	34	39	34
New Zealand	(85–99)	53	21	51	21
United States	(85–00)	17	13	21	15
Japan	(85–00)	29	22	23	20
South Korea	(85–99)	12	12	–	14
Singapore	(85–98)	21	17	–	19
Philippines	(85–96)	24	30	–	4
Taiwan	(85–98)	33	50	–	3
Malaysia	(86–95)	14	12	–	3
South Africa	(85–98)	18	41	–	49
Kenya	(85–95)	42	33	–	35
Zambia	(85–95)	40	58	–	30
Zimbabwe	(85–95)	12	17	–	25
Argentina	(86–95)	67	51	–	73
El Salvador	(85–95)	10	11	–	13
Chile	(85–98)	23	27	–	13

Source: coverage data: Traxler (1994), Ochel (2000) and Visser (2002) for West European data; Prince (1994) for Swiss data; Bureau of Labour Statistics for the US, and Statistics Canada for Canadian data; ILO (1997) and ILO database for other countries.

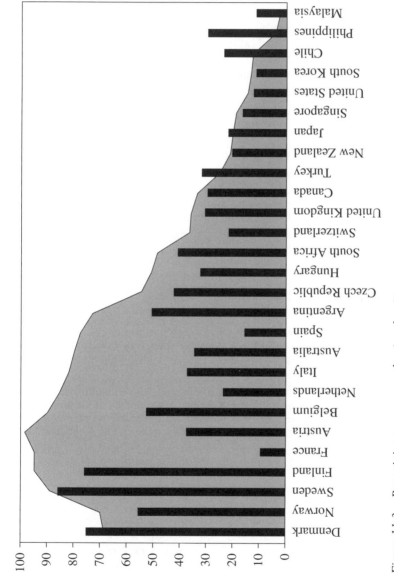

Figure 11.3   Bargaining coverage and union density

11.3. It is possible to note a number of regularities in these data, however. The countries can be divided into four groups:

1. Gravitating towards the 'authoritarian or paternalist' right in Figure 11.3 we find the countries where bargaining coverage is lower than an already low level of union membership, suggesting that some unionized groups are excluded from the right to bargain their wages (for example, in Malaysia, Philippines, South Korea, Turkey, and not shown in the figure: in Mauritius, Panama, Chile, Nicaragua, China, Hong Kong and Taiwan);
2. Moving towards the 'liberal' centre there are those countries with low membership and low coverage, characterized by enterprise bargaining (for example in the United States, Canada, Japan and since the 1990s also in the United Kingdom);
3. Further to the 'employer or state coordinated' left we find countries with coverage rates far 'in excess of' union membership due to a high level of employer organization and/or mandatory extension of sectoral or national agreements (for example in Austria, Australia, Belgium, France, Germany, the Netherlands, Portugal, and Spain), and, finally,
4. Furthest to the 'self-regulating and powerful' left a few countries with high membership and high coverage rates, and fairly centralized bargaining systems until the recent past (in Denmark, Sweden, Finland and Norway).

12. Conclusion

At the beginning of the 1990s there were several reasons to be optimistic about the future of trade unions. In 1992, Denis MacShane, a former official of the International Metal Workers' Federation who was elected European Member of Parliament for Labour, summarized:

> When I first took out a union card 23 years ago there were no trade unions in Spain, Greece, or Portugal, no independent trade unions in Eastern Europe, weak and divided unions in the ex-colonial lands and unions unable to operate under military pressure in Latin America. Now, trade unions of different ideologies exist in many countries, operating at various levels of effectiveness and seeking to function on behalf of their members. (MacShane, 1992)

In this survey I have stressed the important connection between union organization and democracy and highlighted important examples of unions campaigning in the forefront of restoring or obtaining democracy, examples ranging from Brazil and Chile to South Korea, to South Africa. Later in the decade, the optimism of the early 1990s was more tempered. The transition to market economies and democracy in Central and Eastern

Europe proved extremely difficult for unions and many of the new and most vigorous unions who fought repressive and authoritarian regimes in the early decade suffered heavy losses under the pressure of a more liberal economic climate, aggressive non-union management, the rise of the informal sector, and widespread unemployment. The bad news for unions in the later 1990s was that there was not much good news. Worldwide, unionization rates have decreased since 1985.

Some observers from the left (Panitch, 2000; Moody, 1997; Thomas, 1995) have placed their hopes for union revival, and for collective action of labour in general, in the resurgence of 'social movement unionism' and in the 'alliance with NGOs' outside the traditional and shrinking realm of stable (male) wage employment. Encouraging examples can be found in Brazil, South Africa, Mexico or even India, but much of the new unionism or the alliance with women's organizations among the self-employed is fragile and dependent on external and international support. This is not to say that such initiatives are unimportant or that unions should not try to organize outside the formal labour market, but to stress the point that they are up against enormous odds.

In this survey no attention has been given to the role of international and regional trade union federations. Since the demise of the Communist World Federation of Trade Unions in the 1990s, only the International Confederation of Free Trade Unions (ICFTU) and its Christian counterpart, the World Congress of Labour (WCL), have survived as viable organizations (Carew et al., 2000; Pasture, 1999). The ICFTU claims 124 million and the WCL 25 million members – the latter especially in Latin America. In addition there are regional organizations, of which the European Trade Union Confederation (ETUC), with 68 national affiliates from 29 countries and a total membership of over 50 million in 1999, is by far the strongest (Ebbinghaus and Visser, 2000). These international union federations now play an important role in international organizations like the ILO, the OECD or the European Union, in the defence of human rights, in the diffusion of trade union rights and in giving financial and support to struggling trade union organizers around the world. However, international trade unionism is very weak and many obstacles have to be overcome, not only financially. The integration with sectoral organizations is poor; the international movement is dominated by the affiliates from North America and Western Europe, the regional organizations outside Europe are weak and the results in peripheral countries meagre, and the attention to the non-organized informal sector is scant (van der Linden, 2000).

The lobbying role in international organizations is probably the most effective and has received more attention in recent years, even outside the ILO. The chief trade union organizer in the OECD, John Evans, is again optimistic:

The fact that in January 1997 the OECD was ready to censure the Republic of Korea – a new Member – for not living up to commitments on freedom of association and collective bargaining given when it joined the Organization, is highly significant. It did not happen in the case of Mexico's membership of the OECD and would have been unthinkable even five years ago (Evans, 1998, p. 10).

Within its programme for 'Decent Work', the ILO tries to encourage union involvement in social dialogue and tripartite talks with employers and government. Promising examples are found in Western and Eastern Europe, in South Africa, Chile, Singapore and South Korea. These moves away from a more traditional adversarial approach may be in line with attempts to redefine trade unions' productive role in advancing democracy, industry, growth and decent employment. Important as they may be, these exercises in national or industrial responsibility have rarely led to an upsurge in union membership. Experiences with social dialogue in Central and Eastern Europe, South Africa, Chile, Singapore and South Korea, and in many West European countries, have been associated with further losses in union representation, if measured by union membership and density. However, if the indicator is bargaining coverage, the standing of unions in public opinion, the prestige and professionalism of its leaders, these experiences must be judged in a more positive light.

Notes

1. The largest omissions, in terms of population size, are in Asia: Vietnam, Myanmar, North Korea, Cambodia, Laos, Afghanistan, Iran, Iraq, Saudi Arabia and Yemen, in Africa: Algeria, Libya, Sudan, the Democratic Republic of Congo, Madagascar and Angola, in Eurasia: some states of the former Soviet Union, and in Europe: Albania and the independent republics of former Yugoslavia, except Slovenia. In these countries, conditions of dictatorship, repression or civil war make the existence of trade unions, and the collection of data, problematic if not fully impossible.
2. The fact that some trade unions do sometimes organize farm and plantation workers produces only a distortion where the agricultural sector is large and unionization in agriculture is significant. Of all the countries in the dataset these conditions obtain only in Malaysia, where historically and today unions do organize plantation workers (Galenson, 1994, p. 6), and in Italy, where in the recent past unions were involved in the administration of health insurance (Ebbinghaus and Visser, 2000, p. 420).
3. The Economic Survey 1997–98 for India estimated the total labour force at 397.2 million people, of whom only 28 million were covered by basic labour legislation and written contracts.
4. Trade unions in Belgium, Denmark, Iceland, Finland and Sweden are involved in the administration of unemployment benefit claims. Examples of unions as main medical insurance providers include Israel and Taiwan before 1994, and many unions in the former Communist countries.
5. Past examples include countries with authoritarian, state-dominated corporatist systems like Brazil before 1985 and Portugal before 1974, as well as many party-dominated unions in former communist countries. The main current example is China, whose unions raise their revenues from a 0.5 per cent levy on monthly wages and a small tax on the enterprise's wage fund.
6. In some countries this is an impossible task. In Ireland, for instance, 'unions appear to

organise significant numbers of self-employed members', but, as in the case of retired members, there are 'no time series indicators of the share of membership among the self-employed' (Roche and Ashmore, 2001, p.12). UK union statistics pose the same problem. It is therefore that, following Bailey and Kelley (1990), I have discounted reported membership in the UK and Ireland with a fixed deflator of 10 per cent. Comparison with survey data in the 1990s shows that for recent years this may be a reasonable approach.

7. Works councils may be defined as 'institutionalised bodies for representative communication between a single employer ("management") and the employees ("workforce") of a single plant of enterprise ("workplace")' (Rogers and Streeck, 1995, p. 6). The main difference with company unions is that works councils 'are by definition not voluntary associations but established institutions with a representational monopoly. Once established, workers cannot refuse to "join" them or to be represented by them. There is no exit from a works council other than changing one's place of employment' (idem, p. 8). A 'company union', without outside links, and organized on the basis of a closed shop, would come close to being a works council, but such 'in-house unions' are rare (some do exist, however, in Taiwan, Sri Lanka or Singapore).

8. In addition to labour force surveys, it has been possible to use survey data from studies undertaken in the case of Austria, Denmark, France, Germany, the Netherlands, Spain, Italy (some regions), and South Africa, as well as enterprise surveys from Great Britain, Japan, South Korea, Taiwan, Singapore, Hong Kong, Bulgaria, the Czech and Slovak Republics, Hungary, and Poland.

9. The large fall in union membership and density in Portugal – from over 50 per cent in the mid 1980s, and possibly close to 100 per cent during the Salazar dictatorship, to some 25 per cent in the 1990s – deserves special mention. It is a peculiar case in Western Europe, but has exemplary features for what is happening to unions, for instance in Brazil, Mexico, or in the ex-Communist world, who make the transition from a kind of obligatory, quasi tax-based membership to voluntary organization. Before 1974 union membership in Portugal had been compulsory except where it was forbidden, as was the case in the civil service, in agriculture and fishing, and in domestic services. Hence, the post-Salazar unions 'inherited' large membership numbers, but could not retain these members on the basis of voluntary subscription (Pinto, 1990). A similar phenomenon has been observed in Germany, where inherited members from the East left the unions in droves in the years following unification.

10. The ban on union pluralism meant in practice that the newly established, not government controlled union federation which had emerged in the 1980s was banned. Under the new law the ban will be phased out gradually and remain in force in workplace till 2002. The reformed Korean labour law forbids the employer from paying workers while they are on strike, dismissed workers are banned from exercising their right to union membership, and unionization in the public sector and among teachers in private schools remains unlawful (Young-Ki, 1998, p. 67).

References

Akyeampong, Ernest (1997), 'A Statistical Portrait of the Trade Union Movement', *Perspectives on Labour and Income*, Winter, 45–54.

Ali, Syed Hussein (1995), 'Economic Take-off: Trade Unions in Malaysia', in Henk Thomas (ed.), *Globalization and Third World Trade Unions: The Challenge of Rapid Economic Changes*, London: Zed Books, pp. 63–79.

Baglioni, Guido (1990), 'Industrial Relations in Europe in the 1980s', in Guido Baglioni and Colin Crouch (eds), *European Industrial Relations: The Challenge of Flexibility*, London: Sage, pp. 1–41.

Bailey, Richard and John Kelley (1990), 'An Index Measure of British Trade Union Density', *British Journal of Industrial Relations*, 28 (2), 267–270.

Bain, George S. and Robert Price (1980), *Profiles of Union Growth*, Oxford: Basil Blackwell.

Baskin, Jeremy (1996a), 'The Social Partnership Challenge. Union Trends and the Industrial

Relations Challenge', in Jeremy Baskin (ed.), *Against the Current: Labour and Economic Policy in South Africa*, Johannesburg: Ravan Press, pp. 21–40.

Baskin, Jeremy (1996b), 'Unions at the Crossroads: Can They Make the Transition?' *South Africa Labour Bulletin*, 20 (1), 8–16.

Beynon, Huw and José R. Ramalho (2000), 'Democracy and the Organization of Class Struggle in Brazil', in Leo Panitch and Colin Leys (eds), *Working Classes – Global Realities. The Socialist Register 2001*, London: Merlin Press, pp. 219–237.

Bhattacherjee, Debashish (2002), 'Organized Labour and Economic Liberalization in India: Past, Present and Future', in A.V. Jose (ed.), *Organized Labour in the 21st Century*, Geneva: International Institute for Labour Studies, pp. 307–345.

Bhattacherjee, Debashish and T. Datta Chaudhuri (1994), 'Unions, Wages and Labour Markets in Indian Industry, 1960–86', *Journal of Development Studies*, 30 (1), 443–465.

Blowmik, Sharit (1998), 'The Labour Movement in India: Present Problems and Future Perspectives', *Indian Journal of Social Work*, 59 (1), 147–166.

Blum, Albert, Marten Estey, James Kuhn, Wesley Widman and Leo Troy (1971), *White-Collar Workers*, New York: Random House.

Bond, Patrick, Darlene Miller and Greg Ruiters (2000), 'The Southern African Working Class: Production, Reproduction and Politics', in Leo Panitch and Colin Leys (eds), *Working Classes – Global Realities. The Socialist Register 2001*, London: Merlin Press, pp. 89–118.

Breman, Jan (1996), *Footloose Labour*, Cambridge: Cambridge University Press.

Bresser Pereira, Luiz Carlos (1993), 'Economic Reforms and Economic Growth: Efficiency and Politics in Latin America', in Luiz Carlos Bresser Pereira, José Maria Maravall and Adam Przeworski (eds), *Economic Reforms in New Democracies*, Cambridge: Cambridge University Press, pp. 15–76.

Brown, William (1993), 'The Contraction of Collective Bargaining in Britain', *British Journal of Industrial Relations*, 31 (2), 189–200.

Calmfors, Lars, Alison Booth, Michael Burda, Daniele Checchi, Robin Naylor and Jelle Visser (2001), 'The Future of Collective Bargaining in Europe', in Tito Boeri, Agar Brugiavini and Lars Calmfors (eds), *The Role of the Unions in the Twenty-First Century*, Oxford: Oxford University Press, Part 1, pp. 1–155.

Campero, Guillermo (2002), 'Trade Union Responses to Globalization: Chile', in A.V. Jose (ed.), *Organized Labour in the 21st Century*, Geneva: International Institute for Labour Studies, pp. 139–165.

Carew, Anthony, Michel Dreyfus, Geert Van Goethem, Rebecca Gumbrell-McCormick and Marcel van der Linden (eds) (2000), *The International Confederation of Free Trade Unions*, Bern: Peter Lang.

Chang, Clara and Constance Sorrentino (1991), 'Union Membership Statistics in 12 Countries', *Monthly Labor Review*, 114 (12), 46–53.

Chatterjee, Roy (1980), *Union, Politics, and the State. A Study of Indian Labour Politics*, New Dehli: South Asian Publishers.

Checchi, Daniele and Jelle Visser (2002), 'Pattern Persistence in European Trade Union Density', Milan: Centro Interdepartimentale wTw – Work, Training and Welfare, research paper 3.

Chi-Sen, Chen (1998), 'Current Labor Status and Reforms of Labor Legislation in Taiwan', Tokyo: RENGO Research Institute Report, no. 8, 73–81.

Clarke, Simon and Peter Fairbrother (1994), 'Post-communism and the Emergence of Industrial Relations at the Workplace', in Richard Hyman and Anthony Ferner (eds), *New Frontiers in European Industrial Relations*, Oxford: Basil Blackwell, pp. 368–397.

Clegg, Hugh A. (1976), *Trade Unionism and Collective Bargaining: A Theory Based on Comparison of Six Countries*, Oxford: Blackwell.

Cramford, Aaron, Raymond Harbridge and Kevin Hince (1996), 'Unions and Union Membership in New Zealand. Annual Review for 1995', working paper 2/96, Wellington: Industrial Relations Centre (Victoria University).

Crowley, Steve and David Ost (eds) (2001), *Workers After Workers' States*, Lanham, MD: Rowman and Littlefield.

Damachi, Ukandi G. (1992), 'Industrial Relations and African Development', in Tayo Fashoyin (ed.), *Industrial Relations and African Development*, Geneva: IIRA, pp. 11–27.

Deyo, Frederic C. (1989), *Beneath the Miracle: Labor Subordination in the New Asian Industrialism*, Berkeley: University of California Press.

Dovydeniene, Roma (2002), 'Trade Union Responses to Globalization in Lithuania, in A.V. Jose (ed.), *Organized Labour in the 21st Century*, Geneva: International Institute for Labour Studies, pp. 239–277.

Ebbinghaus, Bernard and Jelle Visser (1999), 'When Institutions Matter: Union Growth and Decline in Western Europe, 1950–1995', *European Sociological Review*, 15 (2), 135–158.

Ebbinghaus, Bernard and Jelle Visser (2000), *Trade Unions in Western Europe Since 1945*, London: Macmillan.

Epstein, Edward C. (1989), *Labor Autonomy and the State in Latin America*, Boston: Unwin Hyman.

European Commission (2000), *Industrial Relations in Europe*, Brussels: European Commission, Directorate-General for Employment and Social Affairs.

Evans, John (1998), 'Economic Globalisation: The Need for a Social Dimension', Tokyo: RENGO Research Institute Report, no. 8.

Fashoyin, Tayo (ed.) (1992), *Industrial Relations and African Development*, Geneva: IIRA.

Fashoyin, Tayo (1995), 'Nigeria', in Dennis Briscoe, Miriam Rotham and Raoul Nacamulli (eds), *Industrial Relations Around The World*, Berlin/New York: De Gruyter, pp. 312–326.

Fashoyin, Tayo (1997), 'Economic Liberalisation and Industrial Relations in Uganda', Geneva: ILO, working paper, Task Force on Industrial Relations, January.

Flanagan, Robert (1999), 'Macroeconomic Performance and Collective Bargaining: An International Perspective, *Journal of Economic Literature*, 37 (3), 1150–1175.

Freeman, Richard B. (1986), 'The Effect of the Union Wage Differential on Management Opposition and Union Organizing Success', *American Economic Review,* 76 (1), 92–96.

Freeman, Richard B. and Joel Rogers (1999), *What Workers Want*, Ithaca, NY: ILR Press.

Frege, Carola M. (2002), 'Understanding Union Effectiveness in Central Eastern Europe: Hungary and Slovenia', *European Journal of Industrial Relations*, 8 (1), 53–76.

Frías, Patricio and Jaime Ruiz-Tagle (1995), 'Free Market Economic and Rapid Democratization. The case of Chile', in Henk Thomas (ed.), *Globalization and Third World Trade Unions: The Challenge of Rapid Economic Changes*, London: Zed Books, 130–148.

Galenson, Walter (1992), *Labor and Economic Growth in Five Asian Countries*, New York: Praeger.

Galenson, Walter (1994), *Trade Union Growth and Decline. An International Study*, New York: Praeger.

Galin, Amira (1994), 'Myth and Reality: Trade Unions and Industrial Relations in the Transition to Democracy', in John Niland, Russell Lansbury and Chrissie Verevis (eds), *The Future of Industrial Relations*, Thousand Oaks, CA: Sage and International Industrial Relations Association, pp. 295–306.

Ghose, Ajit (1999), 'Current Issues of Employment Policy in India', *Economic and Political Weekly*, 24 (36), 2592–2608.

Golden, Miriam A. and Michael Wallerstein (1995), 'Unions, Employers and Collective Bargaining: A Report on Data for 16 Countries from 1950 to 1990', paper presented at the annual meetings of the Midwest Political Science Association, Chicago.

Golden, Miriam, Michael Wallerstein and Peter Lange (1999), 'Postwar Trade Union Organization and Industrial Relations in Twelve Countries', in Herbert Kitschelt, Peter Lange, Gary Marks and John Stephens (eds), *Continuity and Change in Contemporary Capitalism*, Cambridge: Cambridge University Press, pp. 194–230.

Greenfield, Gerard (2000), 'Organizing, Protest and Working Class Self-Activity: Reflections on East Asia', in Leo Panitch and Colin Leys (eds), *Working Classes – Global Realities. The Socialist Register 2001*, London: Merlin Press, pp. 239–248.

Hall, Peter and David Soskice (2001), 'An Introduction to Varieties of Capitalism', in Peter Hall and David Soskice (eds), *Varieties of Capitalism. The Institutional Foundations of Comparative Advantage*, Oxford: Oxford University Press, pp. 1–68.

Harbridge, Raymond and Anthony Honeybone (1996), 'External Legitimacy of Unions: Trends in New Zealand', *Journal of Labor Research*, XVII (3), 425–444.

Harbridge, Raymond and Pat Walsh (2000), 'The Evolution of Collective Bargaining in New Zealand', *Labour and Industry*, 11 (1), 1–22.

Harbridge, Raymond, Pat Walsh and David Wilkinson (2001), 'Determinants of Union Growth in New Zealand: Ending the Decline?', Toronto, paper presented at International Conference on Union Growth, 30 April–1 May.

Harriss-White, Barbara and Nandini Gooptu (2000), 'Mapping India's World of Unorganized Labour', in Leo Panitch and Colin Leys (eds), *Working Classes – Global Realities. The Socialist Register 2001*, London: Merlin Press, pp. 89–118.

Hassel, Anke (1999), 'The Erosion of the German System of Industrial Relations', *British Journal of Industrial Relations*, 37 (3), 483–505.

Hensman, Rohini (2000), 'Organizing Against the Odds: Women in India's Informal Sector', in Leo Panitch and Colin Leys (eds), *Working Classes – Global Realities. The Socialist Register 2001*, London: Merlin Press, pp. 249–258.

Hince, Kevin and Martin Vranken (1991), 'A Controversial Reform of New Zealand Labour Law: The Employment Contracts Act 1991', *International Labour Review*, 130 (4), 475–493.

Holmlund, Bertil and Lundborg, Per (1999), 'Wage Bargaining, Union Membership, and the Organization of Unemployment Insurance', *Labour Economics*, 6 (3), 397–415.

Hong, Ng Sek and Malcolm Warner (1998), *China's Trade Unions and Management*, New York: St. Martin's Press.

Hwang, Hueh-Chin (1996), 'The Transformation of Industrial Relations under Democratization in Taiwan, 1987–1996', in IIRA-Asia (1996), *Transformation of Industrial Relations Under Democratization*, Proceedings of the Third Asian Region Congress of the Industrial Relations Research Association, Taipei, Sept. 30–Oct. 4.

ILO (1996), *World Employment Report 1996–97. National Policies in a Global Context*, Geneva: International Labour Office.

ILO (1997a), *World Labour Report 1997–98: Industrial Relations. Democracy and Social Stability*, Geneva, International Labour Office.

ILO (1997b), *Trade Union Experiences in Collective Bargaining in Central Europe. A report of an ILO survey in Bulgaria, Czech Republic, Hungary, Poland, and Slovakia*, Geneva: International Labour Office.

ILO (1998), *World Employment Report 1998–99. Employment in the Global Economy. How Training Matters*, Geneva: International Labour Office.

Iversen, Torben (1999), *Contested Economic Institutions. The Politics of Macroeconomics and Wage Bargaining in Advanced Democracies*, Cambridge: Cambridge University Press.

Jacoby, Sanford M. (1993), 'Pacific Ties: Industrial Relations and Employment Systems in Japan and the United States since 1990', in N. Lichtenstein and H. Harris (eds), *Industrial Democracy in America: The Ambiguous Promise*, Cambridge: Cambridge University Press.

Koonings, Kees, Dirk Kruyt and Frits Wils (1995), 'The Very Long March of History', in Henk Thomas (ed.), *Globalization and Third World Trade Unions*, London: Zed Books, pp. 99–129.

Kuruvilla, Sarosh, Subesh Das, Hyunji Kwon and Soonwon Kwon (2001), 'Asia Trade Unions: Growth and Decline, Organizational Power, and New Strategies', Toronto, paper presented at International Conference on Union Growth, 30 April–1 May.

Lange, Peter and Lynne Scruggs (1999), 'Where Have All Members Gone? Union Density in an Era of Globalization', *Stato e Mercato*, 55, 39–75.

Levin, David A. and Stephen Wing-Kai Chiu (1994), 'Decolonization Without Independence. Political Change and Trade Unionism in Hong Kong', in John Niland, Russell Lansbury and Chrissie Verevis (eds), *The Future of Industrial Relations*, Thousand Oaks, CA: Sage and International Industrial Relations Association, pp. 329–348.

Lim, Hyun-Chin and Suk-Man Hwang (1999), 'After IMF: Labor Realignment Under a Changing Role of the State in South Korea', paper presented at the Eleventh International Meeting on Socio-Economics, Madison WI, 8–11 July.

Linden, Marcel van der (2000), 'Conclusion', in Bart de Wilde (ed.), *The Past and Future of International Trade Unionism*, Ghent: AMSAB-Institute for Social History, pp. 310–317.

Linden, Marcel van der (2001), 'Conceptualizing the World Working Class', Amsterdam, paper presented at Amsterdam (graduate) School for Social Science Research seminar, 22 October.

Lipset, Seymour Martin (1962), 'White-Collar Workers and Professionals – Their Attitudes and Behavior Towards Unions', reprinted in William Faunce (ed.) (1967), *Readings in Industrial Sociology*, New York: Appleton-Century Crofts, pp. 525–548.

Lipset, Seymour Martin (1986), 'Labor Unions in the Public Mind' in Seymour Martin Lipset (ed.), *Unions in Transition: Entering the Second Century*, San Francisco, Institute for Contemporary Studies, pp. 287–321.

Lipset, Seymour Martin and Ivan Katchanovski (1999), 'White-Collar and Professionals – Their Attitude and Behavior Towards Unions II', research paper, Washington DC, George Mason University.

Macredie, Ian and Joanne Pilon (2001), 'A Profile of Union Members in Canada', paper presented at International Conference on Union Growth, Toronto, 30 April–1 May.

MacShane, Denis (1992), 'The New International Working Class and its Organizations', *New Politics*, 4 (1), 134–148.

MacShane, Denis (1994), 'The Changing Contours of Trade Unionism in Eastern Europe', in Richard Hyman and Anthony Ferner (eds), *New Frontiers in European Industrial Relations*, Oxford: Basil Blackwell, pp. 337–367.

Macun, Ian and Andrew Frost (1994), 'Living Like There's No Tomorrow. Trade Union Growth in South Africa, 1979–1991', *Social Dynamics*, 20 (2), 67–90.

Manning, Chris (1995), 'Approaching the Turning Point? Labour Market Change Under Indonesia's New Order', *Journal of Institute of Developing Economies*, 52–81.

Manusphaibool, Chuta (1998), 'Tasks and Challenges for Labour Society in Thailand', Tokyo: RENGO Research Institute Report, no. 8, 82–85.

Mason, Bob (1995), 'Industrial Relations in an Unstable Environment: The Case of Central and Eastern Europe', *European Journal of Industrial Relations,* 1 (3), 341–367.

Meardi, Guglielmo (2002), 'The Trojan Horse for the Americanization of Europe? Polish Industrial Relations Towards the EU', *European Journal of Industrial Relations*, 8 (1), 77–99.

Moody, Kim (1997), *Workers in a Lean World. Unions in the International Economy*, London: Verso.

Nathanson, Roy and Associates (2002), 'Union Responses to a Changing Environment: The New Histadrut – The General Federation of Labour in Israel', in A. V. Jose (ed.), *Organized Labour in the 21st Century*, Geneva: International Institute for Labour Studies, pp. 167–198.

Neumann, László (2002), 'Does Decentralized Collective Bargaining Have an Impact on the Labour Market in Hungary?', *European Journal of Industrial Relations*, 8 (1), 11–31.

Ochel, Wolfgang (2001), 'Collective Bargaining Coverage in the OECD from the 1960s to the 1990s', unpublished paper, Munich: Institute for Economic Research.

O'Donnell, Guilhermo (1973), *Modernization and Bureaucratic Authoritarianism: Studies in South American Politics*, Berkeley: University of California, Institute of International Studies.

Ost, David (1996), 'Polish Labor Before and After Solidarity', *International Labor and Working-Class History*, 56 (1), 29–43.

Ost, David (2002), 'The Weakness of Strong Social Movements: Models of Unionism in the East European Context', *European Journal of Industrial Relations*, 8 (1), 33–51.

Panitch, Leo (2000), 'Reflection on Strategy for Labour', in Leo Panitch and Colin Leys (eds), *Working Classes – Global Realities. The Socialist Register 2001*, London: Merlin Press, pp. 357–392.

Pasture, Patrick (1999), *Histoire du syndicalisme chrétien international. La difficile recherche d'une trousième voie*, Paris: L'Harmattan.

Peetz, David (1998), *Unions in a Contrary World*, Melbourne: Cambridge University Press.

Penninx, Rinus and Judith Roosblad (eds) (2000), *Trade Unions, Immigration and Immigrants in Europe 1960–1993*, New York, Oxford: Berghahn.

Pinto, Mario (1990), 'Trade Union Action and Industrial Relations in Portugal', in Guido Baglioni and Colin Crouch (eds), *European Industrial Relations. The Challenge of Flexibility*, pp. 243–264.

Prince, Jean-Christophe (1994), *L'Impact des conventions collectives de travail en Suisse*, Zürich: Schulthess.

Rama, Martin (1995), 'Do Labour Market Policies and Institutions Matter? The Adjustment Experience in Latin America and the Caribbean', *Labour*, 9, special issue, 243–268.

Regini, Marino (1992), 'Introduction: The Past and Future of Social Studies of Labour Movements', in Marino Regini (ed.), *The Future of Labour Movements*, London: Sage and International Sociological Association, pp. 1–16.

Riddell, Craig W. (1993), 'Unionization in Canada and the United States: A Tale of Two Countries', in David Card and Richard Freeman (eds), *Small Differences That Matter: Labor Markets and Income Maintenance in Canada and the United States*, Chicago: University of Chicago Press, pp. 109–148.

Roche, William K. and Jacqueline Ashmore (2001), 'Irish Unions in the 1990s: Testing the Limits of Social Partnership', in Graham Griffin (ed.), *Changing Patterns of Trade Unionism*, Sydney: Criterion.

Rodrik, Dani (1998), 'Why Do More Open Economies Have Bigger Governments? *Journal of Political Economy*, 106 (5), 997–1033.

Rogers, Joel and Wolfgang Streeck (eds) (1995), *Works Councils*, Chicago: University of Chicago Press.

Rosanvallon, Pierre (1988), *La Question syndicale. Histoire et forme d'une forme sociale*, Paris: Calman-Lévy.

Rose, Joseph B. and Gay N. Chaison (2001), 'Unionism in Canada and the United States in the 21st Century: the Prospects for Revival', Toronto, paper presented at International Conference on Union Growth, 30 April–1 May.

Rothstein, Bo (1992), 'Labour Market Institutions and Working Class Strength', in Sven Steinmo, Kathleen Thelen, and Frank Longstreth (eds), *Structuring Politics. Historical Institutionalism in Comparative Analysis*, Cambridge: Cambridge University Press, pp. 33–56.

Schiphorst, Freek (1995), 'The Emergence of Civil Society: The New Place of Unions in Zimbabwe', in Henk Thomas (ed.), *Globalization and Third World Trade Unions: The Challenge of Rapid Economic Changes*, London: Zed Books, pp. 215–231.

Seidman, Gay W. (1994), *Manufacturing Militance: Workers' Movements in Brazil and South Africa, 1970–1985*, Berkeley: University of California Press.

Shalev, Michael (1992), 'The Resurgence of Labour Quiescence', in Marino Regini (ed.), *The Future of Labour Movements*, London: Sage and International Sociological Association, pp. 102–132.

Smith, Rusell E. (1995), 'Brazil', in Dennis Briscoe, Miriam Rotham and Raouk Nacamulli (eds), *Industrial Relations Around the World*, Berlin/New York: De Gruyter, pp. 47–65.

Song, Ho Keun (2002), 'Labour Unions in the Republic of Korea: Challenge and Choice', in A.V. Jose (ed.), *Organized Labour in the 21st Century*, Geneva: International Institute for Labour Studies, 199–237.

Standing, Guy (1997), 'Labour Market Governance in Eastern Europe', *European Journal of Industrial Relations*, 3 (2), 133–159.

Standing, Guy, John Sender and John Weeks (1996), *Restructuring the Labour Market. The South African Challenge*, Geneva: International Labour Office.

Teulings, Coen and Joop Hartog (1998), *Corporatism or Competition? Labour Contracts, Institutions and Wage Structures in International Comparison*, Cambridge: Cambridge University Press.

Thomas, Henk (1995), 'The Erosion of Trade Unions', in Henk Thomas (ed.), *Globalization and Third World Trade Unions: The Challenge of Rapid Economic Changes*, London: Zed Books, pp. 3–27.

Thomas, Henk, E.A. Ramaswamy, Amrita Chhacchi and Michel Hendriks (1995), 'Three Highly Differentiated Trajectories', in Henk Thomas (ed.), *Globalization and Third World Trade Unions: The Challenge of Rapid Economic Changes*, London: Zed Books, pp. 31–62.

Traxler, Franz (1994), 'Collective Bargaining: Levels and Coverage', *Employment Outlook 1994*, Paris: Organization for Economic Co-operation and Development, pp. 167–194.

Troy, Leo (2000), 'US and Canadian Industrial Relations: Convergent or Divergent?' *Industrial Relations*, 39 (4), 695–713.

Tsuru, Tsuyoshi and James B. Rebitzer (1995), 'The Limits of Enterprise Unionism: Prospects for Continuing Union Decline in Japan', *British Journal of Industrial Relations*, 33 (3), 459–492.

Valenzuela, Samual J. (1992), 'Labour Movements and Political Systems: Some Variations', in Marino Regini (ed.), *The Future of Labour Movements*, London: Sage and International Sociological Association, pp. 53–101.

Vaughan-Whitehead, Daniel (2000), 'The Wage Crunch in Central and Eastern Europe: Past Effects and Future Risks', in Linda Clarke, Peter de Gijsel and Jörn Janssen (eds), *The Dynamics of Wage Relations in the New Europe*, Boston: Kluwer, pp. 103–123.

Venkataratnam, C. S. (1997), 'Indian Industrial Relations', Geneva: International Labour Office, working paper, ILO-Task Force on Industrial Relation.

Verma, Anil, Thomas A. Kochan and Stephen J. Woods (2002), 'Union Decline and Prospects for Revival: Editor's Introduction', *British Journal of Industrial Relations*, 40 (3), 373–384.

Visser, Jelle (1990), 'In Search of Inclusive Unionism', *Bulletin of Comparative Labour Relations*, 18, 5–278.

Visser, Jelle (1991), 'Trends in Trade Union Membership', *Employment Outlook 1991*, Paris: Organization for Economic Co-operation and Development, pp. 97–134.

Visser, Jelle (1992), 'The Strength of Union Movements in Advanced Capitalist Democracies: Social and Organisational Variations', in Marino Regini (ed.), *The Future of Labour Movements*, London: Sage and International Sociological Association, pp. 17–52.

Visser, Jelle (1997), *Global Trends in Unionisation*, Geneva: International Labour Office.

Visser, Jelle (2002), 'Why Fewer Workers Join Unions: A Social Customs Explanation', *British Journal of Industrial Relations*, 40 (3), 403–430.

Wallerstein, Michael and Miriam A. Golden (2000), 'Postwar Wage Setting in the Nordic Countries', in Torben Iversen, Jonas Pontusson and David Soskice (eds), *Unions, Employers, and Central Banks*, Cambridge: Cambridge University Press, pp. 107–137.

Walsh, Pat (1989), 'A Family Fight? Industrial Relations Reform Under the Fourth Labour Government', in Bill Easton (ed.), *The Making of Rogernomics*, Auckland: Auckland University Press, pp. 149–170.

Weinstein, Marc (1995), 'From Co-Governance to Ungovernability: The Reconfiguration of Polish Industrial Relations, 1989–93', in Kirsten Wever and Lovell Turner (eds), *The Comparative Political Economy of Industrial Relations*, Madison, WI: IRRA, pp. 151–180.

Western, Bruce (1997), *Between Class and Market – Post-war Unionization in the Capitalist Democracies*, Princeton, NJ: Princeton University Press.

World Bank (1995), *World Development Report 1995: Workers in an Integrating World*: Oxford: Oxford University Press.

World Bank (1996), *World Development Report 1996: From Plan to Market*, Oxford: Oxford University Press.

Young-Ki, Park (1998), 'Labor Society and the Future of Trade Unions in Korea', Tokyo: RENGO Research Institute Report, no. 8, 60–72.

12 Recent changes in the industrial relations framework in the UK

John T. Addison and W. Stanley Siebert

There will be no going back. The days of strikes without ballots, mass picketing, closed shops and secondary action are over. (Tony Blair, May 1998; see Department of Trade and Industry, 1998, p. 3)

I see trade unions as a force for good, an essential part of our democracy, but as more than that, potentially, as a force for economic success. They are a part of the solution to achieving business success and not an obstacle to it. (Tony Blair, September 1999; see Brown, 2000, p. 305)

1. Introduction

In this chapter we investigate the major changes that have taken place in collective bargaining in the UK in the last two decades, consider their impact, and further address the consequences of union decline. We shall also speculate on the likely course of bargaining arrangements over the first decade of the present century. Much attention will be given over to the ever-changing legal framework within which collective bargaining is set – swings in the legal pendulum from Thatcher through Blair to, potentially much more important, the ministrations of the European Union (EU).

Domestic and international law provide the backbone of our discussion. We will review the main legislative enactments of the Thatcher/Major administrations introduced between 1980–93. We also describe at more leisurely pace the changes engineered by New Labour in the form of the 1999 Employment Relations Act and the prospective Employment Bill. At issue is whether these most recent domestically initiated changes in the law are reversals of the *status quo ante* or tidying up exercises, especially on the equity front. Be that as it may, EU social policy initiatives portend more dramatic changes – and more so for Britain than other member states of the Community.

The extensive nature of the legal changes introduced between 1980 and 1993 has been linked to shifts in the impact of unions on various dimensions of firm performance, as well as the union premium and wage inequality. We review these outcomes. There has also occurred some material improvement in Britain's comparative economic performance, which we also chart. In each case, it is conventional – and in our view correct – to attribute these largely beneficial changes in part to innovations in union

415

law. As usual, however, the devil is in the detail and it would be idle to pretend that we can apportion the component contributions of legislation, deregulation, and globalization.

If domestic legislation were the end of the story, then an economic evaluation of post-1997 developments might simply focus on indicative cost estimates of a modest number of changes, some of which are non-trivial. But one of the first actions of the new administration when it came into office was to sign up to the *Social Chapter*. The social policy agenda of the EU has deep-seated implications for collective bargaining in Britain, so that we have also to address in more detail and perhaps give equal billing to the 'economic consequences of Mr Blair' as we do to those of Mrs Thatcher.

2.   The Thatcher reforms
Legislation[1]
A summary of the laws affecting unionism introduced by Mrs Thatcher and her successors is given in Table 12.1. To give context, the table actually starts with some Old Labour legislation in the form of the *1974 Trade Union and Labour Relations Act* (TULRA) (amended in 1976).[2] This distinctly pro-union legislation was the quid pro quo for union agreement on a voluntary incomes policy. Both TULRA and the Employment Protection Act of 1975 used the concept of unfair dismissal (see note 2) to strengthen the closed shop or union membership agreements (UMAs). This was achieved by removing employment protection from workers who were dismissed for *not* belonging to a union in workplaces where union membership was a condition of employment. In other words, dismissal for non-membership of a union was 'fair' when a firm had a closed shop. This innovation led to the expansion of closed shop to almost 5 million workers in 1980, mainly of the 'post-entry' variety.

The *1975 Employment Protection Act* put in place further measures to 'encourage the extension of collective bargaining'. First, unions were given the right to claim arbitration from the Central Arbitration Committee (CAC) to secure the observance of 'recognized' terms and conditions of employment in an industry. If the CAC identified an employer as engaged in an industry covered by an industry-wide agreement, it could make an award bringing that employer's terms and conditions up to the recognized level. Also under this so-called 'Schedule 11' procedure, in the absence of such terms, unions could claim arbitration to apply the 'general level' obtaining for comparable workers in the district.[3] Second, the Act also provided that the Advisory, Conciliation and Arbitration Service (ACAS) could be called on by a union to make a recommendation that it be recognized by an employer for collective bargaining purposes. Failure on the part of the employer to comply involved the possibility of an arbitration award by the CAC. Overall, ACAS heard about 1600 union claims for recognition over the period 1976–80, when the procedure was operative (ending with the 1980 Employment Act), and has estimated that its efforts resulted in the extension of recognition to about 65 000 workers (ACAS, 1981, p. 99). Although this might seem a small number in the national context, the procedure helped union organizing activities by establishing that public policy was favourable to union organization and in encouraging employers to recognize unions voluntarily to avoid the public scrutiny involving a reference to ACAS (Davies and Freedland, 1993, p. 421).

One of the election pledges of the incoming Conservative government of Mrs Thatcher in 1979 was root and branch union reform. Indeed, successive Conservative administrations passed six important pieces of industrial relations legislation, 1980–93.[4] But at the beginning, Conservative governments felt the need to move cautiously. Under the first piece of legislation, the *1980 Employment Act,* only new UMAs were submitted to a tough electoral hurdle of an 80 per cent majority (existing UMAs were left untouched). At the same time, strike threat power was reduced by removing union immunity from liability for damages when organizing 'secondary' strikes, including coercive union recruitment campaigns and 'blacking' the goods of non-union firms. For the moment, however, the union itself – and in particular union funds – broadly remained immune from all actions for damages. The Act also introduced the idea of secret ballots, which at this stage were only voluntary. A fund was established from which trade unions could be reimbursed for expenditures in connection with such postal ballots. The TUC response was to boycott the scheme. Finally, the legislation abolished statutory union recognition procedures.

The *1982 Employment Act* was much bolder. All UMAs were now required to clear the voting hurdle every five years. Dismissal for non-membership of a union where there was an existing UMA remained lawful, but only if the UMA had secured the necessary majority within the previous five years. Punitive compensation of up to £20 000 was available for individuals adjudged wrongfully dismissed (Deakin and Morris, 1995, p. 445). Measures were also adopted to stop discrimination against non-union workers. Contracts could not be enforced if they specified union-only labour, nor could tenders be awarded on this basis. Relatedly, the Fair Wages Resolution was also rescinded.[5]

The 1982 Act also removed trade unions' blanket immunity from liability for damages for actions in tort. Specifically, the legislation reduced the number of torts for which immunity was given by narrowing the definition of a trade dispute. Moreover, unions would be liable for industrial action left unprotected by the more limited immunities. Prior to the Act, the only

Table 12.1   The course of union legislation

Legislation	Content
1974 and 1976, Trade Union & Labour Relations Acts	Repealed the right *not* to be a union member (except for genuine religious belief). Where a firm and a union negotiate a union membership agreement (closed shop), dismissal of workers for non-membership of union deemed fair. Also, worker had no right to appeal to Industrial Tribunal when dismissed for non-membership in union.
1975, Employment Protection Act	Tightened unfair dismissal rights. Established a Trade Union Certification Officer to certify union independence from management. Established an Advisory, Conciliation and Arbitration (ACAS) Service to investigate, report, and make recommendations for union recognition. Also set up Central Arbitration Committee with enforcement role in recognition procedure and to hear claims from unions in support of extension of terms and conditions of collective agreements.
1980, Employment Act	Statutory union recognition procedures abolished. *New* union membership agreements required to be approved in secret ballot by at least 80 per cent of those entitled to vote. Immunity from damages in tort withdrawn from union officials in cases of secondary industrial action, including action to compel union membership. Fund established to reimburse unions for postal secret ballots on industrial action and union elections. Picketing away from own workplace made unlawful.
1982, Employment Act	All union membership agreements required to be approved in secret ballot every five years, again by not less than 80 per cent of those entitled to vote, or 85 per cent of those voting. Punitive compensation of up to £20 000 to be awarded to workers unfairly dismissed on grounds of non-membership in unions. Contracts requiring union-only labour to be unlawful, as well as tenders awarded on a basis of union-only labour. Trade union funds no longer automatically sheltered from liability for damages in tort with narrowing of immunities. Damages in any proceedings set at up to £250 000 for unions with more than 100 000 members. Fair Wages Resolution (requiring government contractors to pay union rates) rescinded.
1984, Trade Union Act	Secret ballots (either postal or workplace) required prior to industrial action; postal ballot expenses to be reimbursed by the Certification Officer. Also secret ballots required for union executive elections every five years and political funds every ten years.

Table 12.1   (*continued*)

Legislation	Content
1988, Employment Act	Established a Commissioner for the Rights of Trade Union Members (CROTUM) to assist union members with advice and in applications to the High Court. Union members given the right not to be disciplined by their union for failure to support industrial action. Remedies available to union from their union set at up to £8500. It became automatically unfair to dismiss a worker for non-membership of a union irrespective of whether the closed shop had been supported by a ballot. Industrial action to impose a closed shop lost immunity from tort liability.
1990, Employment Act	It was now unlawful to discriminate against non-union members (or union members) at the time of recruitment. Job advertisements could not specify union membership. Any practice under which employment was afforded only to union members presumed to be discriminatory. Unions had to repudiate unofficial industrial action; unofficial strikers could be summarily dismissed; and immunity for industrial action in support of dismissed strikers removed.
1993, Trade Union and Employment Rights Act	No union could refuse to accept anyone into membership (or expel anyone) unless on grounds of the individual's conduct. The union dues check-off to be authorized in writing by each member every three years. Established a Commissioner for Protection against Unlawful Industrial Action (COPUIA) to advise and finance individuals claiming to have been affected by unlawful industrial action who could apply to the High Court for an order against the union to discontinue that action. Tighter restrictions on strike ballots. Wages councils abolished.
1999, Employment Relations Act	Established a statutory union recognition procedure for firms employing more than 20 workers; made it automatically unfair to dismiss strikers during first eight weeks of industrial action; weakened strike balloting rules; and gave the right to be accompanied by a union official in disciplinary interviews. The penalty for unfair dismissal also raised from £12 000 to £50 000. CROTUM and COPUIA abolished.

real remedy for employers was against individual dispute organizers, who would not have the wherewithal to pay substantial damages. Henceforth, the union could be sued for unlawful industrial action – although given the large possible damages to which unions could be exposed, the Act placed an upper limit on damages that could be awarded against unions.

In the wake of the 1982 Act, there was to be a steady increase in legal actions by employers against unions (McKay, 1996) – and also against striking workers. Most legal challenges took the form of the interlocutory injunction; that is, a court order to prevent the onset or continuation of industrial action, issued at the discretion of the High Court pending a full trial. (Note such remedies are precluded as unfair in the USA.) The alternative to the injunction is the action for damages, which was hardly considered before the 1982 Act for the reasons given earlier. By contrast, between 1980 and 1995 there were 201 legal actions against unions, including 166 injunctions (McKay, 1996, pp. 11, 14).

Following the re-election of Mrs Thatcher in 1983, an enduring legislative innovation was the *1984 Trade Union Act*. The legislation developed the balloting idea presaged in the 1982 Act. Secret ballots were now required in three areas: before industrial action, when electing union officials, and for the political levy. Without a ballot, trade union immunity was lost. Such ballots impeded industrial action because the rules were 'extremely complex, technical and, in parts, ambiguous, thus leaving unions vulnerable to potential challenge in the courts on several counts' (Deakin and Morris, 1995, p. 794). The Act and its associated Code of Practice put forward principles governing such matters as the balloting constituency, content of the voting paper, conduct of the ballot, and the time limit (four weeks) within which action had to be taken after a ballot. Approximately one-third of the injunctions taken out since 1980 were based on these balloting provisions (McKay, 1996, p. 16).[6]

In 1988 and 1990 two further Employment Acts were passed. The *1988 Employment Act* followed another election victory for Mrs Thatcher, after a campaign in which the issue of union power had again figured large. This Act sought to remove the ability of trade unions to enforce the closed shop through industrial action. It thus became unlawful to take any form of industrial action to establish or maintain a closed shop, irrespective of whether or not the closed shop had been approved in a ballot. It was now also unfair to dismiss an employee for non-membership in a union, even if that arrangement had been sanctioned by ballot. The legislation also made it 'unjustifiable' for unions to discipline members for refusing to take part in industrial action. The courts were empowered to award up to £30 000 for such infringements (the same amount as obtained in the case of unjustifiable expulsion from a union). For the first time, union members could also take their union to court on the grounds that industrial action had not been the subject of a lawful ballot.

The *1990 Employment Act* then tried a different approach to the closed shop. Hitherto the legislative attack had attempted to eliminate the threat of dismissal based on non-membership. Now attention turned to the point of hire. The Act made it unlawful to discriminate against non-union workers when hiring. By the same token, it was also unlawful to discriminate against union workers when hiring, although employers were entitled to protect themselves against troublemakers. In each case the aggrieved job applicant had to make a complaint to an Industrial Tribunal. A closed-shop agreement, oddly enough, was not in and of itself unlawful (Hendy, 1993, p. 65). The 1990 legislation further circumscribed strike activity by holding unions liable for unofficial action unless that was expressly repudiated. Unofficial strikers could be summarily dismissed by their employers, and any action taken on behalf of these workers lost immunity. Finally, all secondary action was outlawed.

The last piece of Conservative union legislation was the *1993 Trade Union Reform and Employment Rights Act*, which again followed an election victory – albeit sans Thatcher. The Act's most far-reaching change for unions was its requirement for written authorization from union members for the dues check-off every three years. The Act also stipulated that an individual would be free to join any union at the workplace. This clause sought to override trade union procedures preventing unions poaching members from each other (the Bridlington rules). It was felt that the measure would also weaken union control over particular jobs, and thereby lead to increased flexibility at the workplace. In addition to these changes, the legislation tightened balloting rules for industrial action, most notably with respect to the obligation to notify employees. It also abolished wages councils.

Against this backdrop, the election of New Labour in 1997 was inevitably to bring about another policy shift. Yet, as Table 12.1 indicates, its major piece of legislation was not to be enacted for another two years. In the interstices, the new government was only to nibble at the edges as it were; for example, by repealing in 1998 the requirement that the union obtain written authorization from its members for the check-off every three years. We consider New Labour's approach of after reviewing the economic consequences of the Tory reforms, 1980–93.

Economic effects
Even though we shall subsequently have occasion to go behind the following numbers, perhaps the most obvious development on the union front in Britain has been the pronounced decline in unionism in the last two decades

– this after a period of substantial growth. In 1979 some 53 per cent of workers were union members. By 1999 this had fallen to 28 per cent. Correspondingly, there has also occurred a sharp fall in the share of employees whose wages are set by collective bargaining: from 70 per cent in 1980 through 54 per cent in 1990 to around 45 percent in the mid-1990s (see Machin, 2000).[7]

There are a number of explanations for this overall tendency, including the changing structure of the economy and the workforce, macroeconomic developments, increased competitiveness, and changes in union organizing activities. It seems that we can downgrade the importance of compositional factors (such as increases in the proportion of female workers) many of which also applied in the 1970s when unions were growing apace. As for macroeconomic factors, and in particular the business cycle (see Chapter 2 by Schnabel in this volume), these have undoubtedly played a role but in all likelihood a secondary one. This is because the downturn in union recognition reflects an inability of unions to organize new establishments that have been set up since 1980 rather than a process of derecognition (Machin, 2000; Disney et al., 1995). The issue then devolves on why this process of recognition has become more difficult. Freeman and Pelletier's (1990) business cycle model accords the law pride of place, arguing that virtually all of the change in union density, 1980–86, is due to the strictures of British industrial relations legislation. This is probably going too far because some other countries have experienced precipitous declines in union membership without corresponding changes in their legal environment. On the other hand, the decline in coverage in Britain is anomalous and as we have seen the role of the law is direct here. Moreover, once we view the changes in union law as part of a wider reform agenda, the contribution of the law is central and not easily dismissed as permissive.

Turning therefore to the questions of the economic consequences of the decline in unionism, we first review the evidence of union effects on performance at establishment level through time – along the dimensions of productivity and productivity growth, profitability, pay, employment, and plant closings – before examining changes in Britain's macroeconomic performance. Perhaps no micro outcome indicator has attracted greater scrutiny than establishment and firm *productivity*. The early (British) literature points to negative union effects despite contemporaneous estimates of the union–non-union pay differential of 10 per cent (see Machin, 1991). The dominant theme of studies using more recent data, however, is that unionized firms/plants increased their productivity most at the end of the 1980s (and perhaps also in 1979–84) and/or that there is no longer evidence of a union productivity shortfall (see, for example, Addison and Belfield, 2001; Conyon and Freeman, 2001; Moreton, 1999; Fernie and Metcalf, 1995; and

Gregg et al., 1993) But the latter evidence is not overwhelming, leaving us with the more attenuated conclusion that there has been a reduction in the 'disadvantages of unionism' (Oulton, 1990, p. 86) through time. At issue here, apart from the suggestion that inefficient union plants have been evolved out of the system, is whether negative union effects are confined to establishments where there is fragmented bargaining (a regime in which multiple unions bargain separately) (Pencavel, 2002). Another concern is whether negative effects can be overturned in a supportive industrial relations environment (Brown et al., 1997; Chapter 5 by Metcalf in this volume).

The early evidence concerning unions and *profitability/financial performance* points unequivocally to lower profits in unionized workplaces (see, for example, the survey by Metcalf, 1993). The more recent evidence presents a more mixed picture although there is every indication of a decline – even a 'collapse' – in this effect through time (see, in particular, Addison and Belfield, 2001; Menezes-Filho, 1997; Machin and Stewart, 1996). There is thus some disputation as to whether the union effect is still negative and continuing controversy as to the implications of a negative coefficient estimate for the union variable where observed. In the former case, Pencavel (2002) reports that any reduction in financial performance is confined to situations where bargaining is fragmented (but see Menezes-Filho, 1997). This result is in some sense the 'successor' to the hierarchy of union effect observed in earlier data, where stronger adverse profitability effects were observed in closed shop settings or where management recommended unionism to its workers. In the latter case, since there is more evidence for the UK than for the USA that union wage gains come at the expense of excess profits (rather than normal returns), there has been less concern with allocative consequences (see also Chapter 9 by Menezes-Filho and van Reenen in this volume).

The trend of the profitability findings is also consistent with some evidence on the development of the union wage mark up. Thus, studies using *workplace data*, point to a decline in the union premium during the decade of the 1990s after a period of stability (see Stewart, 1987, 1995). Also, the most recent workplace data for 1998 indicate a further diminution of the union premium (see, for example, Bryson, 2002). On the other hand, work using *individual data* indicates much greater persistence in the union markup even if not in the number of workers in receipt of it. Thus, we cannot conclude from the data that the wage premium has withered away. Rather, the indication is that if the reform agenda ushered in a material reduction in the union–non-union differential it was long in coming (see Chapter 7 by Blanchflower and Bryson in this volume).

We next consider the effects of unions on *employment*. Here the key research finding from workplace data is a consistently negative effect of unions on employment, with no real suggestion of any moderation in that effect over time (one exception is the study by Millward et al., 1992). Unions thus seem to retard employment growth. A rule of thumb is that unionized establishments tend to grow by roughly 3 per cent less per year than their non-unionized counterparts (e.g. Booth and McCulloch, 1999; Blanchflower et al., 1991).

There was some concern in the early literature that the union employment effect at this time (1980–84) was simply the result of an abandonment of restrictive practices in the union sector. In other words, the reduction in employment in the union sector might be a one-time affair followed by normal employment growth after some interval in which changes in working conditions had been fully digested. This suspicion gained currency because the union coefficient in the employment change equation of Blanchflower et al. (1991) was found to be sensitive to the inclusion of a variable identifying 'organizational change' at the workplace, a proxy for any such reform of working conditions (see Machin and Wadhwani, 1991). However, in addressing this very problem, Blanchflower et al. report that their union result stands when the union coverage measure is replaced by union density, and that in any event their results for union density also hold up once one splits the sample according to whether or not plants experienced organizational change. Also, as noted, research using more recent data further attests to the robustness of the union employment result in the presence of organizational change, and the negative effect is replicated in panel data (Addison and Belfield, 2002b). Here, then, is one empirical regularity.

The final micro outcome indicator we examine is *plant closings*. The evidence is intriguing in the light of the foregoing. Thus, studies using information on plant closings for 1984–90, linked to union and economic data for 1984, reveal a negative but statistically insignificant association between union recognition and plant closings (Machin, 1995). Moreover, more powerful unions, as proxied by the magnitude of the wage premium or presence of the closed shop, have no incremental effect on closings (Stewart, 1995). But when we come to consider closings data for 1990–98, now linked to union and other information for 1990, the effect of unionism on closings is reversed; that is, the sign of the coefficient estimate for the union variable is now positive and statistically significant (Addison et al., 2001). This broad result hides as much as it reveals. Although reporting a material and robust positive association between either of two measures of unionism – recognition for collective bargaining purposes and union coverage – Addison et al. (2001) find that this holds only for establishments that are part of larger (i.e. multi-establishment) undertakings. For single-plant entities (here firms), the direction of the association is reversed. (All studies support the more general result that single independent plants are less likely to close than their counterparts that are part of multi-establishment undertakings.) The authors interpret the former result as consistent with a decline in union bargaining power in the wake of more than a decade of legislation removing union immunities and regulating union governance, either by emboldening employers in multi-plant enterprises to close unionized establishments, or by weakening union influence over employment in such settings (see Manning, 1993).[8] The single plant result, on the other hand, is rationalized in terms of (differential) union concessions in conjunction with rents.

While not contesting these empirical findings, Bryson (2001) argues that union weakness – presumably accentuated by the legislation – underpins the change in union effect detected in the more recent workplace data. He contends that this development is deleterious – whereas it is implicit in the previous study that the rate of plant closings was earlier suboptimal. For Bryson weak unions are less able to fulfil the collective voice function.[9] He reports that where unions are strong the coefficient estimate for unionism in the plant closings probit equation is no longer statistically significant. Strong unions are variously defined by the presence of the closed shop, and a combination of high union density, extensive bargaining coverage, and accompanying on-site lay union representatives, inter al. In short, the converse situation defines unions that are too weak to be an efficient instrument of collective voice for workers.[10]

This concludes our review of the micro evidence. We preface our discussion of comparative macro effects with some remarks on the British *strikes* record not least since it was the famous 'winter of discontent' that propelled Mrs Thatcher into office. The facts of the matter are that strikes have decreased by a factor of 10 since 1979: the number of stoppages declined from over 2000 a year in the 1970s to around 200 a year during most of the 1990s (Employment Department, 1995, Table 2; ONS, 2001, Table 2).

The union legislation detailed in rows 3 to 8 of Table 12.1 has clearly increased the costs of strikes to unions. Yet these legal challenges to strike action do not speak for themselves. For example, one also needs to know the practicalities, such as how the law has been used by employers. Moreover, on theoretical grounds – and in particular from the perspective of Pareto-optimal accident theories – the main effect of the law should presumably have taken the form of reducing settlements by chipping away at union bargaining power rather than affecting strike frequency (Hirsch and Addison, 1986; Siebert and Addison, 1981). Strike frequency has more to do with factors associated with incomplete or asymmetric information, and hence with miscalculation on the part of either or both sides as to the position of the other's concession curve (see Chapter 4 by Cramton and Tracy in this volume). The legislation is not easily diagnosed in these terms, although the undoubted ambiguities as to what constituted lawful industrial action under the evolving law may have caused unions to be overly cautious in exercising their bargaining power. From a different theoretical perspective the changes in the law narrowing the range of (legal) industrial action may have curbed strikes having a basis in solidaristic and political goals.

Empirical analysis has been unable to disentangle the effects of changes in the law from other factors that have likely reduced strikes, such as heightened unemployment, falling union membership, and compositional factors attendant on the decline of sectors with traditionally high levels of strike activity (see Dunn and Metcalf, 1996). Even though there is no firm indication that the legislation reduced strikes at a given unemployment rate (Blanchflower and Freeman, 1994, p. 57), the general presumption is nonetheless that the influence of the law has increased. Not only did legal challenges in the courts increase, but also management was – at least until comparatively recently – encouraged to use an implied threat of legal action.

Two final empirical regularities might usefully be mentioned. Whatever the theoretical pedigree of the argument, the closed shop has been linked empirically to higher strike propensity, so the decline in the closed shop offers one possible explanation for the observed reduction in industrial action. Perhaps more important, in view of the greater robustness of the empirical association, has been the decline in multiunionism (see Millward et al., 1992, p. 282), with the mechanical effect of decentralized bargaining being countered by a corresponding growth in single-table bargaining (see endnote 7).

The institutional reforms designed to reduce union power were but one component of an internally self-consistent reform package adopted by successive Conservative administrations with a view to improving Britain's poor relative economic performance. These measures included, in addition to the abolition exchange controls and statutory wage-fixing machinery (on the wages council component, see below), a sustained programme of privatization of the nationalized (and heavily unionized) industries, the contracting out of government services to private-sector enterprises, the deregulation of once-regulated industries, and welfare reform (although the scale of the reduction in the replacement rate has been overstated).[11]

Comparing the decade of the 1980s with that of the 1970s, data provided by Blanchflower and Freeman (1994) suggest that these reforms may have succeeded in improving the relative position of the UK vis-à-vis other OECD nations in terms of inflation, growth, and unit labour costs. The authors also observe some domestic improvement in the speed of employment adjustment and in the responsiveness of wages to local conditions. That said, Blanchflower and Freeman do rather accentuate the negative. Apart from the pronounced rise in wage inequality in Britain during the 1980s (examined in more detail below), they note that the reforms were not associated with any improvement in the responsiveness of real wages to unemployment and even appeared to be accompanied by a relative deterioration in unemployment (for males though not for females).

Given that their sample period is 1979–90, the authors do recognize that the legal measures may not have had time to work. Fortunately, an updated treatment is available in the work of Card and Freeman (2002). The authors first assemble information from reputation indices of economic competitiveness/freedom to illustrate the favourable developing position of the UK. It is shown that, at the start of Mrs Thatcher's period in office, Britain occupied a middling rank among OECD countries in terms of the market friendliness of its institutions, but by the end of the 1990s it stood at the top of the rankings. In similar vein, the authors also examine cross-country rankings of labour market institutions – extent of unionization, centralization of bargaining, and employment protection legislation – and again report the tendency towards greater market orientation of such institutions in Britain.

Next, the authors examine trends in GDP per capita (here, per working age adult) for the UK, France and Germany (and the USA), 1960–99, and its decomposition into output per unit of labour and labour input per working age adult. It is shown that after 1979 British output per working age adult grew at a faster rate than in either Germany or France, in sharp contrast to the two decades before then. This turnaround largely reflected rising labour input per capita in Britain, that is, increasing labour force participation (and hours). After 1980 labour productivity (i.e. output per unit of labour input) in the UK grew at approximately the same rate in Britain as in Germany and France unlike in earlier years when British productivity lagged. Interestingly, the poor productivity record of the UK prior to 1979 does not represent 'inadequate' investment, and after 1979 capital again grew at much the same rates in the three European countries. After controlling for the contributions of sectoral shifts and capital, there remains an unexplained growth in UK output per capita and output per working age adult vis-à-vis Germany and France.

In other words, British labour productivity *and* labour force participation rose independently of sectoral shifts and investment propensities in the interval of the Thatcher reform years relative to that country's chief European competitors. Why? Using estimates of the lower productivity of union workers in Britain before 1979, and an assumed elimination of that differential thereafter, Card and Freeman calculate that up to 4.3 percentage points of the gain in productivity (somewhat over one-eighth of the total) can be attributed to the union reforms. They also estimate that two other reforms, privatization and the introduction of profit and share ownership schemes, could have raised productivity by 1.1 and 2.0 per cent, respectively (while the growth in self-employment may have reduced it by 0.4 per cent). Thus, the various reforms of Conservative administrations are estimated to have improved British productivity by 7 per cent, or roughly 0.35 per cent annually. This is in the order of one quarter of the observed difference in growth rates between 1960–79 and 1979–99.[12]

In sum, Mrs Thatcher's reforms appear to have played an important role in Britain's aggregate economic growth. The productivity gap was eliminated and work effort rose. Despite these improvements, there has also occurred a sharp increase in earnings inequality. Because it is conventional to attribute this development in part to union decline (e.g. Machin, 1997; Schmitt, 1995), it requires close scrutiny here.

The rougher edges?
The UK's earnings distribution has admittedly widened considerably over the period since Thatcher attacked the unions. The question arises as to whether there is a connection (see also the contribution in Chapter 8 by Card, Lemieux, and Riddell in this volume). Schmitt (1995, p. 201), for example, noting the 'striking' inverse relation between union density and earnings dispersion, has calculated that the decline in union density could account for 21 per cent of the rise in the pay premium for a university degree, 1978–88, and 13 per cent of the rise in the non-manual differential. Machin (1997, p. 653) has obtained an even larger figure. Comparing 1983 with 1991, he has estimated the male earnings variance would be 40 per cent less if the 1983 levels of union coverage prevailed in 1991.

On the other hand, the emphasis has been changing recently. Gosling et al. (2000, p. 661) do not mention unions in their analysis of the changing distribution of UK male wages. Instead, they emphasize education: the way recent cohorts have improved their acquisition of education, as well as changes over time in the returns to education. Moreover, Card (2001) has pointed out that the equalizing effects of unionism can easily be exaggerated. It is necessary to allow for the fact that unionization effects vary across the wage distribution. He shows that if the *structure* of unionization changes, so that union density falls more over time for the lower paid – as has happened both in the USA and the UK (see below) – then estimates of the equalising tendency of unionization must be reduced.

Let us now detail changes in the structure of unionization over the last twenty years. For the early period, we use the 1983 General Household Survey (GHS) dataset (see also Gosling and Lemieux, 2001; Machin,

1997). The only year in which the GHS included a union membership question is 1983, but this year is early enough to represent the 'golden age' of unionism. For the later period, we use the 1995 Labour Force Survey (LFS), 1995 representing the nadir of the union movement's fortunes. Union status is measured by a similar question in both surveys: 'Are you a member of a trade union or staff association'?[13] And comparable earnings and other background information are also available. We can therefore use these two surveys to span the period in which union power changed most, and can consider the effect of union membership on wages, *ceteris paribus*.

Table 12.2 gives a picture of changes in union membership over the 1983–95 period. The sample is restricted to individuals aged 16–66 years, not self-employed, and with positive earnings. In addition, the wage data have been converted to 1995 values using the retail price index, and observations with hourly wages outside the £1 to £45 range were deleted. The table documents the well-known decline in union membership for both men and women, but shows this decline has been uneven. In 1995, aggregate membership was only 64 per cent of its 1983 level for men, and 71 per cent for women. But the pattern of membership gains and losses varies by education, age and region. Those with degrees have registered the least decline in membership, while the younger workers, and those with least education, have registered the most. The South continues to be the least unionized region, and male membership has fallen faster here than in other regions. Finally, public sector unionization has held up well, particularly for women.

A way of showing how unionization favours the more skilled, following Card (2001), is to define predicted wage percentiles based on the *non-union* wage structure (presumed unaffected by union distortions), and to compare union densities using these percentiles. The picture is given in Figures 12.1 and 12.2, which graph union density by predicted wage percentile for males and females.[14] For males in 1983, we see that union membership is lowest among the least skilled (lowest decile), highest at the third decile, then somewhat lower for the more skilled. The 1995 data show a different pattern, with density falling most among the least skilled, leaving the highest density at the top decile. For females, density has also fallen most among low skill groups, although with some fall at the top decile as well. Thus, unionization appears to have shifted ever more towards benefiting a labour 'elite'.

Table 12.3 has panels for 1983 and 1995, showing how the variance in wages has increased over the period. For men the increase has been nearly 40 per cent, from 0.223 to 0.309, and for women somewhat less, from 0.192 to 0.256. These increases are what we are concerned to explain. The table also shows the variance in wages for union and non-union workers separately. It

Table 12.2   Trade union membership rates, 1983 and 1995

	Men			Women		
	1983	1995	Ratio 95/83	1983	1995	Ratio 95/83
Overall	56.7	36.0	.64	42.1	29.8	.71
By education:						
Degree or equivalent	51.4	40.1	.78	61.7	48.2	.79
Further education	59.9	41.7	.70	65.1	59.2	.91
'A' level or equivalent	54.1	36.7	.68	42.0	26.5	.63
'O' level or equivalent	46.2	24.2	.52	33.5	22.8	.68
Other	57.9	40.3	.70	33.1	22.4	.68
None	62.5	32.9	.53	43.5	21.1	.49
By age (years):						
16–30	44.1	22.7	.52	36.6	21.4	.58
31–55	62.3	42.0	.68	45.0	34.3	.76
56–66	65.9	39.5	.61	45.6	26.5	.58
By colour:						
White	56.4	36.0	.64	42.1	29.6	.70
Non-white	67.4	27.6	.41	46.8	28.9	.62
By region:						
North	64.9	43.4	.67	48.3	35.2	.73
Midlands	57.6	37.3	.65	46.8	27.0	.58
South, incl. London	49.1	29.1	.59	32.0	24.4	.76
Wales	65.0	48.9	.77	52.8	38.8	.73
Scotland	63.5	38.0	.60	55.7	37.7	.68
By sector:						
Private	41.5	27.2	.63	25.8	14.7	.57
Public	85.0	65.7	.78	69.0	58.3	.84
Observations	4440	4063		3535	3770	

Notes: Samples are taken from the 1983 General Household Survey and the 1995 third quarter Labour Force Survey. Samples include respondents aged 16–66 years, who were not self-employed and whose hourly wage was between £1 and £45 in 1995 pounds (1983 wages valued in 1995 pounds according to the retail price index). In the case of the Labour Force survey, the income weights supplied with the data are used.

can be seen that the union wage variance is lower than the non-union – hence the equalizing effect of greater unionization. Interestingly, it can also be seen that while both union and non-union wage variances have risen over time, the union variance for men remains much smaller than the non-union: the union–non-union 'variance gap' remains substantial. Thus, male unions,

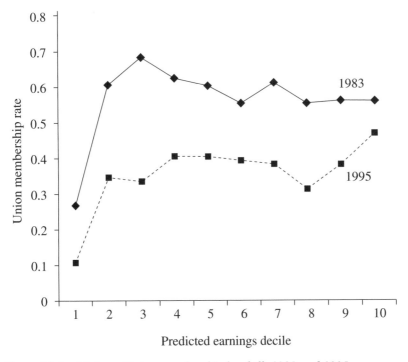

Figure 12.1   Males – Union membership by skill, 1983 and 1995

even though less extensive than heretofore, can still strongly 'standardize' their members' wages.

Table 12.3 also contains information on the union–non-union wage gap, both unadjusted and adjusted for a set of basic human capital variables. The unadjusted wage gaps are always larger than the adjusted gaps, because union workers have higher skills than their non-union counterparts. However, the difference between adjusted and unadjusted wage gaps grows between 1983 and 1995, reflecting the increased unionization of high-skill groups in 1995. The adjusted wage gap falls over time as well, at least for men. However, we must not be too quick to assume that this fall reflects the lower power of male unions, because we have seen that they are still powerful in reducing the union wage variance.

We can now put these facts together to estimate union effects on wage dispersion (Card, Lemieux, and Riddell in Chapter 8 perform similar calculations, and draw comparisons between Canada, the UK and the USA). First, we perform a two-sector calculation, following Freeman (1980, p. 19). Here, the effect of unions on the variance of wages (V) relative to the

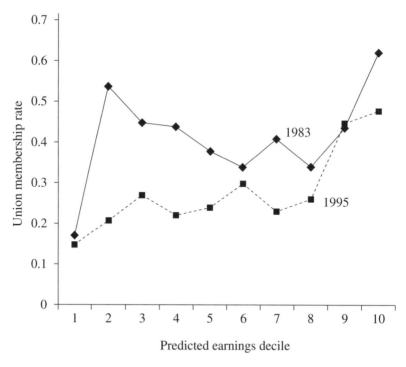

Figure 12.2   Females – Union membership by skill, 1983 and 1995.

variance if all workers were paid according to the non-union sector wage structure (V^*) is:

$$V - V^* = U\Delta_V + U(1-U)\Delta_W^2 ,$$

where U is union density, Δ_V is the union–non-union variance gap, and Δ_W is the union–non-union wage gap. Since unions reduce variance within the union sector, the term $U\Delta_V$ is the negative 'within-sector' effect. The term $U(1-U)\Delta_W^2$ is the positive 'between-sector' effect, reflecting the fact that unions widen wage dispersion by bringing about the union wage gap.

Comparing the size of $V - V^*$ between 1983 and 1995 gives a measure of the effect of unions on wage dispersion.[15] Such a comparison is performed in Table 12.4. Taking the column for men, we estimate that in 1983 unionism reduced wage variance by -0.072. In 1995 the reduction was smaller: -0.060. The implication is that if the 1983 structure of unionization prevailed in 1995, wage variance would be less by 0.019 ($= -0.053 + 0.072$), or 21.1 per cent. For women the effect is similar. In 1983 unionism had a small

Table 12.3 *Wage distributions of union and non-union workers, 1983 and 1995*

	Men		Women	
	Non-union	Union	Non-union	Union
1983				
Overall variance in log wages	0.223		0.192	
Variance log hourly wage	0.289	0.151	0.197	0.147
Mean log hourly wage	1.637	1.854	1.278	1.534
Adjusted union wage gap	0.151		0.197	
(gap controlling for public sector)	(0.126)		(0.160)	
1995				
Overall variance in log wages	0.309		0.256	
Variance log hourly wage	0.355	0.202	0.237	0.216
Mean log hourly wage	1.86	2.05	1.54	1.89
Adjusted union wage gap	0.086		0.205	
(gap controlling for public sector)	(0.082)		(0.177)	

Note: The adjusted union wage gap is the union coefficient from a regression controlling for years of education, years of experience (plus experience squared and cubed), and dummies for non-white, marital status, and five regions (plus a dummy for public sector employment in the case of the bracketed coefficient). See notes to Table 12.2 for sample and hourly wage definitions.

Sources: see Table 12.2.

Table 12.4 Simple estimates of the contribution of declining unionization to wage inequality 1983–95

	Men	Women	Remarks
1983			
Union density, U	.567	.421	From Table 12.2.
Union wage gap, ΔW	.151	.197	Difference between union and non-union wages (Table 12.3).
Union variance gap, ΔV	−.138	−.050	Difference in union and non-union wage variances (Table 12.3).
Union effect, *between* sectors, $U(1-U)\Delta W^2$	.006	.009	Small effect of unions in raising wage inequality by widening mean pay as between union and non-union sectors.
Union effect, *within* sectors, $U\Delta V$	−.078	−.021	Larger effect of unions is to reduce wage dispersion within union sectors.
Total effect	*−.072*	*−.012*	Estimated total effect of unions is to reduce wage variance; for example, for men the reduction is −.072.
1995			
Union density, U	.360	.298	From Table 12.2.
Union wage gap, ΔW	.086	.205	From Table 12.3.
Union variance gap, ΔV	−.153	−.021	From Table 12.3.
Union effect, *between* sectors, $U(1-U)\Delta W^2$	.002	.009	See explanations for 1983 above.
Union effect, *within* sectors, $U\Delta V$	−.055	−.006	See explanations for 1983 above.
Total effect	*−.053*	*.003*	Variance-reducing effect of unions is smaller in 1995 than 1983, and women's unions even increase dispersion in 1995.
Changes 1983–95			
Change in variance of wages	.086	.064	See Table 12.3; for example, for men .086 = .309−.223.
Change in effect of unions	.019	.015	Change in total effect derived above: for example, for men, .019 = −.053−(−.072).

Contribution of unions (%)	21.1	23.4	For example, for men, .211 = .019/.086. Effect of decline in unionization for women is larger than for men, mainly because variance gap has declined so much for women.
Memo item			
Contribution of 'de-unionization' if 1983 U prevailed in 1995 (%)*	36.8	3.1	This number depends mainly on $(U_1 - U_0)\,\Delta_{v1}$, the change in U weighted by the 1995 variance gap. This gap is very small for women, hence the 1.5% figure.

Note: * This number gives the deunionization effect assuming changes only in union density. Thus, (with 1, 0 representing the two years), the effect of deunionization on the 1998 variance is: $\Delta_1 - \Delta'_1 = (U_1 - U_0)\,\Delta_{v1} + [(U_1(1 - U_1) + U_0(1 - U_0)]\,\Delta_{w1}^2$, where $\Delta_1 = V - V^*$, Δ_{v1} = union variance gap in 1995 and Δ_{w1} = union wage gap in 1995.

narrowing effect, but in 1995 actually *widens* the wage variance by 0.003. Hence if the 1983 structure of unionization prevailed, the improvement would be 0.015, or 23.4 per cent.

We now allow for differences in union structure (i.e. coverage, plus wage and variance gaps) by group. Table 12.5 provides the relevant formula, and the results of the calculations. To interpret the results it is worth remembering that in 1983, for both men and women, the wage gap declines nicely by wage decile, so that those with high skills receive hardly any premium, as might be expected. Correspondingly, the variance gap widens at higher wage deciles, showing more skilled non-union workers have very varied jobs, and consequently highly variable pay. But patterns are less definite in 1995. Wage gaps are large for highly skilled workers as well – perhaps indicating that unions have gained more power at this end even while they have lost it at the lower end. The variance gap is also now large at the lower end, with unskilled non-union workers having more variation in pay. This result might reflect the decline in national wage bargaining, which may have spilled over more onto non-union workers in 1983 and thereby reduced pay dispersion.

The estimates in Table 12.5 serve to reduce the impact of declining unionization on wage dispersion. Looking first at men, unions reduce overall wage variance in both years: by −0.043 in 1983 and by −0.41 in 1995. However, as can be seen, the reduction is similar in 1995, which rules out declining unionization as a factor in the widening male wage variance over the 1983–95 period.[16] The main factor behind the greater dispersion-reducing effect of unions in 1995 is the wider variance gaps in 1995. In other words, unions compress pay more in 1995 than 1983. On the other hand, for women, the adjusted and simple estimates are less dissimilar. The dispersion-reducing effect of unions is now estimated to be larger in 1983 (at −0.015) than in 1995 (−0.001). Consequently, we can still allow the decline of women's union density to play some role in the widening of women's wage variance.

These results considering changes in the structure of UK unionism differ from the received wisdom, and would be worth exploring further with other datasets, and over a longer time period.[17] Nevertheless, we should be alert to the possibility that UK unionization, while it has lost members among the less skilled, has to some extent made up for this by gaining members among the skilled. Consequently, the equalizing effects of unions are less than might be thought.

3. New Labour

Prior to its election victory in May 1997, New Labour had signalled its intention to make a number of changes that would affect industrial relations practice and labour law. For example, Mr Blair had promised to recognize

Table 12.5   Adjusted estimates of the contribution of declining unionization to wage inequality, allowing for different union effects across pay deciles

	Men	Women	Remarks
1983			
Variance in log wages	.223	.192	From Table 12.3.
Effect of unions			
Simple	−.072	−.012	From Table 12.4.
Adjusted	−.043	−.015	Allowing for different union impacts across pay deciles
1995			
Variance in log wages	.309	.256	From Table 12.3.
Effect of unions			
Simple	−.053	.003	From Table 12.4.
Adjusted	−.041	−.001	Allowing for different union impacts across pay deciles
Changes 1983–95			
Change in variance of wages	.086	.064	From Table 12.4.
Change in effect of unions			
Simple	.019	.015	From Table 12.4.
Adjusted	−.002	.014	For men, unions have a dispersion-reducing effect in 1995, hence decline of unions has hardly increased dispersion.

Notes: The adjusted formula (allowing for different union effects by skill category) for the effect of unions on the variance of wages (V) relative to the variance if all workers were paid according to the non-union sector wage structure (V^*) is given in Card (2001, p. 298) as:

$$V - V^* = E[u(c)\Delta v(c)] + E[u(c)(1 - u(c))\Delta w(c)^2] + \text{var}[u(c),\Delta w(c)] + 2\text{cov}[W_N(c),u(c)\Delta w(c)],$$

where $u(c)$ is the distribution of union density across the c skill categories, $\Delta v(c)$ is the distribution of variance gaps, $\Delta w(c)$ is the distribution of wage gaps and $W_N(c)$ is the distribution of non-union wage rates. Values are as follows:

	Men		Women	
	1983	1995	1983	1995
$E[u(c)\Delta v(c)]$	−.026	−.033	−.030	−.026
$E[u(c)(1-u(c))\Delta w(c)^2]$	.009	.004	.011	.009
$\text{var}[u(c),\Delta w(c)]$	.003	.001	.001	.002
$2\text{cov}[W_N(c),u(c)\Delta w(c)]$	−.029	−.013	.003	.014
Total	**−.043**	**−.041**	**−.015**	**−.001**

unions at the Government Communications Headquarters (GCHQ).[18] He had also announced his intention to set up a Low Pay Commission, which would resurrect minimum wages but at the national rather than industry level. Moreover, the new administration would adopt a very different attitude to Europe: in June 1997 the new government committed itself to accepting the *Social Chapter*, thereby ending a period of bifurcation in Community social policy.

In this section, we review the main changes – actual and planned – of New Labour, beginning with the new National Minimum Wage, through the 1999 Employment Relations Act, to the prospective Employment Act. The altogether more dramatic changes foreshadowed by the end of two-track social Europe are remitted to section 4.

The National Minimum Wage

In April 1999 a national minimum wage was introduced following the Low Pay Commission's recommendation. This is the first time that the UK has had a *national* minimum. Trade unions have been strong supporters of the concept, aiming to take the minimum wage as a starting point for negotiations for low-paid workers in the usual way (Labour Research Department, 1999, p. 10). Previously there had been an industry-based system of Wages Councils for low-wage industries, set up by the Trade Boards Act of 1909. It had been hoped that these Councils would foster the growth of voluntary collective bargaining in their industries. However, trade unions were never certain whether Wages Councils were helping or hindering such growth (Donovan Commission, 1968, para. 229). Thus, given that the Wages Council system had been abolished in 1993, the move by New Labour and the unions for an alternative system of minimum wage-setting, but on a national basis, seemed natural. The question was seemingly only a matter of how high the bar should be set.

The minimum was initially fixed at £3.60 an hour for those aged 22 years and above (see Table 12.6), with a youth sub-minimum of £3.00 for those aged 18–21 years (17 year-olds and under were not covered), and a development rate of £3.20 for adults in the first six months of a new job with accredited training. The Low Pay Commission (2001, Appendix 1, para. 17) estimated that about 1.5 million workers (6.4 per cent of the workforce) had a pay increase as a consequence. The pay increase was large: those earning less than the minimum in 1998 had an increase of 15.5 per cent, 1998–99, as compared with only 4.6 per cent for everyone else (Low Pay Commission, 2001, para. 3.30).[19] Some sectors were more heavily affected than others. Thus, Machin et al. (2002, Table 2) report in their study of residential care homes that nearly a third of these workers required a pay increase as a result of the minimum.

Table 12.6   Estimates of workers whose pay is raised by the NMW

Date of minimum wage law	Level (age group)	Coverage estimate, 000s (per cent of group)	Remarks
April 1999	£3.60 (22+) £3.00 (18–21)[a]	1401 (6.4) 122 (7.7)	Estimate by Low Pay Commission (2001, Table A1.1) using ONS central estimate from April 1998 NES and LFS[b]
Oct 2000	£3.70 (22+) £3.20 (18–21)	856 (3.8) 81 (4.8)	Estimate using ONS central estimate from April 2000 NES and LFS[c]
Oct 2001	£4.10 (22+) £3.50 (18–21)	1611 (7.0) 97 (5.5)	Estimate using ONS central estimate from April 2001 NES and LFS[c]

Notes:
[a] Youth rate was subsequently raised to £3.20 in June 2000.
[b] The Office of National Statistics (ONS) central estimate methodology using the April New Earnings Survey (NES) and the quarterly Labour Force Survey (LFS) is explained in Studdard and Jenkins (2001).
[c] ONS central estimate low pay distributions for April 2000 and April 2001 are published at the ONS website (ONS, 2002).

The course of the minimum, together with estimates of numbers affected, is shown in Table 12.6. As can be seen, there have been upratings annually. The table presents estimates of the numbers of workers affected by these October upratings calculated on the basis of wage distributions for the previous April (ONS, 2002). In other words, by taking the wage distribution six months prior to a new minimum, we estimate how many workers would have higher pay as a result of the minimum. On this basis, the October 2000 uprating meant that only 977 000 workers had a pay rise (about 4 per cent of the workforce). However, the October 2001 uprating had almost double the impact, with 1.7 million workers (7 per cent of the workforce) having a pay rise. Unions have been complaining about the low coverage of the minimum, and have called for improved uprating together with abolition of the youth rate (Labour Research Department, 2001, p. 12). But Table 12.6 makes it clear that coverage remains significant. It is also important to realise that, although only some 5 per cent of the youth (18–21 years) workforce is covered by the youth minimum, almost 30 per cent of this group would require a pay increase if the adult minimum were required.[20]

As regards impact on employment, the evidence is mixed. The most comprehensive study is by Stewart (2001, p. 29), who finds that introduction of the minimum had zero impact. He compared employment probabilities pre- and post-1999 for those at the minimum, and for those just above the minimum. If the minimum had had any effect, the employment probabilities post-1999 should have been worse for the minimum wage group. But there was no significant difference. (That said, note that this study only looks at employment development a few months after the minimum was introduced, not longer-run effects.) On the other hand, there is strong evidence of displacement effects in particular markets. For example, the Low Pay Commission's 2000 survey of low-paying firms – including hairdressing, cleaning, care homes – found that 40 per cent of the sample registered a 'significant' or 'slight' reduction in staffing levels (Low Pay Commission, 2001, Appendix Table A2.11). Furthermore, the study of residential care homes by Machin et al. (2002, p. 19) detects reductions in both employment and hours following the minimum, with an employment elasticity in the region of -0.15 to -0.40. Particularly striking is the fact that the rate of employment growth of care assistants has fallen to zero since 1999, having increased steadily in the previous five years. Clearly minimum wages can bite.

The 1999 Employment Relations Act

The shape of the government's industrial relations policies became clear with the publication of the White Paper *Fairness at Work* (Department of Trade and Industry, 1998). This emphasized both the domestic and the European dimensions. On the purely domestic front, its main but not exclusive thrust was the establishment of new procedures for collective representation. On the European front, national law would have to reflect decisions taken in the European Union (EU) under the Agreement on Social Policy – now the *Social Chapter* (see section 4). Yet, as indicated by his 'there will be no going back' statement cited at the start of this chapter, Mr Blair was careful to retain the curbs on industrial action and the impediments of the closed shop that he had inherited.

New Labour's amended proposals became law in June 1999. Only the barest bones of the legislation are summarized in the final row entry of Table 12.1; even so, the contrast between the 1999 Employment Relations Act and preceding legislation is sharp. We now add some flesh to these bones, as well as commenting briefly on the 'family friendly' provisions of the Act.

Beginning with the union content, the main element in the legislation is the establishment of a statutory union recognition procedure for all firms employing more than 20 workers in the event that a union claim for recognition (identifying the union and the bargaining unit involved) is rejected, unanswered, or otherwise not negotiated by the employer. In these circumstances, the union can apply to the Central Arbitration Committee (CAC) for recognition, thereby activating a statutory recognition procedure. The CAC has to decide whether the proposed (or indeed some other) bargaining unit is appropriate and whether or not the union has the support of a majority of members of the appropriate bargaining unit. Once the definition of the bargaining unit is decided (and here prime consideration is supposed to be given to its compatibility with 'effective management'), the CAC determines whether the union is able to demonstrate that the majority of unit is in favour of membership. Union recognition will be awarded automatically if the CAC is satisfied that majority of members of the bargaining unit are union members. If not, the CAC has to arrange for a secret ballot. Recognition is granted if a majority of those voting are in favour, providing that they constitute at least 40 per cent of the bargaining unit.

A method of collective bargaining can be imposed by the CAC at the request of either party in circumstances where its award of recognition has not resulted in collective bargaining either because of failure to agree on a method or failure to follow an agreed method, or in the case of voluntary recognition agreements for the same reasons. Here the Act provides for the establishment of a joint negotiating body and a six-step bargaining procedure to cover the determination of pay, hours, and holidays (on an annual basis).

A second major advance for unions ushered in by the legislation is the right for all workers (not just union members) to be accompanied by a trade union representative in grievance and disciplinary hearings. Data from the 1998 Workplace Employee Relations Survey show that, although most firms currently allow employees to be accompanied by a third party, less than one half allow them to choose whoever they wish (Cully et al., 1999, p. 97). As a result, non-union firms are now likely to be faced 'not with a workplace representative, but with a full-time union official who will probably be seeking to maximise recruitment' (IRS, 1999, p. 10). Note that this right to representation is independent of the recognition procedure and applies irrespective of the size of the firm.

Third, although the Act does not alter the basic legal principle that strikes have to be supported by valid ballots, it does relax strike balloting procedures. Thus, for example, unions will no longer be required to furnish employers with the names of members that are being balloted or called out on strike – although the 1993 requirement of seven days' advance notice of a ballot is still required of the union.[21]

Fourth, strikers are specially protected against dismissal. Prior to the Act, even strikers on official strike could be dismissed fairly unless they were able to show that the dismissal was selective and motivated by an anti-union animus. Henceforth, dismissal of those on lawfully organized industrial action will only be fair if the employer can demonstrate that 'reasonable' procedural steps to resolve the dispute have been undertaken – and even then only eight weeks after the striker has been on strike. Employees who believe they have been dismissed unfairly in this regard can petition an employment tribunal. Further, the Act raises the maximum penalty for unfair dismissal from £12 000 to £50 000 (in fact, with special awards, the maximum is closer to £68 000; see IRS, 1999, p. 8). The qualifying service period is also abolished for strikers. (For the workforce as a whole, the qualifying period is reduced from two years to one year.) The clear intention is to ensure little threat of court actions against striking workers in the future.[22]

As was noted earlier, the Act also contains family-friendly measures, defined as policies that enhance family life while making it easier for people to go to work with less conflict between their responsibilities at home and at work (Department of Trade and Industry, 1998, p. 9). In normal circumstances, statutory provision of improved labour standards might be expected to diminish the demand for unionization on the part of workers or reflect decreased unionization. But note that family-friendly measures are essentially part of the corpus of European social policy, which as we shall see contains many directives of direct benefit to union organization. The two main provisions in question pertain to maternity/parental leave and part-time work, transposing into UK law the provisions of two EU directives. In the former area, the Act increases the period of basic maternity leave from 14 to 18 weeks. It also provides the right to additional leave for women with one year of service with their employer (rather than two years as heretofore). Three months' parental leave is also extended to mothers and fathers (and adoptive parents) of children under five, born after 15 December 1999. For their part, the atypical work provisions seek to ensure that part-time workers are treated 'no less favourably' than their full-time counterparts as regards their terms and conditions of employment. These two transpositions phased in under the ERA follow on the heels of the domestic application of much more controversial European legislation in the form of the working time and European Works Council directives.

The Employment Bill

New Labour's Employment Bill was first submitted to Parliament in November 2001 and at the time of writing has yet to become law. Outside of disputes resolution it has little obvious relevance to unions.[23] That the emphasis of the draft legislation lies elsewhere – namely, maternity leave and fixed-term contracts – was nevertheless widely interpreted at the time as indicating that there was no unfinished 'union business'.

The Bill contains maternity leave provisions that extend the amount and duration of paid leave for mothers.[24] These terms are accompanied by paternity leave for fathers (two weeks' paid leave on top of the 13 weeks' unpaid leave under the existing law), again subject to a minimal service (and threshold earnings) requirement, as well as paid adoptive leave of 26 weeks' duration. Each measure is part of New Labour's family-friendly legislation mentioned earlier. Also included under this heading are the proposals pertaining to fixed-term contracts, to be the subject of formal Regulations. These will transpose into UK legislation the provisions of supranational EU legislation (see below) providing no less favourable treatment for workers on fixed-term contracts than for regular employment. Apart from the discrimination component, the Regulations will also set the terms under which such contracts can be extended and the circumstances in which they will instead be deemed converted into open-ended employment. The regulation of atypical work may of course facilitate union membership directly by 'regularizing' it or indirectly by increasing the cost of a substitute for union labour.

Finally, the most important component of the provisions on dispute resolution is the insertion of a statutory three-step disciplinary and grievance procedure into the written contract of employment. The aim here is to reduce the attractiveness of employment tribunals, recourse to which has been running at record levels. Thus, in 1990/91, there had been only about 40 000 employment tribunal applications, but by 2000/01 this had risen to nearly 140 000 – with an embarrassingly fast increase since 1997 (Department of Trade and Industry, 2001a, p. 28). The government thought it could reduce this figure by requiring firms to adopt model 'disciplinary' and 'grievance' procedures, to include details of these procedures in the employee's written statement of employment, and to allow tribunals to take into account, when ruling on compensation, whether this procedure had been properly used (Department of Trade and Industry, 2001b, p. 18). However, as a practical matter, the increase in tribunal applications is mostly fuelled by extra employment rights (and extra entitlement to compensation) rather than to 'bad management'. Accordingly, we doubt whether the measures will succeed in damping down the future course of tribunal applications.

The economic consequences of Mr Blair

Early assessments of the effects of policy shifts are fraught with difficulty (see for example, Coutts et al., 1981). Unbowed, in an early assessment of the proposals in *Fairness at Work*, Minford and Haldenby (1999) argued that the new recognition procedures could result in one million new union members. This calculation is based on a Confederation of British Industry survey of expected claims for recognition. Minford and Haldenby then use the Liverpool macro-model to estimate the costs of the new recognition procedures – and indeed all the regulatory aspects of *Fairness at Work*. Via the projected increase in wage demands in line with increased membership, the disemployment costs of the new recognition procedures are set at half a million workers after two years, which certainly seems too high.

The government's statutory recognition procedures came into force in June 2000 and the signs do point to an increase in recognition. Thus, the number of recognition agreements recorded by the TUC which had doubled in 1999 over 1998, more than doubled again in 2000 to 159 agreements covering 58 233 workers (see TUC 2000, 2001; see also EIRR, 2001). Note also that union membership rose modestly in 2000 for the first time in 20 years.

But New Labour has not sought systemic reform of the Thatcher law legacy. Thus, legislation on the closed shop, the various constraints on industrial action, elections for union officials, and membership rights against the leadership has not been subject to change. Nor for that matter has there been any attempt to alter the financial reporting obligations of unions, or to reinstate the Fair Wages Resolution or the statutory extension of collective bargaining. The new administration can also be said to have been responsive to the needs of industry in seeking to limit the domestic impact of a number of pieces of EU legislation, most notably the Working Time Directive, and in resisting one-size-fits-all draft legislation on European consultative rights (Brown, 2000, p. 304). What we instead have is a so-called *third way*, the elements of which comprise an extension of individual employment rights, a modicum of protection for low-paid workers under the NMW, family friendly or work/life balance policies, and the goal of social partnership or cooperative unionism (facilitated in part through help on recognition).[25]

New Labour's policies have tended to draw more criticism from its friends than its opponents. Thus, its entire programme has been termed minimalist, by virtue of the absence of any unfinished business (i.e. new union legislation) in the current Employment Bill as well as the government's attempts to date to limit the impact of EU directives referred to earlier (Smith and Moreton, 2001). For its part, the government would emphasize the importance of its notion of 'partnership' at the workplace or mutual cooperation.[26] Partnership is certainly the leitmotif of *Fairness at Work*. Witness the statement: 'Within Britain's flexible and efficient labour market, the Government is proposing in this White Paper a framework in which the development of strong partnerships at work can flourish as the best way of improving fairness at work' (Department of Trade and Industry, 1998, p. 8). The other hallmark of the White Paper, at least as conventionally depicted, is the focus on individualism (Brown et al., 2000).

But this is patently not the end of the story. The second quotation of

Mr Blair at the start of this chapter necessarily marks a shift away from individualism. The issue here is one of whether unions facilitate effective partnership. The scene is set for a replay of the old controversy about unions and efficiency in an environment of more cooperation between the two sides of industry which is, to complicate matters analytically, 'in part a symptom of a weakened union movement' (Brown, 2000, p. 308). Interestingly, some of the first salvoes in this controversy are fired in this Handbook (see Chapter 5 by Metcalf in this volume). The second reason is the EU context. Almost irrespective of Mr Blair's acceptance of the EU model, it is the case that domestic law on industrial relations will increasingly be driven by the *acquis communautaire*, to which we now turn.

4.   The European level

Within a month of its election victory New Labour opted in to the Agreement on Social Policy (ASP). The ASP was the device used to save the 1991 Maastricht Treaty in the face of continuing British opposition to pan-European labour standards. The formula chosen was to relegate the terms of what was to have been a Social Chapter to a protocol appended to the treaty. Attached to the protocol was an agreement – the ASP – that noted the intention of the other (at that time) 11 member states to pursue a new route to social policy with the specific exemption of the UK. This process heralded the emergence of what has been called a 'two-track' social Europe; the other track being the standard and narrower treaty route. Labour's return to the fold merged the two tracks. This merger was formalized with the conclusion of the Treaty of Amsterdam in October 1997, which incorporated the provisions of the ASP directly into the main body of the treaty – a Social Chapter after all. What has the UK let itself in for; and, in particular, what are the implications for collective bargaining?

The Agreement on Social Policy

The ASP made two fundamental changes. First of all, it provided for the first time a firm treaty basis for social policy legislation in identifying ten distinct social policy themes, in five of which qualified majority voting (rather than unanimity) would apply.[27] Second, it gave the two sides of industry at European level – the 'social partners' – an elevated role in determining policy.[28] The aim is to have the two sides consulted by the Commission on the possible direction of social policy, and also to 'take over' any legislation and reach a framework agreement between themselves on measures that would duly become binding across the EU. This move towards corporatism might result in better (i.e. employment increasing) policy making,[29] but it does of course also serve to legitimize the activism of the social affairs directorate.

Since ratification of the Maastricht Treaty in 1993, the social partners have had mixed success. They were able to reach agreements on parental leave, part-time work, and (most recently) fixed-term contracts – agreements that were subsequently given the force of law by Council directives. But in all cases where they were unable to reach agreement, the Commission advanced its own proposals. And it was able to secure legislation on European Works Councils (EWCs), the burden of proof in gender discrimination cases and, most recently, the directive on national works councils. The Commission was also to use the standard treaty route, that is, process legislation before all 12 (now 15) member states.[30] In short, both the ASP and the standard treaty routes were used to attend to unfinished (social chapter) business and to advance new proposals.

The immediate effect of New Labour's opt in was that there was a body of European legislation on the books that the UK had had no say in framing and now had to implement.[31] Although formal application of the Treaty of Amsterdam would be delayed until each and every member state had ratified it (May 1999), it proved possible to extend the law to the UK well before then by readopting ASP legislation on a whole-Community basis. Much more important than catch-up, however, was the progression of draft legislation and new initiatives, with the UK rejoining the fold to end the two-track social Europe. Recall that Community social policy now enjoys not only an unambiguous treaty basis but also equal billing with economic integration in the European endeavour.

The skein of EU union-related law

Health and safety consultation   British legislation predating Community social policy required the employer only to consult recognized unions via health and safety committees. However, Council Directive 89/391/EEC of 12 June 1989 established general principles for information, dialogue, 'balanced participation', and training for workers and their representatives. Non-union employees had to be consulted as well. Thus, current British practice, under The Health and Safety (Consultation with Employees) Regulations (SI 1996/1513), requires that employees not in groups covered by union health and safety representatives now have to be consulted – either directly or through elected employee representatives – by their employer. Consultation rights are extensive and range from changes in, say, ways of working that affect employees' health through information on likely risks and remedial action, to training. The implication is that the UK model, which has traditionally required collective bargaining, has become inadequate with the decline in unionism. The Commission perceives a need for wider employee representation, the stimulation of which could well promote unionism as we shall see.

Collective redundancies and transfers of undertakings Community legislation on worker rights in the event of collective redundancies (i.e. mass layoffs) and transfers of businesses was contained in the Commission's first social action plan, and dates from 1975 and 1977, respectively. As in the case of health and safety, both laws call for employee representatives and the provisions are the same in each case.

The current EU law on collective redundancies is Directive 98/59/EC of 20 July 1998. A collective redundancy is defined as a permanent layoff involving 20 or more employees at a single establishment in a 90-day period. Consultation has to cover ways of avoiding the dismissals and mitigating the layoffs and their consequences. It has furthermore to be conducted with a view to reaching agreement and must provide written details on the redundancies to employee representatives. The timing of consultation is a function of the number of layoffs: at least 90 (30) days prior to the first dismissal if 100 or more (between 20 and 99) redundancies are proposed. Penalties for failure to consult are up to 90-days' pay for each affected employee under a protective award issued by an industrial tribunal.

Again until quite recently, UK law made no provision for affected employees not represented by a union. But under the Collective Redundancies and Transfer of Undertakings (Protection of Employment) (Amendment) Regulations 1999 (SI 1999/1925), the employer has now to inform and consult appropriate representatives of these employees, who may be existing representatives – if their remit and method of election or appointment gives them suitable authority from the employees concerned – or newly elected representatives. (If employees fail to elect representatives within a reasonable time then employer has to consult directly with the affected employees.) The new legislation sets down a nine-item set of rules to apply in cases where employee representatives are to be specially elected. For example, the employer has to determine the number of representatives to be elected so that they are sufficient to represent the interests of all the affected employees having regard to the number and classes of those employees, and before an election the employer has to determine the length of office of the representatives which has to be long enough to meet the information and consultation requirements. These requirements can stimulate unionism for two reasons: first, the circumstances of redundancy concentrate the minds of employees and can well tip the scales in favour of union organization; second, the unions should be able to work the complex new rules best.

EU regulations pertaining to transfers of businesses – or 'acquired rights' – have recently been revised as a result of Directive 2001/23/EC of 12 March 2001. The British enabling legislation is The Transfer of Undertakings (Protection of Employment) Regulations 1981 (SI 1981/1794), as amended in 1995 (SI 2587) and 1999 (SI 1925). Abstracting from the changing technicalities of what precisely constitutes a business transfer, the regulations have the effect: first, that employees of the undertaking which changes hands automatically become employees of the new employer on the same terms and conditions; and, second, that representatives of affected employees have a right to be informed about the transfer and to be consulted (with a view to securing their agreement) about any measure contemplated by the old or new employer that will affect these employees.

The provisions on representatives are identical to those described for collective redundancies. Breach of the regulations can result in up to 13 weeks' pay per affected employee. Where the cause of action involves collective redundancies as well as acquired rights, the penalties are in principle additive rather than offsetting.

The EWC Directive   Community draft legislation on transnational works councils dates from 1975, although the present directive stems from the action programme of the Social Charter. Passage of the legislation was delayed by British opposition, so that the European Works Council Directive (94/45/EC of 22 September 1994) was adopted under the ASP. It requires consultative workers' councils in companies with at least 1000 employees in the Community and with at least 150 employees in each of two member states, if requested by employees. Member state implementing provisions had to be in place by September 1996, establishing a formal procedure for the negotiation of an EWC (under Article 6 of the directive). Failure to reach agreement under this procedure within three years would trigger a statutory works council (i.e. after September 1999). By the same token, Article 13 of the directive also recognized voluntary works council arrangements – 'Article 13 agreements' – where these could be concluded prior to the passage of national legislation. Note that the legislation allowed for its review: 'Not later than 22 September 1999, the Commission shall in consultation with member states and with management and labour at European level, review its operation and, in particular, examine whether the workforce thresholds are appropriate with a view to proposing suitable amendments to the Council, where necessary'.

As we have noted, ASP legislation does not apply to the UK. After the British opt in, therefore, it became necessary to extend the law to the UK. This was done in December 1997 via Directive 97/74/EC. The British enabling legislation – the Transnational Information and Consultation of

Employees Regulations 1999 (SI 199/3323) – gave UK-based multinationals until 15 December 1999 to negotiate Article 13 agreements and a further three years to avoid statutory EWCs.[32]

In what sense does this legislation strengthen unions? After all, it gives no role to unions per se; rather, negotiations are via a special negotiating body, the (UK) members of which are elected by secret ballot of the workforce, with no provision for nomination by existing employee representatives. Nevertheless, we know that unions have played a key role in negotiating EWCs (e.g. EIRR, 2000a, p. 22). That said, we also know that the experience with EWCs – admittedly most of which have been Article 13 agreements (i.e. voluntary arrangements) – has been benign and the immediate cost implications seem modest (see, respectively, Addison and Belfield, 2002c; Department of Trade and Industry, 1999). So the issue hinges on the directive's relationship to the information and consultation requirements of the other mandates reviewed here and, relatedly, on the next revision of the law when the Commission is likely to lower the employment size threshold, strengthen the information and consultation rights, and elaborate on the procedures (more meetings, training of EWC members, and enhanced rights to expert assistance). These at least are the recommendations of the ETUC (EIRR, 2000b, p. 21). Finally, there is the vexed issue of the EWC as a springboard for pan-European collective bargaining (see Chapter 13 by Sadowski, Ludewig and Turk in this volume).

The European Company Statute   A thirty-year deadlock on provision for a European Company Statute (ECS) was broken in October 2001 with the adoption in Council of legislation establishing the legal basis of the European Company (Regulation (EC) No. 21257/2001 of 8 October 2001) and its twin covering employee involvement in the new entity (Directive 2001/86/EC of 8 October 2001). The legislation will come into force in October 2004. The European Company is a form of legal entity available on a voluntary basis to companies operating in more than one member state and wishing to take advantage of a unified tax structure. The arrangements for employee involvement in the ECS resemble those for EWCs but there are some important differences that will presumably require early modification of the directive governing the latter. Put simply, the legislation provides for free negotiations between management and employee representatives with the goal of reaching a voluntary agreement on employee involvement arrangements. But management has to initiate the special negotiating body (SNB) procedure, which also differs in a number of respects from the EWC counterpart. In particular, in determining the rules for the election of SNB members, member states can make provision for trade union representatives who need not be employees of the company.

Further, union representatives are explicitly mentioned among the 'experts' that the SNB can request to assist it.

The negotiating process must begin as soon as the SNB is established, and just six months are allowed for negotiations – as compared with three years in the EWC case – although this interval may be extended at the joint request of the two sides. Voluntary agreements have to meet a number of basic conditions as with the EWC (e.g. composition of the 'representative body', frequency of meetings, and financial resources allocated to it) but in addition to information and consultation there is also the possibility of board-level representation. The inclusion of such representation is largely optional but if a single company converts to a European company pre-existing levels of board representation continue to operate.

Failure to reach an agreement again generates a set of standard rules on employee involvement. These not only provide for information and consultation through a 'representative body' – that on occasion exceed the standard set for the statutory EWC – but also for board level representation in certain cases.

National systems for consulting and informing workers – or company works councils   The ECS just described is voluntary, while EWCs pertain to multinationals alone. However, the Community has just passed similar information and consultation requirements that will cover the generality of employers. Directive 2002/14/EC establishing a general framework for informing and consulting employees in the European Community came into force on 23 March 2002. The directive was initially proposed by the Commission in 1997 but as with the ECS its origins go back much further, and can be traced back to the 1972 Fifth Company Law draft directive and its subsequent iterations (Addison, 2000; Addison and Siebert, 1994, 1991).

The directive is to be implemented within three years. At the discretion of the member state, it applies either (a) to undertakings with at least 50 employees in any one member state, or (b) to establishments employing at least 20 employees in any one member state. The UK has chosen the former option, and has also negotiated transitional provisions. Specifically, the UK is permitted in the first instance to restrict the application of the directive until March 2007 to businesses with 150 or more employee and then, for a further year, to businesses with at least 100 employees.

The directive leaves the precise form of mechanism to the member state but requires that employers inform employees about the undertaking's economic situation, and consult them on employment prospects (including threats to employment and anticipatory measures to deal with them) as well as on decisions likely to lead to substantial changes in work organization or contractual relations. Information and consultation provision has to be with 'employee representatives', but these can be defined according to national law and practice. Employers and employees can negotiate procedures for informing and consulting employees that differ from those set out in the directive so long as existing agreements on information and consultation meet their obligations. Finally, the Commission will oversee operation of the directive by March 2007 again with a view to proposing any 'necessary amendments'.

Trade unions have generally been supportive of the directive, although the UK government has been more cautious. For the unions, the directive opens up the possibility of easier organizing, using the works council as a vehicle.[33] More directly, the directive will raise UK employment standards. In the words of one prominent union general-secretary, it will no longer be 'cheaper and easier to sack workers in the UK' (Lyons, 2002, p. 15).[34] In fact, the switch to a broad, permanent and statutory system of workplace representation in the UK should have far-reaching consequences for the pattern of trade unionism. Unions may well become more powerful in wage- and standard-setting centrally along corporatist lines, even if developments at workplace level are less obvious. (Thus, a short-term fillip to membership from employee involvement legislation might not be sustainable longer term.)

The EU Charter of Fundamental Rights   We conclude this review of specific instruments with brief commentary on the little-known EU Charter of Fundamental Rights of September 2000 (for an accessible review of which, see EIRR, 2000c). From our perspective the key features of the Charter are the solidarity clauses of Articles 27 and 28. The former states that 'workers or their representatives must, at the appropriate levels, be guaranteed information and consultation in good time and under the conditions provided for by Community law and national laws and practices'. The latter provides that 'workers and employers, or their respective organizations, have, in accordance with Community law and national laws and practices, the right to negotiate and conclude collective agreements at the appropriate levels and, in cases of conflict, to take collective action to defend their interests, including strike action'.

In both cases, interest has centred on the substitution of the term 'at the appropriate levels' for the 'at all levels' contained in the interim draft. The changes in question, since they do not guarantee more than what already exists under national law – together with the status of the Charter as a non-binding declaration rather than an element of the new Treaty of Nice – are widely viewed as a defeat for unions (e.g. Hendy, 2001). The role of the UK government in spearheading opposition to the Charter is notable – on the grounds that its package of economic and social rights conflicted with the needs of the largely deregulated British labour market. But the Charter is best viewed as a starting rather than end point. As the experience with the 1989 Social Charter demonstrates, non-binding instruments can be used to justify all manner of subsequent interventions.

A summing up   The fact that the UK is now fully obliged to transpose EU directives into national law means that the influence of Europe will increase, even if New Labour will likely seek to weaken their impact. As in the past, the main effect will be on legal regulation of the employment contract rather than on unionism per se (see Addison and Siebert, 1994, 1991; Addison, 2001). Although the emphasis on labour conditions and standards will not diminish, the international dimension seems set to increase in importance and this carries domestic implications for freedom of association and recognition of the right to collective bargaining (see European Commission, 2001a). In addition, the Commission will focus on the consequences of industrial restructuring, one important aspect of which will cover the social responsibilities of companies (European Commission, 2001b). Employee involvement measures complementing those described above are, then, in the offing and these may be expected to further strengthen union influence, if not necessarily at the workplace.

The EU social policy agenda (European Commission, 2000) is an active one, and to faciliate its passage the Commission places particular emphasis on the value of social partner negotiations in 'modernizing and improving employment relations', inter al. To be sure, the partners sometimes refuse to play ball – as in the case of the latest directive on national systems for informing and consulting workers – but the process of social dialogue is ever widening in scope. While the emergence of European collective bargaining may be a long way off, the sustainability of the independence of British collective bargaining procedures seems under greater pressure than ever.

5.   Conclusions

The present chapter has indicated that laws do matter. The aggressive reforms of Mrs Thatcher seem to have reduced union bargaining power, membership, and coverage. But the laws were part of a wider deregulatory agenda that sought tax reduction, denationalization, pension privatization, changes in macroeconomic management, the excision of wage floors and other props to collective bargaining, the abandonment of exchange controls, and a modicum of welfare reform. So contextualized, the union reforms seem to have worked. As cases in point we identified unambiguous improvements in the productivity levels, productivity growth rates, and profitability of union establishments vis-à-vis their non-union counterparts as well as a marked improvement in the nation's aggregate economic growth relative to Germany and France. Not surprisingly, the gains were not recorded overnight. And to be sure there was a downside in the form of widened earnings inequality; the other side of the coin being a faster growth in income. Interestingly, our analysis revealed that the facts of union decline may have contributed rather little to the former development.

That was then and New Labour is now. A case can be made that Mr Blair's domestic agenda has not badly rocked the Thatcher boat, despite some scary initial estimates of the cost of *Fairness at Work*. Admittedly, even if Mr Blair had sought to restore union immunities and set the legislative clock back to 1975, the scope for British unions to influence/dictate events is smaller today than heretofore. As Machin (2000, p. 643) has argued: 'the increasingly powerful "new economy" seems to offer little role or place for trade unions'. But these factors may apply with much less force to the EU as a whole, where there is scope for pan-European (even global) rule making. Indeed, we have conjectured that Mr Blair's acceptance of the Social Chapter will do more to revive British unionism than any item of his domestic agenda. We also incline to the view that he did not fully anticipate the consequences. And there is a precedent here: some two decades earlier Margaret Thatcher accepted an extension of qualified majority voting in the Council of Ministers in return for speedier achievement of *economic* union without fully understanding the consequences for *social* union. Be that as it may, the next issue is whether British unionism is a changed animal, so that the consequences of high density today are anyway very different from yesteryear. Some observers are of the opinion that there has been a sea change and thus see much to commend the greater degree of employee involvement deriving not only from the EU legislation that we have documented but also from New Labour's avowed partnership approach (see Department of Trade and Industry, 2002; Chapter 5 by Metcalf in of this volume). Since research has thus far inadequately informed us as to the efficacy of high performance workplaces and ambitious systems of worker involvement (organic or otherwise), we can at least conclude that these are in fact exciting times for the economic analysis of unions in general and British unions in particular.

Notes

1. This subsection and the next draw on the paper 'Union Security in Britain' (Addison and Siebert, 1998), published in the *Journal of Labor Research*. The authors are indebted to the Journal's editor, James T. Bennett, for permission to use much of this material.
2. Until 1971 unions were protected from common law actions based on restraint of trade through statutory immunities granted under the 1906 Trade Disputes Act (on the immunities system, see Deakin and Morris, 1995, pp. 758ff.) Thus, unions were exempted from all liability in tort and union organizers were protected from certain such liabilities when acting in contemplation or furtherance of a trade dispute. Striking workers for their part

enjoyed no such immunity. In 1971, under the Industrial Relations Act, a Conservative administration offered unions legal rights – including union recognition – rather than immunities in exchange for stricter control of strikes. The legislation attempted to impose a US-style industrial relations framework, with a labour court, a mechanism for recognizing unions which could then form 'agency shops' similar to those permitted by the Taft–Hartley Act of 1947, a set of 'unfair labour practices', including unfair dismissal (for the first time in British law), and legally enforceable collective agreements. The measure was unsuccessful, largely because the Trades Union Congress (TUC) discouraged unions from registering under the Act – although the concept of 'unfair dismissal' remained and has indeed been tightened over the years.

3. Nearly 400 claims a year were being made by unions under the legislation in the late 1970s (ACAS, 1981, Table 10).

4. A further piece of legislation, the 1989 Employment Act, lifted restrictions on the working time of women and young workers, exempted small firms from some employment law, and limited the right to time off with pay for trade union duties.

5. The Fair Wages Resolution dated from 1909. It required all government contractors to pay rates of wages and observe hours of work that were not less favourable than those 'commonly recognised by employers' or those 'which in practice prevail' – which in practice came to mean union rates.

6. Some stiff financial penalties were imposed. Examples include a £650 000 fine on the National Graphical Association in 1984 and the sequestration of £707 000 of the assets of the National Union of Mineworkers (Marsden, 1985, p. 157).

7. Two changes in the *structure* of bargaining have accompanied the decline in union density and coverage. The first is an increasing decentralization or fragmentation of collective bargaining (see Brown et al., 2000; Millward et al., 2000). Enterprise-based bargaining at either company or establishment level has come to dominate industry-level agreements. In those workplaces where collective bargaining was the principal method of pay determination, multi-employer agreements were in the minority by 1998 (46 per cent versus 69 per cent in 1984). But, as we have seen, a clear minority of workers now have their pay set by collective bargaining. In 1998 around 15 per cent of all employees had their pay fixed by collective agreements with more than one employer as compared with the 20 per cent who had their wages determined by collective bargaining at enterprise level (7 per cent at plant level and 13 per cent at some higher level in the organization). The difference is most pronounced in the private sector, where just 4 per cent of employees now have their pay set by collective agreements involving more than one employer.

   The second structural change is a decline in multi-unionism (see, for example, Bryson and Wilkinson, 2002). Negotiations with separate unions or groups of unions are becoming a thing of the past in the private sector. In 1998 of the 21 per cent of private sector workplaces recognizing at least one union for pay bargaining, a little over one-quarter involved multiple unions and of these two-fifths involved separate negotiations. Overall, then, just 2 per cent of all private sector workplaces engaged in separate bargaining with multiple unions or groups thereof.

8. Manning (1993) argues that the requirement for pre-strike ballots – introduced under the 1984 Trade Union Act (see Table 12.1) – has led to a decline in union influence over employment. In multi-plant undertakings, unions could in earlier times keep open unprofitable plants by threatening to strike profitable ones. Requiring unions to ballot members destroys the credibility of this threat because workers whose jobs are not in jeopardy are unlikely to vote for a strike.

9. It will be recalled that collective voice can provide a mechanism for overcoming many of the public goods aspects of the workplace. By aggregating worker preferences, unions can thereby enable firms to choose a more efficient mix of wage and personnel policies. Union voice may also open creative channels of communication with management, and enhance management decision-making. Further, unions that have a say in how worker information is used by management may stimulate the disclosure of pro-productive private information by workers.

10. Interestingly, Bryson (2001) also suggests that strong (weak) unions may be an efficient (inefficient) agent for management as well. Here he is apparently exploiting another public goods dimension of the workplace that arises when there are important complementarities in the production process, even if joint determination of effort does not necessarily imply that the union will be the employer's monitor of the employees.

11. Pencavel (2002) chooses to stress the abandonment of full employment policies.

12. Some corroboration of these results is offered in regressions of levels of and changes in output and employment on (one of) the reputation indices over the interval 1970–95.

13. There is also a union coverage question in both surveys, but the questions are somewhat different. In the GHS the question is: 'Is there a trade union or staff association where you work, which people in your type of job can join if they want to?' In the LFS the question is simply: 'At your place of work, are there unions, staff associations, or groups of unions?'

14. The prediction equation is based on Card's specification (2001, p. 303), and includes education years, dummies for colour, marital status and (4) regions, linear, quadratic and cubed experience, and interactions of five levels of education with linear and quadratic experience. It is fitted to non-union workers only, and then used to assign union and non-union workers into ten equally-sized groups.

15. We follow Card (2001) here. An alternative measure is possible; for example, Gosling and Lemieux (2001, p. 18) compare 1998 with 1983 by computing $\Delta'_1 = V - V^*$ for 1998 given the 1983 level of unionization. The result of this calculation is shown in the Memo item of Table 12.4. This measure holds constant changes in union variance and wage gaps over the period, which seems arbitrary (see also Machin, 1997, p. 652 for a use of this method).

16. Card, Lemieux and Riddell in Chapter 8 attribute somewhat greater impact to declining unionization in the UK than do we. But they, too, find that allowing for changes in the structure of unionization across skill groups greatly reduces this impact.

17. But see Gosling and Lemieux (2001) on the difficulties of time-series union analysis for the UK.

18. In 1984, the Conservative government ended the right to trade union membership at GCHQ, arguing that it conflicted with national security interests – there had been a strike at the centre in 1981, and 14 workers were duly dismissed for refusing to give up their membership.

19. Gosling and Lemieux (2001, Table 3) estimate that the minimum wage, applied to the 1998 distribution, would have reduced the variance of the distribution by 2 per cent for men, and by 6 per cent for women.

20. Using the ONS central estimate from April 2001 NES and LFS, 29.8 per cent of the workforce aged 18–21 years fell below the adult NMW of £4.10.

21. Also, subject to agreement, unions can extend the validity of industrial action ballots from four to eight weeks; the resumption of industrial action after its suspension does not require the usual seven days' notice to the employer; and the courts are to have greater discretion in disregarding accidental failures in the organization of ballots for industrial action.

22. Other aspects of the union legislation that merit mention include the banning of employer blacklists of union activists and the dismissal of union activists, as well as the abandonment of the requirement for periodic ballots for the deduction of union dues from the payroll.

23. The principal exception is the entitlement of shop stewards who advise union members about their training ('learning representatives') to paid time off to carry out their duties, including their own training.

24. The increase in the length of paid maternity leave is material – from 18 to 26 weeks – and the increase in statutory pay (paid for the last 20 weeks) is a little under two-thirds, but the employer can recover most of the cost.

25. For a formal statement on New Labour's third way as applied to industrial relations, see Undy (1999).

26. For the union position on partnership at the workplace, see TUC (1999).

27. The five areas where qualified majority voting apply under the ASP are: health and safety, working conditions, information and consultation rights of workers, gender equality, and the integration of persons excluded from the labour market. Unanimity is stipulated in respect of dismissals protection, freedom of association, conditions of employment for third-country nationals resident in the Community, social security provisions, and financial contributions for manpower instruments; but under the December 2000 Treaty of Nice there has been a further extension of qualified majority voting to cover the first three of these areas.

28. The social partners on the employer side are UNICE and CEEP. UNICE is the French acronym for the Union of Industrial and Employers' Confederations of Europe and CEEP is its public sector counterpart, the European Centre of Public Enterprises. The union side is represented through the ETUC or European Trade Union Confederation.

29. See Teulings and Hartog (1998, p. 308) and Chapters 6 and 14 of this volume on the 'costs of decentralization'. A contrary view is offered by Siebert (2002, p. 8), who points out that corporatist countries generate poor employment performance if we link high levels of collective agreement coverage, taxes, and employment protection legislation to corporatism.

30. Thus, among other things, it secured adoption in Council of the posted workers directive as well as updates to earlier Community legislation dealing with collective dismissals and workers' rights in the event of company transfers (see below).

31. Note that the EU working time mandate (Directive 93/104/EC of 23 November 1993) implemented by the new government in October 1998 is not ASP legislation but rather Social Charter legislation, whose treaty basis was unsuccessfully challenged by the UK. The domestic enabling legislation, delayed by the election, is the Working Time Regulations 1998 (SI 1998, No. 1833).

32. Interestingly, while 111 UK-based undertakings are estimated to be affected by the British enabling legislation, almost as many British multinationals appear to have been covered by the earlier EU legislation by virtue of the scale of their operations in continental Europe while the vast majority of non-UK based multinationals with operations in the UK included their British employees (see Addison and Belfield, 2002c).

33. That said, works councils could admittedly conflict with the traditional trade union principle of single channel communication (see Addison et al., 2000, p. 11).

34. Roger Lyons is General-Secretary of Amicus, the UK's second biggest union. The union was formed by the amalgamation of the MSF (Manufacturing, Science and Finance union) and AEEU.

References

ACAS (1981), *Annual Report 1980*, London: Advisory Conciliation and Arbitration Service.

Addison, John T. (2000), 'European Union Labor Market Directives and Initiatives', in Samuel Estreicher (ed.), *Global Competition and the American Employment Landscape As We Enter the 21st Century*, Boston, MA: Kluwer Law International, pp. 691–738.

Addison, John T. (2001), 'Labor Policy in the EU: The New Emphasis on Education and Training under the Treaty of Amsterdam', *Journal of Labor Research*, 23 (2), 303–317.

Addison, John T. and Clive R. Belfield (2001), 'Updating the Determinants of Firm Performance: Estimation using the 1998 WERS', *British Journal of Industrial Relations*, 39 (2), 341–366.

Addison, John T. and Clive R. Belfield (2002a), 'Unions and Establishment Performance: Evidence from the British Workplace Industrial/Employment Relations Surveys', IZA Discussion Paper No. 455, Bonn: Institute for the Study of Labor, March.

Addison, John T. and Clive R. Belfield (2002b), 'Unions and Employment: The One Constant?', IZA Discussion Paper No. 479, Bonn: Institute for the Study of Labor, April.

Addison, John T. and Clive R. Belfield (2002c), 'What Do We Know About the New European Works Councils? Some Preliminary Evidence from Britain', *Scottish Journal of Political Economy*, 49 (4), 1–27.

Addison, John T. and W. Stanley Siebert (1991), 'The Social Charter of the European

Community: Evolution and Controversies', *Industrial and Labor Relations Review*, 44 (4), 597–625.

Addison, John T. and W. Stanley Siebert (1994), 'Recent Developments in Social Policy in the New European Union', *Industrial and Labor Relations Review*, 48 (1), 5–27.

Addison, John T. and W. Stanley Siebert (1998), 'Union Security in Britain', *Journal of Labor Research*, 19 (3), 495–517.

Addison, John T. and W. Stanley Siebert (2001), 'Union Security in Britain with an Addendum on New Labour's Reforms,' in Samuel Estreicher, Harry Katz and Bruce E. Kaufman (eds), *The Internal Governance and Organizational Effectiveness of Labor Unions: Essays in Honor of George Brooks*, New York: Kluwer Law International, pp. 249–278.

Addison, John T., W. Stanley Siebert, Joachim Wagner and Xiangdong Wei (2000), 'Worker Participation and Firm Performance: Evidence from Germany and Britain', *British Journal of Industrial Relations*, 38 (1), 7–48.

Addison, John T., John S. Heywood and Xiangdong Wei (2001), 'Unions and Plant Closings in Britain: New Evidence from the WERS Panel', IZA Discussion Paper No. 352, Bonn: Institute for the Study of Labor, August.

Blanchflower, David G. and Richard B. Freeman (1994), 'Did Mrs Thatcher's Reforms Change British Labour Market Performance?', in Ray Barrell (ed.), *The U.K. Labour Market – Comparative Aspects and Institutional Developments*, Cambridge: Cambridge University Press, pp. 51–92.

Blanchflower, David G., Neil Millward and Andrew J. Oswald (1991), 'Unionism and Employment Behaviour', *Economic Journal*, 101 (407), 815–834.

Booth, Alison L. and Andrew McCulloch (1999), 'Redundancy Pay, Unions and Employment', *Manchester School*, 67 (3), 346–366.

Brown, William (2000), 'Putting Partnership into Practice in Britain', *British Journal of Industrial Relations*, 38 (2), 299–316.

Brown, William A., Simon Deakin and Paul Ryan (1997), 'The Effects of British Industrial Relations Legislation', *National Institute Economic Review*, 161, 69–83.

Brown, William, Simon Deakin, David Nash and Sarah Oxenbridge (2000), 'The Employment Contract: From Collective Procedures to Individual Rights,' *British Journal of Industrial Relations*, 38 (4), 611–629.

Bryson, Alex (2001), 'Unions and Workplace Closure in Britain, 1990–98', unpublished paper, London: Policy Studies Institute, October.

Bryson, Alex (2002), 'The Union Membership Premium: An Analysis Using Propensity Score Matching', unpublished paper, London: Policy Studies Institute, January.

Bryson, Alex and David Wilkinson (2002), 'Collective Bargaining and Workplace Performance: An Investigation Using the Workplace Employee Relations Survey 1998', Employee Relations Research Series No. 12, London: Department of Trade and Industry.

Card, David (2001), 'The Effect of Unions on Wage Inequality in the U.S. Labor Market', *Industrial and Labor Relations Review*, 54 (2), 296–315.

Card, David and Richard B. Freeman (2002), 'What Have Two Decades of British Economic Reform Delivered?', in Richard Blundell, David Card and Richard B. Freeman (eds), *Seeking a Premier League Economy*, Chicago: University of Chicago Press for NBER.

Conyon, Martin J. and Richard B. Freeman (2001), 'Shared Modes of Compensation and Firm Performance: U.K. Evidence', NBER Working Paper 8448, Cambridge, MA: National Bureau of Economic Research, August.

Coutts, Ken, Roger Tarling, Terry Ward and Frank Wilkinson (1981), 'The Economic Consequences of Mrs Thatcher,' *Cambridge Journal of Economics*, 5 (1), 81–93.

Cully, Mark, Stephen Woodland, Andrew O'Reilly and Gill Dix (1999), *Britain at Work: As Depicted by the 1998 Workplace Employment Relations Survey*, London: Routledge.

Davies, Paul and Mark Freedland (1993), *Labour Legislation and Public Policy*, Oxford: Clarendon Press.

Deakin, Simon and Gillian S. Morris (1995), *Labour Law*, London: Butterworths.

Department of Trade and Industry (1998), *Fairness at Work*, London: HMSO, Cm 3968, May.

Department of Trade and Industry (1999), *Implementation of the Regulations on European Works Councils – Regulatory Impact Assessment*, London: DTI.

Department of Trade and Industry (2001a), *Routes to Resolution: Improving Dispute Resolution in Britain*, London: DTI.

Department of Trade and Industry (2001b), *The Government Response*, London: DTI.

Department of Trade and Industry (2002), 'High Performance Workplaces – the Role of Employee Involvement in a Modern Economy', Discussion Paper, London: DTI, July.

Disney, Richard, Amanda Gosling and Stephen Machin (1995), 'British Unions in Decline: Determinants of the 1980s Fall in Union Recognition', *Industrial and Labor Relations Review*, 48 (3), 403–419.

Donovan Commission (1968), *Royal Commission on Trade Unions and Employers' Associations*, Cmnd. 3623, London: HMSO.

Dunn, Stephen and David Metcalf (1996), 'Trade Union Law Since 1979', in Ian Beardwell (ed.), *Contemporary Industrial Relations: A Critical Analysis*, Oxford: Oxford University Press, pp. 66–98.

EIRR (2000a), 'European Works Councils Update', *European Industrial Relations Review*, 316, 20–22.

EIRR (2000b), 'Commission Issues EWCs Report', *European Industrial Relations Review*, 317, 19–22.

EIRR (2000c), 'Draft EU Charter of Fundamental Rights Agreed', *European Industrial Relations Review*, 322, 14–19.

EIRR (2001), 'Union Recognition Increasing', *European Industrial Relations Review*, 327, 24–27.

Employment Department (1995), 'Labour Disputes in 1994', *Employment Gazette*, 103 (7), 279–289.

European Commission (2000), 'Communication from the Commission to the Council, the European Parliament, the Economic and Social Committee and the Committee of the Regions – Social Policy Agenda', COM (2000) 379 final, Brussels: Commission of the European Communities.

European Commission (2001a), 'Communication from the Commission to the Council, The European Parliament and the Economic and Social Committee – Promoting Core Labour Standards and Improving Social Governance in the Context of Globalisation', COM (2001) 416 final. Brussels: Commission of the European Communities, 18 July 2001.

European Commission (2001b), 'Promoting a European Framework for Corporate Social Responsibility – Green Paper', Luxembourg: Office for Official Publications for the European Communities.

Fernie, Sue and David Metcalf (1995), 'Participation, Contingent Pay, Representation and Workplace Performance: Evidence from Great Britain', *British Journal of Industrial Relations*, 33 (3), 379–415.

Freeman, Richard B. (1980), 'Unionism and the Dispersion of Wages', *Industrial and Labor Relations Review*, 34 (1), 3–23.

Freeman, Richard B. and Jeffrey Pelletier (1990), 'The Impact of Industrial Relations Legislation on British Union Density', *British Journal of Industrial Relations*, 28 (2), 141–164.

Gosling, Amanda and Thomas Lemieux (2001), 'Labor Market Reforms and Changes in Wage Inequality in the United Kingdom and the United States', NBER Working Paper 8413, Cambridge, MA: National Bureau of Economic Research (August).

Gosling, Amanda, Stephen Machin and Costas Meghir (2000), 'The Changing Distribution of Male Wages in the U.K.', *Review of Economic Studies*, 67 (4), 635–666.

Gregg, Paul, Stephen Machin and David Metcalf (1993), 'Signals and Cycles? Productivity Growth and Changes in Union Status in British Companies, 1984–9', *Economic Journal*, 103 (419), 894–907.

Hendy, John (1993), *A Law Unto Themselves: Conservative Employment Laws*, London: Institute of Employment Rights.

Hendy, John (2001), *Union Rights... And Wrongs: The Reform of Britain's Anti-Union Laws*, London: Institute of Employment Rights.

Hirsch, Barry T. and John T. Addison (1986), *The Economic Analysis of Unions – New Approaches and Evidence*, London and Boston, MA: Allen & Unwin.

IRS (Industrial Relations Services) (1999), 'Now We Are Two,' *Employment Trends*, 679, 2–24.

Labour Research Department (1999), 'Minimum Wage Becomes A Reality', *Labour Research*, 88 (4), 10–12.

Labour Research Department (2001), 'Has New Labour Satisfied Unions?', *Labour Research*, 90 (6), 12–14.

Lanot, Guy and Ian Walker (1998), 'The Union/Nonunion Wage Differential: An Application of Semi-Parametric Methods', *Journal of Econometrics*, 84 (2), 327–349.

Low Pay Commission (2001), *The National Minimum Wage: Making a Difference*, Third Report, London: Low Pay Commission.

Lyons, Roger (2002), 'Partners in Productivity', *Financial Times*, 30 July, p. 15.

Machin, Stephen (1991), 'The Productivity Effects of Unionism and Firm Size in British Engineering Firms', *Economica*, 58 (232), 479–490.

Machin, Stephen (1995), 'Plant Closures and Unionization in British Establishments', *British Journal of Industrial Relations*, 33 (1), 55–68.

Machin, Stephen (1997), 'The Decline of Labour Market Institutions and the Rise in Wage Inequality in Britain', *European Economic Review*, 41 (3–5), 647–657.

Machin, Stephen (2000), 'Union Decline in Britain', *British Journal of Industrial Relations*, 38 (4), 631–645.

Machin, Stephen (2001), 'Does It Still Pay to be in or to Join a Union', unpublished paper, Department of Economics, University College London.

Machin, Stephen, Alan Manning and Lupia Rahman (2002), 'Where the Minimum Wage Bites Hard: The Introduction of the UK National Minimum Wage to a Low Wage Sector', unpublished paper, Department of Economics, University College London.

Machin, Stephen and Mark Stewart (1996), 'Trade Unions and Financial Performance', *Oxford Economic Papers*, 48 (2), 213–241.

Machin, Stephen and Sushil Wadhwani (1991), 'The Effects of Unions on Organisational Change and Employment', *Economic Journal*, 101 (407), 835–854.

Manning, Alan (1993), 'Pre-Strike Ballots and Wage-Employment Bargaining', *Oxford Economic Papers*, 45 (3), 422–439.

Marsden, David (1985), 'Chronicle – Industrial Relations in the UK, August–November 1984', *British Journal of Industrial Relations*, 23 (1),139–158.

McKay, Sonia (1996), *The Law on Industrial Action Under the Conservatives*. London: Institute of Employment Rights.

Menezes-Filho, Naercio (1997), 'Unions and Profitability over the 1980s: Some Evidence on Union–Firm Bargaining in the United Kingdom', *Economic Journal*, 107 (442), 651–670.

Metcalf, David (1993), 'Industrial Relations and Economic Performance', *British Journal of Industrial Relations*, 31 (2), 255–283.

Millward, Neil, David Smart and William R. Hawes (1992), *Workplace Industrial Relations in Transition*, Aldershot: Dartmouth.

Millward, Neil, Alex Bryson and John Forth (2000), *All Change At Work?*, London: Routledge.

Minford, Patrick and Andrew Haldenby (1999), 'The Price of Fairness – The Cost of the Proposed Labour Market Reforms,' London: Centre for Policy Studies, June.

Moreton, David (1999), 'A Model of Labour Productivity and Union Density in British Private Sector Unionized Establishments', *Oxford Economic Papers*, 51 (2), 322–344.

ONS (2001), 'Labour Disputes in 2000', *Labour Market Trends*, 109 (6), 301–314.

ONS (2002), Measuring Low Pay, London: Office of National Statistics website http://www.statistics.gov.uk/themes/labour_market/pay_and_earnings/ measuring_low_pay.asp.

Oulton, Nicholas (1990), 'Labour Productivity in U.K. Manufacturing in the 1970s and the 1980s', *National Institute Economic Review*, 132, 71–91.

Pencavel, John H. (2002), 'The Surprising Retreat of Union Britain,' in Richard Blundell, David Card and Richard B. Freeman (eds), *Seeking a Premier League Economy*, Chicago: University of Chicago Press for NBER.

Schmitt, John (1995), 'The Changing Structure of Male Earnings in Britain, 1974–1988', in Richard B. Freeman and Lawrence F. Katz (eds), *Differences and Changes in Wage Structures*, Chicago: University of Chicago Press, pp. 177–204.

Siebert, W. Stanley (2002), 'Notes on Labour Market Flexibility', unpublished paper, Department of Commerce, Birmingham University.

Siebert, W. Stanley and John T. Addison (1981), 'Are Strikes Accidental?', *Economic Journal*, 91 (362), 389–404.

Smith, Paul and Gary Morton (2001), 'New Labour's Reform of Britain's Employment Law: The Devil is not only in the Detail but in the Values and Policy Too', *British Journal of Industrial Relations*, 39 (1), 119–138.

Stewart, Mark (1987), 'Collective Bargaining Agreements, Closed Shops and Relative Pay', *Economic Journal*, 97 (385), 140–156.

Stewart, Mark (1995), 'Union Wage Differentials in an Era of Declining Unionisation', *Oxford Bulletin of Economics and Statistics*, 57 (2), 143–166.

Stewart, Mark (2001), 'The Impact of the Introduction of the UK Minimum Wage on the Employment Probabilities of Low Wage Workers', unpublished paper, Department of Economics, University of Warwick.

Studdard, Nigel and James Jenkins (2001), 'Measuring Low Pay Using the New Earnings Survey and the Labour Force Survey', *Labour Market Trends*, 109 (1), 55–66.

Teulings, Coen and Joop Hartog (1998), *Corporatism or Competition? Labour Contracts, Institutions, and Wage Structures in International Comparison*, Cambridge: Cambridge University Press.

TUC (1999), *Partners for Progress: New Unionism at the Workplace*, London: Trades Union Congress, October.

TUC (2000), *Trade Union Trends: Focus on Recognition*, London: Trades Union Congress, January.

TUC (2001), *Trade Union Trends: Focus on Recognition*, London: Trades Union Congress, January.

Undy, Roger (1999), 'New Labour's "Industrial Relations Settlement": the Third Way', *British Journal of Industrial Relations*, 37 (2), 315–336.

Wood, Stephen and John Godard (1999), 'The Statutory Union Recognition Procedure in the Employment Relations Bill: A Comparative Analysis', *British Journal of Industrial Relations*, 37 (2), 203–244.

13 Europeanization of collective bargaining
Dieter Sadowski, Oliver Ludewig and Florian Turk

1. Europeanization of industrial relations: fact or fantasy?

What is, if any, the impact of EU-European integration on national and supranational actors, legal arrangements and policy processes in the realm of collective bargaining? We use a broad concept of collective bargaining to identify possible European dynamics, embracing all sorts of bipartite or tripartite cooperation and concertation on labour problems, involving both sides of industry and perhaps governmental authorities that are aimed at either resolutions, the preparation and implementation of policies, or binding collective agreements. We ask how collective actors – employers, employees and their respective representatives – react to increasing economic integration. Do they react in different national contexts differently? How do the social partners handle the 'twin pressure of decentralization and internationalization' (Waddington, 2001)? Can we observe a change in the nature of negotiation issues, for example, a change from substantive to procedural issues or from quantitative to qualitative issues? Who is negotiating, and has the level of negotiations changed in terms of European, multi-employer, single-employer plant-level bargaining? Are the national industrial relations in Europe about to be absorbed into supranational industrial relations? Or is the process of Europeanization stalled somewhere between intergovernmentalism and supranational institution building?

Many observers, be they Euro-pessimists or Euro-optimists, imagine European industrial relations only as supranational centralized industrial relations (see Keller and Bansbach, 2001; Keller, 1995; Streeck, 1996, 1994, 1993). But that is not at all compelling. Other developments would also rightly be coined 'European'; for example, a process of convergence of the European national systems, formation of a European supranational collective bargaining system, conclusion of new tripartite social pacts at the national level, the conclusion of new bipartite intersectoral agreements, unilateral initiatives by national social partner organizations aimed at cross-border coordination of collective bargaining or pan-European company bargaining within multinational companies as a reaction towards European integration. Essentially neglecting the conceivable impact of bargaining structures on macroeconomic performance (see Burda, 1999;

Dølvik, 2000), we concentrate on the micro-dynamics of these different processes of Europeanization. These processes may overlap each other, and they may involve spontaneous or government driven developments in various intensities. Their sequence and relative force in our view depend on the interests and the resources available to the three main actors in the European policy arena of industrial relations: the employees, the employers and the governmental institutions. We use the idea of an *optimal collective bargaining area* to analyse the different actors' engagement in a European collective bargaining area or areas. In particular, we seek to answer to the question of why even the extant, admittedly limited authority of the social partners to regulate labour issues is not fully utilized. While resistance on the employers' side is often thought to account for the infant state of European collective bargaining, we also ask from a club-theoretic perspective whether national unions can be expected to have a strong interest in delegating bargaining authority to supranational bodies.

Our analysis proceeds in three steps. In section 2, we give an overview of what has happened in European industrial relations to date. Section 3 outlines the concept of optimal collective bargaining areas that is then applied in section 4 to explain the behaviour of the main actors and to understand their interests and intentions. Section 5 contains our conclusions.

2.   The history of European industrial relations and labour policy: Spontaneous versus driven institution building

In the history of European industrial relations four periods can be distinguished, wherein active periods of Europeanization take turns with rather passive ones. The first period, 1957 to 1972, sees the foundation of the European Economic Union and first approaches and proposals for the establishment of uniform European social policies. The second period, 1972 to 1980, is dominated by the 1974 Social Action Programme, which could serve as a legal basis for subsequent collective bargaining initiatives. Influenced by Prime Minister Thatcher, the years 1980 to 1986 turned out to be a period of deregulation. Many proposals for directives failed to obtain approval in the European Council. With the Single European Act in 1986, qualified majority voting in the European Council was introduced, and in 1989 the Maastricht Treaty provided the social partners to some extent with the means for hard law making.[1] Thus we shall concentrate on the post-Maastricht period.

The voluntary social dialogue of the pre-Maastricht period – beginning in the early 1970s – generated at the intersectoral or interprofessional level joint opinions and declarations (Keller and Bansbach, 2001). The so-called Val Duchesse dialogue, initiated by Jacques Delors, tried to involve the European peak associations of 'management and labour' – mainly the

European Trade Union Confederation (ETUC), the Union of Industrial and Employers' Confederations of Europe (UNICE) and the European Centre for Public Enterprises (CEEP) – in the process of European social policy making. The European Commission aimed for framework agreements as points of reference for national sector and intersectoral bargaining (Keller and Bansbach, 2001; Blanpain, 2000; Falkner, 2000; Kluth, 1998). The Commission even succeeded in introducing a legal framework for binding procedures on the basis of a voluntary agreement signed by the social partners on 31 October 1991, which then became part of the Social Protocol (Keller and Bansbach, 2001), firstly annexed to the Maastricht Treaty and later included in the Amsterdam Treaty (Articles 136–139). These articles provide a procedural framework through which agreements of the social partners could become European directives. The resulting possibility of a process that could be termed 'bargained legislation' (Biagi, 1999) provides the social partner with an instrument to create hard law.

The Maastricht Treaty sometimes appears to mark a watershed at the intersectoral level of the Social Dialogue. The Commission itself comments:

> The entry into force of the new provisions in 1993 launched the cross-industry social dialogue into a new era. The social partners' right to be consulted on proposals in the social field and to opt for agreement-based rather than legislative measures now makes them central players in the European social arena. The 'joint opinions' period has thus gradually given way to the negotiation of European framework agreements. (European Commission, 2000, p. 8; Keller and Bansbach, 2001, p. 422)

To date there are only three voluntary framework agreements concluded: on parental leave (96/34/EC) in 1995, on part-time work (97/38/EC) in 1997 and on fixed-term contracts (1999/70/EC) in 1999, all initiated and pushed by the European Commission. A further negotiation on temporary agency work between ETUC, UNICE/UEAPME (European Association for Craft and SME) and CEEP broke down in May 2001 (EIRO, 2001a).

The low number of agreements is one indicator of the relatively slow progress of European collective bargaining. The directive on the establishment of the European Works Councils (EWCs) clearly illustrates the initiating role of the Commission. After more than 40 pre-Directive EWC-type agreements and several failures (see Figure 13.1 for the three main proposals), the directive was legislated as a result of a Commission's initiative in 1994 (in detail see Lecher et al., 1999; Lamers, 1998; Marginson et al., 1997; Blanpain and Windey, 1994). This new institution might influence the Europeanization of collective bargaining, due to its natural European character. For example, in a recent study Carley (2001) analysed agreements of

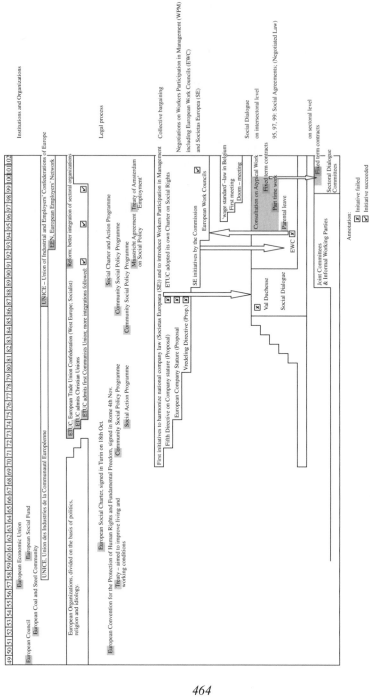

Figure 13.1   Timetable of IR institutional building in the EU

464

EWCs and management in eight multinational companies. He found that this so called Euro-bargaining certainly deals with collective bargaining issues although in most cases core issues such as wages and working time are omitted. The active involvement of EWCs in the protests against restructuring plans of multinational companies, such as in the cases of Renault 1997, ABB Alstom Power 2000 or General Motors 2001, provides another channel of influencing European industrial relations (Carley, 2001; EIRO, 1997).

In the early 1960s, the immediate predecessors of the current sectoral social dialogue evolved. Until the end of 1998, sector dialogues occurred in joint committees and the informal working parties. They had mainly consultative purposes and provided the Commission with information. In 1998, the old structure was replaced by unitary social dialogue committees. According to the Commission, these committees 'shall be consulted on all developments at Community level having social policy implications, and develop and promote the social dialogue at sectoral level' (European Commission, 1998; Keller and Bansbach, 2001, p. 429). In the meantime, sector dialogues led to more than 100 non-binding joint opinions and recommendations (Keller and Bansbach, 2001).

Following the breakdown of the negotiations on temporary agency work at the intersectoral level, the issue was actually negotiated within the framework of the European sectoral social dialogue committee for temporary agency work. On 8 October 2001, Euro-CIETT (the European Committee of the International Confederation of Temporary Work Businesses) and Uni-Europa (the European regional organization of Union Network International), an international organization grouping services and white-collar worker' trade unions, signed a joint declaration on temporary agency work (EIRO, 2001b).

The Commission-driven intersectoral and sectoral social dialogue must be contrasted to more spontaneous initiatives. A famous non-Commission driven approach to a European coordination of collective bargaining at sector level is the initiative of the European Metalworkers Federation (EMF). In the early 1990s the metalworker unions established a network of institutions[2] in order to determine minimum standards, such as the standards on working time and training defined in 1998, and to establish a joint commitment to European guidelines for national collective bargaining with the intention of preventing downward competition (see Schulten, 2002; Schulten, 2001, the former provides also an overview of other European Industry Federations, which is followed by the example of EMF).

Another example for spontaneous cross-border coordination is given by the cooperation between Belgian, Dutch, German, and Luxembourg trade unions, which met in September 1998 in the Dutch town of Doorn. This regional group adopted a joint declaration which emphasized the need for close cross-border coordination of collective bargaining under EU Economic and Monetary Union. Transnational working groups were established, and the parties agreed to exchange information as well as observers regularly, and to meet at annual summit conferences with leading representatives from all major national union organizations from the four countries. In Doorn, the trade unions agreed on a set of joint bargaining guidelines in order to prevent possible downward competition on wages and working conditions. Unions should seek bargaining outcomes at least equivalent to the sum of the development of prices and the increase in labour productivity (EIRO, 1998).

Another example of cross-border collective bargaining is an initiative launched by the German Metalworkers' Union IG Metall, which established a network for collective bargaining in 1997 in order to cooperate with metalworkers' unions of neighbouring countries. Within this network, mutual exchanges of trade union observers, joint information systems and training, as well as common working groups and mutual recognition trade union membership are implemented (for more detail, see Schulten, 2002).

Following the merger of two pharmaceutical companies, the two affected German and French chemical unions agreed to coordinate collective bargaining policy. Other interregional cooperation exists between Austrian, German and Swiss construction workers' unions as well as between some Nordic unions. Schulten (2002, p. 11) points out that interregional cooperation is mostly centred around German trade unions.

These and similar processes also helped to form the collective actors – or social partners in European jargon – themselves. One main actor is ETUC (European Trade Union Confederation), founded in 1973 by 17 national organizations affiliated with the International Confederation of Free Trade Unions (ICFTU). It has since expanded to represent 60 million members (90 per cent of union members within the European Union), who belong to 74 National Trade Union Confederations from 34 European countries and 11 European industry federations. ETUC replaced previous European organizations, divided along political, religious or ideological lines, to represent workers at European level and to foster their interests in the European institutions. It monitors the workers' group in the Economic and Social Committee (ESC) and is represented in the various advisory committees in which the social actors operate (Blanpain, 2000; Ebbinghaus and Visser, 2000).[3] Within ETUC, the delegates of the Executive Committee and Congress come from the affiliated organizations in proportion to their membership, and decisions can only be taken by a two-thirds majority vote.

To maintain its position against its rival organization, the Confédération Européennes des Cadres (CEC), ETUC founded in 1992/93, a joint venture with Euro-Fiet, called Eurocadres, which is a sector organization for white-collar employees. Eurocadres is recognized by the Commission, and it claims to have five million members among managerial and professional staff (ETUC, 1999). Another trade union organization closely affiliated to the ETUC is: EFREP/FERPA (European Federation of Retired and Elderly Persons). In addition, the ETUC coordinates from its headquarters in Brussels the activities of the 39 ITUCs (Interregional Trade Union Councils), which organize trade union cooperation at a cross-border level (Ebbinghaus and Visser, 2000; ETUC, 2002).

ETUC has rather limited financial resources despite a marked improvement following reform in 1991. Since then, the budget increased to nearly 4.4 million euros (or 10 cents per affiliated union member) in 1996 (Dølvik, 1997; Ebbinghaus and Visser, 2000). ETUC is financed by fees from the affiliated union confederations. It has also a relatively small staff – 36 before the 1991 reform, and around 45 since then – compared to constituent national unions and confederations. However, some supporting institutions, such as those for research (ETUI: European Trade Union Institute), training (ETUCO: European Trade Union College and AFETT: European Training of Workers on the Impact of New Technology) and technical standards (TUTB: Trade Union Technical Bureau) are largely funded by the European Commission, as are language and travel support for social dialogue activities (Ebbinghaus and Visser, 2000). Finally, it has to be mentioned that the national unions delegate almost no bargaining authority to the ETUC or the European industry federations (EIFs) notwithstanding their official commitment towards the Europeanization of union action (Turner, 1993; Keller, 1995; Traxler, 1996).

Several EIFs existed at the beginning of the 1990s, of which 14 were affiliated with ETUC (Ebbinghaus and Visser, 2000; Visser and Ebbinghaus, 1992). This total has now shrunk to 11, in part due to mergers among the EIFs (ETUC, 2002). The two largest of these are the European Public Service Unions (EPSU) and the EMF. The different EIFs have varying organizational structures and statutes. Some of them can be regarded as truly European, others organize themselves only at the regional level or as European Committees (Ebbinghaus and Visser, 2000). After the reform of ETUC in 1991 the affiliated EIFs received one third of the delegate votes of the ETUC congress and executive committee. However ETUC support for the EIFS is regarded as half-hearted since the sectoral activities of the latter might undermine the position of the former (Ebbinghaus and Visser, 2000).

With its limited resources, the ETUC attempts to promote transnational and cross-border contact among local union officials and public authorities, but it has to rely on national federations. The resulting Interregional

Trade Union Councils (ITUC) are recognized by ETUC, and have observer status at the ETUC congress since 1991. In recent years ITUCs have also increased and expanded across the EU's eastern border (ETUC, 1999, for an overview see Ebbinghaus and Visser, 2000).

On the employers' side, various associations are active (for an overview see Hornung-Draus, 2001, 1998; Blanpain, 2000; Tyskiewicz, 1991; for the Europeanization of interest representation by specific national business associations, see Wilts 2001). UNICE is the main representative of Europe's employers. Created in 1958, it is the European intersectoral confederation of central national business organizations (industry and employers' organizations), which organizes 34 umbrella business federations from 27 European countries plus six federations as observers. As one of the most prominent social partners at the European level, UNICE is represented in the different European organs (Timmesfeld, 1994; Tyskiewicz, 1991). The sector Euro-associations of business are not incorporated into UNICE, which therefore does not represent any sector interests. In the early 1990s, UNICE initiated an informal European Employers' Network to coordinate employer organizations in order to obviate incoherent social-policy strategies of industry associations (Hornung-Draus, 1998).

Another employers' organization is CEEP, which represents the employers of the public sector. This European organization has both national federations and firms as its members. It was founded by state-owned firms in the common market countries in 1961 because UNICE was unwilling to include them. Given the larger role of politics and state control and more harmonious labour relations, CEEP has shown more willingness through the years to participate in the social dialogue and to agree with the unions than UNICE (Ebbinghaus and Visser, 2000).

A different type of association comprises inter-industry associations, which represent special categories of firms. Predominant among them is UEAPME (European Association for Craft and SME), which was originally formed in 1979 as a result of the amalgamation of various European trade associations and organizations of medium-sized enterprises. Its member organizations currently represent a total of 5 million businesses employing some 20 million people. The organization has a number of committees spanning the major policy areas of the EU. The main stated objectives of UEAPME are to inform its members about developments in European policy, promote joint action on the part of national organizations at European level and ensure that the interests and views of its members are understood and reflected by the EU institutions. In 1998 UNICE and UEAPME signed a cooperation agreement.

A further organization, Eurochambres, represents more than 1500 Chambers of Commerce and Industry, most of them having public law status, and their national organizations in 36 countries, with over 15 million businesses of which 95 per cent are SMEs.

Finally, there are employer organizations that embrace sector Euro-associations such as EuroCommerce (representing retail, wholesale and international trades) or COPA (Committee of Agricultural Organizations in the EC), the associations of agriculture.

How can the European level behaviour of social actors, their doings in some circumstances and their inactivity on other occasions, be explained?

3. Analytical framework: optimal bargaining area

To grasp the logic of the development, we borrow from the economic theory of clubs, pioneered by Tiebout (1956) and Buchanan (1965). We then enrich it with arguments from the theory of optimal currency areas originally developed by Mundell (1961) and McKinnon (1963). It is not only by analogy but also by direct use that we build upon the theory of optimal currency areas. It will serve us in a first step to sketch the macroeconomic frame of any Europeanization of collective bargaining by highlighting its benefits and costs and hence potential tradeoffs.

The fixing of exchange rates within EMU and the euro eliminates one major channel for the adjustment of macroeconomic imbalances. Additionally, fiscal policy cannot serve as an alternative adjustment channel due to the stability pact (Dølvik, 2000; Martin, 1999). In the presence of imbalances, one has therefore to resort to other adjustment mechanisms: to product and factor markets. Mundell pointed out that a high integration of factor markets, including factor mobility and flexible price mechanisms, is crucial for a well functioning currency area. Furthermore, factor markets and especially the labour market have to react in similar ways to monetary impulses across the currency area (ECB, 2002; European Commission, 2002; Burda, 1999).

Even conventional wisdom accepts that there is no common European labour market (Marginson et al., 2001; (Burda, 1999). Persistent barriers such as language, culture, labour law and labour market regulation or policy institutions contribute to low cross-country labour mobility, compared for instance to the states of the USA (Angrist and Kugler, 2002; Heise, 2000; Obstfeld and Peri, 1999; Eichengreen, 1997, 1993; Jovanović, 1997; Decressin and Fatas, 1995). Consequently, the major burden of any adjustment is put on labour costs, including wages, and by implication the burden is put on collective bargaining (European Commission, 2002; Martin, 1999). But how do the labour market institutions cope with such pressures? By developing European-wide institutions and European collective bargaining? Our answer builds upon the analogy between optimal currency areas and optimal bargaining areas (Heise, 2000). The optimal size of a currency area is determined by the tradeoff between gains in the microeconomic efficiency due to reduced transaction costs and the elimination of the exchange rate risk on the one hand, and, on the other hand, the loss of macroeconomic efficiency due to the removal of an adjustment channel and the necessity of pursuing only one monetary policy for all member states. These latter costs depend not only on the differing institutional frameworks in the member countries of the currency union but also on differing preferences with respect to the macroeconomic policy mix. Applying similar efficiency criteria to the question of an optimal area for collective bargaining, one can argue on the one hand that pan-European centralized or coordinated collective bargaining might result in reduced transaction cost. Additionally, a coordinated reaction to the monetary policy of the European Central Bank could reduce adjustment costs resulting from changes in monetary policy (Calmfors et al., 2001; Dølvik, 2000).

On the other hand, there might be increased costs from uniform wage policies for regions that differ widely with respect to labour costs, labour costs increases, GDP per capita or inflation rates and unemployment. The data do indeed vary greatly across Europe: unemployment varies from 2.3 per cent in Luxembourg up to 14 per cent in Spain (Eurostat, 2002), inflation from 0.8 per cent in the United Kingdom up to 3.8 per cent in Luxembourg (Eurostat, 2002) and hourly labour costs in manufacturing industry from €6.2 (Portugal) up to €28.4 in Germany (EIRO, 2002). Changes in remuneration range from −1.3 per cent in Spain up to 3.2 per cent in Sweden (Eurostat, 2002), minimum wages vary from €406 in Spain up to €1290 in Luxembourg (Clare, 2002). (The numbers given here are for the year 2000 except for minimum wages (2001) and hourly wage costs (2000).) Any uniform wage policy across Europe may be expected to hamper the competitiveness of some countries while perhaps improving it for others, creating or aggravating labour market imbalances that would not be mitigated given the low labour migration. Wage uniformity would be likely to nurture macroeconomic imbalances – overheating economies in some countries and increasing unemployment in others.

It is unclear whether a European guideline for wage increases such as a distributive margin – inflation rate plus productivity increase – would secure enough flexibility, because an overall formula does not allow reaction to regional labour market problems, high unemployment or regional exogenous shocks, and is therefore likely to prolong differences in unemployment rates. A more flexible rule would be needed (Dølvik, 2000), but that would also increase the discretionary scope for the national bargaining partners to deviate from the rule in order to improve their own competitive advantage, thereby undermining the rule. This tendency is strong for reasons given below.

Further distributional effects from a European collective bargaining area have to be accounted for, because benefits accruing to one group might be at the expense of others. They might be weighted differently, depending on their incidence, but they will certainly determine the willingness of the single national actors to join European bargaining institutions. The economic theory of clubs is, it seems to us, a promising vehicle for analysing the calculus of different actors to pool resources and/or activities. Clubs are organizations that provide shared collective goods exclusively to their members and spread the costs of these collective goods over these members. Hence everyone who wants to join the club has to calculate the costs and benefits of joining, and the incumbent members have to analyse the marginal cost of admitting another member to the club. Among the costs to be borne are not only the costs of providing the local public good, but also the costs of deviating from some members' preferences in the case of diverging preferences with respect to the public good. We shall scrutinize the cost–benefit calculus of the different actors in the next section in order to derive hypotheses about whether or not these actors have an interest in the Europeanization of collective bargaining, which type of European bargaining they will prefer, and what the resulting collective European bargaining system will look like.

4. The actors' costs and benefits of Europeanizing collective bargaining

4.1. *Employees' organizations as central actor*

In section 2 it was shown that at first sight the European trade union movement is based on a strong and solid organizational infrastructure; a second look, however, revealed that the ETUC and the European industry federations are poorly endowed with financial and personnel resources (Traxler, 1996; Keller, 1995; Turner, 1993). One wonders why the national unions are not able or not willing to organize their European activities in such a way that the scope for bargaining provided by the social protocol is used in order to bring directives on their way?

A club theorist would expect unions to consider not only the gains from economies of scale, reductions in transaction costs and increased union power, before they organize on a pan-European level, but also the costs caused by increased organizational heterogeneity and stronger differences in preferences.

This tradeoff might vary according to different areas of union activity. Besides wage bargaining, unions deal with the collection and distribution of information among members, they have to reconcile differences of interest and articulate the resulting compromises (see Faith and Reid, 1987). If the cost of Europeanizing bargaining, collecting and distributing information, interest mediation and voice activities vary, then the likelihood of

Europeanization will correspondingly vary along these functions. In the following remarks, we therefore try to establish the most important aspects of unions' cost–benefit calculus with respect of Europeanization.

Employees' and unions' incentives for Europeanizing collective bargaining

Race to the bottom   The most prominent reason given in the literature for European collective bargaining or its coordination is the danger of social dumping, wage dumping or a race to the bottom (see, for example, Dølvik, 2000; Ebbinghaus and Visser, 2000; Heise, 2000; Blanpain, 1999; Bordogna, 1996).[4] The absence of a European labour market is to be contrasted with the strongly integrated European product markets. Their integration led to intense competition for market shares, foreign direct investment, and employment among European countries, companies and their workers within the Common Market. This competition is even more severe in the EMU due to the higher market transparency, reduced transaction costs and the elimination of exchange rate risks (Dølvik, 2000). Under these circumstances, high-cost producers will lose market share and employment to low-cost countries and companies as long as the cost differentials are not matched by similar productivity differentials (Streeck, 1997). If employment enters positively in the utility functions of employees and consequently of unions, then employees and unions share to some extent the product market interests of their employers (Traxler, 1996). In this case it can be rational for national unions to negotiate moderate wage increases, namely, below the wage increases in competing countries, and to make concessions on costly working conditions in order to reduce labour costs and increase employment (Martin, 1999). Such a competitive cut in labour costs is equivalent to the classic beggar thy neighbour policy of competitive devaluation under a flexible exchange rate regime (Burda, 1999). As the same behaviour is rational for all unions in the EU, this wage and working condition competition can result in a race to the bottom (see Mahnkopf and Altvater, 1995). The diverse social pacts in the different European countries (see, for example, Hassel, 2001; Fajertag and Pochet, 2000, 1997; Martin, 1999) include elements of such undercutting competition (Hyman, 2002; Dølvik, 2000). It might be most severe within multinational companies (MNC), because management can threaten to relocate production from one European subsidiary to another if employees are not willing to engage in wage concessions (Hyman, 2002; Sisson et al., 2002; Calmfors et al., 2001). In the end, wages and working conditions will have worsened in most or all countries without improvements in the relative competitive situation (see Mahnkopf and Altvater, 1995). One has to expect not just a race to the bottom, but a rat race to the bottom.

In as much as the renationalization through social pacts and the decentralization through company-orientated collective bargaining are triggered by the integration of the Common Market and the EMU, one can regard both processes as forms of Europeanization (Marginson et al., 2001; Martin, 1999).

To avoid the misery of a downward spiral, unions have to follow a strategic imperative (see for example Calmfors et al., 2001; Martin, 1999; Traxler, 1996): they should protect the working conditions and interests of all workers who are competing with each other in order to prevent undercutting. By forming a union on the European level that aims to maximize the utility of the whole European workforce, the negative spillover from a wage cutting country to the other countries is internalized. As mentioned above, this process might be even stronger within MNCs. Stopping the rat race to the bottom is a strong incentive to coordinate collective bargaining at the European level (Calmfors et al., 2001), but as with all public goods, there might be incentives for national unions to deviate from the agreements of such a European bargaining area to gain competitive advantages. Only if national unions were prepared to establish a pan-European club that ensures the compliance of its member unions, would the negotiation task benefit from Europeanization.

Raising rivals' costs   The labour cost and productivity differentials in Europe are substantial: according to Heise (2000), the country with the highest productivity is three times as productive as the country with the lowest productivity. Similar relations can be observed for labour costs (EIRO, 2002). As mentioned previously, the member unions of ETUC have voting rights within ETUC that reflect their size. The bigger a union is, the more voting rights it has, and in a democratic organization voting rights reflect power. This size effect increases the probability that one national union or a group of unions from different countries with similar productivity can influence to some extent the policy of the European peak organization. In such a case they might be tempted to utilize negotiations to raise the labour costs in other countries. If they were successful, market shares and employment would shift to the countries with the more influential unions. This 'raise rivals' costs' strategy is well established in the analysis of firm behaviour and industry structure (Choi and Yi, 2000; Granitz and Klein, 1996; Brennan, 1988; Salop and Scheffman, 1983). It has important implications for collective bargaining (Haucap et al., 2001; Boockmann, 1999) and bears some similarity to the race to the bottom story. Such a risk would impose high costs of organizational centralization on weaker unions, because they would fear losses in employment. The weaker unions should then refuse European coordination or centralization of collective bargaining and a substantial transfer of power to the supranational organization. In equilibrium one would expect as many bargaining areas as groups of similar productivity exist or in a greater bargaining area only a very small power transfer and/or veto rights for all member unions. Even within the Doorn group, for instance, which can be regarded as the most highly coordinated bargaining area in Europe, there is only an exchange of observers without any voting rights, meaning that there is no power transfer. Such a calculus would lead to Europeanization in terms of regionalization whereby these regions could be parts of states, whole states or cross-border regions.

Some observers conceive of the high wage increases in eastern Germany, orchestrated by West German unions and employer associations during the unification process, partly as a result of such a raising rivals' costs approach (see FT.com, 2002). This development most likely harmed the eastern economy and its employment. Similarly, one can view the demands for worldwide labour standards as an attempt to raise the labour cost of developing countries and to protect the employees in the industrialized countries.

Preference costs   A major task for any European peak organization and an indicator of its capacity to organize interests is the formulation, articulation, and implementation of common positions towards relevant topics (Traxler, 1996). Obviously, the more heterogeneous the preferences and the positions of the employees and unions in Europe are, the harder and the more costly this task will become. These costs comprise not only increased organizational and negotiation costs, but also the important cost that arises insofar as members' preferences deviate from the compromised joint position. Club theory again suggests having as many union clubs as (country) groups of homogenous preferences in Europe (Berglas, 1976; Williams, 1966). These preference groups can differ from the productivity groups mentioned in the previous paragraphs; hence, they add another layer of bargaining areas to Europe, which has regional as well as sectoral dimensions. The size and members of these subgroups may also differ between the different union functions and bargaining issues. In the case that these issues should be resolved by a European peak organization it seems probable that along the differing or even conflicting preferences on diverse issues varying coalitions will emerge, blocking each other and the whole peak organization.

Nobody can reasonably doubt the existence of such differences in preferences among employees and unions across Europe. They are the result of cultural, social and historical factors. Thus, most Dutch and Scandinavian unions are in favour of part-time work, while German unions oppose it, still adhering (more or less) to the ideal of the fully-employed male bread winner (Visser, 1998). To take another example, the member unions of the

EMF could not agree on the banning of Sunday work. The German, Belgian and French unions favoured a ban, whereas the Nordic unions opposed it because their national agreements gave their members the right to work on Sundays (Sisson et al., 2002).

A solution to the problem of preference heterogeneity could be sought in the lowest common denominator. However such agreements would erode the national agreements in countries with higher standards (Baumann et al., 1996), reason enough for unions from countries with high standards not to join a pan-European club.

Information exchange   Even without a transfer of power, there are possible benefits from supranational coordination and consultation from improved information flow and learning. By informing each other of collective bargaining outcomes, working conditions, and employer strategies, national unions become equipped with evidence and examples from other countries that might be useful for national collective bargaining and therefore they might improve their bargaining positions. ETUC, for example, provides its members with information about the collective bargaining outcomes in different countries through an annual report on the coordination of collective bargaining (see, for example, ETUC Executive Committee, 2001). Information exchange is particularly intensive within the Doorn group, probably because the similarity of the economic structure of these countries flags increasing returns to information exchange (Calmfors et al., 2001; Ebbinghaus and Visser, 2000). Such information can also be used to learn from each other's experience by analysing and adopting the collective agreements concluded by the other European unions. For example, using a Dutch agreement as a model, Spanish unions signed a contract with an employers' associations to ease dismissal protection in order to bring more people into permanent instead of fixed-term employment (Visser, 1998). The costs of generating such information is usually higher than the cost of distributing it. Hence, the gains will increase with the constituency that receives the information and, as a consequence, information gathering and distribution should be centralized in any process of Europeanization.

Union officials and their interest   Looking from a public-choice perspective, we assume that union officials are not only motivated by their official goals – improving the lives of the union members – but that they are also pursuing to some extent their own selfish interests: personal income, social prestige, benefits and power. How does this influence their engagement in favour of the Europeanization of collective bargaining? Democratically elected union officials should exert the will of the so-called median voter or they will be voted out. But as elections only come up periodically, and informing about the officials' activities is costly for union members, officials have a discretionary scope to pursue their own interests. This scope grows with union size because of rising information costs and greater spread of benefits. There is no strong incentive to control the officials, and the well-known free-rider problem results (Vaubel, 1986). Within transnational unions, language and cultural differences aggravate these problems. Following this reasoning one should expect that officials, who want to increase their discretionary scope, should support the formation of a pan-European union and the European coordinating of collective bargaining.

However, the same assumptions of rational and selfish officials can be used to derive a contradictory hypothesis. The different means of Europeanization, ranging from the formation of a pan-European union over the foundation of cross-border unions to a close coordination of collective bargaining, imply by definition a substantial transfer of power and social prestige from national unions to the European peak organizations. While this would create few highly attractive positions in the peak organizations, it would also devalue most top jobs as well as the second and third tier positions in the national unions. National officials, likely to lose on average from the Europeanization of their organization, will resist it. The near failure of the merger of five German service sector unions into a single one – Ver.di – could be interpreted in such a fashion. The largest of the five unions, the Public Services, Transport and Traffic Union (ÖTV), almost withdrew from the merger because many medium-level officials opposed it. And it seems that this opposition was triggered by the planned reduction of regional districts from 160 to 110, which would have caused a similar reduction of district officials (EIRO, 2001c, 2000). Similar behaviour would lead to resistance of most types of changes and consequently to resistance to any type of Europeanization.

Although the transfer of power from national unions to the supranational level is rather unlikely because competing bureaucracies in general are not willing to surrender competencies (Alesina et al., 2002; Niskanen, 1971), there have been mergers in several countries. In Austria, for example, the metal workers union merged with the textile union. Similar mergers took place in Germany (Waddington, 2001). Most of these mergers, however, saw a small and weak union disappearing in a dominant one (Waddington, 2000). Such union mergers as a last resort are incentive-compatible even from a public-choice perspective.

Legal and institutional obstacles to the Europeanization of collective bargaining

The Europeanization of collective bargaining is not just a matter of the unions' interests and willingness but also of their capacity to Europeanize collective action and negotiations and the limitations caused by legal and institutional restrictions.

In principle, the unions' ability to act on a European level can be restricted by differences in national legal and institutional frameworks and in organizational structures (Keller, 1995). The diversity of national industrial relations systems has persisted into the present (see Table 13.1; see also Dølvik, 2000; Ferner and Hyman, 1998a). We select a few issues to highlight capacity barriers to Europeanization. Major sources of obstacles for cross-border union mergers or even cooperation are national specificities stemming from differing structures, history, concepts and traditions (European Commission, 2002; Burda, 1999; Taylor, 1999). For example, in countries like Denmark, Finland, Germany or Sweden, there are strong and centralized national or at least sector unions; in other countries, the union movement used to be split along political lines (France, Italy, Portugal, Spain) or religious lines (Belgium and to some extent, the Netherlands); and some unions even have formal affiliations to political parties, such as in Great Britain and to some extent in Ireland (Brugiavini et al., 2001). Some of these competing national unions, like the Portuguese CGTP-IN and UGT or the French CGT and CFDT, have rather antagonistic relationships to each other that hamper European coordination (Daley, 1999; Visser, 1998). And frictions still prevail between communist and non-communist unions across Europe and consequently between communist unions and ETUC (Moreno, 2001). These splits in the labour movement are reflected in the extent of the dominance of a single union federation. Each of the largest confederations in Austria, Germany, Greece, the United Kingdom, and Ireland represent more than 80 per cent of the unionized employees, while in Spain, Italy and France the largest federations represent less than 40 per cent (Visser, 1998). The overall union density, too, varies extremely: from below 10 per cent in France to almost 90 per cent in the Scandinavian countries (Ebbinghaus and Visser, 2000; Table 13.1).

Given these differences in structure, ideology, and organizational strength of the national unions, what are the appropriate coordination partners for sector bargaining in countries with unions diversified according to political and religious denominations? How could a pan-European union reconcile such differences in interests and ideology, if most national unions and union federations are not able to do so (Moreno, 2001; Traxler, 1996)? Again, the theory of optimal bargaining areas tells us that a high heterogeneity of structures, interests and relevant institutions in and among the national states is a major source of costs (see Hallett and Weymark, 2002). Through union mergers and conglomerate unions, the national idiosyncrasies and the resulting costs are substantially increased

Table 13.1 Selected characteristics of IR-systems in the EU – I

Country	Percentage of workers covered by collective agreements, mid-90s[a]	Dominant organizational demarcation line, 1990s[b]	Density (net): active union members as percentage of dependent labour force, 1995[b]	Trade union density (the proportion of those in employment who are union members), 2000[c]	Employers coverage: percentage of employees covered in organized firms, 1990s[b]	Collective bargaining: main level, 1990s[b]	Dominant wage bargaining level in the EU, 2000[c]	Extension of agreements through public law, mid-90s[a]
EU 15				30.4				
Austria	97	–	38.9	39.8	100	Sector	Sectoral level	Significant
Belgium	82	Religion	59.8	69.2	80–90	National/sectoral	Intersectoral level	Significant
Denmark	52	Collar-line	75.9	87.5	90–100	Sector	Intersectoral/sectoral level	Absent
Finland	67	Collar-line	78.8	79.0	60–70	National	Intersectoral level	Limited
France	75	Political	8.6	9.1	30–40	Sector/firm	Company level	Significant
Germany	80	Collar-line	26.5	29.7 (1998)	80–90	Sector	Sectoral level	Limited
Greece	n.a.	n.a.	n.a.	32.5	n.a.	n.a.	Sectoral level	n.a.
Ireland	n.a.	Pol. affil.	44.4	44.5	30–40	National/firm	Intersectoral level	Negligible
Italy	n.a.	Political	32.4	35.4 (1998)	70–80	Sector	Sectoral level	Absent
Luxemburg	n.a.	n.a.	n.a.	50.0 (1998)	n.a.	n.a.	Sectoral/company level	n.a.

Netherlands	79	Collar-line/religion	22.9	27.0	70–80	Sector	Sectoral level	Limited
Portugal	80	Political	31.8	30.0 (1999)	30–40	Sector	Sectoral level	Limited
Spain	67	Political	12.5	15.0	60–70	Sector/firm	Sectoral level	Limited
Sweden	72	Collar-line	87.5	79.0	90–100	Sector	Sectoral level	Absent
UK	35	Pol. affil.	32.0	29.0	20–30	Firm	Company level	Absent
		(Great Britain)	(Great Britain)		(Great Britain)	(Great Britain)		

Sources:

[a] Calmfors et al. (2001)
[b] Brugiavini et al. (2001) and EIRO (2001d)
[c] EIRO (2001d)
[d] EIRO (2002)

(Waddington, 2001; Dølvik, 2000; Ebbinghaus, 1999). Additionally, the internal frictions caused by the mergers consume resources that could be used otherwise for cross-border cooperation.

Another problem arises from the differences in national union power. If there should be some agreement on the European level that is not enforced through European directives, then it must be implemented by the national organizations. Although there would be an agreement on the European level there could be still national employers (or even unions as explained above) opposing it. In such a case the implementation of the agreement hinges on the ability of the national unions to enforce it. In such a case some national unions would not be able to compel these agreements, due to the great differences in power, illustrated by some of the figures in Table 13.1. However, such differences in enforcement could be viewed as means of gaining a competitive advantage that will endanger the whole agreement.

Other obstacles stem from the different legal and institutional bargaining frameworks (Traxler, 1996). In some countries the state is involved in collective bargaining on a regular basis. In others it is explicitly excluded; for example in Germany due to the constitutional principle of *Tarifautonomie*. But even without involvement in bargaining itself, the state can influence the outcome in terms of coverage rate by extending the agreements through public law, such as the German *Allgemeinverbindlicherklärung* (*erga omnes regulation*). This path of influence is absent in Sweden, Denmark, and the UK, yet rather important in Austria, Belgium, and France (Table 13.1; Calmfors et al., 2001 or see the different contributions in Martin and Ross, 1990b).

Another important institutional source of variance between European countries resides in the legal regulation of collective action. The types of industrial action that are allowed or forbidden vary widely between the EU countries. For example, in Denmark, Germany, Italy, and the Netherlands the extent of strikes is restricted by so-called proportionality rules, which require a balance between the final goal, the impact, and the extent of a strike (see Table 13.2; see also Calmfors et al., 2001). In some countries general strikes for political reasons are a legitimate part of the political culture (see Italy or Spain in 2002); in other countries such as Germany political strikes are forbidden in general, and the rule is observed.

There is also considerable variance in Europe with respect to the bargaining level, ranging from multi-employer bargaining on the national level through sector level to single-employer bargaining (Table 13.1; Calmfors et al., 2001). Furthermore, some unions are involved in administering the social security system, such as in Scandinavian countries and to a lesser extent in Germany and France (for an overview, see Brugiavini et al., 2001).

Given these differences, what should a joint strategy look like and how should it be implemented?

Obstacles to joint action also arise from crucial differences in legislation on working conditions, such as working time, health and safety regulation, part-time work, dismissals and to a lesser extent wages. This leaves a rather narrow scope of matters not fixed in one of the countries of the envisaged bargaining area and therefore in principle amenable to pan-European collective bargaining. If the Europeanization of collective bargaining were restricted to only those areas negotiable in all member states, then its scope would be narrow, if not minimal. Belgium serves as an extreme example. The Belgian state intervened 1996 by introducing a wage setting system that limited wage increases to just below the average increases in neighbouring countries. Hence, even the negotiability of wages was largely lost (Ebbinghaus and Visser, 2000).[5]

It is a truism that the upcoming enlargement of the EU will increase the heterogeneity of member states and the resulting obstacles for common European collective bargaining (see Martin and Cristescu-Martin, 2001).

Taking stock in between
Looking at unions in Europe from a club-theorists' perspective, we presented contradictory hypotheses about the interest of national unions in a Europeanization of collective bargaining. We also argued that the institutional framework is hindering the development of a coordinated bargaining strategy. Consequently, no one should expect Europeanization in the sense of a pan-European union emerging to undertake pan-European collective bargaining (for the same conclusions, see Calmfors et al., 2001). It should be clear that this negative prognosis is not so much a result of insufficient European harmonization or a lack of European institutions, as alleged by Euro-sceptics. In their view, whether or not European-wide industrial relations can develop depends upon the ability of the European Union to set an institutional framework based on hard law (see, for example Keller and Bansbach, 2001; Keller, 1995; Streeck, 1996, 1994, 1993). We contradict the hypothesis that unions have a more or less natural interest in the centralization of union activities on the European level with the argument that there are important reasons why they should oppose such centralization. Hence, we view the weak interest of national unions to delegate bargaining authority and resources to European actors as another major factor of the slow progress towards a European coordination of collective bargaining.

As outlined, the lack of interest appears to result from a cost–benefit calculus on the part of national unions. The cost–benefit ratio varies between functions and among European sub-areas. Several European cross-border regions have a more similar structure and more closely related problems

Table 13.2 Selected characteristics of IR-systems in the EU – II

Country	Financial resources[a, b]		Legal framework[d] and legal resources
	Employers' associations	Trade unions	
Austria	n.a.	Membership dues[c]	Conclusion of collective bargaining agreements Works councils Consultation rights
Belgium	n.a.	n.a.	Staff representation
Denmark	n.a.	n.a.	Collective bargaining European works councils Right to take industrial actions
Finland	Membership dues Other	Membership dues Other	Recognition of trade union European works council Right to take industrial action
France	n.a.	Membership dues	Compulsory recognition of trade union Other form of staff representation European works council Right to take industrial action
Germany	Membership dues	Membership dues	Right to join a trade union or an employer's association Collective bargaining agreements Work councils European works councils
Greece	Membership dues	Membership dues	n.a.
Ireland	n.a.	Membership dues	No compulsory recognition of trade union

482

			Recognition of trade union European works councils (EWCs) No right to take industrial action
Italy	Membership dues State Other	Membership dues State Other	
Luxemburg	Membership dues Other	Membership dues Other	Compulsory recognition of trade unions No European works councils
			Right to join a trade union Staff representative committee Works councils
			Employee participation in company management
Netherlands	Membership dues	Membership dues Other	Union recognition Right to take industrial action
Portugal	n.a.	Membership dues	Compulsory recognition of trade union European works councils
Spain	n.a.	Membership dues Other	Compulsory recognition of trade union European works councils
Sweden	n.a.	n.a.	Compulsory recognition of trade union Right to take industrial action
United Kingdom	Membership dues	Membership dues	Compulsory recognition of trade union (England and Wales) European works councils (England and Wales) No right to take industrial action (England and Wales)

Sources:
a EIRO (2001e)
b Own compilation on the basis of the research project 'Survey Concerning the Representativity of Social Partners Organizations'
c Traxler (1998a)
d Mayne/ Malyon (2001)

than the corresponding national states. The substantial number of 39 regional cross-border co-operations among unions in 1998 within ITUCs is therefore no surprise (Ebbinghaus and Visser, 2000). Similarly, the benefits of exchanging information – learning from each other and having better arguments during negotiations – are at least sufficient, while the costs are low. No wonder, then, that the ETUC distributes information about what happens in the different countries among its members.

Similarly, the differences within industries are smaller than in the whole economy. Hence, with coordination at the sectoral level fewer costs should therefore be more probable. European sector organizations in the metals and construction industries have taken steps towards the coordination of wage demands (Ebbinghaus and Visser, 2000; Fajertag, 1999; Kuhlmann, 1999), suggesting the distributive margin mentioned above as guidelines for national bargaining. This probably reflects greater homogeneity and stronger competitive pressure within this industry.

Our analysis and the empirical evidence lead to a rather heterogeneous picture of the Europeanization of collective bargaining. Depending on the field of union activity, the negotiation topics and the industry, almost every outcome – ranging from the centralization on the European level over rationalization and industry or sectoral bargaining to company bargaining – is possible and/or exists in reality.

4.2. *The employers*

Where are the employers positioned in the European policy arena? Why would they or their national associations belong to associations at the European level? How much competence and how many resources will be transferred from national employer organizations to the EU level? Even if EU-level structures are present, are they able to organize and to enact their common interests? And what would this imply for the collective regulation of wages and working conditions at the European level?

In section 2, we presented an overview of employer organizations at the European level and their recent developments in the context of the social dialogue as a response to European integration. A key factor in the development of a European strategy for the representation of business interests can be seen in product-market interests. Evidence is provided by the employers' reaction to the introduction and extension of qualified majority voting for European legislation. It became necessary for employers to coordinate their positions and their lobbying at the European level so as to develop a truly European position with which they could convince a number of governments sufficient to constitute a potential blocking minority of their views. Moreover, a multitude of sector- and sub-sector-specific business organizations (FEBI: Fédérations européenes par branche d'industrie) were created to defend the companies' interests in the different stages of the creation of the Single Market. While the original purpose of the FEBI was directed at purely economic matters subject to European legislation, the social dimension of the Single Market included in the Single European Act of 1987, and especially the development of the social dialogue between employers and trade unions at European level, led to increasing involvement of FEBI in social policy issues. Therefore, it is exceedingly difficult to attribute the observed development of mixed associations to labour market or product market interests. What does the theory explain and predict?

The relatively meagre empirical and theoretical literature on employers' associations generally offers two approaches to understand employer collective action: the first focuses on interest, the second on resources as its main explanatory variable of collective action. Interest-related concepts are based on collective action theories (Olson, 1965), on the status of labour and capital and their interrelationship (Offe and Wiesenthal, 1980) or on organization theories (Schmitter and Streeck, 1981). Resource-related approaches to employer collective action focus on the interaction between external and internal power resources of employers' organizations (van Waarden, 1991) and the tensions between governability and associability (Traxler, 2000, 1999, 1998b). In our view, the need for organization as well as organizability decisively determines the employers' approach to industrial relations. Below, the willingness and capability will be linked to the purposes and functions which associations serve, using a club-theoretic framework. Collective-action problems at association level are related to the economic problems of clubs and club goods: with firms as individuals and the clubs being organizations of organizations, the national peak organizations become clubs of clubs. The European organizations are, then, in some cases associations of associations of clubs.

Rationale of employer representation at the European level and organizability

Purposes of collective employer activity   Collective employer activity has four main purposes: opposition to unionism, control of procedures, taking wages out of competition, and responding to state policies. In pursuit of these objectives, associations perform five main functions. These are: representation of employers in collective bargaining (*labour-market interests*), lobbying, public and media relations, provision of a forum for debate, and provision of specialized services (*product-market interests*). The last element includes information, research and advice, education and training, and individual assistance to individual members with disputes. Business associations may specialize in representing either product-market interests (*pure trade associations*) or labour-market interests (*pure employer organizations*); or they may combine both interests (*mixed associations*) (Traxler, 1998b). In both areas, they act on the one hand as lobbies and rent-seeking cartels; on the other hand, they can facilitate the pursuit of club goods in a number of ways, reducing problems of free-riding and resolving prisoners' dilemmas (Crouch, 1999).

The individual employer has three basic reasons to accept collective agreements, which represent the benefits of centralization. These are a show of strength on the part of the trade unions and/or the state, the hope of deriving actual benefits from such settlements, or a wage increase fostered by the employers' associations due to its potential incentives to raise rivals' costs. Standard wages can be used as a barrier to entry to product markets if producers differ in labour productivity (Haucap et al., 1999). Any hope of benefiting from collective bargaining can hardly be based on the labour market itself due to the structurally asymmetrical power relationship and the resulting advantages of individual settlements to employers. Benefits are more likely to stem from the specific product market interests of groups of firms, which prompt them to opt for collective settlements in the labour market (Traxler, 1996). The classic reason for firms being interested in multi-employer bargaining is to reduce competition on working conditions among employers. A cartel arrangement of this kind covering working conditions thus serves to contain competition between firms in product markets. European collective agreements would therefore have to correspond to product market interests of firms. This is the case if European collective agreements offer comparative advantages in global competition. Additional benefits are the provision of public information goods or the reduction of costs of negotiation (transaction costs). The main costs of centralization are preference costs. Differences in preferences are predominantly related to product-market competition and differences in productivity.

Optimal club size   Given this rationale, what is the optimal club size to coordinate and centralize employer's interests? Competing logics put conflicting demands on an association's structure and size. Two tradeoffs, one between the logic of membership and the logic of influence, the other between preferences costs and the benefits of centralization, determine the organizations' production set and the optimal level of centralization of employers' interests. Their optimal size is reached where the marginal benefits of a supplementary activity or member equates their marginal costs.

While the logic of membership represents the association's need to retain its legitimacy in relation to its constituency, the logic of influence follows the strategic requirements for effective interest policy. In the course of transforming individual member interests into collective goals, employer organizations on the national or European level have to demarcate their representational domain in terms of membership and tasks. They must be able to recruit members and they have to make their members comply with associational goals and collective decision (Traxler, 1998b). Attracting members becomes easier, the more closely the domain is suited to a certain group of employers or the better the club good is tailored to the needs of the club's members. In tension with this logic of membership, the strategic imperative for employers demands control over as many segments of the labour market as are covered by concerted union activities. Otherwise, there is a risk of being played off against one another.

Individual firms have more resources than individual employees and sometimes more even than the European employer federations, to push through their preference. That allows them to short-circuit the federations, if necessary. The reduced incentive for collective action among firms forces employers' federations to adopt more particularistic structures than unions have. As a striking example, there is not one single sectoral European employer federation member of UNICE, which means that UNICE is not in a position to standardize the sector interests of firms. Thus a transfer of competences or substantial additional resources from national employer organizations to the EU level has not matched the extension of EU competence through successive revision of the EU Treaty so far. Compared with the amount of work and number of topics covered, the secretariat of UNICE, with a permanent staff of nearly 35 employees, is extremely small. This is less staff than are employed by its counterpart on the workers' side, the ETUC, or by certain sectoral business federations at the European level (Hornung-Draus, 1998).

The recent reform of UNICE's decision-making procedures is a perfect illustration of the transfer of competence. Concerning negotiations under the Social Chapter, results still have to be adopted by consensus of the affected member federations. For entering into negotiations a potentially even more restrictive rule has been introduced: 80 per cent of votes from affected federations must be in favour of negotiations. Another example is the transfer of competence and resources from the FEBI to the EEN. Its competences are simply in the field of information and consultation, to promote convergence of views and positions and to prevent proliferation or duplication of overlapping agreements. Every member federation retains its full autonomy and the right to make its own final decisions (Hornung-Draus, 1998, p. 229).

Employers' organizability

The Europeanization or centralization of collective bargaining is not just a matter of willingness but also of organizability. The organizability can be restricted by differences in the national legal and institutional frameworks and in organizational structures.

Differences in the national legal and institutional frameworks   The diversity of national industrial relations systems and employers' organization has persisted into the present (Table 13.1). The overall coverage rate of employers' organizations varies widely. In Austria, Denmark and Sweden, 90–100 per cent of the employees are covered in organized firms. Otherwise it varies from below 40 per cent in the UK, France, Ireland, and Portugal to almost 70–80 per cent in Finland, Italy, the Netherlands and Spain. A major and general trait of employer representation is given with organizational overlap, dual or multiple memberships even, as mentioned, with rivalry of associations. Many employers belong to associations with different and sometimes conflicting policies on major aspects of industrial relations. The literature on employer associations assumes that overlapping memberships necessarily lead to disunity and fragmentation among employers and within associations (Plowman, 1978; Windmuller, 1984). The involvement of the FEBI in European social policy involved the risk of duplication, fragmentation and incoherence of the employers' position at the European level, although the national member organizations of the FEBI are generally the sectoral members of UNICE's member organizations.

Differences in organizational structures   The ability to organize is further hampered by the dual structure of business representation at national level, where the chambers of industry and commerce (based in most countries on mandatory membership) and voluntary organizations coexist, sometimes cooperating, sometimes competing. The voluntary business organizations exist as a single system in which product-market and labour-market interests are covered by the same organization. Some of the pertinent examples are the CNPF (Conseil national du patronat français) in France, FEB (Fédération des Enterprises de Belgique) in Belgium and VNO–NCW (Verbond van Nederlandse Ondernemingen–nederlands Christeelijk Werkgeversverbond) in the Netherlands (Hornung-Draus, 2001). Or they exist as a dual system, in which economic and social matters are treated by different sets of organizations. This dual structure of voluntary business representation exists in Germany, where social matters are dealt with by the employers' organizations organized by economic sectors, all of which are affiliated to the BDA (Bundesvereinigung der Deutschen Arbeitgeberverbände), and economic matters by trade organizations like the BDI (Bundesverband der Deutschen Industrie) representing the manufacturing industry, the BDB (Bundesverband Deutscher Banken) representing private banks, etc. Dual representation also exists in other countries, like

Denmark, Sweden, Iceland or Turkey. In all European countries, except Austria, the chambers of industry promote product-market interests and are not responsible for social policy, nor do they act as social partners and negotiate with trade unions. The economic chambers therefore cannot become members of UNICE.

In many countries where there were dual organizational structures at the national level a consolidation took place by way of mergers. Examples include Ireland, where the Federation of Irish Employers (FIE) merged with the Confederation of Irish Industry (CII) to become IBEC (Irish Business and Employers' Confederation), and Finland with a similar merger between the employer and business organizations of the Finnish manufacturing industry. In Norway, the consolidation went even further, including in the merger at the national level not only the old employer and business organizations but also the chamber of commerce and craft. The Netherlands presents a somewhat different case in that there exist two horizontal organizations at national level, representing employers and industrial interests, a largely overlapping membership but with ideological differences: the NCW had an explicitly Christian profile, while the VNO was ideologically neutral. They merged to become the VNO–NCW.

Conclusion To sum up, we can identify an employer rationale to join factor-market related clubs to a certain extent. Primarily, this extent hinges on a rationale based on product market interests and characteristics. Costs and benefits of centralization will vary with firm size and product and factor market structure. A club size corresponding to the European Single Market does not seem to be optimal from this perspective. The conclusion of intersectoral agreements, the cross-border coordination of collective bargaining or pan-European company bargaining within multinationals are more reasonable expectations. This negative prognosis is not so much a result of insufficient European harmonization or a lack of European institutions; rather, it hinges on the costs exceeding the benefits to organize collective bargaining in clubs at supranational level. Otherwise, in sectors where labour is mobile across borders, such as construction, civil aviation or road haulage, there might be an employer interest in taking wages and major conditions out of competition on a cross-border basis.

4.3 Governmental institutions

The third main protagonists in European industrial relations are the national governments and the political institutions at the European Level. Governments and parliaments take very different roles in industrial relations:

1. *The role of regulator* The state regulates the economic, political, social, international and legal environment of industrial relations.
2. *The role of employer* The state in itself is a big employer and decides or negotiates the terms of the work relationship together with the other partners in industrial relations.
3. *The role of the labour process coordinator* Labour process coordination can range from very weak attempts to persuade participation in social contract negotiation to corporatist procedures or authoritative intervention.
4. *The role of conflict resolver* The state can intervene in industrial conflicts by arranging conciliation, mediation and arbitration.

Again applying the economic theory of clubs, European directives to harmonize national legal regimes now reveal the problems of collective action between governments. The European Union is a group of countries deciding together on the provision of certain public goods including labour market issues. However, such common decision mechanisms might be useful, because of spillovers, social goals, and to prevent behaviour which would result in rat races (see section 4.1) or other dilemmas. The countries are heterogeneous either in preferences and/or in economic fundamentals. The tradeoff between the benefits of coordination, centralization and/or deepening integration arising from economies of scale or externalities, and the costs from the loss of policymaking independence, and of increased heterogeneity of preferences due to a greater number of members endogenously determines the size, depth, composition, and scope of the union. Hence, there is a tradeoff between enlargement and deepening of coordination. The total benefits and total costs of the formation of international organizations are a function of the amount of cooperative activity. Each national government is trying to maximize its own net gain, the difference between individual costs and benefits.

Which powers are national governments likely to delegate to international agencies? Why should legislators choose not to decide themselves but to delegate decision-making competences to other actors such as international organizations? Rational actors will be ready to transfer as much competence as maximizes the expected net gains. The task, then, is to identify costs and benefits connected with the relevant alternatives. The arguments in politicians' utility functions are popularity, ideology and income. Following the 'law of the inverse salience' and the 'dirty-work hypothesis' (Vaubel, 1986), the national governments are not likely to give away very important powers, namely policy instruments that have a decisive influence on elections. Rather, they will try to get rid of their unpleasant activities, their dirty work. If delegation of powers can create asymmetry between credit and blame attributed to the politician as a result of the policy decision of the delegated body, then such delegation can be beneficial to the politician. Unpopular policies that need to be enacted are delegated to an international body which forces a country to implement the unpopular policy and which cannot be opposed (the so called scapegoat argument). Delegation can be used as a tool to protect one's policies against reversal, to enhance credible commitment and information, and to reduce decision-making costs. Delegation of powers also involves costs. By delegating decision-making powers, legislators decrease ex ante and ex post their impact and control on the policy. There is always the risk that a delegated body drifts away from the preferred position of the national government. In addition there are coordination costs, reversal costs, monitoring costs and the forgoing of utility as a consequence of reduced rent seeking (Voight and Salzberger, 2002).

On the other hand, if the economic theory of bureaucracy applies, the officials in international agencies try to maximize their power; their demand for additional power and resources is unlimited. It follows that international agencies are willing to take any work they can get. European organizations may develop a momentum of their own. In a positive analysis, one will expect that competing bureaucracies may not be willing to give up responsibilities easily; instead, bureaucracies at different levels of government will compete over the allocation of resources and responsibilities (Niskanen, 1971). Thus, the division of labour is not demand determined, but exclusively supply determined (Vaubel, 1986, p. 36).

The bureaucratic competition may lead to excessive centralization in policy areas in which the supranational bureaucracy has managed to gain prerogatives (Alesina et al., 2001). Hence, one might derive from this that the Commission's bureaucratic interest is the main motivation for its interest in European social dialogues and collective bargaining and an explanation for the pushed institution building we have described in section 2. Otherwise, in comparison to national agencies the power of the European agencies is limited. The role of social policy of the European Union has been limited and remains highly decentralized and national: the national industrial relations systems have retained their redistributive social policies, labour law, and collective bargaining as domains within their commanding jurisdiction with the exception of the instrument of bargained legislation.

At the national level, government involvement in wage bargaining institutions has increased. Governments facing tighter constraints related to monetary integration and increasing public debt levels have turned to new forms of income policy in order to control pay bargaining through social pacts (Hassel, 2001; Fajertag and Pochet, 2000, 1997; Martin, 1999). Moreover, wage bargainers in some countries have explicitly started to take note of wage developments in other countries. In the Netherlands, wage bargainers have been careful to keep wage increases below the going German rates, which has resulted in complaints about a Dutch beggar-thy-neighbour strategy. In Belgium, the reference to wage bargaining in the neighbouring states was even legislated by the government (Ebbinghaus and Visser, 2000). In Sweden, the Edin norm was based on European pay developments. Given the extent to which national policy makers lost economic policy options over the last decade due to financial Europeanization, fiscal constraints and monetary integration, it is likely that governments will search for paths to defend and maybe increase their remaining policy autonomy.

5.   Conclusion and some speculation on the development of European collective bargaining

Within our club-theoretic framework of optimal collective bargaining areas, we put forward several conclusions and predictions regarding the process of the Europeanization of collective bargaining.

First, although the main driving forces of the process – increased market integration and more intense competition – are not unique to Europe but instead a global phenomenon, the European development of collective bargaining will precede the developments elsewhere, because the homogeneity of actor preferences inside the EU is higher both along country lines and along class lines, and the market integration in Europe is more highly developed than in other regions due to the European Single Market and EMU.

Second, Europeanization or internationalization does not compellingly require a supranational standardization of collective bargaining and the transnational unification of social actors. In contrast, to safeguard revenues of the economic integration of product and financial markets, flexible factor markets are necessary, for which reason micro-level social actors should not attempt to centralize factor market-based negotiations at the supranational level. In contrast to the literature, the club logic applies not only for employers, but also for employees and national governments. We recognize not so much a lack of ability but rather a limited willingness of both social partners, employers *and* unions, to arrive at European solutions. There is only one actor with a zeal for predominantly European solutions: the European Commission, which pushes most of the agreements and institutional developments. This is in sharp contrast to the Euro-pessimists' view of a lack of interest by the Commission in regulating social matters.

Third, we expect no pan-European collective bargaining in the foreseeable future (see Calmfors et al., 2001; Burda, 1999). A more probable outcome is a differentiated and fragmented collective bargaining system that is not oriented on European borders. Depending on differences in preferences, cost, structure and union function, different bargaining areas and patterns will emerge. For some purposes, like the coordination of wages, bargaining in cross-border areas and the patterns illustrated above might be the most predominant outcome. The Eastern enlargement of the EU will give even more credence to this argument. For other union tasks, like information sharing, European centralization seems to be more efficient. A special case is within-company bargaining. Although not explicitly analysed in this chapter, all the criteria discussed above apply to it. It can be expected that the employee groups within MNCs are more homogenous than the employees across MNCs. Hence, coordination is cheaper and thus more probable within the MNCs. Consequently, European company bargaining is another tier in the Europeanization of collective bargaining (see, for example, Taylor, 1999; Marginson and Sisson, 1996).

These expectations and appraisals regarding the process of Europeanization of collective bargaining are in deep contrast to both of the two main schools of thought, the Euro-pessimists and the Euro-optimists, corresponding to proponents of soft law and hard law. They anticipate a deeper centralization of industrial relation systems, differing only in the perception of the cause of the time lag between economic and social integration. In the neo-corporatist Euro-pessimistic view, whether or not European-wide industrial relations can develop hinges upon the ability of the European Union to set an institutional framework based on hard law. Keller (1995) and Streeck (1994) criticize this lack of a supranational legislation that would protect institutionally the status of trade unions as Euro-social partners. The contents of soft regulation are rather limited and mainly not binding. In short the major barriers to Europeanization are seen in the lack of European institutions and in the self-restraint of the employer associations. Therefore it is a typically corporatist view to regard the Common Market and the principle of subsidiarity as a programme of deregulation opposing social principles and as a strategy of socio-political laissez-faire (see, for example, Streeck, 1996, 1994, 1993; Altvater and Mahnkopf, 1993). Hence European social relations are held to lie outside the possible outcome of integration. Euro-optimists, on the other hand, see soft law or soft regulation as a more positive development (see, for example, Teague, 2000; Kenner, 1999, 1995). This school of thought identifies a delay on the part of trade unions in organizing their activities at a European level as the main obstacle to European industrial relations. The level and the quality of union moves to integration, it is argued here, lag one or two steps behind the process of political and economic integration. Platzer (1991) in particular, points to the poor infrastructural resources as well as to the lack of authority of the European trade union federations (so too does Cella, 1994). The internationalization of markets and the establishment of trading blocs influence the efficiency and the effectiveness of any nationally restricted union policy. The globalization of competition undermines the joint interest of labour and capital to regulate industrial relations. Instead of using a protective strategy to respond to the new situation, their preferred alternative, the argument recommends that the unions should pursue a strategy of trying to extend collective bargaining to the supranational arena. However for the reasons given above, they might lack the willingness to do so, which would also explain why the appropriate organizational structure is lacking at the EU level.

Both the neo-corporatist and the more optimistic literature assume that trade unions are interested in and internally capable of European-level formation. Granted that there are institutional and organizational barriers and a limited authority of the social partners to regulate labour issues, these approaches do not explain why the extant institutional framework is not fully utilized by the actors and why the unions do not devote more resources to their European peak organizations.

Additionally, a fourth factor should not be neglected. The increased market integration and the resulting competitive pressure may lead to regime competition among the member states. Furthermore, as mentioned above, many countries attempt to improve their position in this regime competition by national social pacts. These social pacts very often include official or more informal elements of wage bargaining and other collective bargaining topics. Hence, one can observe a renationalization of collective bargaining in certain areas.

With the enlargement of the EU, the heterogeneity within it regarding economic fundamentals, the preferences of employees and employers, and the structures and traditions of unions will substantially increase. Consequently, the costs of centralization and coordination of collective bargaining will rise at all levels too. Hence the enlargement will aggravate the problems of the Europeanization of collective bargaining, and another fragmenting factor is added to the process.

In sum, Europeanization of collective bargaining is a combination of partly parallel, partly competing and partly complementing processes of centralization, renationalization, regionalization and decentralization.

Acknowledgement

We have to thank Paul Marginson and Martin Schneider for helpful comments and suggestions. We are also indebted to Claudia Görgen, Ioana Nicoletta Roman and Yvonne Zimmermann for their help in searching and summarizing parts of the literature.

Notes

1. 'Soft' law is characterized by its non-binding nature. Dealing with more or less general principles, 'soft' regulations often provide minimum provisions preparing the way for

further negotiations. Examples of this form of agreement are joint opinions, declarations, resolutions, recommendations, proposals, guidelines, codes of conduct, agreement protocols and agreement proper (Sisson and Marginson, 2001). 'Hard' law agreements or 'negotiated laws', in contrast, typically set standard provisions while dealing with specific rights and obligations rather than general principles and include sanctions. In practice, there is no strict dividing line between 'soft' and 'hard' regulation and there might be cases involving both (Sisson and Marginson, 2001; Biagi, 1999).

2. This network includes the EMF Collective Bargaining Committee, Selected Working Parties, the Collective Bargaining Conference, the EMF Summer School, the European Collective Bargaining Information Network (named EUCOB@) and Interregional Cross-Border Collective Bargaining Networks (for a detailed description see Schulten, 2002).

3. In 1974 ETUC admitted most Christian unions in Western Europe. However, it took another 25 years to overcome the remaining divisions between socialist, Christian and Communist union movements and special status organizations like white-collar, public service or professional unions (Moreno, 2001; Ebbinghaus and Visser, 2000).

4. 'Social dumping' is a somehow misleading phrase. Dumping is defined as selling something below its cost or as selling abroad below the price of the home country. Both definitions are not met by collective bargaining and social policy within Europe.

5. It is true that this arrangement was first negotiated by the social partners in the run-up to EMU and then made law. However, the legislation eliminated the opportunity to deviate from this rule at some later point in time.

References

Alesina, Alberto F., Ignazio Angeloni and Frederico Etro (2001), 'The Political Economy of International Unions', Working Paper No. 8645, National Bureau of Economic Research (NBER), Cambridge.

Alesina, Alberto F., Ignazio Angeloni and Ludger Schuhknecht (2002), 'What Does the European Union Do?', Discussion Paper No. 3115, Centre of Economic Policy Research (CEPR), London.

Altvater, Elmar and Birgit Mahnkopf (eds) (1993), *Gewerkschaften vor der Europäischen Herausforderung – Tarifpolitik nach Mauer und Maastricht*, Münster: Westfälisches Dampfboot.

Angrist, Joshua and Adriana Kugler (2002), 'Protective or Counter-productive? European Labour Market Institutions and the Effects of Immigrants on EU natives', Discussion Paper No. 3196, Centre of Economic Policy Research (CEPR), London.

Baumann, Hans, Ernst-Ludwig Laux and Myriam Schnepf (1996), 'Collective Bargaining in the European Building Industry – European Collective Bargaining?', *Transfer*, 2 (2), 321–333.

Berglas, Eitan (1976), 'Distribution of Tastes and Skills and the Provision of Local Public Goods', *Journal of Public Economics*, 6 (2), 409–423.

Biagi, Marco (1999), 'The Role of Social Partners in Europe: From Dialogue to Partnership', *Comparative Labour Law and Policy Journal*, 20, 485–496.

Blanpain, Roger (1999), 'European Social Policies: One Bridge Too Short', *Comparative Labour Law and Policy Journal*, 20, 497–507.

Blanpain, Roger (ed.) (2000), *European Labour Law*, The Hague, London and Boston, MA: Kluwer Law International.

Blanpain, Roger and Paul Windey (eds) (1994), *European Work Councils. Information and Consultation of Employees in Multinational Enterprises in Europe*, Leuven: Uitgeverij Peeters.

Boockmann, Bernhard (ed.) (1999), *Europäische Kollektivverhandlungen. Eine positive ökonomische Analyse*, Baden-Baden: Nomos.

Bordogna, Lorenzo (1996), 'Wage Bargaining and Industrial Relations Under the Single European Currency. The Problem of the Relationships Between EMU and Non-EMU Countries', *Transfer*, (2) 2, 298–316.

Brennan, Timothy J. (1988), 'Understanding "Raising Rivals' Costs"', *Antritrust Bulletin*, 33 (1), 95–113.

Brugiavini, Agar, Bernhard Ebbinghaus, Richard Freeman, Pietro Garibaldi, Bertil Holmlund, Martin Schludi and Thierry Verdier (2001), 'What Do Unions Do to the Welfare State?' in Tito Boeri, Agar Brugiavini and Lars Calmfors (eds), *The Role of Unions in the Twenty-First Century. A Report for the Fondazione Rodolfo Debenedetti*, Oxford: Oxford University Press, pp. 159–292.

Buchanan, James A. (1965), 'An Economic Theory of Clubs', *Economica*, 32 (125), 1–14.

Burda, Michael C. (1999), 'European Labour Markets and the Euro: How Much Flexibility Do We Really Need?', Discussion Paper No. 1232, Centre of Economic Policy Research (CEPR), London.

Calmfors, Lars, Alison Booth, Michael Burda, Daniele Checchi, Robin Naylor and Jelle Visser (2001), 'The Future of Collective Bargaining in Europe', in Tito Boeri, Agar Brugiavini and Lars Calmfors (eds), *The Role of Unions in the Twenty-First Century. A Report for the Fondazione Rodolfo Debenedetti*, Oxford: Oxford University Press, pp. 1–155.

Carley, Mark (2001), '*Bargaining at European level? Joint Texts Negotiated by European Works Councils*', Luxembourg: Office for Official Publications of the European Communities.

Cella, Gian Primo (1994), 'The Viability of Supranational Industrial Relations', *International Industrial Relations Association (IIRA)*, pp. 69–79.

Choi, Jay P. and Sang-Sueng Yi (2000), 'Vertical Foreclosure with the Choice of Input Specifications', *Rand Journal of Economics*, 31 (4), 717–743.

Clare, Richard (2002), 'Minimum Wages in the European Union 2001', *Eurostat – Statistics in Focus – Population and Social Conditions*, Theme 3-5/2001, 1–3.

Crouch, Colin (1999), 'Adapting the European Model: the Role of Employers' Associations and Trade Unions', in Gerhard Huemer, Michael Mesch and Franz Traxler (eds), *The Role of Employer Associations and Labour Unions in the EMU. Institutional Requirements for European Economic Policies*, Aldershot and Brookfield, VT: Ashgate, pp. 27–53.

Daley, Anthony (1999), 'The Hollowing Out of French Unions: Politics and Industrial Relations After 1981', in Andrew Martin and George Ross (eds), *The Brave New World of European Labor. European Trade Unions at the Millennium*, New York, and Oxford: Berghahn Books, pp. 167–216.

Decressin, Jörg and Antonio Fatas (1995), 'Regional Labour Market Dynamics in Europe', *European Economic Review*, 39 (9), 1627–1655.

Dølvik, Jon Erik (1997), *Redrawing Boundaries of Solidarity. ETUC, Social Dialogue and the Europeanization of Trade Unions in the 1990s*, Oslo: Arena, FAFO.

Dølvik, Jon Erik (2000), 'Economic and Monetary Union: Implications for Industrial Relations and Collective Bargaining in Europe', Discussion Paper DWP, No. 2000.01.04, European Trade Union Institute (ETUI), Brussels.

Ebbinghaus, Bernhard (1999), 'European Union Organizations', paper presented at the Fourth European Conference of the European Sociological Association (ESA), organized at Amsterdam, 18–21 August 1999.

Ebbinghaus, Bernhard and Jelle Visser (eds) (2000), *The Societies of Europe. Trade Unions in Western Europe since 1945*, New York: Grove's Dictionaries, and Oxford: Macmillan Reference.

ECB (European Central Bank) (2002), *Labour Market Mismatches in Euro Area Countries*, Frankfurt am Main: ECB.

Eichengreen, Barry J. (1993), 'European Monetary Unification', *Journal of Economic Literature*, 31 (3), 1321–1357.

Eichengreen, Barry J. (ed.) (1997), *European Monetary Unification: Theory, Practice and Analysis*, Cambridge, MA: MIT Press.

EIRO (1997), 'The Renault case and the future of social Europe', (http://www.EIRO.euro-found.ie/1997/03/feature/EU9703108F.html, 30 July 2002).

EIRO (1998), 'Unions in Benelux and Germany favour close transnational coordination of bargaining policy in EMU', (http://www.EIRO.eurofound.ie/1998/10/feature/DE9810278F.html, 27 May 2002).

EIRO (2000), 'Creation of unified service sector union suffers setback at ÖTV congress', (http://www.EIRO.eurofund.ie/2000/11/Feature/DE0011202F.html, 15 March 2002).

EIRO (2001a), 'Temporary agency work talks break down', (http://www.EIRO.eurofound.eu.int/2001/06/InBrief/EU0106215N.html, 27 May 2002).

EIRO (2001b), 'Joint declaration on temporary agency work' in EIRObserver 6'01, page 2 (http://www.EIRO.eurofound.ie/EIRObserver.html, 27 May 2002).

EIRO (2001c), 'Unified Service Sector Union (ver.di) created', (http://www.EIRO.eurofund.ie/2001/04/Featur/DE0104220F, 15 March 2002).

EIRO (2001d), 'Industrial relations in the EU, Japan and USA, 2000', (http://www.EIRO.eurofound.eu.int/2001/11/feature/tn0111148f.html, 27 March 2002).

EIRO (2001e), 'European Employment and Industrial Relations Glossaries', (http://www.eurofound.ie/industrial/industrial_knowledge.htm, 27 March 2002).

EIRO (2002), 'Labour costs – annual update 2001', (http://www.EIRO.eurofund.ie/2002/03/Update/tn0203104u.html, 15 March 2002).

ETUC (1999), *Activity Report 1995–1998*, Brussels: European Trade Union Confederation (ETUC).

ETUC (2002), http://www.etuc.org/en/aboutetuc/default.cfm?CFID=59760&CFTOKEN=40009608.

ETUC Executive Committee (2001), *Annual Report on the Coordination of Collective Bargaining in Europe*, Brussels, ETUI (http://www.etuc.org/ETUI/CBEurope/EurActiv/CBCRep01EN.pdf, 14 July 2002).

European Commission (1998), 'Adapting and Promoting the Social Dialogue at Community Level', Brussels: COM (1998) 322 final.

European Commission (2000), 'Industrial Relations in Europe – 2000', Brussels: COM (2000) 113 final.

European Commission (2002), *Report of the High Level Group on Industrial Relations in the European Union*, Luxembourg: Office for Official Publications of the European Communities.

Eurostat (2002), 'NewCronos' – Database, release date: 21 March 2002, Berlin: Eurostat Datashop Berlin.

Faith, Roger L. and Joseph D. Reid (1987), 'An Agency Theory of Unionism', *Journal of Economic Behavior and Organization*, 8 (1), 39–60.

Fajertag, Guiseppe (1999), 'Collective Bargaining in Europe in 1998: Towards a European Wage Policy', in Emilio Gabaglio and Reiner Hoffmann (eds), *European Trade Union Yearbook 1998*, Brussels: European Trade Union Institute (ETUI), pp. 119–138.

Fajertag, Guiseppe and Philippe Pochet (eds) (1997), *Social Pacts in Europe*, Brussels: European Trade Union Institute (ETUI).

Fajertag, Guiseppe and Philippe Pochet (eds) (2000), *Social Pacts in Europe: New Dynamics*, Brussels: European Trade Union Institute (ETUI).

Falkner, Gerda (2000), 'The Institutional Framework of Labour Relations at the EU Level: Provisions and Historical Background', in Reiner Hoffmann, Otto Jacobi, Berndt Keller and Manfred Weiss (eds), *Transnational Industrial Relations in Europe*, Düsseldorf: Hans-Böckler-Stiftung, pp. 11–28.

Ferner, Anthony and Richard Hyman (1998), 'Introduction: Towards European Industrial Relations?', in Anthony Ferner and Richard Hyman (eds), *Changing Industrial Relations in Europe*, Oxford: Blackwell Publishers and Malden, MA: Blackwell Publishers, pp. xi–xxvi.

FT.com (2002), 'Divide: Unity remains elusive as ever', (http://specials.ft.com/ln/ftsurveys/country/sc22de6.htm, 15 March 2002).

Gardner, Margaret and Gil Palmer (eds) (1992), *Employment Relations*, South Melbourne, Victoria: Macmillan.

Granitz, Elisabeth and Benjamin Klein (1996), 'Monopolization by "Raising Rivals' Costs": The Standard Oil Case', *Journal of Law and Economics*, 5 (1), 1–47.

Hallett, Andrew Huges and Diana N. Weymark (2002), 'The Cost of Heterogeneity in a Monetary Union', Discussion Paper No. 3223, Centre of Economic Policy Research (CEPR), London.

Hassel, Anke (2001) 'The Problem of Political Exchange in Complex Governance Systems: The Case of Germany's Alliance for Jobs', *European Industrial Relations*, 7 (3), 305–323.

Haucap, Justus, Uwe Pauly and Christian Wey (1999), 'The Incentives of Employers' Associations to Raise Rivals' Costs in the Presence of Collective Bargaining', Discussion Papers FS IV 99–6. Wissenschaftszentrum Berlin (WZB).

Haucap, Justus, Uwe Pauly and Christian Wey (2001), 'Collective Wage Setting When Wages are Generally Binding. An Antitrust Perspective', *International Review of Law and Economics*, 21 (3), 287–307.

Heise, Arne (2000), 'Collective Bargaining in the European Union. A Theory of Optimum Wage Areas', *International Scope Review*, 2 (3), 1–23.

Hornung-Draus, Renate (1998), 'European Employer Organizations: Structure and Recent Developments', *Industrielle Beziehungen*, 5 (2), 218–235.

Hornung-Draus, Renate (2001), 'Employers', in György Széll (ed.), *European Labour Relations, Volume1: Common Features*, Hampshire: Gower Publishing Aldershot and Burlington, pp. 314–334.

Hyman, Richard (2002), 'The Future of Unions', *Just Labour*, 1 (1), 7–15.

Jovanović, Miroslav N. (ed.) (1997), *European Economic Integration*, London and New York: Routledge.

Keller, Berndt (1995), 'Towards a European System of Collective Bargaining? Perspectives Before and After Maastricht', in Reiner Hoffmann, Otto Jacobi, Berndt Keller and Manfred Weiss (eds), *German Industrial Relations Under the Impact of Structural Change, Unification and European Integration*, Düsseldorf: Hans- Böckler- Stiftung, pp. 123–146.

Keller, Bernd and Matthias Bansbach (2001), 'Social Dialogues: Tranquil Past, Troubled Present and Uncertain Future', *Industrial Relations Journal*, 32 (5), 419–434.

Kenner, Jeff (1995), 'EC Labour Law: The Softly, Softly Approach', *International Journal of Comparative Labour Law and Industrial Relations*, 15 (1), 33–60.

Kenner, Jeff (1999), 'The EU Employment Title and the "Third Way": Making Soft Law Work?', *International Journal of Comparative Labour Law and Industrial Relations*, 15 (1), 33–60.

Kluth, Michael. F. (ed.) (1998), *The Political Economy of a Social Europe. Understanding Labour Market Integration in the European Union*, Bassingstoke and London: Macmillan Press and New York: St. Martin's Press.

Kuhlmann, Reinhard (1999), 'Coordination of Collective Bargaining Policy in the European Metalworking Sector: A Response to the Challenges Posed by the Euro', in Emilio Gabaglio and Reiner Hoffmann (eds), *European Trade Union Yearbook 1998*, Brussels: European Trade Union Institute (ETUI), pp. 139–150.

Lamers, Josee (ed.) (1998), *The Added Value of European Works Councils*, Bussum, Netherlands: Imprimo.

Lecher, Wolfgang, Bernhard Nagel and Hans-Wolfgang Platzer (eds) (1999), *The Establishment of European Works Councils – From Information Committee to Social Actor*, Aldershot and Brookfield, VT: Ashgate Publishing.

Mahnkopf, Birgit and Elmar Altvater (1995), 'Transmission Belts of Transnational Competition? Trade Unions and Collective Bargaining in the Context of European Integration', *European Journal of Industrial Relations*, 1 (1), 101–117.

Marginson, Paul and Keith Sisson (1996), 'European Collective Bargaining: A Virtual Prospect?', paper presented at the IREC-Conference 'Industrial Relations in Europe: Convergence or Diversification?, organized at the University of Copenhagen, 19–21 September 1996.

Marginson, Paul and Keith Sisson (1998), 'European Collective Bargaining: A Virtual Prospect?', *Journal of Common Market Studies*, 36 (4), 479–504.

Marginson, Paul, Mark Gilman, Otto Jacobi and Hubert Krieger (1997), *Negotiating European Works Councils– An Analysis of Agreements under Article 13*, Dublin: European Foundation for the Improvement of Living and Working Conditions.

Marginson, Paul, Keith Sisson and James Arrowsmith (2001), 'Sector-level Bargaining between Decentralization and Europeanization: Four Countries and Two Sectors

Compared', paper presented at the workshop 'Industrial Relations – An Anachronism?', organized at the University of Tuebingen, 15–16 June 2001.

Martin, Andrew (1999), 'Wage Bargaining Under the EMU: Europeanization, Re-Nationalization or Americanization', Discussion Paper DWP 99.01.03, European Trade Union Institute (ETUI), Brussels.

Martin, Andrew and George Ross (eds) (1999b), *The Brave New World of Labour. European Trade Unions at the Millennium*, New York and Oxford: Antony Rowe.

Martin, Roderick and Anamaria Cristescu-Martin (2001), 'Employment Relations in Central and Eastern Europe in 2000: The Road to the EU', *Industrial Relations Journal*, 32 (5), 480–493.

Mayne, Susan and Susan Malyon (eds) (2001), *Employment Law in Europe*, London, Dublin, and Edinburgh: Butterworth.

McKinnon, Ronald I. (1963), 'Optimum Currency Areas', *American Economic Review*, 53 (3), 717–725.

Moreno, Juan (ed.) (2001), *Trade Unions Without Frontiers. The Communist-oriented Trade Unions and the ETUC*, Brussels: European Trade Union Institute (ETUI).

Mundell, Robert A. (1961), 'A Theory of Optimum Currency Areas', *American Economic Review*, 51 (3), 657–665.

Niskanen, William A. (ed.) (1971), *Bureaucracy and Representative Government*, Chicago: Aldine Publishing.

Obstfeld, Maurice and Giovanni Peri (1999), 'Regional Nonadjustment and Fiscal Policy: Lessons from EMU', Working Paper No. 6431. National Bureau of Economic Research (NBER), Cambridge.

Offe, Claus and Helmut Wiesenthal (1980), 'Two Logics of Collective Action. Theoretical Notes on Social Class and Organizational Form', *Political Power and Social Theory*, 1, 67–115.

Olson, Mancur (ed.) (1965), *The Logic of Collective Action. Public Goods and the Theory of Groups*, Cambridge, MA: Harvard University Press.

Platzer, Hans-Werner (ed.) (1991), *Gewerkschaftspolitik ohne Grenzen? Die transnationale Zusammenarbeit der Gewerkschaften im Europa der 90er Jahre*, Bonn: Dietz.

Plowman, David (1978), 'Employer Associations: Challenges and Responses', *Journal of Industrial Relations*, 10 (3), 237–263.

Salop, Steven C. and David T. Scheffman (1983), '"Raising Rivals" Costs', *American Economic Review*, 73 (2), 267–271.

Schmitter, Philippe C. and Wolfgang Streeck (1981), 'The Organization of Business Interests. A Research Design to Study the Associative Action of Business in the Advanced Industrial Societies of Western Europe', IIM Discussion Paper, IIM and LPM, 81–13, Wissenschaftszentrum Berlin (WZB), Berlin.

Schulten, Thorsten (2001), 'The European Metalworkers' Federation's Approach to a European Coordination of Collective Bargaining. Experiences, Problems and Prospects', in Thorsten Schulten and Reinhard Bispinck (eds), *Collective Bargaining under the Euro. Experiences from the European Metal Industry*, Brussels: European Trade Union Institute (ETUI), pp. 303–332.

Schulten, Thorsten (2002), 'Europeanization of Collective Bargaining. An Overview on Trade Union Initiatives for a Transnational Coordination of Collective Bargaining Policy', Discussion Paper No. 101, Wirtschafts- und Sozialwissenschaftliches Institut in der Hans-Böckler- Stiftung (WSI), Düsseldorf.

Sisson, Keith and Paul Marginson (2001), '"Soft Regulation" – Travesty of the Real Thing or New Dimension?', Industrial Relations Research Unit, University of Warwick.

Sisson, Keith, Jim Arrowsmith and Paul Marginson (2002), 'All Benchmarkers Now? Benchmarking and the "Europeanization of Collective Bargaining"', Working paper 41/02 of the ESRC 'One Europe or Several?' Program, Economic and Social Research Council (ESRC), Swindon.

Streeck, Wolfgang (1993), 'The Rise and Decline of Neo-Corporatism', in Lloyd Ulman, Barry Eichengreen and William T. Dickens (eds), *Labor and an Integrated Europe*, Washington, D.C.: The Brookings Institution, pp. 80–99.

Streeck, Wolfgang (1994), 'European Social Policy After Maastricht: The "Social Dialogue" and "Subsidiarity"', *Economic and Industrial Democracy*, 15 (2), 151–177.

Streeck, Wolfgang (1996), 'Neo-Voluntarism: A New European Social Policy Regime?' Gary Marks et al. (eds), *Governance in the European Union*, London, Thousand Oaks, CA, New Delhi: Sage, pp. 64–95.

Streeck, Wolfgang (1997), 'Citizenship under Regime Competition: The Case of the European Works Councils', Jean Monnet Chair Paper 97/42, European University Institute/ Schuman Centre, Florence.

Taylor, Robert (1999), 'Trade Unions and Transnational Industrial Relations', Discussion Paper DP/99/1999, International Labour Organization's (ILO) International Institute of Labour Studies, Geneva.

Teague, Paul (2000), 'Macroeconomic Constraints, Social Learning and Pay Bargaining in Europe', *British Journal of Industrial Relations*, 38 (3), 429–452.

Tiebout, Charles (1956), 'A Pure Theory of Local Expenditures', *Journal of Political Economy*, 64, 416–24.

Timmesfeld, Andrea (ed.) (1994), *Chancen und Perspektiven europäischer Kollektivverhandlungen. Zur Bedeutung nationaler Interessendivergenzen für die kollektive Handlungsfähigkeit europäischer Dachverbände*, Baden-Baden: Nomos-Verlag.

Traxler, Franz (1991), 'The Logic of Employers' Collective Action', in Dieter Sadowski and Otto Jacobi (eds), *Employer's Associations in Europe: Policy and Organization*, Baden-Baden: Nomos, pp. 29–50.

Traxler, Franz (1995), 'Farewell to Labour Market Associations? Organized vs. Disorganized Decentralization as a Map for Industrial Relations', in Colin Crouch and Franz Traxler (eds), *Organized Industrial Relations in Europe: What Future?* Aldershot and Brookfield, VT: pp. 3–20.

Traxler, Franz (1996), 'European Trade Union Policy and Collective Bargaining – Mechanisms and Levels of Labour Market Regulation in Comparison', *Transfer*, 2 (2), 287–297.

Traxler, Franz (1998a), 'Austria: Still the Country of Corporatism', in Anthony Ferner and Richard Hyman (eds), *Changing Industrial Relations in Europe*, Oxford and Malden, MA: Blackwell, pp. 239– 261.

Traxler, Franz (1998b), 'Employers and Employer Organizations' in Brian Towers and Mike Terry (eds), *Industrial Relations Journal: European Annual Review 1997*, Oxford and Malden, MA: Blackwell, pp. 99–111.

Traxler, Franz (1999), 'Employers and Employer Organizations: the Case of Governability', *Industrial Relations Journal*, 30 (4), 345–354.

Traxler, Franz (2000), 'Employers and Employer Organizations in Europe: Membership Strength, Density and Representativeness', *Industrial Relations Journal*, 31 (4), 308–316.

Turner, Lowell (1993), 'Prospects for Worker Participation in Management in the Single Market', in Lloyd Ulman, Barry Eichengreen and William T. Dickens (eds), *Labor and an Integrated Europe*, Washington, DC: Brookings Institution.

Tyskiewicz, Zygmunt (1991), 'UNICE: The Voice of European Business and Industry in Brussels – A Programmatic Self-Presentation', in Dieter Sadowski and Otto Jacobi (eds), *Employers' Associations in Europe: Policy and Organization*, Baden-Baden: Nomos, pp. 85–101.

Van Waarden, Frans (1991), 'Two Logics of Collective Action? Business Associations as Distinct from Trade Unions: The Problems of Associations of Organizations,' in Dieter Sadowski and Otto Jacobi (eds), *Employer's Associations in Europe: Policy and Organization*, Baden-Baden: Nomos, pp. 51–85.

Vaubel, Roland (1986), 'A Public Choice Approach to International Organizations', *Public Choice*, 51, 39–58.

Visser, Jelle (1998), 'European Trade Unions in the Mid-1990s', in Brian Towers and Mike Terry (eds), *Industrial Relations Journal: European Annual Review 1997*, Oxford and Malden, MA: Blackwell Publishers, pp. 113–130.

Visser, Jelle and Bernhard Ebbinghaus (1992), 'Making the Most of Diversity? European Integration and Transnational Organization of Labour', in Justin Greenwood, Jürgen R.

Grote and Karsten Ronit (eds), *Organized Interests and the European Community*, London: Sage, pp. 206–37.

Voigt, Stefan and Eli M. Salzberger (2002), 'Choosing Not To Choose: When Politicians Choose To Delegate Powers', *Kyklos*, 55 (2), 289–310.

Waddington, Jeremy (2000), 'Towards a Reform Agenda? European Trade Unions in Transition', *Industrial Relations Journal*, 31 (4), 317–330.

Waddington, Jeremy (2001), 'Articulating Trade Union Organization for the New Europe?', *Industrial Relations Journal*, 32 (5), 459–463.

Williams, Alan (1966), 'The Optimal Provision of Public Goods in a System of Local Governments', *Journal of Political Economy*, 74, 18–33.

Wilts, Arnold (2001), 'Europeanization and Means of Interest Representation by National Business Associations', *European Journal of Industrial Relations*, 7 (3), 269–286.

Windmuller, John P. (1984), 'Employer Associations in Comparative Perspective: Organization, Structure, Administration', in John P. Windmuller and Alan Gladstone (eds), *Employer Associations and Industrial Relations: A Comparative Study*, Oxford: Clarendon, pp. 1–23.

14 Contemporary developments in and challenges to collective bargaining in the United States
John Delaney

1. Introduction

To paraphrase Dickens, the start of the twenty-first century represents both the best and worst of times for unions and collective bargaining in the USA. Evidence indicates that workers represented by unions earn considerably more than their non-union counterparts. In 2001, for example, the government data presented below indicate that union members earned nearly 40 per cent more in hourly total compensation than similar non-union workers. At the same time, union density rates have experienced a free fall for the past four decades. This has led to a situation in which less than 10 per cent of US private sector workers were covered by collective bargaining in 2001. These clashing extremes have created a difficult conundrum for organized labour and provide an appropriate backdrop for an examination of the current state of collective bargaining in the USA. The substantial gains negotiated by unions during the last 60 years will likely erode unless organized labour enrolls more members. Unfortunately for unions, none of the strategies developed to revive the labour movement has yet been successful.

In general, the current situation is bleak for unions and bargaining in part because organized labour has not changed with the times. While much of my argument rests on conjecture and speculation, 50 years of declining union density suggests that today's workers may want something different than unions can or are willing to provide. The inability of unions to organize new members, the rigid US legal framework governing collective bargaining, the passage of free trade legislation, and the changing nature of today's workers now threaten to make collective bargaining an anachronism. More important, because unions have been unable to adjust to the new realities of work and workers, some observers are beginning to ask whether the US system of collective bargaining is well suited to satisfying the needs of workers and employers today. Of course, the silver lining of this bleak situation for organized labour is that difficult circumstances are more likely than good ones to generate worker unrest or innovative organizing approaches. Either outcome could stimulate support for unions.

Below, after detailing some recent developments in collective bargaining, I identify several challenges that US unions must confront. The American union movement's success in dealing with these challenges will determine whether it will be revitalized or marginalized in coming years.

2. Collective bargaining trends and developments

The state of the US union movement can be reasonably well assessed by examining four general indicators: (1) union density rates; (2) collective bargaining outcomes; (3) worker unrest and work stoppage data; and (4) information on the social and political role and status of labour unions in America. To focus on recent trends, I examine patterns in these indicators since 1990. Because wide variation has occurred in some of these measures over time and the past decade may not be a representative time frame for analysis, caution should be exercised in generalizing from my assessments. Nonetheless, a consistent pattern emerges from an examination of the four indicators.

Union density in the United States

The common denominator in virtually every recent assessment of unions in the USA is the general decline in union density since the 1950s (see for example, Chaison and Bigelow, 2002; Nissen, 2002; Turner et al., 2001; Katz and Darbishire, 2000; Voos, 1994). Although union density can be measured in different ways, I focus on the percentage of workers covered by collective bargaining agreements instead of the percentage of workers belonging to unions. This density measure includes both union members and non-members working in units covered by bargaining agreements. Accordingly, it provides a clue as to the spread of union bargained gains, as US law requires unions to bargain for all workers (not just union members) in units represented by unions. In the middle of the twentieth century, about 35 per cent of private sector workers and 50 per cent of manufacturing workers in the USA were represented by unions. US Bureau of Labor Statistics (BLS) data reported in Table 14.1 show that the private sector union representation rate dropped below 10 per cent in 2000 and that the representation rate in manufacturing is now less than 16 per cent. More telling, however, is the fact that the representation rate consistently declined during the 1990s. Only in the public sector has the US unionization rate held steady. The Table 14.1 data verify an ongoing pattern of union membership decline.

The general pattern in Table 14.1 is interesting because the union movement made a concerted effort in the 1990s to organize new workers. That effort was successful in some sectors, such as the hotel and hospitality industries (Waddoups and Eade, 2002), but not across sectors. As a result, it

Table 14.1   Union representation rates in the United States, 1992–2001

	Percentage of workers represented by a union			
	Overall (%)	Manufacturing (%)	Private sector (%)	Public sector (%)
1990	18.3	22.2	13.4	43.3
1991	18.2	21.8	13.1	43.3
1992	17.9	21.0	12.7	42.3
1993	17.7	20.3	12.3	43.8
1994	17.5	19.7	12.0	44.7
1995	16.7	18.7	11.4	43.5
1996	16.2	18.3	11.2	43.0
1997	15.6	17.2	10.8	42.3
1998	15.4	16.8	10.3	42.5
1999	15.3	16.6	10.2	42.1
2000	14.9	15.6	9.8	42.0
2001	14.8	15.5	9.7	41.8

Source: US Bureau of Labor Statistics Online Archives.

appears that intensified union organizing has not only failed to increase the representation rate, it has not allowed unions to offset the normal yearly membership losses due to retirements, layoffs, plant closings, and so on. Undoubtedly, without the intensive organizing effort, union representation rates would be lower than Table 14.1 reports. The resulting situation can only be characterized as desperate for organized labour in the USA. Despite some notable organizing victories in recent years, unions have been losing members overall. The pattern of decline raises questions about the future viability of the labour movement. Table 14.1 also indicates that unions are increasingly becoming a public sector phenomenon. This situation is not good for the union movement. Job growth has been concentrated in the private sector over the past decades. This pattern is not likely to change. Given the high union density rates in government workplaces, unions may be approaching the upper bound of potential public sector unionization. Further, during times of tight budgets, unions may also face pressure from government entities to reduce costs and improve performance. Whereas public employee unions have been insulated from some of the forces depressing unionism in the private sector, such as the relocation of facilities to other nations, recent signs suggest new threats on the horizon. For example, the US Supreme Court recently decided that the use of school vouchers to support education in religious schools does not violate the US constitution (*Zelman* v. *Simmons-Harris*, 2002). Similarly, President Bush, in §730 of a bill creating a US Department of Homeland Security, proposed limiting the unionization and civil service rights of that agency's workers (see President's Homeland Security Department Proposal, 2002). These developments have the potential to influence significantly the circumstances and job situations faced by public school teachers and federal employees in the future.

There has been much speculation about the causes of union decline. In general, the trend seems to be the result of a complex interplay of forces, including changing worker sentiments, globalization, and outdated labour laws (see Kochan, 2000; Fiorito and Maranto, 1987). Significantly, the decline of unionism has coincided with the growth of employment systems relying on teams and employee involvement (see Katz and Darbishire, 2000, pp. 18–21). Survey research indicates that employees today desire such work systems (Freeman and Rogers, 1999). As a result, it is unsurprising that businesses have adopted a variety of work practices over the past two decades that have provided employees with information and input into the organization (Gittleman et al., 1998; Osterman, 1994). These work practices are not necessarily new or limited to the non-union sector (Ichniowski et al., 1989). Indeed, some studies have suggested that the adoption of a variety of work practices, such as employee involvement, profit sharing, information sharing, and so on may produce greater returns in union firms than in non-union ones (see Schwochau et al., 1997; Cooke, 1994). This may help explain why the survival rate for participation programmes in unionized firms is high relative to the survival rate in non-union firms (see Eaton, 1994). Still, unions have been unable to capitalize on these findings to organize more workers.

Union representation rates have also been affected by changes in the general economy. For example, union density has declined as the service sector of the economy has grown. Unions have historically been less successful organizing service sector employees than manufacturing employees. As US manufacturing jobs have disappeared, unions have lost members.

Despite the push by the AFL-CIO to increase organizing activity in the 1990s, the number of employees involved in union certification elections on an annual basis has declined for many years. Although the union movement has increased attempts to secure unionization through means other than an election (e.g. card check agreements, neutrality pledges from employers), those efforts still lag traditional organizational approaches (see Eaton and Kriesky, 2001). This means that in recent years, new union members are less likely to have voted for a union in an election than to have obtained a job at a company that was already organized. In other words, union security arrangements enlist these new members, who are required to pay union dues in order to keep their job. It is not known whether these members are less loyal to their unions than individuals who vote for a union in an election. If such a loyalty difference exists, it may suggest that existing research overstates unionized workers' sentiments for unions.

The extent of union density and represented workers' loyalty to the labour movement are important issues because they affect union bargaining power and bargaining outcomes. Declining union power is inevitable when membership has eroded. How a potential power reduction translates into outcomes may also influence organized labour's ability to recruit new members.

Bargaining outcomes in the 1990s
The trend in union bargaining gains during the 1990s is not as clear as the trend in union membership density. On the one hand, evidence indicates that union members continue to earn more than similar non-members. Table 14.2 provides BLS data on average hourly compensation for union members and non-members. Across total compensation, wages, benefits, and health insurance, the data show that union members earned about 42 per cent, 26 per cent, 87 per cent, and 227 per cent more, respectively, than non-members in 2002. This is evidence of a substantial union wage premium, one that is much larger than the historic 15 per cent differential estimated by Lewis (1963) and generally accepted by researchers. Table 14.3 reports information on median weekly earnings by union status. It reveals an average union wage premium of about 30 per cent over the years 1990–2001. Notably, the union premium grew from 1990–94 and declined thereafter. In 2001, Table 14.3 suggests that union members earned about 24 per cent more than non-members. While the average union premium varies slightly across the Tables 14.2 and 14.3 data sources, it is sizeable in each case. Unsurprisingly, the premium is larger for benefits than wages, which may occur because taxes are lower on benefits than on wages. In general, the large union pay advantage should be a useful recruiting tool in campaigns seeking to unionize workers. For the same reason, the union pay premium likely encourages employers to fight such organizing efforts.

Because the union wage premiums reported above are not adjusted to account for workers' characteristics and skills or government data collection methods, the differentials must be cautiously interpreted. Adjustment for the attributes noted will reduce the union premiums. While the exact effect of adjustments is unclear, a careful examination by Hirsch et al. (2002) has suggested that the current union wage premium seems to be between 15 per cent and 20 per cent (see also Chapter 7 by Blanchflower and Bryson in this volume). The debate about the size of the union wage premium notwithstanding, it is important to note that evidence shows that union workers earn more than similar non-union

Table 14.2 Average hourly compensation by union membership status

	Union workers				Non-union workers			
	Total compensation $	Wages $	Benefits $	Health insurance $	Total compensation $	Wages $	Benefits $	Health insurance $
1990	18.78	12.47	6.30	–	14.22	10.52	3.70	–
1991	19.76	13.02	6.75	1.63	14.56	10.78	3.79	0.78
1992	21.09	13.63	7.46	1.89	15.22	11.21	4.01	0.86
1993	21.86	13.98	7.88	2.07	15.76	11.52	4.24	0.92
1994	23.26	14.76	8.51	2.28	16.04	11.70	4.34	0.94
1995	22.40	14.42	7.99	2.09	16.26	11.90	4.35	0.90
1996	23.31	14.93	8.38	2.05	16.61	12.23	4.39	0.88
1997	23.48	15.13	8.34	2.01	17.21	12.75	4.46	0.95
1998	23.59	15.38	8.22	1.97	17.80	13.21	4.58	0.86
1999	24.75	16.21	8.53	2.02	18.20	13.54	4.66	0.89
2000	25.88	16.87	9.01	2.17	19.07	14.18	4.89	0.95
2001	27.80	18.36	9.45	2.26	19.98	14.81	5.18	1.04
2002	29.42	19.33	10.09	2.57	20.79	15.38	5.41	1.13

Note: Wages and benefits may not sum to total compensation because of rounding in BLS calculations. The benefits column includes health insurance, which component is entered separately to show the pattern it displays over time across the union and non-union sectors.

Source: Bureau of Labor Statistics web site (*http://www.bls.gov/ncs/ect/sp/ecbl0013.pdf*).

Table 14.3   Median weekly earnings for workers represented by a union and non-union workers

	Represented by union ($)	Non-union ($)	Union/Non-union differential (%)
1990	493	386	27.7
1991	506	400	26.5
1992	541	413	31.0
1993	569	426	33.6
1994	587	432	35.9
1995	598	447	33.8
1996	610	462	32.0
1997	632	478	32.2
1998	653	499	30.9
1999	667	516	29.3
2000	691	542	27.5
2001	712	575	23.8
Change, 1990–2001	44.4%	49.0%	–
Average union premium, 1990–2001	–	–	30.4%

Source: US Bureau of Labor Statistics web site
(http://www.bls.gov/schedule/archives/all_nr.htm#UNION2).

workers. That circumstance should operate to encourage individuals to join unions or seek unionized jobs.

Consideration of the union pay premium in the private sector adds insight to the compensation data reported in Tables 14.2 and 14.3. The union wage premium in the private sector has varied more substantially than the overall union wage premium. As noted above, some of the variation is due to data collection methods (see Hirsch et al., 2002). In a 1997 National Compensation Study survey, for example, BLS reported that the overall union–non-union wage differential was 4.3 per cent. Notably, the same survey indicated that the union–non-union wage differential for blue-collar workers was almost 38 per cent and that non-union white-collar workers earned about 3 per cent more than white-collar union workers (US Bureau of Labor Statistics, 1997)! Although the union premium increased somewhat in subsequent National Compensation Study surveys, the general pattern suggests that unions have been able to secure substantially higher compensation for employees with lower skill levels, but not for higher skilled or service sector employees. This pattern likely encourages employers to fight unionization efforts among lower-paid workers and dis-

Table 14.4   Union and non-union compensation cost indices, 1989–2000

	Union workers	Non-union workers
1989	100.0	100.0
1990	104.1	105.5
1991	108.8	110.1
1992	114.0	113.8
1993	119.1	117.7
1994	123.0	121.7
1995	125.8	125.2
1996	129.7	128.7
1997	131.8	132.8
1998	135.3	137.8
1999	139.0	142.5
2000	144.4	149.1
2001	149.5	155.3

Notes: Indices for the month of June are used for all years.
See http://www.bls.gov/web/echistry.pdf.

Source: US Bureau of Labor Statistics Web Site.

courages employees in high skill jobs and growing segments of the economy from joining unions. In turn, this one–two punch will likely reinforce and perhaps accelerate the decline in union density.

Underlying some of the variation highlighted in the compensation data is the fact that non-union workers' pay has risen at a more rapid rate in recent years than has pay for unionized workers. Table 14.4 reports BLS compensation cost index information for the years 1989–2001. The pattern in Table 14.4 is consistent with a trend that began in the early 1980s. Although union workers earn more than non-union workers, the average compensation gap is declining.

The data presented in Tables 14.2 to 14.4 suggest some potential inconsistencies. In particular, if non-union workers are getting larger compensation increases than union workers, why is the union wage premium so large? Ignoring the measurement issues noted by Hirsch and his associates, as union density has diminished in general, it is likely that the remaining pockets of union members represent the strongest union segments. These segments may have unique attributes that endow them with significant bargaining power. Accordingly, these segments are able to negotiate lucrative outcomes, magnifying the union–non-union wage differential. At the same time, the large union wage premiums contribute to employers' willingness to fight unionization. Whereas the union wage premium is still large, a continued decline in union membership at some point will smother the union compensation premium as substantial non-union competition will pressure union employers to make job, employment and pay adjustments. Alternatively, high paying union jobs could become so scarce that the differential – however large – is meaningless to the average worker in search of employment.

Some noteworthy bargaining events and outcomes in the 1990s reinforce the view presented above. For example, the Teamsters union successfully negotiated good contracts with United Parcel Service in 1997 and 2002. In the former case, a well-coordinated strike effectively shut down the package delivery firm for 15 days and resulted in a new contract providing substantial gains to workers. For example, UPS agreed to create 10000 new full-time jobs by combining part-time positions. It also agreed to limits on its ability to subcontract work and promised to negotiate with the union over safety issues, such as the maximum weight of packages transported by drivers. Compensation increased by about 15 per cent and the firm agreed that its pension plans would remain part of the Teamsters' multi-employer pension fund (Ginsbach et al., 1997). In the 2002 negotiation, although a strike was averted, the union achieved additional gains for unionized UPS workers. The firm agreed to increase compensation by 22 per cent over six years and to create an additional 10 000 new jobs. The agreement means that the average package delivery driver will earn more than $28 per hour in the new contract's last year (Hirschman and Krupin, 2002). Clearly, UPS workers have benefited handsomely from the employment terms negotiated by their union with the package carrier. Such outcomes are not always the case.

In 1997, American Airlines' pilots, represented by the Allied Pilots Association reached an impasse in bargaining with the carrier. The pilots' strike was halted after less than one hour, however, by a Presidential Order convening an emergency board to work with the parties to develop an agreement. Eventually, the pilots and the company reached an agreement, which was reluctantly accepted by the union. Because of dissatisfaction with the results, the pilots engaged in a 'sickout' early in 1999. The job action by the pilots forced the airline to cancel nearly 5000 flights and disrupted travel for 450 000 travellers (Peltz and Gregory, 1999). Because the pilots continued the sickout after a federal judge ordered them back to work, the judge imposed a fine of over $45 million on the union, its president and vice-president for contempt of court. The fine, which had to be paid to the company, was based on the judge's estimate of the amount of revenue lost by the airline during the time the union violated the back-to-work order (Bloomberg News, 2000). While the union appealed the judge's decision, it continued to have difficult relations with American. In September 2000, the union rejected a contract extension proposal from the

Table 14.5   Work stoppages in the United States, 1990–2001

	Number of major work stoppages	Number of workers involved (000s)	Days idled (000s) by work stoppages	Days idled as a percentage of estimated total working time (%)
1990	44	185	5926	0.02
1991	40	392	4584	0.02
1992	35	364	3989	0.01
1993	35	182	3981	0.01
1994	45	322	5021	0.02
1995	31	192	5771	0.02
1996	37	273	4889	0.02
1997	29	339	4497	0.01
1998	34	387	5116	0.02
1999	17	73	1996	0.01
2000	39	394	20419	0.06
2001	29	99	1151	0.00

Note: Annual data are reported.

Source: US Bureau of Labor Statistics web site
(http://www.bls.gov/news.release/wkstp.toc.htm).

company that included forgiveness of the fine. When the US Supreme Court refused to overturn the judge's decision, the union was forced to arrange a payment schedule with the company; the union paid $20 million immediately and will pay $25.5 million plus interest over a 15-year period (Houston Chronicle News Services, 2001). Along with an abortive job action by Major League Umpires in 1999 (see Dworkin and Posthuma, 2002), the dispute between American Airlines and its pilots represented the most serious union bargaining miscalculation during the past decade.

Labour peace: The decline of the strike
Observers have regularly reported that a strike is a relatively rare event. While this comment has been meant to imply that the vast majority of negotiations result in voluntary agreements, its meaning has become literal today. Table 14.5 reports BLS data on major work stoppages (defined as strikes involving 1000 or more workers) over the years 1990–2001. In addition, Figure 14.1 depicts the Table 14.5 data and provides a line denoting the linear trend in strike activity over the period. In combination, Table 14.5 and Figure 14.1 indicate that the absolute number of major work stoppages is quite small today – one-tenth of what they were 25 years ago – and that the trend in strike activity continues to be negative. Because the government

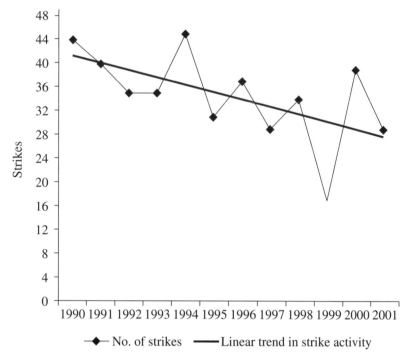

Figure 14.1   Major work stoppages, 1990–2001

no longer compiles information on strike activity in smaller units, the trend in major work stoppages cannot be verified as representing all strike activity. It is likely, however, that the trends are similar and that fewer work stoppages are occurring today than took place in the past.

Scholars have made numerous assertions on why strike activity has declined (LeRoy, 2001, 2000, 1995; LeRoy and Johnson, 2001). Often cited is the notion that US labour law gives employers considerable power in strike situations. For example, employers can impose their last offer if an impasse in negotiations occurs and it is lawful to replace permanently any employee who walks off the job during an economic strike. Faced with the possibility of job loss, it is asserted, unionized workers are reluctant to strike in the absence of overwhelming bargaining power.

More important than the number of stoppages, the trend in strike activity, and the interpretation of observers, is the fact that US workers and residents today know very little about strikes. The data reported in Table 14.5 and Figure 14.1 suggest that US citizens have little exposure to major strikes. As a result, people have little perspective on the reality of picketing, going without pay, and being out of work that goes hand in hand with the execution of a strike. Instead, people have developed a romanticized or Hollywood vision of a work stoppage. There is little exposure to the hardship and difficulty associated with a work stoppage. In turn, it may be much more difficult for workers to conduct a successful strike when they have little sense of the sacrifices a strike requires. The lack of understanding probably contributes to the declining trend in strike activity, as workers increasingly do not have the stomach to suffer the hardships required to prevail in a work stoppage. If the collective withholding of labour is the ultimate weapon of a union, the trend in US strike activity over the past decade suggests that organized labour has lost its capacity to pressure most employers into concessions. It will be difficult for unions to sustain their compensation premium or organizational efforts in such an environment.

It has been asserted that union workers are more likely than non-union workers to exercise 'voice' (see Freeman and Medoff, 1984). The notion underlying the concept of voice is that union workers will express their discontent through a variety of methods rather than quitting their jobs. Voice has been conceptualized to explain at least a portion of grievance activity, turnover, support for management, and other manifestations of unrest at work (see Batt, Colvin and Keefe, 2002; Boroff and Lewin, 1997; Schwochau et al., 1997).

Because measures of worker unrest tend to be less precise than data on strikes, it is difficult to provide an assessment of worker unrest during the past decade. Voice in the form of unrest can reflect many things, ranging from union organizing activity through dissatisfaction with working conditions to concerns over exposure to hazardous substances. In light of this, inferences on worker unrest must generally be drawn from fragmentary databases and isolated studies. One relevant study was produced by the US Occupational Safety and Health Administration (OSHA) in response to a US Congressional request.

During the 1990s, members of Congress complained that OSHA inspected many more work establishments experiencing labour unrest than establishments without unrest. It was alleged that workers were filing complaints so that the employers with which a problem existed would be punished by an OSHA inspection visit. At the request of Congress, the General Accounting Office (GAO) issued a report on this subject (US Government Accounting Office, 2000). In the report, the GAO used information from several sources, including the National Labor Relations Board and the Federal Mediation and Conciliation Service to estimate the number of establishments with and without labour unrest during the years 1994–98. In particular, labour unrest was presumed to exist in establishments experiencing union organizing activities, unfair labour practice charges, efforts to

Table 14.6   Labour unrest in the USA, 1994–98

	1994	1995	1996	1997	1998
Total establishments	6620651	6761169	7008812	7057794	7354744
Establishments with labour unrest	22086	22138	20932	22202	20721
Percentage of establishments with labour unrest	0.033%	0.033%	0.030%	0.031%	0.028%
Major work stoppages as percentage of establishments with labour unrest	0.020%	0.014%	0.018%	0.013%	0.016%

Source: Calculated from US General Accounting Office, 2000.

decertify or remove a union, and work stoppages. Table 14.6 presents information calculated from the GAO report. Using the GAO's measure, far less than 1 per cent of US establishments experienced labour unrest in any year during the mid-1990s. While strike activity cannot be disaggregated from the measure, the number of major work stoppages represents much less than 1 per cent of the number of establishments that experienced labour unrest 1994–98. Accordingly, it is unlikely that the GAO's measure of labour unrest is a simple mirror of strike activity. Although the GAO's measure is far from ideal, it suggests that US establishments experienced a generally tiny, albeit steady, amount of unrest during the mid-1990s.

As noted, many opinions have been offered on why the amount of strike activity has declined in the USA. Scant attention has been paid, however, to the possibility that workers simply prefer more cooperation and less confrontation today than was the case in the past. For example, Richard Freeman and Joel Rogers (1999) surveyed US workers to assess their views on many work-related subjects. Freeman and Rogers reported that while workers want more opportunities to participate at work individually and in groups (p. 4), they desired cooperative, positive relations with managers (p. 5). Indeed, over 80 per cent of respondents indicated that they preferred 'a cooperative management to a powerful workplace organization' (p. 58). If workers prefer cooperative relationships at work, their support for organized unrest, such as strikes and job actions, is likely lower now than was the case in the past. In short, there are fewer manifestations of labour strife today, and that is how employees prefer it.

Table 14.7 *Political action committee contributions (in millions of dollars) to candidates by committee type*

| Election cycle | Committee type | | | | |
	Labour union ($)	Corporation ($)	Trade group ($)	Total contributions ($)	Labour/Total contributions (%)
1991–92	41.4	–	–	–	–
1993–94	41.9	69.6	52.9	189.6	22.1
1995–96	48.0	78.2	60.2	217.9	22.0
1997–98	44.6	78.0	62.3	219.9	20.3
1999–00	51.6	91.5	71.8	259.8	19.9

Source: US Federal Election Commission Reports

Other measures of union vitality: political action and public support
Organized labour's activity in the political arena increased substantially during the decade of the 1990s. While the future of the union movement has been regularly questioned in recent years, there is no basis for questioning the vitality of organized labour in the area of campaign finance. Unions are active participants in the political marketplace. Table 14.7 reports that union contributions to candidates for public office grew about 25 per cent during the past decade and that political action committees affiliated with labour donated about one-fifth of the contributions to candidates over that period. Some recent evidence suggests that the data in Table 14.7 dramatically understate the involvement of unions in politics. For example, Masters (in press) reported unions' 'soft money' political expenditures increased from about $4.3 million in the 1991–92 election cycle to $53.1 million in the 1999–2000 cycle. By cleverly calculating all union political expenditures in the 1999–2000 election cycle, Masters estimated that unions spent nearly $272 million (or five times their PAC contributions) in 2000. While this amount represents a small proportion of the total expenditures on the 2000 election, it illustrates that the union movement is currently investing in a strategy of political action. Troy (2001, p. 245) has also voiced this sentiment, asserting that the labour movement has adopted a new approach, 'a redirection from emphasizing its trade union function – organizing the unorganized – to political action'. Although this observation appears to be accurate, it remains to be seen whether political expenditures will payoff for a union movement running out of members. For more than a century, researchers have documented

the political activities of organized labour and illustrated how unions have sought to use the political process to amplify bargaining power (see Masters, in press; Bennett and Taylor, 2001; Delaney et al., 1999; Masters and Delaney, 1987; Seidman et al., 1958; Hudson and Rosen, 1954; Webb and Webb, 1897).

Public opinion and support of the US labour movement has varied over time. Over the years 1987–99, for example, Gallup polls indicate that approximately 25 per cent of respondents reported a great deal or quite a lot of confidence in organized labour. In general, the amount of public confidence in unions is similar to the amount of public confidence in many other US institutions, such as business corporations. It has been suggested that in recent years people are expressing more positive views of unions than was the case over the past few decades. For example, high school seniors have reported that unions are doing a good or very good job (US Bureau of Justice Statistics, 2000). In 2002, news reports of corporate scandals will likely raise the public image of unions. Whether or not organized labour's improved public standing is maintained over time, public support does not ensure union revitalization. If stable public support materializes, it may aid unions by supporting organizing efforts. But unions still face the burden of giving workers a compelling reason to join a labour organization. Over the past decade, such a reason has proved to be elusive.

Overview: the current state of US unions
Current trends and measures suggest an exceedingly difficult situation for unions in the USA. Evidence suggests that organizing efforts in the private sector have been unsuccessful and that job growth in the public sector, where unions have organized workers, is likely to be small in the foreseeable future. While unionized workers still receive better remuneration than non-union workers, compensation for non-union employees has been growing at a more rapid rate in recent years. There is a scarcity of high-paying union jobs. Strike activity has dwindled to near non-existence. Unions have focused substantial attention on the political arena. Organized labour has achieved some success there, especially in protecting union-favourable law from repeal. While some signs have emerged that unions are receiving a stronger public vote of confidence, such sentiment could take years to translate into tangible union gains. In short, US unions must find a way to deal with current challenges effectively or there will be few unions in the future. In light of the labour movement's challenges, this is a tall order.

3.   Current challenges to US unions and collective bargaining
Several factors must be kept in mind when making an assessment of the challenges faced by unions and collective bargaining in the USA. First, it

is critical to remember that bargaining patterns and results vary considerably across industries and sectors. That is one reason why some unions can score huge bargaining victories at the same time that other unions struggle to achieve gains. Although this variation has always existed, it is potentially more important in an age of declining union density. In particular, large union compensation premiums may exist for some union jobs, but those jobs are likely to be scarce. For example, workers in the auto industry continue to benefit from strong bargaining power, earning excellent compensation packages as a result. But employment in unionized auto plants is under pressure. More importantly, union workers in some industries have been forced to make concessions in instances where market forces and non-union competition create pressure to reduce wages. This has happened to truckers, newspaper workers, and meatpacking workers in the 1990s (see Clark et al., 2002). Accordingly, the challenges faced by unions vary somewhat across industries.

Variation also exists within industries, often because of occupational skill differences. For example, airline pilots have secured more generous contracts than flight attendants, mechanics, and customer service representatives. This variation is consistent with differences in union bargaining power. Such differences are largely explained by factors summarized by the Hicks–Marshall laws of elasticity of the derived demand for labour (Hicks, 1966; Marshall, 1923). In certain occupations, great bargaining power exists because of employee skill levels, solidarity, or some other unique attribute. In other occupations or sectors, bargaining power is low or non-existent. Accordingly, although employees in a specific industry face similar challenges due to industry forces, they may face other dissimilar challenges due to other developments.

Second, notwithstanding observable variation, evidence suggests that unions have had difficulty winning traditional job actions levelled against employers in recent years. As was noted above, strike activity has been low in recent years, and this has likely reduced employers' fear of strikes. It has also created an environment in which the general public has little conception of what a strike is or does. Without a credible strike threat, unions are hard pressed to negotiate attractive contract packages. If union compensation differentials decline, the benefit of joining a union also declines. Admittedly, union–management cooperation and labour peace can benefit firms and unions in some instances, such as has occurred recently in the telecommunications industry. Overall, however, unions must pose a credible strike threat if they are to secure satisfactory outcome packages.

Third, the overall state of the labour movement likely contributes to a situation in which unions and collective bargaining are in the news less often today than was the case in the past. For unions, the lack of public attention compounds a difficult situation and makes it easy for the public to forget about organized labour altogether. Another aspect of this trend, however, is that stories on union corruption or union political activities are not offset by positive stories on union members and leaders, the benefits created by unions, or the gains to society that result from bargaining. The media's emphasis on negative stories on organized labour could force unions to spend money on public relations activities that were unnecessary in the past. It could also force organized labour to identify and report 'accountability' metrics that the general public can understand and assess.

Fourth, and as has been stressed above, underlying much of the collective bargaining difficulty faced by unions is organized labour's inability to enroll new workers. Despite a large shift of resources into organizing over the past decade, unions have few victories about which to brag. Although this led the AFL-CIO recently to replace its organizing chief, speculation has arisen that the labour federation is giving up on the idea that organizing gains on a large-scale basis can be achieved in the foreseeable future (see Masters, in press). Consistent with the speculation, even where unions have achieved organizing success, victories have occurred in industries or occupations that may have only limited upside potential for the labour movement. For example, unionizing graduate student teaching and research assistants at US universities will likely provide fewer future organizing opportunities than did the unionization of the automobile industry 70 years ago.

These general factors affect the nature of the challenges faced by collective bargaining and unions in the USA. They illustrate that some challenges may be temporal and some lasting. It is not yet possible, however, to determine the extent to which historical bargaining patterns and trends continue to apply. Several developments deserve attention because they have the potential to alter bargaining processes and outcomes. Specifically, collective bargaining may be substantially affected by changing workforce conditions and worker expectations, outmoded labour laws, the imbalance created when unions organize on a national basis and markets operate globally, and international terrorism.

The changing nature of work

The nature of work has changed in recent years, both because of advancing technology and the acceleration of service sector job growth. In Drucker's (1993) words, society has moved from an industrial economy to a knowledge economy. This fundamental change has created a situation in which jobs will require a different set of skills. Many of the skills will be individualized and may not be related to production processes or equipment. Some skills will be technical and require training and certification.

And some skills that were unimportant in the past, such as communication and teamwork proficiencies, are becoming very important in this new environment. Market pressures for efficient operation in a knowledge economy mandate that even low-level employees possess skills that were not required in the past. Because some of the skills now required by employers are in short supply, firms have altered their employee mix to alleviate the problem. For example, hospitals and health care facilities have changed the duties of licensed and certified employees, such as nurses, giving those individuals more supervisory responsibilities over groups of lower-paid assistants who have lower skill levels. This has meant that nurses spend less time treating patients and more time supervising other employees. In such instances, it is not known whether workers become less interested in union membership. Even if it is assumed that employees demand for unionization remains the same in such cases, under labour law rules, their supervisory status may cause them to lose their bargaining rights.

In addition, market pressure has intensified the pace of work in most industries and workplaces. Employers in some industries have used this pressure to reduce the extent of unionization. For example, unionized workers in the telecommunications industry tend to be concentrated in the wireline segment of the industry. This segment is growing more slowly than other segments and relies on older technologies that may be replaced (Keefe and Batt, 2002). The general situation creates a dilemma for unions. Since workers need to possess increasingly sophisticated skills to meet employers' expectations and primary and secondary schools do not appear to provide those skills, unions may use their training expertise to attract new members. Unions may also discover an opportunity for organizing and bargaining in the rising pace of work that is apparent in many industries. Employees may seek representation to lessen the pace. At the same time, global competition has intensified the nature of work in many industries and organizations. Union efforts to lessen the intensity of work, accordingly, could create a situation in which a firm is unable to survive. Organized labour's efforts to change situations in firms will not alter the market pressure to compete. Thus, if unions successfully restricted work output, it could increase the outsourcing of union jobs to non-union locations in the USA and other nations. Unions cannot ignore the dramatic changes that are occurring in the nature of work. They must walk a thin line between protecting workers and allowing employers to be profitable in an increasingly competitive world.

Changes in the workforce and workers' expectations
Ironically, although an increase in the intensity of work should cultivate employees' interest in unions, it is not apparent that workers desire representation. Freeman and Rogers (1999) contended that almost all of the union

members in their study and about one-third of the non-members were interested in maintaining or acquiring some form of union representation (pp. 68–70). It is noteworthy that survey respondents generally indicated they preferred some form of representation that worked cooperatively with employers (p. 5) and that 'existing institutions – from unions to EI [employee involvement] committees to government regulations – are either insufficiently available to them or do not go far enough to provide the workplace voice they want' (p. 154). For a variety of reasons, workers today wish to participate at work. The existence of this desire for participation has been cited to support speculation that declining union density is due to constraints such as antiquated labour laws or unfair tactics by employers.

There is another potential explanation. Although unions seemingly benefit from the sentiments expressed by those in the Freeman and Rogers' survey, today's employees may simply not desire organized labour's traditional approaches. If unions are seen as opposing employers, they may be viewed as a sub-optimal solution to the problem of employee voice. This may mean that employees may want representation, but not by a traditional union. Similarly, employees may want voice into matters outside the traditional scope of bargaining in the USA (i.e. wages, hours, and other terms and conditions of employment). They may wish input into the design of products, the selection of supervisors, or the processes used to produce a product or provide a service. If so, collective bargaining as currently practised will not provide the outcomes employees seek. Because research on this subject is scarce, little is known about what employees really want from cooperative interaction with employers. Without more information, it is unwise to assume they want a traditional bargaining approach or relationship.

Because collective bargaining has developed a specific character over time, it has not adequately adjusted to the changing desires of workers. Ironically, whereas union leaders often seek leverage to pressure employers into making concessions, today's workers may disdain the use of such an approach. If this is the case, the harder union leaders fight to achieve bargaining gains, the less non-union employees may prefer unions.

The outdated nature of prevailing US labour law
For many years, labour leaders and some academics have criticized US labour law as being unfriendly to unions (see Friedman et al., 1994). These commentators have argued that decisions by the National Labor Relations Board (NLRB) and US courts regularly favour the interests of employers, non-union workers who do not seek union representation, and conservative groups. Indeed, this has been one of the primary arguments used to explain the lack of union success in organizing new workers or negotiating

good contracts. While research supports the notion that political appointments influence the decisions of the NLRB (Cooke et al., 1995; Cooke and Gautschi, 1982), the general criticisms reflect the great rancour that exists between labour and management (see Delaney et al., 1985). Over time, that animosity seems to have grown. For example, in recent years, it has been argued that the politicization of workplace relations has prevented even minor changes in the existing system of laws covering employee–employer interactions. Leaders in the field of industrial relations have argued that it is time to create a new social contract – one that aligns today's workforce with the institutions and regulations that govern it (Kochan, 2000). Kochan's concern is based on the growing problems arising from a mismatch between many Great Depression era laws and the reality of today's occupational structures, global competition, and changing preferences.

The problem is not one faced by unions alone. Section 8(a)(2) of the National Labor Relations Act (NLRA) makes it an unfair labour practice for an employer 'to dominate or interfere with the formation or administration of any labor organization or contribute financial or other support to it'. Because section 2 of the law defines a labour organization as 'any organization of any kind, or any agency or employee representation committee or plan, in which employees participate and which exists for the purpose, in whole or in part, of dealing with employers concerning grievances, labor disputes, wages, rates of pay, hours of employment, or conditions of work', a great number of the teams unilaterally established by employers in the USA are illegal. Because teamwork has become so important in recent years, this has created numerous problems for firms. Accordingly, employers have sought a labour law change that would make a variety of employer-supported teams and team structures legal. But the Team Act – the legislative amendment supported by employers to solve this problem – has not been enacted because of widespread opposition from labour groups. Even the high-profile group appointed by President Clinton to investigate labour law problems and recommend solutions (the Dunlop Commission) was unable to provide consistent guidance on the issue of teams. Indeed, partisan reactions to the recommendations of the Dunlop Commission created a situation in which no policy changes resulted from the Commission's work (see Kochan, 1995).

Whether or not changes are made in the current system or employers exploit current laws, some aspects of US labour law create significant problems for unions. First, increasingly, the law covers a smaller proportion of the potential workforce. This has occurred because employment growth has been greater in jobs that are excluded from the NLRA, such as managers and independent contractors, than in jobs that are covered by the Act. As exclusions grow, the power of traditional collective bargaining declines. It

has been argued that because of the increase in managerial and professional work, the decline in manual labour, and the increase in managerial
duties for all sorts of employees, the NLRA has become relevant to fewer
and fewer workers over the years (Sockell, 1989). Exclusion has occurred
because labour tribunals view many of today's employees as managers,
independent contractors, or supervisors, among other things. An example
of this phenomenon is a series of recent US Supreme Court cases addressing whether nurses are employees covered by the NLRA or managers who
are not covered (see *NLRB* v. *Hospital and Retirement Corporation of
America*, 1994; *NLRB* v. *Kentucky River Community Care*, 2001). As most
nurses direct the work of other health care employees, the Court has
increasingly defined them as managers who are excluded from coverage by
the NLRA. To the extent that job skill requirements continue to increase
and other jobs routinely contain some supervisory duties, precedent suggests that a larger share of the workforce will be excluded from coverage by
US labour laws. This is critically important because the widespread use of
teams by employers often gives employees some say in decisions that are
viewed as managerial decisions. Accordingly, it is inevitable that future
interpretations of the NLRA will exclude more occupations from coverage.
Excluded employees will find it difficult to organize and bargain using traditional approaches.

Second, as suggested above, the scope of bargaining outlined by the
NLRA – covering wages, hours, and other terms and conditions of employment – increasingly excludes issues that are important to unions and
employers. Essentially, the existing scope of bargaining permits the establishment of an economic arrangement between employers and unions.
Internal union affairs are left for unions alone to regulate and employers
have a virtual monopoly on decisions involving the business and where it
should go in the future. At a time when the nature of jobs has changed and
employees often have broader responsibilities, the existing scope of bargaining is increasingly out of step with employees' desires. This probably
reduces employees' interest in traditional union representation.

Whereas many researchers have focused in recent years on legal impediments to unions in organizing campaigns, the declining scope of coverage
under the NLRA and the narrow scope of bargaining are potentially more
significant problems. The structure of the economy is changing in ways that
will accelerate exclusions. It is not unrealistic to presume that over time the
economy – and its effect on exclusions – would make irrelevant any union-
favourable changes in rules regarding organizing. In addition, the narrow
scope of bargaining creates a situation in which collective bargaining provides few benefits for employers and increasingly ignores issues of concern
to workers. These factors likely create pressures in all industries to avoid

union representation. They also create a need for unions to develop ways of organizing workers outside the traditional channels.

Despite union leaders' complaints that NLRA procedures covering organizational activities are unfair, unions have engaged in few efforts to organize outside of the NLRA and researchers have offered little advice on the likely success of such operations. History appears to have been forgotten; prior to the passage of the NLRA, unions organized workers without guaranteed elections and other protections. Pre-1935 approaches could be used today to organize any employees who are excluded from the Act. Although it seems to be assumed that such efforts are impossible and doomed to failure, organizing outside the NLRA may soon be one of the few avenues open to unions interested in representing workers. The current situation makes it likely that some organizing and bargaining efforts outside the scope and protection of the NLRA are inevitable in coming years. Success in such efforts may allow unions to revitalize themselves and improve their image in society. To be successful in such efforts, unions must find ways to connect with workers – as they did in the 1930s.

National unions in a global marketplace
In the past, unions were successful in part because they were able to 'take wages out of competition'. When most or all employers in an industry or market paid the same union wage scales, employers needed to compete on other dimensions. Today, in a global marketplace, it is increasingly impossible for a US union – or any national union for that matter – to take wages out of competition. Firms regularly transfer operations to other countries to lower costs and improve economic results. This illustrates a dilemma faced by the world's labour movement. Firms are increasingly organized on a global basis while unions are organized on a national or local one. This makes it difficult for unions to deal effectively with competitive decisions made by businesses. Moreover, global business organization ensures that labour laws favourable to unions in a particular country will likely come under pressure over time as businesses respond to the perceived disadvantage of such laws and relocate operations to other nations.

Unions have adopted several approaches to improve their success in a global environment. Political pressure has been used to include clauses in free trade agreements that offer specific labour and environmental protections. For example, the North American Free Trade Agreement (NAFTA) includes side agreements on labour standards designed to protect workers' rights in the US, Canada, and Mexico. Although it has proved difficult to enforce and police these side agreements, their existence indicates that organized labour is cognizant of the threat to unions that globalization represents. Unions have also merged or consolidated within nations to gain efficiencies of scale in organizing and servicing members. This approach does not solve the dilemma of globalization, but it allows unions to operate more efficiently and in so doing aids in efforts to address multinational businesses. In some instances, unions have collaborated with other interest groups to place external pressure on firms. Joint efforts with management have even been undertaken to achieve mutually beneficial outcomes (e.g. UPS and Teamsters officials lobbied jointly to gain new air routes to China). But organized labour has made only limited efforts to cooperate with labour movements in other countries (e.g. labour federations in France and the Netherlands have recently supported the efforts of the US union UNITE to pressure the French firm Pinault-Printemps-Redoute to respect its workers' unionization rights in a plant in Indiana). Until union movements coordinate their efforts more effectively on a global basis, however, employers will have an advantage over unions. Because a variety of forces make it difficult for unions to collaborate, organized labour will likely remain in a suboptimal situation for many years. If unions coordinate efforts transnationally, however, it may be possible for national unions to achieve more success in negotiations with employers.

September 11 and terrorism
The terrorist attacks on 11 September 2001, and subsequent anthrax mailings, will potentially have lasting effects in all US industries. In addition, the attacks raised issues that will affect unions and collective bargaining. While it is obvious that the airline, public safety, trucking, and electric utility industries will face new rules, restrictions, and precautions, no industry will be exempt from concern over terrorism. Many union employees work in the industries mentioned. Many others work in the telecommunications, petrochemical, leisure and hospitality, professional sports, health care, and dockworking industries. The potential for terrorism will have direct effects on operations in these and other industries and will likely make certain job-related (and bargaining) issues more salient than they were in the past. A variety of indirect effects on unions and bargaining may also arise.

The threat of terrorism will cause changes in rules, security, and operations in many industries. For example, in the airline industry, security concerns have become paramount. Because the concerns are grave, airline unions will seek to bargain over security matters. Pilots have already sought permission to carry weapons and some airlines have installed stun guns in airline cockpits. Considerable interest has arisen in other areas too, such as training in self-defence, passenger threat assessment, and general security protocols. Such concerns could lead to changes in airline hiring policies beyond governmentally mandated background checks of employees. Because many of the new security procedures imposed by the US government seem to be inconsistent across airports, impose delays, and inconvenience passengers (greatly, in some cases), demand for air travel has fallen. This will generate employee and union attention because a sustained decline in demand could lead to layoffs or reduced compensation or both. As a result, union leadership in these areas could garner employee and public support. Unions have long negotiated over issues related to safety and training. A successful approach to these issues in bargaining could allow airline unions to gain widespread public support, which would aid the union movement generally, and increase air passenger traffic. At the same time, it will take considerable union pressure to affect these issues given the role assumed by the government for security. This means that union political action will be an important lever in efforts to address airline employees' safety concerns.

The terrorist attacks also had a variety of indirect effects on unions and bargaining. For example, the hospitality industry was especially hard hit as members of the Hotel and Restaurant Employees Union (HERE) suffered approximately 88 000 layoffs – 11 per cent of the total number of layoffs attributed to September 11 – as a result of decreased travel after the attacks (see Waddoups and Eade, 2002). While the travel and hospitality industry had rebounded somewhat by the summer of 2002, many workers have not yet been recalled. Moreover, the decline in attendance and emergent need for higher levels of security in prominent resorts and theme parks will certainly influence the substance and tenor of bargaining in unionized hospitality establishments into the foreseeable future.

Some consequences of the attacks could be helpful to organized labour. For example, security has become a great concern in the trucking industry and public utility industries. Issues such as who holds permits to transport hazardous waste, whether Mexican drivers should be granted full access to US highways, and how power plants and reservoirs should be guarded will be raised in unions' bargaining and political efforts. These concerns could aid organized US truckers enormously if they delay the implementation of NAFTA provisions on trucking. They could also aid union apprenticeship programmes by creating a preference for workers who have received formal certification for sensitive jobs (e.g. electricians, nuclear technicians). The situation could also create more willingness from the government to encourage union–management cooperation and partnerships. In such an environment, joint union–management initiatives regarding security in various industries could create a basis for future union growth.

The response of the US government to September 11 also includes an ominous problem for unions. Specifically, President Bush has sought to restrict the bargaining and civil service rights and protections of workers employed by the Department of Homeland Security (President's Homeland

Security Department Proposal, 2002). To the extent that the government continues to seek such restrictions on workers' rights and protections in the name of homeland security, organized labour faces a serious challenge. If legislators and courts accept the government's arguments, longstanding civil service and collective bargaining rights could be unilaterally suspended. Unions will be required to expend considerable political capital to forestall the administration's proposal. If they fail to do so, it is possible that long-standing unionization and bargaining rights in sensitive industries or occupations could also be targeted for elimination.

4. Conclusions

Overall, the state of collective bargaining in the US in 2002 is mixed, though on average it is declining. While this situation is not due to the inability of collective bargaining to produce gains, evidence that bargaining is under duress increasingly exists. As I have stressed, the problem is fuelled fundamentally by the labour movement's inability to organize new workers. With few exceptions, union organizing efforts have not offset yearly membership losses due to plant closings, layoffs, and retirements. Despite the contentions of some observers (e.g. Freeman and Rogers, 1999), there appears to be little clamour for bargaining from the individuals who could benefit most from it. This means that power is still a central theme in any analysis of collective bargaining in the US private sector. But union power has eroded to a point that it may never recover to a critical mass.

Although the general trends are negative for unions, considerable variation exists in the prevailing status of bargaining across US industries. This ensures that occupations with strong bargaining power by virtue of their special skills or difficulty of replacement (such as pilots) will likely continue to negotiate favourable outcomes in the short term. Unionized individuals in other occupations, however, face increasingly difficult times in their efforts to secure bargaining gains. This situation suggests a mixed future for unions and collective bargaining.

Union bargaining power still exists in industries that have maintained union density in core jobs (e.g. autos, telecommunications). Even in those industries, however, unions face challenges. In the auto industry, the UAW must develop a way to organize new facilities (often foreign transplants that locate in parts of the US that have been traditionally unsympathetic to unions). The union must also work with Big Three employers to increase their market share. Such cooperation will create a dilemma for the union as it will face pressure from members to steer the gains of cooperation to members rather than managers or shareholders. Unless enough of the gains go to the firms, however, corporate investment in unionized plants will likely decline. As a result, failure to walk this thin line effectively will make the UAW's future dimmer than it could be. This issue will be especially salient in the next several years as Japanese firms seek to gain market share in segments of the industry that have driven profits for the Big Three (e.g. SUVs and large pickup trucks).

In telecommunications, the challenge is to ensure that firms allow unionized workers to participate in segments of the market that are growing, such as wireless communications and Internet protocol communications rather than assigning such work to non-union employees. While unions in this industry will also face pressure from both firms and employees, they will be required to lobby in concert with firms for regulatory actions that help the industry. As unions have long been active politically, joint efforts with employers could lead to enhanced options for unionized telecom employees. At a minimum, telecom firms will be less hostile to unions because of the need for labour's lobbying help before government regulatory bodies.

Although the specific challenges differ across industries, unions uniformly must find a way to enroll new members and gain public support. Depending on the circumstances facing specific unions, the approaches taken may include labour–management cooperation, productivity bargaining, or deunionization. In truth, unions in every industry face significant pressure to change. Minor adjustments have not made organized labour stronger in recent years. When John Sweeney swept into power at the AFL-CIO, there was hope that increased emphasis on organizing would help the labour movement grow. The investment of money and people in organizing, however, has not produced better outcomes than occurred under Lane Kirkland. Simultaneously, campaign finance reform legislation threatens to weaken somewhat unions' political power. This is problematic given that union political efforts have offset to some extent labour's organizing woes. Ultimately, it is necessary to ask whether the product unions are offering to potential members is an attractive one. Because unions have taken different approaches across industries to address this issue, observers may wish to focus on how individual unions have sought to make their product more attractive. Ironically, the bleak nature of the situation faced by unions may be the impetus necessary for change and revival. How individual unions respond will provide a clue as to the labour movement's future. That future is tied inextricably to the rise of talented new union leaders – ones who are ready to jettison practices and even tradition if necessary to create a revival.

Many forces are outside the control of unions. For example, recent court decisions mean that bargaining could be negated for employees who have a managerial component in their normal duties. Depending on whether courts view team-based arrangements as creating a managerial component in a job, it is possible that even more positions will be excluded from the

NLRA. In the past, national boundaries placed severe restraints on organized labour. Today, unions have reached a point where international combinations present one of the few opportunities to revitalize the labour movement. Despite the external threats and difficult general situation, unions can still control their destiny. A critical first step in the direction of seizing control will be an effort to change the nature of unionism. The absence of change in collective bargaining, the subjects of bargaining, the approaches taken in bargaining, and so on, signal labour's dilemma. Collective bargaining has become an institution that can deliver only a narrow range of (primarily) economic outcomes for workers. It is unable to address business decisions directly. It often includes antagonistic interactions. It relies on laws permitting the negotiation of contracts compelling covered non-members to pay union representation fees. And union leaders are no longer assumed to be the good guys.

The political situation in the USA will likely diminish the power of the union movement in the near term. As a result, there is a great need for visionary union leadership today, as well as the identification of mechanisms other than collective bargaining that will aid and protect the interests of workers.

References

Batt, Rosemary, Alexander J.S. Colvin and Jeffrey Keeffe (2002), 'Employee Voice, Human Resource Practices, and Quit Rates: Evidence from the Telecommunications Industry', *Industrial and Labor Relations Review*, 55 (4), 573–594.

Bennett, James T. and Jason E. Taylor (2001), 'Labor Unions: Victims of Their Political Success?', *Journal of Labor Research*, 22 (2), 261–273.

Bloomberg News (2000), 'Court Says Pilots Still Owe Money to American Over Work Stoppage', *Houston Chronicle*, September 23, p. 2.

Boroff, Karen E. and David Lewin (1997), 'Loyalty, Voice, and Intent to Exit a Union Firm: A Conceptual and Empirical Analysis', *Industrial and Labor Relations Review*, 51 (1), 50–63.

Chaison, Gary and Barbara Bigelow (2002), *Unions and Legitimacy*, Ithaca, NY: ILR Press.

Clark, Paul F., John T. Delaney and Ann C. Frost (eds), (2002), *Private-Sector Collective Bargaining*, Champaign, IL: Industrial Relations Research Association.

Cooke, William N. (1994), 'Employee Participation Programs, Group-Based Incentives, and Company Performance: A Union–Nonunion Comparison', *Industrial and Labor Relations Review*, 47 (4), 594–609.

Cooke, William N. and Frederick H. Gautschi (1982), 'Political Bias in NLRB Unfair Labor Practice Decisions', *Industrial and Labor Relations Review*, 36 (4), 539–549.

Cooke, William N., Aneil K. Mishra, Gretchen M. Spreitzer and Mary Tschirhart (1995), 'The Determinants of NLRB Decision-Making Revisited', *Industrial and Labor Relations Review*, 48 (2), 237–257.

Delaney, John T., David Lewin and Donna Sockell (1985), 'The NLRA at Fifty: A Research Appraisal and Agenda', *Industrial and Labor Relations Review*, 39 (1), 46–75.

Delaney, John T., Jack Fiorito and Paul Jarley (1999), 'Evolutionary Politics? Union Differences and Political Activities in the 1990s', *Journal of Labor Research*, 20 (3), 277–295.

Drucker, Peter (1993), *Post-Capitalist Society*, New York: HarperCollins.

Dworkin, James B. and Richard A. Posthuma (2002), 'Professional Sports: Collective

Bargaining in the Spotlight', in Paul F. Clark, John T. Delaney and Ann C. Frost (eds), *Private-Sector Collective Bargaining*, Champaign, IL: Industrial Relations Research Association, pp. 217–261.

Eaton, Adrienne E. (1994), 'The Survival of Employee Participation Programs in Unionized Settings', *Industrial and Labor Relations Review*, 47 (3), 371–389.

Eaton, Adrienne E. and Jill Kriesky (2001), 'Union, Organizing under Neutrality and Card Check Agreements', *Industrial and Labor Relations Review*, 55 (1), 42–59.

Fiorito, Jack and Cheryl L. Maranto (1987), 'The Contemporary Decline of Union Strength', *Contemporary Policy Issues*, 5 (4), 12–27.

Freeman, Richard B. and James L. Medoff (1984), *What Do Unions Do?*, New York: Basic Books.

Freeman, Richard B. and Joel Rogers (1999), *What Workers Want*, Ithaca, NY: ILR Press.

Friedman, Sheldon, Richard W. Hurd, Rudolph A. Oswald and Ronald L. Seeber (eds) (1994), *Restoring the Promise of American Labor Law*, Ithaca, NY: ILR Press.

Ginsbach, Pam, Michelle Amber and Barney Tumey (1997), 'Teamsters Preparing for Ratification Vote as Tentative Contract Ends 15-Day Strike', *Daily Labor Report*, August 20, pp. AA-1–AA-3.

Gittleman, Maury, Michael Horrigan and Mary Joyce (1998), 'Flexible Workplace Practices: Evidence from a Nationally Representative Survey', *Industrial and Labor Relations Review*, 52 (1), 99–115.

Hicks, John R. (1966), *The Theory of Wages*, 2nd edn, New York: St. Martin's Press.

Hirsch, Barry T., David A. Macpherson and Edward J. Schumacher (2002), 'Measuring Union and Non-union Wage Growth: Puzzles in Search of Solutions', paper presented at the Middlebury Economics Conference, Middlebury College, Middlebury, VT.

Hirschman, Dave and Stephen Krupin (2002), 'UPS, Union Both Satisfied: Teamsters Win 10,000 New Jobs', *Atlanta Journal and Constitution*, July 17, p. 1D.

Houston Chronicle News Services (2001), 'Pilots Union Agrees to Reimburse American Over Sickout in 1999', *Houston Chronicle*, April 28, p. 3.

Hudson, Ruth Alice and Hjalmar Rosen (1954), 'Union Political Action: The Member Speaks', *Industrial and Labor Relations Review*, 7 (3), 404–418.

Ichniowski, Casey, John T. Delaney and David Lewin (1989), 'The New Human Resource Management in US Workplaces: Is it Really New and is it Only Nonunion?', *Relations Industrielles*, 44 (1), 97–119.

Katz, Harry C. and Owen Darbishire (2000), *Converging Divergences: Worldwide Change in Employment Systems*, Ithaca, NY: ILR Press.

Keefe, Jeffrey and Rosemary Batt (2002), 'Telecommunications: Collective Bargaining in an Era of Industry Reconsolidation', in Paul F. Clark, John T. Delaney and Ann C. Frost (eds), *Private-Sector Collective Bargaining*, Champaign, IL: Industrial Relations Research Association pp. 263–310.

Kochan, Thomas A. (1995), 'Using the Dunlop Report to Achieve Mutual Gains', *Industrial Relations*, 34 (3), 350–366.

Kochan, Thomas A. (2000), 'Building a New Social Contract at Work: A Call to Action', *Perspectives on Work*, 4 (1), 3–12.

LeRoy, Michael H. (1995), 'The Changing Character of Strikes Involving Permanent Striker Replacements, 1935–1990', *Journal of Labor Research*, 16 (4), 423–437.

LeRoy, Michael H. (2000), 'Creating Order out of Chaos and Other Partial and Intermittent Strikes', *Northwestern University Law Review*, 95 (1), 221–270.

LeRoy, Michael H. (2001), 'The Formation and Administration of Labor Policy by the NLRB: Evidence from Economic and ULP Strike Rulings', *Journal of Labor Research*, 22 (4), 723–737.

LeRoy, Michael H. and John H. Johnson IV (2001), 'Death by Lethal Injunction: National Emergency Strikes Under the Taft–Hartley Act and the Moribund Right to Strike', *Arizona Law Review*, 43, 63–134.

Lewis, H. Gregg (1963), *Unionism and Relative Wages in the United States: An Empirical Inquiry*, Chicago: University of Chicago Press, Chapter 2.

Marshall, Alfred (1923), *Principles of Economics*, 8th edn, London: Macmillan.

Masters, Marick F. (2002), 'Unions in 2000: A Strategic Choice Perspective', in press, *Journal of Labor Research*.

Masters, Marick F. and John T. Delaney (1987), 'Union Political Activities: A Review of the Empirical Literature', *Industrial and Labor Relations Review*, 40 (3), 336–353.

Nissen, Bruce (ed.) (2002), *Unions in a Globalised Environment: Changing Borders, Organizational Boundaries, and Social Roles*, Armonk, NY: M.E. Sharpe.

NLRB v. *Hospital and Retirement Corporation of America*, 511 US 571 (1994).

NLRB v. *Kentucky River Community Care*, 532 US 706 (2001).

Osterman, Paul (1994), 'How Common is Workplace Transformation and Who Adopts It?', *Industrial and Labor Relations Review*, 47 (2), 173–187.

Osterman, Paul (2000), 'Work Reorganization in an Era of Restructuring: Trends in Diffusion and Effects on Employee Welfare', *Industrial and Labor Relations Review*, 53 (2), 179–196.

Peltz, James F. and Stephen Gregory (1999), 'Pilots' Sickout Causes Huge Problems for Holiday Travel', *Los Angeles Times*, February 13, p. A1.

President's Homeland Security Department Proposal (2002), http://www.whitehouse.gov/deptofhomeland/bill/hsl-bill.pdf.

Schwochau, Susan, John Delaney, Paul Jarley and Jack Fiorito (1997), 'Employee Participation and Assessments of Support for Organizational Policy Changes', *Journal of Labor Research,* 18 (3), 379–401.

Seidman, Joel, Jack London, Bernard Karsh and Daisy L. Tagliacozzo (1958), *The Worker Views His Union*, Chicago: University of Chicago Press.

Sockell, Donna (1989), 'The Future of Labor Law: A Mismatch Between Statutory Interpretation and Industrial Reality', *Boston College Law Review*, 30, 987–1026.

Troy, Leo (2001), 'Twilight for Organized Labor', *Journal of Labor Research*, 22 (2), 245–259.

Turner, Lowell, Harry C. Katz and Richard W. Hurd (eds) (2001), *Rekindling the Movement: Labor's Quest for Relevance in the 21st Century*, Ithaca, NY: ILR Press.

US Bureau of Justice Statistics (2000), *Sourcebook of Criminal Justice Statistics*, Washington, DC: Bureau of Justice Statistics, Table 2.85.

US Bureau of Labor Statistics (1997), *National Compensation Study: Occupational Wages in the United States, 1997 – Bulletin 2548,* Washington, DC: BLS, http://www.bls.gov/ncs/ncspubs.htm#Compensation.

US General Accounting Office (2000), *Worker Protection: OSHA Inspections at Establishments Experiencing Labor Unrest* [GAO/HEHS-00–144], Washington, DC: General Accounting Office, http://www.gao.gov/new.items/he00144.pdf.

Voos, Paula (ed.) (1994), *Contemporary Collective Bargaining in the Private Sector*, Madison, WI: Industrial Relations Research Association.

Waddoups, C. Jeffrey and Vincent H. Eade (2002), 'Hotels and Casinos: Collective Bargaining During a Decade of Expansion', in Paul F. Clark, John T. Delaney and Ann C. Frost (eds), *Private-Sector Collective Bargaining*, Champaign, IL: Industrial Relations Research Association pp. 137–177.

Webb, Sidney and Beatrice Webb (1897), *Industrial Democracy*, London: Longman, Green.

Zelman v. *Simmons-Harris*, 536 US (June 27, 2002).

Index

ABB Alstom Power 465
active manpower policy 350
activists 373
adoptive leave 443
Advisory, Conciliation and Arbitration
    Service (ACAS), UK 238, 416–17,
    418
Africa 366, 375, 388–91, 396
age
    and membership 27–9, 362
    and wages 219, 224–5, 226–7, 228,
    235–7, 261, 263
agency work 463, 465
Agreement on Social Policy (ASP), EU
    416, 438, 440, 445–6, 448
agriculture sector 366, 469
air traffic controllers 109
aircraft production 118, 133
airline industry 141, 524–5
All-Chinese Federation of Trade
    Unions (ACFTU) 388
Allied Pilots' Association 510–11
American Airlines 510–11
American Federation of Labor-
    Congress of Industrial
    Organizations (AFL-CIO) 339,
    505, 518, 527
anarcho-syndicalist unions 335
Angola 389
anti-inflation board, Canada 107–8
Antiga 395
apartheid 391
apprenticeship programmes 525
Arab countries 388
arbitration 382, 416–17
Argentina 394, 395, 396, 399, 402, 403
Asia 366, 382–8
Asian crisis 1999 386
Australia
    bargaining 122, 248, 401, 402, 403,
    404
    income inequality 233
    industrial relations 119, 122, 158,
    160, 174

union density/membership 20, 21,
    23, 24, 26, 29, 31, 120, 374, 382,
    383, 402, 403, 404
political role of unions 353–4
productivity 129, 131, 139, 142,
    165
technological diffusion 315, 319
wages 207, 208–9
Australian Bureau of Statistics 373
Australian Workplace Industrial
    Relations Surveys (AWIRS) 139,
    208
Austria
    bargaining 401, 402, 403, 404, 466,
    477
    income inequality 233
    industrial relations 174, 184, 478,
    480, 482, 488, 489
    political role of unions 341, 344,
    347, 357
    union density/membership 376,
    398
    union wage premium 207, 209–11,
    212, 231, 402, 403
    unions 476
    welfare state 359
automobile industry 120, 517, 518,
    526
Azerbaijan 380

ballots 417, 421
    see also postal ballots; secret ballots
Baltic states 381
Banda, Dr Hastings 391
Bangladesh 385, 387
banking sector 488
bargaining 3, 85–113
    Australia 122, 248, 401, 402, 403,
    404
    Austria 401, 402, 403, 404, 466, 477
    Belgium 404, 465–6, 492
    Canada 401, 402, 403, 404
    China 408
    Denmark 402, 403, 404, 477

bargaining (*continued*)
  economic and political environment
    3, 183–8
  Finland 248–9, 404
  France 248, 402, 403, 404
  Germany 120, 122, 164, 190, 248,
    303, 401, 404, 465–6
  Italy 402, 403
  Japan 120, 173, 303, 401, 402, 403,
    404
  Luxembourg 465–6, 478, 482
  Malaysia 404
  Netherlands 402, 403, 404, 465–6,
    492
  New Zealand 190, 382, 401, 402, 403
  Norway 248–9, 404
  optimal bargaining areas 469–71
  Philippines 402, 403, 404
  Portugal 404, 482
  South Africa 401, 402, 403, 404
  South Korea 402, 403, 404
  Spain 184, 402, 403, 404
  structure and environment 61–76,
    176–80
  Sweden 190, 248–9, 402, 403, 404,
    477, 479, 480, 492
  Switzerland 401, 402, 403, 466
  Taiwan 402, 404
  Turkey 404
  UK 120–1, 190, 401, 402, 403, 404,
    477, 480
  USA 120, 180, 190, 401, 402, 403,
    404, 502–28
bargaining agenda 53, 60
bargaining conduct 48–53
bargaining coordination 176–80
bargaining coverage 367, 400–5
bargaining outcomes, USA 506–11
bargaining power 30, 53, 126
bargaining scope 53–61, 71–2, 522
Belarus 366, 379, 380
Belgium
  bargaining 404, 465–6, 492
  employee preferences 475
  income inequality 233
  industrial relations 174, 478, 480,
    481, 482
  union density/membership 376, 378,
    396, 398, 402, 403
  political role of unions 341, 344, 347

unemployment insurance 33–4
unions 477
Benelux countries 378
'between-sector' effect 256, 260, 286–7
'Big Plane' 133
Bismarck countries 347
'blacking' of goods 417
Blair, Tony 415, 436, 453
  reforms of 436–45
blue-collar workers 362
  Sweden 340
  and membership 30, 362, 400
  union wage premium 204, 209, 218,
    260, 508
Bolivia 395, 396, 399
Botswana 391, 392
Brazil
  productivity 325, 327
  union density/membership 394, 395,
    399, 405
  union wage premium 209–10, 212,
    231
Bretton Woods system 360
Bridgestone/Firestone tyre plant
  133–4
Bridlington rules 421
British Household Panel Survey
  (BHPS) 204, 271
British Social Attitudes Surveys
  (BSAS) 222, 223
Bulgaria 379, 380
Bundesverband der Deutschen
  Industrie (BDI) 488
Bundesverband Deutscher Banken
  (BDB) 488
Bundesvereinigung der Deutschen
  Arbeitgeberverbände (BDA) 488
Bush, George 504–5, 525
business associations 468, 484, 485–6,
  488
business cycles 25–6, 201, 422
business transfers 447–8
business unions 339

Callaghan, James 346
Cameroon 392
campaign finance reform legislation,
  USA 527
Canada
  bargaining 401, 402, 403, 404

gender and unionisation/wages 261, 263, 265, 268, 270, 273, 274, 275, 282–3

income inequality 233, 259, 275–89

industrial relations 119, 174, 248

investment 151, 152, 166

labour disputes 101, 105–6, 107–9, 110–11

political role of unions 353–4

productivity 130, 134, 165, 326–7

research and development 309, 310

skill groups 273–4, 287

technological diffusion 315, 318

union density/membership 249, 366, 374, 375, 381, 383, 398, 400, 402, 403

union wage premium 120, 134, 209–11, 212, 231, 249, 263

wage dispersion 260

wage structure 247, 261–2, 263, 274, 282–3

workers' rights 523

Canadian General Social Survey (GSS) 208

Canadian Labour Force Survey (CLFS) 276, 277

Cape Verde 392

capital equipment 123, 142, 150, 166

capital flexibility 299

capital markets, internationalisation of 361

capital, return on 141, 142

capital-labour substitution 154

Catholic parties 336, 340

Catholic unions 340, 341

Central Arbitration Committee (CAC), UK 416–17, 441

Central America
  informal employment sector 369
  membership 366, 391–6

central banks, institutional independence of 186–7, 188, 192

Central Europe 368, 379, 404–6, 406

centralized bargaining 69–71, 120, 190, 248, 358, 404
  and economic and monetary policy 353, 357
  and fiscal policy 185, 187

and wage demands 176

and wage-setting 74, 75, 173–4, 352

Germany 164

studies of 177, 178, 180

versus decentralized systems 68

Centre Party, Germany 341

Centre-left parties 346, 348

Centre-right parties 336

CGT, France 341, 477

chambers of commerce and industry 468–9, 488–9

Charter of Fundamental Rights 2000, EU 451–2

chemical unions 466

'Cheshire cat' unions 55

Chile
  union campaigns 404–6
  union density/membership 402, 403, 406
  union wage premium 209–11, 212, 231

China
  bargaining 404
  informal employment sector 369
  union density/membership 366, 384, 385, 386, 388, 397, 399

Christian Democratic Union (CDU/CSU),Germany 341

Christian trade unions 357

Christian-democrat parties 357

Christian-Democratic Party, Germany 336

Clinton, Bill 521

closed economies 293

closed shops 16, 34, 35, 62, 76, 158
  and financial performance 146, 166, 423
  and plant closings 424, 425
  decline of 426
  legislation 373, 416, 418, 420, 421

club theory 471

coal industry 51

collective bargaining
  contracts 175–83
  coverage and representation 247–9, 400–5
  economic and political environment of 183–8
  empirical evidence on 104–9

collective bargaining (*continued*)
structure and coordination 176–80
systems 173–5
EU legislation on 451–2
Europe 9–10
USA 502–28
collective bargaining, Europeanization
of 461–94
collective employer activity 485–6
collective objective function 51
collective redundancies 447–8
Collective Redundancies and Transfer
of Undertakings (Protection of
Employment) (Amendment)
Regulations 1999 447
collective voice 124, 125, 137, 147, 148,
163, 165
Colombia 395
Commissioner for Protection against
Unlawful Industrial Action
(COPUIA), UK 419
Commissioner for the Rights of Trade
Union Members (CROTUM),
UK 419
Committee of Agricultural
Organizations in the EC (COPA)
469
common product markets and
standardization of wages 252–3
Communist parties 340, 341
Communist trade unions 357, 379,
477
Communist World Federation of
Trade Unions 405
company-level bargaining 190
company-orientated collective
bargaining 473
compensation packages 205
competitive markets 61
compulsory arbitration 382
compulsory membership *see* closed
shops
concession bargaining 93
Confédération Européenes des Cadres
(CEC) 466–7
Confédération Française
Démocratique du Travail (CFDT),
France 477
Confédération Générale Italienne du
Travail (CGIL), Italy 341

Confederation of British Industry
443–4
Confederation of Independent Trade
Unions in Bulgaria (CITUB)
379
Confederation of Irish Industry (CII)
489
conflict payoffs 64, 67
conflict, reduction of 46
conglomerate unions 477
Congo 389
Congress of South African Trade
Unions (COSATU) 391
Congress Party, India 387
Conseil national du patronat français
(CNPF) 488
Conservative government, UK 351
reforms of 416–36
conservative parties 345
Conservative Party, Australia 382
Conservative Party, UK 337
construction sector
bargaining 120, 484
wage differentials 218
construction workers' unions 466
consultation, national systems for
450–1
Continental Europe
bargaining 248
productivity 295
research and development 328
cooling-off periods 101–2, 108–9,
110–11
cooperative industrial relations 121,
147–8, 155, 157, 160–1, 166
and partnership agreements 158
cooperative ownership 133
cooperative working 520
coordinated bargaining
arrangements 70, 176–80, 181,
187, 189, 190
and economic performance 5
coordinated market economies 381
coordination improvement 46
corporatism 184–5
cost of living (COLA) clauses, USA
93, 180–1
cost–benefit considerations of
membership 19, 21, 27, 33
Costa Rica 395

costs
  of disputes 91, 92, 96–100, 103–4,
    107, 109–11
  of membership 17
  to unions 14–15
Côte d'Ivorie 303
councils of workers 335, 348
Cournot
  competition 72–3, 74
  duopoly 300
craft unions 338–9, 356, 384
  and restrictive practices 127–8
  and standards of workmanship 125
craft workers 158
cross-border cooperation 465–6, 480,
  484
cross-border union mergers 477
'cross-hauling' 74, 75
cross-national analyses of unionisation
  32–5, 36
cross-sectional analyses of union
  membership 26–32
Cuba 394, 395
Current Population Survey (CPS),
  USA 201, 202, 207, 212, 213, 214,
  218, 276–7
cyclical nature of wage gaps 228–30
cyclical patterns of strikes 105–6
Cyprus 209, 210, 211, 212, 231, 390
Czech Republic 379, 380, 402, 403

Data Handbook on European Unions
  368
decentralized bargaining systems 67,
  68–9, 72, 74, 120–1, 122, 164, 173,
  176, 182, 187–8, 190, 192, 352–3,
  384
  versus centralized systems 68
decline, macro-determinants of 20–6
Delors, Jacques 462–3
decommodification of labour 355
democracy, transition to 394
democracy, union campaigns for
  404–6
democratic class struggle and party
  linkages 345–7
Democratic Party, USA 336, 339
democratization, South Korea 386
Denmark
  bargaining 402, 403, 404, 477

employers' associations 488, 489
employment insurance 33
income inequality 233
union density/membership 207, 212,
  376, 378, 396, 398, 402, 403
union wage premium 231, 402, 403
wage indexation 181
welfare provision 355, 356
Department of Homeland Security,
  USA 505
  protection of workers 525–6
Department of Trade and Industry,
  UK 238, 440
deregulation 352, 353
developing countries 369–70, 374
direct action 355
disability pensions 358–9
disagreement payoffs 62, 63, 64
disciplinary procedure 419, 420, 441–2,
  443
discrimination
  against non-union workers 417,
    419
  against union workers 419, 421
  on gender 446
dismissal
  of non-union workers 417, 418, 419,
    420, 421
  of striking workers 419, 441–2
disputes, fixed costs of 97–100
dockworkers 126, 141
Dominican Republic 395
Doorn group 465–6, 474, 475
Dunlop Commission, USA 10, 148,
  521

East Asia 375, 382, 384, 397
Eastern Europe
  democratization 378–9, 404–6
  membership 368
  political role of unions 354, 406
economic analysis of unions 1, 2, 5–6
economic effects
  of Conservative reforms, UK
    421–36
  of Labour reforms 443–5
economic environment of bargaining
  183–8
economic integration 73–4
economic liberalization 384

economic management 351
economic models of union behaviour
3, 44–81
economic performance and
coordinated bargaining 5
economic policy 349–54, 360–1
Ecuador 395, 396
Edin norm 492
educational qualifications
and union wage premium 270–1
and wage inequality 206, 217, 218,
219, 220, 224–5, 226–7, 261, 262,
263, 277–8
efficiency-enhancing role of unions 46
efficient bargaining model 56, 57, 58,
59–60, 71, 72
Egypt 389, 390
El Salvador 395, 402
electoral process of membership, USA
220–21, 248
employee grievances/preferences 46
employee involvement committees
(EIs) 162–4, 520
employees' incentives, Europeanization
of collective bargaining 472–6
employer representation 347–8, 485–7
employers 484–5
joint understandings with 338
selection of workers 199
employers' associations
Europe 462–5, 467, 468–9, 482–3,
493
North America 381
diversity in 488–9
employers' organizability 487–92
employment
effect of minimum wage on 439–40
Employment Acts 1980, 1982, 1988 and
1990, UK 417, 418, 419, 420, 421
employment and Keynesianism 349–51
employment behaviour 46
Employment Bill, UK 442–3
employment contracts 190
Employment Contracts Act 1991, New
Zealand 382
employment growth 21, 24, 167, 521
employment legislation 120
employment protection 121–2
Employment Protection Act 1975, UK
416, 418

Employment Relations Act 1999, UK
415, 419, 438, 440–2
employment tribunals 442, 443
employment, creation of 352
employment, terms and conditions
520, 522
employment, unions influence on
58–60, 423–4
Enron 141
enterprise bargaining 382, 386, 404
enterprise unions 121, 342, 388
and performance 121, 138, 155, 158,
160–1, 166
entrepreneurial firms 121, 143–4, 166
environment of bargaining 61–76
equal pay 182
erga omnes mechanisms 400–1, 480
Eritrea 391, 392
Estonia 380, 381
Ethiopia 391, 392
ethnicity 27, 28, 29, 30
and membership 397–9
and wages 209, 218, 219, 224, 225,
235, 236, 257
Euro-Fiet 467
Euro-sceptics/optimists 13, 481, 492
Eurocadres 467
Eurochambres 468
EuroCommerce 469
Europe, industrial relations and labour
policy 462–9
see also European Union
European Association for Craft and
SME (UEAPME) 463, 468
European Central Bank (ECB) 188,
361, 470
European Centre for Public
Enterprises (CEEP) 10, 463, 468
European Commission 362, 463,
465
European Committee of the
International Confederation of
Temporary Work Businesses
(Euro-CIETT) 465
European Company Statute (ECS)
449–50
European Employers' Network 468
European Federation of Retired and
Elderly Persons (EFREP/FERPA)
467

European industry federations (EIFs)
465, 467
European intersectoral confederation
of central national business
organization 468
European Metalworkers Federation
(EMF) 465, 467, 475
European Monetary Union (EMU)
188–9, 192, 351–2, 360, 469, 472,
473, 492
European Public Service Unions
(EPSU) 467
European Trade Union College
(ETUCO) 467
European Trade Union
Confederation (ETUC) 10, 361,
405, 449, 463, 467–8, 471, 475,
477, 484, 487
Economic and Social Committee
(ESC) 466
member unions of 473
European Trade Union Institute
(ETUI) 467
European Training of Workers on the
Impact of New Technology
(AFETT) 467
European Union 9–10, 378
Agreement on Social Policy (ASP)
416, 438, 440, 445–6, 448
Charter of Fundamental Rights
2000 451–2
collective bargaining 401, 471–84
Directive 89/39/1/EEC 446
Directive 94/45/EC 448
Directive 96/34/EC 463
Directive 97/38/EC 463
Directive 97/74/EC 448
Directive 98/59/EC 447
Directive 1999/70/EC 463
Directive 2001/23/EC 448
Directive 2001/86/EC 449
Directive 2002/14/EC 450
Economic and Social Committee
348, 361
European Company (Regulation
(EC) No 21257/2001 449
European Works Council (EWC)
446, 448–9, 463
Fifth Company Law draft directive
1972 450
industrial relations frameworks
445–52
Maastricht Treaty 354, 359, 361,
445, 446, 462, 463, 490, 492, 493,
494
Single European Act 1986 462
Social Action Programme 1974 462
Social Chapter 416, 438, 440, 445,
452, 487
Social Dialogue 463
Stability and Growth Pact 354, 359,
360, 361
Treaty of Amsterdam 445, 446,
463
Treaty of Nice 451
union related law 446–52
voluntary framework agreements
463
Working Time Directive 444
Europeanization of collective
bargaining 461–62
costs and benefits of 471–2
incentives for employees and unions
472–6
legal and institutional obstacles to
476–85
Europeanization of economic and
monetary policy 361–2
Evans, John 405–7
exchange rate policies 189
exchange rates 469, 472
expected utility function 49, 51, 52
external bargaining structure 62,
65–71

factor markets 469, 492
Fair Wages, Resolution, UK 417, 418,
444
Fairness at Work, Department of
Trade and Industry 440, 443–4,
453
Family Expenditure Survey (FES), UK
271
family-friendly policies 442, 443
'featherbedding' 46, 295
Federal Mediation and Conciliation
Service, USA 513
Federal Reserve Bank, USA 351
Fédération des Enterprises de Belgique
(FEB) 488

Federation of Independent Unions,
    Russia 379
Federation of Irish Employers (FIE)
    489
Fédérations européenes par branche
    d'industrie (FEBI) 484–5, 488
female workers
    income inequality 261, 263, 264–9,
        271, 272, 275, 276, 279–86, 432–6
    skill groups 270, 274
    training 162
    union density/membership 207, 270,
        275, 278–9, 362, 396, 397, 429–31,
        432, 436
    union wage premium 205, 208–9,
        218–19, 225–28, 246
financial markets 295–6
financial performance 140–9, 166–7
    Germany 144
    and union wage mark up 423
Finland
    bargaining 248–9, 404
    income inequality 233
    industrial relations 174, 477, 478,
        482
    union density/membership 207, 376,
        378, 398, 402, 403, 404
Firestone 133–4
firm-firm bargaining 50
firms
    closure of 167
    legislation 449–50
    new 73
    relocation 472, 523
    restructuring 465
    size 15, 30, 137, 299
    standardization of wages 252
    willingness to pay 86
fiscal policy 185–8, 469
fixed-term contracts 442, 443, 463,
    475
Ford Motors 133–4, 248
foreign direct investment 73–6, 388
formal employment sector 368, 369,
    394
fragmented bargaining 121, 423
France
    bargaining 248, 402, 403, 404
    economic growth 427
    industrial relations 174, 478, 488

political role of unions 336, 340–1,
    344, 350–1, 361, 477
union density/membership 212, 373,
    375, 377, 398, 402, 403
union wage premium 209–11
welfare state 359
Fratia, Romania 379
free market unions 379
free trade agreements 523
free-riders 15–18, 25, 34, 77, 80, 370,
    382, 476
fringe benefits 205
frustration-aggression approach to
    membership 19
full employment, commitment to 345,
    349–50
full-time workers, union wage premium
    219, 224, 226–7, 237
functional representation 347–8

G-7 countries 135, 375
Gabon 391, 393
game-theoretic intuition 64
gender discrimination 446
gender gap
    membership 397, 400
    union density 400
    wages 249–51, 279, 286, 287, 400
    see also female workers; male
        workers
General Accounting Office (GAO),
    USA 513–14
General Confederation of Portuguese
    Workers (CGTP-IN), 477
General Household Survey (GHS),
    UK 271, 276, 277, 428–9
General Motors 465
general strikes 359, 480
general unions 339, 436
German Bundesbank 187, 188, 351,
    353
German Confederation of Trade
    Unions (DGB), Germany 336,
    341, 347
German Metalworkers' Union (IG
    Metall) 466
Germany
    bargaining 120, 122, 164, 190, 248,
        303, 401, 404, 465–6
    employee/union preferences 474–5

employers' organizations 488
financial performance 144
income inequality 233
industrial relations 119, 129, 136,
    155, 162–4, 174, 478, 482
innovation 315, 317
investment 121, 153, 154
labour costs 470
monetary policy 188
political role of unions 336, 341–2,
    343–4, 346, 347, 357, 480
productivity 131, 136–7, 147–9, 165,
    166, 427
research and development 306, 309,
    313–14, 328
technological diffusion 315, 317,
    319
union density/membership 20, 22,
    23, 24, 26, 27, 28, 29, 120, 375,
    376, 398, 402, 404
union structure 343–4, 476, 477
union wage premium 209–11, 212
welfare state 359
works councils 121, 129, 136–8,
    162–4, 167, 335
Ghana 389, 391, 392, 397, 399
Ghent system 33, 35, 347
global terrorism 524–6
globalization 73–4, 183
    and national unions 523–4
go-slows 64
Gorbachev, Mikhail 379
governance 133, 159
Government Communications
    Headquarters (GCHQ), UK 438
government elections 346–7
    funding of 515–16
government, delegation of powers
    490–1
governmental institutions 489–92
governments
    and union membership 34
Great Depression 349, 521
Greece
    industrial relations 477, 478, 482
    informal employment sector 369
    union density/membership 377
grievance procedure 125, 443
gross domestic product (GDP) 427
growth, macro-determinants of 20–6

Guatemala 394, 395
Guinea 393
Guyana 395

Hanover Firm Panel, Germany 137,
    148, 164
Harvard School analysis 46, 125, 127
health and safety 125, 446–7, 524–6
Health and Safety (Consultation with
    Employees) Regulations (SI
    1996/1513), UK 446
health care workers 522
health insurance 389
Heckman estimator 199–200
Hicks-Marshall laws 517
high tech firms 143
high-cost countries 472
high-involvement management (HIV)
    practices 121, 132, 133, 143, 157
highly skilled workers
    recruitment 273
    wages 256, 272–3, 289
    'hold-up' problems 296–9
holdouts 87–93, 99, 104, 109, 112, 113
Honduras 395
Hong Kong 382, 384–6, 404
Hospital and Retirement Corporation
    of America 522
hospitality industry 503–4, 525
Hotel and Restaurant Employees
    Union (HERE), USA 525
Huizinga-Sorensen result 74
human capital, investment in 155,
    161–2
human resource management (HRM)
    132, 158, 159
Hungary 379, 380, 402, 403

Iceland 374, 376, 378, 489
ideology 31
immigrant workers 388, 389
income inequality 275–87, 428, 437
    literature on 256–75
    trends in 288–9
incomes policies 190–2, 345, 351, 416
independent workers' organisations,
    Russia 379
India
    informal employment sector 369,
    396

India (*continued*)
  self-employment 384
  union campaigns 405
  union density/membership 385, 387, 396, 397, 399
Indian National Trades Union Council 387
individual contracting 382
Indonesia 382, 385, 386, 387
industrial action 420–1
  and productivity 122, 123, 146
  legislation 417, 420–1, 480
  see also strikes
industrial discontent 344–5
industrial production and strikes 106
industrial relations
  adversarial style of 123–4, 129, 165
  and macroeconomic performance 120
  and wage structure 246
  Australia 119, 122, 158, 160, 174
  Austria 174, 184, 478, 480, 482, 488, 489
  Belgium 174, 478, 480, 481, 482
  Canada 119, 174, 248
  changes in 25
  cooperative style of 126, 127
  Denmark 174, 478, 480, 482
  Europe 445–52, 462–9
  European Union 478–9
  Europeanization of 461–2
  Finland 174, 477, 478, 482
  France 174, 478, 488
  Germany 119, 129, 136, 155, 162–4, 174, 478, 482
  Greece 477, 478, 482
  Ireland 478, 482, 488, 489
  Italy 174, 478, 482, 488
  Japan 119, 129, 158, 174
  Luxembourg 478, 483
  Netherlands 174, 479, 480, 483, 488, 489
  Norway 174, 489
  Portugal 479, 483
  Spain 475, 479, 483
  Sweden 174, 483, 488, 489
  Switzerland 174, 184
  Turkey 489
  UK 9, 119, 127, 134–5, 154–5, 174, 184, 202, 378, 382, 416–45, 479, 483, 488

  USA 202, 10–11
  see also cooperative industrial relations
Industrial Tribunals, UK 418, 421
industrial unions 187, 256, 257, 356–7
  and restrictive practices 127–8
industrialization 337, 338
industrialized countries
  and strikes 109
  collective bargaining and macroeconomic performance 172–93
industrializing countries 382
industry federations 466
industry-level bargaining 147–8, 303
industry-wide bargaining 248
inequality and unions, literature on 256–75
inflation
  and collective bargaining 190
  and strikes 93, 107
  and unemployment 350–1, 352
  and union membership 21, 25
  in Europe 470
informal employment sector 389, 396, 405
  rise and size of 369–70
information exchange 471–2, 475, 484
information improvement 46
initial public offerings (IPOs) 143, 145
innocent bystander provision, USA 102–3, 107
innovation 7, 329
  economic studies of 315
  empirical issues in relationship with unions 301–27
  theoretical models of union impact 294–301
institution building 462–9
institutional determinants of unionisation 32–5
institutional structures, differences in 488–9
institutional obstacles, Europeanization of collective bargaining 476–81
interactionist approach to membership 19
interest groups, unions as 337, 344

intermediate bargaining systems 173, 187

internal bargaining structure 62–4, 65, 76

International Confederation of Free Trade Unions (ICFTU) 405

International Confederation of Temporary Work Businesses 465

International Labour Organization (ILO) 366, 387, 400
'Decent Work' programme 406
Labour Report 368
World Employment Report 1998–1999 369–70

International Metal Workers' Federation 404

International Monetary Fund 360

International Social Survey Program (ISSP) 209

international trade 73–6

international trade union federations 405, 465, 466

International Typographical Union (ITU) 52

Interregional Trade Union Councils (ITUCs) 467–8, 484

interventionist state traditions 337–8

investment 4, 149–54
and financial performance 141
and labour productivity 122, 123
in human capital 161–2
in research and development 296–301
relative factor price effects 295

Ireland
industrial relations 478, 482, 488, 489
political role of unions 477
union density/membership 374, 376, 398

Irish Business and Employers' Confederation (IBEC) 489

Israel 389, 390, 399

Italy
bargaining 402, 403
income inequality 234
industrial relations 174, 478, 482, 488
informal employment sector 369

political role of unions 336, 340, 341, 344, 362, 477
union density/membership 375, 376, 396, 398, 402, 403
union wage premium 209–11, 212, 369
wage indexation 181
welfare state 359–60

Japan
bargaining 120, 173, 303, 401, 402, 403, 404
financial performance 145–6, 158, 160–1
industrial relations 119, 129, 158, 174
innovation 298, 295
investment 153, 154
labour disputes 105
political role of unions 342
productivity 131, 138, 144, 158, 160, 165–6
union density/membership 375, 382, 384, 385, 397, 398, 401, 402, 403
union wage premium 120, 207, 209–11, 231
works councils 121, 129

Japanese Trade Union Confederation (RENGO) 342

job flexibility 157

job regulation *see* work rules

job security 18

job-changers 273

joint consultative councils 154

joint understandings with employers 338

Jordan 390

Kentucky River Community Care 522

Kenya 389, 391, 392, 402

Keynesianism 344–5, 349–51

Kirkland, Lane 527

knowledge economy 518–19

knowledge production function 301

Kohl, Helmut 347

Korea 399, 406

KOS federation, Czechoslovakia 379

labour agreements 87–91, 93, 101, 103
and compensation 92

labour contracts, Japan 298
labour cost flexibility 189, 192
labour costs 358–9, 469–71, 472
Labour Courts 125
labour demand function 53–4, 56, 58, 59
labour disputes 86–113
    costs of 91, 92, 96–100, 101, 103–4, 107, 109–11
    duration of 96, 101, 105, 106, 108, 110
    see also strikes
Labour Force Surveys (UKLFS) 222, 223, 224, 225, 276, 277, 429
Labour government, UK 346, 350
    reforms of 436–45
labour legislation
    and strikes 103, 109
    changes in 25
    European Union 445–52
    USA 512, 520–3
labour legislation, UK 416–21, 436–43
    economic effects of 421–36, 443–5
labour market boards 344
labour market policies 347, 356
labour market policy funds 337
labour market rivalry 73
labour market-product market links 155–7
labour mobility 469, 489
labour movement 336
Labour Party, Australia 382
Labour Party, Israel 389
Labour Party, UK 336, 337, 339, 346
    see also New Labour
labour policies
    and labour disputes 94, 101–4, 109–12
    effects on welfare 109–11
    Europe 462–9
    impact on collective bargaining 108, 173–4
labour productivity 122–39
Labour Relations Board, Canada/USA 248
Labour Standard 186–7
labour turnover 125, 161, 163
labour, decommodification of 355
labour-intensive industrialization 384

labour–management cooperation 527
labour-management relations 132, 143
labour market–product market links 121–2, 140
labour-market interests, collective bargaining 485–6
Labour/Alliance coalition government, New Zealand 382
'last-in, first-out' employment rule 50
Latin America
    informal employment sector 369
    international trade unions 405
    membership/density 366, 375, 391–6
    productivity 327
layoffs 525
leader-follower model 71
Left wing parties 340
legal frameworks, differences in 488
legal obstacles, Europeanization of collective bargaining 476–85
legislation, European Union 446–52
Lenin, Vladimir Ilyich 388
Lesotho 391, 392
liberal democracies 335, 336, 355, 360
liberal market economies, union decline in 381–2
liberal state traditions 338–9
liberal-republican political traditions 340–1
Liga, Hungary 379
Lithuania 380
lobbying 344, 348–9, 405–7, 484, 527
lockouts 64, 91
Low Pay Commission, UK 438, 439, 440
low-cost countries 472, 523
low-skilled workers
    and multi-unions 158
    and selection 273
    and wages 257, 263, 270, 274, 275, 289
'Luddism' 294–5
Luxembourg
    bargaining 465–6, 478, 482
    industrial relations 478, 483
    unemployment 470
    union density/membership 376
Luxembourg Income Study 206, 207

Maastricht Treaty 354, 359, 361, 445,
446, 462, 463, 490, 492, 493, 494
macro-determinants of membership
20–6, 35
macroeconomic effects of unions 4–5
macroeconomic management 344–5
macroeconomic performance, influence
of collective bargaining 172–93
MacShane, Denis 404
Major, John 415
Major League Umpires, USA 511
Malawi 392
Malaysia
bargaining 404
union density/membership 385, 386,
399, 402, 403
union structure 382
male workers 362, 426
and selection 273, 275
income inequality 257, 261, 263–72,
288, 289–90
training 162
union density/membership 27, 207,
270, 278–9, 362, 429–31
wage premium 205, 208, 209,
218–19, 224–5, 226–8, 235–7,
279–87, 432
Mali 393
Malta 390
management
behaviour of 124, 125–6, 137, 149
role of 157–8
management opposition 17, 24, 30–1
management staff unions 373–4
managerial competence 164
managerial staff 467, 522
managerial X-inefficiency 46
manual workers 362
decline in 522
status of 355
union density/membership 17–18,
30, 362, 400
wage differentials 208
wage premium 219, 223, 224, 226–7,
237
manufacturing sector
and investment 151–2, 154
and strikes 105, 106, 107, 108, 109
and wage councils 164
income inequality 257, 260

labour costs 470, 503, 504, 505
productivity/financial performance
129, 132, 133, 134–5, 137, 138–9,
145–6, 157
trade organisations 488, 489
union density/membership 127, 362,
396, 397–400
wage premium 218, 219, 224, 226–7,
237
Marcos, Ferdinand 386
market power 73
Marshallian laws 56, 256
maternity leave 442–3, 463
Mauritania 393
Mauritius 391, 392, 404
McDormick Deering 257
median voter mechanism 50
Meiji Restoration, Japan 342
membership 2–3, 8–9
Africa/Middle East 388–91
and collective bargaining coverage
247–9
Asia 382–8
Australia 20, 21, 23, 24, 26, 29, 31,
120, 374, 382, 383, 402, 403, 404
Austria 376, 398
Belgium 376, 378, 396, 398, 402, 403
Brazil 394, 395, 399, 405
Canada 249, 366, 374, 375, 381, 383,
398, 400, 402, 03
Central/Latin America 391–6
Chile 402, 403, 406
China 366, 384, 385, 386, 388, 397,
399
comparisons 368–9
composition 362, 367
costs and benefits 197–8, 220–21
decline in 220–21, 381–2
Denmark 207, 212, 376, 378, 396,
398, 402, 403
determinants of 13–36
Europe 375–81
explanation of 76–80
Finland 207, 376, 378, 398, 402, 403,
404
France 212, 373, 375, 377, 398, 402,
403
Germany 20, 22, 23, 24, 26, 27, 28,
29, 120, 375, 376, 398, 402, 404
Greece 377

membership (*continued*)
  in liberal market economies 381–2
  India 385, 387, 396, 397, 399
  Ireland 374, 376, 398
  Italy 375, 376, 396, 398, 402, 403
  Japan 375, 382, 384, 385, 397, 398,
    401, 402, 403
  Luxembourg 376
  Malaysia 385, 386, 399, 402, 403
  meaning and counting of 370–5
  Mexico 366, 394–5
  Netherlands 20, 23, 26, 27, 29, 30,
    374, 376, 378, 398, 400, 402, 403,
    404
  New Zealand 381, 382, 383, 398, 403
  Norway 209, 211, 212, 231, 374, 376,
    398, 402, 403
  Philippines 382, 385, 386, 402, 403
  poaching 421
  Portugal 377, 402, 488
  Russia 366, 368, 379, 380
  Singapore 382, 384, 385, 402, 403
  social sciences explanations for
    18–20
  South Africa 374, 391, 399, 402, 403
  South Korea 382, 384, 385, 386, 397,
    402, 403
  Spain 377, 378, 398, 402, 403, 477,
    488
  Sweden 374, 376, 397, 398, 402, 403
  Switzerland 377, 398, 402, 403
  Taiwan 382, 384, 385, 402
  Turkey 389, 390, 402, 403
  UK 17–18, 20, 22, 24, 25, 27, 28, 31,
    120, 127, 175, 249, 270, 271–2,
    374, 375, 376, 381, 398, 400, 402,
    403, 421–2, 429, 430–1
  USA 20, 22, 24, 25, 27, 28, 31, 120,
    263, 366, 374, 375, 381, 383, 396,
    397, 398, 400, 402, 403, 503–6
Mercosur 368
merger of unions 476, 477, 480, 523–4
metals industries 484
metalworkers unions 465, 466, 476
Mexico
  informal employment sector 369,
    405
  union density/membership 366,
    394–5
  workers' rights 523

micro-determinants of membership
    26–32
Middle East 384, 388–91
migrant workers 386, 388
minimum wage 248, 288, 438–40, 470
mining industry 396
Monetarism 351–4
monetary policy 185–8, 352–4,
    469–71
monitoring role of unions 124
monopoly firms 54–5, 62, 140–1, 300
monopoly unions 53, 127, 145, 163,
    298–9
morale 46, 125
Morocco 389, 390
Mozambique 389, 392
Mugabe, Robert 391
multi-employer bargaining 190, 480,
    486
multi-employer national award system,
    New Zealand 382
multi-establishment firms 424–5
multi-unionism 121, 124, 129
  and bargaining 128
  and product markets 135–6, 149,
    165, 166
  and profitability 146, 147, 158, 160
multi-year collective bargaining
    agreements 181
multinational companies (MNCs) 465,
    473, 493, 524
  and relocation 472, 523
multiple union agreements 63–4
Murdoch, Rupert 294
mutual aid pacts 103

Namibia 391, 392
Nash wage bargaining 55, 59, 62–3, 64,
    67, 69, 72, 75
National Bureau of Economic
    Research (NBER), USA 212
  Matched Outgoing Rotation Group
    (MORG) 213, 214, 215, 216, 218
National Centre for Social Research,
    UK 238
National Child Development Study
    (NCDS), UK 271
National Confederation of Hungarian
    Trade Unions (MSzOSz),
    Hungary 379

National Dock Labour Scheme, UK 127, 141
National Economic Development Council (NEDC), UK 350
national economic policy councils 347
national employers' associations 484–5
National Health Insurance Law, Israel 389
National Labor Relations Act (NLRA), USA 11, 521, 522, 523, 528
National Labor Relations Board (NLRB), USA 221, 513, 520, 521
National Minimum Wage, UK 438–40
national unions in a global marketplace 523–4
national/sectoral agreements 404, 475
nationalized industries 141
Nazi Party, Germany 341
neo-corporatist incomes policies 345
neo-liberal governments 360
Netherlands
    bargaining 402, 403, 404, 465–6, 492
    income inequality 234
    industrial relations 174, 479, 480, 483, 488, 489
    political role of unions 341, 344, 347, 477
    union density/membership 20, 23, 26, 27, 29, 30, 374, 376, 378, 398, 400, 402, 403, 404
    union preferences 474–5
    union wage premium 209–11, 212
    welfare state 359
New Deal, USA 339, 349
New Labour 415, 421, 436–45, 453
New Order regime, Indonesia 386
new technology 294–5
    diffusion of 315–26
New York Stock Exchange 143
New Zealand
    bargaining 190, 382, 401, 402, 403
    income inequality 207
    industrial relations systems 174
    labour policies 186
    political role of unions 353
    union density/membership 381, 382, 383, 398, 403
    union wage premium 209–11, 212, 402, 403

Nicaragua 394, 395, 404
Niger 391
Nigeria 389, 391, 393
Nigerian Congress of Labour 391
non-agricultural workers 368, 369, 396
    union density rates 371–2
non-cooperative bargaining 3, 87, 97, 104
non-cooperative game theory 63
non-manual workers
    training 162
    wage differentials 219, 224, 226
non-manufacturing industries *see* service industries
non-union employment 183, 190, 353, 370
non-union sector 190
    wage dispersion 251–3
    wage structure 247, 255–6
non-union workers
    and discrimination 420–1
    and strikes 103–4
North American Free Trade Agreement (NAFTA) 368, 523
    provisions on trucking 525
Norway
    bargaining 248–9, 404
    income inequality 233
    industrial relations 174, 489
    political role of unions 355, 356
    union density/membership 209, 211, 212, 231, 374, 376, 398, 402, 403
    union wage premium 209, 210, 231
    wages 181, 182

observed skills 202
occupational associations *see* craft unions
occupational pensions 359
Occupational Safety and Health Administration (OSHA), USA 513
OECD 120, 157, 302, 353, 368, 369
    and international union federations 405
    and technological diffusion 325
    and union density 211
    and union pluralism 386
    Employment Outlook 120

oligopolistic industries 299
one-party governments 389
open shops 16, 202, 373
    and unionization 16, 17, 18, 76–7, 80
optimal collective bargaining areas 462
OPZZ, Poland 379
ordinary least squares (OLS) 200, 201,
    204, 303, 305
Organization for Economic
    Cooperation and Development
    see OECD
organizational structures, differences in
    488–9
over-manning 123
overtime working 123

Pakistan 384, 385, 387
Panama 395, 404
Panel Survey of Income Dynamics 202
Paraguay 395, 399
Pareto's law 56, 77, 297, 425
part-time workers
    and union preferences 474
    legislation 442, 463
    union density/membership 30, 397
    wage premium 219, 223, 224, 226
partnership agreements 158
party linkages and the democratic class
    struggle 345–7
patents 300, 301, 302–3
paternity leave 442, 443, 463
pattern bargaining 71, 120
pay-as-you-go pension schemes 359
PDS, Germany 341
peer pressure 30
pensioners rights/interests 362, 396
pensions 359
perestroika 379
personnel management 122
Peru 395
Philippines
    bargaining 402, 403, 404
    union density/membership 382, 385,
        386, 402, 403
Phillips curve 350, 351, 352
picketing 418
Pinault-Printemps-Redoute 524
Pinochet, General Augusto 396
plant closures 202, 424
plant-based unions 387

plant-level bargaining 64, 190
plants, life cycle of 8–9, 12
Poland 379–81, 399
policy approaches to union
    macroeconomic impacts 189–92
policy networks 348
Policy Studies Institute, UK 238
political behaviour of unions,
    historical origins 337–44
political campaigns 336
political environment of bargaining
    183–8
political exchange 344–5
political factors of membership 18–20
political independence of unions 338
political parties, alliances with 336–7
political process, unions involvement in
    344–54
political role of unions 7–8
    Australia 353–4
    Austria 341, 344, 347, 357
    Belgium 341, 344, 347
    Canada 353–4
    France 336, 340–1, 344, 350–1, 361,
        477
    Germany 336, 341–2, 343–4, 346,
        347, 357, 480
    historical origins of 337–44
    Ireland 477
    Italy 336, 340, 341, 344, 362, 477
    Japan 342
    Netherlands 341, 344, 347, 477
    New Zealand 353
    Philippines 477
    Portugal 377
    Sweden 340, 345–6, 350, 355, 356,
        357
    Switzerland 341, 344, 355
    UK 336, 337, 338–9, 340, 343, 346,
        349, 350, 351, 353–4, 356, 479
    USA 336, 339, 349, 351, 353–4
political segmentation of unions 344
political strikes 335, 480
politically fragmented/unified trade
    unions 343, 477
Portugal
    bargaining 404, 482
    industrial relations 479, 483
    labour costs 470
    political role of unions 477

union density/membership 377, 402, 488
union wage premium 209–11, 231
post-war economies 350–1
postal ballots 417
preference costs 474–5, 486
pressure groups, unions as 362
price controls 351
and strikes 103, 107
price rules 190–1
price-setting 72–3
print-workers 294
private incentive good model 77
private information 86, 87, 91, 97, 104
private sector
China 388
financial performance/productivity 139, 143
income inequality 271–2
union density/membership 143, 278, 397
USA 503–4, 508, 526
union wage premium 213, 216, 219, 224, 226, 235
pro-labour governments 185–6, 192
Prodkepa, Bulgaria 379
product demand 66
product market characteristics 68, 70–1
product market competition 65, 67, 68, 73, 121, 127, 135, 143, 155, 157, 167
product market spillovers 75
product market structure 46
product market–labour market links 121–2, 140, 155–7
product quality 133–4
production industries, membership 366
production, capital intensity of 124
productivity 122–39, 272–3
of workers 272–3
productivity growth 294, 326–7
Professional Air Traffic Controllers' Organization (PATCO) 109
professional associations 374
professional occupations 397, 400, 467, 522
profit maximization 50, 51, 52, 73
profit schemes 428
profitability 104–5, 121, 304
and union wage mark up 423

in imperfect financial markets 295–6
psychological factors of membership 18–20
public image of unions 348–9
public institutions 337
public policies, influence on 337, 344
public policy institutions 189–90
public sector
Canada 381
employers' representation 468
Europe 396, 400, 467
income inequality 271–2
Indonesia 386
UK 429
union density/membership 30, 127, 397
USA 278, 503–4, 505, 516
wage differentials 218, 219, 224, 226, 228, 235
union wage premium 218, 219, 224, 226, 228, 235
Public Services, Transport and Traffic Union (ÖTV), Germany 476
public support for unions, USA 515–16
public utility industries 141, 525
publicity for unions 517–18

quantity-setting 72–3

radical unions 337–8
Räte, Germany 335
rational-choice approach to membership 19
Reagan, Ronald 360
real wages 21, 24–5, 181, 187
impact of bargaining arrangements 176–8
recruitment costs 125
recruitment legislation 419
recruitment, employer 199
recruitment, union 19, 32, 33, 221, 337, 417
USA 503–4, 518, 522–3, 526, 527
redundancies 358, 360
collective 447–8
reference groups 32
reference values 52
reference wages 54, 58
reformist unions 337–8

regional trade union federations 405
Rehn-Meidner model 350
relative factor price effects on
    investment 295
relative wages structure 5–6, 124, 197,
    249–56
religious segmentation of unions 344,
    477
relocation of firms 472, 523
Renault 465
rent capture 46, 47
rent-maximization 50, 51, 52–3, 59,
    66–7, 71
replacement workers 87, 97–100, 101,
    108, 109, 110–11, 134, 367
representation rights 27
    grievance/disciplinary hearings 441
research and development (R&D)
    301–15
    strategic investment in 149–50, 151,
        299–301
reservation wages 67
restrictive work practices 122–3, 126,
    424
retention 33
retired workers' unions 467
retirement, incentives for 358
revenues, of unions 14–15
right to bargain 404
right to organize 337
right-to-manage 53–4, 55, 56, 57, 58,
    59, 60, 61, 71, 297, 300, 327
right to vote 338
risk aversion 51, 58
Romania 379, 380
Roosevelt, Franklin D 339
Russia
    union density/membership 366, 368,
        379, 380
    workers' councils 335

Saltsjöbaden national agreement 340
saturation effect 24
Scandinavia
    bargaining 173, 177, 184, 190, 248–9
    labour federations 182
    union density/membership 397–8,
        477
    political parties 345, 355
    social security systems 480

union preferences 474–5
'Schedule 11' procedure, UK 416
Schröder, Gerhard 347
screening bargaining model 111–12
Second Post-war Settlement 335,
    349–51
secondary picketing 103
secondary strikes 417, 421
secret ballots 417, 418, 420, 441
sector level bargaining 121, 477
sectoral collective bargaining 370
sectoral social dialogue 465
self-employed workers' unions 373, 374
self-employment 374, 396, 405
semi-skilled workers 261
Senegal 391, 392
sequential bargaining model 58–9,
    60–1
service sector 362, 366, 400, 505
    and strikes 103, 105, 108
    growth of 518–19
    income inequality 257–8, 260
    investment 151
    productivity/financial performance
        129, 145
    USA 508–9
    wage differentials 218, 219, 220, 224,
        226
service sector unions 476
    and employee benefits 15–16
share ownership schemes 428
shipbuilding industry 299
shop stewards 124–5
sickness pay 205, 356
'sickouts' 510–11
signalling bargaining model 111–12
Singapore
    social dialogue 406
    union density/membership 382, 384,
        385, 402, 403
Single European Act 1986 462
Single European Market 354, 360, 378,
    489, 492
Single Market Programme (SMP) 74
single union agreements 63–4
single union workplaces 135–6
single-employer bargaining 480
single-firm single-union bargaining 65
single-union pairs 61, 62
skill demarcations 150

skill differentials 257, 272–3
skill groups 202, 277–8
    and income inequality 260, 261, 270,
        271, 275, 277, 287
    and selection 272–3
    and wages 205, 217, 246, 253–5,
        255–6, 279
    see also highly skilled workers; low
        skilled workers; skilled workers
skill shortages 519
skilled workers, bargaining power of
    526
skills, unobserved 255–6
Slovakia 379, 380
Slovenia 379–80
small and medium-sized enterprises
    (SMEs) 137, 302, 468
Social Action Programme 1974 (EU)
    462
Social and Economic Council,
    Netherlands 347
Social Chapter 416, 438, 440, 445, 452,
    487
social composition of union density
    396–400
social contracts 184, 191, 521
social custom 25, 27, 32, 77–80
    and unionization 15–18, 35–6
Social Democratic Party
    Germany 336, 341, 346, 347
    Sweden 350
social dialogue 462–3, 465
social factors of membership 18–20
social insurance 339, 347
'social movement unionism' 405
social pacts 354, 472, 473, 491, 494
social policy 354, 361–2, 445–6, 485
Social Policy Research Unit (SPRU),
    UK 303, 315
social progress, campaigns for 336
Social Register 2001 394
social sciences explanations for
    membership 18–20, 35
social security 356, 357, 480
social security boards 344
social security funds 337
social services, as employer 357–8
social welfare programmes 394
social-democratic parties 345, 346–7,
    355, 357–8, 378

Socialist government, France 351
Socialist Party, Japan 342
Socialist Party, Sweden 340, 346
Socialist Register 2001 394
Socialist unions 341
Solidarity, Poland 379, 381
Sotsprof, Russia 379
South Africa
    bargaining 401, 402, 403, 404
    social dialogue 406
    union density/membership 374, 391,
        399, 402, 403
    union wage premium 209
South Korea
    bargaining 402, 403, 404
    democratisation 386
    union density/membership 382, 384,
        385, 386, 397, 402, 403
    social dialogue 406
    union campaigns 404–6
    union wage premium 209
South-East Asia
    informal employment sector 369
    union density/membership 382, 384,
        386
sovjets, Russia 335
Spain
    anarcho-syndicalist unions 335
    bargaining 184, 402, 403, 404
    income inequality 234
    industrial relations 475, 479, 483
    informal employment sector 369
    unemployment 470
    union density/membership 377, 378,
        398, 402, 403, 477, 488
    union wage premium 209–11, 212,
        231
    wages 470
Sri Lanka 385, 387
Stability and Growth Pact, Europe
    354, 359, 360, 361
stagflation 351
state-run industries 360
status, differences in 157
steel industry 257
Stone–Geary utility function 49–53
stoppage of work provision, USA
    102–3, 107
strategic research and development
    299–301

strikes
  and pay 16, 87, 91, 102, 107
  costs of 425–6
  dismissal of workers 441–2
  empirical evidence on 104–9
  legislation on 335, 394, 426
  proportionality rules 480
  USA 511–16, 517
structure of bargaining 61–76
structure–conduct–performance
    framework 47, 48
Suharto 386, 387
supply and demand 13–14, 27
Supreme Court, USA 504, 511, 522
surplus capture 63
surplus creation 46
Survey of Union Membership (SUM),
    Canada 276, 277
Surveys on Work Arrangements (SWA)
    276
Swaziland 392
Sweden
  bargaining 190, 248–9, 402, 403, 404,
    477, 479, 480, 492
  income inequality 233
  industrial relations systems 174, 483,
    488, 489
  political role of unions 340, 345–6,
    350, 355, 356, 357
  unemployment insurance 33
  union density/membership 374, 376,
    397, 398, 402, 403
  union wage premium 209–11, 212,
    402
  wages 181–2, 470
Sweeney, John 527
Switzerland
  bargaining 401, 402, 403, 466
  industrial relations 174, 184
  union density/membership 377, 398,
    402, 403
  political role of unions 341, 344, 355
Syria 390

Taiwan
  bargaining 402, 404
  union density/membership 382, 384,
    385, 402
Tanzania 391, 392
Tarifautonomie 480

tax-based incomes policies (TIPs) 192
Team Act, USA 521
team working 157
  USA 521, 522, 527–8
Teamsters union, USA 510, 524
technological diffusion 294, 315–26
  Australia 315, 319
  Canada 315, 318
  Germany 315, 317, 319
telecommunications industry 519, 527
terrorism 524–6
textile unions 476
Thailand 382, 385, 386, 387
Thatcher, Margaret 122, 327, 360, 415,
    427, 452
  reforms of 416–36, 452–3
threat payoffs 93–7
threats 64
'Tiger' economies 382, 386
time-series analyses of union
    membership 20–6
Tobit model 306
tort, actions in 417
total quality management (TQM) 132,
    133
Trade Boards Act 1909, UK 438
trade policies 74–5
trade protection 74
Trade Union Act 1984, UK 418, 420
Trade Union and Employment Rights
    Act 1993, UK 419
Trade Union and Labour Relations
    Act (TULRA) 1974 and 1976,
    UK 416, 418
trade union confederations 248–9,
    466
trade union councils 467
Trade Union Reform and Employment
    Rights Act 1993, UK 421
Trade Union Technical Bureau
    (TUTB) 467
Trades Union Congress (TUC), UK
    337, 339, 346, 444
  partnership agreements 158
traditional approaches of unions 520
training 161, 162, 465, 467, 519, 525
  investment in 299
Transfer of Undertakings (Protection
    of Employment)
    Regulations 1981 448

transfers of undertakings 447–8
transitional economies 378–9, 404–6
transnational economic policy 360–1
Transnational Information and
    Consultation of Employees
    Regulations 1999 448–9
transnational unions 476
transnational works councils 448–9
Treaty of Amsterdam 445, 446, 463
Treaty of Nice 451
trucking industry 141, 525
trust, and unionisation 31
Tunisia 389, 390
Turkey
    bargaining 404
    industrial relations 489
    informal employment sector 369
    union density/membership 389, 390,
        402, 403
Turkish Federation of Employers 389
two-threat bargaining model 65, 107
two-way trade 74, 75
tyre manufacturing 118, 165

Uganda 389, 391, 392
UK
    bargaining 120–1, 402, 403
    closed shops 17, 34, 158, 166, 419
    collective bargaining 190, 401, 404,
        477, 480
    Conservative Party reforms 416–36
    employment 167
    financial performance 141, 142, 144,
        146–7, 164, 165, 166
    gender and wages 263, 266, 269, 270,
        271–2, 284–5
    income inequality 234, 270, 271,
        275–89, 288–90
    industrial relations 9, 119, 127,
        134–5, 154–5, 174, 184, 378, 382,
        479, 483, 488
    innovation 298, 303, 321, 322, 315,
        328, 329
    investment 121, 151–2, 161–2, 165,
        166
    Labour Party reforms 436–45
    'Luddism' 294–5
    multi-unionism 129, 139, 147, 158,
        160
    nationalized industries 141

political role of unions 336, 337,
    338–9, 340, 343, 346, 349, 350,
    351, 353–4, 356, 479
productivity 126–7, 130, 134–6, 139,
    157–8, 165, 166, 167, 323, 325,
    326–7
research and development 302, 303,
    306, 307, 308, 309, 310, 313–14,
    315, 328–9
shop stewards 124–5
strikes 106, 109, 417, 418, 419, 420,
    421
technological diffusion 316, 318–19,
    321
union density/membership 17–18,
    20, 22, 24, 25, 27, 28, 31, 120, 127,
    175, 249, 270, 271–2, 374, 375,
    376, 381, 398, 400, 402, 403
union structure 158–60
union wage premium 222–3, 228–30,
    267, 263, 266, 269, 271–2
wage differentials 222–8
wage dispersion 431–6
wage structure 247, 248, 249, 262
welfare state 359, 360
UK Labour Force and British Social
    Attitudes Surveys 207
Ukraine 366, 379, 380
uncoordinated bargaining
    arrangements 176, 187–8
underemployment 389
unemployment
    affect on membership 21, 24
    among males 105–6
    and economic policy 360
    and monetarism 352
    and union density/ membership 396
    and union wage premium 228–30,
        231–2
    Europe 426, 470
    impact of bargaining arrangements
        176–80
    USA 205
unemployment benefits 347–8, 356
    for striking workers 102–3
unemployment insurance 33, 34, 356,
    373
unfair dismissal 416, 442
Uni-Europa 465
unification of unions 343–4

union behaviour, economic models of
3, 44–81
union collaboration 524
union confederations 477
union decline, macro-determinants of
20–6
union density
and research and development 151,
309, 315, 327
and social composition 396–400
and union wage effects 220, 231–2
Australia 20, 21, 23, 24, 26, 29, 31,
120, 374, 382, 383, 402, 403, 404
Austria 376, 398
Belgium 376, 378, 396, 398, 402, 403
Brazil 394, 395, 399, 405
Canada 249, 366, 374, 375, 381, 383,
398, 400, 402, 403
Chile 402, 403, 406
China 366, 384, 385, 386, 388, 397,
399
Denmark 207, 212, 376, 378, 396,
398, 402, 403
Europe 211
France 212, 373, 375, 377, 398, 402,
403
Germany 20, 22, 23, 24, 26, 27, 28,
29, 120, 375, 376, 398, 402, 404
Greece 377
India 385, 387, 396, 397, 399
influence on economy 175–80, 190
Ireland 374, 376, 398
Italy 375, 376, 396, 398, 402, 403
Japan 375, 382, 384, 385, 397, 398,
401, 402, 403
Luxembourg 376
Mexico 366, 394–5
Netherlands 20, 23, 26, 27, 29, 30,
374, 376, 378, 398, 400, 402, 403,
404
New Zealand 381, 382, 383, 398, 403
Norway 209, 211, 212, 231, 374, 376,
398, 402, 403
Philippines 382, 385, 386, 402, 403
Portugal 377, 402, 488
Russia 366, 368, 379, 380
Singapore 382, 384, 385, 402, 403
social composition/within-nation
variation of 396–400
South Africa 374, 391, 399, 402, 403

South Korea 382, 384, 385, 386, 397,
402, 403
Spain 377, 378, 398, 402, 403, 477,
488
Sweden 374, 376, 397, 398, 402, 403
Switzerland 377, 398, 402, 403
Taiwan 382, 384, 385, 402
Turkey 389, 390, 402, 403
UK 17–18, 20, 22, 24, 25, 27, 28, 31,
120, 127, 175, 207, 249, 270,
271–2, 374, 375, 376, 381, 398,
400, 402, 403, 421–2, 429–30
USA 20, 22, 24, 25, 27, 28, 31, 120,
207, 263, 366, 374, 375, 381, 383,
396, 397, 398, 400, 402, 403,
503–6, 526
union effect 306–7
Union Générale des Travailleurs
(UGT), Portugal 477
union growth, macro-determinants of
20–6
union incentives, Europeanizing of
collective bargaining 472–6
union membership agreements
(UMAs) 416, 417
union membership *see* membership
Union Network International 465
union objective function 49, 51
Union of Automobile Workers (UAW),
USA 339, 526–7
Union of Industrial and Employers'
Confederations of Europe
(UNICE) 10, 463, 468, 487, 488,
489
union officials 475–6
and productivity 138–9, 161
behaviour of 298
see also shop stewards
union political behaviour, history of
337–44
union power 480
changes in 476
union preferences 53, 474–5
union recognition 73, 375, 417, 418,
440–1, 443–4
and financial performance/
productivity 138, 140, 156, 158
and shareholder wealth 143
union representation 347–8
in collective bargaining 400–5

union shops *see* closed shops
union status, endogeneity of 305–6
union structure and organisation
    158–61
union tax 394
union wage effects 197–238
union wage mark up 423
union wage premium
    Austria 207, 209–11, 212, 231, 402,
       403
    Brazil 209–10, 212, 231
    Canada 120, 134, 209–11, 212, 231,
       249, 263
    Chile 209–11, 212, 231
    cyclical nature of 228–37
    Denmark 231, 402, 403
    France 209–11
    Germany 209–11, 212
    Italy 209–11, 212, 369
    Japan 120, 207, 209–11, 231
    Netherlands 209–11, 212
    New Zealand 209–11, 212, 402, 403
    Norway 209, 210, 231
    Portugal 209–11, 231
    South Africa 209
    Spain 209–11, 212, 231
    Sweden 209–11, 212, 402
    UK 222–8, 228–30, 267, 263, 266,
       269, 271–2
    USA 212–22, 228–30
union wage-setting behaviour 74
union–firm bargaining 50, 51, 53, 56,
    65, 71, 73
union–firm pairs 61, 66, 68–70, 72,
    74–5
union-friendly political parties 338
union-managed unemployment
    insurance 33
union–management relations 145, 157,
    166, 525
union–party links 343–4
union-related law, European Union
    446–52
unionism 366–406
    collective voice of 124, 125, 137, 147,
       148, 163, 165
    disadvantages of 423
    forms of 127–8
    supply and demand 13–15
unionization 13–36

and collective bargaining 175–6
    management attitudes to 76
    decline in 270
    structure of 428–9
unionized monopoly/duopoly 61, 71,
    72, 74
unionized oligopoly 60, 65–8, 71, 73,
    74–6
unions and entry 73
unions, challenges for 360–3, 516–26
unions, economic analysis of 1, 2
unions, efficiency-enhancing role of 46
unions, origins of 335–6
unions, impact on wage structure 6–7
unions, links with management 157–8
unions, macroeconomic effects of 3–5
unions, monitoring role of 165
unions, political role of 7–8, 335–63
unions, political strength of 337
unions, size of 367, 473, 476
unions, theoretical foundations of
    economic theory 48
unions, voting rights 473–4
unions, weakness of 425, 473–4
unitary social dialogue committees 465
UNITE, USA 524
United Automobile Workers, USA 248
United Parcel Service (UPS), USA
    510, 524
universal insurance systems 355
universal suffrage 338
University of Essex, Data Archive
    238
unobserved skills 255–6, 263, 272–5
unofficial action 419, 421
unskilled workers 339, 436
    membership 279
    wage differentials 208, 279
upstream-downstream bargaining 50,
    65, 73
urban labour markets 257
Uruguay 395, 396
US Federal Reserve 187
USA
    bargaining 51, 180
    collective bargaining 93, 102, 103,
       104–5, 106, 107, 109, 120, 180,
       190, 401, 402, 403, 404, 502–28
    financial performance 141, 142–3,
       144, 145, 165, 166, 167

USA (*continued*)
  gender and wages 261, 262, 263, 264,
    267, 270, 271, 272, 273–4, 275,
    280–1
  income inequality 233, 234–5, 258,
    270, 275–87, 288–90
  industrial relations 10–11, 119,
    154–5, 157–8, 174, 184, 295
  innovation 293, 295, 298, 315
  investment 150–1, 152, 162, 165,
    299, 308, 316–17
  labour disputes 104–5, 106, 107, 108,
    109
  labour legislation, USA 512, 520–3
  nationalized industries 141
  political role of unions 336, 339,
    349, 351, 353–4
  productivity 12, 129, 130, 132, 133,
    157–8, 164, 165, 323, 324–5,
    326–7, 427
  research and development 302, 307,
    308, 310–12, 328
  technological diffusion 318, 320–1
  unemployment insurance 102–3
  union density/membership 20, 22,
    24, 25, 27, 28, 31, 120, 263, 366,
    374, 375, 381, 383, 396, 397, 398,
    400, 402, 403, 503–6
  union shops 34, 158
  union structure and organization
    158
  union wage premium 216, 228–30
  unions, state of 516
  wage differentials 212–22
  wage distribution 431–2
  wage structure 247, 248, 249, 262,
    274, 287
  welfare state 359, 360
utilitarian utility function 49–53, 72

Val Duchesse dialogue 462–3
Várgas, Getúlio 394
Venezuela 395, 396, 399
Verdi, Germany 476
Verbond van Nederlandse
  Ondernemingen – nederlands
  Christeelijk Werkgeversverbond
  (VNO-NCW) Netherlands 488,
  489
vertical market relations 65

Vietnam 382
voice mechanisms 46, 121, 126, 133,
  155, 161, 163, 513, 520
  see also collective voice
voluntary membership *see* open shops
voluntary social dialogue 462–3
voting rights 338

wage bargaining 87–100, 111–12
wage bill maximization 48–9, 50
wage compression 181–2
wage concession function 109
wage controls
  and strikes 103, 107
wage demands 186, 187
wage differentials 14, 15, 31, 65, 68,
  182, 198–201, 422–36, 431–6, 502,
  506–11
  UK 222–8
  USA 212–22
  worldwide 207–12
wage dispersion 181–2, 251–5, 260,
  287, 428–36
wage distribution, UK 428–36
wage increases, deferred 180–1
wage indexation 181
wage inflation 361
wage moderation 73, 345, 472
wage policies 469
wage restraint 183, 184, 187, 188, 351,
  352, 353, 357, 361
wage rules 190–1
wage scales 523
wage setting 17, 75, 202, 352, 481
wage strategies 296–9
wage structure 6–7, 246–90
wage–employment outcomes 56
wage-maximization 52, 58
Wages Councils 421, 438
wages, Europe 470–1
Wagner Act 248
war-of-attrition bargaining model 112
Weimar Republic 341
welfare 109–11
welfare benefits 18
welfare state 339, 354–60
  as employers 357–8
West Asia 384
Western Europe 359–60
  collective bargaining 401

dialogue with unions 406
  membership 368, 369, 375, 378, 405
Western governments 350
white trade unions 391
white-collar workers 362
  roles of unions 346
  status of 355, 357
  union density/membership 30, 340,
    400, 467
  union wage premium 204, 217, 260
  USA 508
wild cat strikes 64, 340
'winter of discontent' 346, 425
'within sector' effect 260, 286
women's organizations 405
work practices, USA 505, 514
work rules 123, 125, 145, 150
work to rule 64, 88, 91
work, changing nature of 518–19
worker benefits 17–18
worker dissatisfaction 31, 513–14
worker preferences 125
worker utility function 51
workers' earnings capacity 199
workers' expectations 519–20
workers, exploitation by unions 124
workers, selection of 199, 272–3
workforce
  and cooperation 88
  changes in 519–20
working class and direct action 335
working conditions, legislation on 481

working practices 125, 129, 132
working time 465, 475
Workplace Employment Relations
    Surveys (WERS), UK 135–6, 142,
    146–7, 238, 441
workplace governance 159
Workplace Industrial Relations
    Surveys (WIRS), UK 154, 261
workplace presence 32, 33, 34
Workplace Relations Act 1997,
    Australia 382
Works Constitution Act (1972),
    Germany 136, 137, 148, 163
Works Constitution Reform Act
    (2001), Germany 162–4
works councils 34, 448–9, 450–1
  and productivity/performance 121,
    125, 136–7, 147–9, 154, 155, 165,
    167
  and research and development 309
  see also European Works Councils
    (EWCs)
World Congress of Labour (WCL)
    405
World Trade Organization 360, 368
WorldCom 141
worldwide unionism 366–406

Xerox 141

Zambia 389, 391, 392, 402
Zimbabwe 391, 392, 402